ALTERNATIVE VISIONS OF THE INTERNATIONAL LAW ON FOREIGN INVESTMENT

Muthucumaraswamy Sornarajah
(Photograph: David Tan, 2015)

ALTERNATIVE VISIONS OF THE INTERNATIONAL LAW ON FOREIGN INVESTMENT

Essays in Honour of Muthucumaraswamy Sornarajah

Edited by

C.L. LIM

University of Hong Kong and Keating Chambers, London

CAMBRIDGE
UNIVERSITY PRESS

CAMBRIDGE
UNIVERSITY PRESS

University Printing House, Cambridge CB2 8BS, United Kingdom

Cambridge University Press is part of the University of Cambridge.

It furthers the University's mission by disseminating knowledge in the pursuit of education, learning and research at the highest international levels of excellence.

www.cambridge.org
Information on this title: www.cambridge.org/9781107139060

First published 2016

Printed in the United Kingdom by Clays, St Ives plc

A catalogue record for this publication is available from the British Library

Library of Congress Cataloguing in Publication data
Sornarajah, M., honouree. | Lim, C. L. (Chin L.), editor.
Alternative visions of the international law on foreign investment : essays in honour of Muthucumaraswamy Sornarajah / edited by Chin Leng Lim.
New York Cambridge University Press, 2016.
LCCN 2015042969 | ISBN 9781107139060 (hardback)
LCSH: Investments, Foreign (International law) | BISAC: LAW / International.
LCC K3830 .A425 2016 | DDC 346/.092–dc23
LC record available at http://lccn.loc.gov/2015042969

ISBN 978-1-107-13906-0 Hardback

CONTENTS

FIGURES

TABLES

CONTRIBUTORS

NATHALIE BERNASCONI-OSTERWALDER, lic.iur, LLM Georgetown, admitted to the Basel Bar, is Program Leader and Senior International Lawyer, Investment and Sustainable Development Program, International Institute for Sustainable Development (IISD).

HONGRUI CHEN, PhD (Xi'an Jiaotong University), is Lecturer at the School of Law, Xi'an Jiaotong University, China.

JEAN HO, PhD (Cambridge), LLM (Panthéon-Sorbonne), LLM (NYU), is Assistant Professor at the Faculty of Law, National University of Singapore.

CHIN LENG LIM of Keating Chambers, London, is Professor of Law at Hong Kong University; a member of CPEC, tasked to advise Hong Kong's commerce secretary; Lionel A. Sheridan Visiting Professor at NUS and Visiting Professor at King's College London.

HOWARD MANN is Associate and Senior International Law Advisor at the International Institute for Sustainable Development and is the lead author of IISD's Model International Agreement on Investment for Sustainable Development. He represented IISD in the amicus curiae intervention in *Methanex Corp.* v. *United States.*

PETER MUCHLINSKI is Professor of International Commercial Law, SOAS, University of London.

DAVID MUSAYELYAN, LLM (Taiwan National University), is Research Associate to Professor Trakman.

ANIRUDDHA RAJPUT is Advocate at the Supreme Court of India; Research Associate, Center for International Law; and Member of the Expert Group constituted to comment on the Model Bilateral Investment Treaty of 2015 by the Law Commission of India.

KARL P. SAUVANT is Resident Senior Fellow, Columbia Center on Sustainable Investment, a joint centre of Columbia Law School and the Earth Institute at Columbia University, New York. He was formerly Director of UNCTAD's Investment Division.

DAVID SCHNEIDERMAN is Professor of Law and Political Science at the University of Toronto. He is the author of "Constitutionalizing Economic Globalization: Investment Rules and Democracy's Promise" and "Resisting Economic Globalization: Critical Theory and International Investment Law".

WENHUA SHAN, PhD (Xiamen), PhD (Cambridge), attended Trinity College, Cambridge, and is the Ministry of Education Changjiang Chair Professor of International Economic Law and Dean at Xi'an Jiaotong University. He is Senior Fellow at the Lauterpacht Centre at Cambridge and Professor of Law at the University of New South Wales.

KYLA TIENHAARA is Research Fellow at the Regulatory Institutions Network (RegNet), Australian National University.

LEON TRAKMAN, LLM, SJD (Harvard), is Professor of Law and formerly Dean at the University of New South Wales.

TODD TUCKER is a Gates Scholar at the University of Cambridge's Centre of Development Studies.

GUS VAN HARTEN is Associate Professor at Osgoode Hall Law School. He is the author of "Investment Treaty Arbitration and Public Law", "Sovereign Choices and Sovereign Constraints" and "Sold Down the Yangtze: Canada's Lopsided Investment Deal With China".

KENNETH J. VANDEVELDE, JD (Harvard), PhD (California), is Professor of Law at, and the former Dean of, the Thomas Jefferson School of Law in San Diego.

JIANGYU WANG is Associate Professor at the Faculty of Law, National University of Singapore.

PREFACE

International economic law is a branch of public international law. Its subfields, however, have taken on the appearance of disconnected specialist subjects over the years, not least in the world of international legal practice with its Gattologists, Bitologists and sovereign debt workout specialists. In recent decades, the international law on foreign investment especially risked becoming unmoored from sovereign legal relations. Sornarajah, however, always took the classical view of a subject rooted in the sources and systems of public international law. Without being sovereign-centric he views the law as being as much a product of sovereign will as it is the result of economic change. His conclusions sometimes appeared incongruous with economic globalisation, transnational legal innovation, the explosion since the 1990s of private claims before investment tribunals and even the practice of these tribunals. But as Gus van Harten says here, Sornarajah "has pursued independent critical scholarship in international investment law for a longer time than any other living specialist in the field and has done so with patience and grace", and the current backlash against investor-state arbitration is a tribute to the viewpoint which he has long held.

Whichever side one takes in the current debates, it is the right time for a book which explores Sornarajah's views. This book attempts to do so in light of recent withdrawals from the Washington Convention, and a growing epidemic of ongoing national "reforms" of investment treaties and the institution of investor-state dispute settlement as it is currently understood. The backlash against investor-state arbitration, appearing in different shades in different places, is now no longer confined to a number of Latin American nations. Large economies – Indonesia, India and the European Union among them – are taking a broadly similar turn. From Kuala Lumpur to K Street, from Potsdamer Platz to the Palais d'Egmont, protests have taken place around the globe against ongoing mega-regional investment treaty negotiations.

A critical introduction to these complex, contemporary developments is also required, and it is hoped that this book will be of interest and use to students and scholars, government international law counsel and policy-makers, private legal counsel and arbitrators alike. The contributors come from varied backgrounds in the making, implementation, evaluation and contestation of treaty policies and from the worlds of treaty-making, professional law teaching, public interest lawyering, international law litigation and arbitration practice. Many, though not all, have been Sornarajah's fellow-travellers. Nonetheless, we have put these writings together to honour a friend and colleague whose life's work foreshadowed, and was in any case devoted to explaining, the philosophy cementing the latest turn of events.

While scholars as eminent as Yale's Michael Reisman counsel continuing global economic integration, and reject a return to the old days of the New International Economic Order or outright reversion to protectionism and mercantilism, Sornarajah rejects depictions of the law as a part of the unbreakable march of economic globalisation. Here is the kind of modern contest between alternative visions of the law which this book also tries to explain.

Muthucumaraswamy Sornarajah might sometimes have seemed out of place, dancing to the beat of a different drummer. Yet he was always taken seriously, and his time has come. This book is an attempt to recreate the drumbeats he heard, reveal the subject he sees and show the paths to which his drums lead.

C.L. Lim
Typhoon Season, 2015
HKSAR, China

ACKNOWLEDGEMENTS

My principal debt is to the authors of this volume who selflessly and so enthusiastically set other urgent matters aside to meet a harsh writing schedule. The chapters arrived quickly and fell equally swiftly into place. They have inspired me with their professionalism, camaraderie and good cheer.

Joel Lee, sometime Vice-Dean of the law school at the National University of Singapore, first alerted me to Professor Sornarajah's coming statutory retirement. The idea for the book was conceived in one evening. It would have remained no more than an evening's conversation without the enthusiasm and support of Simon Chesterman, Dean of the NUS law school. Professor Sornarajah made his papers available to me, and the University of Hong Kong's Human Research Ethics Committee granted timely approval to work on them. I thank Simon Young, Associate Dean at HKU, for his advice on the ethical issues, and Michael Hor, our Dean in Hong Kong, for his constant encouragement.

Still, we would not have come this far without Finola O'Sullivan, whose capacity to digest lengthy correspondence while travelling and whose decisiveness in setting an immediate course of action meant that while our project came together with great intensity of purpose, the proposal itself received the early attention of Cambridge University Press. There followed thoughtful and helpful comments and suggestions from two perceptive and careful anonymous referees. They improved upon the original scheme. Joe Ng at the Press steered our project on its onward journey with consummate navigational skill and thoughtfulness.

I have been a fortunate law teacher. Zachary Korman, a native Texan and Lord President Cooper Memorial Prize Scholar at Edinburgh, devoted long hours over many months as my assistant. He kept a weather eye open in respect of every detail from six thousand miles, joined me in reading through the manuscript and making corrections. Zack prepared the table of treaties, legislation and cases. Justine So, now in practice, perhaps suspecting that ideas quickly dreamt up are liable to evaporate, ensured that I could commence the whole project armed only with a phone.

There were other well wishers. Sornarajah's portrait which appears in this book was taken by David Tan, Vice-Dean at NUS, following arrangements made by Jean Ho.

My wife, Lyn, bore a lost holiday with her usual aplomb. Work for this book was completed while I was Lionel A. Sheridan Visiting Professor at NUS, for which I am indebted to the Class of '61.

LIST OF TREATIES, NATIONAL LEGISLATION, CASES AND AWARDS

Treaties and Other Instruments*

* Note that a useful web-site which makes the texts of bilateral investment treaties (BITs) freely and easily accessible is UNCTAD's "Investment Policy Hub" at <www.investment-policyhub.unctad.org>. Similarly for the investment chapters of free trade agreements (FTAs), the WTO maintains a useful "RTA Information System" at <www.rtais.wto.org>. WTO treaties are also available at <www.wto.org>.

United Nations General Assembly Resolutions

National Legislation by Country

China

Ecuador

India

United Kingdom

United States

International Cases

Arbitral Awards

National Cases by Country

Canada

Czech Republic

France

India

Nigeria

Singapore

United Kingdom

United States

PART I

1

The worm's view of history and the twailing machine

C.L. LIM

Introduction

Muthucumaraswamy Sornarajah devoted his career to the study of the international law on foreign investment. In the later part of that career, he turned his attention to a critique of economic neo-liberalism. Using the language of film and photography, he called it "the worm's view of history".[1] He is, for this and other reasons, often regarded as a member of the radical Third World Approaches to International Law (TWAIL) movement.[2] This chapter introduces the reader to Sornarajah's work.[3] I aim to describe his writings over the years in the hope of conveying a flavour of the issues, themes and concerns which so preoccupied him. Subsequent chapters go on to develop upon a broad range of his concerns. These collected writings are offered to him on the occasion of his formal and statutory, albeit not his substantive, retirement from the National University of Singapore.[4] It is also the right time for a book on, and for, Sornarajah. Many of the ensuing chapters seek to capture the

[1] M. Sornarajah, "Power and Justice: Third World Resistance in International Law", (2006) 10 *SYBIL* 19, 26.

[2] Although Sornarajah is a sympathist, this is something which he rejects together with any association with the New Haven School of International Law. I make this plain at the outset since in this book, in this chapter and the concluding chapter, I shall be making frequent references to both TWAIL and Yale. TWAIL is a scholarly movement which is said to have grown out of the graduate research community at the Harvard Law School, but for a longer historical view, see D.P. Fidler, "Revolt Against or from Within the West? TWAIL, the Developing World and the Future Direction of International Law" (2003) 2 *Chinese JIL* 29, 32. See also C.L. Lim, "Neither Peacocks Nor Sheep: T.O. Elias and Postcolonial International Law" (2008) 21 *Leiden JIL* 295.

[3] His friends simply call him "Sorna".

[4] Formerly the University of Singapore, and before that the University of Malaya in Singapore.

current moment in the field as a global backlash against investor-state arbitration continues to unfold.

Viewed in time and against its background events, Sornarajah's body of work may be distinguished from that of a previous generation. His writings cannot be reduced to that historical attempt, following the wave of post-war, post-colonial nationalisations of the 1960s and 1970s, to shape a New International Economic Order (the "NIEO"). He had started writing only after these events, by which time many in the West had considered the efforts of the 1960s and 1970s to have failed. Third World scholars were no longer on the offensive, but they were easily characterised as ideological radicals which time and events had passed. Sorna's writings during this period were marked by subsequent global events instead, and this "post-NIEO" work evolved accordingly. Our story begins in the 1980s when the Cold War was drawing to a close and the economic globalisation era was about to begin. Borrowing a few lessons from biographical history and historical biography, I will also attempt to describe the subsequent backlash against globalisation which had begun in earnest in the late 1990s,[5] culminating in the 2008 Global Financial Crisis.

Turning to the larger field of international law, more specifically the use of its sources, international investment law had shifted from having an uncertain basis in the changing state of customary international rules – grown from the contending practices of industrialised and developing states – to the emergence of a worldwide network of bilateral investment treaties (BITs).[6] In between, there had been various experiments. For a moment, the whole field threatened to shift away from a strict basis in the public international law rules of state responsibility towards a new hybrid form.[7] This had been the result of an attempt to marry public international law rules to contractual commitments. It included the attempt to turn ordinary contractual promises into a new form of public international law promise, and to adapt the principles and

[5] See J. Stiglitz, *Globalisation and Its Discontents* (London: Penguin, 2002), generally.

[6] The book which marked that change was Rudolf Dolzer's and Margerete Stevens' *Bilateral Investment Treaties* (Hague: Kluwer, 1995). See further, C.L. Lim, "The Strange Vitality of Custom in the International Protection of Property, Contracts, and Commerce", in Curtis A. Bradley (ed.), *Custom's Future: International Law in a Changing World* (Cambridge: CUP, in press).

[7] S.W. Schill, "W(h)ither Fragmentation? On the Literature and Sociology of International Investment Law" (2011) 22 *European Journal of International Law* 875–908, available on Global Law Books at www.globallawbooks.org/reviews/detail.asp?id=712 to which page references are here made, 12, 16.

techniques of private commercial arbitration to the settlement of public, non-contractual disputes. Some saw promise in contract and private law because of the uncertainties surrounding international custom. However, by the 1980s a new, worldwide regime of thousands of international investment treaties had become firmly established, even in the Third World. As treaty law gained ascendance, contractual innovations were no longer so sorely required by international capital to assure its protection when abroad. In time, the process of settling investment disputes also became treaty-based, by which I mean that a claim could be brought before arbitration even in the absence of a breach by the host state of any existing investment contract. The most important work which private law did, however, in the attempt to create a modern international investment system was to extend the teachings of commercial arbitration to a new form of treaty-based claim. Eventually, contract, its role for now largely spent, ceased to be as important in supplying either the cause of action or in binding the parties to arbitration.[8]

Sornarajah's work began on the arbitration of disputes involving state contracts with foreign investors.[9] But his training as an international lawyer meant that he also had an acute appreciation of the hierarchy of legal norms. This led him to remain true to his subject, in the face of the rapid developments just described, and to favour the controlling role of public international law precepts and doctrines over the private law precepts of the commercial arbitration lawyer.[10] He considered commercial arbitration's doctrines especially unsuitable for their adaptation *holus*

[8] Commercial arbitration had earlier been used in disputes over foreign investment contracts; see M. Sornarajah, *International Commercial Arbitration* (Singapore: Longman, 1990). Subsequently, the growing popularity of investment treaty arbitration under the North American Free Trade Agreement (NAFTA) marked the emergence of arbitrations which proceeded without an arbitration clause in a contract, or "arbitration without privity", J. Paulsson, "Arbitration without Privity" (1995) 10 *ICSID Rev-FILJ* 232. This development had begun earlier in *SPP* v. *Republic of Egypt* (the "Pyramid Oasis" Case) (1991) 16 YB Comm Arb. 28, which had concerned a unilateral promise of arbitration under a national investment promotion law. This insight was applied to BIT undertakings to arbitrate in *AAPL* v. *Sri Lanka*, ICSID Case No. ARB/87/3 (1990); 4 *ICSID Rep*. 245 (1991); 6 *ICSID Rev-FILJ* 526 (1991), 30 *ILM* 577, the first BIT arbitration; Paulsson, "Arbitration without Privity", 234–236. Sornarajah calls this insight the "original sin", M. Sornarajah, *Resistance and Change in the International Law on Foreign Investment* (Cambridge: CUP, 2015), 139.

[9] See Sornarajah's *International Commercial Arbitration*, generally.

[10] Indeed, even the new arbitral jurisprudence which subsequently emerged with the explosion of BIT-based arbitration has at best only an uncertain effect on public international law doctrine; see, however, A. Bjorklund, "Investment Treaty Arbitral Decisions as *Jurisprudence Constante*", in C.B. Picker *et al.* (eds.), *International Economic Law: The*

bolus (in their entirety) to the settlement of what essentially were disputes over the application of public international law rules on foreign investment. Rather, his view reflected a traditional conception of international economic law as that body of law dealing with the economic relations of states.[11]

This is the Sornarajah whom most readers know.

Muthucumaraswamy Sornarajah

Muthucumaraswamy Sornarajah was born on 24 April 1942 in Manipay, located in the Northern district of Jaffna.[12] Jaffna was the principal city of the Tamil people of Ceylon (now, Sri Lanka). Only weeks before, Japan, fresh from its conquest of Singapore, had carried out the terrifying Easter Sunday Raid on Ceylon, which in 1948 went on to gain independence as a dominion. As a schoolboy, he attended the Royal College in Colombo, the "Eton of Ceylon", and was among the last to be taught Latin and Greek, subjects then entrusted by the Royal College to Mr E.F.C. Pereira. It was not an easy time, for tension had commenced between the majority Sinhalese and the minority Tamil races. Sorna recalls being tutored with equal devotion by both Sinhalese and Tamil masters, and to have been shaped almost exclusively by Sinhalese teachers. He had been a rebellious child who when made to stand outside the classroom as punishment would do so on his head in order to better torment his schoolmaster.[13] Sorna was to be as quick subsequently in his understanding of the exploitation of normative ambiguity and to develop a habit of turning things on their head, but I shall not rush the story.

In 1948, the Immigration Act was passed, denying citizenship to Indian Tamils who had worked on Ceylon's tea estates. By 1956, Sinhalese had also been made the sole national language. It had the effect

State and Future of the Discipline (Oxford: Hart, 2008), 265; *contra* Sornarajah, *Resistance and Change*, 50, 53.

[11] Professor McRae has attributed this classic view to Georg Schwarzenberger, Ignaz Seidl-Hohenveldern and the 1971 Colloque d'Orlèans; D.M. McRae, "The Contribution of International Trade Law to the Development of International Law" (1998) 275 *RdC* 99, 120–122.

[12] The account in this section has relied on access to Professor Sornarajah's private papers at the author's request. The use of these papers is governed by Hong Kong University's rules on research ethics in the conduct of non-clinical research on human subjects. I am grateful to Professor Sornarajah, and to the relevant university committee for granting me their permission.

[13] There is no mention in his private papers of the name of this kindly school teacher.

of depriving young Tamils of access to careers in the public service which, traditionally, had presented an alternative to working in the tea estates. Sorna's own maternal grandfather had joined the Malayan Civil Service where by 1896 there had emerged a common system of recruitment through the Far Eastern Cadetships for the Ceylonese, Malayan and Hong Kong services.

In 1958, the first anti-Tamil riots began.[14]

Sorna's home was not spared the violence although in a fit of athleticism rarely to be seen later in life, he managed to save it from being burned to the ground by swinging onto the roof to kick away the petrol bombs. The boy of 16 years and his old grandmother fled. Together with his family, he went from one and thereafter to another refugee camp.[15] Fortunately, he was soon to win entry to the University of Ceylon, eventually graduating LLB with a rare First Class Honours. The university became a sanctuary. The *Mahaveli Ganga* ran through it with – if you could just imagine the place through Sorna's own description – waterfalls from the hills which surrounded the campus forming rivulets which fed that great river. The head of school was Professor Nadarajah who taught from R.W. Lee's book on Roman Dutch Law and presented a virtual annotation of it.[16] For all three years there, Sorna was taught by Mr Rajah Goonesekere, "an Oxford-trained lawyer" Sorna remarks in his private papers, and subsequently the principal of the Law College. It was he who left a lasting impression upon his student, and it is Mr Goonesekere to whom Sorna attributes his own method of teaching ex tempore with few notes. As for style, Sorna saw cause for emulation there too – mastery of the law is a pre-requisite but opinions are to be freely ventured. He became, in due course, Mr Goonesekere's successor at the University of Ceylon, teaching the subjects the latter had taught.

His first teacher in international law, however, was that titan, Dr Chittharanjan Felix ("C.F.") Amerasinghe, who at the time was completing his own work on state responsibility for injuries to aliens. A privileged

[14] T. Vitachi, *Emergency '58: The Story of the Ceylon Race Riots* (London: André Deutsch, 1959).

[15] I have mentioned all of this as it seems extreme adversity deriving from ethnicity, and national circumstances is not unusual in the making of international lawyers, and the point could have some value for future research. As Sornarajah has observed in his private papers, the pattern of events described here is of course also familiar to those elsewhere in the Commonwealth.

[16] R.W. Lee, *The Elements of Roman Law*, 4th ed. (London: Sweet & Maxwell, 1956).

young Sorna was granted access to Dr Amerasinghe's unfinished chapters,[17] sparking an early love for our subject.

He eventually attended the Yale Law School (LLM) and was to be much influenced by the policy science method developed there, notwithstanding his lifelong ambivalence towards that approach which I shall mention later. He also attended the federal University of London, graduating both LLM and PhD, where his courses – which were mainly in international law with a smattering of criminal law – were split between those offered at King's College on the Strand, and the London School of Economics nearby on Houghton Street. It was common at the time, although less so now, that international lawyers were given a place to teach in a law school on condition that they could also make themselves useful by teaching a bread-and-butter legal subject. Sorna had obtained an assistant lectureship at the University of Ceylon beforehand. His agreement with the university was that he would be responsible for the teaching of criminal law. The fact that permission to read for a PhD degree had been granted meant also that it had to be done in a hurry, in time for him to return to his duties in November of 1970 at the University of Ceylon. Again, this was not uncommon for those who had nascent teaching careers. In any case, it justified a decision to write on what he already, largely, knew of the criminal law. He had not, in his view, the luxury to properly pursue research in international law. What England did, however, was to confirm in his mind that it was international law that he wanted to do, that and a lifelong membership of the British Labour Party.

In later life, Sorna was awarded a higher doctorate (LLD) by London University. As required by the statutes for the degree, it was awarded on the basis of his collected works in international law.

His teaching career, as I mentioned, had already begun earlier in 1966, as an assistant lecturer at the University of Ceylon, and he was subsequently promoted to the position of Lecturer in Law. These were eventful years, tumultuous politically, but which resulted nonetheless in three articles on criminal law-related matters in the *International and Comparative Law Quarterly* (*ICLQ*) and an agreement to constitute what became a long and happy marriage for the past 40-odd years. He did eventually get to teach international law when his former teacher, C.F. Amerasinghe, left to pursue a subsequently distinguished career at the World Bank. But Ceylon was then

[17] C.F. Ameransinghe, *State Responsibility for Injuries to Aliens* (Oxford: Clarendon, 1967).

already in the grip of violence resulting from the *Jathika Vimukthi Peramuna*'s ("The Race's Salvation Front's") racial politics. Sorna recalls that in response, the Government "callously eliminated ... many thousands of youth, both innocent and guilty ... Among them were many university students."[18] In any event, eventually, communalist politics took over. Government facilities were reserved for the Sinhalese, the sons of the soil, and Buddhism became the state religion. It was cause for discomfort that the sixth-century Buddhist text, the *Mahavamsa*, which preached that the killing of Tamils is not a sin, had by then become a schoolchild's textbook.[19] It influenced the sort of history taught in the schools and played a role in entrenching majoritarian communalism.[20]

Sorna served on the Senate of the University of Ceylon, and as Proctor of the University of Colombo in which capacity he had been responsible for student discipline during that very difficult time. It was as I had mentioned the time of the uprising of the Jathika Vimukthi Peramuna, which attracted many Sinhalese university students. As Proctor, Sorna came into contact with these students. He recalls that:[21]

> After the ruthless crushing of the uprising by the military, many of the students, some of them innocent of any participation in the movement, did not turn up for lectures. This was a sad and haunting event. The brutality of the army that was unleashed on the Tamils later had started much earlier with communal politics seeping into the universities in Sri Lanka.

Sorna eventually made the decision in 1974 to continue his career at the University of Tasmania, joining the Department of Law there as a lecturer following an interview with Professor Derek Roebuck. Life for Tamil academics had become too difficult in his native land and here was a kindly man offering the chance of escape.[22]

The early foundations of his reputation as an international lawyer were laid during those happy Tasmanian years. He continued to write for the

[18] Correspondence with Professor Sornarajah, 23 June 2015.

[19] B.R. Rubin, *Cycles of Violence: Human Rights in Sri Lanka since the Indo-Sri Lanka Agreement* (Washington, DC: Asia Watch, 1987), 128.

[20] As described to the author, correspondence with Professor Sornarajah, 23 June 2015.

[21] *Id.*

[22] In light of his experiences, Sornarajah has, throughout his career, maintained a deep interest in the issues of self-determination, secession and minority rights in international law, and has played a pivotal role in relation to these matters. That, however, is not the subject of this collection.

ICLQ, and had begun work on the international law on foreign investment which eventually became *The Pursuit of Nationalised Property*.[23] The Tasmania faculty at the time was destined to become an illustrious lot. At the time, it included Frank Bates, Norman Palmer and Don Chalmers. By 1985, Sorna had served for four years as the head of the department but in 1986, by which time there was one book, a further edited work and eleven articles in the *ICLQ*, he decided to join the National University of Singapore as an associate professor.

In Singapore, he was eventually promoted to full professor in 1995, having produced the *International Law on Foreign Investment* in 1994, which the very distinguished reviewer in the *British Yearbook of International Law* considered worthy of becoming a classic.[24] Classic or not, it immediately became a new subject in the law school curriculum. Sorna subsequently assumed the present title of C.J. Koh Professor of Law. He kept up with his international links; with the United States as a visiting professor at the American University at Washington, and with visiting appointments at the Lauterpacht Centre in Cambridge, the world-leading Centre for Petroleum and Mineral Law at the University of Dundee and a period spent at the Max Planck Institute. He engaged in policy work as a consultant to the United Nations Conference on Trade and Development, serving in several well-known roles. He also occupied himself in capacity-building work in Vietnam and Sri Lanka under the auspices of the United Nations Development Programme and the World Bank.

While his academic reputation is known widely, Sorna's prestigious practice as an arbitrator and counsel also deserves mention. He had qualified to practise law in Sri Lanka, in England and Wales, and before the Supreme Court of Singapore. Today, his name crops up regularly in the usual discreet soundings taken over long-distance telephone calls. But he does not speak about these professional roles.[25] He was co-arbitrator (with Messrs Schwebel and Cardenas) in *Perusahaan Umum Listrik*

[23] M. Sornarajah, *The Pursuit of Nationalised Property* (Dordrecht: Nijhoff, 1986). See also M. Sornarajah (ed.), *The South West Dam Case: The Legal and Political Issues* (Hobart: University of Tasmania, 1983).

[24] M. Sornarajah, *The International Law on Foreign Investment*, 1st ed. (Cambridge: CUP, 1994). This book is, hereinafter, referred to as "Foreign Investment". Subsequent editions are referred to with an indication of the particular edition. For the review, see E. Denza, "Book Review" (1994) 65 *BYIL* 483, 484.

[25] Perhaps that is fitting for a scholar-practitioner, whose sensibilities and needs are rather different from those of practitioner-scholars in the field of arbitration practice.

Negara (Electricity Board of Indonesia) and the Republic of Indonesia v. *PT Paiton Energy Company* (1999) (the "PT Paiton" arbitration),[26] and had served as sole arbitrator in other arbitrations. He enjoyed sitting in arbitrations with Lord Hoffman and Lord Phillips. Sorna was also lead counsel for the claimants in *Yaung Chi Oo Ltd* v. *The Government of the Union of Myanmar* (2002), heard before three distinguished arbitrators (Messrs Sucharitkul, Crawford and Delon).[27] That dispute had involved the naked seizure of an investment by the Burmese army, and Sorna hoped to convert the case into one which would expose military atrocities in Myanmar. He served as counsel in *Merbok Hilir Ltd* v. *Board of Investment (Sri Lanka)* (ICC Arbitration) and he also served as an expert largely on the side of states, producing an extensive opinion in *El Paso* v. *Argentina*,[28] an experience he particularly enjoyed, and also in *Council of Canadians and Ors.* v. *Canada* in which the Council of Canadians and the Canadian Union of Postal Workers had challenged the constitutionality of the North Atlantic Free Trade Agreement's (NAFTA's) investment rules.[29]

He is, however, a full-time law teacher whose love – to paraphrase Lord Bramwell – is not of fees,[30] and whose title of professor is not a mere enticement for them.[31] A professor involved in the private dispensation

[26] See M. Sornarajah and R. Arumugam, "An Overview of the Foreign Direct Investment Jurisprudence", in Denis Hew (ed.), *Brick by Brick: The Building of an ASEAN Economic Community* (Singapore: ISEAS, 2007), 144, 160.

[27] *Yaung Chi Oo Trading Pte. Ltd.* v. *Government of the Union of Myanmar*, ASEAN I.D. Case No. ARB/01/1, 31 March 2003 (2003); 8 ICSID Reports 463 (2003); 42 ILM 430. This arbitration is well known for it stands for the effectiveness of having an "admissions model" BIT requiring approval of an investment for the investment to qualify as such. On this point, see also *Rafat Ali Rizvi* v. *Indonesia*, ICSID Case No. ARB/11/13, 16 July 2013 (Griffith President, Donoghue, Sornarajah), para. 61. *Yaung Chi Oo* is discussed in some detail in Sornarajah and Arumugam, "An Overview of the Foreign Direct Investment Jurisprudence", 163 *et seq.*

[28] Legal Opinion of M. Sornarajah, *El Paso* v. *Argentina*, ICSID Case No. ARB/03/15, 5 March 2007. The dispute, as is well known, arose from the Argentinian economic crisis, the consequent devaluation of the currency and the subsequent "pesification" policy. Although Sornarajah's argument regarding the absence of standing in minority shareholders was eventually rejected, his argument on the necessity defence was upheld and this had an effect on other Argentinian cases.

[29] Affidavit of M. Sornarajah, Ontario Superior Court of Justice, Court File 01-CV-208141.

[30] *Salt* v. *Marquess of Northampton* [1892] AC 1, 18–19 ("But the piety or love of fees of those who administered equity have thought otherwise").

[31] In the practising community, use of the title is now widespread, even among those who one might suppose would have considered academic life wearisome and the idea of having substantive writing commitments to be professionally hazardous. This is not to say that the field as a whole is not fortunate to have many eminent academic experts.

of commercial justice is nothing new under the sun, but Sorna is noticeably mindful of the value of a reputation acquired for scholarly and professional impartiality.[32]

Overview of Sornarajah's works

State investment contracts

Aside from *The Pursuit of Nationalised Property*, Sornarajah's early major works were on state contracts, in the contexts of international joint ventures and the settlement of investment contract disputes through commercial arbitration. These other early books are perhaps less well known, especially when compared to his *International Law on Foreign Investment*. However, the thrust of his later works cannot be properly understood without some appreciation of his earlier writings.

Sorna's concerns had been disciplinary at the outset, having much to do with the evolution of specific doctrines in the field. He wrote at a time when investment disputes were typically contractual. If he has been less than enthusiastic about our current attempts to expand treaty protection, it is because of his view that absent solid customary rules, contractual commitments are often still required to pin down the obligations states might owe to investors and that here lie doctrinal limits to what contract can do which cannot always be cured by treaty law.[33]

It was only when Sorna's views became more fully developed that he proceeded to mount his current theoretical attack on economic neo-liberalism.[34] We should therefore separate his earlier doctrinal writings from this latest theoretical effort.

As I have tried to suggest, Sorna's first concern had been to reveal and develop the international law on foreign investment, especially from the time when public international law precepts were only beginning to be

[32] It is sometimes uncritically accepted that a person whose writings reveal little might be more desirable than an ample scholar in the field. Perhaps one cannot be so naïve about competing professional concerns, for it is unlikely that the risk of challenges based upon issue conflicts will disappear. See further, *Urbaser* v. *Argentina*, decision on Claimant's Proposal to Disqualify Professor Campbell McLachlan, ICSID Case No. ARB/07/26, 12 August 2010. Yet it would be a shame for the most qualified writers to suppress their scholarship as a result. *Cf.* Sornarajah's views on scholarship and the practising profession in his *Resistance and Change*, 61.

[33] *Supra* note 7, and Chapters 13 and 14.

[34] His writings on economic neo-liberalism are now expanded in his latest book; Sornarajah, *Resistance and Change*.

adapted to mixed arbitrations. The rules on the protection of foreign-owned property, starting with the upheavals of the Russian and Mexican revolutions, were subsequently thrown into disarray after the Second World War. There had previously been feeble references in the doomed Havana Charter to the protection of foreign investments and its likely effect on capital flows,[35] but it is at least well known that both Harry Dexter White and John Maynard Keynes, the architects of the Bretton Woods design, had favoured closed capital accounts.[36] Capital found its way abroad eventually,[37] but only after the protection of foreign investments in the minerals and extractive sectors were left out of the design of the multilateral international economic system. Subsequently, a wave of post-war nationalisations by the newly decolonised developing nations took place. Settled law did not play a dominant role in the eventual practice which developed from negotiating lump-sum settlements instead.[38] Furthermore, these nationalisations became bound up with a fierce debate over global reform of the norms concerning expropriation, particularly the standard of compensation. This debate was to play out concurrently in the multilateral diplomatic arena, chiefly in the United Nations General Assembly,[39] and before arbitration tribunals. The Libyan experience at the time is a good illustration of this. In any event, customary international law became torn between the interests and demands of the industrialised capital-exporting nations on the one side and the emergent Third World on the other. Starting with the German–Pakistani treaty of 1959, the movement towards concluding BITs proceeded alongside this development as capital sought better protection. That movement did so largely according to the private design of Hermann Abs and Lord Shawcross, and the efforts of the Organisation for Economic Co-operation and Development (OECD).[40]

[35] Chiefly, in Articles 11(1)(b) and 12; see A. Lowenfeld, *International Economic Law*, 2nd ed. (Oxford: OUP, 2008), 482–483. See further, S. Wolf, "The Regulation of Foreign Direct Investment under WTO Agreements – Is There Still a Case for a Multilateral Agreement on Investment?", in C. Tietje (ed.), *International Investment, Protection and Arbitration* (Berlin: BWV, 2008), 71, 74–75.

[36] See further, C.L. Lim and B. Mercurio, "The Fragmented Disciplines of International Economic Law after the Global and Financial Crisis: An Introduction", in C.L. Lim and B. Mercurio (eds.), *International Economic Law after the Global Crisis: A Tale of Fragmented Disciplines* (Cambridge: CUP, 2016), 1, 8, 12; D.E. Moggridge, *Maynard Keynes: An Economist's Biography* (London: Routledge, 1992), 673.

[37] *Id.*, 12 et seq. [38] Lowenfeld, *International Economic Law*, 485. [39] *Id.*, 486–493.

[40] See R. Dolzer and C. Schreuer, *Principles of International Investment Law*, 2nd ed. (Oxford: OUP, 2012), 8.

The Washington Convention of 1965,[41] driven by the efforts of Aron Broches, also subsequently became an important part of the development of a global system for the protection of foreign investment. According to Broches' scheme, the standards of protection were to be derived from the BITs but the dispute settlement apparatus was to be supplied by the Convention instead.

There was to be another twist to the story for while the movement towards having BITs gained pace, contract became – ultimately – a temporary device to bridge the gap then existing between custom and treaty. This caused ever-bolder innovations in contractual design and drafting and also in the pleadings of claimants in third-party disputes.[42]

Sorna's early books – *International Commercial Arbitration*, which had been published in 1990, and *Law of International Joint Ventures*, which appeared in 1992 – focused on investment contracts, an interest he had also developed from teaching international business transactions.[43] These early Singapore works were written not long after his Tasmanian monograph, *The Pursuit of Nationalised Property*, published in 1986, in which he had welcomed the emergence of the international law of development,[44] and adopted a view of expropriations law which was broadly similar to that taken by the Third World nations. *Pursuit* also included treatment of the way the domestic courts handled expropriation claims, leading Sornarajah to develop an early interest in the law on foreign state immunity and Acts of State.[45]

Broadly speaking, his interests evolved from an interest in international customary rules to an interest in domestic judicial remedies, and subsequently to the formulation of international contracts and the arbitration of contractually based investment disputes. He had written a noteworthy article in 1979, entering the fray on that great question of the day – the standard of compensation for expropriation.[46] It was a work on what then were recent developments. The full-blown critique of

[41] Convention on the Settlement of Investment Disputes between States and Nationals of other States, 18 March 1965, 575 UNTS 159, also known as the "ICSID" or "Washington" Convention.

[42] See further, Lim, "Strange Vitality".

[43] See Sornarajah, *International Commercial Arbitration*, v; M. Sornarajah, *Law of International Joint Ventures* (Singapore: Longman, 1992), vii.

[44] Sornarajah, *Pursuit*, 14.

[45] This is a field in which, notably, he has not – or not yet – developed his interest into book-length form.

[46] M. Sornarajah, "Compensation for Expropriation: The Emergence of New Standards" (1979) *13 JWTL* 108.

economic neo-liberalism which we have today only came much later. In between time has – and did – upset many fighting faiths,[47] and Sornarajah set out to track the development of legal doctrine roughly from the 1980s to the present time; over a span of 35 years.

There is no doubt where Sorna fell, at least as a scholar, when it came to the debate between the Third World countries and the industrialised countries during the 1960s and 1970s.[48] Yet part of the reason for his preference for the "Third World viewpoint" was shaped by a search for doctrinal bedrock. Sorna's project was not ideological. Rather, it was doctrinal with, as we shall see, a social–scientific dimension.

He had begun mapping out the development of international legal doctrine according to a particular social science methodology just when the pendulum was swinging anew in favour of the industrialised nations. This may have contributed to his reaction against that swing. It was an important time, following the doubt which until then had been cast on classical nineteenth-century views on the protection of foreign-owned property.

The International Law on Foreign Investment *in the age of normlessness*

The International Law on Foreign Investment eventually appeared in 1994. To Sornarajah, it was still a time of doctrinal uncertainty although there was a widespread perception that the Third World governments were already in full retreat. Subsequently, Third World unity would be broken altogether by the pragmatic demand for capital and investments. Against that background, however, some of his early readers concluded – to quote Matthew Arnold – that Sornarajah's work was only a melancholy, long, withdrawing roar.[49] But it would have been a mistake to think that *International Law on Foreign Investment* had only occupied itself with a historical subject.

[47] *Abrams* v. *United States* 250 US 616 (1919), *per* Holmes J. (dissent) ("time has upset many fighting faiths").

[48] T. Wälde, "Book Review", *Int'l Bus Lawyer*, September 1996, 393, 394.

[49] Matthew Arnold's "Dover Beach", in J. Wain (ed.), *The Oxford Library of English Poetry*, Vol III, Darley to Heaney (Oxford: OUP, 1986), 166, 167. American legal textbook writers take the view that by then the Washington Consensus had already triumphed, see (e.g.) R.H. Folsom *et al.*, *International Business Transactions: A Problem-Oriented Coursebook*, 11th ed. (St Paul, MN: West, 2012), 5. The late Andreas Lowenfeld, *International Economic Law*, 468, had put it more gently by writing that "[i]n the 1980s the fundamentals began to change".

As we have seen, the 1960s–1980s witnessed attempts by Western industrialised nations to introduce greater protection and stability for investments abroad to counter the previous efforts of the new nations of the Global South. The new nations were, in Henry Kissinger's sense,[50] a revolutionary force and were almost certainly seen at the time to have been a dangerous and destabilising force against what the developed nations viewed to be the legitimate world order.

Following the groundwork laid by the BITs and the Washington Convention, the arbitration of BIT disputes had also emerged by the early 1990s, but to Sornarajah, especially, the world had yet to settle the proper arrangements for decolonisation's aftermath. The new devices which the industrialised nations fashioned were no doubt restrained in their own view, and these as I said had initially been contractual in nature. However, by the early 1990s both NAFTA and the Energy Charter Treaty presaged a new beginning for the industrialised world's viewpoint.[51]

Sorna had been quick to notice the shift from customary international law protection of foreign property to contractual means of protection, but at least at the time of the first edition of *International Law on Foreign Investment* the subsequent explosion of investment arbitration under BIT investor-state dispute settlement had yet to occur. The contractual devices which mainstream scholars in the industrialised West advocated were chiefly of two kinds – (1) "internationalised" contractual instruments, and (2) contractual dispute settlement clauses.

Internationalised contractual commitments

While, as we have seen, international law's governance of contested expropriations went through a period of post-war uncertainty which lasted into the 1980s,[52] attempts were made from the 1960s onwards to elevate the host state's contractual commitments to the level of international law protection. This took the form of an innovative idea – that of

50 H.A. Kissinger, *A World Restored: Metternich, Castlereagh and the Problems of Peace, 1812–1822* (London: Phoenix, 2000), 3 (". . . it is the essence of a revolutionary power that it possesses the courage of its convictions, that it is willing, indeed eager, to push its principles to their ultimate conclusion. Whatever else a revolutionary power may achieve therefore, it tends to erode, if not the legitimacy of the international order, at least the restraint with which such an order operates").

51 Paulsson, "Arbitration without Privity", 233.

52 Lowenfeld, *International Economic Law*, 484–485.

the internationalised contract,[53] for which the basis was said to lie outside the domain of municipal law altogether. Instead, the basis of the new internationalised contractual device was said to lie in the international doctrine of *pacta sunt servanda*. According to this view, it mattered not that a private contract with a foreign state could not amount to a treaty, the important point was that international law also required agreements to be honoured. The internationalised contract was to become a Janus-faced conceptual device, having an "internal" and an "external" aspect.[54]

In its internal aspect, it consisted of the drafting of specialised contractual clauses. These were chiefly (1) *stabilisation clauses* – existence of which was said to be indicative of internationalisation – which, while they chose a governing national law, sought to insulate national rules from future changes on the basis that obedience to such clauses was required by international law;[55] (2) *choice of law clauses*, which were express attempts to remove any connection between the host state's laws and the contract;[56] and, finally, (3) *arbitration clauses* in state contracts, which it was anticipated would not only remove the dispute from the reach of the host state's domestic courts but also forestall claims to foreign state immunity before the courts of third states. The existence of an arbitration clause was said to be indicative of internationalisation.[57]

The external aspect, in turn, consisted of evidence of internationalisation which is extraneous to the contract. This – according to the well known *Texaco* v. *Libya* Award – included consideration of the benefits which the foreign investment would have brought to the developing country, the long-term duration of investment contracts and the financial magnitude of the investment.[58]

Sornarajah mounted a fierce challenge to all these devices and arguments.[59]

53 See (e.g.) A. McNair, "The General Principles of Law Recognised by Civilised Nations" (1957) 33 *BYIL* 1; I. Seidl-Hohenveldern, "Recollections of Alfred Verdross" (1994) 5 *EJIL* 98, 102; F.A. Mann, *Studies in International Law* (Oxford: OUP, 1972), 143; A. von Mehren, "Special Substantive Rules for Multistate Problems" (1974) 88 *Harv. L. Rev.* 347.

54 Sornarajah, *Pursuit*, 85.

55 See (e.g.) *Kuwait-Aminoil Award*, 24 March 1982 (1982) 21 ILM 976, 94–97, 102; also reproduced in Lowenfeld, *International Economic Law*, 507–508.

56 Sornarajah, *Pursuit*, 101 *et seq.*

57 *Id.*, 98 *et seq.* See also the arbitrator's famous view in *Texaco v. Libya*, (1977) 53 ILR 389 (1978), 17 ILM 1, paras. 40–45.

58 *Texaco* v. *Libya* (1977) 53 ILR 389 (1978); 17 ILM 1 (Dupuy, sole arbitrator); Sornarajah. *Pursuit*, 86.

59 For a summary today of these earlier criticisms which he had made, see further, M. Sornarajah, *The International Law on Foreign Investment*, 3rd ed. (Cambridge: CUP. 2010), 279–299.

From contractual to treaty-based arbitration clauses

I have already mentioned contractual arbitration clauses, and Sorna's objection to the view that somehow these could, according to Verdross and others, "internationalise" the underlying contract.[60] Such contractual clauses presaged an even more radical eventual device, namely, treaty (i.e. BIT) arbitration clauses which contained the promise of the host state to submit to arbitration without requiring any immediate contractual nexus with the foreign investor.[61] Ultimately, as BITs – the bilateral investment treaties referred to earlier – grew in popularity, treaty arbitration clauses became an altogether new basis of consent to arbitration; notwithstanding the fact that such treaties were only concluded between the home and the host state.

Sorna's objection was that this not only offended the doctrine of privity of contract but also that, as in the case of *Fedax* v. *Venezuela*, where holders of promissory notes had transferred the notes to new holders in order to enjoy BIT protection,[62] the result was a grant of third-party rights to an unascertainable class of persons.

Against the complex of contractual "Internationalising" devices

In 1994, Sornarajah's focus remained contractual, and he argued against all these devices – stabilisation, choice of law and arbitration clauses – and the arguments justifying their use. His critics may not agree with him, but the point I wish to make is that, at the time when he first expressed these views, the devices themselves were still relatively new legal innovations. Viewed in their proper historical context, Sorna's

60 Sornarajah, *Pursuit*, 98, citing Verdross for saying that a state contract containing an arbitration clause "is not a contract governed by the legal order of a state, but a new legal order established by the common will of the parties on the basis of the principle pacta sunt servanda and other general principles of law governing contracts", A. Verdross, "Quasi-International Agreements and International Economic Transactions" (1964) 18 *YBWA* 230, 234–235.

61 Absence of such a nexus was to be cured by the subsequent notification of the investor's intent to arbitrate. This is readily accepted in ICSID arbitration where enforcement is also not a difficulty. As for non-ICSID arbitration, notification in writing may be claimed to be sufficient to fulfil the writing requirement of the Convention on the Recognition and Enforcement of Foreign Arbitral Awards of 1958, 10 June 1958, 330 UNTS 38 (New York Convention), and of any corresponding national law of the seat of the arbitration. However, Sornarajah has asked if tribunals should allow such claims, in the absence of a specific treaty commitment by the host state, such as in the case of the Washington Convention, to allow arbitration without privity.

62 *Fedax NV* v. *Venezuela* (1998) 37 ILM 1378.

arguments were directed against what he saw as proposals for a new form of law. This should be kept especially in mind when ascribing certain "old-fashioned" views to Sornarajah today. To a great extent his continuing criticism of these devices involves an implicit and pragmatic concession that, notwithstanding his own views, many international lawyers and legal practitioners seem strangely content to embrace the validity and efficacy of such devices.

Why then have his views been so remarkably consistent – or put more bluntly, unchanging – throughout? To answer that question, we would need to understand Sornarajah's thoughts on the nature and methods of international lawyering.

New Haven

We need to know his legal methodology. In *International Law on Foreign Investment*, Sornarajah commences with the claim that the field can no longer be explained through positivist legal analysis.[63] Equally, "idealistic theories" based upon "morality and conscience" are unreliable in a situation where "value systems of somewhat equal moral validity are in collision". So long as the Western industrialised view was under assault from the new developing states, there was the risk of a legal vacuum unless "decision makers and scholars" set upon the task of proposing acceptable norms.[64] Sorna considered the law to be in a "normless state".[65] However, he appears to draw back some 16 pages on, saying that "[t]he fact that the law is presently mired in conflict does not show the absence of law" and that "[i]n each situation a set of principles will have to prevail" on the basis of a "confluence or convergence" between the basic rules of the systems of the developed and developing states.[66]

Nonetheless, Sorna's concern was to point out that "[w]hat is passed off as custom by the different contending groups can hardly satisfy the stringent standards required by international law".[67]

These are telling passages which need to be understood before we conclude that Sornarajah's views reflect some simple, obstinate denial of subsequent legal developments.[68] Rather, his view was that,

[63] Sornarajah had at first been trained in the orthodox, doctrinal fashion by Dr Chittharanjan Felix Amerasinghe (C.F. Amerasinghe) at the University of Ceylon.

[64] Sornarajah, *Foreign Investment*, 3–4. [65] *Id.*, 4. [66] *Id.*, 20. [67] *Id.*, 21.

[68] A key example of such "obstinacy" has been a denial of the ability of the sovereign from making a binding unilateral commitment *sans* concomitant treaty obligation (e.g.

notwithstanding the absence of settled law, one could commence a search for acceptable doctrines.[69] Put simply, the law is something to be prescribed, not discovered, and as we will also see, his view of international investment law is that it will never become fully settled. There is an inherent tension between competing values in the law which will cause, what he calls, "the pendulum" to swing to and fro between competing views over time. What propels the pendulum is the pressure of opposing social forces.[70]

Sornarajah's search for acceptable doctrines was influenced by a particular method championed by his professors at the Yale Law School. In a seminal 1959 article, Myres McDougal and Harold Lasswell had advocated a forward-looking or "policy-orientated" approach to law. This required a healthy dose of scepticism towards legal claims generally,[71] which was fostered by the new mood of American Legal Realism that prevailed at the time. As a critic once observed of McDougal and William Burke, "the authors appear to regard their task as that of constructing rather than finding the law".[72]

To be sure, Sorna never fully converted to the Yale method. He had been taught at the University of Ceylon that having "a solid basis in law", which is only to be discovered under the stringent conventional requirements for the formation of custom, was a prerequisite to any sound legal

through legislation) to a private investor; *id.*, 86–87. That passage remains unchanged, Sornarajah, *Foreign Investment*, 3rd ed., 90–91. But even this point has been misrepresented. He had, in these same pages, accepted from the time of the first edition that whether or not states can bind their future laws under contract is a "hotly debated issue" – see page 91 of the third edition, reproducing the same passage which first appeared on page 87 of the first edition. However, we find one reviewer saying that Sornarajah had seriously doubted the idea that sovereign states can bind themselves to multinational corporations, and that on the flip-side this raises a real problem for the host state which wants to attract foreign investment; A. Guzman, "Book Review" (1995) 6 *EJIL* 612, 613.

69 Professor Peter Muchlinski, who is a contributor to this volume, criticised this aspect of Sornarajah's work as being too idealistic, for there was simply little hope of consensus in the field; P. Muchlinski, "Book Review" (1996) 59 *MLR* 482, 483.

70 In the final chapter to this volume, I go on to call this his "Newtonian" view of the law.

71 M.S. McDougal and H.D. Lasswell, "The Identification and Appraisal of Diverse Systems of Public Order" (1959) 53 *AJIL* 1, 5.

72 P. Allott, "Language, Method and the Nature of International Law" (1978) 45 *BYIL* 79, 121. A student of Lasswell and McDougal ("L & M") put it this way: "Conflict resolution, thus, is part of the L & M board game including pre-emptive resolution by evaluating a policy before it goes into effect"; C.W.T. Stephenson, *Transparency Cantos: Values for Human Dignity: Lasswell and McDougal* (Washington, DC: Torquilstone Press, 2002), 7. I thank Mr Charles W.T. Stephenson for handing me this privately printed work.

reasoning.[73] His discovery of normlessness in the protection of foreign investments, however, was to liberate him. Now, he could freely combine the need for careful surveys of the law according to the traditional positivist method with the radical Yale approach. It was the age of rock and roll, and our legal scholar took to it.

Notwithstanding its roots in American Realism, the Yale method was also an offspring of Poundian social engineering,[74] essentially opposed to mere exposition of the law.[75] Harvard's Roscoe Pound, for whom "mechanical jurisprudence" led to "backwardness of law in meeting social ends",[76] had earlier popularised the following view in the law schools and at the Bar:[77]

> I have suggested thinking of jurisprudence as a science of social engineering . . . It is an organized body of knowledge with respect to the means of satisfying human demands, securing interests, giving effect to claims and desires, with the least friction and the least waste, so far as these things can be brought about by the legal order . . . As one of the social sciences, jurisprudence has for its field to discover what part of this task may be achieved or furthered by the legal order and how.

One description of the Yale approach puts it this way: "Its aim would be to find an answer to which all can assent rationally, not because others

[73] Sornarajah's private papers (on file).

[74] J. Herget, *American Jurisprudence 1870–1970: A History* (Houston: Rice, 1990), 225. Pound had been an influential dean at the Harvard Law School, albeit described as an "unfortunate choice"; J. Seligman, *The High Citadel: The Influence of Harvard Law School* (Boston: Houghton Mifflin, 1978), 57 *et seq.*

[75] R. Pound, *Social Control through Law* (New Haven: Yale, 1942), 112–116; R. Pound, *Jurisprudence*, Vol. 1 (St Paul, MN: West, 1959), 463 *et seq*, 543. The late Ronald Dworkin drew, however, a distinction between "sociologists" like Pound, and law school "instrumentalists" like Lasswell and McDougal; R. Dworkin, *Taking Rights Seriously* (London: Duckworth, 1977), 3–4, as did William Twining who pointed out that Lasswell's and McDougal's exactitude in comparison to Pound made them rather successors to Bentham and cousins of English analytical jurisprudence, albeit "seduced by the scientific analogy too far away from informed common sense"; W. Twining, *Karl Llewelyn and the Realist Movement* (London: Weidenfeld & Nicolson, 1973), 385–386. Be that so, my point is simply that the similarities between Poundian sociological jurisprudence and Lasswell's and McDougal's "Law, Science and Policy" approach shared a broad similarity of purpose despite intricate differences of method, rigour, and language. Both focus on the tasks to be performed by law, not as the study of a body of rules and principles.

[76] R. Pound, "The Need of a Sociological Jurisprudence" (1907) 19 *The Green Bag* 612; quoted in Seligman, *The High Citadel*, 49–50.

[77] Pound, *Jurisprudence*, Vol. 1, 545

have assented to it in the past, but because it seems right and sensible for the situation as it now is."[78]

For the Yale or "New Haven" approach, the idea that the law may be found logically presupposed the need for choice and selection, or to use another Poundian phrase, it was no mere mechanistic exercise in slot machine justice. This begs the preliminary question of how such choices ought to be made – choices about what the law ought to be. To those who say "But that is not the same thing as finding the law", proponents of the Yale method ask: "Why, what makes you so sure, when we look at all those patterns of past legal claims and decisions, that what you now claim to be the law isn't in fact just another choice?" Accordingly, because rules are merely an accumulation of such trends of past decisions, discovering what the rule is becomes a kind of decision or choice, taking into account the context in which such decisions need to be made and differences of observational standpoint.[79] Reminiscent of Pound but perhaps expressed with greater rigour than the calm words of a gentler age, the New Haven view urges that consideration should be given to the "humanitarian, moral and social purposes of the law" such that the trends of past decisions are themselves to be interpreted with such "desired outcomes" in mind.[80] In making choices about which trends of past decisions are valuable, one therefore ends up asking what is reasonable in light of what humanity would consider to be "desirable human values".

We need turn only to Sorna's sudden burst of reflection in his first book, *The Pursuit of Nationalised Property*, to find the earliest clues to New Haven's influence:[81]

> The task of the lawyer in this area then is to identify the community expectations which have been expressed and assess which set of claims best accord with the achievement of these expectations.

Sornarajah's detractors today may not always acknowledge that the quarrel is not with conflicting reports of what "the law" is but with an

[78] Allott, "Language, Method and the Nature of International Law", 123.

[79] To the English and Commonwealth common law mind, these two dimensions – past decisions and the forward-looking aspect of law – were subsequently presented by the late Ronald Dworkin, working within the tradition of English analytical jurisprudence, as "conventionalism" and "pragmatism"; R. Dworkin, *Law's Empire* (Harvard: Belknap), Chas. 4 and 5.

[80] R. Higgins, *Problems and Process: International Law and How We Use It* (Oxford: OUP, 1994), 3–6.

[81] Sornarajah, *Pursuit*, 315.

underlying theoretical approach instead,[82] born of a time when the law was in a high state of fluidity.

As Sorna's body of work started to form in the earlier part of the 1990s, the ground beneath him shifted, again. During the 1980s the position of Third World governments began to change. By the early 1990s, NAFTA and the Energy Charter Treaty were also beginning to emerge, and disputes like the *Pyramid Oasis Case* and *AAPL* v. *Sri Lanka* pointed a new way forward for investment treaty arbitration under the thousands of BITs which had by then come into being.[83] All this reached a highpoint sometime before the advent of the Global Financial Crisis, particularly during the "roaring '90s", as Sornarajah once called that period.

As Sorna attempted to prescribe the way forward, the view of the industrialised nations had become firmly established through a combination of the end of the Cold War, the continued popularity of BITs, which settled the standards of treatment of foreign investors and their investments, and the emergence of BIT-based investment treaty arbitration, which gave such a boost to international law firm disputes practices. Where once he wrote to fill a void with "proposals *de lege ferenda*", today we find a voluminous arbitral jurisprudence – much of which was only produced from the 1990s – and which, when compared to some of Sorna's proposals for future "acceptable norms", strike an apparently discordant note.[84]

Here then are the causes of the break between what Sorna viewed to be sound legal principle and the current legal-professional viewpoint in the international investment arbitration community. In light of the explosion of arbitral activity, practitioners now felt comfortable with the passive task of searching out seemingly authoritative and controlling doctrines in search of support for whatever position one might seek to advance, with the aid of plum pronouncements from the dense thicket of arbitral awards.[85]

[82] Of all his reviewers, it was his former teacher C.F. Amerasinghe who pointed out Sornarajah's underlying methodology; see C.F. Amerasinghe, "Book Review" (1996) 11 *ICSID Review* 240, 242. He also notes Sornarajah's ambivalence towards a full-blown application of the New Haven methodology, *id.*, 243.

[83] See earlier, above.

[84] This is not to say that Sornarajah's work does not contain proposals for yet other areas which have received scant regulation, such as the regulation of multinationals and the notion of home state liability; for a reviewer who was alive to these forward-looking aspects of Sornarajah's project, see D. French, "Book Review" (2005) 76 *BYIL* 557, 557.

[85] Nathalie Bernasconi's chapter in this volume discusses this point, and she points to the contrast between such arbitral practice and the accepted method for discovering customary international law rules.

Only a generation ago thoughts of such a routine professional method would have been naïve. It must be recalled again that Sorna's long journey in search of acceptable policy proposals had been conceived during a time of normlessness;[86] a time during which the 'controlling norms' which now evoke his criticism did not – in his view at least – even exist. Put differently, it was not the present practical, legal situation which had occupied his focus and attention, and it is certainly not today's arbitration practitioners in the field to whom he originally spoke. More importantly, there was an underlying, though partially hidden,[87] methodology to Sornarajah's work. That method, as I had mentioned earlier, marries legal prescription with legal discovery.[88] Changing views about acceptable doctrine may not after all fit with the best policy prescription.

Legal trends come and go, propelled by larger forces, but it is the scholar's job to stand still.

Banished to the margins?

Things are now changing again, as I shall go on to explain, but for a while at least some scholars treated Sornarajah's writings as a curious form of marginalia, questioning the role of his work in laying the foundations for "today's mainstream investment law literature". According to one such criticism,[89] the mainstream literature which we now have was first formed by events that only began in 2004. This is an astonishing claim; but according to that view, our present literature consists of two critical areas of focus – investment treaties and investment arbitration. Together,

[86] Even non-positivists must employ what is at least a "thin positivist methodology", by which we mean the idea of common methods of legal identification without recourse to morality, or in this case proposals of policy; see J. Finnis, "The Truth in Legal Positivism", in R.P. George (ed.), *The Autonomy of Law: Essays on Legal Positivism* (Oxford: OUP, 1996), 195.

[87] The reader might ask: "But why does he bury the key to unlocking his 'code' so deeply?" I believe there are two aspects to this. First, Sornarajah, like others of the New Haven milieu, appears to have reacted unfavourably to the way the New Haven School always seemed to come out in favour of the United States' policy choices on the large issues of the day. The curious reader might wish to turn to Sornarajah, *Pursuit*, 315. There is a reasoned explanation for the seemingly apologetic nature of some of the New Haven School's prescriptions, but that is not the subject of this book and I put it aside. Secondly, the New Haven vocabulary is specialised, cumbersome, and often near-impenetrable to outsiders, or as Professor William Twining put it, it risks coming across as "wearisome, or too pretentious, or unpalatable in some other way" even though "[t]he theory deserves better of its critics"; Twining, *Karl Llewelyn and the Realist Movement*, 386.

[88] Or at least attempts to do so.

[89] Schill, "W(h)ither Fragmentation?"

they represent a convergence of public international law and international commercial arbitration as fields of knowledge and a meeting of public international lawyers and the arbitration community as scholarly and practitioner communities. The new scholarly mainstream emerged, according to this view,[90] from the foundations first laid by a trilogy of works by Dolzer and Stevens on investment treaties in 1995,[91] Brower and Brueschke in their 1998 work on the Iran–US Claims Tribunal[92] and by Professor Schreuer in his monumental commentary on the ICSID Convention which was published in 2001.[93] In other words, Sorna's *International Law on Foreign Investment* appeared only to have clung obstinately to a bygone age:[94]

> Sornarajah's monograph on *The International Law of Foreign Investment*, first published in 1994, still embeds investment law in the struggle between capital-exporting and capital importing countries. Writing from a developing-country perspective, he presents international investment law principally as a reflection of a power struggle in North–South relations. This power struggle, in his view, eventually led to the rejection of multilateral investment protection treaties by developing countries as a group, and the increasing conclusion of BITs towards the end of the Cold War and beyond.

Yet the *International Law of Foreign Investment* has also adapted to changes in the field and it has evolved rapidly through successive editions. After all, the New Haven method must take recent decisional trends into account. From such social facts, its practitioners – of whom Sornarajah is at least an outlying member – plots the likely future trajectory of current legal developments before prescribing a preferred policy choice. However, the prescription of preferred policy choice may wholly contradict the apparent direction of current trends,[95] as that prescription will ultimately be sought to be justified by values common to all, not just some part of, humanity. Such universal values are – or are said to be – discoverable through sociological analysis.[96]

[90] *Id.*, 8–10. [91] Dolzer and Stevens, Bilateral Investment Treaties.

[92] Which had focused not only upon the influence of the tribunal on the formation of customary international law but crucially also on matters of arbitral procedure. See C.N. Brower and J.D. Brueschke, *The Iran–United States Claims Tribunal* (Hague: Nijhoff, 1998).

[93] C. Schreuer, *The ICSID Convention – A Commentary* (Cambridge: CUP, 2001).

[94] Schill, "W(h)ither Fragmentation?", 8, footnotes omitted.

[95] L. Chen, *An Introduction to Contemporary International Law: A Policy-Oriented Perspective* (New Haven: Yale, 1989), 20–21.

[96] For criticisms, see J. Stone, *Visions of World Order* (Baltimore: Johns Hopkins, 1984), 29–30, and Sornarajah himself in *Pursuit*, 315. But it is also important to note that rules are

This is all a roundabout way of saying that each successive edition of Sornarajah's book accounted for these movements in the "legal facts". One example is Sorna's rejection of the international minimum standard of treatment in 1984, in the first edition. That had appeared in the first footnote on page 83, the opening page of the chapter on "Controls by the Host State". In the second edition, that part of the footnote had been removed. Again, in the second edition, which was published in 2004, Sornarajah writes in the opening lines of the first paragraph of the Preface:[97]

> The international law on foreign investment has witnessed an explosive growth since the last edition. The decade had witnessed a proliferation of bilateral and regional investment treaties, and a dramatic rise in litigation in such treaties.

In the third edition, he says:[98]

> Since the second edition of this book, the international law on foreign investment has witnessed such enormous activity that a new edition is justified within five years. The number of arbitration awards based on investment treaties has increased, resulting in several books written solely on the subject of investment treaty arbitration.

The point is not that he was not alive to change, but that he saw these changes as mere epiphenomena. The latest developments are only the latest stage in an ongoing legal process. Rather than having drifted away from the mainstream,[99] he has been visibly concerned about the underlying motivations for fragmenting the field. In the third edition, he wrote:[100]

no better; Higgins, *Problems and Process*, 7. Sornarajah himself viewed the Yale approach as something designed to promote American foreign policy, and which was couched in an inscrutable language. What he derived from it was that the law has been made in various stages somewhere in the past, and that it continues to be used instrumentally to promote the policy preferences of those in power.

97 M. Sornarajah, *The International Law on Foreign Investment*, 2nd ed. (Cambridge: CUP, 2004), xv.

98 Sornarajah, *Foreign Investment*, 3rd ed., xv.

99 Unlike in the field of popular musical criticism this is intended to carry a negative connotation. See A. Huber, "Mainstream as Metaphor: Imagining Dominant Culture", in S. Baker *et al.* (eds.), *Redefining Mainstream Popular Music* (London: Routledge, 2013), 3.

100 Sornarajah, *Foreign Investment*, 3rd ed., xv. See also Sornarajah, *Resistance and Change*, 2, footnote 5.

> This work has held the area of the law together without fragmenting it any further. The carving out of an international law on foreign investment itself may have furthered fragmentation in international law. Yet, the aim was to ensure that the base remained clearly in international law principles. That aim does not appear to have been preserved in many of the later works which sought to carve out further areas as free-standing ones. The original niche of this work remains unaffected. It seeks to establish the foundations of the law clearly in the international law rules on state responsibility and dispute resolution rather than approach it with the central focus on investment treaties and arbitration which seems to have attracted the practitioner more than the scholar.

In contrast, saying a "customary and treaty law regime" has been replaced by a "treaty and customary law regime" would represent little advancement. Consider that dead horse, about the possible effect of the modern proliferation of BITs on customary law formation.[101] It would be odd to call this a "treaty question" today rather than one about the proper ascertainment of customary rules.[102] Or take the fact that the proper relationship between BIT clauses and the minimum customary standard of treatment remains contentious.[103] It cannot be suggested that by calling this a "BIT interpretation problem", rather than a question about the continued relevance of custom, constitutes any real advancement.[104]

To be sure, legal practice is now characterised by treaty talk, expressed in the controlling environment of third-party investment arbitration;[105]

101 See, on this long-standing debate, F.A. Mann, "British Treaties for the Promotion and Protection of Investments" (1981) 52 *B.Y.I.L.* 241, 249; J.E. Alvarez, "A BIT on Custom" (2009) 42 *NYU Jo Int'l L & Pol* 17, 76, drawing on Andreas Lowenfeld's earlier work.

102 *Cf.* M. Sornarajah, "State Responsibility and Bilateral Investment Treaties" (1986) 20 *JWTL* 79, 91–92.

103 For the NAFTA Article 1105(1) cases, see *Mondev* v. *USA*, ICSID Case No. ARB(AF)/99/2, Award, 11 October 2002; *ADF* v. *USA*, ICSID Case No. ARB(AF)/00/1, Final Award, 9 January 2003. For a non-NAFTA case, where an express reference to custom is not "embedded", as Jason Yackee puts it, in the definition of the fair and equitable treatment clause, see *Siemens* v. *Argentina*, ICSID Case No. ARB/02/08, Award, 6 February 2007, para 291. *Contra Tecmed* v. *Mexico*, ICSID Case No. ARB(AF)/00/2, Award, 29 May 2003. See further, J.W. Yackee, "Controlling the International Investment Law Agency" (2012) 53 *Harv. ILJ* 391, 428–429; *contra* Patrick Dumberry, "The Emergence of a Consistent Case Law: How NAFTA Tribunals have Interpreted the Fair and Equitable Treatment Standard", 30 October 2013, available at kluwerarbitrationblog.com.

104 Schill does not say, however, that the "broader international law framework" has become unimportant, *cf.* Schill, "W(h)ither Fragmentation?", 19.

105 Schill, "W(h)ither Fragmentation?", 12 ("international investment law was no longer the broader perspective still taken by Sornarajah, but the substantive and procedural aspects of the law applicable to and within investor-state arbitration under international investment treaties").

but two things should be kept in mind. First, Sornarajah eschewed descriptive legal scholarship, choosing instead to analyse the developing and industrialised country tensions as but one aspect only of a larger analysis of patterns of subjectivities in the interactions of key international participants. Members of the Yale school tend to focus on what they call, in their social-scientific parlance, "participants", "perspectives", "situations", "base values", "strategies" and "outcomes".[106] Rather than having employed a crude North–South framework of analysis,[107] Sorna viewed these "shaping factors" against a broad canvass, which included questions about the historical setting, the conflicting economic theories, the identity and nature of the key actors be they states, multinationals or non-governmental actors, the allocation of risks and – of course – the sources of law.[108] Secondly, his major contribution was to explain just how the law is shaped by ever-changing trends.[109]

As if to prove the point, Sorna's resistance to disciplinary fragmentation is now supported by a reverse trend; indeed, a fierce backlash in the current treaty practices of states and against the institution of investor-state arbitration itself.[110] It is this latest reversal which has occupied several contributors in this volume.

His critics, without a longer and more comprehensive view of the field, spoke without the same comprehensive regard for the dynamic nature of the subject.

Disputes are part of the investment process

Sornarajah's employment of the Yale legal-sociological method also emerged in his *Settlement of Foreign Investment Disputes* in 2000. He began by defining the social problem, and in turn, he defined the nature

[106] M. Reisman, "McDougal's Jurisprudence: Utility, Influence, Controversy" (1985) 79 *Proc. ASIL* 266, 273; Chen, *An Introduction to Contemporary International Law*, 16.

[107] I do not mean to say that the conflict of interests between the North–South divide is not, by itself, a worthy subject; for an excellent treatment in the manner of the New Haven approach, see R. Higgins, *Conflict of Interests* (London: Bodley Head, 1965), 47.

[108] Sornarajah, *Foreign Investment*, 3rd ed., 33 *et seq.*

[109] I am not saying that Schill ignores the recent backlash against investor-state dispute settlement, but that he ignores it in his assessment of Sornarajah's writings. *Cf.* Schill, "W(h)ither Fragmentation?", 24–25.

[110] The New Haven methodology insists that "we must compare many examples of trend before we can build up a body of scientific knowledge"; H.D. Lasswell and M.S. McDougal, "Legal Education and Public Policy: Professional Training in the Public Interest" (1942) 52 *Yale L.J.* 203, reproduced in McDougal *et al.*, *Studies in World Public Order* (New Haven: Yale, 1960), 53, 55.

of foreign investment contract disputes.[111] This form of agreement is no ordinary contract precisely because of the element of state regulatory control over the private transaction.[112] *Settlement* proceeded to outline the factors shaping the law. First, as I have mentioned, the investment contract is no garden variety contract due in part to its long duration and, in the other part, to the fact that one party involved is a sovereign. Then, there are the actors and interests involved – the host state, private investor and the investor's home state – whose interaction means that the transaction itself involves a complex competition between private-sovereign and sovereign-to-sovereign interests and objectives. The private actor itself is no garden variety private actor but a multinational corporation whose true nature should also be understood. Eventually, non-governmental international moral entrepreneurs too emerged. In *Settlement*, Sorna detailed the causes of investment contract disputes. These included the interest in protecting the foreign investor, the creation of the dispute settlement regime, the different interests involved and the different methods of dispute settlement.[113] This is standard New Haven methodology for delineating the focus of inquiry by identifying the shaping forces of the law as a continuing process of participant expectations and their involvement in choice-making.[114]

Settlement was ultimately about understanding "the significance of the subject of dispute settlement in understanding the process of foreign investment".[115] It was a necessary but only an intermediate step towards understanding the subject of international investment law.

The larger work of synthesis

Sornarajah's studies on dispute settlement, which commenced with *Pursuit* and led to *International Commercial Arbitration* before

111 The focus on foreign investment transactions probably suggests that the book could just as easily have been called, and the corresponding problem defined as, the settlement of "foreign investment transaction disputes" but that would also have been a mouthful.

112 M. Sornarajah, *The Settlement of Foreign Investment Disputes* (Hague: Kluwer, 2000), 4–5. The book, to be sure, is not what we find so commonly today, a tome on the subject of investment arbitration which for Sornarajah is but one means of the larger problem of the settlement of foreign investment disputes.

113 *Id.*, 4–20. On "transnational moral entrepreneurs", see C. Harding and C.L. Lim, "The Significance of Westphalia: An Archaeology of the International Legal Order", in C. Harding and C.L. Lim (eds.), *Renegotiating Westphalia* (Hague: Nijhoff, 1999), 1, 8 *et seq.*

114 Chen, *An Introduction to Contemporary International Law*, 17.

115 Sornarajah, *Settlement*, 23.

culminating in *Settlement*, ultimately required a larger work of synthesis. That larger work was 1994's *The International Law on Foreign Investment*, which now verges upon a fourth edition.

That work has changed, sometimes quite remarkably, over the years. The chapter on BITs – beginning with the second edition – now precedes that on multilateral treaties. In the first edition, Sorna had already referred to the "importance" of BITs.[116] There also emerged a new chapter on the breach of treaty treatment standards as a cause of action because, as he explained, with the "spelling out" of the standards of treatment through the proliferation of BITs, a new head of liability – breach of treaty treatment standards – had also emerged. Previously, there was largely only one head, namely, "takings of property".[117] Of course, such standards have today been subjected to much arbitral examination which has also expanded their scope.[118]

As for the growth in arbitral jurisprudence, there appeared, in the second edition, a table of cases, and by the third edition, two new chapters were written. They now precede a fresh chapter first introduced in the prior edition on breach of treatment standards. The two new chapters are those on "contract-based" arbitration and "treaty-based" arbitration. Sornarajah explains that investment treaty arbitration was now an important subject, but that "before the emergence of the investment treaty system in 1959, there was an earlier system of investment protection which the multinational corporations had virtually devised by themselves" and that "this system worked entirely on the basis of contractual structures".[119] It is a pithy reference to his own past writings

[116] Sornarajah, *Foreign Investment*, 1st ed., 225. Guzman's complaint, "Book Review", generally, is perhaps slightly different and appears to concern the underestimation of the benefits, in economic efficiency terms, which BITs will bring.

[117] Sornarajah, *Foreign Investment*, 2nd ed., 315. *Cf.* Paulsson, "Arbitration without Privity", 233.

[118] See Nathalie Bernasconi-Osterwalder's chapter in this volume. Of the distinct "sub-heads", or "sub-sub-heads", the notion of legitimate expectation has been particularly controversial. See *Tecmed* v. *Mexico* (Award) (2004) 43 ILM 133, 173; see also *MTD Equity Sdn Bhd & anor* v. *Chile* (Award) (2005) 44 ILM 91, 105–106, 122. For cases which show an absence of a specific representation, see *International Thunderbird Gaming Corp* v. *Mexico*, UNCITRAL (NAFTA), Award, 26 January 2006, para. 147. See further, A.R. Sureda, *Investment Treaty Arbitration – Judging under Uncertainty* (Cambridge: CUP. 2012), 77; J. Crawford, "Treaty and Contract Claims in Investment Arbitration – 22nd Freshfields Lecture" (2008) 24 *Arb Int'l* 351, 372; Sornarajah, *Resistance and Change*, 257, 272 *et seq.*

[119] Sornarajah, *Foreign Investment*, 3rd ed., 276–277.

from *International Commercial Arbitration* to *The Settlement of Foreign Investment Disputes.*[120]

He was hardly inclined to dismiss contractual disputes, for in practice "[v]irtually every foreign investment entry is accomplished through a contract, except where entry is made through a merger or acquisition".[121] Admittedly, if the current trend of inserting pre establishment rights – i.e. national treatment for the establishment of a foreign investment, or more plainly, investment market access – continues, the situation could change. However, one cannot treat investment treaty arbitration as something which is novel or new, for its genesis, and therefore its proper understanding, lies in investment contract arbitration.[122]

Notwithstanding the changing shape of writings in the field and the creation of the abundant literature on BITs and investment treaty arbitration, Sornarajah's writings have charted the scholarly field through all these changes and attempted to keep the field itself whole and in a systematic order, in contrast with the claim of his critics that the "mainstream" of the subject is now to be found in the more practitioner-orientated literature on investment treaty arbitration, practice and procedure.[123] The field of international investment law is hardly spent, together with its troublesome concerns about finding some accommodation between opposing interests against a global landscape which has seen one or the other viewpoint rise only to fall again in the throes of great global events over the course of virtually the last hundred years.

[120] Jean Ho and I have adopted and kept the investment contract/investment treaty typology in our survey of the field, see C.L. Lim and J. Ho, "Investment Arbitration", *Oxford Bibliographies*, available at oxfordbibliographies.com.

[121] *Id.*, 277. [122] *Id.*

[123] The reasons for which would be commercial; *cf.* Schill, "W(h)ither Fragmentation?", 13 ("a viable option for a career path in private practice"), 16 (unlike the public international lawyers, today's commercial arbitration lawyers "write primarily for arbitration practitioners"). This is not to deny the great importance of having today's impressive range of excellent works on investment arbitration. My observations are confined only to how we view "mainstream scholarship" on international investment law, or more precisely, how we should not be so quick to select and dismiss parts of the genre in some metaphysical search for the scholarly "mainstream". If anything, the time has come for works which would assemble all the parts carefully. But Schill is not alone in this criticism; see J.F. Murphy's review of the first edition, (1995) 89 AJIL 666, although Murphy's claim that BITs will prevent investment disputes, rather than Sornarajah's view that the shift by developing countries in the mid-90s towards attracting foreign capital will reverse itself, has now been proven to be wholly incorrect. Even so, Sornarajah was plainly aware that BITs "will be looked upon as the best way of securing investment protection", *Foreign Investment*, 276.

For Sornarajah, one can attempt to produce a dispassionate and historically informed analysis but still draw conclusions that may be unwelcome.[124]

The pendulum swings anew

Seen from the perspective of the first publication of *The International Law on Foreign Investment*, the growth in investment claims, which began in the late 1990s, had transformed a specialised area of the international law of state responsibility into a booming legal industry. This industry elicits multimillion dollar fees for advice and representation in connection with spectacularly large claims. It has ushered in an era where the 'professors' are now often full-time practitioners with adjunct academic titles of various kinds, where practitioner guides have claimed the status of mainstream scholarship and impartiality risks being defined by the uncritical acceptance of the new tropes of arbitral reasoning. But now, that whole cavalcade of factors joined to the locomotive of economic globalisation has encountered stiff popular political resistance.

The nature of our professional setup has also had its complexities. An unsuccessful challenge was recently mounted against a distinguished arbitrator and professor who sat on the board of a bank, which, it was alleged, had at least some interest in the dispute,[125] and against another distinguished arbitrator – a former professor – who, in advising in a dispute against the respondent had pleaded an award he had given while presiding over a dispute involving the same respondent.[126] At the level of national treaty behaviour, attempts in ongoing treaty negotiations which continue to seek to beat a path to such tribunals are now running into

[124] This is not to deny unconscious bias. At a technical level, Jürgen Kurtz has remarked upon the fact that Sornarajah has paid rather less attention to the "liberal concepts" of most favoured nation (MFN) and national treatment (NT); see J. Kurtz (2005) 4 World Trade Review 324, 332. See also Muchlinski's book review, 483. Amerasinghe, on the other hand, commented upon Sornarajah's harsh tone towards some Western writers, particularly towards F.A. Mann and Richard Lillich, even if he thought the criticisms were fair; Amerasinghe, book review, 243. However, the late Thomas Wälde wrote that Sornarajah "exposes numerous hypocrisies in the Western position" and that "[i]n the treatment of issues and argument, he pays full attention to the voices from the Third World – often ignored by many biased or arrogant academic writers from the Western countries"; Wälde, book review, 393, 394. Similarly, Murphy concluded that: "A strength of his study is that he makes a largely successful effort to present a balanced picture of the arguments advanced on both sides"; Murphy, review of the first edition, 666.

[125] *EDF* v. *Argentina*, ICSID Case No. ARB/03/23, Challenge Decision, 25 June 2008.

[126] *Investment Treaty News*, 17 January 2007.

political quicksand. Battles over investor-state dispute settlement provisions in the Trans-Pacific Partnership negotiations, and the Trans-Atlantic Trade and Investment Partnership negotiations, now take place in the streets,[127] in treaty negotiating rooms, through the political institutions in state capitals[128] and in the supranational institutions of Europe.[129]

In recent years, Sorna has turned his scholarly attention to the social and economic causes of this latest turn of events. The result is that the articulation of his views on economic neoliberalism has become clearer.[130] It would be more appropriate to return to this subject in the concluding chapter of this book for in between there is still much other explanation to be done.

Essays for Muthucumaraswamy Sornarajah

The occasion and the reversal in the field

In this volume, we have set out to honour M. Sornarajah by putting together a body of critical writings in the field of the international law of foreign investment. I have already mentioned that we are again, as when Sorna had first commenced writing, at an inflection point in our debates about international investment treaties and investor-state arbitration. There is now not only considerable scholarly debate but also in the larger scheme of things a widespread, global public backlash.[131] These essays were written against that background, which has witnessed withdrawals from the Washington Convention and the initiation of national reviews

127 See H. Farrell, "People are Freaking Out about the Trans Pacific Partnership's Investor Dispute Settlement System. Why Should You Care?", *Washington Post*, 26 March 2015, available at www.washingtonpost.com.

128 See G. Sargent, "Is TPP Trade Deal a Massive Giveaway to Major Corporations?", *Washington Post*, 27 April 2015, available at www.washingtonpost.com.

129 See "Commission Floats ISDS Reform Ahead of EU Ministerial Trade Talks", 6 May 2015, available at www.euractiv.com.

130 Sornarajah, *Resistance and Change*, 43–70.

131 Sornarajah welcomed the emerging force of Western NGOs as allies joined in common cause but still, and especially during the George W. Bush years, they were perhaps not more than a peripheral force in the broader scheme of things, the failure of the Multilateral Agreement on Investment notwithstanding. Fortunately for the arbitration profession, there was little of immediate practical effect that the NGO community could do to influence the proliferation of disputes based on the vast number of treaties which have for long been in existence.

of existing treaties by various developing nations from Southeast to South Asia and Latin America.[132]

As Sorna once put it in conversation,[133] "the pendulum has begun to swing again".

The structure of the book

This book begins with a defence of the liberal vision by one of its most prominent and respected voices. Ken Vandevelde is well known as an international treaty practitioner and scholarly authority on the investment agreements of the United States[134] and so to him fell the role of promoter of the faith. In his chapter, he explores the origins of the contemporary international law of foreign investment in liberal economic and political theory. He argues that the law rests on three principles – (1) investment neutrality, or the principle that the state ought to be neutral and leave the allocation of capital to market forces, (2) investment security, or the sanctity of investment-related property and contractual rights, and (3) market facilitation, which he defines as the principle that the state should provide conditions required for the market to function properly. Ken adds that the law should promote the rule of law, and he takes us back to the United States' post-war effort to craft investment-related provisions in accordance with that vision. Leon Trakman and David Musayelyan proceed in their chapter to describe where things now stand. In particular, they focus on a shift in state sentiment, "from investor protections embodied in investment treaties to reliance on domestic courts to resolve investor-state disputes".[135] Their analysis comes at the right time by focusing on the "growing rejection" of investor-state arbitration; but it also picks up on a strand which has emerged in Sornarajah's latest writings.[136] Leon and David trace this shift in sentiment to the initiative of a handful of Latin American states (Bolivia, Ecuador and Venezuela) before spreading to countries as varied as Australia, South Africa, India, Indonesia and, possibly, now Germany

[132] M. Waibel *et al.* (eds.), *The Backlash against Investment Arbitration: Perceptions and Reality* (Hague: Kluwer, 2010).

[133] Quoted with permission.

[134] K.J. Vandevelde, *U.S. International Investment Agreements* (New York: OUP, 2009).

[135] See Chapter 3.

[136] For Sornarajah's declaration that, in terms of the shifting interests of the developed and developing nations, the shoe is now on the other foot, see M. Sornarajah, "Sovereign Wealth Funds and the Existing Structure of the Regulation of Foreign Investments" (2011) 1 *Asian JIL* 267.

and France. What characterises this present trend is a commonly shared sense that domestic courts are friendlier to domestic public policies: a sense of the "chilling effect" that investor-state arbitration might have on public-interest legislation and the potentially crippling effect of investment claims brought by highly financed and forceful foreign investors.

The subsequent chapters, some of which may be read in direct response to Ken's opening chapter, traverse a vast terrain. The sequence of topics is intended to serve as a useful critical introduction to the field at the present time, and to mirror Sornarajah's own concerns. They range from discussion of the restrictive scope which current investment treaty practice generally accords to developing countries' policy or regulatory space to discussion of the complex arbitral jurisprudence on internationalised contracts and umbrella clauses, the sociological aspects of resistance to neoliberalism, past and continuing efforts to reform international investment law and the emergence of ancillary global regulatory issues, ranging from the regulation of transnational corporations to the regulation of sovereign wealth funds.

And thus, Part II explores our sense that the field is beginning to emerge anew from the current backlash. Gus Van Harten, who together with David Schneiderman was among the first scholars to view investment treaty arbitration from a governance perspective,[137] jolts the reader by asking whether there ought to be reform at all, rather than outright withdrawal.[138] Gus discusses the record of reform, beginning with NAFTA reform in 2001 and, more recently, by the European Commission in connection with the EU–US Trans-Atlantic Trade and Investment Partnership (TTIP) negotiations and the EU–Canada Comprehensive Economic and Trade Agreement. He argues that the results have been dismal. Reform has failed to deal with the lack of balance and reciprocity in the allocation of rights and responsibilities between investor and host state. Reform has also failed to address investor-state arbitration's shortcomings. The answer, he proposes, is withdrawal. The Canadian constitutional lawyer David Schneiderman's subsequent chapter resumes this line of inquiry. David observes that lawyers and scholars in the field have been unwilling to admit the

[137] Schill, "W(h)ither Fragmentation?", 26.

[138] Which reminded this author of the central story in Derrick Bell, *Afrolantica Legacies* (Chicago: Third World Press, 1998).

impending threat to the system[139] and have chosen to view the backlash as only a public relations problem.[140]

The next two contributions are more optimistic and focus on the promising nature of newer forms of treaty and codes of conduct. Peter Muchlinksi, an early staunch supporter of this book, discusses the Common Market for Eastern and Southern Africa's (COMESA) 2007 Common Investment Area Agreement (CCIA). In asking if this is what new investment agreements ought to look like, he echoes Sornarajah's own interest in discovering or designing a new, more balanced generation of investment treaties. The CCIA contains investor-state dispute settlement provisions which, Peter argues, offer a new model of how we might take into account the types of problems mentioned earlier. Similarly, Karl Sauvant draws our attention to home state governance of transnational corporations (TNCs) and the host countries' perspective under the United Nations Code of Conduct on Transnational Corporations. Sornarajah has shown a long-standing interest in the issue, most famously once drawing fire from Peter Muchlinski.[141] Although the Code negotiations did not succeed,[142] Karl explains that it is a work-in-progress which has at least "crystallised the basic configuration of interests of the principal stakeholders and key issues", and thereby showing where the obstacles lie in future talks.[143]

In Part III of the book the reader will be introduced to Sorna's "worm's view" of the world, as opposed to what he calls "the eagle's view" (i.e. neoliberal economic ideology).[144] Neoliberalism is an ideology which had emerged during the 1980s which reached its height with the end of the Cold War and the rise of economic globalisation and American hyperpower, before culminating in the 2007–2008 Global Financial Crisis. Today, the worm's view instead is on the ascendant accompanying what Fareed Zakaria called "the rise of the rest",[145] namely, the "BRIC", "BRICS", and now "CIVETS" nations in the likes of Indonesia and Egypt. These latter nations in particular have been the subject of ongoing

[139] See Chapter 5.

[140] For similar view in the trade law field, which I have attributed to James Bacchus but which is also rightly associated with Pascal Lamy's policy as Director of the World Trade Organization, see C.L. Lim, "East Asia's Engagement with Cosmopolitan Ideals under its Trade Treaty Dispute Provisions" (2011) 56 *McGill LJ* 821, 832.

[141] Muchlinski, "Book Review", 483. [142] See also Chapter 15. [143] See Chapter 7.

[144] The terms appear to have been derived from photography and cinematic technique. The worm's-eye view viewed from a low angle, from below, is compared to the bird's-eye view from above.

[145] F. Zakaria, *The Post-American World, and the Rise of the Rest* (London: Penguin, 2009).

attention in respect of the proposed "termination" of their BITs.[146] We also see the emergence of a yet unsettled configuration of new international power relationships. Consequently, the essays in Part III reflect these underlying changes in world order. Aniruddha Rajput discusses India, which recently joined the backlash by publishing its March 2015 Draft Model BIT. Here we see an India smarting from its engagement with investor-state arbitration in the *White Industries* dispute where an investment tribunal had found that inordinate delays within the Indian legal system had violated an investor's BIT rights through the operation of a most favoured nation (MFN) clause.[147] As I mentioned, India has now produced the March 2015 Draft Model BIT.[148] Anir explains that India, nonetheless, continues to face complex questions about the proper inter-relationship between investment arbitration and traditional forms of settlement, the Indian courts and India's existing legal framework. For now, the March 2015 Draft would rid India's investment treaties of MFN and fair and equitable treatment (FET) clauses and carve out taxation issues from the scope of India's future BITs.

Wenhua Shan and Hongrui Chen offer a timely account in the next chapter of changes in China's investment treaty practice at a time when China's capital exports and imports are now evenly matched, and as China advances towards the conclusion of a new generation of Chinese investment treaty with the United States in the midst of continued economic liberalisation and reform of its system of governance. They paint a picture of a large country on the move. Their account is timely because few understand the minute design changes which are likely to occur as China's treaty practice coalesces around a new, "fourth generation", Chinese Model BIT ("China BIT 4.0"). Theirs is a hard-headed account of China's fundamentals, and they ask – Would not China's treaties be balanced in light of its equivalent role as capital exporter and importer today? Some Chinese scholars have suggested a two-track BIT programme, with one set of treaties for those from whom China imports

146 See e.g.J. Feris, "Challenging the Status Quo – South Africa's Termination of Its Bilateral Trade Agreements", *International Arbitration Newsletter*, DLA Piper, 10 December 2014, available at www.dlapiper.com. R. Beckman *et al.*, "BIT by BIT in Indonesia", Norton Rose Fulbright, October 2014, available at www.nortonrosefulbright.com.

147 L.E. Peterson, "India is Held Liable for Investment Treaty Breach Due to Protracted Judicial Delays Suffered by Foreign Investors", *Investment Arbitration Reporter*, 7 February 2012; P. Ranjan, "The White Industries Arbitration: Implications for India's Investment Treaty Programme", *Investment Treaty News*, 13 April 2012.

148 See B. Giaretta and A. Kishore, "The Changing Landscape of Investment Treaty Protection in India", *Ashurst*, April 2015, available at www.ashurst.com.

capital and another for which it exports capital. Shan and Chen criticise this notion as a "morally indecent" suggestion.

The subsequent chapters in the volume turn instead to current issues of treaty design, jurisprudence and doctrine. They deal with such treaty standards which have drawn the greatest debate – expropriation and FET treatment clauses in particular, including the emergent doctrine of the protection of investors' legitimate expectations and pre establishment national treatment clauses. Kyla Tienhaara and Todd Tucker discuss how direct takings of property have become rare but that, as Sornarajah had predicted following *Methanex* v. *USA*,[149] claims today for creeping, indirect or regulatory expropriation have become responsible for the current backlash against treaty-based investor-state arbitration. That backlash, they argue, is fuelled by fear of overbroad interpretations by arbitrators of the protective effect of expropriation clauses. Sorna had decried indirect expropriation for its tendency to fragment international legal regulation. It does so by subordinating environmental, health and social policies to international investment law. Tienhaara and Tucker assess Sornarajah's prediction and trace the way expropriation clauses have been framed since *Methanex*.

Howard Mann, a distinguished public interest lawyer often associated with the *Methanex* dispute, turns to the conscious destruction of economic development policy space through the grant of investors' rights, where newer treaty clauses are not so much the protectors of pre-existing rights but generators of new types of rights. He draws comparisons between the General Agreement on Trade in Services (GATS), NAFTA's negative-list market access provisions and a host of other treaties on the question of market access; amongst these are the approaches by COMESA, ASEAN and Singapore's and Europe's current treaty trajectories. Such provisions have an impact on joint venture requirements, South Africa's minority empowerment policies, state-owned enterprises and the development of national champions. Bearing in mind that the ability to bring an investor-state dispute depends in the first place upon treaty design, "[t]he broad result is that investment treaties are becoming more supportive of the rights of existing capital owners to extend and expand their capital base, while precluding governments from adopting policies and tools aimed at

149 *Methanex Corporation* v. *United States of America*, Final Award of the Tribunal on Jurisdiction and Merits, 3 August 2005; M. Sornarajah, "A Law for Need or a Law for Greed? Restoring the Lost Law in the International Law of Foreign Investment" (2006) 6 *International Environmental Agreements: Politics, Law and Economics* 329.

broadening the base of economic development and inter-generational equity."[150]

The next chapter by Nathalie Bernasconi-Osterwalder turns to FET and minimum standard of treatment (MST) clauses. These, she argues, were rarely well understood by host states, which still underestimate their effect today. Sornarajah had previously addressed the vagueness of FET clauses in response to a 2004 OECD report, noting that at least in the older treaties where states did not commit to investor-state arbitration by tribunals of compulsory jurisdiction one simply could not assume, as a matter of treaty intent, that host states had casually committed themselves to the "capricious discretion" of an arbitral tribunal.[151] Today, the FET standard has in fact become the most popular legal ground on which claims are now based, enjoying a strong success rate for investors in comparison with the other forms of treaty clauses. Her diagnosis mirrors Sornarajah's – that host states have not succeeded in limiting the scope of arbitral discretion.[152]

Part IV of this book is separated from Part III for it contains two chapters which focus specifically on Sorna's long-standing interest in investment contracts. My chapter explores Sornarajah's ambivalence towards umbrella clauses. On the one hand, such clauses intend what theories of the internationalisation of state contracts intend. However, no principle prevents the scope of a treaty clause from being extended to the breach of an investment contract. The problem, however, is that there is a mass of conflicting, and unsettled, jurisprudence which may in part have been caused by tribunals contending that an umbrella treaty clause internationalises the whole underlying investment contract. Viewed, however, as garden variety treaty clauses which are to be construed normally, no theoretical problem arises; in which case at least some of the policy objections against umbrella clauses also fall away. Jean Ho's chapter (Chapter 14) goes on to discuss Sornarajah's scepticism about the internationalisation of state contracts. She puts the question squarely – Can state responsibility be engaged for breach of contract? In her chapter, she argues that Sornarajah's three principal objections to the internationalisation of state contracts have foreshadowed corresponding

[150] See Chapter 11.

[151] M. Sornarajah, "The Fair and Equitable Standard of Treatment: Whose Fairness? Whose Equity?", in F. Ortino *et al.* (eds.) *Investment Treaty Law: Current Issues Volume II: Nationality and Investment Treaty Claims and Fair and Equitable Treatment* (London: BIICL, 2007).

[152] See Chapter 12.

developments in the law. Firstly, modern-day arbitral tribunals do not elevate all contractual breaches to treaty breaches when applying umbrella or FET clauses. Secondly, because state contracts today admit the possibility of unilateral changes, this could suggest the demise of stabilisation clauses. Finally, the supposition that state contracts should be carved in stone in order to render adequate investor protection is false.[153] Jean's argument is that internationalisation has become increasingly incompatible with the law of state responsibility for contractual breach.

Part V, entitled "The International Regulation of State Capitalism", contains a stand-alone chapter by Jiangyu Wang, which sets out to examine an issue which Sorna has been concerned with of late – the emergence and international regulation of state capitalism and sovereign wealth funds (SWFs). The SWF is a complex creature, being government linked and controlled while engaging in ordinary commercial life. He discusses its controversial nature from the viewpoint of the host states in which the funds are invested and the fact that SWF activities are a ready source of tension between home and host state. Jiangyu devotes considerable attention to the non-binding conciliatory principles and guidelines which have since emerged, and he discusses their prospective value as a basis for deeper regulation.

The final chapter explores Sornarajah's latest work, in which he provides an account not only of the law but also the social forces which move it. There, I set out to explain Sornarajah's legal method in its mature form, show how his doctrinal work was fed by legal-sociological analysis[154] and show how his views – driven by his adopted method – evolved with actual changes occurring on the legal and global landscape. It was as if he had a machine which, at the one end, sucks in the actual changing patterns of global economic, treaty and other behavioural events and detects the emergence of fresh doctrinal arguments and moves by proponents of economic neoliberalism.[155] With a final push of the button, our imaginary machine churns out doctrinal counterarguments at the other end. As Sorna toiled away at the machine, the pendulum swung first in favour of the industrialised nations and the new doctrinal

[153] *Id.*

[154] His approach to legal reasoning was "trans-Atlantic" and iconoclastic, combining both formal and substantive methods of reasoning; see P.S. Atiyah and R.S. Summers, *Form and Substance in Anglo-American Law* (Oxford: Clarendon, 1984), 28–32.

[155] M. Sornarajah, "Mutations of Neo-Liberalism in International Investment Law" (2011) 3 *Trade, Law & Development* 203, 205.

arguments supporting this latest triumph of capital. The machine churned out Sorna's counterarguments, and this has in part contributed to the identification of Sornarajah as a "Twailer",[156] signifying an association with the TWAIL movement, but it was really more a function of the machinery that he employed.

I have chosen the image of a "Twailing Machine" which performs these jobs as it would not be entirely accurate to treat Sorna's method as having any greater resemblance with the methods of the TWAIL movement. TWAIL is possessed by history, colonial history in particular.[157] History is important to Sornarajah, as is the importance of effecting an egalitarian shift, understanding the relationships between the Third World and the industrialised nations and understanding the relationship between law and power. However, colonial history has no special explanatory force for Sornarajah. His task has been to map and shape the development of doctrine and to examine doctrine's utility and effects within the field of the international law on foreign investment. I also use the image of the "Machine", to suggest a seeming automaticity,[158] in depicting Sornarajah's production of doctrinal counterarguments.[159] This machine we might imagine connects to or interfaces with the Yale method at the one end, at which global events and facts are fed into it, and a more contemporary mode of critical legal scholarship at the other end, where the machine spews out doctrinal countermoves reminiscent of the Critical Legal Studies Movement.

I have mentioned also that Sorna's legal-sociological method has of late become more sophisticated. At the one level, the current backlash

[156] See Sornarajah, "Mutations", generally.

[157] A. Anghie, *Imperialism, Sovereignty and the Making of International Law* (Cambridge: CUP, 2005), is the indispensable work in this regard; see also Antony Anghie and Bhupinder Chimni who have tried to show how "doctrines of international law had been created through the colonial encounter", in "Third-World Approaches to International Law and Individual Responsibility in Internal Conflicts" (2003) 2 *Chinese JIL* 77, 84, 84.

[158] For Pound on traditional doctrinal argument as "slot machine jurisprudence", see R. Pound, *Law and Morals*, 2nd ed (Chapel Hill, NC: University of North Carolina Press, 1926), 46 ("It was an eighteenth-century idea that a body of enacted law might be made so complete and so perfect that the judge would have only to select the exact precept made in advance for the case in hand, and then mechanically apply it"), 55 ("the futility of nineteenth-century attempts to make courts into judicial slot machines"); L.A. Fennell, "Between Monster and Machine: Rethinking the Judicial; Function" (1999) 51 *South Carolina L Rev* 183, 196.

[159] For the idea of a neat production of counter-doctrinal moves, see (e.g.) R.W. Gordon, "Critical Legal Studies as a Teaching Method, Against the Background of the Intellectual Politics of Modern Legal Education in the United States" (1989) 1 *Leg Ed Rev* 6.

promises to change the exact nature of the kinds of detailed, doctrinal arguments that tribunals will confront and employ, and I shall say more about some of these newly emergent doctrines in the last chapter of this book.[160] But at another level, Sornarajah's sociological jurisprudence – which had fairly passively applied sociological insights to the study of law – has also become more comprehensive, verging on becoming a sociology of law which seeks to explain social change itself through the study of law. As the final chapter will show, he has since developed a theory about how legal change provokes forceful social reactions and how these reactions in turn unleash countervailing social forces which beget further legal change.

Sornarajah has adapted his sociological method as his legal understanding has begun to shape his views about the interactions between transnational and international participants, and of larger social forces, in the international investment field. As Jerome Frank once wrote, "[n]ow the true art of the lawyer is the art of legal modification".[161] The twailing machine alone is no longer sufficient, even if it remains necessary. In his latest book, Sornarajah has endeavoured to provide a "theory of resistance and change" in accordance with his earlier writings. He observes that the changes that have taken place in the international law on foreign investment result from a clash between power and justice[162] and that ours is once more an era of impending change driven by the prospect of economic neoliberalism's demise.

Yet, we must first begin at the beginning with the law's origins and doctrines before returning – only at the end of this book – to Sornarajah's latest turn towards a full-blown legal sociology.[163]

[160] Sornarajah's recent turn towards theory began with a sense of a "changing paradigm"; Sornarajah, "Power and Justice", 23. It appears to owe something to Kuhn's influence; T.S. Kuhn, *The Structure of Scientific Revolutions*, 2nd ed. (Chicago: University of Chicago, 1970).

[161] J. Frank, *Law and the Modern Mind* (New York: Tudor, 1936), 10.

[162] A theme developed in an article which the present author had elected to publish; Sornarajah, "Power and Justice".

[163] In the final chapter of this book, "The Many-Headed Hydra and Laws that Rage of Gain".

2

The liberal vision of the international law on foreign investment

KENNETH J. VANDEVELDE

Introduction

The modern international law of foreign investment, by which I mean the law established by a network of more than 3,000 international investment agreements,[1] was founded on a vision of political and economic liberalism. Although it is common to date the origin of this network to a bilateral investment treaty (BIT) concluded in 1959 between Germany and Pakistan,[2] that seminal BIT was to a considerable extent a distillation of provisions that had appeared more than a decade earlier in a series of friendship, commerce, and navigation (FCN) treaties concluded by the United States in the years after 1945. Thus, it is in these FCN treaties, drafted to reflect the liberalism of Franklin Roosevelt's New Deal and Harry Truman's Fair Deal, that we may find the founding liberal vision of the modern international law on foreign investment.

The argument in this chapter proceeds in eight sections. This introduction constitutes the first section. In "US postwar FCN treaties as a reflection of liberal principles," I demonstrate how the US postwar FCN treaties were intended to promote liberal principles. In "Defining liberalism," I define liberalism for the purposes of my argument. In "Fashioning a liberal investment regime," I show how the liberalism of the New Deal and Fair Deal was reflected in the US postwar FCN treaties, the substance of which was largely replicated in the first BIT program, inaugurated by Germany in 1959. In "The emergence of neoliberalism," I discuss the impact on international investment treaty law of the emergence of neoliberalism. In "Assessing the liberal vision today," I assess the

1 As of the end of 2014, UNCTAD had identified 3,268 international investment agreements. United Nations Conference on Trade and Development, IIA Issues Note: Recent Trends in IIAs and ISDS, February 2015.

2 Treaty between the Federal Republic of Germany and Pakistan for the Promotion and Protection of Investments, signed 25 November 1959, 457 U.N.T.S. 23 (1963).

relationship between international investment law as it exists today and liberalism. In "Liberalism and its critics," I comment on some of the criticisms of the liberal vision of the international law on foreign investment. Finally, I close with the "Conclusion."

This chapter focuses heavily upon US treaty practice for two reasons. First, one of the chapter's central theses is that the modern international law of foreign investment originated in US postwar FCN treaty practice and reflects the New Deal/Fair Deal liberalism of the 1940s, which necessitates an inquiry into US practice. Second, this chapter considers the influence of neoliberalism on investment treaty law, and the United States was a leading proponent of neoliberalism at the time that it launched its BIT program, suggesting that any such influence may be found, at least in part, by examining the US BITs.

US postwar FCN treaties as a reflection of liberal principles

The United States concluded its first FCN treaty, with France, in 1778.[3] For more than a century and a half, the United States continued to negotiate FCN treaties primarily to establish a legal basis for trade and maritime relations between the United States and its treaty partners.[4]

The Second World War effected a hiatus in US FCN treaty negotiations, during which the Roosevelt and Truman administrations prepared to inaugurate a new series of FCN treaties, one in which a primary purpose would be to promote and to protect US investment abroad.[5] The United States had compelling reasons to promote outward investment. With peace imminent, the Roosevelt administration feared that millions of workers formerly employed in the war effort would be unable

[3] Treaty of Amity and Commerce, United States-France, signed 6 February 1778, 8 Stat. 12, T.S. No. 83.

[4] From 1778 through the end of the Truman administration, the United States concluded 130 such treaties. Herman Walker, Jr., "Provisions on Companies in United States Commercial Treaties" (1956) 50 *American Journal of International Law* 373, 374 n. 4.

[5] On the US postwar FCN treaty program, *see* Robert R. Wilson, *United States Commercial Treaties and International Law* (New Orleans, LA: Hauser Press, 1960); Robert Wilson, *The International Law Standard in Treaties of the United States* (Cambridge, MA: Harvard University Press, 1953); Harry Hawkins, *Commercial Treaties and Agreements: Principles and Practice* (New York: Rinehart, 1951); Herman Walker, "Modern Treaties of Friendship, Commerce and Navigation" (1958) 42 *Minnesota Law Review* 805; Herman Walker, "Treaties for the Encouragement and Protection of Foreign Investment: Present United States Practice" (1956) 5 *American Journal of Comparative Law* 229; Robert Wilson, "Postwar Commercial Treaties of the United States" (1949) 43 *American Journal of International Law* 262.

to find employment in a peacetime economy, plunging the nation back into another Great Depression. Although many of these workers could be employed in producing goods to meet pent-up domestic demand unmet during the war years, the Roosevelt administration did not believe that domestic demand would be sufficient to absorb the entire supply of labor.[6] The solution was to employ in production for export those who could not find work supplying domestic demand.[7] This solution confronted the problem that neither the countries of Europe devastated by the war nor the countries of the economically underdeveloped continents of Africa, Asia, and South America possessed the dollars that they would need to purchase US exports.[8] Consumers outside the United States could obtain dollars, however, through US investment in their economies. US investment would supply an immediate infusion of foreign exchange and, to the extent that it increased the productive capacity of an economy, could bolster exports to the United States that would provide a further means for acquiring dollars.[9] The United States committed itself to a policy of promoting economic reconstruction and development abroad through outward foreign investment.

American businesses seeking to establish investment enterprises abroad faced numerous impediments, among them cultural and linguistic barriers, fear of foreign domination, inadequate transportation and communications facilities, unreliable power supplies, poorly trained workers, economic fragility, political instability, and inadequate legal protection. The US Government harbored no illusions that it could remove all of these impediments to outward foreign investment.[10]

[6] Alan Lawson, *A Commonwealth of Hope: The New Deal Response to Crisis* (Baltimore: Johns Hopkins University Press, 2006), 238. Lawson describes a "widespread expectation" that the depression would return once the "artificial prosperity" induced by war ended.

[7] James F. Byrnes, the director of war mobilization, expressed the consensus when he wrote in 1945, "We Must Export Goods if We Are to Provide Jobs for All Our Workers," *New York Times* (2 January 1945), 12.

[8] Memorandum In Reply to the President's Letter of 9 April 1943, National Archives and Records Administration, Record Group 43, ITO Subject Files, Box 37, Folder marked "Foreign Investment Policy (I)."

[9] Executive Committee on Economic Foreign Policy, Memorandum headed "Subcommittee on Foreign Investment Policy," dated 26 June 1945, National Archives and Records Administration, Record Group 43, ITO Files, Box 38, Folder marked "FIP Documents."

[10] For example, during negotiation of the US FCN treaty with South Korea, the State Department instructed the US embassy in Seoul to avoid giving the impression that conclusion of the treaty "would necessarily be immediately productive of increased private United States investment." The Department explained that "[t]he main function of the treaty, insofar as investment is concerned, is to provide assurances that the juridical conditions affecting foreign investment are favorable and will remain so. The treaty

Inadequate legal protection, however, was one impediment that it could address through investment-related provisions in its FCN treaties. The State Department significantly revised the model FCN treaty that it had used before the war to include new provisions to protect foreign investment, while retaining a few previously existing provisions that had protected US property abroad.

In describing its new FCN treaties, the United States routinely referred to them as embodiments of liberal principles. For example, a 1946 State Department publication explained that the FCN treaty program was "designed to provide a legal framework, based on liberal principles and adapted to modern conditions affecting international intercourse, for mutually advantageous relations between two countries over a long period of time."[11] Similarly, a decade later, in submitting the US FCN treaty with Nicaragua to the president, the Department of State explained that the treaty "expresses the common faith of the two countries in liberal principles."[12]

The State Department believed that the FCN treaties provided for US businesses operating abroad the same kinds of protections that the US Constitution provided to businesses, both American and foreign, operating in the United States.[13] The US postwar FCN treaties, with their new investment provisions, were intended to project American liberal principles abroad. Indeed, President Harry Truman's famous Point Four proposal, under which the United States would provide technical assistance to other countries to promote economic development, was hailed as an extension of Truman's Fair Deal to the rest of the world.[14] Following the announcement of the Point Four program, the Truman administration treated the postwar FCN treaties explicitly as an element

cannot be expected to remove important investment impediments of a non-juridical character." Department of State Telegram to US Embassy, Seoul, 12 October 1953, National Archives and Records Administration, Record Group 59, Department of State File No. 611.95B4/10–253.

[11] Memorandum by Vernon G. Setser headed, "Status of Commercial Treaty Program," dated 5 November 1946, National Archive and Records Administration, Record Group 59, Department of State File No. 711.002/11–546.

[12] Letter dated 6 March 1956, from Acting Secretary of State Herbert Hoover, Jr., to President Dwight Eisenhower, NARA, Record Group 59, Department of State File No. 611.174/3–656.

[13] *Department of State Bulletin*, Vol. 24, No. 618 (7 May 1951), 746.

[14] *The Washington Post* (21 January 1949), 1. *The Washington Post's* headline read, "Truman Proposes 'Fair Deal' Plan for the World."

of that program and thus part of the extension of New Deal/Fair Deal liberalism to Europe and the developing world.[15]

Defining liberalism

My account requires that I define the term "liberalism" as I use it here. As I will show, the concept of liberalism has both a political and an economic dimension, although rarely was that distinction drawn by US FCN treaty negotiators.

Liberalism began in the mid-seventeenth century as a political doctrine. John Locke theorized that all persons were born in a state of nature with equal liberty.[16] Therefore, no person could exercise dominion over another without the latter's consent. In a state of nature, each person's liberties were in constant danger of infringement by others. To protect their liberties, individuals consented to the creation of a state with power to protect each against the other through legislation for the common good. The danger existed, however, that a state created to protect liberty would become too strong and would itself become an oppressor. One preventative was constitutionalism, the idea that the state itself is subject to fundamental law.

Political liberalism, then, encompassed at least three principles of relevance here. The first principle is that the state exists to protect individual liberty. The second is that the state possesses the power to regulate for the common good. The third is that state regulatory power is limited by the rule of law. I will refer to these as the liberty principle, the regulatory principle, and the legality principle, respectively.

As this brief summary of Locke's liberal political theory suggests, the regulatory principle exists in tension with the liberty principle. That is, state regulatory power threatens, but is also limited by, the liberty of the individual. The tension is mediated by the legality principle, under which law establishes boundaries between the regulatory principle and the liberty principle, putting it in tension with each of these other two principles.

15 For example, during a press conference held on 13 July 1949, Secretary of State Dean Acheson explained that the US FCN treaty with Italy was "designed to stimulate a mutually advantageous flow of capital and technology which is in line with basic objectives of the Point Four program." Telegram dated 13 July 1949, from the Secretary of State to the US mission in Rome, National Archives and Records Administration, Record Group 59, Department of State File No. 711.652/7–1349.

16 John Locke, *Second Treatise of Government* (London: Awnsham Churchill, 1689).

Meanwhile, in 1776, Adam Smith published his *Wealth of Nations*, laying the theoretical foundations for an economic liberalism.[17] Smith argued that an economy achieves maximum productivity by allowing competitive markets, rather than the state, to allocate resources so that the most efficient producers prevail. Smith wished not to minimize state action but to eliminate state action that gave preferences to inefficient producers. Indeed, Smith acknowledged that markets will not adequately provide certain goods or services and, therefore, the state should provide them. He identified national defense and the administration of justice, among others, as functions best performed by the state. Economic liberalism thus recognizes that the state has a responsibility to protect property and contract rights.

Applied to investment policy, economic liberalism includes three principles.[18] The first is the principle that the market rather than the state should allocate capital, the principle of investment neutrality. The second is the principle that the state should protect property and contract rights, the principle of investment security. The third is that the state should ensure the proper functioning of the market and should act where the market is inadequate, the principle of market facilitation. Like the three principles of political liberalism, these three principles of economic liberalism exist in tension with each other. For example, a state seeking to ensure that a market is competitive may exercise the principle of market facilitation to prohibit a merger of two enterprises, thereby intruding upon the principle of investment neutrality.

As different dimensions of liberalism, the three principles of political liberalism and the three principles of economic liberalism that I have identified are analogs. The liberty principle, which seeks to preserve individual freedom of action, is the analog to the principle of investment neutrality, under which the state leaves investors free to put capital to its most productive use. The regulatory principle, which acknowledges the power of the state to regulate for the common good, is the analog to the principle of market facilitation, which acknowledges that states should act where markets are not functioning adequately. The legality principle, under which state regulation is constrained by the rule of law, is the

[17] Adam Smith, *An Inquiry into the Nature and Causes of the Wealth of Nations* (London: W. Strahan and T. Cadell, 1776).

[18] I have developed this argument more thoroughly in Kenneth J. Vandevelde, "The Political Economy of a Bilateral Investment Treaty" (1998) 92 *American Journal of International Law* 621.

analog to the principle of investment security, under which property and contract rights are protected by law.

Although the principles of political and economic liberalism are analogous, they are not the same. Political liberalism originated as a theory to promote liberty, while economic liberalism originated as a theory to promote economic productivity. A state committed to political liberalism, in the exercise of the regulatory principle, may choose to pursue policies that are calculated to promote ends other than increasing economic productivity, such as setting labor or environmental standards or providing protection against market instability. Furthermore, even where a liberal polity pursues a policy of promoting economic productivity, it will find that economic liberals can differ over the precise balance to be struck among the principles of economic liberalism to achieve that goal. Some economic liberals may regard a particular market failure as necessitating state regulation, while others may believe that state regulation would worsen the situation. Economic liberalism does not provide an unambiguous answer to every question of how best to promote productivity.

As this discussion suggests, a state committed to political liberalism may choose among a variety of concrete economic policies, both because it may choose to pursue goals in addition to economic productivity and because, even where it chooses to promote economic productivity, the best means to that end may be uncertain. Thus, for example, in the early history of the United States, many of the states adopted economic policies that embraced an activist, regulatory state. They conferred monopolies, they chartered private corporations in which they invested state funds, and they extensively regulated the private sector to protect the public interest.[19]

By the middle of the nineteenth century, however, states were abandoning their experiments with state capitalism and deregulating their economies. At the end of the century, when some of the effects of industrialization drove Populist and Progressive demands for increased regulation at both the state and the federal levels, such reforms were denounced as a departure from classic liberal principles.[20] During that same period, neoclassical

19 *See, e.g.*, Oscar Handlin and Mary Flug Handlin, *Commonwealth: A Study of the Role of Government in the American Economy: Massachusetts, 1774–1861* (Cambridge, MA: Harvard University Press, 1969); Carter Goodrich, *Government Promotion of American Canals and Railroads, 1800–1890* (New York: Columbia University Press, 1960); and William J. Novak, *The People's Welfare: Law and Regulation in Nineteenth Century America* (Chapel Hill: University of North Carolina Press, 1996).

20 *See* Arnold M. Paul, *Conservative Crisis and the Rule of Law: Attitudes of Bar and Bench, 1887–1895* (Gloucester: Peter Smith, 1960).

economists provided theoretical support for a laissez-faire policy by proposing models of economic behavior in which markets self-regulate by always returning to an equilibrium point, which meant that state regulation, including regulation of the type practiced earlier in the century, was unnecessary and even pernicious.[21] The US Supreme Court invalidated a number of reforms on the ground that they violated individuals' liberty of contract.[22] That is, the Supreme Court interpreted the Constitution so that the principles of legality and liberty seemed to compel adherence at least in part to neoclassical economic liberalism.

The Great Depression led to a reconsideration of liberalism. Lord John Maynard Keynes challenged the neoclassical models, arguing that markets could find an equilibrium point at which unemployment was unacceptably high and that only state intervention to stimulate demand would reduce unemployment.[23] Franklin Roosevelt's New Deal saw a failed market economy and sought to remedy that failure through a broad exercise of the regulatory principle and its analog, the market facilitation principle, experimenting variously with state capitalism, increased spending, and greater government oversight of the economy.[24] The US Supreme Court reconsidered the legality principle as it had been understood in prior decades and revised constitutional doctrine to limit constitutional impediments to New Deal economic policies.[25] Roosevelt regarded his more regulatory state not as a curtailment of the liberty principle but as a means to greater freedom. As he explained in his 1944 State of the Union address, "true individual freedom cannot exist without economic security and independence. 'Necessitous men are not free men.'"[26] Indeed, while expanding the regulatory principle with respect to economic matters, the Supreme Court in the 1930s and 1940s

[21] The foundational figures of neoclassicism include Alfred Marshall, William Stanley Jevons, Carl Menger, Leon Walras, and John Bates Clark.

[22] The classic case is *Lochner* v. *New York*, 198 U.S. 45 (1905), in which the US Supreme Court invalidated a state law that limited the working hours of bakers.

[23] *See* Robert Skidelsky, *Keynes: The Return of the Master* (New York: Allen Lane, 2009).

[24] *See* Alan Brinkley, *The End of Reform: New Deal Liberalism in Recession and War* (New York: Knopf, 1995); Jordan A. Schwartz, *The New Dealers: Power Politics in the Age of Roosevelt* (New York: Knopf, 1993); Ellis W. Hawley, *The New Deal and the Problem of Monopoly: A Study in Economic Ambivalence* (Princeton: Princeton University Press, 1966).

[25] In its 1937 decision in *West Coast Hotel* v. *Parrish*, 300 U.S. 379 (1937), the Supreme Court approved a state minimum wage law similar to one previously held unconstitutional in its 1923 decision in *Adkins* v. *Children's Hospital*, 261 U.S. 525 (1923). This decision is generally regarded as signaling the end of the Court's *Lochner* era. After *West Coast Hotel*, the Court invalidated no further New Deal legislation.

[26] Franklin Roosevelt, State of the Union Address, 11 January 1944.

strengthened the liberty principle with respect to other matters,[27] such as freedom of speech[28] and freedom of religion.[29] Roosevelt, in one of his famous fireside chats, responding to criticisms that the New Deal was, variously, socialist, communist or fascist, asked his listeners, "Have you lost any of your rights or liberty or constitutional freedom of action and choice?"[30] Alluding to the Bill of Rights, he told his listeners to "ask yourself whether you personally have suffered the impairment of a single jot of these great assurances."[31]

Fashioning a liberal investment regime

The US postwar FCN treaties

It was in this context that the Roosevelt and Truman administrations launched the US postwar FCN treaty program as the first series of bilateral investment treaties. In this section, I turn to the question of how the investment provisions of the US postwar FCN treaties reflected New Deal/Fair Deal liberalism.

The US postwar FCN treaties strengthened the liberty principle by protecting the rights of Americans abroad in ways that reflected the kinds of protections afforded by the US Constitution. They included, among others, provisions protecting freedom of religion,[32] freedom of press,[33] and due process of law.[34] The United States took these provisions

[27] *United States* v. *Carolene Products*, 304 U.S. 144 (1938) (upholding a federal prohibition on filled milk but cautioning that a more exacting scrutiny may be applied in certain cases, such as those involving alleged violations of the Bill of Rights).

[28] *West Virginia Board of Education* v. *Barnette*, 319 U.S. 624 (1943) (holding that a requirement that school children recite a pledge of allegiance to the US flag violated their freedom of speech).

[29] *Everson* v. *Board of Education*, 330 U.S. 1 (1947) (holding that the First Amendment to the Constitution erected a "wall of separation between church and state").

[30] Franklin D. Roosevelt, Fifth Fireside Chat, 28 June 1934, *reprinted in* William D. Pederson, *The FDR Years* (New York: Facts on File, 2006), 340, 341.

[31] *Id.*

[32] For example, Article II(3) of the US FCN treaty with the Netherlands provided that "Nationals of either Party, within the territories of the other Party, shall be permitted . . . (b) to enjoy liberty of conscience [and] (c) to hold both private and public religious services."

[33] For example, Article II(3) of the US FCN treaty with the Netherlands provided that "Nationals of either Party, within the territories of the other Party, shall be permitted . . . (d) to gather and to transmit material for dissemination to the public abroad; and (e) to communicate with other persons inside and outside such territories by mail, telegraph and other means open to general public use."

[34] For example, Article III(2) of the US FCN treaty with the Netherlands provided that "If, with the territories of either Party, a national of the other Party is taken into custody . . . [s]uch

seriously. For example, during FCN treaty negotiations with Pakistan, the State Department instructed its embassy there that "[p]rotection [of] civil rights [is] of fundamental importance to [the] people and Government in [the] US where such rights [are the] subject [of] strong constitutional guarantees and [the] Department cannot agree to any language which could be construed as compromising those rights."[35]

The analog to the liberty principle in the realm of investment policy is the principle of investment neutrality. In fact, the US postwar FCN treaties rested on the belief that investment flows should be guided by market principles.[36] That is, these treaties advanced significantly the principle of investment neutrality. In particular, the US postwar FCN treaties granted to nationals and companies of each party national and most favored nation (MFN) treatment with respect to the right to engage in various economic activities, such as manufacturing, commerce, and finance.[37] Engaging in these activities, of course, included the establishment of investment. The same language also guaranteed that each party would accord national and MFN treatment to nationals and companies of the other party during the conduct of their business activities.

Yet, the principle of investment neutrality, as one would expect in a document reflecting New Deal liberalism, was certainly not absolute in the US postwar FCN treaties. In the economic sphere, the New Deal recognized that the state possessed a robust regulatory power, which

national shall: (a) receive reasonable and humane treatment; (b) be promptly informed of the accusations against him; (c) be brought to trial as promptly as is consistent with the proper preparation of his defense; and (d) enjoy all means reasonably necessary to his defense, including the services of competent counsel of his choice."

35 Telegram dated 14 January 1955, from the Department of State to the US embassy in Karachi, NARA, Record Group 59, Department of State File No. 611.90D4/1–1455.

36 Herman Walker, a leading negotiator of the US postwar FCN treaties during both the Truman and the Eisenhower administrations, noted explicitly that the FCN treaty "was based on the principle that free market conditions should govern investment decisions." State Department Despatch dated 29 June 1959, National Archives and Records Administration, Record Group 59, State Department File No. 611/514/6–2959.

37 For example, Article VII(1) of the US FCN treaty with the Netherlands provided that "Nationals and companies of either Party shall be accorded national treatment with respect to engaging in all types of commercial, industrial, financial and other activity for gain (business activities) within the territories of the other Party ... Moreover, enterprises which they control ... shall in all that relates to the conduct of the activities hereof, be accorded treatment no less favorable than that accorded like enterprises controlled by nationals and companies of such other Party." Article VII(4) provided that "Nationals and companies of either Party, as well as enterprises controlled by such nationals and companies, shall in any event be accorded most-favored-nation treaty with reference to the matters treated in the present Article."

could, and in the FCN treaties did, limit the principle of investment neutrality. First, as already seen, the right to engage in economic activities was only the right to do so on a nondiscriminatory basis. The state was free to exclude private investment from any sector of the economy, as long as the exclusion was nondiscriminatory. Second, even this right to nondiscrimination existed only with respect to the activities specifically listed. Third, within the sectors of the economy listed, the US postwar FCN treaties carved out specific matters in which national treatment did not apply.[38] These sectors were those in which the states or the federal government had existing discriminatory laws. Fourth, in some treaties, particularly with less developed countries, the United States did not even seek to obtain a guarantee of national treatment with respect to the establishment of investment.[39]

Provisions in the US postwar FCN treaties relating to the security of investment were extensive and are quite recognizable to those familiar with the BITs. The FCN treaties included a guarantee of fair and equitable treatment,[40] most constant protection and security,[41] and, as already noted, a promise of national and MFN treatment following establishment of an investment. They prohibited arbitrary or discriminatory treatment,[42] required prompt, adequate, and effective compensation for expropriation,[43] restricted the host state's power to impose

[38] For example, Article VII(2) of the US FCN treaty with the Netherlands provided that "Each Party reserves the right to limit the extent to which aliens may within its territories establish, acquire interests in, or carry on enterprises engaged in communications, air or water transport, banking involving depository or fiduciary functions, or the exploitation of land or other natural resources."

[39] This was true, for example, in the US postwar FCN treaties with Ethiopia and Iran.

[40] For example, Article I of the US FCN treaty with the Netherlands provided that "Each Party shall at all times accord fair and equitable treatment to the nationals and companies of the other Party, and to their property, enterprises and other interests."

[41] For example, Article VI(1) of the US FCN treaty with the Netherlands provided that "Property of nationals and companies of either Party shall receive the most constant protection and security within the territories of the other Party."

[42] For example, Article VI(3) of the US FCN treaty with the Netherlands provided that "Neither Party shall take unreasonable or discriminatory measures that would impair the rights or interests within its territories of nationals and companies of the other Party, whether in their capital, or in their enterprises and the property thereof, or in the skills, arts or technology which they have supplied."

[43] For example, Article VI(4) of the US FCN treaty with the Netherlands provided that "Property of nationals and companies of either Party shall not be taken within the territories of the other Party except for a public interest, nor shall it be taken without the prompt payment of just compensation. Such compensation shall be in an effectively realizable form and shall represent the equivalent of the property taken; and adequate provision shall have been made at or prior to the time of taking for the determination and payment thereof."

exchange controls[44] unless its foreign exchange position so required,[45] and protected an investor's right to employ key personnel[46] and to gain access to local courts.[47] Disputes concerning the interpretation or application of the treaty were to be submitted to the International Court of Justice (ICJ).[48]

The Germany–Pakistan BIT

Although the US postwar FCN treaties could justifiably be regarded as the first bilateral investment treaties, they differed profoundly from later BITs in that they were not limited to investment matters. The modern

[44] For example, Article XII(2) of the US FCN treaty with the Netherlands provided that "Neither Party shall impose exchange restrictions . . . except to the extent necessary to maintain or restore adequacy in its monetary reserves, particularly in relation to its external commercial and financial requirements." Further, Article XII(1) guaranteed to nationals and companies of each Party national and MFN treatment "with respect to payments, remittances and transfers of funds or financial instruments . . ." In addition, Article VII(3) provided that "Exchange restrictions shall not be imposed by either Party in a manner unnecessarily detrimental or arbitrarily discriminatory to the claims, investment, transport, trade, and other interests of nationals and companies of the other Party, or to the competitive position thereof."

[45] For example, Article XII(2) of the US FCN treaty with the Netherlands permitted exchange controls "to the extent necessary to maintain or restore adequacy in [a party's] monetary reserves . . ." Article VII(3) further provided that "If either Party imposes exchanges restrictions in accordance with paragraph 2 of the present Article, it shall, after making whatever provisions may be necessary to assure the availability of foreign exchange for goods and services essential to the health and welfare of its people, make reasonable provision for the withdrawal, in foreign exchange in the currency of the other Party, of (a) the compensation [for expropriated property], (b) earnings, whether in the form of salaries, interest, dividends, commissions, royalties, payments for technical services, or otherwise, and (c) amounts for amortization of loans, depreciation of direct investments, and capital transfers to the extent feasible, giving consideration to the special needs for other transactions."

[46] For example, Article VIII(1)(a) of the US FCN treaty with the Netherlands provided that "Nationals and companies of either Party shall be permitted to engage, within the territories of the other Party, accountants and other technical experts, executive personnel, attorneys, agents, and other specialists of their choice."

[47] For example, Article V(1) of the US FCN treaty with the Netherlands provided that "Nationals and companies of either Party shall be accorded national treatment with respect to access to the courts of justice and to administrative tribunals or agencies within the territories of the other Party, in all degrees of jurisdiction, both in pursuit and in defense of their rights."

[48] For example, Article XXV(2) of the US FCN treaty with the Netherlands provided that "Any dispute between the Parties as to the interpretation or application of the present Treaty, not satisfactorily adjusted by diplomacy, shall be submitted to the International Court of Justice, unless the Parties agree to settlement by some other pacific means."

network of BITs – treaties that promote and protect foreign investment and do little else – traces its origin to the BIT concluded by Germany and Pakistan in 1959.[49]

When Germany concluded its first BIT, most of that treaty's provisions had antecedents in the US postwar FCN treaties. Article 1 granted a right of establishment, but subordinated it to local law, a much weaker version of the right guaranteed in the US postwar FCN treaties. Article 2 prohibited discrimination against foreign investment, while Article 3 required "protection and security" for investment and compensation for expropriated investment. Articles 4, 5, and 6 guaranteed a right of transfer of capital and returns. Article 12 provided for state–state dispute settlement, either through state–state arbitration or, if both parties agreed, ICJ adjudication. All of these provisions had antecedents in the US postwar FCN treaties.

The Germany–Pakistan BIT did contain two new substantive provisions of note. The first, which appeared at Article 3(3), required national and MFN treatment with respect to compensation for losses due to armed conflict, revolution or revolt. The second, which appeared at Article 7, required each party to observe any other obligation it may have entered into with regard to covered investments.

The Germany–Pakistan BIT did not include a provision guaranteeing to investment fair and equitable treatment, although such a provision would soon appear in Germany's other BITs.[50] That provision has been interpreted to include both a guarantee of nondiscrimination and protection for the investor's legitimate expectations resulting from assurances by the host state.[51] Thus, some of the substance of the two new substantive obligations of the Germany–Pakistan BIT appeared in the US

[49] Germany–Pakistan BIT, *supra* note 2.

[50] The provision appeared, for example, in German's 1961 BIT with Thailand.

[51] On the interpretation of the fair and equitable treatment standard, *see* Iona Tudor, *The Fair and Equitable Treatment Standard in the International Law of Foreign Investment* (Oxford: OUP, 2008); Katia Yannaca-Small, "Fair and Equitable Treatment Standard," in Katia Yannaca-Small (ed.), *Arbitration Under International Investment Agreements: A Guide to the Key Issues* (Oxford: OUP, 2010); Kenneth J. Vandevelde, "A Unified Theory of the Fair and Equitable Treatment Standard" (2010) 43 *New York University Journal of International Law and Politics* 43; Rudolf Dolzer, "Fair and Equitable Treatment: A Key Standard in Investment Treaties" (2005) 39 *International Lawyer* 87; Christoph Schreuer, "Fair and Equitable Treatment in Arbitral Practice" (2005) 6 *Journal of World Investment and Trade* 357; Barnali Choudhury, "Evolution or Devolution? Defining Fair and Equitable Treatment in International Investment Law" (2005) 6 *Journal of World Investment and Trade* 297.

postwar FCN treaties under the requirement of fair and equitable treatment or the restriction on expropriation.[52]

The Germany–Pakistan BIT was, of course, only the first of thousands of international investment agreements that would be concluded worldwide. It set the pattern, however, for the BIT programs inaugurated by other European countries during the 1960s and 1970s and these, in turn, set the pattern for the entire network of international investment agreements. Although the language would evolve, the kinds of provisions seen in Germany's early BITs – guarantees of a right of admission subject to local law, nondiscriminatory treatment (particularly for losses from war and civil disturbance), fair and equitable treatment, full protection and security, the observance of obligations with respect to investment, compensation for expropriation, and free transfers and consent to state–state arbitration – largely defined the content of the European BITs, at least until the incorporation of consent to investor-state arbitration at the end of the 1960s.[53] Thus, to say that the early German BITs included few provisions that did not have antecedents in the US postwar FCN treaties is to say that the early European BITs collectively included few provisions that did not have antecedents in the US postwar FCN treaties. The global network of more than 3,000 international investment agreements rests on the foundation of the US postwar FCN treaties, drafted and negotiated as a projection of New Deal/Fair Deal liberalism.

The emergence of neoliberalism

The election of Ronald Reagan in 1980 signaled a shift in the United States from New Deal/Fair Deal liberalism to neoliberalism, a version of liberalism that had emerged during the 1970s. Neoliberals argued that the economic problems of the 1970s – notably high unemployment accompanied by high inflation – were the result of excessive state regulation and called for a shrinkage of the state.[54] Thus, the liberty principle and its analog, the investment neutrality principle, should receive the widest application, meaning that states should defer to decisions made by

[52] As discussed further, in note 75, the effect of the observance of obligations provision is contested, which complicates any effort to compare it with the fair and equitable treatment provision.

[53] I have traced the appearance of these provisions and the evolution in their language in Kenneth J. Vandevelde, *Bilateral Investment Treaties: History, Policy and Interpretation* (Oxford: OUP, 2010).

[54] *See generally* David Harvey, *A Brief History of Neoliberalism* (Oxford: OUP, 2007).

private actors in the market. At the same time, states should confine the regulatory principle and its analog, the market facilitation principle, to the narrowest possible circumstances by the deregulation of the economy. Taxes should be reduced, thereby limiting resources available to the state, and budgets should be balanced to prevent the use of debt to finance government expenditures. State enterprises should be privatized.

The rise of neoliberalism in the 1970s coincided with the inauguration of the US BIT program, although there was no causal relationship. The United States had continued to negotiate FCN treaties into the 1970s but had not successfully concluded a treaty since 1966.[55] Meanwhile, several European countries had successfully concluded scores of BITs similar to the 1959 BIT between Germany and Pakistan.[56] Accordingly, in 1977, the United States decided to launch its own BIT program to emulate the successful BIT programs of several European countries. The United States ceased negotiating FCN treaties, offering countries that expressed an interest in negotiating an FCN treaty the opportunity to negotiate a BIT instead.

The United States drafted a model BIT comprising modified versions of the investment provisions of its postwar FCN treaties, with a few provisions borrowed from the European BITs, most notably a provision consenting to arbitration of investment disputes with investors, a provision committing each party to observe any obligations into which it had entered with respect to investments, and a provision on losses attributable to war or civil disturbance, and with a few novel provisions not in any BIT, most notably a prohibition on performance requirements.[57]

Thus, the US BITs followed closely the vision of investment treaty policy underlying the US postwar FCN treaties. Most of the provisions in the US model BIT traced their origin to those FCN treaties. In launching its BIT program, the United States sought not to change its investment

55 The United States concluded its last FCN treaty, with Thailand, on 29 May 1966.

56 By the 1977, when the US inaugurated its BIT program, European countries that had initiated BIT programs included Germany, France, Switzerland, the Netherlands, Italy, the Belgium-Luxembourg Union, Sweden, Denmark, Norway, the United Kingdom, and Austria.

57 Although President Carter approved the BIT program in 1977, the first successful negotiations did not occur until 1982. A copy of the US model BIT adopted in 1982 may be found at Appendix A of Kenneth J. Vandevelde, *U.S. International Investment Agreements* (Oxford: OUP, 2009), 236–237. The model was revised in 1983 and the 1983 model formed the basis of most of the successful US BIT negotiations of the 1980s. Thus, the 1983 model, which may be found at Appendix B of that same work, will be treated here as typical of the US BITs of the 1980s.

treaty policy but to find a treaty instrument that would continue its postwar investment treaty policy and that would be easier to conclude than an FCN treaty. Although US investment treaty provisions had grown out of New Deal/Fair Deal liberalism, these provisions could also accommodate the neoliberal economic policies of the Reagan administration, particularly because the provisions did not require a treaty party to exercise its regulatory power and because they included the strongest commitment to investment neutrality that it was feasible to negotiate at that time.

In drafting their new model BIT, US officials suffered some doubt regarding whether the model should include a commitment to investment neutrality as strong as that which had appeared in the US postwar FCN treaties. Some of those involved in the interagency drafting process advocated omitting the obligation of national treatment with respect to the establishment of investment, believing that in the prevailing political climate few other countries would agree to that obligation. That view did not prevail, however, in part because of a desire not to retreat from the obligations contained in the FCN treaties.[58] Ultimately, the United States drafted a model BIT that incorporated a potentially stronger commitment to investment neutrality than had appeared in its postwar FCN treaties, although it then bargained away some of the stronger language in negotiations, particularly during the 1980s. For example, while the right of nondiscriminatory treatment with respect to establishment in the US BITs applied in principle to all investment, an apparent broadening of the provision relative to that in the FCN treaties, the US BITs allowed each party to designate in an annex sectors of the economy to which the right of national treatment would not apply, thereby inviting potentially more qualifications than had appeared in the FCN treaties, where the excepted sectors were the same for both parties and were identified in the treaty text. Similarly, the transfers provision in the US BITs applied to transfers into and out of the host country (contrary to the counterpart provision in the FCN treaties, which addressed only remittances) and no longer included in every case a balance of payments exception. At least in the 1980s, however, the United States on several occasions agreed during particular negotiations to include such an exception.[59] Furthermore, the US BITs included a limited prohibition on performance requirements,

[58] Vandevelde, *U.S. International Investment Agreements*, 236–237.

[59] Of the ten US BITs concluded during the 1980s, four included an exception for periods of low foreign exchange reserves. These were the BITs with Egypt, the Democratic Republic of the Congo, Bangladesh, and Turkey.

which was an innovation in BIT practice, but the United States also agreed in several negotiations in the 1980s to substantially qualify that prohibition as well.[60]

The substance of the investment security provisions that appeared in the US postwar FCN treaties changed little in the US BITs. The most notable changes in the investment security provisions came in the form of the addition of three new provisions, requiring the observance of obligations with respect to investment, addressing losses from war and civil disturbance, and consenting to investor-state arbitration. Although fully consistent with neoliberalism, these new provisions in US treaty practice were not neoliberal innovations. The observance of obligations provision had appeared in the 1959 Germany–Pakistan BIT[61] and duplicated at least in part protection provided by the US postwar FCN treaties.[62] The provision on losses from war and civil disturbance largely duplicated protection already provided by other BIT provisions and also had antecedents reaching back to the 1959 Germany–Pakistan BIT.[63] An investor-state arbitration provision had first appeared in BITs in the late 1960s before the emergence of neoliberalism,[64] and such a mechanism had been proposed at least as early as 1948, during the Truman administration.[65] If the US BIT had more investment security provisions than the US postwar FCNs in some respects, then that fact owed far more to US emulation of European practice dating back to 1959 than to a shift from New Deal liberalism to neoliberalism.

While the emergence of neoliberalism did not result in a reconceptualization of the content of US investment treaties, it did contribute to one

[60] Of the ten US BITs concluded during the 1980s, six modified the prohibition on performance requirements so that the parties were required only to seek or endeavor to avoid performance requirements. These were the BITs with Egypt, Morocco, the Democratic Republic of the Congo, Bangladesh, Haiti, and Turkey.

[61] Germany–Pakistan BIT, *supra* note 2, Art. 7. [62] See text *supra* at notes 51–52.

[63] Vandevelde, *U.S. International Investment Agreements*, 432–433.

[64] The first BIT to provide for investor-state arbitration was a 1968 treaty between the Netherlands and Indonesia. Under Article 11 of that treaty, each of the parties undertook to submit to the jurisdiction of ICSID upon demand on an investor of the other party. Agreement on Economic Cooperation, Indonesia-Netherlands, 7 July 1968. The first BIT that set forth the parties' consent (as opposed to their promise to consent) was concluded between Italy and Chad the following year. Accord en vue de proteger et favoriser les investissements de capitaux, Chad-Italy, 11 June 1969. *See generally* Antonio R. Parra, *The History of ICSID* (Oxford: OUP, 2012), 133.

[65] International Law Association, Draft Statutes of the Arbitral Tribunal for Foreign Investment and of the Foreign Investment Court (1948), *reprinted in* United Nations Conference on Trade and Development, 3 International Investment Instruments: A Compendium 259 (Geneva, 1996).

profound change in international investment law. For reasons that I have discussed extensively elsewhere, the events of the 1980s – including the emergence of neoliberalism, the collapse of the Soviet Union, the Third World debt crisis and the successful example of several East Asian economies – created pressures that led developing countries and transitional economies to seek foreign investment with unprecedented enthusiasm and to embrace the conclusion of BITs as one means of encouraging inward foreign investment.[66] The result is that the rate at which BITs were concluded increased more than tenfold. While fewer than 400 BITs worldwide had been concluded during the 30 years from 1959 to 1989,[67] during the next 15 years some 2,000 BITs would be concluded.[68]

Furthermore, because developing and formerly socialist countries were actively seeking investment, they were more willing both to conclude BITs and to demand fewer changes to the language of the model BITs proposed by capital-exporting countries. This was particularly notable with respect to the investment neutrality provisions. For example, by the early 1990s, the US BITs rarely contained a balance of payments exception,[69] and they consistently included a robust prohibition on performance requirements.[70] The investment security provisions of the US BITs had encountered far less resistance in the 1980s than the investment neutrality provisions and the United States continued in the 1990s to be able to obtain agreement on these provisions with few qualifications.

Assessing the liberal vision today

The foregoing discussion has shown that in the 1940s the United States sought through the negotiation of postwar FCN treaties to create an international investment regime based on New Deal/Fair Deal liberalism and that these treaties laid the foundation for the network of more than 3,000 international investment agreements. In this section, I will assess

[66] Kenneth J. Vandevelde, "Sustainable Liberalism and the International Investment Regime" (1998) 19 *Michigan Journal of International Law* 373.

[67] UNCTAD, *World Investment Report 2008* (Geneva, 2008), 9.

[68] UNCTAD, Recent Developments in International Investment Agreements (2007–June 2008), IIA Monitor No. 2 (2008).

[69] Of the 35 US BITs signed during the 1990s, only three have a balance of payments exception. These are the BITs with Tunisia, Sri Lanka, and Jamaica.

[70] Of the 35 US BITs signed during the 1990s, only the US BIT with Tunisia lacks a firm commitment not to impose performance requirements. That BIT provided, at Article II (6), that the parties shall "endeavor not to impose" performance requirements.

the extent to which the contemporary international law of foreign investment reflects that liberal vision.

As has been seen, the principles of liberalism exist in tension with each other. Thus, there is no single liberal version of an international investment agreement. Different investment agreements, all in the liberal tradition, may strike somewhat different balances among the principles of liberalism. Our assessment, then, involves identifying how the international law of foreign investment reflects each of the principles of liberalism.

The single most visible principle in the network of international investment agreements is the legality principle and, its analog, the investment security principle. As I have argued elsewhere, the legality principle, i.e., the principle of the rule of law, can be regarded as comprising at least five more specific norms: reasonableness, nondiscrimination, security, transparency, and due process.[71]

Nearly the whole of a contemporary international investment agreement falls within these five rule of law norms. The prohibition on unreasonable or discriminatory measures reflects, obviously, the norms of reasonableness and nondiscrimination. The requirements of national and MFN treatment also reflect the norm of nondiscrimination. The guarantee of full protection and security, the observance of obligations provision (which protects contract rights), the provision requiring compensation and imposing other conditions on the expropriation of property, and the right of free outward transfer of capital and returns all reflect the norm of security. Provisions requiring publication of laws relating to investment reflect the norm of transparency. The investor-state and state–state arbitration provisions and the provision on judicial access all reflect the norm of due process. The fair and equitable treatment provision incorporates all five norms.[72]

In short, the contemporary international law on foreign investment is largely based on the principle of legality and its analog, the principle of investment security. Investment treaties, above all else, exist to bring foreign investment within the protection of the rule of law.

Indeed, the current network of international investment agreements actually reflects a stronger commitment to legality and investment security than did the US postwar FCN treaties because of the inclusion of provisions for investor-state arbitration. Such provisions help to ensure

[71] Vandevelde, "A Unified Theory of the Fair and Equitable Treatment Standard," 43.
[72] *Id.* at 53–53.

that other treaty provisions subjecting host state treatment of foreign investment to the rule of law, many of them dating back to the US FCN treaties of the 1940s, are effective.

The investment neutrality principle, while prominent in the US BITs, has won far less acceptance in the BIT practice of most other countries. Although a right to nondiscrimination with respect to establishment has become increasingly common, it still appears in a small minority of existing international investment agreements and appears in only a relatively small number of model BITs.[73] Rather, the more common practice is to grant a right of establishment in accordance with the law of the host state, in effect a commitment only to adhere to domestic law, which might impose substantial restrictions on the establishment of investment. Furthermore, in many international investment agreements, the transfers provision protects the right to repatriate capital and returns but does not apply to transfers into the host country.[74] The performance requirements provision has become more common but still appears in only a relatively small minority of international investment agreements. Thus, the typical international investment agreement makes little provision for investment neutrality. It protects investment that is allowed by the host state but does not require the host state to open its economy to foreign investment.

As noted earlier, particularly since the end of the 1980s, countries throughout the world have chosen to remove many of their barriers to international capital movements and to seek to attract foreign investment, even if international investment agreements do not require them to do so.[75] Furthermore, international investment agreements do promote market allocations of capital insofar as they provide greater protection for investment once established and, thereby, diminish one impediment to international capital movements, the lack of effective legal protection for foreign investment in the host country.[76] Thus, the

[73] I have been able to find such a provision in the model BITs of eight countries: Bolivia, Canada, Finland, Italy, Kenya, Norway, Peru, and the United States.

[74] Vandevelde, *Bilateral Investment Treaties*, 319.

[75] For example, UNCTAD reported that during the last 9 months of 2014, 82 percent of investment policy measures taken at the national level were directed at removing barriers to, and promoting, foreign investment. The same report, which includes data back to 2000, indicates that the "vast majority" of investment policy measures taken throughout the reporting period were for purposes of removing barriers to, or promoting, foreign investment. United Nations Conference on Trade and Development, Investment Policy Monitor No. 13, January 2015.

[76] The question of the extent to which international investment agreements are actually associated with increased international investment flows is a matter of continuing debate.

expansion in the network of international investment agreements has been accompanied by greater investment neutrality in practice.

International investment agreements virtually never require states to exercise their regulatory power or, in particular, to take action to address inadequacies or failures in the market. They, nevertheless, do recognize the regulatory principle and its analog, the principle of market facilitation, insofar as they leave the treaty parties with very broad discretion to exercise their regulatory power within their domestic jurisdiction. Indeed, the provisions of the current network of international investment agreements, when properly interpreted, impose on host states few restrictions on their regulatory discretion not already reflected in US law.[77] Nor should this be surprising. As has been noted, US policy, when it drafted the investment provisions of the postwar FCN treaties that formed the basis for the current international law on foreign investment, was to project US constitutional and legal principles onto the rest of the world.[78] Thus, the international law on foreign investment leaves states with the discretion to exercise a robust regulatory principle.

As this discussion suggests, the current international law on foreign investment, both because of its weak commitment to investment

See, e.g., Karl P. Sauvant and Lisa E. Saches (eds.), *The Effect of Treaties on Foreign Direct Investment: Bilateral Investment Treaties, Double Taxation Treaties, and Investment Flows* (Oxford: OUP, 2009).

77 For a recent detailed discussion of the similarity between US law and the international law of foreign investment, *see* Parvan P. Parvanov and Mark Kantor, "Comparing U.S. Law and Recent U.S. Investment Agreements: Much More Similar Than You Might Think," in Karl P. Savant (ed.), *Yearbook of International Investment Law and Policy 2010–2011* (Oxford: OUP, 2012). Assessing the equivalency between US law and the provisions of international investment agreements is complicated by the fact that the meaning of certain provisions of international investment agreements, most notably the provision requiring parties to observe obligations into which they have entered with respect to investment, is contested. The contributions to this volume by Jean Ho and C.L. Lim address this issue. *See also* Rudolf Dolzer and Christoph Schreur, *Principles of International Investment Law*, 2nd ed. (Oxford: OUP, 2012), 168–175; Andrew Newcombe and Lluis Paradell, *Law and Practice of Investment Treaties: Standards of Treatment* 438 (Alphen aan den Rijn: Kluwer Law International, 2009); Jeswald W. Salacuse, *The Law of Investment Treaties* (Oxford: OUP, 2010), 280–283; Katia Yannaca-Small, "What About This 'Umbrella Clause'?," in Katia Yannaca-Small (ed.), *Arbitration Under International Investment Agreements: A Guide to the Key Issues* (Oxford: OUP, 2010), 479; Vandevelde, *Bilateral Investment Treaties*, 263–269.

78 This policy was reaffirmed in 2002, when Congress enacted legislation establishing as a negotiating objective in free trade agreements the conclusion of investment chapters that provided no greater substantive rights for foreign investors in the United States than US investors possessed under US law. Bipartisan Trade Promotion Authority Act, P.L. 107–210, Section 2102(b)(3), codified at 19 U.S.C. 3802(b)(3).

neutrality and because of the broad regulatory discretion that it leaves, can scarcely be regarded as creating or requiring a neoliberal investment regime. International investment agreements, taken as a whole, do not demand market allocations of capital. Nor do they limit host state regulatory discretion to such an extent as to force states to adopt a neoliberal domestic policy. More specifically, nothing in the current network of international investment agreements requires privatization or prohibits deficit financing. For the most part, these treaties prohibit regulatory actions only to the extent that such actions are arbitrary or discriminatory, violate prior undertakings or assurances by the state, are inconsistent with due process, or are so severe as to be expropriatory. Additional disciplines apply to certain limited circumstances. For example, the power to impose exchange controls may be limited, as may the power to require that indigenous personnel be appointed to senior management positions. Again, however, such provisions hardly compel a neoliberal economic policy. While the typical international agreement does not require a neoliberal economic policy, it does not preclude one either and its provisions can to some extent advance such a policy.

Liberalism and its critics

The liberal vision of international investment law promoted by the United States since the end of the Second World War has always met with opposition. In the early years, the chief targets of opponents and the most difficult provisions to negotiate were the investment neutrality provisions, more specifically, those provisions that removed barriers to capital movements, that is, those relating to the right of establishment and the free transfer of capital. Some 30 years later, when the United States inaugurated its BIT program, those provisions – along with the prohibition on performance requirements – again were among the most difficult to negotiate. The liberal idea that markets should allocate capital remains contested,[79] and even the United States includes exceptions to the principle in its international investment agreements.

The principle of legality and its analog, the principle of investment security, have met resistance as well. Much of this resistance arose, however, only in the late 1990s, following the submission of several investment disputes to investor-state arbitration, particularly under the

[79] For example, Howard Mann's contribution to this volume criticizes provisions that limit the imposition of performance requirements.

North American Free Trade Agreement.[80] A number of nongovernmental organizations (NGOs), most notably environmental groups, feared that the substantive provisions of the BITs would provide a basis for investor-state arbitral tribunals to award compensation to investors that suffered loss as the result of environmental regulations.[81] Since then, other NGOs have raised similar concerns that legitimate, nondiscriminatory regulatory measures would subject host states to demands for compensation from investors or that the mere prospect of a demand for compensation would chill the enactment of such measures.

Opposition to the legality principle in the BIT increasingly has manifested itself as opposition to investor-state arbitration.[82] Critics express the fear that investor-state arbitral tribunals, in deciding claims of investment treaty violations by investors, will interpret the provisions of these treaties more expansively than the treaty parties intended, thereby impairing the regulatory principle.[83] Some have called for the deletion of provisions most susceptible of misinterpretation or for the insertion of clarifying language that would reduce the likelihood of misinterpretation,[84] and, in fact, the United States revised its model BIT in 2004 to address many of these concerns. Other critics have concluded that the best way to avoid misinterpretation is to abolish or sharply limit the jurisdiction of investor-state arbitral tribunals.[85] Many critics would

[80] The cases that drew the special attention of these NGOs were *Methanex* v. *United States*, involving a ban on a gasoline additive, *Metalclad* v. *Mexico*, involving a refusal to permit operation of a solid waste facility, *S.D. Myers* v. *Canada*, involving a ban on the export of certain toxic chemicals, and *Ethyl Corporation* v. *Canada*, a ban on interprovincial trade in or the import of a gasoline additive.

[81] *See* Jack J. Coe, Jr., "Taking Stock of NAFTA Chapter 11 in Its Tenth Year: An Interim Sketch of Selected Themes, Issues, and Methods" (2003) 36 *Vanderbilt Journal of Transnational Law* 1381; Jeffrey Atik, "Legitimacy, Transparency and NGO Participation in the NAFTA Chapter 11 Process," in Todd Weiler (ed.), *NAFTA: Investment Law and Arbitration: Past Issues, Current Practice, Future Prospects* (New York: Transnational Publishers, 2004).

[82] This volume offers ample evidence of that fact. The contributions by Leon Trakman, Gus van Harten, David Schneiderman, and Peter Muchlinski all raise criticisms of investor-state arbitration.

[83] For example, the contributions of Kyla Tienhaara and Todd Tucker to this volume describe the concern that tribunals will interpret the concept of expropriation too broadly, resulting either in a narrowing of host state regulatory discretion or a chilling effect. Leon Trakman's contribution also discusses the possible chilling effect of international investment agreements.

[84] Leon Trakman's contribution to this volume suggests some modifications to treaty language.

[85] *See, e.g.*, International Institute for Sustainable Development, Investment-Related Dispute Settlement: Reflections on a New Beginning (Winnipeg 2015). Gus Van

return international investment law to the mid-1960s, when nearly all of the substantive norms that are present in most BITs had been developed, but investors lacked an effective remedy for violation of those norms, thus rendering treaty protections largely illusory in practice.

Those who first sought to create a treaty-based liberal investment regime – one in which foreign investment was protected by the rule of law – believed it vital that treaty principles be enforceable through binding, third-party dispute settlement.[86] In their mind, binding, third-party dispute settlement in accordance with law was an indispensable element of the rule of law.[87] Seeking to promote the ICJ as an instrument of the international rule of law, the drafters of the US postwar FCN treaties chose adjudication before that court as the mechanism by which treaty rights would be enforced. By the 1970s, however, dissatisfaction with the available means of enforcing treaty obligations led one capital-exporting state after another to provide in its BITs for investor-state arbitration.

The liberal vision does not, of course, require a particular dispute settlement mechanism. Rather, it requires that disputes be settled in a manner that is readily accessible, that decides disputes in accordance with applicable law and due process, and that provides an effective remedy without undue delay. A dispute settlement mechanism that does not meet those criteria will undermine the rule of law that the investment treaty regime was intended to create and that the liberal vision requires. Investor-state arbitration has become ubiquitous in international investment agreements not because it is a perfect system

Harten's contribution to this volume describes the case for withdrawal from the systems of investor-state arbitration, while David Schneiderman's contribution argues that the system itself is in peril. Peter Muchlinski's contribution suggests ways to reform investor-state arbitration that would reduce the number of claims brought to arbitration.

86 As the State Department instructed its chief negotiator during negotiations with the Sultanate of Muscat and Oman, "Such a provision [for adjudication of treaty disputes before the International Court of Justice] is necessary for two reasons in particular. First, the basic security of United States investments in that country requires a binding assurance that disputes affecting such investments shall have available, if needed, a forum where settlement may be had in accordance with the principles of international law and free from political pressure." Department of State telegram dated 2 December 1957, to the US Consulate General in Dhahran, National Archives and Records Administration, Record Group 59, Department of State File No. 611.86E4/10–257.

87 "The appearance of this clause in the FCN treaties establishes in the clearest possible manner the principle of the rule of law and of objectivity in the carrying out of treaty obligations . . ." Briefing Paper by Herman Walker titled "Compromissory Clause" and dated 29 September 1954, National Archives and Records Administration, Record Group 59, Department of State File No. 611.62A4/9–2454.

of dispute settlement but because capital-exporting states have believed that it comes closer to satisfying these criteria than any of the alternatives.

Conclusion

The current international law of foreign investment originated in a series of US postwar FCN treaties first negotiated in the years immediately after the Second World War on the basis of a liberal political and economic vision. This was a vision in which the rule of law mediates between state regulatory power and investor freedom. The model for this vision was the set of US constitutional principles that created the legal framework for New Deal liberalism. American negotiators, in promoting their postwar FCN treaties, hoped to project these principles onto the rest of the world. This is the vision that underlies now familiar norms such as the guarantees of fair and equitable treatment, full protection and security, national and MFN treatment, prompt, adequate, and effective compensation for expropriation, and free transfer of payments related to an investment, the prohibitions on unreasonable or discriminatory measures, and binding, third-party dispute settlement in accordance with applicable international law and due process. This is the vision that provides the interpretive context for these provisions.

The emergence of neoliberalism in the 1970s and its ascension in the 1980s resulted in calls for a diminished state, one that privatized enterprises and refrained from regulating them. While the investment provisions dating from the US postwar FCN treaties and the BITs of the 1960s permitted the adoption of neoliberal policies, they did not require such policies. Neither did the emergence of neoliberalism result in any fundamental shift in the text of the BITs being concluded worldwide. The significance of neoliberalism was that it was an important element in a constellation of events that prompted states that traditionally had opposed the liberal vision to consent to the conclusion of BITs and to do so with minimal changes to the models drafted by developed countries. In short, the ascendancy of neoliberalism greatly expanded the number of countries participating in the contemporary regime of international investment law, but it did not significantly alter the content of the specific treaty provisions that constituted the regime itself. Nevertheless, the explosion in the number of international investment agreements in the wake of the ascendance of neoliberalism and the ability of investment treaty provisions to advance some neoliberal goals have linked the current international law on foreign investment with neoliberalism in the minds of many.

The liberal vision underlying the international law on foreign investment faces some formidable challenges, both from those who oppose it in principle and from those who fear its misapplication in practice. Resistance to the liberal vision from the beginning has sharply limited provisions on investment neutrality, preserving for host states almost unlimited discretion to regulate inward capital movements, even if they have increasingly declined to exercise that discretion. More recent fears that investor-state arbitral tribunals will misinterpret investment treaty provisions intended to promote the rule of law have led critics to call for the deletion or modification of substantive protections and for the omission of consent to investor-state arbitration. In short, concerns about the possible erosion of the regulatory principle at home have led critics to call for, in effect, a virtual abandonment of efforts to promote the legality principle abroad.

Those who laid the foundation for the contemporary international law on foreign investment in the 1940s believed that they had drafted a set of provisions that reserved to the host state a robust power to regulate, while promoting economic development and the rule of law worldwide. The product of their labor endures some 80 years and 3,000 investment agreements later, but the liberal vision on which their work was founded remains controversial.

3

Caveat investors – where do things stand now?

LEON TRAKMAN AND DAVID MUSAYELYAN

Introduction

This chapter focuses on a perceptible shift in international investment law from investor protections embodied in investment treaties to reliance on domestic courts to resolve investor-state disputes. Professor Sornarajah has written at length on the future of investor-state arbitration (ISA). According to Sornarajah, ISA represents the asymmetric protection of foreign direct investment.[1] This system privileges powerful business interests and holds strong sway over the regulatory power of weaker states. Feeling the potential vicissitude of the investor-state dispute resolution system which they had created, developed states are now retreating from the expansive protections that they had previously provided to outbound investors.[2] Citing examples of countries such as the United States, Australia, Canada and the European Union (EU), Sornarajah argues that the legitimacy of ISA is seriously questioned. Envisioning a world where investors may devise their forms of dispute resolution subject to domestic constraints, Sornarajah further argues that ISA will be replaced by a more state-centric system of investor-state dispute resolution.[3]

In fact, the ISA has received critical coverage in the academic literature on account of its potential to unduly favour investors over domestic public policies directed at public health, environmental protection and

[1] M. Sornarajah, "Starting Anew in International Investment Law", (2012) 74 *Vale Columbia Center on Sustainable International Investment* 1, available at: http://ccsi.columbia.edu/files/2014/01/FDI_74.pdf.

[2] M. Sornarajah, "Mutations of Neo-Liberalism in International Investment", (2011) 3(1) *Trade L. & Dev* 203.

[3] See above note 1.

national security.[4] These concerns are covered at length in the other chapters of this volume and are only briefly examined in the third section of this chapter. More pertinent to this discussion is the fact that a number of states have rejected ISA and require foreign investors to bring their grievances to the local courts of host states.

Initially, for example, ISA was rejected by Ecuador, Bolivia and Venezuela. More recently, a number of major market economies have pledged to abolish ISA. These states are Australia, India, Indonesia and South Africa. Some EU member states are also considering reforming their ISA-granting agreements. Taking these recent developments into consideration, where do things stand now with regard to ISA? This issue is the subject of this discussion.

The actual or potential rejection of ISA by major developed free market economies lends support to Sornarajah's thesis. However, while discontent with ISA is certainly identifiable, this chapter does not envision a wholesale abolition of that system. As will be demonstrated here, the initial furore against ISA has subsided. In fact, even the states that have pledged to terminate ISA have either abandoned their initial position or have not taken concrete actions to articulate their desired investment regimes. Thus, while agreeing with Sornarajah that investment treaties are becoming more balanced between foreign investors and states, the authors of the present volume predict the continuation of the existing ISA regime.

The goal of this chapter is to demonstrate how states struggle to uphold their rejection of ISA and analyse the types of regulatory regimes they have implemented in light of their disaffection with it. To this end, the second part of this chapter engages in a general overview of states that have chosen to restrict ISA and the manner in which they chose to limit it. The third section examines some of the commonly cited reasons for excluding ISA, followed by a defence from the proponents of the ISA system. The fourth section examines the treaty-making behaviour of states following the rejection of ISA. The final section explains the resilience of ISA.

The new wave of discontent against ISA

Looking back to the years between 2007 and 2014, one would be hard-pressed not to consider the possibility of ISA falling out of favour among policy makers in some domestic states. Within a span of just a few years, a

[4] See below Section III.

number of states had announced that they will no longer provide ISA in future agreements, while others vowed to terminate their existing treaties.

In order to accurately appreciate the significance of these events, it is important to view them in light of the broader ISA treaty-making practice. Although ISA is now frequently provided for in various investment facilitation agreements, the practice did not become standardised until the early 1990s. Furthermore, although ISA provisions are present in the majority of investment agreements, a number of states have continued to negotiate ISA selectively. For example, the Free Trade Agreement (FTA) between Australia and the United States required foreign investors to rely on the domestic courts of the host state to resolve their disputes.[5] Brazil never signed the International Centre for Settlement of Investment Disputes (ICSID) Convention and has, traditionally, excluded ISA in its investment facilitation agreements. Finally, Japan has negotiated for ISA selectively, most recently agreeing to exclude it in its FTA with Australia.[6]

More so, states have routinely qualified the way ISA is applied to them. This was particularly common during the first generation of Bilateral Investment Treaties (BITs) when states reserved extensive regulatory powers and accorded limited protections to inbound investors. For example, in acceding to the ICSID Convention in 1993, China adopted a number of reservations and restricted the scope of ISA under its early Model BITs, upon which its negotiated BITs were modelled.[7] In particular, China did not grant ISA tribunals the jurisdiction to determine whether an expropriation has occurred, in addition to declining to provide national treatment to foreign investors. It also restricted ISA to

[5] That Treaty provided for investors of either partner state to have access to the domestic courts of the other, based on the rationale that the courts in both the countries adhered to a "rule of law" tradition. See, e.g., P. Drahos and D. Henry, "The Free Trade Agreement Between Australia and the United States", (2004) 328 *Brit Med J* 1271; W.S. Dodge, "Investor-State Dispute Settlement between Developed Countries: Reflections on the Australia-United States Free Trade Agreement", (2006) 39 *Vand. J. Transnat'l L* 1 (commenting on the exhaustion of local remedies).

[6] See Ministry of Foreign Affairs of Japan, *Japan-Philippines Economic Partnership Agreement* September 2006 at: www.mofa.go.jp/policy/economy/fta/philippines.html. See generally, S. Hamamoto and L. Nottage, "Foreign Investment In and Out of Japan: Economic Backdrop, Domestic Law, and International Treaty-Based Investor-State Dispute Resolution", 8(5) *TDM*, available at: www.transnational-dispute-management.com/article.asp?key=1766.

[7] On the development of China's model investment agreements, see W. Shan and N. Gallagher, "China", in C. Brown (ed.), *Commentaries on Selected Model Investment Treaties* (Oxford: OUP, 2013), chapter 4.

determining the nature and extent of compensation. China also stipulated that foreign investors had to resort to domestic administrative review before referring their cases to ISA. In addition, it imposed a waiting period of 3–9 months in order to provide parties with the opportunity to reach a settlement. Only after having exhausted local remedies and these waiting periods could foreign investors initiate ISA proceedings against a host state.[8] It should be noted that, although China's latest model treaty is still in the drafting stages, commentators believe that the Model BIT will restrict investors' rights and access to ISA, comparatively to its previous Model BIT, which granted significant protections to foreign investors.[9]

Similarly, the latest US Model BIT upon which the Chinese Model BIT may draw has extended the scope of a state's right to engage in regulatory expropriation. It has restricted the rights of foreign investors under standards of fair and equitable treatment, minimum standards of justice and national treatment, and provided for a subjective national security test by which state parties to BITs define their own national interests, as distinct from being based on objective criteria.[10] In addition, the US Model BIT reserves the rights of state parties to impose governmental measures to protect public health, environmental safety and related public interests. Reflecting the desire of American policy makers to restrict the rights of foreign investors, the US–Peru FTA subjects foreign investors to greater regulation by the host state.[11]

These examples demonstrate that ISA has been continuously evolving to accommodate the delicate balancing act of states wishing to attract

[8] L. Trakman, "China and Investor-State Arbitration", in *China, Trade and Investment* (Cambridge: CUP, 2014); L. Trakman, "China and Investor-State Arbitration", (2012) UNSW Law Research Paper No. 2012-48 available at: http://ssrn.com/abstract=2157387.

[9] See, e.g., W. Shan and S. Zhang, "An Inquiry on US 2012 Model BIT and Its Acceptability for China", (2013) 5 *Modern Law Science* 201; W. Shan, N. Gallagher, and S. Zhang, "National Treatment for Foreign Investment in China: A Changing Landscape", (2012) 27 *ICSID Review* 120 at para. 229. But see the US–China BIT, which subjects the admission of FDI to both MFN and national treatment clauses. See R. Dolzer and M. Stevens, *Bilateral Investment Treaties* (Hague: Martinus Nijuhoff Publishers, 1995), 49.

[10] See United States Model Bilateral Investment Treaty (2012) at: www.ustr.gov/sites/default/files/BIT%20text%20for%20ACIEP%20Meeting.pdf. On the illustrative measure of 'investment' in the US Model BIT, see K.S. Gudgeon, "United States Bilateral Investment Treaties: Comments on Their Origin, Purposes, and General Treatment Standards", (2012) 4 *Berkeley Journal of International Law* 105.

[11] See *Peru Trade Promotion Agreement*, US–Peru, 12 April 2006 (entered into force 1 February 2009) Article 10.21; *Free Trade Agreement*, US–Colombia, 22 November 2006 (entered into force 15 May 2012) Article 10.21; *Free Trade Agreement*, Korea–US, 30 June 2007 (approved by Congress, 12 October 2011) Article 11.21.

foreign investment, while, at the same time, retaining regulatory control over national assets. Thus, access to ISA could be described as cyclical, with states qualifying it according to their national priorities.

Owing to its fluid nature, ISA has always been a controversial subject within international trade law, with volumes of academic works devoted to the study of its merits and pitfalls. However, the debate over the value of ISA has become particularly pronounced in recent years on account of a number of states withdrawing from the forerunning ISA centre, the ICSID.[12] Although ICSID is just one of several arbitration centres available to investors, the majority of *known* investment-related disputes have been submitted to the ICSID for arbitration.[13] Thus, the unprecedented withdrawals from the organisation had pushed ISA into the mainstream news, giving rise to the speculated end of ISA.

The recent backlash against ISA can be traced back to Latin America. In 2007, Bolivia withdrew from the ICSID, gaining the dubious distinction of being the first state to repudiate the Convention.[14] Bolivia's actions gave rise to a host of procedural and legal issues in relation to the termination of the Treaty and the status of ISA provisions in Bolivia's other agreements.[15] Naturally, the case received prominent coverage in media and academia. This is especially so, considering that a number of other regional economies – Cuba, Nicaragua, Ecuador and Venezuela – have pledged to follow and terminate their membership in the ICSID.

However, by 2010, only Ecuador had issued its notice of termination.[16] Not long after Ecuador's withdrawal from the ICSID Convention, the Australian Government issued its Policy Statement, stating that it would no longer agree to the adoption of international investment arbitration in

[12] See, e.g., ICSID, "List of Contracting States and Other Signatories of the Convention (as of 18 April 2012)" at: http://icsid.worldbank.org/ICSID/FrontServlet?requestType=ICSIDDocRH&actionVal=ShowDocument&language=English.

[13] International Centre for Settlement of Investment Disputes, "ICSID Caseload–Statistics (Issue 2012–2)" at: http://icsid.world bank.org/ICSID/FrontServlet?requestType=ICSIDDocRH&actionVal=CaseLoadStatistics.

[14] On Bolivia's denunciation and withdrawal from the ICSID, see ICSID News Release, *Bolivia Submits a Notice under Article 71 of the ICSID Convention* (16 May 2007).

[15] See generally, United Nations UNCTAD, "Denunciation of the ICSID Convention and BITs: Impact on Investor-State Claims" (2019) 2 IIA Issue Note.

[16] On Ecuador's withdrawal from the ICSID, see ICSID News Release, *Ecuador Submits a Notice under Article 71 of the ICSID Convention* (9 July 2009): https://icsid. worldbank .org/ICSID/FrontServlet?requestType=CasesRH&actionVal=OpenPage&PageType=AnnouncementsFrame&FromPage=NewsReleases&pageName=Announcement20; K. Nowrot, "International Investment Law and the Republic of Ecuador: From Arbitral Bilateralism to Judicial Regionalism", (2011) 1 *Transnational Dispute Management* 5.

its bilateral and regional trade agreements.[17] Unlike Bolivia and Ecuador, Australia did not choose to withdraw from the ICSID and, presumably, intended to retain its existing BITs. The 2011 Policy Statement had only provided that Australia would no longer negotiate treaty protections 'that confer greater legal rights on foreign businesses than those available to domestic businesses' or rights that would 'constrain the ability of the Australian Government to make laws on social, environmental and economic matters in circumstances where those laws do not discriminate between domestic and foreign businesses'.[18]

Although Australia has abandoned its controversial position on ISA after the defeat of the Gillard Government in 2012, in favour of a pragmatic treaty-by-treaty approach, the 2011 Policy Statement has ignited fierce debate over the future of investment protections. After all, Bolivia and Ecuador did not have extensive investment networks. Increasingly inward-looking, these two states have initiated a number of nationalisation campaigns under the leadership of left-leaning governments advocating economic self-reliance. Comparatively, Australia had prospered from the increased FDI inflows and dedicated major efforts towards expanding its trade network. Furthermore, it has a healthy market economy with a stable political system. Thus, Australia's rejection of ISA came as a major shock to the legal community.

Because Australia was the only developed state to categorically reject ISA, a major line of inquiry was whether Australia would set a new trend in the regulation of FDI.[19] Would other developed countries follow suit in rejecting ISA? Perhaps of greatest concern was a fear that ISA had lost its legitimacy, even with the states that had previously benefited from the system. Was Australia just the precursor to regulatory revisionism that was to come?

Those hoping to see a global backlash against ISA were disappointed. In 2013, the repudiation of ISA appeared to be primarily a Latin American project. Parallel to the events in Australia, in 2012, Venezuela and Argentina announced their plans to withdraw from the

[17] C. Emerson, "Trading Our Way to More Jobs and Prosperity" (2011), available at: www.acci.asn.au/getattachment/b9d3cfae-fc0c-4c2a-a3df-3f58228daf6d/Gillard-Government-Trade-Policy-Statement.aspx (hereinafter, Policy Statement); See J. Kurtz, "Australia's Rejection of Investor–State Arbitration: Causation, Omission and Implication", (2012) 27(1) *ICSID Review* 65–86.

[18] Policy Statement, above note 17.

[19] L. Trakman, "Investor State Arbitration or Local Courts: Will Australia Set a New Trend?" (2012) 46(1) *Journal of World Trade* 83–120.

ICSID Convention. The foreign ministry of Venezuela was quite vocal in its criticism of ISA, stating that '[acceding to ICSID was] a decision of a provisional and weak government, without popular legitimacy, and under the pressure of transnational economic sectors involved in the dismantling of Venezuela's national sovereignty'.[20] Venezuela's withdrawal was finalised in July 2012. In addition, Venezuela terminated its BIT with the Netherlands.[21]

Although supporters of Australia's 2011 Policy Statement were anticipating more-developed nations rejecting ISA, South Africa is the only other country with attributes of a developed state to reject ISA at the time of writing.[22] In formulating its foreign policy, South Africa has followed Australia's approach, stating that it would not provide for ISA in its future agreements, but without ending its membership in the ICSID. However, it terminated a number of its pre-existing BITs.[23]

In 2014, Indonesia indicated that it would seek to terminate its BIT with the Netherlands, which was due to expire in July 2015. The Netherlands embassy in Jakarta further noted that the Indonesian Government had indicated that it intended to terminate all 67 of its BITs.[24] Finally, at around the same time, India announced that it intended to review its BIT system and is considering excluding ISA from its future agreements or, at the very least, would require investors to exhaust domestic remedies before submitting disputes to international arbitration.[25] At the time of writing, the exact policy position of these two countries remains unclear.

20 Ministry of Foreign Affairs Statement on ICSID Repudiation, available at: www.mre.gov.ve/index.php?option=com_content&view=article&id=18939:mppre&catid=3:comunicados&Itemid=108 (in Spanish).

21 Netherlands–Venezuela, Bolivarian Republic of BIT (1991).

22 L.E. Peterson, "South Africa Pushes Phase-out of Early Bilateral Investment Treaties after at Least Two Separate Brushes with Investor State Arbitration' (23 September 2012), available at: www.iareporter.com/articles/20120924_1.

23 N. Peacock and H. Ambrose, "South Africa Terminates Its Bilateral Investment Treaty with Spain: Second BIT terminated, as Part of South Africa's Planned Review of Its Investment Treaties" (21 August 2013), Herbert Smith Freehills Dispute Resolution Arbitration Notes, available at: http://hsfnotes.com/arbitration/2013/08/21/south-africa-terminates-its-bilateral-investment-treaty-with-spain-second-bit-terminated-as-part-of-south-africas-planned-review-of-its-investment-treaties/.

24 Netherlands Embassy in Jakarta, Indonesia, "Termination Bilateral Investment Treaty", available at: http://indonesia.nlembassy.org/organization/departments/economic-affairs/termination-bilateral-investment-treaty.html.

25 D. Sikarwar, "Government to Draft Model Treaty on MNCs' Mediation Rush", *The Economic Times* (9 August 2013), available at: http://articles.economictimes.indiatimes.com/2013-08-09/news/41240891_1_bipa-international-arbitration-white-industries-australia/; E. Jung,

On the basis of the brief survey provided, a number of preliminary observations are in order. First, various media outlets often refer to the events between 2007 and 2014 as a major shift in global practice in which a large number of states are abandoning ISA.[26] As was indicated earlier, the evidence does not warrant this view. Although a minority of states have pledged to limit ISA, only three countries have terminated their obligations under the ICSID Convention. Other countries dissatisfied with ISA are likely to restrict ISA in their future agreements. How this will unfold remains to be seen. Notably, a small minority of states is attempting to terminate their existing BITs. The unilateral repudiation of investment agreements appears to be more common among the states that had terminated their ICSID membership. This varied approach to restricting access to ISA is summarised in Table 3.1.

While each of these approaches carries with it unique legal questions and challenges, this section emphasises that there has not been a unified movement against ISA.

Furthermore, the recent movement against ISA should be viewed against the broader context of current ISA treaty-making practice. At the time of writing, no other states have expressed their desire to abandon ISA. Global trends suggest that ISA continues to grow in popularity, contrary to the recent backlash against it. For example, a major study conducted in 2012 by the OECD concluded that out of the 1,600 BITs analysed, only 6.8 per cent did not provide for ISA.[27] Treaty statistics from 2013 further illustrate the resilience of ISA. In 2014, 27 new investment agreements were concluded, the majority of which provide for ISA.[28] Furthermore, some 42 cases were initiated at the ICSID in 2014; close to half of these cases were initiated against developed states.[29] This

"India Plans to Abolish ICSID Clause in FTAs", *The Bilaterals* (6 April 2012), available at www.bilaterals.org/?india-plans-to-abolish-isd-clause.

[26] See e.g. *The Economist*, "The Arbitration Game" (11 October 2014), available at: www.economist.com/news/finance-and-economics/21623756-governments-are-souring-treaties-protect-foreign-investors-arbitration; J. Eaton, "Multiple Countries Reject Investor-State (2013 Update)", *The Sierra Club of Canada* (25 January 2014), available at: www.sierraclub .ca/en/main-page/multiple-countries-reject-investor-state-2013-update, www.bilaterals.org/?india-plans-to-abolish-isd-clause.

[27] D. Gaukrodger and K. Gordon, "Investor-State Dispute Settlement: A Scoping Paper for the Investment Policy Community" (2012) OECD Working Papers on International Investment, 11.

[28] UNCTAD, *World Investment Report 2014* (Switzerland, 2014), 115.

[29] Above note 28.

Table 3.1 *Approaches to restricting ISA*

	Terminated membership in the ICSID	Terminated BITs containing ISA	Will exclude ISA from future agreements
Australia	No	No	Case by case*
Bolivia	Yes	Yes (5)	Yes
Ecuador	Yes	Yes (11)	Yes
India	No	No	Unclear
Indonesia	No	Yes (1)	Unclear
South Africa	No	Yes (4)	Yes
Venezuela	Yes	Yes (1)	Yes

* See Section IV.

indicates that foreign investors have confidence in proceedings against developed and not only developing states.

Although Sornarajah views ISA as a tool of powerful capitalist states, developing countries invariably have opted for ISA in concluding BITs and FTAs. China is an illustrative example of ISA's lasting appeal.[30] As a developing country, China was initially cautious about adopting ISA and sought to limit recourse to it.[31] However, in recent years, China has expanded the scope of ISA, particularly in its bilateral agreement with Canada and its trilateral agreement with Japan and Korea.[32] In addition to signing a myriad of BITs, China has also extended investor protections to protect its growing outbound investors from the regulatory defences of host states.[33]

30 An example of China's endorsement of arbitration under the ICSID convention and UNCITRAL is contained in Articles 5 and 9 of the Germany–China BIT, which came into force on 11 December 2005. Article 10(2) includes an umbrella clause providing that each state party shall respect its treaty obligations relating to investors from the other state party.

31 See W. Shan, "China and International Investment Law", in L.E. Trakman and N.W. Ranieri (eds.), *Regionalism in International Investment Law* (Oxford: OUP, 2013).

32 China has over 130 BITs, becoming the state with the second largest number of BITS signed after Germany, which has signed the most BITs. For an overview of China's BITS, see generally, China FTA Network, *FTA News Release*: http://fta.mofcom.gov.cn/english/index.shtml.

33 On China's shifting position in regard to investment arbitration, see generally V. Bath and L. Nottage (eds.), *Foreign Investment and Dispute Resolution Law and Practice in Asia* (New York: Routledge, 2011).

Second, it is important to examine whether a new regulatory culture is emerging in Latin America. This view is advocated by Sornarajah, but there is limited evidence to support this idea.[34] Although three Latin American countries have recently rejected ISA, they do not reflect a regional trend. For example, while Argentina had initially supported Venezuela's initiative and in 2012 proposed a parliamentary bill to terminate ICSID, at the time of writing, no decision has been made with regard to its withdrawal.[35] It is reasonable to suggest that the recent decisions rendered in Argentina's favour and the ongoing negotiations with the ICSID and the IMF mediated by the United States have encouraged Argentina to reconsider its policy.[36] Similarly, although Cuba and Nicaragua have proclaimed their intention to repudiate the ICSID Convention, at the time of writing, neither one has made formal arrangements to leave the treaty. Cuba has not terminated its investment agreements, while Nicaragua terminated only one of its agreements.

The foregoing analysis does not deny the possibility that a number of states are dissatisfied with ISA. As was noted earlier, states continuously balance their BITs to support national priorities. This balance is a moving target and it is expected that treaty drafters will re-evaluate their existing agreements.

Arguments for and against ISA

A number of common themes run across all critical studies of ISA. Conceptually, criticisms of ISA fall into three categories: the potential of ISA to promote 'regulatory chill', the inherent bias of ISA in favour of developed states and the quality of arbitral decisions.

Indeed, the commonly cited reason as to why states have become more critical of ISA is the conviction that it will produce a regulatory chill, meaning that the threat of an ISA claim by a foreign investor will discourage states from engaging in public interest regulation.[37] This has become a pressing issue for a number of developed countries

[34] Sornarajah, "Mutations of Neo-Liberalism in International Investment Law", 210.

[35] The proposed bill is available at: www1.hcdn.gov.ar/proyxml/expediente.asp?fundamentos=si&numexp=1311-D-2012 (in Spanish).

[36] Buenos Aires Herald, "US Sees Progress in Talk Between Argentina and IMF, ICSID" (30 April 2014), available at: www.buenosairesherald.com/article/158335/us-sees-progress-in-talks-between-argentina-and-imf-icsid.

[37] See K. Tienhaara, "Regulatory Chill and the Threat of Arbitration: A View from Political Science", in C. Brown and K. Miles (eds.), *Evolution in Investment Treaty Law and Arbitration* (Cambridge: CUP, 2012), 606–628.

attempting to institute better environmental- and health-related public policies. As will be discussed in the final section of this paper, disputes surrounding public policy have prompted some states to repudiate ISA.

Indeed, public policy litigation is a highly sensitive issue that stands at the forefront of investment facilitation. This concern is reinforced by the fact that grounds for annulling an ISA award, such as under the ICSID Convention, are limited to procedural issues and challenges to the impartiality of arbitrators or conflicts of interest. Owing to the specificity of the grounds for annulment, ISA decisions are rarely set aside, and awards are usually considered to be final and binding upon the parties.[38]

A further concern among some developing countries, not limited to Latin America, is that ISA awards will favour investors from developed states over developing countries and that various ISA conventions such as the ICSID will perpetuate those disadvantages.[39] This is the argument posed by the Latin countries discussed in the previous section of this chapter.

Opponents of ISA argue that domestic courts are better suited to resolve disputes involving host states and foreign investors. On a broad level, domestic courts are aware of the unique challenges faced by the host state. The judicial system is often regarded as a key arm of government in a democracy; judges are appointed by the government or democratically elected. Thus, domestic courts possess the mandate and the sensitivity to domestic conditions surrounding disputes over public policy initiatives.

Furthermore, domestic proceedings are seen to be more conducive to a fair and just decision than an arbitral tribunal sitting in a foreign jurisdiction. Specifically, domestic trials are ordinarily open to the public; they provide for third-party submissions and verdicts are often reached by juries. Detailed judgments are usually published and freely available to

[38] See M. Bernardo, R. Cremades, and B. Cremades y Asociados, "The Use of Preliminary Objections in ICSID Annulment Proceedings", *Kluwer Arbitration Blog* (4 September 2013) available at: http://kluwerarbitrationblog.com/blog/2013/09/04/the-use-of-preliminary-objections-in-icsid-annulment-proceedings-2/.

[39] These concerns are not entirely novel. They were reflected in the Calvo Doctrine enunciated decades ago by the Argentine Republic. That doctrine stipulated that domestic authorities, not limited to local courts, should resolve disputes including matters arising over FDI that had previously been submitted to international tribunals. See, generally, W. Shan, "From North-South Divide to Private-Public Debate: Revival of the Calvo Doctrine and the Changing Landscape in International Investment Law" (2007) 27(3) *Nw J Int'l L & Bus* 631; B. Cremades, "Resurgence of the Calvo Doctrine in Latin America" (2006) 7 *BLI* 53.

ordinary citizens. Finally, to ensure that the process remains fair, the losing party is provided with a right to appeal a decision to a higher court. As a result, domestic courts are viewed as being most qualified to reach informed decisions, take account of the legitimate interests of litigants and consider important public policy considerations involved in the issue.

When the quality of justice is measured against these criteria, ISA appears to be inadequate. Aspects of ISA proceedings are often confidential; third-party interventions in ISA proceedings are subject to restrictions; and ISA awards are sometimes unpublished or published in part only.[40] While ISA parties generally have the option to modify ISA proceedings including opening them to the public, such decisions require the explicit consent of both sides, which is difficult to achieve by investor-state parties already engaged in a dispute.

Furthermore, given that ISA disputes are often decided by commercially trained international arbitrators who, arguably, lack adequate appreciation of domestic conditions, ISA has the potential to produce over-extensive awards in favour of foreign investors at the expense of 'host' states. Illustrating the risks of ISA awards bankrupting a foreign investor is the frequently cited Loewen case, in which an ISA tribunal upheld a punitive damage jury determination against a Canadian funeral home, under Chapter 11 of the North American Free Trade Agreement, leading to that company's insolvency.[41]

While supporters of ISA admit these deficiencies, they emphasise that many of the above-mentioned criticisms also apply to domestic legal systems. For example, although ISA proceedings are resource intensive and can lead to unreasonable awards based on domestic public policy, litigation in domestic courts can be equally costly and may deliver

[40] See L. Trakman, "The ICSID in Perspective", in Trakman and Ranieri (eds.), above note 32 at 253.

[41] On the Loewen case, see, for example, C. Brower and S. Lee, "NAFTA Chapter 11: Who then should Judge? Developing the International Rule of Law under NAFTA Chapter 11", (2001) 2 *Chi J Int'l L* 193–195; J.J. Coe Jr., "Domestic Court Control of Investment Awards: Necessary Evil or Achilles Heel within NAFTA and the Proposed FTAA" (2002) 19 *J Int'l Arb* 185; D.A. Gantz, "An Appellate Mechanism for Review of Arbitral Decisions in Investor-State Disputes: Prospects and Challenges" (2006) 39 *Vand J Transnat'l L* 39. But see W.S. Dodge, "Case Report: Waste Management, Inc v Mexico", (2001) 95 *AJIL* (presenting the case for modelling Chapter 11 on the WTO appellate process). See also G.R. Saxonhouse, "Dispute Settlement at the WTO and the Dole Commission: USTR Resources and Success", in R.M. Stern (ed.), *Issues and Options for U.S.-Japan Trade Policies* (Ann Arbor: University of Michigan Press, 2002), 363.

devastating blows to foreign investors, including allegedly excessive damage awards. This is illustrated, somewhat ironically, by the ISA tribunal in the Loewen case which upheld a punitive damage jury award reached in a domestic US court.[42]

In addition, prioritising domestic courts over ISA on grounds that ISA tribunals diverge in applying standards of treatment, such as 'fair and equitable' treatment to the foreign investors, ignores the extent to which domestic courts apply a diverse range of domestic rules of evidence and procedure to resolve disputes against states.[43] Domestic courts also domesticate conceptions of public policy differently.[44] The argument is that ISA can limit the nuanced impact of different domestic legal systems and cultures on FDI, such as the different influence of civil, common and customary laws.[45] Furthermore, ISA can reduce reliance on competing domestic rules of evidence and procedure, such as adversarial evidentiary rules in common law systems and inquisitorial methods of adducing evidence in civil law systems.[46]

Similarly, even though ISA awards are sometimes difficult to challenge, ISA annulment proceedings are not necessarily under-inclusive because they are limited to procedural matters. Asserting that appeals from domestic courts are wider in scope than annulment proceedings also ignores the extent to which domestic judicial systems diverge over the grounds for allowing an appeal.

The debate over regulatory chill is more complex, often due to the sensitive nature of the claims that are submitted to arbitral courts. From the perspective of investors, ISA obviates the need to seek domestic law remedies, which may be seen to be less impartial than international investment arbitration.[47] ISA can also confer substantive protections,

[42] On the Loewen case, see Brower and Lee, above note 41.

[43] For a debate on this issue, see L.E. Trakman and M. Sornarajah, "A Polemic: The Case For and Against Investment Liberalization", in Trakman and Ranieri (eds.), above note 32 and Appendix at 499.

[44] On such issues, see generally, Foreign Investment Review Board, *Current International Investment Issues – OECD Investment Committee:* www.firb.gov.au/content/international_investment/current_issues.asp?NavID=60.

[45] On the significance of legal cultures, including regionally, in international investment law, see C.B. Picker, "International Investment Law: Some Legal Cultural Insights", in Trakman and Ranieri (eds.), above note 32 at 120.

[46] See L.E. Trakman, "Legal Traditions and International Commercial Arbitration", (2006) 17(1) *Am Rev Int Arb* 119–120, 126–128.

[47] See Kurtz, "Australia's Rejection of Investor–State Arbitration: Causation, Omission and Implication", 65; Trakman, "Investor State Arbitration or Local Courts: Will Australia Set a New Trend?" *JWT* 46(1) (2012), 83.

such as most-favoured-nation (MFN) or national treatment on foreign investors under international investment law.

Host states may also benefit from ISA. Resort to ISA can limit the perceived social and political costs associated with domestic litigation, including by allowing the disputing parties to control public access to proceedings. Owing to these advantages, ISA serves as a 'delocalised' process of resolving disputes between foreign investors and host states. Outbound investors can rely on ISA, not only in response to states providing for ISA in their BITs and FTAs, but also in response to home-state investors trying to avoid the domestic courts and laws of particular host states.

It is also difficult to argue that foreign arbitral tribunals are incapable of rendering a fair and accurate decision in cases involving public policy initiatives. On the contrary, ISA arbitrators may be more experienced than domestic court judges, since the majority of the cases they hear are related to investment matters. ISA tribunals are likely to have a firmer grasp of principles of investment law and public international law.[48] They are also likely to apply a more uniform system of international investment laws and procedures than domestic laws and procedures that diverge across different legal systems. ISA arbitrators, in being drawn from different national backgrounds, are conceivably less prone to prioritise domestic public policies than some domestic courts in some host states.

Thus, while a small number of ISA arbitrators are repeatedly appointed from a list of panellists nominated by member states, it is difficult to infer that domestic litigation is preferable on grounds that domestic judges are appointed by nation states.[49] In fact, from the perspective of institutional learning, this arrangement may be more favourable to norm assimilation because the same stakeholders make up the institution. These career arbitrators are not insulated from ideas and often respond to global trends in and concerns of the international community. Reflecting this is the famous US–Shrimp/Turtle World Trade Organization (WTO) case, where a panel based its decision on the 'evolving interpretation' of WTO law.[50] It is important to note that the ICSID and the United Nations Conference on Trade and

[48] See, for example, S. Franck, "The Legitimacy Crisis in Investment Treaty Arbitration: Privatizing Public International Law through Inconsistent Decisions" (2004–2005) 73 *Fordham L R* 1543–1544; G.A. Alvarez and W.W. Park, "The New Face of Investment Arbitration: NAFTA Chapter 11", (2003) 28 *Yale J Int'l L* 365.

[49] See L.E. Trakman, "A Plural Account of the Transnational Law Merchant", (2011) 2(3) *TLT* 335.

[50] WT/DS58/AB/R (12 October 1998).

Development (UNCTAD) have continuously emphasised the need to accommodate developmental and sustainable policies of states and have undertaken significant organisational initiatives to uphold these priorities. Thus, it is difficult to argue that arbitrators are inherently pro-business without any awareness of global trends and issues.

Finally, although ISA arbitrators are not working under a multilateral investment treaty and are not bound by precedent, it has become a standard practice for arbitrators to routinely reference past decisions of various arbitral tribunals. In fact, over the 30 years of ICSID and United Nations Commission on International Trade Law (UNCITRAL) decision-making, ISA jurisprudence has acquired a sophisticated degree of coherence.[51] This is a significant accomplishment since ISA decisions are ad hoc and bind only the direct parties to the dispute, and ISA tribunals often diverge in applying international investment laws, such as the state defence of 'necessity' to specific ISA disputes.[52]

Finally, concern over the lack of transparency of some ISA proceedings is directly relevant to the wishes of disputing parties. Confidentiality in ISA proceedings was historically determined by the disputing parties. An important reason why ISA is attractive to foreign investors, and sometimes state parties, is because it was traditionally closed to the public. This avoided media coverage often associated with the publicised decisions of domestic courts of law and the concern of disputing parties not to suffer reputational damage arising from the disclosure of sensitive information,

[51] On the variability of international investment treaty law, see S.W. Schill, *The Multilateralization of International Investment Law* (Cambridge: CUP, 2009), 363; but compare M. Sornarajah, "The Case Against an International Investment Regime", in Trakman and Ranieri (eds.), above note 32 at 475.

[52] On allegedly inconsistent ICSID decisions in a series of investment claims against Argentina, commencing with the *CMS, Enron* and *Sempra* cases, see *CMS Gas Transmission Co* v. *The Argentine Republic (Award)* (ICSID Arbitral Tribunal, Case No. ARB/01/8, 12 May 2005); *Enron Creditors Recovery Corporation and Ponderosa Assets, L.P.* v. *Argentine Republic (Award)* (ICSID Arbitral Tribunal, Case No. ARB/01/3, 22 May 2007); *Sempra Energy International* v. *The Argentine Republic (Award)* (ICSID Arbitral Tribunal, Case No ARB/02/16, 28 September 2007). See further, A. Reinisch, "Necessity in International Investment Arbitration – An Unnecessary Split of Opinions in Recent ICSID Cases? Comments on CMS v. Argentina and LG&E v. Argentina" (2007) 8 *JWIT* 191; S.W. Schill, "International Investment Law and the Host State's Power to Handle Economic Crises: Comment on the ICSID Decision in LG&E v. Argentina" (2007) 24 *J Int'l Arb* 265; M. Waibel, "Two Worlds of Necessity in ICSID Arbitration: CMS and LG&E" (2007) 20 *Leiden J Int'l L* 637. See C. Peinhardt and T. Allee, "Devil in the Details? The Investment Effects of Dispute Settlement Variation in BITs", in Karl Sauvant (ed.), *Yearbook on International Investment Law & Policy 2010–2011* (Oxford: OUP, 2011), 833–854.

not limited to adverse determinations. However, in recent years, the nature of ISA has changed to provide greater public awareness of and participation in ISA proceedings. ISA tribunals have repeatedly opened hearings to the public, with the support of the investor-state parties, given sensitivity about the need for transparency in redressing public–private disputes on matters of public interest. Consequently, there is now far greater public access to ISA proceedings and records than there was a decade ago.[53] For example, the ICSID now provides for third-party intervener status in ISA proceedings and for the publication of ISA awards.[54]

Regardless of whether ISA proceedings remain closed or open to the public, disputing parties are generally allowed to issue statements on their positions to the public, provided that these statements do not disclose information marked in proceedings as 'confidential'. Those statements may be sufficient to keep the public informed and focused on issues of national significance. Furthermore, these public releases may also provide incentives for both disputing parties to open ISA proceedings to the public in order to offset the impact of a statement by one disputing party in the absence of a public record.

In summary, both ISA and domestic courts have advantages and drawbacks. Both mechanisms for resolving investor-state disputes will have their supporters. At times, foreign investors will prefer the intimate setting of an arbitral tribunal and, at other times, they will opt for the expediency of domestic courts owing to their confidence in the local legal system.

Furthermore, whether ISA is more efficient or fairer than domestic litigation will depend on the normative values and risks that are ascribed to each. For example, if normative priority is given to legal coherence, the risk of ISA tribunals and domestic courts adopting narrow literal methods of treaty interpretation in order to arrive at coherent results by coherent means, apply to both. Similarly, the risk of domestic courts and ISA tribunals adopting purposive methods of interpretation will

[53] See, for example, A. Antonietti, "The 2006 Amendments of the ICSID Rules and Regulations and the Additional Facility Rules" (2006) 21 *ICSID Rev – Foreign Invest L J* 427; E. Baldwin, M. Kantor, and M. Nolan, "Limits to Enforcement of ICSID Awards" (2006) 23 *J Int'l Arb* 1.

[54] On this amendment to the ICSID Rules, see Antonietti, above note 53. See also Statement by the OECD Investment Committee, *Transparency and Third-party Participation in Investor-State Dispute Settlement* (June 2005), available at: www.oecd.org/daf/inv/investment-policy/34786913.pdf.

hinge on the purpose each ascribes to an applicable investment law. Both domestic courts and ISA tribunals may construe treaties liberally but ascribe different purposes to those treaties. Domestic courts may highlight the need to protect domestic public policy values. On the other hand, ISA tribunals may highlight the need to protect the commercial interests of foreign investors.

If normative priority is given to investment expertise, ISA arbitrators are likely to have a greater comprehension of investment law than most domestic judges.[55] If emphasis is given to the transparency of legal procedures, ISA will once again prevail over the choice of domestic courts in jurisdictions that have problematic corruption transparency indexes and rule of law scores.[56] In issue is that domestic courts and ISA tribunals are not only likely to accord priority to different normative values but also likely to differentiate among those values from one case to another. If priority is given to the binding force of precedents, as common lawyers conceive of it, ISA arbitrators who subscribe to precedent are also likely to treat past ISA awards as binding on them.[57]

As a result, it is difficult to conclude that domestic courts and ISA tribunals are likely to subscribe to one or another normative preference. Even the presupposition that ISA tribunals are more likely to prioritise the commercial interests of foreign investors, while domestic courts are more likely to prioritise the public policy concerns of the 'host' state is not self-evident.[58]

The result is that it is easier to draw broad quantitative than qualitative distinctions between the normative proclivities of domestic courts and

[55] On the expertise of investor-state arbitrators, among various other factors in support of ISA, see generally, C. Dugan, D. Wallace, Jr., and N. Rubins, *Investor-State Arbitration* (New York: OUP, 2008); P. Muchlinski, F. Ortino, and C. Schreuer (eds.), *Oxford Handbook of International Investment Law* (Oxford: OUP, 2008); C. McLachlan, L. Shore, and M. Weiniger, *International Investment Arbitration: Substantive Principles* (Oxford: OUP, 2008).

[56] On Transparency International's Corruption Perceptions Index 2014, see Transparency International, Corruption Perceptions Index 2012, available at: www.transparency.org/cpi2014/results. On doubts about the reliability of such indexes, see T. Thompson and S. Anwar, "Transparency International's Corruption Perceptions Index: Whose Perceptions Are They Anyway?", March 2005: http://siteresources.worldbank.org/INTWBIGOVANTCOR/Resources/TransparencyInternationalCorruptionIndex.pdf.

[57] See, for example, C. Schreuer and R. Dolzer, *Principles of International Investment Law* (Oxford: OUP, 2008), 357.

[58] On the ICSID Panels of Arbitrators and Conciliations, see ICSID, *Search ICSID Panels:* https://icsid.worldbank.org/ICSID/FrontServlet?requestType=ICSIDDataRH&reqFrom=Main&actionVal=PanelStates&range=A~B~C~D~E.

ISA tribunals. As a quantitative measure, ISA jurisprudence is likely to be more consistent in scope of application than a multiplicity of different domestic laws applied by local courts to govern foreign investment in light of localised laws and procedures.[59] However, if one takes into account qualitative measures, the extent of that consistency will depend on the value priorities that are ascribed to domestic courts and ISA tribunals in discrete cases.

Investment agreements of states dissatisfied with ISA

This section investigates investment treaty-making behaviour of states that have repudiated ISA, assessing their policies since that repudiation. In particular, it aims to determine whether those states have been consistent in their policy direction and analyses their subsequent investment agreements.

For organisational purposes, these states are divided into two groups: states that repudiated the ICSID Convention and states that have retained their membership in the ICSID but have chosen alternative avenues to restrict ISA.

States that have retained their membership in the ICSID

Countries in this category have been inconsistent in their foreign policy direction with regard to ISA. As will be discussed next, a number of these states have reversed their initial rejection of ISA and continue to provide for ISA to varying degrees in their investment agreements.

Australia

Australia has undergone a major policy shift on ISA since its 2011 Policy Statement against adopting ISA. Consistent with that policy, in 2012 it signed an FTA with Malaysia, choosing to exclude ISA from the investment chapter of the agreement, requiring both parties to resolve investor-state disputes in the local courts.[60] While Malaysia is considered to be a developing country with an evolving legal system, the Australian Government did not draw a distinction between countries with allegedly strong and weak legal systems in formulating its post-ISA investment policy.[61] Thus, exclusion of ISA from the FTA with Malaysia served as a

[59] On the development of international investment norms around conceptions of efficiency, see Foreign Investment Review Board, above note 44.

[60] The official website of *The Malaysia–Australia Free Trade Agreement* (hereinafter, MAFTA) is www.dfat.gov.au/trade/agreements/mafta/Pages/malaysia-australia-fta.aspx.

[61] Policy Statement, above note 17.

credible demonstration of the Australian government's commitment to move away from ISA, regardless of whether doing so would benefit or harm its own investors operating abroad including in Malaysia.

However, the subsequent change in the Federal Government of Australia has resulted in a near U-turn in Australia's policy towards ISA. On coming to power in September 2013, the Abbott Government announced that it would consider negotiating ISA selectively.[62] It is difficult to conclude with certainty whether this policy direction represented a mere face-saving gesture in light of the Policy adopted by the previous administration or a real commitment to negotiate ISA on a case-by-case basis, given the absence of a pre-determined pattern in the current Government's ISA negotiations beyond a commitment not to decide a priori in favour of or against ISA.

The result is that Australia had completed FTA negotiations with China, Japan and Korea, each containing an investment chapter.[63] Agreements with Korea, and apparently China as well, have provided for ISA, while the agreement with Japan does not offer ISA.[64]

On the surface, the lack of ISA in the agreement with Japan confirms Australia's selective approach to negotiating ISA. However, scholars believe that the lack of ISA in the agreement with Japan is partly due to Japan's neutrality towards ISA on the account of its legal culture.[65] Furthermore, according to Article 14.19 of the FTA, the State Parties are required to conduct a review of the investment chapter in the fifth year of the agreement, or earlier if both sides agree. The Article further states that, if Australia enters into any multilateral or bilateral

[62] Australia Government, Department of Foreign Affairs and Trade, "Trade and Investment Topics – ICSID", available at: www.dfat.gov.au/trade/topics/Pages/isds.aspx.

[63] The official website of *The China–Australia Free Trade Agreement* (hereinafter, ChAFTA) is www.dfat.gov.au/trade/agreements/chafta/Pages/australia-china-fta.aspx; The official website of *The Korea–Australia Free Trade Agreement* (hereinafter, KAFTA) is www.dfat.gov.au/trade/agreements/kafta/Pages/korea-australia-fta.aspx; The official website of *The Japan–Australia Economic Partnership Agreement* (hereinafter, JAEPA) is www.dfat.gov.au/trade/agreements/jaepa/Pages/japan-australia-economic-partnership-agreement.aspx; The official text of ChAFTA has not been released at the time of writing.

[64] KAFTA Article 11.16 para. 1 (a), (b), (c) and (d); JAEPA Article 14.6 paras. 1 and 2. The ChAFTA legal text has not been made public at the time of writing. However official press releases have confirmed that the agreement will provide for ISA. See, http://trademinister.gov.au/releases/Pages/2014/ar_mr_141117.aspx.

[65] This view is advocated by Luke Nottage. See, L. Nottage, "Why No Invest-State Arbitration in the FTA with Japan", *East Asian Forum* (9 April 2014), available at: www.eastasiaforum.org/2014/04/09/why-no-investor-state-arbitration-in-the-australia-japan-fta/.

international agreement providing for a mechanism for the settlement of an investment dispute between Australia and an investor of another or the other party to that agreement, both sides will be obliged to establish an equivalent mechanism under the Japan–Australia Economic Partnership Agreement (JAEPA) and must begin their negotiations within 3 months following the date on which the other agreement enters into force.[66] Because Australia's FTA with China provides for ISA, the provision in the JAEPA will be triggered as soon as the FTA with China enters into force.[67] Thus, Australia will be obligated to negotiate a similar agreement with Japan.

To further demonstrate Australia's uncertainty over ISA, it is unclear how Australia considers the legal system of its trade partners in relation to ISA. For example, in the official press release following its negotiations with China, Australia noted that '[ISA] will enable Australians to invest in China with greater confidence'.[68] Presumably, this was done partially in response to China's developing legal system. However, Korea has a sophisticated legal system with strong legal capacity. Yet, ISA was provided for in both the agreements, suggesting that Australia is conceivably relying on ISA essentially as a bargaining chip to negotiate for other favourable terms.

Having demonstrated Australia's evolving position on ISA, we now examine its recently concluded agreements. The analysis of these agreements reveals a number of similarities that are reflected in Australia's vision of ISA.

Summarising the investment chapter of the soon-to-be released China–Australia FTA, the Australian Department of Foreign Affairs and Trade noted that the 'the ICSID provisions contain strong safeguards to protect the Australian Government's ability to regulate in the public interest and pursue legitimate welfare objectives in areas, such as health, safety and the environment'.[69] This emphasis on rebalancing investor and state rights is also evident in Australia's FTA with Malaysia, Korea and Japan. These agreements create a number of innovations in order to minimise these risks and exercise a certain degree of control over the vital sectors of its economy.

First, the investment chapters in the agreements with Korea, Japan and Malaysia contain MFN clauses; however, they explicitly provide that

[66] JAEPA Article 14.19 para. 2. [67] Above note 65. [68] Above note 65.
[69] Above note 65.

these clauses do not apply to dispute resolution.[70] The rationale for including this qualification is twofold. First, specific to the FTA with Malaysia, the exclusion of dispute resolution will block investors from both sides from arguing that ISA provisions should apply to them, because other investment agreements signed by Australia and Malaysia provide for ISA. Second, the exclusion of dispute resolution from MFN will allow Australia to qualify ISA without challenges from foreign investors who will cite beneficial agreements and sidestep Australia's attempts to limit the ambit of ISA.[71] As such, these provisions indicate an important treaty modification on the part of Australia in order to effectively circumscribe the scope of ISA protections.

Second, all three agreements provide extensive provisions on the minimal standard of treatment. These agreements state that the state parties must provide that this minimal standard is in accordance with the customary international law minimum standard of treatment of aliens, including fair and equitable treatment and full protection and security. However, all three agreements clarify this standard by providing definitions of such treatment. These agreements note further that such treatment shall not require treatment in addition to or beyond that which is required by the defined standard, and shall not create additional substantive rights.[72]

Third, in all three agreements, the state parties provide a list of non-conforming measures that may be maintained in perpetuity, provided they are outlined in the annexes. Specific sectors of the economy and a number of state-owned entities are included in these exceptions.[73] However, other exceptions may be adopted by the parties to these agreements. In the case of JAEPA, it is explicitly noted that a state party may even impose new and more restrictive exceptions.[74] However, nothing

[70] KAFTA Article 11.4 para. 2, footnote 35; JAEPA Article 14.4; MAFTA Article 12.5 footnote 20.

[71] See e.g., *Emilio Augustin Maffezini* v. *The Kingdom of Spain* (ICSID Case No. ARB/97/7) where an investor cited MFN provision in another treaty in order to avoid the mandatory period for consultations and negotiations before gaining a right to initiate arbitral proceedings. The panel agreed with the investor because the MFN in the BIT did not exclude arbitral proceedings.

[72] KAFTA Article 11.5 para. 2; JAEPA Article 14.5 note 1; MAFTA Article 12.7 para. 2 (c).

[73] JAEPA Article 14.10 para. 1 (a) (b) (c) and (d), Annex 6 (Non-Conforming Measures Relating to Paragraph 1 of Articles 9.7 and 14.10) and Annex 7 (Non-Conforming Measures Relating to Paragraph 2 of Articles 9.7 and 14.10).

[74] JAEPA Article 14.10 para. 4.

forbids the state parties from adopting such restrictions in the other agreements as well.

The agreement with Korea creates an innovative provision, further strengthening the exceptions outlined in the annexes. According to that agreement, if a party's defence is based on the annexes, the arbitral panel must suspend its proceedings and refer both parties to the Joint Committee in charge of the FTA for the final determination on the defence.[75] The decision of the Joint Committee is final and binding on the arbitral panel.[76] This provision is probably included to ensure that undue judicial activism by the panels should not force state parties to renegotiate carve-out exceptions to investor protections.

In addition to these annex-specific measures, the parties to all the above agreements may adopt or enforce measures for the protection of public morals and public order, necessary to protect human, animal or plant life, health or for the purpose of the conservation of living or non-living exhaustible natural resources. Additional exceptions are possible in cases where a party must secure compliance with laws or regulations or for the protection of national treasures of artistic, historic or archaeological value.

These GATT Article XX-inspired measures are frequently found in investment agreements. Improving upon this well-established drafting practice, JAEPA clarifies when these measures are applicable and what they may include.[77] The implementation of these measures could well become problematic. In particular, each party will need to ensure that such measures are not applied in a manner that would produce arbitrary or unjustifiable discrimination between covered investments or investors of the other party and other investments or investors, where like conditions prevail or constitute a disguised restriction on investment.

With regard to the regulation of ISA, at the time of writing, only Australia's FTA with Korea contains provisions regulating ISA, as is illustrated next. As was already indicated, the FTA with China has not been made public, pending its ratification. Although only one agreement is available for analysis, the ISA provisions under the Korea–Australia Free Trade Agreement (KAFTA) serve as an excellent example of Australia's current approach to regulating ISA.

Of some importance, according to the latest UNCTAD study of ISA, states have two options in drafting ISA clauses. They may employ a

[75] KAFTA Article 11.23 para. 1. [76] KAFTA Article 11.23 para. 2.
[77] JAEPA 14.15 (a) (b) (c) and (d).

minimalist approach and participate in ISA proceedings according to the rules of the forum selected by the disputing party. Alternatively, they may be more expansionist, providing detailed guidelines regulating ISA proceedings.[78]

Without a doubt, the FTA with Korea falls within the latter expansionist category. In general, the agreement employs a number of treaty innovations which seek directly to address common concerns voiced towards ISA. Some of these provisions are discussed next.

First, the FTA with Korea attempts to pre-empt an ISA dispute before it reaches the stage of arbitration and exclude frivolous claims. Parties are bound by a cooling off period of 6 months, and investors are required to provide a state party with a written notice containing its intention to submit a claim to an arbitral tribunal.[79] This notice must be submitted 90 days before an arbitral filing.

Second, there is a significant effort by treaty-makers to ensure that the proceedings are transparent. According to the KAFTA, all hearings are open to the public.[80] Furthermore, parties are obliged to release all relevant documents (the notice of intent, the notice of arbitration, pleadings, memorials and briefs submitted, minutes or transcripts of the hearings of the tribunal, orders, awards and its decisions) to the general public.[81] This transparency rule is subject to the standard protection that is accorded to confidential information.[82]

With regard to *amicus curiae* briefs, the KAFTA is less explicit. According to the Article 11.20 para. 5, 'after consulting the disputing parties, the tribunal may allow a party or entity that is not a disputing party to file a written *amicus curiae* submission with the tribunal'. It is not entirely clear if a tribunal may allow *amicus curiae* submissions on its own volition without the consent of the disputing parties owing to the confusion surrounding the 'after consulting the disputing parties' phrase.

The FTA with Korea includes another notable textual innovation that deserves closer analysis. According to Article 11.20 para. 13,

> [if] a separate, multilateral agreement enters into force between the Parties that establishes an appellate body for the purposes of reviewing awards rendered by tribunals constituted pursuant to international trade or investment arrangements to hear investment disputes, the Parties shall

[78] UNCTAD, *Investor-State Dispute Settlement, UNCTAD Series on International Investment Agreements II* (Switzerland 2014), 170.

[79] KAFTA Article 11.16 para. 2. [80] KAFTA Article 11.21 para. 2.

[81] KAFTA Article 11.21 para. 1 (a) (b) (c) (d) (e).

[82] KAFTA Article 11.21 para. 4 (a) (b) (c) (d).

> strive to reach an agreement that would have such appellate body review awards rendered under Article 11.26 in arbitrations commenced after the multilateral agreement enters into force between the Parties.[83]

According to Article 11.20 of the KAFTA, both parties are obligated to enter into good-faith negotiations and attempt to establish an appellate mechanism. A strict interpretation of Article 11.20 suggests that the parties are not obligated to actually successfully create such a mechanism. Regardless, the unique nature of this Article and its ambitious goals reflect the desire of the parties to contemplate such an appellate mechanism.

In summary, the analysis of Australia's recent investment agreements indicates its readiness to provide for ISA. Having negotiated ISA in its agreements with China and Korea, Australia will have to provide a similar mechanism for the resolution of investment disputes between states and private parties in its agreement with Japan.

In essence, rather than rejecting ISA, Australia is increasingly qualifying the way ISA is applied. Reflecting its concerns with public policy litigation, Australia is attempting to balance its treaties to allow a moderate degree of state control over ISA on economic and political grounds by curtailing or limiting investor rights in certain sectors of the economy. Further attempting to improve ISA, Australian and Korean treaty drafters have taken an expansionist approach and added extensive provisions clarifying the conduct of arbitral proceedings. In all probability, similar ISA provisions will be present in the FTA with China and with Japan.

India and Indonesia

The behaviour of India and Indonesia has been similarly inconsistent with regard to ISA. First, neither country has articulated its approach to regulating ISA. Second, both states have maintained the status quo with regard to their existing investment treaties. Although Indonesia has allowed its BIT with the Netherlands to lapse, it has not terminated its other agreements. India has not terminated any of its agreements at the time of writing.

Second, although Indonesia has not concluded any investment agreements at the time of writing, India has recently signed an investment facilitation agreement with ASEAN.[84] Broadly, the agreement does not create any significant innovations with regard to transparency or the

[83] KAFTA Article 11.20 para. 13.

[84] Agreement for Trade in Services and Agreement on Investment under the Framework Agreement on Comprehensive Economic Cooperation between the Association of

conduct of arbitral proceedings and leaves the specifics to the relevant ISA tribunal. Thus, the treaty is largely minimalist in its regulation of arbitral proceedings. This treaty drafting approach differs significantly from Australia's FTA with Korea. The Agreement is analysed next.

One major feature of the Agreement lies in its endeavour to pre-empt arbitral proceedings and resolve all disputes at the early stage in proceedings. Specifically, the Agreement requires both parties to engage in negotiations. In fact, the parties are unable to proceed to arbitration without first submitting a notice requesting consultations.[85] This is somewhat different from Australia's FTA with Korea, which only suggests consultations during the cooling-off period, but does not oblige the contracting parties to engage in any particular ADR method.

Having exhausted the cooling-off period of 180 days, parties under the India-ASEAN Agreement have the option of proceeding to arbitration. A party intending to initiate arbitration must provide a written notice 90 days before the filing for arbitration.[86] The agreement provides the standard fork-in-the-road provision by excluding all other forums once a particular forum has been selected.[87] Finally, a substantive portion of the Agreement is devoted to disposing of frivolous claims.[88] All other substantive issues in relation to the conduct of proceedings are left to the respective forum.

With regard to transparency, the India–ASEAN Agreement is particularly conservative. According to the treaty, 'the disputing party may make public the final awards and decisions of the tribunal'.[89] A strict interpretation of this provision suggests that the parties do not have an obligation to disclose these documents. Finally, nothing is stated with regard to *amicus curiae* submissions or the role of experts in arbitral proceedings.

In order to retain regulatory control over the economy, the agreement between India and ASEAN includes a list of reservations submitted by all sides. Once again these reservations may continue in perpetuity, with the possibility of adding new exceptions to the Annexes. Furthermore, the Agreement contains the standard provision on general exceptions in

Southeast Asian Nations and the Republic of India (India–ASEAN Agreement). The full text of the agreement is on file with the author.

85 India–ASEAN Agreement Article 20 para. 7.

86 India–ASEAN Agreement Article 20 para. 8 (b).

87 India–ASEAN Agreement Article 20 para. 7.

88 India–ASEAN Agreement Article 20 paras. 12, 13, 14 and 15.

89 India–ASEAN Agreement Article 20 para. 17.

nearly identical language as found in the Australia–Korea FTA.[90] One notable addition to the list of exceptions is a provision on 'safety'.[91] No explanation or definitions are provided regarding this provision.

The Agreement further clarifies that fair and equitable treatment does not include any additional obligations.[92] The approach to regulating this provision is identical to the drafting language utilised by Australia.

Curiously, the agreement between India and ASEAN does not contain MFN provisions in relation to ISA in a manner that was articulated in Australia's latest investment facilitation agreements. Rather than taking a firm position on the issue, the Agreement notes that 'a party shall not be obliged to extend to the investors of another Party the benefits or privileges arising from customs union, free trade agreement or a similar bilateral, regional or international arrangement of which party is or may become a member'.[93]

Aware of the judicial activism that is sometimes exercised by arbitral tribunals, the Agreement creates a modest safeguard against expansive treaty interpretation. Specifically, according to Article 19, the arbitral tribunal or the responding party may request a joint interpretation of a provision that is the subject of a claim. The result of that interpretation is binding on the arbitral tribunal.[94] Somewhat similar to the clause found in the Australia–Korea FTA, this provision may be used by the responding state to promote a diplomatic resolution of the dispute in a manner that would be acceptable to the signatories. Finally, Annex 2 of the agreement provides that, if an alleged measure falls under a category of security exceptions, the issue will have no standing before the arbitral tribunal.[95]

In summary, the Agreement between India and ASEAN is relatively modest in the ambit it accords to ISA. Rather than enhance the ISA regime, it appears that the state Parties were more concerned to create a list of exceptions and carve-outs, leaving the conduct of arbitration to the relevant arbitral rules. As an added layer of security, that Agreement permits the disputing parties to interpret it during the course of an arbitration. However, this process is not automatic. In other aspects, the Agreement is representative of the existing ISA-granting treaties discussed earlier.

[90] See, e.g. India–ASEAN Agreement Article 4 paras. 1–6, India–ASEAN Agreement Article 21.

[91] India–ASEAN Agreement Article 21 para. 1 (c) (iii).

[92] India–ASEAN Agreement Article 3.

[93] India–ASEAN Agreement Article 3 para. 3.

[94] India–ASEAN Agreement Article 20 para. 19.

[95] India–ASEAN Agreement Annex 2.

The aforementioned analysis suggests that India and, to greater extent, the ASEAN countries have maintained the status quo and have not significantly altered their ISA regulatory regimes. This is particularly evident in India's approach to ISA in its treaties. India has neither refused ISA nor has it requested foreign investors to rely on domestic remedies before resorting to ISA. Furthermore, supporting India's reliance on the status quo is its recent bilateral investment treaty with the United Arab Emirates. Although that Agreement has not been released to the public, official media outlets suggest that it is largely an old generation agreement that provides for ISA without significant textual innovations.[96]

It should be noted that India is currently negotiating a major free trade agreement with Australia. This will create an interesting negotiating dynamic between these two countries. Will Australia insist on including an investment chapter in this particular agreement? One of the goals articulated by Australia is that 'an FTA could facilitate and encourage investment by reducing barriers, increasing transparency and enhancing investment protections'.[97] India is frequently subjected to ISA claims, most of which relate to taxation measures. Furthermore, India's legal system is somewhat underfunded and is still transitional. In this particular case, Australia may find itself in a paradoxical position. On one hand, it negotiates ISA selectively and should sympathise with a state like India if it pursues a similar regulatory policy. On the other hand, business interests in Australia will likely lobby the Australian Government for significant protections, especially considering possible scepticism over the effectiveness of India's domestic courts in resolving claims.

South Africa

At the time of writing, South Africa is the only state that has consistently resisted ISA. It has terminated four of its BITs. It has not signed any new investment facilitation agreements.

[96] K. Singh, "India–UAE Agreement, Why Such Desperate Haste", *Global Research* (6 January 2014), available at: www.globalresearch.ca/india-uae-investment-agreement-why-such-desperate-haste/5363937; K. Singh, "What Can India Learn from Its Investment Treaty with the UAE?", *East Asian Forum* (4 December 2014), available at: www.eastasiaforum.org/2014/12/04/what-can-india-learn-from-its-investment-treaty-with-the-uae/

[97] Status of the negotiations is available at: http://dfat.gov.au/trade/agreements/aifta/Pages/australia-india-comprehensive-economic-cooperation-agreement.aspx.

States that have repudiated the ISCID

States that have repudiated the ICSID have been much more consistent in their treaty-making behaviour. Since repudiating ISA, these states that have repudiated the ISCID have undertaken to terminate their existing BITS. Ecuador and Bolivia have been most active in this regard. These two states have terminated most of their investment facilitation agreements. Comparatively, despite its passionate rhetoric, Venezuela has only terminated one of its BITS at the time of writing. Neither state has concluded any subsequent investment facilitation agreements. This inaction could be explained by the ongoing financial instability in these countries. Their economic woes have become more pronounced with the fall in oil prices in the last quarter of 2014. As a result, it is difficult to identify the types of investment facilitation agreements these states will draft in the future, as such agreements are not yet available.

Why ISA has retained its resilience

The foregoing analysis demonstrates that a number of states that were previously committed to abandoning ISA have reversed their policy directions. At the time of writing, only Bolivia, Ecuador, South Africa and Venezuela remain committed to repudiating ISA. Therefore, one may ask, why has ISA retained its resilience?

First, it is important to note that all of the countries summarised in Table 3.1 have been subject to politically and economically charged ISA claims. Thus, politics and economics have been inherently related to intense disaffection with ISA at the time. Political considerations have discouraged target states from being inactive when they face multibillion dollar investor claims over what is popularly perceived to be 'good policy initiatives'. By repudiating ISA, these states send a signal to their domestic constituents and the international community, expressing their displeasure with the state of affairs. This in turn may tame foreign investors who will attempt to resolve disputes with the host states through consultations, thus avoiding public scrutiny and the cost of dispute resolution.

The downside to this strategy lies in the fact that it is inconsistent with the broader interests of states to attract FDI on account of the reactionary nature of that strategy. This explains why the Australian administration, elected in 2013, revised its policy direction on ISA.

Priding itself on being focused on prosperity, however, it did not face the political pressures of the previous administration. Thus, it had far less to lose in reverting back to the status quo and endorsing ISA, albeit on a case-by-case basis. India and Indonesia face similar dilemmas. India remains subject to a very large number of ICSID claims. While the previous administration there had attempted to respond to this by publicly repudiating ISA, the recent Modi Government has not articulated any specific policy direction. Nevertheless, one reason why ISA remains resilient is because the disaffection with ISA is often politically motivated.

Second, critics of ISA often equate ISA with the ICSID and misunderstand the manner in which ISA operates under different trade and investment agreements. The doubtful argument is that repudiating ICSID will shield states from claims by investors. However, the ICSID is only one forum for the resolution of investor-state disputes. Although a state repudiating the ICSID Convention will not be subject to ICSID obligations, foreign investors are frequently provided with multiple fora for filing claims against host states. The ICSID is somewhat unique in that it provides very limited avenues for appeals, usually only on procedural grounds. Other arbitral fora are subject to the New York Convention on the Recognition and Enforcement of Foreign Arbitration Awards, which allows domestic courts to set aside an arbitration award on various grounds. A state that has significant control over its local judiciary may feel more confidence in its ability to nullify a foreign judgment. However, independent judiciaries may enforce a foreign judgment based on its merits.

This fact explains why states that have repudiated the ICSID convention have begun to terminate their investment treaties. This was the only way in which those states could ensure that no arbitral proceedings would be initiated against them in different fora. Once again this strategy has limited benefits. As is discussed in other articles, most BITs now include survival clauses, meaning that the treaty will remain in force for a number of years following its termination. Although short-term political considerations may encourage states to terminate their investment treaties as a show of action, such a policy is likely to have a minimal impact on treaty practice due to such survival clauses. Thus, one reason why ISA remains popular is owing to a very extensive infrastructure created by states with extensive pre-existing agreements that provided for ISA. With the limited number of states repudiating

ISA in new treaties, it is unlikely that there will be any significant shift in this treaty practice.

Related to the above-mentioned argument, ISA remains highly popular. Although Sornarajah views ISA as inherently biased against developing states, his view overlooks imbalances in power among states, including among developing states. First, developing states come in all sizes and are often able to bargain with developed states for favourable treaty provisions. This is particularly true in the case of China. Unofficial reports of negotiators suggest that China insisted on including ISA in its agreement with Australia. A similar position was taken by Korea. Both of these countries are resource-reliant and employ various powerful state-owned entities or SOEs and conglomerates in their search for investment opportunities abroad. These entities are viewed with suspicion by host states, which explains why China and Korea wish to arbitrate in a neutral third-party forum, notably through ISA, and why states falter in formulating investment-facilitation agreements that exclude ISA.

Notably too, even small economies may formulate powerful treaty negotiating platforms. For example, although ASEAN economies are small, when united, they represent a powerful regional force. Increasingly, that organisation into a regional block allows the resulting institution, such as ASEAN, to conclude agreements that its member states consider more favourable, such as in providing for ISA.

Finally, ISA has retained its popularity, because there is still no conclusive evidence that its deficiencies cannot be addressed through treaty modification. Rather than excluding ISA, states are now increasingly relying on treaty modification to create space for public policy. This trend is evident in Australia's recent trade agreements, particularly, its FTA with Korea. India has similarly undertaken this approach, although to a lesser extent. Remarkably, the behaviour of Australia and India replicate global trends, with a number of states qualifying access to ISA in their latest agreements to ensure greater transparency and fairness. This ability to tweak the existing ISA governance eliminates the need to undertake radical reforms.

Conclusion

This paper set out to explore the current state of play in international investment law by analysing the behaviour of states that rejected ISA. As this paper demonstrates, the movement against ISA has subsided. Rather than repudiating the existing system, even those states who favoured repudiation are increasingly relying on various treaty revisions to balance their investment facilitation agreements. Thus, there is very limited movement in favour of abolishing ISA as a whole.

Analysis of recently concluded treaties in this chapter acknowledges Sornarajah's concerns over involving states in arbitral proceedings. However, attempts by state parties to subvert ISA proceedings have been very limited in fact. First, the ability of state parties to 'hijack' arbitral proceedings risks transforming an arbitral process into essentially a dispute between states. This is likely to result in a legal quagmire, not least of all over the ambit of treaty protections accorded to foreign investors by a pre-existing treaty. Beyond these issues, states may find themselves in difficult negotiating positions. After all, states have devised ISA in some measure to disengage from investment disputes and to focus on high politics. If home state intervention in disputes between host states and foreign investors grows, states will find themselves increasingly politically and economically embroiled in such conflicts. In addition, power politics and gun-boat diplomacy may once again come into play. However, states well appreciate that spats between them over processes for resolving investor-state disputes may strain political alliances and undermine their long-term relationships. Thus, it is likely that states will use 'hijacking provisions' in treaties rarely.

Furthermore, states conceptualise their role in arbitral proceedings differently. For example, Australia appears to be particularly concerned with transparency and is attempting to introduce greater openness in the arbitral process. Comparatively, India and ASEAN are mostly concerned with preserving the list of security exceptions in their treaties and do not prioritise the actual arbitral process as part of their ISA reforms.

In addition, rather than witness a decline of ISA, foreign investors are likely to be subject to provisions in investment treaties that identify priorities in which host states may intervene in the public interest. However, given the problematic nature of some of these national interest priorities and the prospect of foreign investors bringing ISA actions, host states are likely to invoke such priorities with caution.

What is also likely to evolve is greater institutional support for transparent ISA proceedings. There is already broad consensus that ISA proceedings could, and should, be more open to the general public. As this chapter has argued, such transparency will add further benefits to ISA proceedings over resort to national courts.

Whatever the future of ISA may be, this chapter suggests that ISA will not be radically different from the present regulatory order. Nor, arguably, should the determination be otherwise.

PART II

4

Reforming the system of international investment dispute settlement

GUS VAN HARTEN

Introduction

Should a country withdraw from investment treaties or sign more of them based on a "reformed" version of investment treaty arbitration? That question has faced commentators on investment treaty arbitration, which I will call ISDS (for investor-state dispute settlement) in this chapter, for at least a decade.[1] It has also faced governments with greater urgency as more foreign investor lawsuits have been launched and larger awards issued against states.

In this chapter, I examine the question by reviewing the European (and United States) reform program in ISDS, evidenced especially by reforms adopted by North American states in the early 2000s and more recently by the European Commission in its proposals for a Europe–United States Transatlantic Trade and Investment Partnership (TTIP) and a Canada–Europe Comprehensive Economic and Trade Agreement (CETA).[2]

[1] I adopt the label ISDS because it is the one used by the European Commission, although I use the term here to refer to the more precise concept of investment treaty arbitration. Despite this concession in the choice of terms, I do not wish to downplay the role of arbitration, in contrast to mediation or negotiation/settlement under threat of arbitration, as the compulsory and binding element in any broader definition of ISDS.

[2] Canada–European Union: Comprehensive Economic and Trade Agreement (CETA): Consolidated CETA Text, available online: Department of Foreign Affairs and International Trade (Canada) www.international.gc.ca/trade-agreements-accords-commerciaux/agr-acc/ceta-aecg/text-texte/toc-tdm.aspx?lang=eng (last accessed 8 October 2014); European Commission, "Public Consultation on Modalities for Investment Protection and ISDS in TTIP" (undated) [the consultation text], available online: European Commission http://trade.ec.europa.eu/doclib/docs/2014/march/tradoc_152280.pdf (last accessed 8 October 2014); all page number references are to the online pdf version in which the pages are not numbered. This chapter is based in part on a submission I provided to the Commission as part of the consultation. The discussion does not incorporate proposals for ISDS reform subsequent to those outlined in the documents cited here.

I argue that this official reform program has not addressed basic flaws in ISDS, especially its lack of balance in the allocation of rights and responsibilities and its lack of independence, fairness, and subsidiarity in adjudicative process and institutional structure of ISDS. Thus, the reform movement of the major Western powers appears to support the case for other states to pull out of investment treaties and ISDS, if they wish to avoid its flaws. Likewise, the lack of commitment to genuine reform appears to affirm Professor Sornarajah's longstanding critical position in the field.

Professor Sornarajah's contribution

Any academic who has taken an independent and critical perspective on ISDS has walked a trail blazed by Sornarajah. I will provide a short anecdote to flag this point. When I was a doctoral student at the London School of Economics I attended a talk at which Sornarajah spoke alongside another panel member who, unlike him, was praiseful of ISDS. When I spoke to Sornarajah afterward, he mentioned that the other panel member, an ISDS arbitrator, had told him after the talk that he felt like hitting Sornarajah for his constant criticism of ISDS and that Sornarajah had responded that if it happened he would hit him right back. Presumably, the statements were in jest yet the anecdote reminds me of how defensively some ISDS practitioners react to ideas supporting the case for serious reform of ISDS. In my own experience, that reaction was generated primarily by my (I thought) conservative call in 2007 to replace ISDS arbitrators with judges owing to their final authority over public law. Considering Sornarajah's more wide-ranging and fundamental critique of ISDS, the consistency of his scholarship appears all the more impressive.[3]

Ironically, my own thoughts about making ISDS judicial was an issue on which Sornarajah and I tended to differ. After studying the institutional setup of investment treaty arbitration, it seemed to me that an international investment court was desirable because it could deliver a fair, independent, open, and basically sensible – in a way that ISDS is not – means to resolve international disputes about egregious mistreatment or

[3] e.g. M. Sornarajah, *International Law on Foreign Investment* (Cambridge: CUP, 1994); "The Retreat of Neo-Liberalism in Investment Treaty Arbitration", in C. Rogers and R. Alford (eds.), *Developments in Investment Arbitration* (New York: OUP, 2009); *Resistance and Change in the International Law on Foreign Investment* (Cambridge: CUP, 2015).

egregious misconduct of foreign investors. I stress this second type of dispute, about misconduct of foreign investors, to make the point that a judicial process should be accompanied by substantive as well as institutional and procedural reforms to address the great imbalance in today's global economy between foreign investor rights, on the one hand, and foreign investor responsibilities and the state's right to regulate, on the other.

Yet, even with that proviso, I suspect that Sornarajah would still have serious reservations about the idea of an international investment court, such as on the powerful objections that it will serve to institutionalize a flawed system, would replicate and entrench existing imbalances, and would have little more than a quixotic hope of achieving the fairness and balance that I had in mind. Better then to convey a consistent message that investment treaties are flawed because of the unfair, slanted, and undemocratic arrangement of power that they create. As Sornarajah has put it at a general level, international law and ISDS must not become "the means by which hegemonic states impose principles on the basis of a pretense such as a higher standard of civilization or better standards of governance"; rather, it is "best to start anew" by recognizing the "competing interests of the sustainable use of resources, the pursuance of social interest in the health and welfare of communities, human rights considerations in the conduct of business, and corporate social responsibility."[4]

As it happens, I am myself coming around to Sornarajah's perspective, for two reasons. The first is the widespread and, to me, still surprising hostility of many in the ISDS industry to proposals for basic reform aimed at judicialization. Perhaps I was naïve from the start but even the wildest dreamer can observe only so many ducks, weaves, quarter-steps, misleading public claims, and behind-the-scenes lobbying maneuvers before coming to doubt the willingness of power brokers in the industry to accept the need for fundamental change to make the system tolerable, even if only from a conventional rule-of-law point of view. The second reason for this pessimism about the prospect for meaningful reform is the refusal of major Western governments to take up the opportunities to adopt modest improvements that are clearly required from the same rule-of-law perspective. Instead, one creative and evasive argument after another[5] has been offered to the public for maintaining the power of

[4] M. Sornarajah, "Starting Anew in International Investment Law", Colombia FDI Perspectives, No. 74 (16 July 2012).

[5] For an example in the European context, see G. Van Harten, "Creative Accounting and the Sales Pitch for ISDS", *EurActiv* (6 March 2015).

ISDS arbitrators to review, on the say-so of a foreign investor and in a highly questionable process, anything that a sovereign does and then potentially to reassign millions or even billions of dollars in public funds to very large companies and very wealthy individuals.[6] It is such a far-out situation that, in my experience, many decision-makers or journalists who are unfamiliar with ISDS at first find it hard to believe that the system works the way it does, and so they should, and it is a fair hyperbole to say that – after a fuller story of ISDS is told – it can sometimes take smelling salts to get the unsuspecting listener off the ground.

Flaws in the official reform model

In this chapter, I elaborate on my second reason for pessimism about the prospects for meaningful reform. That is, I argue that reform proposals advanced, most recently in Brussels and based on the history of ISDS in North America, fall well short of what is needed and, thus, suggest a lack of a commitment to addressing obvious flaws in ISDS. The focus of my criticism is the European Commission's approach to ISDS, represented especially by the public text of the Canada–EU CETA, and the Commission's advocacy of that position in a public consultation document issued in 2014.[7] Essentially, the Commission's approach reflects the North American' read US Trade Representative, model of ISDS, delineated after 2000 under NAFTA and in subsequent US investment treaties.[8] As I will show, this specimen of the reform model can be defended – if one takes seriously the flaws in ISDS as an unfair and imbalanced means of adjudication – only through dubious reasoning that seems designed to hide the unjustified privileging of foreign investors and the scandalous transfer of power away from legislatures and courts to for-profit lawyers sitting as arbitrators.

[6] I refer to the privileging of these foreign investors in particular on the basis that they were apparently the beneficiaries of over 90% of the ordered compensation in ISDS up to the spring of 2014. G. Van Harten, "Who Was Awarded Compensation in Past ISDS Awards?", *Blog Post* (28 March 2015), available at: gusvanharten.wordpress.com.

[7] Note 2 above. I comment on more recent reform proposals from the European Commission in "Key Flaws in the European Commission's Proposals for Foreign Investor Protection in TTIP", Osgoode Legal Studies Research Paper No. 61/ 2015 (November 2015), http:/ssrn.com/abstract=2692122.

[8] e.g. Free Trade Commission (NAFTA), *Notes of Interpretation of Certain Chapter 11 Provisions* (31 July 2001), online: Government of Canada www.international.gc.ca/trade-agreements-accords-commerciaux/topics-domaines/disp-diff/NAFTA-Interpr.aspx (last accessed 4 October 2014); Dominican Republic-Central America-United States Free Trade Agreement, 19 USCS S. 4011 (2005) (CAFTA), Article 10.5(2) and (3) and 10.21, Annex 10-B, and Annex 10-C.

Originally, the reform model I criticize here came about when Canada, the United States, and Mexico apparently realized at a higher political level that they had given ISDS arbitrators the power of the public purse for virtually anything each country might do in its sovereign role – such as pass legislation, issue a supreme court decision, and other not-trifling matters – and, strikingly, that this power could be exercised in secret and without involvement by any party except for the foreign investor and national government of the country whose exercise of sovereignty was challenged.[9] Somehow, the transfer of power under NAFTA had apparently been missed by all but a small number of persons responsible for the deal's investment chapter and, elsewhere, for ISDS-based agreements like the Energy Charter Treaty and numerous other investment treaties concluded en masse in the decade before the explosion of foreign investor lawsuits began in the late 1990s.[10]

Following from this realization, a reform effort by the North American governments managed to achieve a mostly open ISDS process; a very limited form of participation in the ISDS process by other affected parties, albeit only at the arbitrators' discretion; and a few leaky plugs of expansive readings given to foreign investor rights by the arbitrators in early NAFTA cases.[11] Yet, other glaring issues of unfairness, lack of independence, and substantive imbalances were left untouched, and even the problem of ISDS confidentiality has lingered owing to closed-door settlements involving regulatory changes or payouts of public money based on an ISDS process that heavily favors foreign investors over other interests.[12]

Faced with this backdrop for ISDS reform, is it right as an academic researcher to keep emphasizing what seemed like a reasonable proposal to make ISDS judicial and hope that one day – through eventual judicial reinterpretation or states' actions – that a fair and balanced

[9] G. Van Harten, "Five Justifications for Investment Treaties: A Critical Discussion" 2 *Trade, Law and Development* 19, 53–54.

[10] Energy Charter Treaty (annex I of the Final Act of the European Energy Charter Conference) (Lisbon, 17 December 1994; 34 ILM 373). For information on investment treaties concluded by countries during the peak period for new investment treaties in the 1990s, see UN Conference on Trade and Development (UNCTAD), Investment Policy Hub, http://investmentpolicyhub.unctad.org/.

[11] Free Trade Commission (note 8 above).

[12] e.g. For a report on the estimated number of ISDS settlements, which are nearly always based on confidential terms, see United Nations Conference on Trade and Development, *International Investment Agreements Issues Note – Recent Trends in IIAs and ISDS* (Geneva: UNCTAD, February 2015).

multilateral system of investment regulation and dispute settlement might emerge? Or should one make clear that ISDS does not seem to be getting better and the only viable option for self-defense by a country is to pull out of the treaties that create ISDS, even if a state has to wait for years to remove completely the risks and constraints created by ISDS?

European Commission's adoption of the official reform model

The rest of this chapter proceeds by examining more closely some recent verifiable example of the official reform movement. In particular, I highlight a series of claims by the European Commission – in a public consultation document in 2014 – to ballyhoo its "reformed" approach to ISDS in the proposed TTIP and in the public text of the proposed Canada–Europe CETA. A series of representative claims by the Commission is laid out with an explanation of weaknesses or occasional strengths of each claim. The claims are organized according to five criteria, which, I suggest, should be used to judge proposals for ISDS reform fairness, independence, openness, balance, and subsidiarity (focusing on the last two). This list of criteria is not meant to be exhaustive. For example, one could also consider this criterion for evaluating a version of international investment adjudication that fit all of the other five criteria:

- Does the proposal provide a compelling justification, based on clear and reliable evidence, for using an international judicial process instead of other institutions and processes to resolve foreign investment disputes?

This last criterion operates at a broader level than the ones I discuss in this chapter; that is, it points to reasons for transferring power from existing institutions to a new, or at least newly applied, mechanism for resolving international disputes: an international judicial process that allows for private claims by foreign investors against states in their sovereign role – based on the rights and protections usually enunciated in investment treaties – even with a duty to exhaust alternative remedies in domestic or existing international courts or contract-based forums and even with a formal balance in the allocation of rights and responsibilities related to foreign investment. This larger issue is well beyond the scope of this chapter in part because it seems so distant from current detailed debates about ISDS reform.

Thus, the chapter now leaves behind this blue-skies evaluation to focus on basic criteria of fairness, independence, openness, balance, and subsidiary and, then, on the finer details – tiny and cloudy side alleys, if one were to abuse the metaphor – of the Commission's inadequate reform proposal. This particularly focused approach is necessary because, even in its approach to reform, the Commission did not discuss the option of using a judicial process instead of for-profit arbitration to resolve foreign investment disputes.[13] Put differently, in its consultation document, the Commission did not ask, why is investor-state arbitration needed at all? To answer that question rigorously would require a careful framing of the question and a comprehensive assessment of a range of economic, political, social, and legal aspects of the use and impact of ISDS. For example, the consultation would have needed to examine:[14]

- the costs and benefits of ISDS in broad terms;
- the implications of ISDS for principles such as democratic choice, regulatory flexibility, and market efficiency;
- the compatibility of ISDS with values and criteria of judicial decision-making;
- the relative utility and role of alternative means – such as domestic and European courts, state-to-state adjudication, and market mechanisms including investment contracts and risk insurance – to protect foreign investors.

Because the Commission's consultation was not framed to address these issues, it was not designed to collect information and evidence that would cast doubt on or contradict common assertions by ISDS proponents that, for example, ISDS encourages investment, contributes to jobs and growth, encourages "good governance," and so on;[15] that states were well-informed when they entered into earlier treaties that create ISDS;[16] that foreign

[13] For a discussion of the Commission's recent proposals for an "investment court system", see note 2 above.

[14] A starting point for such an analysis is L.N. Skovgaard Poulsen, J. Bonnitcha, and J. Webb Yackee, *Analytical Framework for Assessing Costs and Benefits of Investment Protection Treaties* (London: LSE Enterprise, March 2014).

[15] e.g. Prime Minister of Canada, "Canada-China Foreign Investment Promotion and Protection Agreement (FIPA)", *News Release* (8 February 2012) (on file with author); B. Kingsbury and S. Schill, "Investment-State Arbitration as Governance: Fair and Equitable Treatment, Proportionality and the Emerging Global Administrative Law" IILJ Working Paper 2009/6 (Global Administrative Law Series) (19 August 2009).

[16] e.g. L. Herman, "China Investment Treaty No Sell-Out", *Financial Post* (2 October 2014); Van Harten (note 9 above), 41.

investors – including huge multinationals – are at a disadvantage relative to domestic investors and citizens in a state's politics;[17] that domestic courts in one or another country (or even in all countries) mistreat or discriminate against foreign investors;[18] that arbitrators have increasingly applied investment treaties in a more restrained or balanced way;[19] and that ISDS is an independent and neutral process of adjudication.[20]

Therefore, before continuing with an examination of the Commission's reform model, it should be stressed that, without a compelling and evidence-based case for creating special rights and privileges for foreign investors relative to other actors, there is no reason to incorporate ISDS into any treaty. Giving a special status to any actor in law or access to public funds, especially the largest companies and wealthiest individuals in the world, calls for a clear justification based on evidence that doing so will deliver a public benefit to outweigh the disadvantages to other actors and costs to the public. Otherwise, one would proceed with a massive expansion of the scope of ISDS – for instance, using the US economy as a rough proxy, TTIP would extend ISDS coverage of international investment flows by about 300 percent in comparison to current ISDS coverage based on existing treaties[21] – without a careful review of the serious risks to public funds and constraints on

[17] For a discussion of the underlying claim, see E. Aisbett, "Foreign Firms: Powerful or Persecuted?" Proceedings of the German Development Economics Conference No. 39 (2010); D. Schneiderman, *Resisting Economic Globalization* (New York: Palgrave Macmillan, 2013) 123–127.

[18] e.g. consultation text (note 2 above) 9 and 11.

[19] For a discussion, see G. Van Harten, *Sovereign Choices and Sovereign Constraints: Judicial Restraint in Investment Treaty Arbitration* (Oxford: OUP, 2013), 153, chapter 6.

[20] e.g. J. Paulsson, *Denial of Justice in International Law* (Cambridge: CUP, 2005), 265; C.N. Brower and L.A. Steven, "Who Then Should Judge? Developing the International Rule of Law under NAFTA Chapter 11" (2001) 2 *Chi JIL* 193; C.N. Brower and S.W. Schill, "Is Arbitration a Threat or a Boon to the Legitimacy of International Investment Law" (2009) 9 *Chi JIL* 471

[21] Measured by the amount of FDI flows to which the treaty would apply, TTIP alone is more significant than all the existing treaties combined. For example, TTIP would cover 50–60% of investment flows in and out of the United States. Besides TTIP, a few other treaties pursued by the Commission or the United States – the Trans-Pacific Partnership, EU–China investment treaty, and US–China investment treaty – appear likely to expand the coverage of investor-state arbitration from 15% to 20% to more than 80% of investment flows. These approximate figures were calculated based on the existing investment treaty coverage of country-by-country inward and outward FDI flows for the United States in 2012 from the data provided in Organisation for Economic Cooperation and Development (OECD), "StatExtracts: FDI Flows by Partner Country", available online: http://stats.oecd .org/Index.aspx?DataSetCode=FDI_FLOW_PARTNER. The figures do not account for the possibility of forum-shopping by foreign investors, which is difficult to measure, and

voters and regulators; to the principle of a level playing field for all market actors; and to established structures of public accountability, regulatory flexibility, fair adjudication, and judicial independence.

Why arbitrators not judges?

Turning to the criteria for evaluating ISDS reform proposals, I note three items that are essential for a judicial process in the final resolution of the legality of sovereign conduct and award of public funds in relation to foreign investment. They are as follows.[22]

The first criterion is institutional independence. The process would need to incorporate the conventional institutional safeguards of judicial independence, such as secure tenure, a set salary, an objective method of case assignment, and prohibitions on outside work as a lawyer. These safeguards are otherwise present in courts as a means to alleviate public concern about potential bias. At present, ISDS does not include such safeguards.

The second criterion is procedural fairness. The process would need to allow a party, besides the claimant investor and respondent (national) government, whose rights or interests are affected by the adjudication to have full standing in the process. Otherwise, the adjudicator would not be required and in a position to hear all sides in the dispute. At present, ISDS does not provide this basic right to all affected parties.

The third criterion is open courts. The process would need to adopt a presumption that all documents and hearings are presumptively public, subject to specifically enumerated and judicially approved exceptions, in order to enable public accountability and support the other two above-mentioned criteria. At present, ISDS is not open in this way, and, in some instances, even the mere fact of the arbitration is kept secret.

I discuss elsewhere[23] – and summarize here – the near-complete failure of the Commission's approach to satisfy the criteria of fairness and

handled in different ways by arbitrators and existing treaties, but may expand existing coverage of investor-state arbitration.

22 For an elaboration of these concepts, see G Van Harten, "Investment Treaty Arbitration, Procedural Fairness, and the Rule of Law", in S.W. Schill (ed.), *International Investment Law and Comparative Public Law* (Oxford: OUP, 2010); G Van Harten, *Investment Treaty Arbitration and Public Law* (Oxford: OUP, 2007), 159–175.

23 G. Van Harten, "The EC and UNCTAD Reform Agendas: Do They Ensure Independence, Openness, and Fairness in Investor-State Arbitration?" in M. Krajewski and S. Hindelang (eds.), *Shifting Paradigms in International Investment Law: More Balanced, Less Isolated, Diversified Approaches* (Oxford: OUP, in press).

independence as well as the significant, but by themselves inadequate, improvements on the criterion of openness.

On procedural fairness, the Commission's model provides full standing rights for the claimant investor and respondent government, but not for any other party whose rights or interests – such as reputational interests – are affected by the decision-making.[24] These other parties cannot participate fully, making the process unfair in the most basic way. The Commission alludes to this unfairness but does not address the problem. In a discussion of openness (the Commission uses the term transparency), the Commission stated, "[i]nterested parties from civil society will be able to file submissions to make their views and arguments known to the ISDS tribunal."[25] Thus, the Commission endorsed a form of *amicus* representation, as practiced in some other contexts of ISDS and as based, in the CETA, on the UN Commission on International Trade Law *Rules on Transparency in Treaty-based Investor-State Arbitration.*[26] This form of representation allows an outside party, at the discretion of the arbitrators, to participate in the proceedings – as the Commission says, to "file submissions" – to the extent permitted by the arbitrators.[27] It allows a tribunal to hear from a party where the arbitrators consider it useful, but it does not require the tribunal to give full standing to any party with a direct interest in the proceeding alongside the other parties.[28] In actual arbitrations, *amicus* status has been granted rarely and with important restrictions.[29] As a result, the Commission has authorized arbitrators to decide disputes without requiring them to hear

[24] CETA (note 2 above), Article X.3 (definition of "disputing parties").

[25] Consultation text (note 2 above), 11.

[26] CETA (note 2 above), Article X-35(1)(b)(ii); UN Commission on International Trade Law (UNCITRAL), *Rules on Transparency in Treaty-Based Investor-State Arbitration* (New York: United Nations, 2014), Article 4.

[27] N. Blackaby and C. Richard, "Amicus Curiae: A Panacea for Legitimacy in Investment Arbitration?", in M. Waibel *et al.* (eds.), *The Backlash against Investment Arbitration* (Austin: Wolters Kluwer, 2010), 259–266.

[28] P. Wieland, "Why the Amicus Curia Institution is Ill-Suited to Address Indigenous Peoples' Rights before Investor-State Arbitration Tribunals: Glamis Gold and the Right of Intervention" (2011) 3 *Trade, Law & Dev't* 334, 344–345, 359–360; E. Levine, "Amicus Curiae in International Investment Arbitration: The Implications of an Increase in Third-Party Participation" (2012) 29 *Berkeley J Int'l L* 200, 208–214; A. Salazar, Defragmenting International Investment Law to Protect Citizen-Consumers: The Role of Amici Curiae and Public Interest Groups (Osgoode Hall Law School Comparative Research in Law & Political Economy Research Paper No. 6/2013, 2013), 4–8.

[29] Wieland (note 28 above), 341–344.

evidence and arguments from all affected parties. Put differently, it has authorized arbitrators to decide disputes in a procedurally unfair way.

With respect to judicial independence, the Commission acknowledged, in its consultation text, issues of independence and impartiality in ISDS in a discussion of arbitrator ethics, conduct, and qualifications. The Commission stated softly "[t]here is concern that arbitrators on ISDS [investor-state dispute settlement] tribunals do not always act in an independent and impartial manner."[30] Yet, the Commission did not mention the longstanding role of institutional safeguards in ensuring an adjudicator's independence and impartiality. Instead, the Commission narrowed the issue by focusing on arbitrator conduct at the individual level[31] and proposed the use of rules to govern arbitrator conduct instead of institutional reforms.[32] To complement the rules on arbitrator conduct, the Commission proposed to allow conflict of interest challenges to arbitrators.[33] This emphasis on individual conduct of arbitrators sidestepped important problems of independence due to the institutional structure of ISDS. The Commission's proposed code of conduct is not a substitute for institutional safeguards; among other issues, it relies on executive officials instead of a judicial process to police the code.[34]

The Commission's failure to ensure institutional independence calls into question its wider reform agenda. Difficulties emerge whenever the Commission envisions decision-making that should be fair and independent. For instance, the Commission plans to address the problem of frivolous ISDS claims by giving arbitrators the power to decide whether a case, in which they stand to earn significant income, should proceed.[35] This creates an obvious conflict of interest; frivolous claims should be vetted by an actor who does not have a financial stake in the outcome of the decision to vet. Alternatively, the Commission promotes its proposed textual clarifications of the treaties by saying "the decisions of arbitral tribunals are only as good as the provisions that they have to interpret and apply."[36] In this respect, the Commission downplays the arbitrators' record of exploiting treaty ambiguity to expand their role and power.[37] Textual clarifications may be helpful, but there is always ambiguity left behind, and the ambiguity remains in the hands of arbitrators. A more

[30] Consultation text (note 2 above), 12.
[31] Consultation text (note 2 above), 12 (emphasis added).
[32] Consultation text (note 2 above), 13. [33] Consultation text (note 2 above), 13.
[34] CETA (note 2 above), Article X.25(10). [35] Consultation text (note 2 above), 14.
[36] Consultation text (note 2 above), 8. [37] Van Harten (note 19 above).

pertinent statement would be that the arbitrators' decisions are "only as good" as the process by which they are appointed and make their decisions. The absence of institutional safeguards means that all outcomes in the Commission's model of ISDS will be tainted, regardless of the underlying text. These examples highlight how a flaw in the institutional design – allowing for-profit arbitrators instead of financially detached judges to supervise sovereigns – undermines the integrity of ISDS systematically.

Finally, on openness, the Commission in its consultation text acknowledged and responded to the lack of openness in ISDS. The Commission stated that the lack of openness jeopardizes the legitimacy and accountability of the system, prevents interested stakeholders from being informed about the process, and undermines consistency and predictability.[38] In turn, the Commission provided, in the CETA, for all ISDS documents and hearings to be made public.[39] The publication of documents is near-comprehensive in that it includes the foreign investor's request for consultations or arbitration, the submissions of parties, and all tribunal decisions.[40] That said, the proposal also has limitations. Most importantly, in the CETA, the Commission has left it to arbitrators instead of judges to decide whether documents should be redacted or hearings closed.[41] Although this is as much an issue of independence as openness, a decision not to open documents or hearings to the public should be based on a judicial process. All arbitrators who seek reappointment may see claimants at some level as their customers and claimants, as well as states, sometimes oppose openness for self-serving reasons. As an aside, in many past cases, arbitrators have erred in favor of confidentiality instead of openness.[42] Another problem with the Commission's approach is that an ISDS claim can be brought, and a settlement reached involving payment of public money and regulatory changes, off the public record. To address this concern, the Commission would need to make clear that the fact and terms of a settlement reached by a state, after the invocation of the treaty by a foreign investor, must be reported to the

[38] Consultation text (note 2 above), 10. [39] CETA (note 2 above), Article X.33.

[40] CETA (note 2 above), Article X.33(1), which incorporates the UNCITRAL, *Rules on Transparency in Treaty-Based Investor-State Arbitration* (above note 26), as supplemented by CETA Article X.33(2).

[41] CETA (note 2 above), Article X.33(5).

[42] e.g. *SD Myers* v. *Canada* (Procedural Orders No. 3 and 11, 10 June 1999 and 11 November 1999), UNCITRAL Rules; *Pope & Talbot* v. *Canada* (Merits, Phase 2, 10 April 2001), 13(4) World Trade and Arb Mat 61.

Commission and made public. Despite these limitations, the Commission has taken more significant steps to address the lack of openness, following in the tracks of the post-2000 North American reform model, than in the case of other flaws.

Lack of balance and subsidiarity

I turn now to two other criteria that go beyond the internal process of ISDS. These criteria involve formal questions about the structural design of international adjudication. I examine these criteria in more depth than the criteria discussed in the previous section and refer to them loosely as balance and subsidiarity.

The first criterion is balance in the allocation of rights and responsibilities between states and foreign investors. To be formally balanced, I suggest the model would need to affirm the right to regulate of states and include responsibilities for foreign investors, alongside their rights, that are actionable in the same manner as their rights. ISDS has elaborate and highly enforceable foreign investor rights – and corresponding responsibilities for states – but lacks a clear affirmation of the right to regulate and lacks substantive and actionable responsibilities for foreign investors.[43] I see this version of "balance" as a formalistic or thin version of the concept because, with the exception of the clarity of any affirmation of the state's right to regulate, it does not avert to the content or extent of the respective substantive rights and responsibilities.

The second criterion is subsidiarity to other venues. If ISDS were to be respectful of other institutions and avoid becoming overloaded, the model would need to supplement, not replace, other venues for dispute resolution.[44] The primary other venues that are available are domestic courts, contractually agreed forums, and any more suitable form of international dispute resolution. To date, ISDS has typically been applied by arbitrators in ways that facilitate parallel ISDS claims under an investment treaty, alongside these other venues.[45]

Notably, in its consultation text, the Commission framed balance in ISDS in the context of a relationship between the protection of foreign investors and the state's right to regulate.[46] In this section, I take a somewhat broader

[43] For a cautious approach to the issue of foreign investor responsibilities, see P.T. Muchlinski, *Multinational Enterprises & the Law*, 2nd ed. (Oxford: OUP, 2007), chapter 3.

[44] G. De Búrca, "The Principle of Subsidiarity and the Court of Justice as an Institutional Actor" (1998) 36 *Common Market L Rev* 217.

[45] Van Harten (note 2 above), chapter 5.

[46] Consultation text (note 2 above), 2 and 8.

view of balance by examining the allocation of rights and responsibilities not only between foreign investors and the state but also simply for each of these types of actor. Yet, whichever approach one adopts, the Commission's approach does not make ISDS balanced.

Rights and responsibilities of states

States assume wide-ranging responsibilities under investment treaties. These include the responsibilities to submit to ISDS arbitrator power and pay compensation as ordered by the arbitrators where they decide that the state failed to treat a foreign investor fairly and equitably, did not pay sufficient compensation for an expropriation, discriminated in favor of domestic investors, or inappropriately limited transfers of capital, for example.[47] However, these responsibilities are rarely if ever accompanied by a clear affirmation of the state's right to exercise its regulatory role in relation to foreign investors.[48]

Investment treaties could easily affirm the state's right to regulate alongside the state's responsibilities. For this right to be balanced against and roughly equivalent to the state's responsibilities, it would need to be affirmed as a general substantive right of the state. That is, it would need to be stated clearly in the treaty without broad limitations – such as a circular requirement for the right to be exercised consistently with the treaty[49] – and applied to all of the state's obligations to protect foreign investors.

One example of an affirmation of the right to regulate in general is found the European Convention on Human Rights (second paragraph of Article 1 of Protocol 1):[50]

> The preceding provisions [on property protection] shall not, however, in any way impair the right of a State to enforce such laws as it deems necessary to control the use of property in accordance with the general interest or to secure the payment of taxes or other contributions or penalties.

[47] e.g. CETA (note 2 above), Articles X.6, X.9, X.11, and X.12.

[48] For an in-depth and innovative discussion, see J.A. VanDuzer, P. Simons, and G. Mayeda, *Integrating Sustainable Development into International Investment Agreements: A Guide for Developing Countries* (London: Commonwealth Secretariat, 2012), 287–398.

[49] e.g. North American Free Trade Agreement (NAFTA) (17 December 1992; 32 ILM 296 and 605; entered into force 1 January 1994), Article 1114 (made circular by the phrase "otherwise consistent with this chapter").

[50] Convention for the Protection of Human Rights and Fundamental Freedoms (the European Convention on Human Rights [ECHR]) (4 November 1950; Eur TS 5, 213 UNTS 222; entered into force 3 September 1953).

Another example is Article 12 of the proposed Havana Charter of 1948:[51]

> . . . a Member has the right: (i) to take any appropriate safeguards necessary to ensure that foreign investment is not used as a basis for interference in its internal affairs or national policies; (ii) to determine whether and, to what extent and upon what terms it will allow future foreign investment; (iii) to prescribe and give effect on just terms to requirements as to the ownership of existing and future investments; (iv) to prescribe and give effect to other reasonable requirements with respect to existing and future investments . . .

These examples affirm the right to regulate in different ways, but both show that states can affirm the right to regulate alongside the state's responsibilities to protect property or to ensure foreign investor security. It is a question of whether states want to do so.

In its consultation text, the Commission said that it wants to affirm the right to regulate. For example, the Commission mentioned a "specific EU objective" in the treaties "to strengthen the balance between investment protection and the right to regulate."[52] It also noted its aim "to make sure that the Parties' right to regulate is confirmed as a basic underlying principle."[53] If that was the aim, however, the Commission failed to achieve it in the Canada–Europe CETA.

In the CETA investment chapter, the right to regulate is not stated at all, let alone clearly as a right of the state. Obviously, it is not enough in legal terms for the Commission to declare its intent to affirm the right to regulate in a public consultation document but not in the treaty itself. Likewise, it is not enough to do so as part of an aspirational statement in a preamble of the treaty or to mention it in CETA chapters other than the investment chapter.[54] Indeed, a mention of the right in the CETA preamble and then elsewhere in the treaty appears to damage the reliability of the right to regulate in the investment chapter, by creating an inference that the parties to the treaty wished to make the right substantive and effective only in the other chapters that mentioned it. As a result, the CETA falls well short of balancing the right to regulate against the state's responsibilities to protect foreign investors.

[51] Final Act of the United Nations Conference on Trade and Employment: Havana Charter for an International Trade Organization (the Havana Charter), UN Conference on Trade and Employment, UN Doc 1948 II.D.4.1 (1948).

[52] Consultation text (note 2 above), 2. [53] Consultation text (note 2 above), 2.

[54] e.g. CETA (note 2 above) Preamble, Chapter 24 (Article 2), and Chapter 25 (Article X.4), which incorporate the right to regulate into the CETA's preamble, chapter on trade and labor, and chapter on trade and environment, respectively, but not its investment chapter.

Instead of following this straightforward route to affirm the right to regulate, the Commission talked in its consultation text about textual clarifications for some of the state's responsibilities to protect foreign investors. For example, the consultation text states that the European Union "is introducing modern and innovative provisions clarifying the meaning of those investment protection standards that have raised concerns."[55] The Commission's reliance on textual clarifications was not new, if that was the intended meaning of "modern and innovative." Indeed, they were the main response of Canada and the United States in their post-2001 reforms of NAFTA (although never again since that time).[56]

More importantly, as a way to affirm the right to regulate, the Commission's textual clarifications were inadequate, misleading, and unreliable. To illustrate, the Commission in the CETA arrived at moderating language for one of the state's obligations: the responsibility to compensate foreign investors for an indirect expropriation.[57] This language supports, to an uncertain degree, the state's regulatory flexibility in the case of the expropriation standard. Yet, it is also limited because it (a) does not apply to other state obligations in the treaty; (b) has important qualifiers that allow arbitrators at their discretion to maintain an expansive pro-claimant investor approach; (c) is open to a significant loophole due to the Commission's approach to most favored nation (MFN) treatment; and (d) maintains power in the hands of arbitrators who have demonstrated themselves broadly disinclined to an approach based on the general balancing of foreign investor rights against the rights of other actors or the state's right to regulate.

Therefore, the textual clarification of any single substantive provision cannot effectively safeguard the right to regulate, even for that single provision alone. If the Commission wanted to affirm the right to regulate, it would need to do so clearly for all of the treaty's obligations for states and in all areas of decision-making.

Worse, the Commission's characterization of its textual clarification of fair and equitable treatment (FET) was dangerous and misleading if the purpose was to safeguard the right to regulate.[58] First, the Commission claims to have ensured a closed list in the definition of this wide-ranging standard as a means to preclude the arbitrators from continuing to

[55] Consultation text (note 2 above), 2. [56] Note 7 above.

[57] CETA (note 2 above), Article X.11 and Annex X.11; consultation text (note 2 above), 2 and 7.

[58] CETA (note 2 above), Article X.9; consultation text (note 2 above), 5–6.

interpret the standard expansively to favor claimants.[59] Yet, the Commission did not include obvious language to remove the arbitrators' ability to decide that the FET standard is not closed under the relevant CETA obligation.[60] Second, the Commission stated that it "intends to ensure that the [FET] standard is not understood to be a 'stabilisation obligation', in other words a guarantee that the legislation of the host state will not change in a way that might negatively affect investors."[61] Yet, the Commission did not reproduce this stated intention at all, let alone clearly and unequivocally, in the CETA's FET language. Third, while claiming that it wanted to constrain the arbitrators' expansive approach to FET, the Commission actually expanded FET relative to its established customary meaning before ISDS arbitrators arrived on the scene about 20 years ago.[62] Indeed, it seems that the Commission wanted Canada to move away from the NAFTA states' position of limiting FET to its customary meaning.[63] This broad approach to FET in the CETA indicates that the Commission actually wanted to expand FET – to meet partway the adventurous position of ISDS arbitrators in their past awards – and to limit further the right to regulate.[64] Thus, the Commission appears to have tried to reassure the public in its consultation text, while burying significant concessions on the right to regulate and arbitrator power in the details of the treaty.

[59] e.g. M. Sornarajah, "Evolution or Revolution in International Investment Arbitration? The Descent into Normlessness", in C. Brown and K. Miles (eds.), *Evolution in Investment Treaty Law and Arbitration* (Cambridge: CUP, 2011), 650–652; R. Kläger, *"Fair and Equitable Treatment" in International Investment Law* (Cambridge: CUP, 2011), 116–119.

[60] For example, the word "only" is not included before the word "where" in the phrase "A Party breaches the obligation of fair and equitable treatment referenced in paragraph 1 where . . ." in Article X.9(2) of CETA (note 2 above).

[61] Consultation text (note 2 above), 6.

[62] For an overview, see S. Montt, *State Liability and Investment Treaty Arbitration* (Oxford: Hart, 2009), ch 6.

[63] Compare e.g. Free Trade Commission (note 8 above), which reflects the post-2001 Canadian treaty position and limits the content of fair and equitable treatment and full protection and security to their meaning in customary international law. See G. Van Harten, "The Canada-China FIPPA: Its Uniqueness and Non-Reciprocity", in J. Currie and R. Provost (eds.), *Canadian Yearbook of International Law* (Vancouver: UBC Press, 2013), 56–57, for an outline of the investment treaties of Canada that include the relevant limiting language on FET and full protection and security since 2001.

[64] Furthermore, the Commission's approach incorporates an aspect of FET – legitimate expectations – that was invented or transplanted by arbitrators (CETA Article X.9(4)). Besides technical problems with the CETA definition, the broad problem with the concept of legitimate expectations is that it can be used to frustrate or preclude legitimate changes to legislative, government, or judicial decisions.

The Commission's clarifications of indirect expropriation and FET were misleading for another reason. Even if they helped to safeguard the right to regulate, the clarifications are undermined by the Commission's approach to MFN treatment.[65] In the consultation text, the Commission acknowledged the danger of MFN treatment that:[66]

> investors may be able to claim that they are entitled to benefit from any provision of another agreement that they consider to be more favourable, which may even permit the application of an entirely new standard of protection that was not found in the original agreement.

Thus, the Commission signaled that any effort to moderate the state's responsibilities to foreign investors could be jeopardized by the arbitrators' ability to use MFN treatment in order to import new or more broadly worded state obligations from other treaties. The Commission said further: "[o]n the 'importation of standards' issue, the EU seeks to clarify that MFN does not allow procedural or substantive provisions to be imported from other agreements."[67] In spite of this claim, the Commission appears not to have ensured clear language in the CETA to close this potential MFN loophole. The relevant language in the CETA uses clear language to preclude the importation of procedural provisions but not substantive provisions from other agreements.[68] For substantive provisions, the CETA language allows that MFN treatment can be used to import substantive obligations from another treaty if there are "measures adopted by a Party pursuant to such obligations."[69] This last phrase is vague; for example, does the passage of a general law merely to implement another treaty in domestic law qualify as a measure that has been adopted by a Party "pursuant to" the substantive obligations in that treaty? It seems quite possible that the answer is yes. Furthermore, European states have concluded numerous other treaties which contain very broad language on the obligations of states to protect foreign investors, and North American countries have similarly broad language in numerous pre-2001 treaties.

Despite the Commission's claim to the contrary,[70] the CETA text endorses an opportunity for arbitrators to continue to use MFN treatment to import substantive provisions from other treaties. This aspect of the CETA text, thus, jeopardizes all the treaty's textual clarifications of

[65] For an outline of this MFN loophole, see Van Harten (note 63 above), 27–34.
[66] Consultation text (note 2 above), 4. [67] Consultation text (note 2 above), 4.
[68] CETA (note 2 above), X.7(4). [69] Ibid. [70] Consultation text (note 2 above), 4.

indirect expropriation, FET, and other substantive provision.[71] The MFN treatment clause would also jeopardize a clear affirmation of the right to regulate, as the other European treaties do not contain that affirmation. To preserve the right to regulate effectively, MFN treatment would need to be removed from the treaty or limited to the domestic regulatory treatment of foreign investors instead of treatment arising from another treaty.

Besides its inadequate textual clarifications, the Commission relies heavily on exceptions, reservations, and carve-outs to protect the state's right to regulate.[72] This really is not a good sign. Such devices are inherently limited. First, they give the right to regulate an inferior legal status in relation to the state's obligations to protect foreign investors. The general stance under the treaty is to protect foreign investors unless the state can establish an exceptional case for exercising the right to regulate. The reliance on exceptions is about prioritizing, not balancing. Second, exceptions, reservations, and carve-outs rarely extend to all state obligations in the treaty.[73] As a result, arbitrators usually have other ways to find a treaty violation despite the presence of a focused exception for the right to regulate. Third, most exceptions are limited to a particular sector or area of decision-making, thus exposing other sectors and areas to the threats that the exception would otherwise counter. For example, why is ISDS an unacceptable threat to "competition matters" but not health or environmental matters?[74] Exceptions, reservations, and carve-outs are simply not a substitute for a clear affirmation of the right to regulate.

As another example of the Commission's unsubstantiated or erroneous claims about the right to regulate, the Commission stated that "most bilateral investment agreements refer to 'investments made in accordance with applicable law'" and continued that:[75]

> [t]his reference has worked well and has allowed ISDS tribunals to refuse to grant investment protection to investors who have not respected the law of the host state when making the investment (for example, by structuring the investment in such a way as to circumvent clear prohibitions in the law of the host state, or by procuring an investment fraudulently or through bribery).

[71] CETA (note 2 above) Article X.9(5) and 6) and Annex X.11.

[72] Consultation text (note 2 above) 8.

[73] e.g. CETA (note 2 above) Articles X.14 and Annex X.11.

[74] Consultation text (note 2 above), 8.

[75] Consultation text (note 2 above), 3.

However, the Commission did not refer to a single treaty or arbitration award to substantiate its claim on this point. My own systematic research clearly contradicts the Commission's claim.[76] Even if one accepted the claim, why would the Commission allow the same arbitrators who expanded FET so widely, for example, to stay in control of the right to regulate? If the Commission did not want foreign investments that circumvent domestic law, or depend on fraud or bribery, to be protected under the treaty, why not say so clearly in the treaty? The Commission has not done so in the CETA and, likewise, has not proposed to affirm clearly the right to regulate. In these ways, the Commission's approach fails to address a basic imbalance in the allocation of states' rights and responsibilities.

There are other examples of the limitations of the Commission's approach to the right to regulate. The essence of the matter is that the Commission implied in a public document that it would safeguard that right of the state but did not do so in the most obvious way: by affirming clearly the right to regulate in the actual text of the CETA. For the Commission, the right to regulate appeared to be more a spin device to promote its ostensibly reformed version of ISDS than an actual aim in the CETA negotiation.[77]

Rights and responsibilities of foreign investors

Foreign investors enjoy a wide range of rights and protections under investment treaties. Yet, as a rule, foreign investors do not have corresponding responsibilities to respect international standards of

[76] In the dataset reported in G. Van Harten, "Arbitrator Behaviour in Asymmetrical Adjudication: An Empirical Study of Investment Treaty Arbitration" (2012) 50 *OHLJ* 211, with several research assistants I coded awards up the spring of 2010. One of the coding tasks was to identify how ISDS arbitrators appeared to allocate the responsibility for showing that an investment was not permissible due to alleged noncompliance with domestic law or alleged corruption. We found nine cases in which that issue was resolved. The resolutions in six of these cases appeared not to support the Commission's claim that language on compliance with applicable law "has worked well" to avoid circumvention of domestic law or counter fraud or bribery [*Olguín* v. *Paraguay* (8 August 2000, para 28); *Swembalt* v. *Latvia* (23 October 2010, para 32–35); *Aguas del Tunari* v. *Bolivia* (21 October 2005, para 188–192 and 204); *Desert Line Projects* v. *Yemen* (6 February 2008, para 99, 102, 105–106, 109, and 116); *Rumeli* v. *Kazakhstan* (29 July 2008, para 318–329); and *Siemens* v. *Argentina* (where Argentina was reportedly not permitted to introduce evidence and argument on the issue of alleged corrupt activities by the claimant)], whereas three cases appeared to support the claim [*Yaung Chi Oo* v. *Myanmar* (31 March 2003, para 27 and 53–63); *Fraport* v. *Philippines* (16 August 2007, para 315, 319, 327, 333, 343–348, 350–356, 394–396, 402, and 404); *Plama* v. *Bulgaria* (27 August 2008, para 112–139)].

[77] For a discussion of the Commission's recent proposals on the right to regulate, see n 7 above.

appropriate conduct in their treatment of workers, consumers, shareholders, or the environment, for example. This disparity makes ISDS imbalanced in a very basic way. The Commission's failure to acknowledge this issue of imbalance is a flaw in its reform agenda. The Commission's handling of the issue also demonstrates some of the ways in which its approach does not satisfy the related criterion of subsidiarity.

There are different ways to address the imbalance between the rights and responsibilities of foreign investors. As a very modest starting point, the treaties could allow states to bring claims against any foreign investor or a related company that brings a claim in circumstances where the investor has not met a specific standard of good corporate conduct.[78] This would be a very modest step because it would not give the state a right, alongside that of foreign investors, to initiate a proceeding against a foreign investor. Likewise, it would not give any such right to a private party that was harmed by a foreign investor and denied justice in domestic courts and domestic law. Yet, there is no sign that even this step has been pursued by the Commission, the US or Canadian governments, or any other Western governmental actor that plays a major role in the negotiation of investment treaties.

In its consultation text, the Commission did not mention any need to include responsibilities for foreign investors in the TTIP or CETA. It said only that "foreign investors, just as domestic ones, must fully respect the domestic legal regime of the host country."[79] This begs a question that is not discussed here: what if the domestic legal regime of a country does not offer justice or is not reasonably available to the victims of a foreign investor's misconduct? It also contrasts with the Commission's strong emphasis on the potential mistreatment of foreign investors as a rationale for ISDS. Thus, it is instructive to examine the Commission's stated justifications for giving a special status to foreign investors and for expanding arbitrator power at significant public expense. The special treatment of any actor entails costs for others; here, the costs include the potential redirection of public funds, the shifting of state priorities, and the distortion of markets in favor of those foreign investors able to finance an ISDS lawsuit.

[78] The state's right could not be limited – as presently for potential counterclaims by states in ISDS – only to the issues raised in the investor's own claim. Likewise, unlike counterclaims, it would have to allow for an enforceable damages award against the company.

[79] Consultation text (note 2 above), 2.

According to the Commission, ISDS is needed in the TTIP and CETA to protect foreign investors from discrimination and abuse in the United States and Canada (and presumably in Europe) and that investment treaties guarantee:[80]

> fundamental principles of treatment [that] are reflected in the rights that democratic governments grant to their own citizens and companies (such as no expropriation without compensation, access to justice, protection against coercion and harassment, non-discrimination), but [that] are *not always* guaranteed for foreigners or foreign companies (my emphasis).

In addition:[81]

> Despite the general solidity of developed court systems such as the US and the EU, *it is possible* that investors will not be given effective access to justice, e.g. if they are denied access to appeal or due process, leaving them without any effective legal remedy. ISDS is therefore necessary to allow legitimate claims to be pursued (my emphasis).

In both of these statements, the Commission avoids an obvious point: foreign companies in general are protected in domestic courts and domestic law. The Commission's concern is that foreign investors are "not always" protected and that "it is possible" that they will not have effective access to justice in any country. If one accepts that these issues of periodic and possible mistreatment of foreign investors are so important as to require a response premised on an extremely powerful form of international adjudication, then the logical solution is to allow international claims in such cases of mistreatment only. Why should foreign investors not be required to go to domestic courts if they are unable to show that the courts would not provide access to justice, compensation for expropriation, and so on?

The duty to resort to the domestic courts, where they offer justice and are reasonably available, applies customarily in international law and in other international courts and tribunals where individuals can bring claims against a state.[82] The Commission's approach – building on a Western European legacy of lopsided investment treaties – allows foreign investors to bring international claims without resorting to domestic courts. However, the Commission offers no evidence that domestic courts in any country do not provide effective protection for foreign

[80] Consultation text (note 2 above), 2. [81] Consultation text (note 2 above), 9.

[82] e.g. S. D'Ascoli and K.M. Scherr, "The Rule of Prior Exhaustion of Local Remedies in the International Law Doctrine and Its Application in the Specific Context of Human Rights Protection", EUI Working Paper LAW No. 2007/02.

investors. In effect, the Commission assumes that domestic courts fail systematically to offer justice in Canada, the United States, and Europe. If those countries are on that list, then we can guess that – in the Commission's eyes – domestic courts fail to offer justice in every other part of the world too. Even more absurdly, the Commission's position assumes that ISDS is institutionally independent and procedurally fair in the manner of a court, which, as I noted earlier in this chapter, it clearly is not.

One might also assert that domestic courts in general take too long or are otherwise insufficient to protect foreign investors. If that is true, why not replace courts with arbitrators for everyone, including domestic persons and foreigners who are not investors? Clearly, domestic actors may suffer just as much or more – for example, when deprived of their physical liberty for years while awaiting trial – than a foreign investor. Even to pose the question reveals the radical proposition lying behind ISDS: the replacement of domestic law and courts with an enclave legal status and exceptionally powerful adjudicative mechanism for foreign investors alone.

Remarkably, in its consultation text, the Commission claimed to "favor" domestic courts for resolving investor-state disputes.[83] It clearly has not done so, at least in the most obvious way, by expecting foreign investors to go to domestic courts where they offer justice and are reasonably available. The Commission offered this defense of its proposal to let the foreign investors sidestep domestic courts: "[d]omestic remedies would be preferable, but TTIP provisions cannot be invoked directly in front of a national court."[84] In addition:[85]

> It is often the case that protection offered in investment agreements cannot be invoked before domestic courts and the applicable legal rules are different. For example, discrimination in favour of local companies is not prohibited under US law but is prohibited in investment agreements. There are also concerns that, in some cases domestic courts may favour the local government over the foreign investor e.g. when assessing a claim for compensation for expropriation or may deny due process rights such as the effective possibility to appeal. Governments may have immunity from being sued.

These are weak and puzzling rationales for giving foreign investors a general right to skirt domestic courts in all cases. Leaving aside the

[83] Consultation text (note 2 above), 12. [84] Consultation text (note 2 above), 9.
[85] Consultation text (note 2 above), 11.

absence of any specific examples or serious analysis to back the Commission's claims, it is true that, in some countries, treaties cannot be invoked directly in domestic courts without an implementing statute to incorporate the treaty into domestic law. In addition, legal rules obviously often differ between domestic law and treaties or among domestic legal systems. Are these not simply features of the distinction between the domestic and international spheres and of the division of the world into states? Put differently, the Commission's rationale for ISDS boils down here to the trite point that there is more than one state in the world. If one is meant to justify special protections for foreign investors – and the ensuing risks to public budgets and constraints on the state's regulatory role – then the case for ISDS on this basis is presumptuous. That is, it is based on a vague assertion that there might be a lack of protection for foreign investors because legal systems differ.

This rationale for ISDS also leads to the answer elaborated earlier: foreign investors – unlike anyone else – should not be given access to ISDS and, then, on top of it, be excused from having to show that domestic legal systems and domestic courts are inadequate or that domestic courts would "favor the local government," to use the Commission's words, in an inappropriate way and, in doing so, deny access to justice. It is not enough for the Commission merely to say "[t]here are ... concerns" that mistreatment of foreign investors "may" take place in order to conclude that mistreatment will happen in any case, let alone systematically, in a country.

The Commission proposed other reforms to address flaws in ISDS. In each case, the reform preserves the special status of foreign investors and the exceptional power of arbitrators. For example, the Commission said that it sought to address the problem of multiple claims by foreign investors by introducing a limited fork-in-the-road clause.[86] Essentially, the CETA version of the clause tracks the NAFTA version, which merely requires foreign investors to pursue monetary remedies either in ISDS or domestic courts, but not in both.[87] This approach in effect allows foreign

[86] Consultation text (note 2 above), 12.

[87] CETA (note 2 above), X.21(1)(f) and (g). To be clear, this is not a duty to exhaust local remedies or a true fork-in-the-road clause. Even if it was, based on the past case-law the former and especially the latter should not be viewed as a reliable way to avoid parallel proceedings when left in the hands of arbitrators with a financial stake in allowing a treaty claim to proceed. Arbitrators have in most cases not given effect to fork-in-the-road clauses, highlighting the weakness of the Commission's reliance on these mechanisms and more broadly on textual clarifications to limit arbitrator power; Van Harten (note 19 above), 147–150.

investors to have their cake and eat it too. They can pursue public compensation in arbitration where compensation is – remarkably – the primary remedy, and they can pursue nonmonetary remedies in domestic courts where compensation is typically not the primary remedy.[88]

If the Commission wanted to prevent multiple claims, it would need to address the arbitrators' near-universal refusal to stay ISDS proceedings in the face of a parallel proceeding in domestic courts, in another international forum, or in a contractually agreed forum. Parallel proceedings run the risk of wasted resources on litigation and conflicting decisions. To facilitate them in the context of a contractually agreed alternative forum contradicts principles of party autonomy and sanctity of contract.[89] The problem could be addressed (a) by requiring foreign investors, before an international claim can be brought, to exhaust reasonably-available remedies in domestic courts and (b) by requiring arbitrators to stay their proceedings when a parallel claim has been or could be brought in a contractually agreed forum or another international forum, when the treaty claim is factually connected to a claim in the other forum, and when the foreign investor or a closely related party is or could be a claimant in the other forum. The Commission has not proposed or done either of these things.

These issues of subsidiarity return us to the deeper question about the balancing of foreign investors' rights and responsibilities. In particular, what if the domestic legal system or domestic courts are inadequate to protect victims of foreign investors? One can imagine scenarios in which a domestic actor, another foreigner, or another foreign investor may suffer greatly because of the misconduct of a foreign company. Yet, those actors would be limited to the supposed ghetto of domestic law and domestic courts, with no right to initiate a claim and obtain compensation from a state or a foreign investor at the international level. Foreign investors' responsibilities are the (neglected) other side of foreign investment disputes.[90] The stark inequality in the treatment of other actors who face serious forms of abuse highlights the system's fundamental imbalance.

On this issue, the Commission justified foreign investors' special status by comparing their protections under TTIP to the protection of property in democratic societies, saying:[91]

88 Van Harten (note 19 above), 113–114. 89 Ibid., 143–147.
90 VanDuzer, Simons, and Mayeda (note 48 above).
91 Consultation text (note 2 above), 7–8.

> In democratic societies, the right to regulate of states is subject to principles and rules contained in both domestic legislation and in international law. For instance, in the European Convention on Human Rights, the Contracting States commit themselves to guarantee a number of civil and political rights. In the EU, the Constitutions of the Member States, as well as EU law, ensure that the actions of the state cannot go against fundamental rights of the citizens.

Actually, this appeal to fundamental rights of citizens points to the imbalance in ISDS. By definition, investment treaties discriminate in favor of foreign investors and against all other actors whose rights or interests are affected by relevant conduct of the state, including its decisions on the regulation of foreign investors.[92] Unlike foreign investors, everyone else can protect his or her property or other rights only through human rights adjudication in domestic and regional institutions. On the other hand, as discussed earlier, the Commission's presumption is that these other institutions are so inadequate for foreign investors that even the usual duty to exhaust local remedies should never apply if a foreign investor prefers to bring an ISDS claim.

The inequality of treatment creates significant advantages for foreign investors. Their access to ISDS gives them, among other things, (a) more widely enforceable awards against states than in human rights adjudication; (b) the potential for much more public compensation – to date, even tens of billions of dollars – than in human rights adjudication; (c) the enjoyment of protections that are not balanced by countervailing aspects of human rights adjudication such as a statement of the state's right to regulate or the need to balance other human rights; (d) the power, unlike human rights complainants, to take part in the make-up of the tribunal; and (e) a decision-making process in which the adjudicator has a financial interest to favor foreign investors, especially deep-pocketed companies, on the assumption that an arbitrator who seeks reappointment would wish to encourage claims in order to support the growth of the marketplace for ISDS services.[93] The Commission does not acknowledge any of these aspects of the conflict between ISDS and human rights; rather, its reform proposal

[92] The Commission's statement (ibid., 4) that its approach would ensure a level playing field between foreign and local investors is inaccurate. The CETA (note 2 above) non-discrimination standards (Article X.6 and X.7) require, like other investment treaties, that foreign investors receive "no less favorable treatment" than either domestic or third-state investors. Thus, the CETA expressly allows for more favorable treatment and an unlevel playing field in favor of the foreign investors.

[93] Van Harten (note 19 above), 159–162.

would extend that conflict into the relatively new domain of developed-to-developed country relations.

A quick example should illustrate the problem. In the era of ISDS, a foreign national who is tortured by state officials cannot bring an international claim against the state, at least without going first to domestic courts.[94] However, the foreign national could bring a vastly more potent ISDS claim if he or she owned assets in the state – and qualified as a foreign investor – though, in that case, only to the extent that the torture affected his or her position as an asset owner and not merely as a human being. In contrast, if a foreign investor's staff were to torture its domestic employees with the state's collaboration, none of the employees could bring an international claim against the company or its officers. Likewise, the employees could not bring a claim against the state for failing to protect them, without going to domestic courts first. I find it hard to describe that as anything but an absurd elevation of foreign investors' rights and protections over everyone else's.

Conclusion

The Commission's endorsement of the official ISDS reform model has a few positive elements, but, overall, it is a failure if the aim was to ensure fairness, independence, balance, or respect for the role of domestic institutions. The official model does not affirm clearly the state's right to regulate. It does not introduce actionable responsibilities for foreign investors alongside their rights. It does not require foreign investors to resort to domestic courts unless the courts have been shown not to offer justice. In turn, the Commission's approach discriminates in favor of foreign investors by giving them a special status in their relationship to legislatures, governments, and courts and against other rights holders and the public interest. The Commission takes positive steps on the issue of openness but it does not address the lack of institutional independence and procedural fairness in ISDS. By consolidating and expanding ISDS, the Commission's approach actually makes those problems much worse.

In some respects, it is easy to criticize the official agenda to consolidate and expand ISDS. The design of ISDS has so many weaknesses that one could write books about how they undermine claims that ISDS delivers a

[94] e.g. Convention against Torture and Other Cruel, Inhuman or Degrading Treatment or Punishment, GA Res. 39/46, annex, 39 UN GAOR Supp. (No. 51) at 197, UN Doc. A/39/51 (1984); 1465 UNTS 85 (entered into force 26 June 1987), Articles 21(c) and 22(4)(b); ECHR (note 51 above), Article 35(1).

fair and independent means of adjudication, balance in investor-state relations, or respect for the role of regulators and courts. The challenge as a researcher sometimes lies in deciding where to begin and how long to spend on each issue.

On the other hand, it can be quite challenging – even as an academic, let alone as a practitioner – to criticize ISDS. One confronts a lot of flak from others who appear, to me at least, dead set on defending and promoting ISDS in spite of its lack of fairness, independence, balance, and so on. That can make the researcher's role more rewarding but also more difficult. While there are stories I could tell about such flak, I mention it only to say that Sornarajah could no doubt tell a lot more. He has pursued independent critical scholarship in international investment law for a longer time than any other living specialist in the field and has done so with patience and grace. It is a tribute to his work that some countries appear now to have chosen the path of withdrawal from ISDS instead of the well-worn and increasingly tired road to "reform."

5

The paranoid style of investment lawyers and arbitrators: investment law norm entrepreneurs and their critics

DAVID SCHNEIDERMAN

Introduction

Members of the investment law and arbitration bar – investment law's norm entrepreneurs[1] – have displayed a curious fury in response to their critics.[2] The response is curious because, given the relative success of investment law in cabining state authority, the bar would have been expected to wallow in this triumph. Indeed, given that success, criticism would be expected, even if it is unwelcome. Investment lawyers and arbitrators operate, after all, in the contentious field of privatized dispute resolution, maintaining a watchful gaze over the permissible scope of state action. Why would not this attract the sort of heightened scrutiny experienced when national high courts resolve disputes about the appropriate ambit of public authority? Yet, investment law's norm entrepreneurs seem threatened by this scrutiny, having recourse to hyperbolic discourse that vilifies critics. What might explain the intemperate nature, even paranoid style, of these leading members of this international law bar?

Some 50 years ago, political scientist Richard Hofstadter described a "paranoid style in American politics." This style was characterized by "heated exaggeration, suspiciousness, and conspiratorial fantasy."[3] While

[1] Cass R. Sunstein is credited with introducing the idea of norm entrepreneur in "Social Norms and Social Roles" (1996) 96 *Columbia Law Review* 903 at 909.

[2] By criticism, I am referring to work that puts into doubt the merits of the legal regime. This critique might be immanent or it might take an external view. I am not, therefore, referring to those who critique the system in order to make it work better, whom we might call reformers.

[3] Richard Hofstadter, "The Paranoid Style in American Politics," *Harpers* (November 1964) 77–86, online at http://archive.harpers.org/1964/11/pdf/HarpersMagazine-1964-11-0014706

there may have been some element of "truth and reality" to this rhetorical expression in American political life, over-the-top denunciations were meant to fend off "threats to a still established way of life" – a means of "manning the barricades of civilization."[4] In which case, observed Hofstadter, the paranoiac will want to fight things to the finish, demanding "total triumph" over the designated enemy. Often that enemy will have special means of control or an "effective source of power: he controls the press," for instance, or "has unlimited funds."[5] Such enemies needed to be vanquished.

While the response of the investment arbitration bar does not perfectly mirror the paranoiac style, it appears to exhibit some of its defining characteristics. Lawyers and arbitrators are manning the barricades to fight "falsehoods" that are being spread by critics. They are in combat with opponents who misrepresent their achievements, exaggerate the failings of investor-state dispute settlement (ISDS), peddle falsehoods to media outlets, and gain the ear of sympathetic rent-seeking politicians. Investment lawyers and arbitrators, by contrast, are virtuous actors, promoting a version of "civilized justice" that represents the "depoliticization" of investment disputes.[6] I propose, in this chapter, to inquire into the presence of this paranoid style in the investment arbitration context.

I turn first to a few examples of this debased rhetoric in action and, then, describe circumstances that might account for it (in "Irreversible?" section). The substance of that critique, which has provoked this angst amongst the investment law crowd, is best represented by the rich body of scholarship authored by M. Sornarajah, whose contributions this volume celebrates. After cataloguing key elements of that critique (in "When things fall apart" section), I reflect on the reasons why investment lawyers may have less reason to worry (in "Conclusion" section). I conclude by suggesting that this attribution of conspiracy and falsehood on the part of critics – to be charged with nothing but "empty rhetoric" – flies not only in the face of the facts but reflects more poorly on the accusers than on their targets.

.pdf?AWSAccessKeyId=AKIAJXATU3VRJAAA66RA&Expires=1428328257&$Signature=nH3jTDh31wGsIb4LTYlUte6D1fc%3D (accessed 5 April 2015).

4 Hofstadter, "The Paranoid Style in American Politics," 79, 81, 82.

5 Hofstadter, "The Paranoid Style in American Politics," 85.

6 See David Schneiderman, "Revisiting the Depoliticization of Investment Disputes," in *Yearbook on International Investment Law and Policy*, 2010–11 (Oxford: OUP), 693–714.

Irreversible?

As investment arbitration spread in the roaring nineties and then into the aughts, investment lawyers had good reason to feel confident about the future. International investment law would provide the security of the "rule of law" for generations to come. Standards of protection might change, admitted Elihu Lauterpacht, but "it seems much less likely that the procedural advances will be reversed." "It is an old maxim that freedom once conferred cannot be withdrawn," observed Lauterpacht, and "so, I believe, it is likely to be with the freedom that has now been given to individuals to assert their rights on the international plane."[7] Even if treaties can be rescinded on relatively short notice, established investments continue to take advantage of treaty protections for 10–15 years, on average, into the future. Even denunciations of the Convention on the Settlement of Investment Disputes Between States and Nationals of Other States (ICSID) will not have quite the desired effect for established investments. Such methods, Christoph Schreuer writes, are not likely to give rise to "quick and decisive results."[8] The legal order appears to be irreversible.

Despite these exhibitions of confidence, investment law's norm entrepreneurs continue to worry. They have issued intemperate screeds, accusing critics of being "misguided," and spreading "lies." Take, by way of example, the final chapter of arbitrator Jan Paulsson's book *Denial of Justice in International Law*. There Paulsson describes critics of investment arbitration as "shrill," "misdirected," "propagandists," appealing to "public prejudice." [9] Arbitrator Charles N Brower, with coauthor Sadie Blanchard, alleged that critics invoke "ideologically driven polemics," having "no discernable basis in reality," based on "nothing more than empty rhetoric," and at bottom "ignorant" – all of this in the first third of their paper.[10] The International Bar Association has issued a

[7] Elihu Lauterpacht, "International Law and Private Foreign Investment" (1997) 4 *Global Legal Studies Journal* 259 at 276.

[8] Christoph Schreuer, "The Future of Investment Law," in Mahnoush H. Arsanjani, Jacob Katz Cogan, Robert D. Sloane, and Siegfried Wissner (eds.), *Looking to the Future: Essays on International Law in Honour of Michael W. Reisman* (Leiden: Martinus Nijhoff Publishers, 2011), 787–803 at 794; also Frederico M. Lavopa, Lucas E. Barreiros, and M. Victoria Bruno, "How to Kill a BIT and Not Die Trying: Legal and Political Challenges of Denouncing or Renegotiating Bilateral Investment Treaties" (2013) 15 *Journal of International Economic Law* 869–891.

[9] Jan Paulsson, *Denial of Justice in International Law* (Cambridge: CUP, 2005) at 233.

[10] The Honourable Charles N. Brower and Sadie Blanchard, "What's in a Meme? The Truth About Investor-State Arbitration: Why It Need Not, and Must Not, be Repossessed by States" (2014) 52 *Columbia Journal of Transnational Law* 689 at 699, 711, 717, 720.

statement correcting "erroneous information [that] is subverting the debate" over the future of ISDS,[11] while a Swedish Member of the European Parliament, Christopher Fjellner, has issued what he calls the "#ISDS challenge." This is in response to the critics' "blatant ignorance" – they are guilty of spreading "nothing but myths and lies."[12] One is prompted to ask: why all of this overheated rhetoric? As in most political contests, each side will overplay its own strengths while downplaying those of the opposing side. Yet similarly overheated rhetoric has not been embraced by critics – most have not been as ready to have recourse to this sort of attack.[13]

There may be some ground for this exhibition of frustration. Recent events underscore the seemingly shaky ground upon which investment arbitration continues to operate. The German government has expressed concern over ISDS, threatening to scuttle ratification of the Canada–EU trade and investment treaty (CETA) and talks leading toward a Transatlantic Trade and Investment Partnership with the United States (TTIP).[14] French and German political ministers indicated, at one stage, that the inclusion of ISDS would render such a deal unacceptable to Europe, precipitating a proposal for an investment court by the EU Commission.[15] Democratic presidential candidate Hillary Clinton denounced ISDS in her precampaign memoirs.[16] The libertarian think

[11] "IBA issues fact-correcting statement on ISDS" at www.ibanet.org/Article/Detail.aspx?ArticleUid=1dff6284-e074-40ea-bf0c-f19949340b2f (last accessed 13 May 2015).

[12] "Do you dare to challenge me in the #ISDSchallenge?" at www.fjellner.eu/the-isdschallenge-single-handedly-taking-on-the-anti-isdsers/ (last accessed 13 May 2015).

[13] This is not an empirical claim, but an impressionistic one, based on my having followed this literature closely since 1994. The worst that I could find in one recent publication that has prompted negative reaction from many investment lawyers refers to investment arbitrators as "ambulance chasers" (the analogy is explained at 19), "hypocritical" (at 48) and "allegedly neutral" (at 71), and investment arbitration as a "money-making machine" (at 15). See Pia Eberhardt and Cecilia Olivet, *Profiting from Injustice: How Law Firms, Arbitrators and Financiers are Fuelling an Investment Arbitration Boom* (Brussels/Amsterdam: Corporate Europe Observatory and the Transnational Institute, November 2012) online at http://corporateeurope.org/sites/default/files/publications/profiting-from-injustice.pdf (last accessed 15 May 2015).

[14] Stefan Wagstyl, "Germany to Block Investor Protection Rules: Free Trade Pacts," *Financial Times* (26 September 2014), 6; Shawn Nonnan and Stefan Wagstyl, "Transatlantic Trade Talks Hit Snag," *Financial Times* (14 March 2014).

[15] James Kanter, "Europe's Trade Chief Calls for More Study on Proposed Pact With U.S.," *The New York Times* (13 January 2015) and EU "Commission Draft Text TTIP – Investment" online at http://trade.ec.europa.eu/doclib/docs/2015/september/tradoc_153807.pdf (accessed 26 October 2015).

[16] Hillary Rodham Clinton, *Hard Choices* (New York: Simon & Shuster 2014), 509–510. It "giv[es business interests] or their investors the power to sue foreign governments to

tank the Cato Institute issued a "Free Trade Bulletin" calling ISDS "an unnecessary, unreasonable, and unwise provision to include in trade agreements."[17] An earlier Cato policy paper argued that "a rationale for the current set of international investment rules is difficult to articulate."[18] Columnist for the *Financial Times*, John Kay, observed that the threat of investor litigation "can have a chilling effect" and suggested that it would be much easier to sell TTIP "if ISDS were no longer a part of it."[19] The erstwhile conservative weekly, *The Economist*, even expressed doubts about investment treaties that grant to "foreign firms a special right to apply to a secretive tribunal of highly paid corporate lawyers for compensation whenever a government passes a law to, say, discourage smoking, protect the environment, or prevent a nuclear catastrophe."[20]

This will not have been the first time that investment treaty arbitration has moved into the center of the public sphere.[21] It is the first time, however, that conservative publications have piled on, resulting in the uncomfortable feeling that investment law's norm entrepreneurs are losing control of the narrative regarding the benefits that allegedly flow from third-party adjudication.

When things fall apart

Professor Sornarajah anticipated this turn of events some time ago. He argued that international investment law was unstable from the start and predicted that it would fall into crisis once capital-exporting states began withdrawing their support. Although investment law norm entrepreneurs generally are dismissive of Professor Sornarajah's claims – it is not apparent that they have read his work closely or at all – he has helpfully

weaken their environmental and public health rules, as Philip Morris is already trying to do in Australia," she wrote.

[17] Daniel Ikenson, "A Compromise to Advance the Trade Agenda: Purge Negotiations of Investor-State Dispute Settlement," Cato Institute Free Trade Bulletin No. 57 (4 March 2014) at 1 online at http://object.cato.org/sites/cato.org/files/pubs/pdf/ftb57.pdf (accessed 20 April 2015).

[18] Simon Lester, "Liberalization or Litigation? Time to Rethink the International Investment Regime," Cato Institute Policy Analysis No. 730 (8 July 2013) at 10 online at http://object.cato.org/sites/cato.org/files/pubs/pdf/pa730_web.pdf.

[19] John Kay, "Free Trade Should Not Put Democracy in the Dock," *Financial Times* (4 February 2015), 7.

[20] "Investor-State Dispute Settlement: The Arbitration Game," *The Economist* (11 October 2014).

[21] See discussion in David Schneiderman, *Resisting Economic Globalization: Critical Theory and International Investment Law* (Houndmills: Palgrave Macmillan, 2013) at 80–81.

detailed the circumstances giving rise to their hyperbolic tendencies and paranoid style. In this part, I turn to each of his claims.

Unstable?

One of the dominant rationales offered to justify investment treaty arbitration has been the uncertainty and unpredictability of host state legal orders. Yet, international investment law, at its inception, has never been able to formulate a stable and predictable set of norms to guide state, and even investor, behavior. The norms not only have been vague and uncertain, even when their content has been filled in by investment tribunals, but also remain perpetually in movement.

Investment lawyers, nevertheless, maintain that the regime brings stability and predictability to relations that can be fraught with conflict. This is accomplished by having investment arbitrators "foist" their preferred interpretations on unsuspecting states, Sornarajah writes: "A principle discovered, a magic wand is waved by a person with suitable esoterica and, hey presto, the principle becomes international law."[22]

Consider, for instance, the content generated by arbitrators to fill in the international minimum standard of treatment. As no treaties describe the content of that standard, Sornarajah identifies three elements from the cases on state responsibility that might have guided interpretation: standards of compensation in the case of expropriation, responsibility for destruction or violence by non-state actors, and denials of justice.[23] The first two elements are typically singled out in investment treaties as independent standards of protection. This leaves denials of justice, which few tribunals have felt bound to read restrictively. Instead, the minimum standard of treatment is declared by tribunals to include the "body of concordant practice" represented by the contemporary investment treaty regime.[24] The so-called old "first track," represented by standards associated with principles of diplomatic protection, has been overtaken by a "second track" having to do with the treatment of

[22] M. Sornarajah, "Power and Justice in Foreign Investment Arbitration" (1997) 14 *Journal of International Arbitration* 103 at 118.

[23] M. Sornarajah, *The International Law on Foreign Investment*, 3rd ed. (Cambridge: CUP, 2010) at 346.

[24] *Mondev International Ltd* v. *United States*, Award, ICSID Case No. ARB(AF)/99/2 (11 October 2002) at para. 117.

aliens "in relation to business, trade and investments," which is "much more liberal."[25]

In this last quoted award, the Merrill and Ring tribunal was bringing the North Atlantic Free Trade Agreement's (NAFTA's) fair and equitable treatment standard into the discussion, as it is expressly mentioned as an element of the minimum standard of treatment in Article 1105. Here again, there is little to guide the work of arbitrators other than the treaty's "object and purpose" and their own preferred policy outcomes. For this tribunal, the standard "protects against all such acts or behavior that might infringe a sense of fairness, equity and reasonableness," standards which cannot be defined with precision.[26] This is considered too narrow an approach according to more recent NAFTA tribunals. What is preferred is the standard articulated by the Waste Management tribunal, which includes conduct that is, among other things, "arbitrary, grossly unfair, unjust or idiosyncratic," a standard which is "to some extent a flexible one."[27]

That there was no previously discernible content to this standard was clear even to its supporters.[28] F.A. Mann admitted that "[a]lthough these may be familiar terms, they have hardly ever been judicially considered." Mann anticipated modern trends by opining that the language of unfair and inequitable treatment "is a much wider conception" than arbitrary, discriminatory, and abusive treatment and "might readily include such administrative measures in the field of taxation, licenses and so forth."[29] There are seemingly few constraints on arbitrators as they continually move opaque and evolving standards in directions more restrictive for state policy.

[25] *Merrill & Ring Forestry LP* v. *Canada*, Award, Ad hoc – UNCITRAL Arbitration Rules (2010) at para. 205.

[26] *Merrill & Ring* at para. 210.

[27] *Waste Management Inc.* v. *Mexico*, ICSID Case No. ARB(AF)00/3 (2004 April), paras. 98, 99 quoted approvingly in *Clayton* v. *Canada*, PCA Case No. 2009–04 (17 March 2015), para. 442.

[28] Archival research on the origins of FET in American treaty practice reveals that it was never intended to provide a substantive standard of treatment but, instead, was meant to be a gap filler that would promote fairness between state parties. See Mona Pinchis, "The Forgotten Purpose of 'Fair' and 'Equitable Treatment' Clauses in Post-War United States Commercial Treaties" (25 May 2015 draft) [unpublished].

[29] F.A. Mann, "British Treaties for the Promotion and Protection of Investments" (1981) 52 *British Yearbook of International Law* 241 at 243.

Expansionist?

It is precisely in this direction that arbitrators have taken interpretation of the fair and equitable treatment (FET) standard. It is part of a phenomenon that Sornarajah labels "expansionary trends" in investment treaty arbitration.[30] Lacking even less specific content than the minimum standard of treatment, arbitrators have conscripted the standard to award compensation to investors in all variety of circumstances, including when states are experiencing nearly complete financial collapse (as in Argentina in 2001). After all, they decree, a promise is a promise.[31] A doctrine of legitimate expectations, for this reason, has been read into FET even in circumstances where no specific commitment was made to investors – nothing, that is, beyond the statutory and regulatory regime in place when an investor enters into the host state jurisdiction to conduct its business. States are also liable in circumstances where a government specifically encourages an investor, even though the government cannot guarantee that the investment will sail through the requisite environmental review process.[32]

This latitudinarian tendency has resulted in FET overtaking expropriation as an easily available standard of treatment irrespective of the circumstances.[33] This is because FET borrows elements of what rises to the level of a compensable event, namely, the extent to which the regulation interferes with reasonable investment-backed expectations. Other prerequisites for finding a compensable event that gives rise, in American parlance, to a "regulatory taking" are omitted.[34] This renders an FET claim easier to make when compared to an alleged expropriation. It is for this reason that Fietta envisages tribunals preferring to find breaches of

[30] M. Sornarajah, "A Coming Crisis: Expansionary Trends in Investment Treaty Arbitration," in Karl Sauvant (ed.) *Appeals Mechanism in International Investment Disputes* (Oxford: OUP, 2008), 39–77.

[31] Mortimore and Stanley report that 54% of the Argentinian population was living below the poverty line in the aftermath of the economic collapse. See Michael Mortimore and Leonardo Stanley, "Has Investor Protection Been Rendered Obsolete by the Argentinian Crisis" (2006) 88 *CEPAL Review* 15 at 25 online at http://socinfo.eclac.org/revista/noticias/articuloCEPAL/4/26314/LCG2289iMortimoreStanley.pdf (last accessed 20 February 2015).

[32] *Clayton* v. *Canada* at 448, 449.

[33] This paragraph draws on David Schneiderman, "Legitimacy and Reflexivity in International Investment Arbitration: A New Self-Restraint?" (2011) 2 *International Journal of Dispute Management* 471 at 487.

[34] Namely, whether the diminution in value is attributable to the government conduct together with the character of the government action. These were initially articulated by US Supreme Court in Penn Central Transportation Co v New York City, 438 US 104, 124–125 (1977).

FET over the "more fundamental and demanding expropriation standard."[35] The *Sempra* tribunal suggested moving precisely in this direction: "on occasion the line separating the breach of the fair and equitable treatment standard from an indirect expropriation can be very thin . . . In case of doubt, however, judicial prudence and deference to state functions are better served by opting for a determination in the light of the fair and equitable treatment standard."[36] *Sempra* underscores the fact that the fair and equitable treatment is serving similar functions as the ground of expropriation but without having to meet the more substantial and lasting deprivation typically associated with a compensable taking.[37]

Recent empirical work shows that investment tribunals show little restraint when interpreting the FET standard – the expansion of the standard "has been widespread not to say epic."[38] Sornarajah has described these expansionary trends as "the product of the dominance of economic liberalism and [so] must be regarded as passing fashions."[39] I evaluate below how "passing" a phenomenon this may be, but there is little doubt that it has contributed to lingering doubts about investment arbitration's legitimacy.

Bias?

Do latitudinarian tendencies point in the direction of arbitral bias in favor of powerful capital-exporting states and their patrons? One of the exemplary contributions that Sornarajah has made to the field is to bring into the discussion of investment arbitration notions of power.[40]

[35] Stephen Fietta, "Expropriation and the 'Fair and Equitable Treatment' Standard: The Developing Role of Investor's 'Expectations' in International Investment Arbitration" (2006) 23 *Journal of International Arbitration* 375 at 385.

[36] *Sempra Energy International* v. *Argentina*, Award, ICSID Case No. ARB/02/16 (2007) at para. 301.

[37] *Pope & Talbot Inc* v. *Government of Canada* (2001), 13 World Trade and Arbitration Materials 61 at paras. 100–102. For further discussion see Schneiderman, "Legitimacy and Reflexivity in International Investment Arbitration," 471.

[38] Gus Van Harten, *Sovereign Choices and Sovereign Restraints: Judicial Restraint in Investment Treaty Arbitration* (Oxford: OUP, 2013) at 101–102 and fn. 151. The rise in FET claims is chronicled in Chapter 10.

[39] Sornarajah, *The International Law on Foreign Investment* at 17.

[40] On the necessity of such discussion in the context of investment arbitration, see David Schneiderman, "Power and the Production in Global Legal Pluralism: An International Political Economy Approach," in Amanda Perry-Kessaris (ed.), *Socio-Legal Approaches to International Economic Law: Text, Context, Subtext* (Abingdon: Routledge, 2013), 98–117.

As a form of privatized dispute resolution, investment arbitration has empowered economic actors, and their home states, to argue that host states should be disciplined for breach of investment treaty standards that would never, in the past, have been tolerated by those home states.[41] This is an illustration, for Sornarajah, of how "private power can be used to formulate norms with claims to be principles of international law."[42] In a biting passage, he writes that the rise of this legal order:

> indicates not only the power of multinational corporations to create law but also the existence of avenues through which international law can be used as an instrument of private power through weak sources of law such as the awards of arbitral tribunals and the writings of highly qualified publicists. The role of the latter, who are but individuals with partialities to certain views either because they believe firmly in them or because it is lucrative to do so, requires a view of international law not as a scientifically neutral discipline but as a manipulable device which serves the interests of power.[43]

Sornarajah has quipped that, by imposing arbitrators' preferred solutions to resolve investment disputes, the "[o]nly general principle that seems to be indicated by these awards – if it could, indeed, be dignified by the term, principle – is that the big boy always wins."[44]

Sornarajah does not purport to be making an empirical claim about arbitral tendencies but, rather, a more general observation. Of course, the big boys cannot always win. If they did, states would withdraw en masse and the system would collapse. Instead, arbitrators, it can be said, are reflexive and strategic actors who are aware that a principal audience for their awards are states themselves. As the principal authors of the legal order, states must be kept relatively content if the system is to be maintained over time and with their continued cooperation. Hence, it would be a mistake to confuse latitudinarian tendencies in interpretation with the observation that investors always win. The data coming out of the

[41] Compared, for instance, with US domestic law. See, for instance, discussion in Lise Johnston and Oleksander Volkov, "Investor-State Contracts, Host-State 'Commitments' and the Myth of Stability in International Law" (2013) 24 *The American Review of International Arbitration* 361–415.

[42] Sornarajah, *The International Law on Foreign Investment* at 62.

[43] Sornarajah, *The International Law on Foreign Investment* at 305.

[44] Sornarajah, "Power and Justice" at 118. Also M. Sornarajah, "The Neo-Liberal Agenda in Investment Arbitration: Its Rise, Retreat and Impact on State Sovereignty," in Wenhua Shan *et al.* (eds.), *Redefining Sovereignty in International Economic Law* (Portland: Hart Publishing, 2008).

International Centre for the Settlement of Investment Disputes (ICSID), for instance, reveal that investors win their adjudicated claims about 46 percent of the time.[45]

Susan Franck has sought to empirically refute claims about bias in investment arbitration but her results are inconclusive.[46] In a study of 159 final awards as of 2012, she could not find any "reliable link" between investment arbitration outcomes and development status.[47] Although she is not able to definitively refute concerns about bias, she curiously rushes to a normative defense of investment arbitration. A content analysis of 140 decisions on jurisdiction suggests otherwise. Investment arbitrators, Van Harten shows, are more likely than not to take jurisdiction over an investor's claim, particularly in cases where investors make their home in capital-exporting states. The study offers "tentative support for expectations of systemic bias in investment treaty arbitration" but does not purport to show "actual bias."[48] Van Harten's study also underscores Sornarajah's claims about expansionary trends. Arbitrators rarely express any deference when weighing investor rights again state interests.[49] Arbitrators, moreover, are likely to interpret substantive protections generously when claimants are from capital-exporting states such as the United States (US), United Kingdom (UK), and France and take a

[45] International Centre for the Settlement of Investment Disputes, "The ICSID Caseload – Statistics (Issue 2015–1)" at 14 online at https://icsid.worldbank.org/apps/ICSIDWEB/resources/Documents/ICSID%20Web%20Stats%202015-1%20(English)%20(2)_Redacted.pdf (accessed 21 April 2015).

[46] On the basis of a sample of 52 cases, as of 2007, she claimed that investment arbitration "functions fairly" and that outcomes bear no relationship to developmental status of arbitrators or respondents, in Susan D. Franck, "Development and Outcomes of Investment Treaty Arbitration" (2009) 50 *Harvard Journal of International Law* 435 at 435, 487. There are reasons, however, to be cautious about her conclusions given the size and sample of her study. See discussion in Gus Van Harten, "The Use of Quantitative Methods to Examine Possible Bias in Investment Arbitration," in *Yearbook on International Investment Law & Policy 2010–2011* (New York: Oxford University Press, 2012), 859–881, and her rejoinder in Susan D. Franck, Calvin P. Garbin, and Jenna M. Perkins, "Response: Through the Looking Glass: Understanding Social Science Norms for Analyzing International Investment Law," in *Yearbook on International Investment Law & Policy 2010–2011* (New York: Oxford University Press, 2012), 883–916.

[47] Susan D. Franck, "Conflating Politics and Development? Examining Investment Treaty Arbitration Outcomes" (2014) 55 *Virginia Journal of International Law* 13 at 60.

[48] Gus Van Harten, "Arbitrator Behaviour in Asymmetrical Adjudication: An Empirical Study of Investment Treaty Arbitration" (2012) 50 *Osgoode Hall Law Journal* 211 at 233–234.

[49] Gus Van Harten, *Sovereign Choices and Sovereign Restraints* at 91.

more restrictive approach when investors are from elsewhere.[50] The data go to show that there is a systematic tendency to serve the interests of investors from powerful capital-exporting states.

Crisis?

All of these systemic features are contributing to what Sornarajah describes as a system in "crisis."[51] States in the developing South increasingly wish to distance themselves from its strictures. The government of Ecuador, for instance, withdrew from the convention that grants jurisdiction to ICSID.[52] Ecuador also denounced 11 Bilateral Investment Treaties (BITs) that proved less than fruitful to the Ecuadorian economy[53] and is on track to denounce another 26 BITs (acting upon the advice of Professor Sornarajah).[54] The new Ecuadorean constitution furthermore provides that no jurisdiction will be ceded to international arbitration concerning commercial and contractual disputes.[55] The South African Department of Trade and Industry (DTI) undertook a wholesale review of its BIT framework, observing that the current model of investment treaty, borrowed from the UK, did not serve well South Africa's constitutional project of societal reconciliation in the face of apartheid's legacy of economic inequality.[56] The government of South Africa, therefore, quietly decided to delegate to an interministerial cabinet committee responsibility for determining whether any new BITs should be signed and existing ones terminated or renegotiated based

[50] Gus Van Harten, *Sold Down the Yangtze: Canada's Lopsided Investment Deal With China* (Toronto: International Investment Arbitration and Public Policy, 2015) at 121.

[51] Sornarajah, "A Coming Crisis," 73.

[52] International Centre for the Settlement of Investment Disputes, "Ecuador Submits a Notice under Article 71 of the ICSID Convention" (9 July 2009) available online at http://icsid.worldbank.org/ICSID/FrontServlet?requestType=CasesRH&actionVal$=OpenPage&PageType=AnnouncementsFrame&FromPage=Announcements&pageName=Announcement20 (accessed 15 May 2010).

[53] United Nations Conference on Trade and Development (UNCTAD), *World Investment Report 2009: Transnational Corporations, and the Infrastructure Challenge* (New York and Geneva: United Nations), 32.

[54] "International Commission That Analyzes 26 Bilateral Investment Treaties Will Recommend To End Agreements" (6 August 2014) online at www.andes.info.ec/en/news/international-commission-analyzes-26-bilateral-investment-treaties-will-recommend-end (accessed 1 April 2015).

[55] Article 422.

[56] South Africa, Department of Trade and Industry, "Bilateral Investment Treaty Policy Framework Review: Government Position Paper" (June 2009) online at www.thedti.gov.za/ads/bi-lateral_policy.pdf.

upon a new model that better fit South Africa's "peculiar circumstances."[57] South Africa has not offered alternative treaty text but has instead tabled a new investment promotion and protection bill and has participated in a process, under the auspices of the South African Development Council (SADC), to draft a new and alternative treaty text.[58] Even India, which actively signed onto 82 BITs (72 are in force) and 4 Free Trade Agreements (FTAs) with investment chapters, is expressing misgivings. Following upon a second investment arbitration loss against Australia-based White Industries for delay in paying out an earlier $4 million arbitration award together with a swath of new claims,[59] India struck a cabinet-level committee to review its BIT policy. A draft model treaty recently was released for discussion that departs significantly from standard model treaty text by abandoning the most favored nation treatment, cabining the minimum standard of treatment to egregious behavior and limiting compensation in cases of expropriation and nationalization.[60] However one describes the current conjuncture, doubts about the system have gained ground, generating the conditions for change of unprecedented proportions in some locales.

Doubts have not been confined to the global South. Those in the developed North either have relaxed standards of protection or are threatening withdrawal from the system. Such responses have been prompted because instruments seemingly designed to discipline

[57] Xavier Carim, "Lessons from South Africa's BITs Review," *Columbia FDI Perspectives No 109* (25 November 2013), www.vcc.columbia.edu/content/lessons-south-africa-s-bits-review.

[58] Republic of South Africa, "Promotion and Protection of Investment Bill" (22 July 2015) online at http://www.parliament.gov.za/live/commonrepository/Processed/20150908/609997_1.pdf (last accessed 27 October 2015); South African Development Community (SADC), "SADC Model Bilateral Investment Treaty Template with Commentary" (July 2012) online at www.iisd.org/itn/wp-content/uploads/2012/10/SADC-Model-BIT Template-Final.pdf (last accessed 29 October 2012).

[59] These include four disputes launched by investors following upon a court-ordered cancellation of a number of 2G telecom licenses because of an unconstitutional and arbitrary process of granting licenses without auction. See Kavaljit Singh, "Treaties That Gave Away the Store," *The Hindu* (27 April 2012) online at www.thehindu.com/opinion/lead/treaties-that-gave-away-the-store/article3357429.ece (last accessed 29 October 2012).

[60] India, "Model Text for the Indian Bilateral Investment Treaty" online at: https://mygov.in/sites/default/files/master_image/Model%20Text%20for%20the%20Indian%20Bilateral%20Investment%20Treaty.pdf (accessed 31 March 2015) discussed at Luke Eric Peterson, "Analysis: India Invites Comments on Draft Model Investment Treaty; Text Offers Radical Departure, and Calls to Mind Norway's Past Efforts at Revision," *Investment Arbitration Reporter* (24 March 2015).

developing states now are being used to target developed ones. "Now that the boot is on the other foot," Sornarajah sardonically observes, "it is beginning to feel the pinch quite a bit."[61] Reform of the US model treaty was prompted by the Loewen Group dispute, a failed challenge to an enormous damages award issuing out of a Mississippi jury trial.[62] Loewen's pending dispute prompted Congress to enact the Trade Promotion Authority (TPA) Act of 2002. The Act directs that foreign investors be accorded no greater rights than US citizens under the US constitution and that the executive branch negotiate investment treaties that limit the scope of investor protections concerning nationalization of expropriation. In the subsequent 2004 US–Australia trade and investment agreement, ISDS was omitted, and it appears that it was Australia that insisted upon this omission.[63] This presaged a change in Australian government policy in 2011 when the Gillard Government announced that it would no longer "support provisions that would confer greater legal rights on foreign businesses than those available to domestic businesses."[64] Precipitated by a threatened dispute over Australia's plain packaging of cigarettes law, the new Australian government relaxed this policy. It is now open to including ISDS, although the mechanism continues to attract controversy.[65] A recent Australian–Korean investment treaty includes the contentious dispute settlement mechanism, but its scope is qualified by exceptions having to do with measures concerning public welfare, health, and the environment.

Even Germany, which inaugurated the modern investment treaty and signed the greatest number of investment treaties, is having second thoughts. As a result of the contentious investment dispute launched by Vattenfall, precipitated by the phase out of nuclear power production in

[61] Muthucumaraswamy Sornarajah, "The Case Against a Regime on International Investment Law," in Leon E. Trakman and Nicolai W. Ranieri (eds.), *Regionalism in International Investment Law* (Oxford: OUP, 2013), 475–498 at 476.

[62] *Loewen Group Inc and Loewen* v. *United States* (2003), "Award," ICSID Case No. ARB (AF)/98/3.

[63] Trade and Environment Policy Advisory Committee (TEPAC) "Report on the U.S.-Australia Free Trade Agreement" (12 March 2004), Attachments 1 & 2.

[64] Department of Foreign Affairs and Trade, Australia, "Gillard Government Trade Policy Statement: Trading our Way to More Jobs and Prosperity" (14 April 2011) at 14, www.acci.asn.au/getattachment/b9d3cfae-fc0c-4c2a-a3df-3f58228daf6d/Gillard-Government-Trade-Policy-Statement.aspx.

[65] See documents collected at the Australian Government, Attorney General's Department, "Tobacco Plain Packaging – Investor-State Arbitration" at www.ag.gov.au/Internationalrelations/InternationalLaw/Pages/Tobaccoplainpackaging.aspx (accessed 1 April 2015).

Germany by the year 2022,[66] German officials, affiliated with the Social Democratic Party, have indicated that they will resist the introduction of ISDS in TTIP talks. As mentioned earlier, this imperils successful ratification of CETA and negotiations leading toward EU investment agreements with other states and regions. With French officials expressing similar misgivings, the EU Commission, which has proposed a new standing investment court, modeled upon WTO dispute resolution, as a way out of the impasse[67] bracketed the question of investor-state in future EU agreements. There might be further impediments down the road, including the question of whether the European Court of Justice will tolerate having arbitral tribunals usurp functions performed heretofore exclusively by that Court.[68]

Crisis? What crisis?

In this part, I question whether the system of investment arbitration is on the verge of collapse. I suggest, instead, that the system has a resilience that can withstand many (perhaps not all) of the pathologies identified in the section "When things fall apart." In what follows, I identify a number of factors that mitigate the crisis tendencies imperilling its future. They turn out to be quite formidable.

Neoliberalism

There is, first, the spread of neoliberal rationality that has accompanied, and has helped to facilitate, the rise of investment treaty arbitration. Neoliberal thought has evinced an impressive ability to structure political possibilities and constrain the discursive space for political alternatives on a global scale. Yet, the matrix of policy options associated with neoliberalism provides no fixed blueprint for society. They instead reveal a fluid concoction with no real consensus about the appropriate limits to state action. Neoliberalism's curse, Peck observes, "has been that it can

[66] *Vattenfall AB and others* v. *Federal Republic of Germany* (ICSID Case No. ARB/12/12).

[67] See EU, "Commission Draft Text TTIP – Investment" and "Investments in TTIP and Beyond – Towards an International Investment Court") online at https://ec.europa.eu/commission/2014-2019/malmstrom/blog/investments-ttip-and-beyond-towards-international-investment-court_en (accessed 5 May 2015).

[68] Steffen Hindelang, "Does Foreign Investment Protection Deliver Juridical Stability? How CETA's Investment Chapter Could Come to Grief in the European Court of Justice," paper presented to the Faculty of Law Workshop, University of Toronto (2 February 2015).

live neither with, nor without the state."[69] Indeed, state functions, if diminished in some domains, get redirected into other spheres. Contemporary markets, it is said, are "thoroughly policed."[70]

Suzanne Sawyer's ethnographic account of indigenous peoples' response to the ascendance of neoliberalism in Ecuador is instructive in this regard. She describes the Ecuadorian state as having been "redefined" such that it intervened in productive ways to ensure legislative and institutional outcomes congenial to multinational oil companies. These interventions, in turn, sparked growing, nation-wide, indigenous political movements, resulting in the production of "transgressive" political subjects.[71] Such policies have given rise to so much political volatility, one could conclude that it has resulted in newer and ever expanding modes of regulation.[72]

If neoliberalism has gone through several distinct iterations over time and across continents, it reveals a discernible unity in so far as it is preoccupied with supervising state functions so that they follow market edicts.[73] This amounts to a subversion of the classical liberal account: rather than states supervising markets, markets supervise states.[74] In the course of so doing, neoliberalism's triumph is "extinguishing the agent, the idiom, and the domains through which democracy – any variety of democracy – materializes."[75] The overall success of neoliberalism in shaping public policy in most places around the world cannot be overstated. Its policy spokesmen continue to have immense influence in the construction of "common sense." Judge Stephen Schwebel, for this reason, treats critics as improbably interrupting the inevitable course of history. Could it be that 180 states, he writes, have been "misguided . . .

[69] Jamie Peck, "Remaking Laissez-Faire" (2008) 32 *Progress in Human Geography* 25.

[70] Bernard Harcourt, *The Illusion of Free Markets: Punishment and the Myth of Natural Order* (Cambridge: Harvard University Press, 2011), 17.

[71] Suzanne Sawyer, *Crude Chronicles: Indigenous Politics, Multinational Oil, and Neoliberalism in Ecuador* (Durham: Duke University Press, 2004), 116, 93.

[72] L. Zamosc, "The Ecuadorian Indian Movement: From Politics of Influence to Politics of Power," in N.G. Postero and L. Zamosc (eds.), *The Struggle for Indigenous Rights in Latin America* (Brighton and Portland: Sussex Academic Press, 2004), 132.

[73] "There are now many varieties and nuances of neoliberalism, but if we stay with that fundamental preference for the market over the state as a means of resolving problems and achieving human ends, we shall have grasped the essence," in Colin Crouch, *The Strange Non-Death of Neoliberalism* (Cambridge: Polity, 2011), 7.

[74] Michel Foucault, *The Birth of Biopolitics: Lectures at the College de France, 1978–79*, translated by Graham Burchell (Houndmills: Palgrave Macmillan, 2005), 116.

[75] Wendy Brown, *Undoing the Demos: Neoliberalism's Stealth Revolution* (New York: Zone Books, 2015), 79.

and that it has taken a think tank here and a group of professors there, or labor union officials here, and environmental proponents there, to reveal to the world the error of their ways?"[76] There simply is no standing in the way of the neoliberal juggernaut. The "fantastic suppositions of neoliberal ideology," Jodi Dean writes, "have become part of the air we breathe, elements of our most fundamental assumptions about how the world works."[77] In the face of an ongoing global recession, it bespeaks of a discursive and institutional vigour that is difficult to overcome. Neoliberal agents could not have secured this kind of supremacy, however, without the ongoing complicity of states. Institutionalizing neoliberalism requires a great deal of work. State actors, to this end, have been energetically working to maintain neoliberalism's supremacy.[78]

States

State power undoubtedly has, in some measure, been capped by the institutionalization of neoliberal rationality. There is a single path to economic success, it is said, and it is the one taken up previously by capital-exporting states. This mandates that states open their borders to all manner of trade and investment, irrespective of their impact on local economic actors. Much of this narrative turns out to be mythical: economically advanced states had in place many measures, such as import substitution, to nurture their own economies which would run afoul of today's strictures.[79]

Political power, consequently, is dampened, if not significantly inhibited, by legal constraints associated with the neoliberal legal project. Admittedly, some policy space is preserved, but this will enure principally to those states that contribute to the development of those norms, namely, economically powerful ones.[80] For those having less access to

[76] Judge Stephen M. Schwebel, "Keynote Address: In Defence of Bilateral Investment Treaties," in Jan Albert van den Berg (ed.), *Legitimacy: Myths, Realities, Challenges* (ICCA Congress Series No. 18) (New York: Kluwer Law International) at 10.

[77] Jodi Dean, *Democracy and Other Neoliberal Fantasies* (Durham: Duke University Press, 2009), 73.

[78] On the distinction between hegemony and supremacy, see Stephen Gill and A. Claire Cutler (eds.) *New Constitutionalism and World Order* (Cambridge: CUP, 2011), 1–21.

[79] See generally Ha-Joon Chang, *Kicking Away the Ladder: Development Strategy in Historical Perspective* (London: Anthem Press, 2002).

[80] Linda Weiss, "Global Governance, National Strategies: How Industrialized States Make Room to Move Under the WTO" (2005) 12 *Review of International Political Economy* 723 at 724.

the means by which "universal" norms are determined,[81] they are expected to fall into line and follow the rules that have been dictated to them on their behalf.[82] Deviation from the standard norm will not be tolerated.

There certainly remain state functions to be performed, and these will principally have to do with smoothing the path for the spread of markets. If other state functions have been curtailed, even in economically powerful ones, this curiously has been accomplished with the complicity of states themselves. They turn out to be both the authors and subjects of neoliberal discipline. State complicity is key, then, to the construction and maintenance of regimes such as the one governing foreign investment. This is the "great paradox" of arbitration, described by Jan Paulsson: "that it seeks the cooperation of the very public authorities from which it wants to free itself." [83] States engage in a variety of discursive strategies that help to smooth over legitimacy problems that arise from disabling state power.[84] They aim to provide cover for the contradictory path that states have taken up in the promotion of neoliberal legal discipline on a global scale.

For some state actors, maintaining the role of double agent has proven to be an unstable state of affairs. Some, consequently, have sought reform if not a complete withdrawal from the system. No real reform of the system is likely without the complicity of capital-exporting states, however. In his first term, President Obama directed that such a reevaluation take place, tasking an Investment Subcommittee of the US State Department's Advisory Committee on International Economic Policy (ACIEP) to recommend a way forward. On the contentious questions, the committee was hopelessly divided,[85] and its recommendations resulted in no "material changes" to US BIT practice.[86] Nor have national

[81] Pierre Bourdieu, *Pascalian Meditations* (Stanford: Stanford Unversity Press, 2000), 71.

[82] David Schneiderman, "The Global Regime of Investor Rights: Return to the Standards of Civilized Justice?" (2014) 5 *Transnational Legal Theory* 60–80.

[83] Jan Paulsson, *The Idea of Arbitration* (Oxford: OUP, 2013), 30.

[84] I have argued elsewhere that such strategies rely upon ideas associated with comparative advantage, consumer freedom, and rule of law promotion. See Schneiderman, *Resisting Economic Globalization*, 36–40.

[85] See "Report of the Subcommittee on Investment of the Advisory Committee on International Economic Policy Regarding the Model Bilateral Investment Treaty" (30 September 2009) at www.state.gov/e/eb/rls/othr/2009/131098.htm (last accessed 6 April 2015).

[86] Mark Kantor, "Little Has Changed in the New US Model Bilateral Investment Treaty" (2012) 27 *ICSID Review* 335–778 at 343.

high courts proven to be reliable stewards of change on this front. Canadian courts have had an opportunity to consider the ways in which the North American Free Trade Agreement constrains the capacity of federal and provincial governments and usurps functions ordinarily performed by constitutionally authorized courts. Judges have shown a marked disinterest in these constitutional connections, describing international and domestic laws as being "distinct legal systems that operate in different spheres."[87] The US Supreme Court also has had occasion to consider the relationship between investment arbitration and judicial review, hearing an appeal from a District Court of Appeals decision vacating an arbitral award that dispensed with the treaty requirement that investors first seek recourse in Argentinian courts. The US Supreme Court, reversing the lower court ruling, effectively liberated arbitrators from the supervisory jurisdiction of the US legal system.[88]

Investment law norm entrepreneurs

Of course, the institutions of neoliberal legality, and the investment legal order in particular, would not have successfully achieved global take-up without the aid of an enthusiastic and influential corps of promoters. These investment law norm entrepreneurs – whether they are academics, lawyers in private practice, professional arbitrators, or even government lawyers – help to actively promote the spread of investment treaty norms. For these agents, international investment law represents the norms of "good governance," norms that they prefer to guide and constrain state actors.

Investment lawyers, as a consequence, have been actively participating in debates in the public sphere over the merits of investment treaties. In Canada, controversy over Parliamentary ratification of a Canada–China BIT resulted in a number of lawyers coming forward to argue in favor of the merits of the agreement. These legal experts, it turned out, were

[87] *Council of Canadians et al.* v. *Canada (Attorney General)*, 2005 CanLII 28426 (Ontario Superior Court of Justice) at ¶ 41. See discussion in David Schneiderman, "Investor Rights and the Judicial Denial of the Neoliberal Constitutionalism," in *Liber Amicorum for Harry Arthurs* (McGill-Queen's University Press, in press).

[88] *BG Group PLC* v. *Republic of Argentina*, 572 U.S. __ (2013). Justice Breyer, who delivered the opinion of the Court, analogized investment arbitration to the review of labor arbitration under US law. See discussion in Stephen Breyer, *The Court and the World: American Law and the New Global Realities* (New York: Alfred A. Knopf, 2015), 179–192.

lawyers who have, or whose firms have, a financial interest in expanding the market for their legal services. In most every such instance, the lawyers involved failed to disclose that interest.[89] A new self-described "think tank," the European Federation for Investment Law and Arbitration (EFILA), sprung up in 2014 with the sole purpose of blocking any serious reform of investment arbitration. Investment treaty reforms should always tilt in the direction of protecting investors, after all, EFILA contends, "the main purpose of investment agreements is to protect their rights."[90] This is a lobby group funded by some of the leading investment arbitration firms in the world and by clients that have profited from investment treaty arbitration.[91]

This is not to say that the arguments of investment lawyers, arbitrators and their lobby groups are motivated solely by financial gain. I am reluctant to claim that every seemingly rational act is prompted by a promise of economic gain.[92] Rather it is to say that investment law's norm entrepreneurs are always quick to point out that this fact typically motivates the actions of others. In these disputes, it is always everyone else – whether they be politicians, campesinos, NGOs, national courts, or investors – who is motivated by self-interest. This is never true of those responsible for defining and expanding the field of investment arbitration.

The regime is premised upon a distrust of authority – other than the authority wielded by the investment arbitration bar. Even if many of these actors have previously been closely connected to the government (former Canadian cabinet minister and leading arbitrator Marc Lalonde comes to mind), the aim is to trim the sails of what governments can do.

89 David Schneiderman and Gus Van Harten, "Self-Interested Lawyers and the Canada-China FIPA," *The Toronto Star* (25 November 2012). Van Harten unpacks their arguments in detail in *Sold Down the Yangtze*.

90 "EFILA final response to the EU Commission's consultation on investment protection and investor-to-state dispute settlement (ISDS) in the Transatlantic Trade and Investment Partnership Agreement (TTIP)" (7 December 2014) at 5 online at http://efila.org/wp-content/uploads/2014/07/EFILA_TTIP_final_submission.pdf (last accessed 14 May 2015).

91 See Fabian Flues, Pietje Vervest, Cecilia Olivet, and Pia Eberhardt, *Lawyers Subverting the Public Interest* (Amsterdam/Brussels: Transnational Institute, Friends of the Earth Europe and Corporate Europe Observatory, April 2015) online at http://corporateeurope.org/sites/default/files/efila_report-web.pdf (last accessed 14 May 2015).

92 See Pierre Bourdieu, "Is a Disinterested Act Possible?," in Pierre Bourdieu (ed.), *Practical Reason* (Stanford: Stanford University Press, 1998), 75–91. Yet it cannot be said that this field is exempt from economic calculation.

It is reasonably clear by now that these actors exhibit a suspicion of government action and of the product of political processes.[93] Describing "an avalanche of legislation" in modern developed legal systems, Jan Paulsson declares that this cannot "sensibly be called 'law'," not "in the sense intuitively accepted by citizens deserving to be obeyed ... Such rules may be seen as no more deserving of obedience than any other manifestation of power."[94] This remarkable admission represents well the disdain for political and regulatory authority that gets channeled in investment arbitration.

Weber understood that the spread of what he called formal legal rationality, which delivers the security and predictability necessary for the capitalist system to thrive, relied on the delivery of professional legal knowledge primarily at universities. It is in the course of legal education that formally rational and value-free norms can be transmitted and then put into practice by trained legal professionals.[95] It should come as no surprise, then, that leading universities of the North Atlantic are staffed by academics who vigorously champion investment arbitration. A simple glance at the table of contents of the new leading journals in the field or the flood of texts and edited volumes since the late 2000s reveals that much of the professoriate teaching and writing in the field are enthusiastically championing the spread of investment law while seeking to accelerate, albeit while improving, its output.

As I have acknowledged, no doubt many sincerely believe that this system is preferred over its alternatives. The dirty little secret (it is actually not so little or so secret[96]) is that many aim to complement their university incomes with lucrative part-time work. Hence the phenomenon of full-time law professors carrying on boutique legal practices in the area of investment law, typically acting as a paid consultant or preferably, and with enough seniority, as an arbitrator. Not all succumb to these pressures to conform, but many do. There seems little doubt that institutions of higher learning are thereby deeply implicated in the spread and maintenance of international investment law's legal order. They are

[93] David Schneiderman, "Investing in Democracy? Political Process and International Investment Law" (2010) 60 *University of Toronto Law Journal* 909.

[94] Paulsson, *The Idea of Arbitration*, 102.

[95] Max Weber, *Economy and Society: An Outline of Interpretative Sociology*, edited by Gunther Roth and Claus Wittich (Berkeley: University of California Press, 1978) 775–776.

[96] See Eberhardt and Olivet, *Profiting from Injustice*, c. 6.

perhaps, as Weber described the relation of legal education to the rise of formal legal rationality, "more important than any other factor."[97]

Tin ears?

It turns out that even those academics, typically of a younger generation, who are offering proposals for reform are coming under attack from more established voices in the arbitration world. Brower and Blanchard chastise Anthea Roberts, for instance, for proposing that states, if dissatisfied with arbitral tendencies, steer investment treaty interpretation by clarifying treaty terms or issuing interpretive directives but not, she insists, by dictating outcomes.[98] This kind of proposal, Brower and Blanchard complain, places too much power in the hands of states whom should be bound by treaty commitments. "To cavalierly wave aside that function of treaties by invoking sovereign prerogatives," they declare, "is to replace international law with pure politics."[99] Jason Yackee's important research contributions reveal little or no correlation between signing BITs and new inward investment, yet these are dismissed by Brower and Blanchard as "unreliable" and "unsophisticated," seemingly, because they do not like his findings.[100] They favor other competing studies because those "findings line up with the ways that one would expect investment treaties to operate."[101] In support they cite one such study[102] that Yackee has thoroughly disassembled.[103]

There have been ever-increasing calls for the adoption of proportionality analysis as a means of generating legitimacy for the system in the

[97] Weber, *Economy and Society*, 776.

[98] Anthea Roberts, "Power and Persuasion in Investment Treaty Interpretation: The Dual Role of States" (2008) 104 *American Journal of International Law* 179–225 at 192–193. See also Jason Webb Yackee, "Controlling the International Investment Law Agency" (2012) 53 *Harvard International Law Journal* 391.

[99] Brower and Bouchard, "What's in a Meme? The Truth About Investor-State Arbitration" at 773.

[100] Brower and Blanchard, "What's in a Meme? The Truth About Investor-State Arbitration," 704, 706.

[101] Brower and Blanchard, "What's in a Meme? The Truth About Investor-State Arbitration," 708.

[102] Eric Neumayer and Laura Spess, "Do Bilateral Investment Treaties Increase Foreign Direct Investment to Developing Countries?" (2005) 33 *World Development* 1567–1585.

[103] Jason W. Yackee, "Bilateral Investment Treaties, Credible Commitment, and the Rule of (International) Law: Do BITs Promote Foreign Direct Investment?" (2008) 42 *Law & Society Review* 805–831; Jason W. Yackee, "Do Bilateral Investment Treaties Promote Foreign Direct Investment? Some Hints from Alternative Evidence" (2011) 51 *Virginia Journal of International Law* 397–441.

eyes of states and citizens. Undertaking review of state action along the lines of many high courts around the world – weighing ends against means – will increase the likelihood of investment arbitration's long-term survival, it is claimed.[104] Like other proposals for reform, proportionality analysis has not been taken up enthusiastically. On those occasions where arbitration tribunals have done so, they have performed that function in a less than satisfying manner.[105]

Such prejudgment, and enthusiasm, about the expected benefits of investment treaty practice and arbitration do not generate encouraging signs of reform. Indeed, they make it difficult to conceive of norm entrepreneurs seeing the field evolving in any meaningful way. If arbitration is, as Paulsson characterizes it, a "quest for civilized closure,"[106] then it is hard to see how this opens up any sort of conversation about how to improve the system other than along procedural lines (i.e. doing away with the unilateral appointment of arbitrators).[107] Even modest proposals, having to do with such things as appellate review, for instance, are not well received.[108] Generally, the system is working well, they maintain, so why change it? It will only continue to improve with the passage of time.[109]

104 See Benedict Kingsbury and Stephan Schill, "Investor-State Arbitration as Governance: Fair and Equitable Treatment, Proportionality and the Emerging Global Administrative Law," in Benedict Kingsbury *et al.* (eds.), *El Nuevo Derecho Administrativo Global en América Latina: Desafíos Para las Inversiones Extranjeras, La Regulación Nacional y el Financiamiento Para ed Desarrollo* (Buenos Aires: RPA, 2009), 221–294 online at www.iilj.org/GAL/documents/GALBAbook.pdf (Accessed 15 May 2010), and Alec Stone Sweet, "Investor-State Arbitration: Proportionality's New Frontier" (2010) 4(1) *Law & Ethics of Human Rights* 47.

105 Erlen M. Leonhardsen, "Looking for Legitimacy: Exploring Proportionality Analysis in Investment Treaty Arbitration" (2012) 3 *Journal of International Dispute Settlement* 95–136.

106 Paulsson, *The Idea of Arbitration*, 13.

107 Paulsson takes this up in his *The Idea of Arbitration*, 276–283. See also the modest procedural reforms proposed by arbitrator Stephen Schwebel in "In Defense of Bilateral Investment Treaties," *Columbia FDI Perspectives No. 135* (24 November 2014) online at http://ccsi.columbia.edu/files/2013/10/No-135-Schwebel-FINAL.pdf (last accessed 15 May 2015).

108 See Schwebel, "Keynote Address: In Defence of Bilateral Investment Treaties," 9–10. For the negative response of US business to EU Trade Commissioner Cecilia Malmström's proposal for a permanent international investment court, see Tom Fariless, "EU Proposes New Trans-Atlantic Court for Trade Disputes," *Wall Street Journal*, 16 September 2015.

109 Jan Paulsson, "Avoiding Unintended Consequences," in Karl P. Sauvant and Michael Chiswick-Patterson (eds.), *Appeals Mechanism in International Investment Disputes* (New York: OUP, 2008), 241–265.

Conclusion

There is no question that investment arbitration is at a crossroads. Political actors within capital-exporting states are having second thoughts about the vast legal apparatus that is destabilizing state authority in the interests of ensuring predictability and profitability for foreign investors. The likelihood of the system falling apart, however, seems unduly optimistic on the part of critics. A more likely outcome is continued retreats on the part of some states and continued expansion of the treaty system on the part of other states. It is true that Social Democrats in Germany may be able to redirect German investment treaty policy in new directions, and that this could have significant implications for the future of the legal order. At the same time, as I have argued earlier, there are powerful currents pushing in an opposing direction. With a worldwide web of thousands of BITs and multilateral treaties with investment chapters currently in force, and new ones being signed, it seems less likely that the system will collapse in on itself. Indeed, it would take a Herculean effort to dispose of it.

What then explains the fury of investment law's norm entrepreneurs? Sure, there might be some element of "truth and reality" to their concerns as was the case in Hofstadter's study,[110] but why the debased and angry rhetoric? There are multiple points of disagreement, to be sure, but are they such that critics should be accused of spreading lies and mistruths? Moreover, if norm entrepreneurs are as confident as they claim to be about the benefits of the system in which they are complicit in constructing, why this petulance directed at detractors? It looks like nothing but "total triumph" over the designated enemy will suffice.[111] It mimics, in a sense, Schmitt's insistence upon friend/enemy groupings – moments that exhibit the "most intense and extreme antagonism" – as being the "high points of politics."[112]

All of which says more about the acrimonious tone of the norm entrepreneurs than about the quality of the critics' arguments canvassed in the section "When things fall apart." What is unfortunate is that this form of "condemnation" works "against self-knowledge," Judith Butler warns.[113] It generates a moral chasm, ensuring that dialogue is uncivil

[110] Hofstadter, "The Paranoid Style in American Politics," 81.
[111] Hofstadter, "The Paranoid Style in American Politics," 85.
[112] Carl Schmitt, *The Concept of the Political*, translated by George Schwab (Chicago: The University of Chicago Press, 1996), 29, 67.
[113] Judith Butler, *Giving an Account of Oneself* (New York: Fordham University Press, 2005), 46.

and nonreciprocal. It forecloses options that have the effect of displacing privileged access by lawyers and arbitrators to determining the content of investment law. It turns out that investment law's norm entrepreneurs are manning the barricades not of civilization but of a power over which they are in fear of losing.

6

The COMESA Common Investment Area: substantive standards and procedural problems in dispute settlement

PETER MUCHLINSKI

Introduction

The Common Market for Eastern and Southern Africa (COMESA) is an organisation of 20 African states established in 1994, replacing the previous Preferential Trade Area between the members.[1] Since its inception, COMESA has taken an active role in the economic integration of its members. In 2000, the COMESA Free Trade Area was established.[2] On 22 and 23 May 2007, the twelfth Summit of COMESA Authority of Heads of State and Government, held in Nairobi, Kenya, adopted the Investment Agreement for the COMESA Common Investment Area (CCIA Agreement).[3] According to COMESA, 'the CCIA Agreement is a precious investment tool whereby the COMESA Secretariat contemplates to create a stable region and good investment environment, promote cross border investments and protect investment, and thus enhance COMESA's attractiveness and competitiveness within COMESA Region, as a destination for Foreign Direct Investment (FDI), and in which

An earlier version of this paper was delivered at the 4th Alternative Dispute Resolution in Africa Conference, Cairo, Egypt, 29–31 July 2008. See SOAS School of Law Research Paper No. 11/2010, http://papers.ssrn.com/sol3/papers.cfm?abstract_id=1698209.

[1] COMESA member States are: Burundi, Comoros, Democratic Republic of Congo (DR Congo), Djibouti, Egypt, Eritrea, Ethiopia, Kenya, Libya, Madagascar, Malawi, Mauritius, Rwanda, Seychelles, Sudan, Swaziland, Uganda, Zambia and Zimbabwe. The Founding Treaty can be accessed in French at www.comesa.int/competition/wp-content/uploads/2014/04/130724_COMESA_TREATY_FR.pdf; English version at: http://investmentpolicyhub.unctad.org/Download/TreatyFile/2422.

[2] See COMESA Secretariat, *COMESA in Brief*, 3rd ed. (Lusaka, April 2007) at para. 7.

[3] CCIA Agreement available at http://investmentpolicyhub.unctad.org/Download/TreatyFile/3092. A printed version is available in Martins Paparinskis, *Basic Documents on International Investment Protection* (Oxford: Hart Publishing, 2012) at 442–464.

domestic investments are encouraged'.[4] Among the key pillars of the Agreement is the 'settlement of investment disputes through negotiations and arbitration mechanism'.[5] It is the purpose of this chapter to examine the CCIA Agreement and the investor-state dispute settlement (ISDS) mechanism that this treaty has put in place. It will do so not only through an examination of procedural structures but also by considering the interaction between these and the substantive claims that can be brought by an investor under the Agreement.

This examination is especially valuable given that, in recent years, the debate on the reform of International Investment Agreements (IIAs) has shifted towards greater acceptance of the need for reforms that take into account the needs of sustainable development. At the core of this process lies the fear that an unaccountable, privatised system of ISDS prioritises investor rights over other equally important policy goals. This may cause a disconnect between the avowed purpose of IIAs as vehicles for economic development and their actual impact as a means of stifling legitimate governmental action that seeks to further the various social and environmental goals inherent in the concept of sustainable development.[6]

Against this background, UNCTAD has produced its comprehensive *Investment Policy Framework for Sustainable Development* (IPFSD).[7] It too expresses concern over investor-state arbitration, saying that ISDS can create unjustified liabilities and high procedural costs. Together, these put a significant burden on defending host countries and exacerbate concerns over the balance between investor protection and the preservation of national policy space for development, especially in the case of less-developed host countries.[8] In addition, ISDS claims have been used by investor claimants in hitherto unanticipated ways to challenge measures adopted in the public interest (such as measures to promote social equity, foster environmental protection or protect public health) showing that 'the borderline between protection from political risk and undue interference with legitimate domestic policies

[4] COMESA, 'Investment Agreement for the CCIA: Legal Tool for Increasing Investment Flows within the COMESA' (2007) (original on file with author).

[5] Ibid.

[6] See further M. Sornarajah, *The International Law on Foreign Investment*, 3rd ed. (Cambridge: CUP, 2010) at 24–232.

[7] See UNCTAD, *Investment Policy Framework for Sustainable Development* (New York and Geneva: United Nations, 2012) UN Pub. UNCTAD/DIAE/PCB/2012/5 available at: http://unctad.org/en/PublicationsLibrary/diaepcb2012d5_en.pdf.

[8] Ibid. at 39–40.

is becoming increasingly blurred'.[9] Accordingly, UNCTAD asserts that this problem needs a solution involving treaty design that looks at options both in ISDS provisions and in the scope and application of substantive clauses.[10]

In a similar vein, the Commonwealth Secretariat has published an extensive study authored by three leading Canadian legal scholars entitled *Integrating Sustainable Development into International Investment Agreements: A Guide for Developing Countries* (the Guide).[11] As with the UNCTAD IPFSD, the Guide lays the problem with current IIAs at the feet of the outcomes of ISDS claims.[12] The proposed solution is again to rebalance new IIAs taking into account such concerns.[13]

The CCIA Agreement is, in a sense, a precursor to these initiatives but has become a relatively neglected model. Indeed, the COMESA website no longer contains a link to this document![14] Yet, it is fair to say that the CCIA Agreement is a significant model for these purposes, in that it proposes an approach that is sensitive to the realities of developing states and of the particular conditions that influence approaches to international commercial arbitration in Africa. Given that the majority of IIAs are based on developed country or developed regional models, this requires that serious attention be paid to the CCIA Agreement in the wider investment law community. It offers an alternative formulation and points to how future generations of IIAs might be drawn up so as to provide, in the words of the Agreement, 'investors with certain rights in the conduct of their business within an overall balance of rights and obligations between investors and Member States'.[15]

[9] Ibid. at 40. [10] Ibid.

[11] J. Anthony VanDuzer, Penelope Simons, and Graham Mayeda, *Integrating Sustainable Development into International Investment Agreements: A Guide for Developing Countries* (London: Commonwealth Secretariat, 2012) (cited as VanDuzer *et al.*) available at: www.iisd.org/pdf/2012/6th_annual_forum_commonwealth_guide.pdf. This study is also published as a Commonwealth Secretariat book *Integrating Sustainable Development into International Investment Agreements: A Guide for Developing Country Negotiators* (London: Commonwealth Secretariat, 2013). See too OECD Informal Ministerial Meeting on Responsible Business Conduct, *Investment Treaty Law, Sustainable Development and Responsible Business Conduct: A Fact Finding Survey* (Paris: OECD, 26 June 2014) available at www.oecd.org/investment/2014RBCMinisterial-TreatyRBC.pdf.

[12] VanDuzer *et al.* in note 11 at 7. [13] Ibid.

[14] See http://programmes.comesa.int/index.php?option=com_content&view=$article&id=111&Itemid=149. The main link is to the UNCTAD website in note 3.

[15] CCIA Agreement in note 3 Article 11.

This chapter will proceed in three stages. First, so as to set the scene, the wider contemporary debate on the problems of ISDS, and their proposed solutions, will be examined so as to explain the background against which the dispute settlement provisions of the CCIA Agreement were finalised. It is clear from the face of these provisions that they seek to offer a new approach to ISDS, which takes into account the types of problems that will be outlined later. The second part of this chapter will offer a detailed analysis of the ISDS procedures in the CCIA Agreement. The third part will then consider the types of claims that an investor can make under the Agreement. There are numerous innovations in the substantive provisions of the Agreement that will have a significant effect on the subject matter of possible claims and, thus, on their admissibility before a tribunal whose jurisdiction is based on the Agreement.

Current issues in investor-state dispute settlement

The main feature of ISDS under IIAs has been the rapid rise of litigation during the first years of the twenty-first century. According to the most recent UNCTAD figures, in 2013, investors initiated at least 56 known investor-state cases. The total cumulative number of the known treaty-based cases reached 568 by the end of 2013. The majority of these disputes were filed with International Centre for the Settlement of Investment Disputes (ICSID) (or the ICSID Additional Facility) (62 per cent) and under the arbitration rules of the United Nations Commission on International Trade Law (UNCITRAL) (28 per cent). The overwhelming majority of cases were brought by investors from the developed countries (85 per cent), three quarters of which were brought against developing and transition economies, of which countries in Latin America and the Caribbean accounted for the largest share. African countries accounted for 10 per cent of respondents, although the number of cases against developed countries also reached 26, a significant number.[16]

Much of this increase can be attributed to the bringing of over 30 cases against Argentina in the aftermath of its financial crisis in 2001/2002 and in the extension of the ICSID Additional Facility Rules to North American Free Trade Agreement (NAFTA) arbitrations.[17] Equally, the

[16] UNCTAD, *World Investment Report 2014* (New York and Geneva: United Nations, 2014) at 124–125.

[17] On the Argentine cases see Carlos E. Alfaro and Pedro M. Lorenti, 'The Growing Opposition of Argentina to ICSID Arbitral Tribunals: A Conflict between International and Domestic Law?' (2005) 6 *JWIT* 417. On NAFTA arbitrations see further www

fact that a very large number of IIAs, mostly bilateral investment treaties (BITs), have been concluded since the 1980s (current UNCTAD estimates place the number of concluded IIAs at 3,236 – 2,902 BITs and 334 other IIAs – at the end of 2013[18]) has created more opportunities for investors to bring treaty-based claims. Furthermore, investors are beginning to understand the value of treaty claims in situations where they feel they have no effective local legal or other remedies to settle their differences with the host country. This is partly because of the rise of specialist international investment lawyers and their entrepreneurship in seeking out clients who could bring treaty-based claims. Whatever the actual reasons may be, a sharp rise in investment treaty-based litigation has caused a number of concerns that are central to the development of dispute settlement procedures and remedies in this area.[19]

On the part of investors, the foremost concern is whether the dispute settlement provisions in IIAs are truly effective in protecting their rights and interests. While claims can be brought, awards are often far lower than the sum claimed. For example, in the case of *TECMED* v. *Mexico*, in its award rendered in May 2003, the tribunal found that the governmental measure at issue violated the full protection and security standard and to be expropriatory. The compensation awarded ($5.5 million), however, was far below the amount claimed ($52 million).[20] Equally, in the awards against Argentina under the US–Argentina BIT of 1991, the tribunals that found against Argentina, nonetheless, held that their award of damages would take account of the reality of the economic crisis that Argentina was facing.[21] Thus, investors' claims will be considered in the

.naftaclaims.com and for critical background see IISD/WWF, *Private Rights, Public Problems A Guide to NAFTA's Controversial Chapter on Investor Rights* (Winnipeg: IISD, 2001).

18 UNCTAD, *World Investment Report 2014* in note 16 at 114.

19 See further Van Duzer *et al.* in note 11 at 399–404 for a detailed analysis of the costs and benefits of ISDS.

20 *Tecmed* v. *Mexico* ICSID Case No. Arb (AF)/00/2 Award of 29 May 2003, 43 ILM 133 (2004).

21 Thus in *Sempra Energy International* v. *Argentine Republic* ICSID Case No. ARB/02/16 Award 28 September 2007 at http://ita.law.uvic.ca/documents/SempraAward.pdf the tribunal stated: 'The Tribunal does not believe that the issue here is one of lowering the standards of protection set under the Treaty or the law. This being said, however, the manner in which the law has to be applied cannot ignore the realities resulting from a crisis situation, including how a crisis affects the normal functioning of any given society. This is the measure of justice that the Tribunal is bound to respect. The Tribunal will accordingly take into account the crisis conditions affecting Argentina when determining the compensation due for the liability found in connection with the breach of the Treaty standards Award.' (at para. 397). See also *CMS Gas Transmission Co* v. *Argentina* ICSID

full context of the surrounding circumstances. As one tribunal has put it, BITs 'are not insurance policies against bad business judgments'.[22]

On the part of host countries, concerns have been expressed, first, as to the risk of large awards being made against them.[23] For example, in the case of *CME* v. *Czech Republic*, an award of some $350 million was made. This raises serious concerns about the legitimacy of such large awards. However, given the fact that most awards fall significantly below the amount claimed, this award may be somewhat out of line with mainstream practice.[24] On the other hand, had the Argentine cases all gone against Argentina, it has been estimated that Argentina would have faced a bill of some $80 billion.[25] It is hard to see how a host country could ever pay such a sum. The social implications of such a payout could be disastrous and would lead to complex negotiations about debt financing and reconstruction as no other route would exist for such sums to be found.

A second concern for host states is that international arbitral tribunals lack the legitimacy of a court of law and, therefore, ought not to have the responsibility to pronounce upon the legality or otherwise of governmental action. Indeed, their power to do so may result in an illegitimate interference with the host country's right to regulate and could lead to 'regulatory chill' in that host country authorities would make decisions not based so much on the wider public interest but rather with a view to avoiding liability to investors under an applicable IIA.[26] In some cases, this could lead to decisions that favour investor rights over other equally

Case No. ARB/01/8 Award of 12 May 2005, 44 ILM 1205 (2005) at paras. 165–166, 240: '[the] reality of the crisis . . . cannot be ignored . . . facts do not eliminate compliance with the law but do have a perceptible influence on the manner in which the law can be applied'.

22 *Maffezini* v. *Spain* Case No. ARB/97/7 award of 13 November 2000: 16 ICSID Rev-FILJ 248 (2001) at para. 64.

23 See UNCTAD in note 7 at 40.

24 *CME* v. *Czech Republic* award of 13 September 2001 and the parallel London award of *Lauder* v. *Czech Republic*, of 3 September 2001, can be accessed at www.cetv-net.com. The Stockholm award was challenged by the Czech Republic before the Svea Court of Appeals in *Czech Republic* v. *CME Czech Republic BV*. The Court of Appeals turned down the Czech challenge and upheld the award, including the approach taken to the calculation of damages based on the market value principle: SVEA Court of Appeals Judgment of 15 May 2003: 42 ILM 919 (2003); see too the Introductory Comment by Thomas Waelde: 42 ILM 915 (2003).

25 See William W. Burke-White and Andreas von Staden, 'Investment Protection in Extraordinary Times: The Interpretation and Application of Non-Precluded Measures Provisions in Bilateral Investment Treaties' (2008) 48 *Va.Jo.Int'l.L.* 307 at 311.

26 See UNCTAD in note 7 at 39–40.

important, if not superior, claims upon the regulatory obligations of public authorities.

A third major concern for host countries is the risk that particular cases will give rise to multiple claims from the same multinational corporate group, causing an excessive amount of time and resources being devoted to defending such claims. This occurred in the CME litigation against the Czech Republic, where both the Netherlands-based holding company of the entity undertaking the investment in the Czech Republic and the owner of the parent company brought separate proceedings in separate venues arising out of the same facts.[27] Corporate groups are not seen as a single entity for these purposes.[28] This raises concerns that the group as a whole might seek to use its ability to bring multiple claims as a means of putting pressure on the host country to admit liability. This point has been made in relation to the aforementioned multiple claims against the Czech Republic. However, in those proceedings, the Czech Republic decided against arguing for a consolidation of the claims. On the other hand, different entities in the group will have different interests to protect, and so to assimilate these parties and these claims may well deprive multinational groups of important legal rights that ensure the proper operation of the investment.[29]

Other stakeholders apart from investors and host countries have also entered the debate on ISDS. In particular, certain Western non-governmental organisations (NGOs) have been vocal critics of the procedures involved in such cases.[30] Their concerns centre on the issue of whether all

[27] See *CME* v. *Czech Republic* and *Lauder* v. *Czech Republic* in note 13. See further 'Who Wins and Who Loses in Investment Arbitration? Are Investors and Host States on a Level Playing Field? – The Lauder/Czech Republic Legacy' (2005) 6 *JWIT* 59–77; Charles Brower and Jeremy Sharpe, 'Multiple and Conflicting International Arbitral Awards' (2003) 4 *JWI* 211.

[28] See *CMS Gas Transmission Company* v. *Argentina* ICSID Case No. ARB/01/8 decision on jurisdiction 17 July 2003 available at www.worldbank.org/icsid/cases or 42 ILM 788 (2003) at para. 80. See too *Azurix* v. *Argentina* ICSID Case No. ARB/01/12 decision on jurisdiction 8 December 2003 available at www.worldbank.org/icsid/cases or 43 ILM 262 (2004) at paras. 86–90.

[29] See further Christoph Schreuer *et al.*, *The ICSID Convention: A Commentary*, 2nd ed. (Cambridge: CUP, 2009) at p. 384.

[30] Among the most knowledgeable in the field is the Canadian-based International Institute for Sustainable development (IIISD). See for example, IISD Publications Centre Comments on ICSID Discussion Paper, 'Possible Improvements of the Framework for ICSID Arbitration' (Howard Mann, Aaron Cosbey, Luke Eric Peterson, Konrad von Moltke, IISD, 2004); IISD www.iisd.org/publications/pub.aspx?pno=667, and Center for International Environmental Law (CIEL) Revising the UNCITRAL Arbitration Rules to Address Investor-State Arbitrations (revised version – December 2007) www.iisd.org/

the relevant stakeholder groups that might be affected by the operation of an investment and the outcome of possible litigation between the investor and host country can know of that process and have a meaningful input into it so as to ensure that their perspective is considered by the tribunal. This position challenges the legitimacy of arbitral tribunals, often composed of private practitioners who have no official capacity other than an appointment by the parties, as deciders of major public policy issues. In this regard, the NGOs share the same concerns as host countries about regulatory chill and the inhibition of legitimate regulatory decisions.

On a more technical level, this perspective demands greater transparency about the existence of arbitral proceedings, a significant number of which take place in secret, openness of hearings and transparency of documentation, as well as greater accountability of arbitrators for their decisions. In addition, rights of third parties to appear as *amici curiae* are advocated. The issue of legitimacy is further elaborated by concern over the impartiality of arbitrators, many of whom may act as counsel in other cases whose outcome can be affected by the outcome of the case in which they are arbitrators. This leads to demands for stricter rules on the appointment and eligibility of arbitrators. Finally, as regard the increasing number of public awards that are inconsistent and confusing in their interpretation of treaty provisions, this position has advocated the establishment of a system of appellate review of awards.

Such concerns led ICSID itself to consider reforms including prompt publication of awards where the parties exercise their right to permit such publication, more open procedures allowing access to proceedings for interested third parties and a possible ICSID appeals facility.[31] Some of these reforms were instituted in the latest changes to the Arbitration

pdf/2008/investment_revising_uncitral_arbitration_dec.pdf. See too William Greider, 'Invalidating the 20th Century: How the Right Is Using Trade Law to Overturn American Democracy' (15 October 2001) 273(11) *The Nation* 21, who focuses on NAFTA dispute settlement in particular, displaying how much this has caused anxiety in North American political circles. More recently, opposition has focused on the ISDS provisions of proposed the Trans-Atlantic Trade and Investment Partnership Agreement: for a summary, see European Commission Staff Working Document Report *Online Public Consultation on Investment Protection and Investor-to-State Dispute Settlement (ISDS) in the Transatlantic Trade and Investment Partnership Agreement* (Brussels, 13 January 2015 SWD (2015) 3 final (TTIP)) at http://trade.ec.europa.eu/doclib/docs/2015/january/tradoc_153044.pdf.

31 See ICSID Secretariat, *Possible Improvements of the Framework for ICSID Arbitration* (Discussion Paper, 22 October 2004); ICSID Secretariat, *Suggested Changes to the ICSID Rules and Regulations* (Working Paper, 12 May 2005).

Rules in 2006, allowing, in particular, for third-party participation in ICSID arbitration at the discretion of the tribunal after the consultation of both parties.[32]

Given the context of this chapter, some further concerns relating to the use of investor-state arbitration in Africa must be highlighted.[33] International commercial arbitration has been viewed with some suspicion in Africa in the past. This is due to a number of factors, the most important being the colonialist roots of this system of dispute settlement.[34] In particular, in colonial times, disputes over international trade transactions would be controlled by the standard terms of trade exchanges and trade associations dominated by colonialist business interests. These systems of arbitration were internal to these bodies. Accordingly, Africans were largely kept out of these bodies and, so, could not know how these systems worked. In addition, the main national arbitration laws of the time were based on old precedents from the metropolitan legal system. After gaining independence, these laws were not replaced, resulting in obsolete procedures that did not reflect the state of the art in commercial arbitration.[35]

Further difficulties arise out of the historical lack of participation in the development of international commercial arbitration on the part of Africans. Many of the major international institutions dealing with international commercial arbitration were founded before the majority of African states had achieved independence. Thus, their rules and procedures were determined without an African presence.[36] This contributed to an essentially Western view of what proper arbitral procedures were and to the further reinforcement of limited African knowledge on the subject. In addition, after decolonization, the newly independent African states concentrated on issues of political self-determination and sovereignty, culminating in calls for a New International Economic Order (NIEO) in the early 1970s.[37] They did not prioritise the reformulation of international commercial law, including international arbitration, further entrenching

[32] See Arbitration Rules Rule 37(2) in *ICSID Convention, Regulations and Rules* (ICSID/15, 10 April 2006 available at https://icsid.worldbank.org/apps/ICSIDWEB/resources/Documents/2006%20CRR_English-final.pdf).

[33] See especially Amazu A. Asouzu, *International Commercial Arbitration and African States: Practice, Participation and Institutional Development* (Cambridge: CUP, 2001) and Samson L. Sempasa 'Obstacles to International Commercial Arbitration in African Countries' (1992) 41 *ICLQ* 387.

[34] See Asouzu previous note at 416 *et seq.*

[35] See Sempasa in note 33 at 391.

[36] Asouzu in note 33 at 420–421; Sempasa ibid. at 395.

[37] Sempasa ibid. at 390 and 394.

the distance between this method of dispute settlement and African laws and practices.

Linked to these sovereignty concerns, newly independent African states expressed misgivings about the value of international commercial arbitration as a means of settling their commercial disputes. Given that, in the early post-colonial period, most economic activity was conducted by the state,[38] there was little interest in the practices and procedures of international commercial arbitration, a system designed to provide redress for disputes between private commercial parties. This situation occurred at the same time as the rise of foreign direct investment by multinational enterprises in African states. Such investments often involved major projects in natural resource extraction or infrastructure development and were governed by concession contracts, which provided for delocalised international arbitration. Such procedures were seen as an imposition on the state by the foreign investor, who had the upper hand in bargaining power over the host country when the concession was given.[39] Moreover, this feeling of external imposition was exacerbated by foreign investors' general suspicion towards the domestic courts and judiciary of the newly independent African states. Investors felt, rightly or wrongly, that national laws and procedures could not be trusted to deliver justice in countries where the state was the dominant presence in business and which appeared prone to authoritarian rule and widespread corruption.[40] Unfortunately, such attitudes are still commonly encountered today, placing a brake on the willingness of foreign investors to use local laws and dispute settlement systems and on their lawyers to advise such a course of action.[41]

More recently, attitudes towards international commercial arbitration have been changing in Africa. In particular, as the market-based model of economic development has become increasingly accepted by African states,[42] the need to ensure that commercial arbitration is available and is based on modern and effective procedural foundations has increased.[43]

[38] Asouzu in note 33 at 30. [39] Sempasa in note 33 at 393.

[40] See Asouzu in note 33 at 35, 37–38, 105–108, 425.

[41] For a strong critique of this prejudice see generally Asouzu in note 33.

[42] See for example the COMESA Treaty (in note 1) Article 151 'Creation of an Enabling Environment for the Private Sector' and Article 152(1) 'Strengthening the Private Sector': 'The Member States shall endeavour to adopt programmes to strengthen and promote the role of the private sector as an effective force for the development, progress and reconstruction of their respective economies.'

[43] See further Dr. C.J. Amasike (ed.), *Strengthening of Arbitration and ADR Institutions and Centres in Africa as a Catalyst for Foreign Investment* (Nigeria: Arbitration and

The response has been to pass more modern arbitration laws, some of which are based on the UNCITRAL Model Arbitration Law of 1985,[44] and to accede to the New York Convention on the Recognition and Enforcement of Arbitral Awards of 1958 (The New York Convention)[45] and the Washington Convention on the Settlement of Investment Disputes Between States and Nationals of Other States, 1965 (the ICSID Convention).[46] In addition, regional arbitration centres have been established in Cairo and Lagos.[47]

Against this background, as will be shown in the next two sections, the CCIA Agreement represents a challenging new departure. As noted in the introduction to this chapter, it provides a system of investor-state arbitration that seeks to reconcile the concerns of the investors, African host countries and other stakeholders in the fair and effective resolution of disputes through regional dispute settlement mechanisms. It offers to the investor the choice of international arbitration based on a balance of rights and obligations between them and the respondent state. In this regard, the CCIA Agreement can be viewed as a significant response to the concerns of investors about local remedies, while at the same time structuring the available substantive types of claims to ensure that legitimate state rights to regulate are not unduly curtailed and that the rights and interests of significant third parties are not ignored.

Investor-state dispute settlement procedures under the CCIA Agreement

Dispute settlement is governed by Part Three of the CCIA Agreement, which offers two principal methods of dispute settlement: state-to-state and investor-state. The former does not normally extend to issues directly arising out of investor claims in most IIAs.[48] However, the

Alternative Dispute Resolution in Africa, Yaliam Press, 2007), and Dr. C.J. Amasike (ed.), *Building a Contemporary and an Effective Arbitration and ADR in Africa* (Nigeria: Arbitration and Alternative Dispute Resolution in Africa, The Regent (Printing and Publishing) Ltd., 2005).

[44] See Asouzu in note 33, ch. 5. [45] See ibid., ch. 6.

[46] The Washington Convention on Settlement of Investment Disputes Between States and Nationals of Other States 1965: 4 ILM 524 (1965); 575 UNTS 159 extensively discussed in relation to Africa in Asouzu in note 33 Part 4.

[47] See Asouzu in note 33 Part 2.

[48] See UNCTAD Investor-State Dispute Settlement (UNCTAD Series on Issues in International Investment Agreements II, New York and Geneva, United Nations, 2014) at 18. Available at http://unctad.org/en/PublicationsLibrary/diaeia2013d2_en.pdf.

CCIA Agreement does allow the home state of a COMESA investor to bring a claim where, 'the respondent has breached an obligation under [the CCIA Agreement], and that the claimant or its investor has incurred loss or damage by reason of, or arising out of, that breach'.[49] The precise scope of this provision is unclear as regard claims brought where the investor suffers loss or damage. For the most part, investor-state disputes will be settled under the investor-state provisions. It would appear that, in certain cases, presumably those not covered by ISDS, a right to diplomatic protection of the investor is permitted. Given the rather uncertain nature of diplomatic protection as a device for the protection of foreign investors, it is unlikely that this procedure will be much used.[50]

ISDS is open only to COMESA investors. According to Article 1(4) of the CCIA Agreement, this includes a natural or juridical person of a Member State, 'making an investment in another Member State, in accordance with the laws and regulations of the Member State in which the investment is made'. For the purposes of this definition, 'natural person' means a person having citizenship of a Member State in accordance with its applicable laws and regulations, and 'juridical person' means 'any legal entity duly constituted or otherwise organised under the applicable laws and regulations of a Member State'. A juridical person owned or controlled by a foreign investor will not qualify as a COMESA investor unless 'it maintains substantial business activity in the Member State in which it is duly constituted or organised'. This requires 'an overall examination, on a case-by-case basis, of all the circumstances, including, *inter alia*: the amount of investment brought into the country; the number of jobs created; its effect on the local community; and the length of time the business has been in operation'.[51] The availability of ISDS is thus limited to investors from other COMESA Member States. Accordingly, a non-COMESA investor would need first to establish a subsidiary, branch or other legally recognised form of business association in a COMESA country so as to benefit from this procedure. In addition, the non-COMESA investor would have to comply with the substantial business activity requirement, which introduces an 'effective link' type of nationality test.[52]

[49] CCIA Agreement in note 3 Annex A Article (2) (1).

[50] On which see further Peter T. Muchlinski, *Multinational Enterprises and the Law*, 2nd ed. (Oxford: OUP, 2007) at 704–707.

[51] CCIA Agreement in note 3 Article 4 (1).

[52] On which see the *The Nottebohm Case (Liechtenstein* v. *Guatemala)* I.C.J. Reports 1955, 4; David Harris, 'The Protection of Companies in International Law in the Light of the

Before either type of dispute settlement mechanism can be invoked, the CCIA Agreement demands use of other dispute settlement techniques. Thus, Part Three begins with Article 26 on negotiation and mediation. According to Article 26, the claimant, whether a state or COMESA investor, is required to issue a notice of intention to initiate a claim to the other potential disputing party. A minimum six-month cooling-off period is imposed between the date the notice is given and the date a party may formally initiate a dispute. Article 26(3) asserts that, '[t]he parties shall seek to resolve potential disputes through amicable means, both prior to and during the cooling-off period'. In this, the CCIA Agreement follows the extensive practice in IIAs to provide for the use of informal dispute settlement methods in the first place.[53] The CCIA Agreement goes on to mandate mediation where the parties fail to agree on an alternative means of dispute settlement. The mediator is chosen by the parties from the COMESA list of mediators or by the President of the COMESA Court of Justice where the parties cannot agree. This procedure does not affect the minimum cooling-off period. If the parties accept a mediation ruling, it becomes immediately binding upon them.[54] This is an innovative development in IIAs. It places alternative dispute resolution (ADR) at the heart of the dispute settlement process. It also allows the parties time before they go to arbitration. In this, it may discourage needless litigiousness, something that has become a rather unwelcome development under IIAs in more recent times. This approach is also supported by UNCTAD in its IPFSD, as ADR can help to prevent an escalation of conflict, preserve the investment relationship and promote a sensible, cheaper, faster and more flexible solution.[55]

Should amicable negotiation or mediation under Article 26 fail, arbitration may be resorted to in accordance with the requirements of Article 28 of the CCIA Agreement. Claims are restricted to Part Two of the Agreement, which deals with investor rights and obligations. Investors cannot bring claims based on the general obligations of Member States or

Nottebohm Case' (1969) 18 *ICLQ* 275 at 285–295. This approach to corporate nationality was rejected by the International Court of Justice in the *Case Concerning The Barcelona Traction, Light and Power Company, Limited* (New Application: 1962) (*Belgium* v. *Spain*) Second Phase, Judgment of 5 February 1970, I.C.J. Reports 1970, 3. However, the ICSID Convention (in note 46) uses a simpler control test of corporate nationality in Article 25 (2)(b) on which see further Muchlinski in note 50 at 726–731.

[53] See, for further examples, UNCTAD in note 7 at 55–57. See too VanDuzer *et al.* in note 11 at 428.

[54] CCIA Agreement in note 3 Article 26(4)–(6).

[55] See UNCTAD in note 7 at 56–57.

the institutional provisions under Part One.[56] A three-year limitation period is imposed on the bringing of claims.[57] The investor must assert that the respondent state, in whose territory the investor has made an investment, has breached an obligation under Part Two and that the investment has incurred loss or damage by reason of, or arising out of, that breach.

The investor is given the choice of a number of dispute settlement fora under Article 28:

(a) to the competent court of the Member State in whose territory the investment has been made;
(b) to the COMESA Court of Justice in accordance with Article 28(b) of the COMESA Treaty; or
(c) to international arbitration:
    (i) under the ICSID Convention, provided that both the home state of an investor and Member State in whose territory the investment has been made are parties to the ICSID Convention;
    (ii) under the ICSID Additional Facility Rules, provided that either the non-disputing Party or the respondent is a party to the ICSID Convention;
    (iii) under the UNCITRAL Arbitration Rules; or
    (iv) under any other arbitration institution or under any other arbitration rules, if both parties to the dispute agree.

This range of choice is typical of modern dispute settlement clauses in IIAs.[58] In addition, Article 28 introduces what is termed 'arbitration without privity' in that, as paragraph 4 clarifies:

> Each Member State consents to the submission of a claim to arbitration under this Agreement in accordance with its provisions. Each investor, by virtue of establishing or continuing to operate or own an investment subject to this Agreement, consents to the terms of the submission of a claim to dispute resolution under this Agreement if he exercises the right to bring a claim against a Member State under this Agreement.

56 CCIA Agreement in note 3 Article 10.

57 By Article 28 (2) of the CCIA Agreement, 'No claim shall be submitted to arbitration if more than three years have elapsed from the date on which the COMESA investor first acquired, or should have first acquired, knowledge of the breach and knowledge that the COMESA investor has incurred loss or damage.' UNCTAD also suggests a three-year limitation period: UNCTAD in note 7 at 56. See too VanDuzer *et al.* in note 11 at 410.

58 See further UNCTAD in note 48 at 62–65 and see Antonio Parra, 'Provisions on the Settlement of Investment Disputes in Modern Investment Laws, Bilateral Investment Treaties and Multilateral Instruments on Investment' (1997) 12 *ICSID Rev-FILJ* 287.

By this provision, each Contracting State makes a unilateral offer of arbitration, which is accepted by the investor when they make the choice to use one of the methods of arbitration listed. For example, should the investor choose ICSID arbitration in writing, usually by filing a claim with ICSID, the Contracting State will be deemed to have consented to the tribunal's jurisdiction in accordance with Article 25 of the ICSID Convention.[59] This approach to consent has been termed 'arbitration without privity' in that the host country makes an offer to all foreign investors, which can be subsequently accepted by any investor involved in a dispute with that country, thereby obviating the need for a prior arbitration agreement between them.[60]

Article 28 makes the choice of the investor final and exclusive. By paragraph 3, '[i]f the COMESA investor elects to submit a claim at one of the fora set out in paragraph 1 of this Article, that election shall be definitive and the investor may not thereafter submit a claim relating to the same subject matter or underlying measure to other fora.' This is known as a 'fork-in-the road' clause. Such 'fork-in-the-road' clauses have been the subject of arbitral interpretation before ICSID.[61] The key issue concerns whether the dispute submitted by the investor to the national courts or tribunals is one that invokes a claim of a breach of the applicable IIA or whether it is an independent cause of action that raises no such issue.[62] If the national claim is identical to the international claim made before the ICSID Tribunal, then the jurisdiction of the latter body has been excluded by the investor's choice under the fork-in-the-road provision. However, questions that can only be determined under the applicable national law of the host country, such as whether a licence has been properly refused or a tax properly charged, can only be considered before national courts or tribunals in the first instance. Such determinations do not, of themselves, raise any issues as to the breach of an IIA. Accordingly, a choice of national tribunal by the investor in such a case will not operate to oust ICSID jurisdiction where the investor subsequently brings a separate claim alleging breach of the CCIA Agreement.[63]

[59] This was accepted in the Report of the Executive Directors on the Washington Convention, para. 24: see 4 ILM 524 (1965) at 527. See further, Schreuer *et al.* in note 29 at 198–221.

[60] See Jan Paulsson, 'Arbitration Without Privity' 10 (1995) *ICSID Rev-FILJ* 232.

[61] See the discussion in Schreuer *et al.* in note 29 at 365–367; UNCTAD in note 48 at 86–90 and VanDuzer *et al.* in note 11 at 415.

[62] See *Genin* v. *Estonia* ICSID Case No. ARB/99/2 award of 25 June 2001 available at www.worldbank.org/icsid/cases or 17 ICSID Rev-FILJ 395 (2002) at paras. 331–333.

[63] See Muchlinski in note 50 at 697.

The reference of an issue of national law to the relevant national dispute settlement body should not preclude a subsequent international claim being brought under the treaty for an alleged violation of its protection provisions, on the ground that such a claim relates to the investment protected under the applicable treaty and is separate from the underlying national legal dispute. In such a case, there can be no fork-in-the-road, as there is no identity of subject-matter in the two legal proceedings. In addition, it is not open to the host country to avoid its responsibility under international law by relying on an exclusive jurisdiction clause in a contract with the investor if the national claim is not only based exclusively on the investment contract but also raises issues as to the conformity of governmental action with the IIA.[64]

The remaining provisions of Article 28 introduce significant innovations into the arbitral procedure, which seek to respond to concerns over the lack of transparency and third-party participation in arbitral proceedings and to balance the rights and obligations of investors in relation to their right to bring claims. On the first of these issues, Articles 28(5) to (7) introduce the public availability of all documents related to the arbitration and open public hearings on both procedural and substantive issues, both of which are subject, on the part of the tribunal, to such exceptional steps as are necessary to protect confidential business information.[65] In addition, the arbitral tribunal shall be open to the receipt of *amicus curiae* submissions. This is to be done in accordance with the process set out in Annex A in relation to state-to-state disputes with necessary adaptation for application to investor-state disputes.[66]

Article 8 Annex A deals with *amicus curiae* submissions. It is rather a general provision which leaves much to be determined.[67] It asserts that,

64 See Muchlinski ibid. See further *Compania de Aguas Aconquija SA and Compagnie Generale des Eaux (Vivendi)* v. *Argentina* ICSID Case No. ARB/97/3 award of 21 November 2000 available at www.worldbank.org/icsid/cases or 40 ILM 426 (2001) at paras. 53–55 upheld by the Ad Hoc Annulment Committee in *Compania des Aguas del Aconquija SA and Vivendi Universal (Formerly Compagnie Generale des Eaux)* v. *Argentina* ICSID Case ARB/97/3 decision on annulment 3 July 2002 available at www.worldbank.org/icsid/cases or 41 ILM 1135 (2002). at paras. 38–42.

65 CCIA Agreement in note 3. By Article 28(5): 'All documents relating to a notice of intention to arbitrate, the settlement of any dispute pursuant to Article 28, the initiation of an arbitral tribunal, or the pleadings, evidence and decisions in them, shall be available to the public.' See further UNCTAD in note 48 at 121–125.

66 Ibid., Article 28(8) and see further UNCTAD ibid. at 125–127 and Van Duzer *et al.* in note 11 at 428.

67 CCIA Agreement in note 3 Annex A Article 8. By para. 3, 'The CCIA Committee may establish and make available to the public a standard form for applying for status as

'[t]he tribunal shall have the authority to accept and consider *amicus curiae* submissions from a person or entity that is not a disputing party (the "submitter")'.[68] Thus, the tribunal is not bound to accept such a submission but has discretion over whether to do so. According to paragraph 3 of Article 8, '[t]he CCIA Committee may establish and make available to the public a standard form for applying for status as amicus curiae. This may include specific criteria which will help guide a tribunal in determining whether to accept a submission in any given instance.' Therefore, more detailed guidance on how this discretion is to be used must await the formulation of such guidelines, which is not mandatory given the non-binding language used in this paragraph.[69] The submissions shall be provided in English, French or Portuguese or in the principal language of the host state. To ensure the identity and affiliation of the submitter, the submission 'shall identify the submitter and any Party, other government, person, or organization, other than the submitter, that has provided, or will provide, any financial or other assistance in preparing the submission'. Submissions may relate to any matter covered by the CCIA Agreement that is relevant to the claim before the tribunal. Again the tribunal will be the judge of what is or is not relevant.

This provision is not a very strong assertion of *amicus curiae* rights given the high degree of discretion left to the tribunal. However, this is consistent with, for example, current practice at ICSID, where third-party submissions will only be admitted at the discretion of the tribunal after consultation with both parties.[70] Equally, it is more detailed than such provisions in other IIAs. For example, Article 28(3) of the US–Rwanda BIT of 2008 simply states, '[t]he tribunal shall have the authority to accept

amicus curiae. This may include specific criteria which will help guide a tribunal in determining whether to accept a submission in any given instance.'

68 CCIA Agreement ibid., Annex A Article 8.

69 Some guidance as to what could be included in such guidelines can be obtained from Article 39(4) of the Canadian Model Foreign Investment Protection Agreement: 'In determining whether to grant leave to file a non-disputing party submission, the Tribunal shall consider, among other things, the extent to which: (a) the non-disputing party submission would assist the Tribunal in the determination of a factual or legal issue related to the arbitration by bringing a perspective, particular knowledge or insight that is different from that of the disputing parties; (b) the non-disputing party submission would address a matter within the scope of the dispute; (c) the non-disputing party has a significant interest in the arbitration; and (d) there is a public interest in the subject-matter of the arbitration.' Available at http://ita.law.uvic.ca/documents/Canadian2004-FIPA-model-en.pdf.

70 See note 31.

and consider *amicus curiae* submissions from a person or entity that is not a disputing party'.[71] On the other hand, the Canadian Model Foreign Investment Protection Agreement of 2004 has a detailed provision on this issue.[72] While such provisions serve to increase transparency and stakeholder participation, they may also have the effect of burdening the parties to the dispute, who may be obliged to respond to arguments made by the *amicus curiae*, and to force parties to settle or refuse to settle based on public pressure rather than on the basis of the applicable legal rules.[73] However, this consequence may be required so as to ensure that investor-state disputes involving major public interest issues take account of those issues as well as narrow rules of law. It also reinforces the need to consider revising IIAs to ensure that the balance of rights and obligations is not geared too far in favour of investors without also considering the host country's regulatory responsibilities and the effects of investor rights on third-party rights.

As to the issue of balance between the rights and obligations of investors, Article 28(9) contains a significant innovation in IIA practice. It states that:

> A Member State against whom a claim is brought by a COMESA investor under this Article may assert as a defence, counterclaim, right of set off or other similar claim, that the COMESA investor bringing the claim has not fulfilled its obligations under this Agreement, including the obligations to comply with all applicable domestic measures or that it has not taken all reasonable steps to mitigate possible damages.[74]

This provision must be read in conjunction with Article 13, which states that 'COMESA investors and their investments shall comply with all applicable domestic measures of the Member State in which their investment is made'. It is under national law that a balancing of rights and responsibilities can be drawn up. Failure to observe applicable national law would take the investor's claim outside the realm of the dispute settlement provisions of the CCIA Agreement. Some recent arbitral

[71] US–Rwanda BIT 19 February 2008 at www.ustr.gov/assets/Trade_Agreements/BIT/Rwa/asset_upload_file743_14523.pdf. This provision is repeated in the 2012 US Model BIT Article 28(3) see www.state.gov/documents/organization/188371.pdf.

[72] See Canada FIPA in note 69, Article 39.

[73] See UNCTAD, *Investor State Dispute Settlement and Impact on Investment Rulemaking* (New York and Geneva: United Nations, 2007) at 86–87.

[74] CCIA Agreement in note 3 Article 28 (9). On counterclaims, see further UNCTAD in note 48 at 115–119. The UNCTAD IPFSD also considers the use of counterclaims for violation of host state law: UNCTAD in note 7 at 58 and see too VanDuzer *et al.* in note 11 at 394–398.

awards have considered similar formulations in BITs. Some BITs contain wording to the effect that the definition of an investment covered by the agreement is one made 'in accordance with host state law'.[75] This can confirm that both foreign and domestic investors have to observe local law and that only those investments that are compliant with local law can obtain protection under the BIT, including any applicable laws on entry and establishment of foreign investment. Thus, a tribunal can refuse jurisdiction over a dispute where the investor has acted in a fraudulent manner that renders the obtaining of an investment contract illegal under the law of the host state, by reason of breaches of good faith and unjust enrichment rules.[76] Equally, where the investor obtains a contract in knowing violation of nationality of ownership requirements under the host state laws, this can take the dispute outside the protection of the BIT.[77] On the other hand, violations of the host state law after the entry of the investment cannot go to jurisdiction but only to the merits of the claim.[78]

The remaining provisions of Part Three deal with enforceability of awards, the maintenance of a roster of COMESA arbitrators and the governing law in disputes. As to enforceability, the CCIA Agreement requires that, 'Member States shall adopt such domestic rules as are required to make final awards enforceable in domestic legal proceedings in their states'.[79] Unlike the ICSID Convention, there is no automatic recognition of awards as if they were decisions of a court of law.[80] However, the execution of the ICSID award will be governed by the laws concerning the execution of judgments in force in the state where execution is sought.[81] This includes the applicable law relating to a

[75] For example the BIT between Chile and New Zealand states that 'investment' means any kind of asset or rights related to it, 'provided that the investment has been made in accordance with the laws and regulations of the Contracting party receiving it . . .' cited in UNCTAD, *Bilateral Investment Treaties 1995–2006: Trends in Investment Rulemaking* (New York and Geneva: United Nations, 2007) at 9. For more recent examples see UNCTAD in note 48 at 117–118.

[76] See *Inceysa Vallisoletana SL* v. *El Salvador* ICSID Case No. Arb/03/26 Decision on Jurisdiction 2 August 2006 available at http://ita.law.uvic.ca/documents/Inceysa_Vallisoletana_en_001.pdf. See for analysis Christina Knahr, 'Investments "in Accordance with Host State Law"' (September 2007) 4(5) *Transnational Dispute Management* available at www.transnational-dispute-management.com.

[77] See *Fraport AG Frankfurt Airport Services Worldwide* v. *The Philippines* ICSID Case No. Arb/03/25 Award of 16 August 2007 available at http://ita.law.uvic.ca/documents/FraportAward.pdf; see too Knahr, 'Investments "in Accordance with Host State Law"'.

[78] Ibid. at paras. 344–345. [79] CCIA Agreement in note 3 Article 29.

[80] See ICSID Convention in note 46, Article 54. [81] Ibid., Article 54(3)

foreign state's immunity from execution.[82] Thus, the respondent state still enjoys the protection of the law of sovereign immunity as applied in the enforcing state.[83] In practical terms, therefore, the enforceability of an ICSID award is subject to the overriding principle of protecting the property belonging to a foreign sovereign, which is used for sovereign rather than commercial purposes, against execution, this being the most commonly applicable rule found in the national laws.[84] By contrast, the COMESA rule is rather in the form of a harmonisation measure, which leaves much open to the national legislative organs. With that being said, it is highly unlikely that the law of sovereign immunity could be disregarded. It is likely that the Member State concerned might pass a specific statute giving automatic recognition to the COMESA award but subject to overriding the national laws on the recognition of international arbitral awards. In this regard, the question of whether or not the Member State is a signatory of the New York Convention would be a relevant consideration. There appears nothing on the face of the CCIA Agreement to alter the application of that Convention to COMESA Awards. More pressing is the issue of whether the national law of the Member State recognises and applies the New York Convention.[85]

[82] Ibid., Article 55.

[83] See for example the US case *LETCO* v. *Government of Liberia* 650 F. Supp. 73 (SDNY 1986), 26 ILM 695 (1987) *aff'd* memo No. 86–9047 (2d Cir, 19 May 1987). See too Georges Delaume, 'Sovereign Immunity and Transnational Arbitration,' in J. Lew (ed.), *Contemporary Problems in International Arbitration* (London: Queen Mary College Centre for Commercial Law Studies, 1986), 313. In *SOABI (SEUTIN)* v. *Senegal* (France, Cour de Cassation, 11 June 1991), 30 ILM 1167 (1991), it was held that a foreign state that has consented to ICSID arbitration has thereby agreed that the award may be granted recognition (*exequatur*) which, as such, does not constitute a measure of execution that might raise issues pertaining to the immunity from execution of the state concerned. The ICSID Convention provided an autonomous and simple system of recognition, which excluded domestic rules concerning recognition of foreign awards. The Award in *SOABI* v. *Senegal* is reproduced in 6 ICSID Rev-FILJ 125 (1991).

[84] See for example *AIG Capital Partners Inc and another* v. *Republic of Kazakhstan (National Bank of Kazakhstan intervening)* [2005] EWHC 2239 (Comm) [2006] 1 All ER 284 (QBD) where it was held that the property of a state's central bank or monetary authority was subject to state immunity under s.14(4) of the State Immunity Act 1978 and, so, could not be used to satisfy an ICSID award, even if such property was being held by third parties on behalf of the central bank or monetary authority.

[85] See further Asouzu in note 22 who notes at 208 that relatively few African countries have adopted the New York Convention. As of the time of writing (June 2008) of the COMESA Member States (see note 1) only Djibouti, Egypt, Kenya, Madagascar, Mauritius, Zambia and Zimbabwe had ratified the New York Convention; see, www.uncitral.org/uncitral/en/uncitral_texts/arbitration/NYConvention_status.html.

As to the roster of arbitrators, the COMESA Secretariat shall maintain such a roster of 'qualified arbitrators from which parties to an arbitration under this Agreement may select arbitrators'.[86] This follows ICSID practice where a panel of suitably qualified arbitrators is also established. Again, much is left open, such as the composition of the arbitral tribunals, the types of qualifications required of a member of the roster and the procedures for appointment of individual tribunals. Other IIAs have more detailed provisions on this issue.[87]

Finally, as regard the governing law, by Article 31 of the CCIA Agreement:

> When a claim is submitted to an arbitral tribunal, it shall be decided in accordance with this Agreement, the COMESA Treaty, national law of the host state, and the general principles of international law.

The choice of governing law has been a contentious issue in the investor-state arbitration.[88] Normally, the law of the host country is the law applicable to an investment contract between the investor and the host state. However, this may not preclude all applications of international law. Indeed, in interpreting Article 42 of the ICSID Convention, ICSID tribunals have consistently held that national law will apply only to the extent that it is consistent with the general principles of international law.[89] For example, it would not be open to the host state to exclude the international law relating to expropriation, as embodied in a BIT, by reference to an inconsistent national law.[90] Indeed, the ad hoc Annulment Committee in the case of *Wena Hotels* v. *Egypt* went a step further and held that, in an appropriate case, a tribunal could apply the law of the BIT, to the exclusion of the national law, under the terms of Article 42(1) in the absence of agreement as to the proper law between the parties.[91]

[86] CCIA Agreement in note 3 Article 30.

[87] See for example the US–Rwanda BIT in note 71 Article 27; Canada Model FIPA in note 69 Articles 29–31.

[88] See further UNCTAD in note 48 at 127–138 and VanDuzer *et al.* in note 11 at 424.

[89] ICSID Convention in note 46 Article 42(1): 'The Tribunal shall decide a dispute in accordance with such rules of law as may be agreed by the parties. In the absence of such agreement, the Tribunal shall apply the law of the Contracting State party to the dispute (including its rules of the Conflict of Laws) and such rules of international law as may be applicable.' See *Amco Asia* v. *Indonesia* resubmitted case 89 ILR 580 at 594 para. 40 (1992).

[90] See *Compania del Desarrollo de Santa Elena* v. *Costa Rica* ICSID Case No.ARB/96/1 award of 17 February 2000, 15 ICSID Rev-FILJ 169 (2000) at para. 64.

[91] ICSID Case No. ARB/98/4 Decision of the *ad hoc* Committee 28 January 2002, 41 ILM 933 (2002) at paras. 40–41.

The CCIA Agreement appears also to use international law as a corrective standard. Although there is a hierarchy of norms working down from the specific provisions of the Agreement, the COMESA Treaty, and national law to the general principles of international law, this cannot be read as somehow limiting international legal review of the other provisions. An international tribunal cannot accept a plea from the respondent state that provisions of its own law, or deficiencies in that law are an answer to a claim against it for an alleged breach of international law.[92] This principle was affirmed by the ICSID Tribunal in *Southern Pacific Properties (Middle East) Limited* v. *Arab Republic of Egypt*,[93] and this approach is likely to inform the interpretation of Article 31 of the CCIA Agreement, subject to one further issue. Given that COMESA is creating a supranational legal order not unlike that of the European Union, it is arguable that international law can apply only to the extent that this serves to develop the supranational order. The two are not necessarily identical. Thus, a COMESA tribunal might be fully entitled to depart from general international law where the express terms of the CCIA Agreement or of the COMESA Treaty diverge from this. On a procedural level, this is unlikely to cause difficulties as a COMESA tribunal will be an international tribunal that must follow the rules of international law in the conduct of its procedures.

By contrast, in relation to substantive protection of investor rights, the specific provisions of these treaties, rather than the much contested international minimum standard of protection for aliens and their property, will be the correct guide for determining the scope of the rights and obligations of COMESA investors. This is especially so given the development orientation of the fundamental aims of COMESA, which may not be entirely compatible with the traditional concept of the international minimum standard, with its stress of the protection of investor rights.[94] This proposition is possibly controversial, but it is hard to see how else Article 31 of the CCIA Agreement can be read given the nature

[92] By Article 27 Vienna Convention on the Law of Treaties 1969: 'A party may not invoke the provisions of its internal law as justification for its failure to perform a treaty . . .' Similarly, by Article 3 of the International Law Commission Articles on State Responsibility 2001: 'The characterization of an act of a State as internationally wrongful is governed by international law. Such characterization is not affected by the characterization of the same act as lawful by internal law' (ILC Report of 53rd Sess. ILC (2001) GAOR 56th Sess, Supp. 10).

[93] Award on the Merits 20 May 1992: 32 ILM 933 (1993).

[94] See COMESA Treaty in note 1 Article 6, which states: 'The Member States, in pursuit of the aims and objectives stated in Article 3 of this Treaty, and in conformity with the

of the substantive rights of action that a COMESA investor might enjoy. They do not necessarily coincide with the international minimum standard but rather create a COMESA standard of protection.

Substantive rights of action under the CCIA Agreement

It has already been noted that investors can only bring claims in relation to an alleged infringement of their rights under Part Two of the CCIA Agreement. Part Two contains the main standards of protection found in most IIAs, although with some important adaptations that will be considered further.[95] In particular, the fair and equitable treatment standard of the non-discrimination provisions and the expropriation clause warrant closer attention. The other substantive provisions of Part Two on the transfer of assets, movement of labour and compensation for losses raise no significant new issues. Their formulations conform to standard IIA practice and need not be further discussed here. The protection of Part Two extends only to investments of COMESA investors, which have been

Treaty for the Establishment of the African Economic Community signed at Abuja, Nigeria on 3 June 1991, agree to adhere to the following principles:

(a) equality and inter-dependence of the Member States;
(b) solidarity and collective self-reliance among the Member States;
(c) inter-State co-operation, harmonisation of policies and integration of programmes among the Member States;
(d) non-aggression between the Member States;
(e) recognition, promotion and protection of human and peoples' rights in accordance with the provisions of the African Charter on Human and Peoples' Rights;
(f) accountability, economic justice and popular participation in development;
(g) the recognition and observance of the rule of law;
(h) the promotion and sustenance of a democratic system of governance in each Member State;
(i) the maintenance of regional peace and stability through the promotion and strengthening of good neighbourliness; and
(j) the peaceful settlement of disputes among the Member States, the active cooperation between neighbouring countries and the promotion of a peaceful environment as a pre-requisite for their economic development.'

On the controversy surrounding the international minimum standard of treatment see Charles Lipson, *Standing Guard: Protecting Foreign Capital in the Nineteenth and Twentieth Centuries* (Berkeley, CA: University of California Press, 1985). See too for a statement by the International Court of Justice expressing concern over this issue *Case Concerning The Barcelona Traction, Light and Power Company* in note 41 at paras. 89–90.

95 They are: fair and equitable treatment (Article 14), transfer of assets (Article 15), movement of labour (Article 16), national treatment (Article 17), most favoured national treatment (Article 19), expropriation (Article 20) and compensation for losses (Article 21).

duly registered with the relevant investment authority in the host country and which have been made either before or after entry into force of the CCIA Agreement.[96] It covers only disputes involving claims that have arisen since the entry into force of the Agreement.[97] Thus, the CCIA Agreement has no retroactive force and claims that arose before its entry into force will have to be dealt with by other means.

Turning to the substantive rights, the right to fair and equitable treatment has a distinctive formulation that introduces a degree of judicial review of the state administrative action.[98] According to Article 14(1) of the CCIA Agreement, ' [f]air and equitable treatment includes the obligation not to deny justice in criminal, civil, or administrative adjudicatory proceedings in accordance with the principle of due process embodied in the principal legal systems of the world'. By Article 14(2), this is said to prescribe 'the customary international law minimum standard of treatment of aliens as the minimum standard of treatment to be afforded to covered investments and does not require treatment in addition to or beyond what is required by that standard'. The final sentence of Article 14(2) is a direct reference to a controversy that arose under the fair and equitable treatment standard in the NAFTA. In the NAFTA arbitration *Pope and Talbot* v. *Canada*, the tribunal asserted that the fair and equitable treatment standard is 'additive' to the international minimum standard.[99] On the other hand, the NAFTA Free Trade Commission issued a Note of Interpretation on 31 July 2001, which rejected any notion that Article 1105 of NAFTA contained any elements that were 'additive' to the international minimum standard.[100] The CCIA Agreement affirms the view that the fair and equitable treatment standard can be equated with the international minimum standard. However, Article 14(3) continues:

> For greater certainty, Member States understand that different Member States have different forms of administrative, legislative and judicial systems and that Member States at different levels of development may

[96] CCIA Agreement in note 3 Article 12 (1) and (2). [97] Ibid., Article 12 (3).

[98] See generally UNCTAD, *Fair and Equitable Treatment: A Sequel* (New York and Geneva: United Nations, 2012).

[99] See *Pope and Talbot* v. *Canada* Award on the Merits of Phase 2, 10 April 2001 at para. 110 available on www.naftacliams.com.

[100] The Note of interpretation was considered to be mandatory by the Tribunal sitting on the damages award in the *Pope and Talbot Case*: see *Pope and Talbot* v. *Canada* award in respect of damages, 31 May 2002, available on www.naftaclaims.com or 41 ILM 1347 (2002). This was confirmed in *Loewen* v. *United States* ICSID Case No. ARB (AF)/98/3 award of 26 June 2003: 42 ILM 811 (2003) at para. 128.

> not achieve the same standards at the same time. Paragraphs 1 and 2 of this Article do not establish a single international standard in this context.

This is a departure from the traditional notion of the international minimum standard as an absolute standard of treatment and introduces a degree of flexibility in its interpretation based on the level of development of the respondent country. In this regard, Article 14 appears to curtail significantly the protection afforded to an investor in relation to maladministration as it provides a novel defence, unknown in the general international law, to the effect that the host country can plead its level of development as an explanation for poor administrative practices. This is not an approach that will find favour with investors, but it is an understandable attempt to curtail unreasonable claims.

Indeed, there is some arbitral case law that suggests that the specific conditions in the host country are a factor that tribunals can take into account when assessing whether a BIT has been infringed. Thus, the tribunal, in the *CMS Case* held that account should be taken of the effect of abnormal conditions prompted by the economic crisis in Argentina in assessing the scope of protection afforded to the investor by an investment treaty.[101] It continued:

> The crisis had in itself a severe impact upon the Claimant's business, but this aspect must to some extent be attributed to the business risk the Claimant took on when investing in Argentina, this being particularly the case as it related to decrease in demand. Such effects cannot be ignored as if business had continued as usual. Otherwise both parties would not be sharing some of the costs of the crisis in a reasonable manner and the decision could eventually amount to an insurance policy against business risk, an outcome that, as the Respondent has rightly argued, would not be justified.[102]

Such concerns may be relevant in special cases, such as transitional economies, economies in crisis and, possibly, highly underdeveloped countries or failing states. However, the actual condition of the host country cannot be used as an excuse for bad governance where the host country is able to offer high standards of administrative action but fails to do so. It may be rather too easy for a host country to use this argument in justifying its own regulatory shortcomings. Thus, some limits need to be developed to this argument. So far, the existing case law remains relatively unclear.[103]

[101] *CMS* v. *Argentina* in note 21 at para. 244. [102] Ibid., para. 248.

[103] See further Nick Gallus, 'The Influence of the Host State's Level of Development on International Investment Treaty Standards of Protection' (2005) 6 *JWIT* 711. Gallus

Turning to the national treatment, this covers both pre-entry and post-entry treatments and is subject to a comprehensive 'like circumstances' test.[104] In addition, the national treatment provision is subject to a negative list of exceptions and qualifications under Article 18 of the CCIA Agreement.

Most favoured nation (MFN) treatment extends to pre- and post-entry treatments and is subject to the same 'like circumstances' test as national treatment.[105] It is subject to the common exceptions relating to regional integration agreements and taxation conventions that are found in most MFN provisions in IIAs.[106] MFN shall not apply to investment agreements entered into by Member States with non-Member States prior to the entry into force of the CCIA Agreement. This ensures that COMESA investors will be unable to use the MFN clause to extend the operation of agreements with non-COMESA countries into the CCIA Agreement. The latter is the sole basis of rights for COMESA investors in the region, and it cannot be supplemented by rights from pre-existing investment treaties concluded with non-Member States.

The expropriation provision in Article 20 is worded so as to protect legitimate regulatory actions of the host country from challenge under the dispute settlement provisions.[107] Thus, compulsory intellectual property licences or the revocation, limitation or creation of intellectual property rights are outside its protection to the extent that such measures are consistent with applicable international agreements on intellectual

notes that there has been a significant number of BIT-based ICSID cases in which the developing host country's level of development was not taken into account. However, in *AMT* v. *Zaire* (ICSID Case No. ARB /93/1 award of 21 February 1997: 36 ILM 1531 (1997)) the issue was relevant to the determination of compensation, where the claimant was found to have been aware of local conditions (at paras. 7.14–7.15).

104 See CCIA Agreement in note 3 Article 17.

105 See further UNCTAD, *Most-Favoured Nation-Treatment: A Sequel* (New York and Geneva: United Nations, 2010).

106 CCIA Agreement in note 3 Article 19.

107 Ibid., Article 20. See too Article 23(3), which provides for a special procedure in relation to claims for expropriation based on a tax measure: 'An investor that seeks to invoke Article 20 with respect to a taxation measure must refer to the Secretary General of the COMESA at the time that it gives its notice of intention to arbitrate under Article 28 the issue of whether that taxation measure involves an expropriation. The Secretary General shall ask the competent authorities of the host state and home state whether they do not agree to consider the issue or, having agreed to consider it, fail to agree that the measure is not an expropriation within a period of six months of such referral, in which case the investor may submit its claim to arbitration, if the other conditions of Article 28 have been fulfilled as well.' See further UNCTAD, *Expropriation: A Sequel* (New York and Geneva: United Nations, 2012).

property.[108] In addition, a measure of general application shall not be considered an expropriation of a debt security or loan solely on the ground that the measure imposes costs on the debtor that cause it to default on the debt.[109] On a more general level, Article 20(8) states:

> Consistent with the right of states to regulate and the customary international law principles on police powers, bona fide regulatory measures taken by a Member State that are designed and applied to protect or enhance legitimate public welfare objectives, such as public health, safety and the environment, shall not constitute an indirect expropriation under this Article.

This provision is an important restatement of the limits of investor protection under the law relating to expropriation. Recently concern has been expressed that, with the extension of IIA provisions on expropriation to indirect or regulatory takings, legitimate exercises of regulatory power taken for essential policy reasons might fall foul of investor claims, thereby weakening the ability of the host state to regulate and leading to 'regulatory chill'.[110] Other more recent IIAs have also included provisions distinguishing between a legitimate regulation and a regulatory taking, and the CCIA Agreement continues this trend.[111] One notable issue arising here is whether the legitimacy of the measure in question will be considered in the light of its proportionality to the regulatory aim being pursued. Such an approach is taken in the Canadian FIPA.[112] It remains to be seen if COMESA tribunals might apply a similar principle or whether they will emphasise the right to regulate and give to the host country a large measure of discretion in interfering with investor rights. Finally, Article 20(9) requires that the host country give to the investor a right to judicial or administrative

[108] Ibid., Article 20 (6). [109] Ibid., Article 20 (7).

[110] See further Muchlinski in note 50 at 587–596.

[111] See for example the US–Rwanda BIT in note 71 Article 6 and Annexes A and B. In Annex B para. 4 (b): 'Except in rare circumstances, non-discriminatory regulatory actions by a Party that are designed and applied to protect legitimate public welfare objectives, such as public health, safety, and the environment, do not constitute indirect expropriations.' This approach is reproduced in the 2012 US Model BIT in Annex B in note 71. See too Canadian FIPA in note 69 Article 13 and Annex B(13) (1) (c): 'Except in rare circumstances, such as when a measure or series of measures are so severe in the light of their purpose that they cannot be reasonably viewed as having been adopted and applied in good faith, non-discriminatory measures of a Party that are designed and applied to protect legitimate public welfare objectives, such as health, safety and the environment, do not constitute indirect expropriation.'

[112] See previous note.

review of any act of expropriation and valuation of compensation under national law. Such review will take into account the requirements of Article 20. This is not an exhaustion of local remedies requirement as the provision does not mandate the use of such procedures prior to making a claim under Article 28 of the CCIA Agreement.

Article 22 of the CCIA Agreement adds a general exceptions clause, which serves to reinforce the host state's right to regulate in the areas listed provided that 'such measures are not applied in a manner which would constitute a means of arbitrary or unjustifiable discrimination between investors where like conditions prevail, or a disguised restriction on investment flows'.[113] This approach follows the structure of Article XX of the GATT and introduces a 'chapeau', outlining a test of the legitimacy of a measure in relation to the aims of the Agreement. The reference to 'disguised restrictions on investment flows' is similar to the GATT Agreement, which refers to an arbitrary and unjustifiable discrimination and disguised restrictions on trade.[114] Under the GATT, this has been interpreted as introducing a 'least trade restrictive' test for regulatory measures requiring the protection of Article XX.[115] COMESA tribunals could develop a similar approach by applying a 'least investment restrictive' test. This would involve examining whether

[113] CCIA Agreement in note 3 Article 22(1). Article 22 goes on to say that, 'nothing in this Agreement shall be construed to prevent the adoption or enforcement by any Member State of measures:

(a) designed and applied to protect national security and public morals;
(b) designed and applied to protect human, animal or plant life or health;
(c) designed and applied to protect the environment; or
(d) any other measures as may from time to time be determined by a Member State, subject to approval by the CCIA Committee.

2. Nothing in this Agreement shall be construed to prevent a Member State from adopting, maintaining or enforcing any measure that it considers appropriate to ensure that investment activity in its territory is undertaken in a manner sensitive to the principles outlined in sub-paragraphs 1(a) to (c) above.
3. Nothing in this Agreement shall be construed to:

(a) preclude a Member State from applying measures that it considers necessary for the fulfillment of its obligations under the United Nations Charter with respect to the maintenance or restoration of international peace or security, or the protection of its own essential security interests; or
(b) require a Member State to furnish or allow access to any information the disclosure of which it determines to be contrary to its essential security interests.'

[114] See too for a similar formulation Canada FIPA in note 69 Article 10.

[115] See United States-Standards for Reformulated Gasoline and Conventional Gasoline WTO Appellate Body adopted 20 May 1996 WT/DS2/AB/R at 22–29.

the policy aim in question could have been achieved with less interference to the investor's rights or to their investment.

Finally, Articles 24 and 25 of the CCIA Agreement provide procedures involving the CCIA Committee in relation to emergency safeguard measures necessitated by threats of serious injury to the economy of a Member State caused by economic liberalisation and temporary balance of payments measures, respectively.[116] Member States undertaking such measures are required to notify the Committee. Again the content of these provisions owe more to the GATT than to other IIAs, which do not in general contain such provisions. In relation to investor-state disputes, these provisions provide a means of dispute avoidance as they allow the Committee to act as an adjudicator of the conformity of the host state measures with the CCIA Agreement. This can prevent the alternative situation where the host Member State passes measures unilaterally, and should the measures cause loss to the investor, then the latter will bring a claim. This occurred in relation to disputes concerning Argentina's emergency measures in response to the peso crisis in 2000–2001, resulting in a large number of BIT-based arbitrations.[117] It is not entirely clear whether decisions made under Articles 24 and 25 can form the basis of a claim by the investor. Although these provisions are located in Part Two of the CCIA Agreement, it appears that investors cannot challenge the determination of the CCIA Committee as its power to make such a determination is granted by Article 7(2)(b), which is in Part One of the CCIA Agreement; as noted earlier, investors are specifically excluded from making claims concerning issues arising out of Part One. However, the private sector representatives can be present at CCIA Committee meetings as ex officio members and to that extent can have an input.

Concluding remarks

This chapter has examined the new ISDS provisions of the CCIA Agreement. This is a significant departure in IIA practice as it represents a developing country arrangement and not one between a developed and developing country, as is usual in relation to the majority of BITs. Therefore, it is a significant example of what developing countries in Africa see as the proper approach to this field of dispute settlement. In this, it should act as a counter-example to the developed country-dominated models of IIAs and

[116] CCIA Agreement in note 3 Articles 24 and 25.
[117] On which see Burke-White and von Staden note 25.

to offer a new departure for analysis of how future IIAs should be structured. That said, it reflects certain new developments taken from the US and Canadian Model BITs, in particular, which are also seen in some of the UNCTAD and Commonwealth Secretariat reform provisions. This may indicate the gradual emergence of a new international consensus about the balance of rights and obligations on the part of the host country in IIAs, giving to it more flexibility in carrying out legitimate regulatory action. Where the CCIA Agreement goes further, however, is in balancing investor obligations against the host country obligations. This is still a very tentative development, and it is rather limited compared to certain NGO initiatives in this field.[118] However, it does represent a new departure in IIA practice and one that may develop more fully over time. What the CCIA Agreement does not do, in contrast to the US and Canadian Models, is provide extensive and detailed procedural provisions on ISDS. In addition, many important issues are left unaddressed, such as the consolidation of multiple claims and appellate review. However, this should not detract from the fact that the CCIA Agreement offers a great deal of food for thought about the further evolution of ISDS issues in future generations of IIAs.

[118] See for example the Canadian-based International Institute for Sustainable Development (IISD), *IISD Model International Agreement on Investment for Sustainable Development Negotiators Handbook* (April 2005 revised April 2006) www.iisd.org/pdf/2005/investment_model_int_handbook.pdf. The Model Agreement is reproduced in 20 ICSID Rev-FILJ 91 (2005).

7

Lessons from the negotiations of the United Nations Code of Conduct on Transnational Corporations and related instruments

KARL P. SAUVANT

Some 40 years ago, in 1977, the United Nations began negotiations on the United Nations Code of Conduct on Transnational Corporations (TNCs). It was the first effort to arrive at comprehensive and balanced rules governing the rights and responsibilities of governments and TNCs. The negotiations ended unsuccessfully in 1993, against the background of an accelerating trend to liberalize national foreign direct investment (FDI) regulatory frameworks to attract such investment and the proliferation of bilateral investment treaties to protect such investment. In parallel to these negotiations (and subsequent to them), successful negotiations were also undertaken in the Organisation for Economic Co-operation and Development (OECD) on Guidelines for Multinational Enterprises (adopted in 1976); in the International Labour Organization (ILO) on the Tripartite Declaration of Principles Concerning Multinational Enterprises and Social Policy (adopted in November 1977); and in the United Nations Conference on Trade and Development (UNCTAD) on The Set of Multilaterally Agreed Equitable Principles and Rules for the Control of Restrictive Business Practices (adopted in December 1980); these instruments dealt with specific aspects of the activities of TNCs.

While not involved in the United Nations Code negotiations themselves, Professor Sornarajah did write about the Restrictive Business Practices Set.[1] Moreover, although the United Nations Code negotiations came to naught, they crystallized the basic configuration of interests of

[1] See, M. Sornarajah, "Towards an International Antitrust Law" (1982) 22 *Indian Journal of International Law* 1–29.

the principal stakeholders and the key issues associated with them. They also laid bare a number of the obstacles that governments seeking a multilateral investment instrument need to overcome. Many of these are still with us today and await an international solution.

This chapter distills the lessons learned from these negotiations.[2] The experience of these negotiations and the lessons learned from them are of immediate relevance to the current international investment negotiations.

* * * * *

A global phenomenon requires a global response. Moreover, this response needs to reflect the principal interests of all the major stakeholders. The fundamental issues put on the international agenda some 40 years ago in the context of the United Nations Code negotiations have, if anything, become more salient, given the expansion of the number of TNCs and the rapid growth of FDI. To be sure, substantial progress has been made since then, not only in understanding the nature and impact of TNCs and their foreign investments but also through a proliferation of various instruments applicable to them. But, a comprehensive overarching framework has eluded us so far, a framework governing international investment as the most important vehicle for bringing goods and services to the foreign markets and integrating the production systems of individual economies.

What can we learn from the experience of the United Nations Code negotiations and the negotiations of related instruments for the establishment of such a framework?

The first lesson is that any effort to negotiate a binding comprehensive multilateral instrument, which defines in a balanced manner the rights and responsibilities of countries and TNCs on all important issues related to international investment, requires careful preparation before the actual negotiations begin. While the lack of such preparations was not decisive for the eventual failure of the United Nations Code negotiations (after all, the governments had largely agreed on the guidelines part of the

[2] The text that follows is the adapted concluding section of Karl P. Sauvant, "The Negotiations of the United Nations Code of Conduct on Transnational Corporations: Experience and Lessons Learned" (2015) 16 *Journal of World Investment and Trade* 11–87, available at: www.works.bepress.com/karl_sauvant/. That article also addressed the following questions: Why did these negotiations start and how did they unfold? What were the underlying interests? What were the OECD, ILO, and UNCTAD negotiating experiences on these issues? Why could negotiators not arrive at an agreement on a United Nations Code? Where do we stand today? What could bring about change?

draft, and they had reached consensus on the OECD, ILO, and UNCTAD instruments), it was an issue when it came to the more specific and technical treatment provisions. Negotiators need to be fully aware of the many difficult technical issues, the advantages and disadvantages of various trade-offs, the implications key provisions have for their national policy-making, the costs of violating provisions of any agreement, etc. A careful preparatory process is advisable for the negotiation of any international investment instrument, and it must be a process that is transparent and inclusive.[3]

Moreover, any effort of this complexity and magnitude presents a major challenge in today's environment.[4] While a comprehensive instrument provides more scope for trade-offs, it also requires that the interests of all the principal stakeholders need to be accommodated across a wide area of issues. Today, this is more difficult than it was 40 years ago. At that time, the principal stakeholders were governments, TNCs and trade unions. Today, one needs to add various vested interests, including practitioners of international investment law (i.e. the international investment arbitration profession), parliamentarians, and various non-governmental organizations. Important economic and political interests are at stake. Reaching consensus is also difficult, because new issues have arisen since the time of the United Nations Code negotiations, broadening the scope of negotiations and increasing the complexity of the subject matter on which agreement needs to be reached. These new issues range from such specific matters as abusive treaty shopping and whether state-owned enterprises need special rules; to the question of where the boundaries are of individual firms (especially in regard to supply chains) and the functioning of the ISDS mechanism; to such fundamental issues as to whether the purpose of the investment regime requires a reorientation toward sustainable international investment.[5] But, then, if a

[3] A prime example here is the process that led to the adoption of the "Guiding Principles for Business and Human Rights."

[4] See in this context the failed negotiations within the OECD of a Multilateral Agreement on Investment and the unsuccessful effort to deal with international investment in the WTO.

[5] Defined as FDI that makes a maximum contribution to the economic, social, and environmental developments of countries and takes place within mutually beneficial governance mechanisms (e.g. in the case of contracts) while being commercially viable. For an early effort to reorient international investment treaties toward sustainability, see the model treaty prepared by the International Institute on Sustainable Development: Howard Mann, Konrad von Moltke, Luke Eric Peterson, and Aaron Cosbey, *IISD Model International Agreement on Investment for Sustainable Development* (IISD, 2006), available at www.iisd.org/pdf/2005/investment_model_int_handbook.pdf. More recently,

comprehensive multilateral agreement is too difficult to achieve, a plurilateral or regional approach could be pursued, an approach in which a significant number of committed key players begin negotiations and invite others to join if and when they are ready to do so.

On the other hand, the rapid adoption of the OECD Guidelines, the ILO Tripartite Declaration, and the UNCTAD Restrictive Business Practices Set – all three negotiated in the shadow of the beginning United Nations Code effort – suggests that it may be easier to focus on specific aspects of the *problematique*, with a manageable agenda. This would involve negotiating issue-specific instruments, be they focused on treatment issues, guidelines, or any other aspect related to international investment. In such circumstances, a more limited range of interests is typically involved, and stakeholders may be more forceful and focused in moving the negotiations forward.[6] However, all the three instruments mentioned at the beginning of this paragraph are voluntary. Still, these three instruments represent the principal concrete legacy of the United Nations Code effort, apart, of course, from having brought the issue prominently and permanently on the international agenda and having helped to clarify many of the key issues involved.

The OECD, ILO, and UNCTAD instruments also show the importance of mutual self-interest, pressure that "something needs to be done" and political will. In the case of these three instruments, there was initially considerable pressure on governments and common self-interest (even if for different reasons) to take action, creating the political will to enter negotiations. Even then, however, there needs to be sufficient overlap of interest between key players in order to move the process forward and to a successful conclusion. However, as the United Nations Code negotiations showed (which also began under conditions of overlapping interest, pressure, and political will), it is difficult to maintain political will and overlapping interest over time, especially when circumstances change, pressure dissipates, and the general consensus about the overall objectives of the negotiations (guidelines and treatment) is fragile.

UNCTAD has pursued this issue through its Investment Policy Framework for Sustainable Development; see UNCTAD, *World Investment Report 2012: Towards a New Generation of Investment Policy* (Geneva: UNCTAD, 2012), ch. IV.

6 Specific issues addressed in the United Nations Code later became the subject of separate instruments; see, e.g. the *Guiding Principles on Business and Human Rights: Implementing the United Nations "Protect, Respect and Remedy Framework"* (United Nations Human Rights Office of the High Commissioner, 2011).

The iron needs to be struck while it is hot – which was done in the case of the instruments mentioned at the beginning of this paragraph.

Furthermore, even if an instrument is voluntary, its scope, content, implementation mechanism, and standing can be strengthened over time. This was the case for the OECD Guidelines, through the availability of a clarification mechanism, the strengthening of the implementation mechanism, the opening up of the implementation mechanism to other interested parties (especially, nongovernmental organizations), and the expansion of the topics covered. In the case of the ILO Declaration, an implementation mechanism was agreed upon after the original instrument was adopted and cross-references to new instruments negotiated in the framework of the ILO (e.g. on core labor standards) were added, expanding the reach of this particular instrument. (In the case of the UNCTAD Set, however, these possibilities were not utilized.) While this does not change the voluntary character of an instrument, it can make it more effective. Moreover, even voluntary instruments can be strengthened, for instance, by referring to them in binding international agreements. Finally, standards agreed to at the international level, even if voluntary, can become hard law in a national context, as happened, for example, with the Dodd Frank due diligence process provisions on conflict minerals in the United States,[7] which are based on the OECD voluntary due diligence instrument. This also suggests that, to whatever extent voluntary instruments exist, they should be used to the fullest extent possible.

The availability and strength of an implementation (or follow-up) mechanism becomes, therefore, crucial to making an instrument effective, as absent such a mechanism, a text alone risks becoming worthless. Follow-up can consist of a review of an instrument in regular intervals, as in the annual discussions of the ILO Tripartite Declaration and the review conferences of the UNCTAD Set that takes place every 5 years. The follow-up is stronger if a dedicated body has been established with the mandate to clarify issues that arise under the instrument, as was done in the case of the OECD and (although less effectively) in the cases of the ILO Tripartite Declaration. Moreover, an implementation mechanism can be upgraded over time, as in the case of the OECD Guidelines through the strengthening of the role of the National Contact Points. It was their implementation mechanisms, developed over time in the case

[7] *See* Dodd-Frank Wall Street Reform and Consumer Protection Act, Pub. L. 111–203, 124 Stat. 1376 (21 July 2010), Section 1502.

of the OECD Guidelines and the active work of the ILO and UNCTAD secretariats, that made these instruments relatively effective by establishing forums for discussion and creating institutional homes and self-interest on the part of the organizations involved, including to promote the use of the respective instruments.

A crucial ingredient making the voluntary OECD – and ILO – instruments relatively effective was that key constituencies, in these cases, particularly, trade unions, had access to the implementation mechanisms of both the organizations in order to present cases/issues that involved possible violations of what had been agreed upon. In the case of the ILO Tripartite Declaration, workers' representatives played the key role. In the case of the OECD Guidelines, the majority of cases/issues initially brought for clarification were tabled by trade unions. Moreover, eventually, nongovernmental organizations obtained access to the OECD's implementation mechanism and used this access fully. Nongovernmental organizations made these two instruments, and especially the OECD Guidelines, "living instruments." Hence, access by key stakeholders to the implementation mechanism of any voluntary instruments agreed upon is likely to help ensure the effectiveness of these instruments.

It appears appealing to seek to negotiate a binding comprehensive multilateral instrument that, in a balanced manner, addresses the rights and responsibilities of all the major stakeholders on all important issues related to international investment, contained in a rational structure. But, absent a catalytic event, a grand design of this nature may be a bridge too far in the foreseeable future. The more likely approach to succeed – already successfully pursued at the beginning of the United Nations Code negotiations – may be an issue-specific approach, a pragmatic approach to seek agreement on aspects of the regulatory framework governing TNCs and their activities for which there is shared self-interest, pressure, and political will, in whatever forum that is most promising. Progress could be sought both regarding the treatment and guidelines aspects of a comprehensive regulatory framework. Part of such an approach could also be to seek a "hardening" of soft law (i.e. voluntary) instruments; the OECD Guidelines are a case in point, covering, as they do, over four-fifths of the world's FDI stock. Even if the resulting instruments are not perfect, they provide a platform on which further agreement can be built, especially, if there is a strong implementation mechanism that also provides access to nongovernmental groups.

Such an approach can also benefit from what appears to be a somewhat cyclical nature of rulemaking regarding international investment, with the pendulum swinging sometimes in favor of one type of instrument and at other times in favor of another type. Thus, during the 1970s and at the beginning of the 1980s, the watchword was "control," while during the later 1980s and the 1990s, the watchwords were "liberalization" at the national level and "protection" at the international level. Since 2000, national policies have become more nuanced,[8] while international instruments consisting of guidelines have been strengthened and new ones have been added, and some international investment agreements have become more cautious while also aiming for more liberalization.

Rulemaking may, therefore, be haphazard, messy, and uneven, depending on what is needed and what is feasible in a given constellation of interests and forces. But, hopefully, an overall regime is put in place over time that, through the combination of various instruments, becomes a regime that covers, comprehensively and in a balanced manner, the various aspects of the relationship between the governments and TNCs.

The international investment regime is in constant flux, but its evolution does not follow a preordained trajectory.[9] It should be helpful that the positions of key stakeholders – host and home country governments – have become less confrontational today than they were when the United Nations Code negotiations took place, and when the debate was essentially along North–South lines. Most importantly, a great number of developing countries and economies in transition are today themselves outward investors, and a number of them are among the most important home countries. As a result, especially the biggest among them define their own position in international investment agreements no longer solely (or primarily) as host countries interested in preserving their policy space, but increasingly also as home countries seeking to protect the investments of their firms abroad. Conversely, developed countries have "discovered" that they are important host countries – including for investments from emerging markets – and, in that position, seek to protect their policy space.

[8] This is reflected in the number of national policy changes related to foreign direct investment that make the regulatory framework less welcoming for such investment, as reflected, e.g. in the creation of screening mechanisms for national security purposes.

[9] On the evolution of the regime, *see* Jose E. Alvarez and Karl P. Sauvant, with Kamil Gerard Ahmed and Gabriela P. Vizcaino (eds.), *The Evolving International Investment Regime: Expectations, Realities, Options* (Oxford: OUP, 2011).

Still, the basic challenges that the United Nations Code negotiators faced remain. They include bridging the basic interests of key stakeholders, reconciling the application of national and international investment law governing foreign investment, finding the right balance between the rights and responsibilities of investors and governments, and having a dispute-settlement mechanism that is acceptable to all. Added to that is the challenge to make the international investment regime supportive of sustainable development, the world's most important economic policy challenge for the years ahead.

Improving the regime requires great effort, a considerable amount of time, and even more patience. Above all, improvements in the international investment regime need to be in the interest of governments, both in their capacity as home and host countries, and other key stakeholders, to give it the legitimacy and robustness that every international regime requires to be viable in the long run. While Professor Sornarajah's first choice may not be to have an international investment regime in the first place, such considerations might well find favor with him as a basis for improving the current regime. The experience gained during, and the lessons learned from, the negotiations of the United Nations Code and related instruments should be of help in reaching this objective.

PART III

8

India and investment protection

ANIRUDDHA RAJPUT

Introduction

Professor Sornarajah has keenly observed and commented upon the economic rise of India and China and its consequences for the regime of international investment law.[1] He has commented vividly upon the regime of international investment law, the attitude toward foreign investment, local conditions, and the rule of law in these countries.[2] Through a comparative analysis of the legal protection of foreign investment in these countries, he has highlighted the similarities and differences between these two regimes. Projecting the similarities, Professor Sornarajah considers that both countries have adopted inconsistent stands at the global, bilateral, and domestic levels. At the global level, they have consistently resisted formulation of rules promoting liberalization and the protection of foreign investors. At the World Trade Organization (WTO), they have ensured that the talks on including investment protection in a multilateral instrument do not continue and have even succeeded in removing the topic from the agenda for further discussions in the future. In contrast, at the bilateral level they have not shunned from entering into investment treaties and free trade agreements with investment protection chapters.[3] Their unwillingness to negotiate investment protection at the multilateral level obliterates the prospects of a multilateral framework for investment protection. The major difference between the two countries is the manner in which they have regulated the regime and the extent to which they have obtained optimum benefit for their domestic economies. India has always exercised

[1] M. Sornarajah and Jiangyu Wang (eds.), *China, India and the International Economic Order* (Cambridge: Cambridge University Press, 2010).
[2] M. Sornarajah, "India, China and Foreign Investment," in M. Sornarajah and Jiangyu Wang (eds.), *China, India and the International Economic Order* (Cambridge: CUP, 2010).
[3] Ibid., 133–134.

control over the conditions of entry. These conditions are sector specific and, over time, have been liberalized to a certain degree. Some sectors need permission, whereas in others, direct investment is possible.[4] China has adopted a far more liberal approach, as compared to the cautious approach of India.[5] China adapted its policies successfully to achieve the maximum benefit from the regime. Initially, the dispute resolution clauses were limited to questions of compensation and did not cover breach of substantive standards. This allowed extensive inflow of investment without the threat of investment claims. Once China became a capital-exporting state, it altered the treaty clauses allowing investors to sue the host state for violations of investment treatment standards. However, India, on the other hand, failed to adopt such proactive policies and was, therefore, left behind in the race for foreign investment.

In the early phases after independence, India adopted a skeptical approach toward foreign investment. This was a caution dictated by the experiences of its colonial past. In the first phase, the emphasis of the Indian economy was on self-reliance. The Government adopted a policy of import substitution rather than export promotion.[6] A more liberalized attitude toward foreign investment was a forced choice. In the early 1990s, India suffered a severe balance of payment crisis. In response, a spate of economic reforms were introduced in 1991. The Bilateral Investment Treaty (BIT) program was commenced in 1994. In the early stages, India's experience with investor-state dispute resolution was scant. The only experience was a claim filed by Dabhol Power Company under the India–Mauritius BIT. The claimant had challenged the decision of the Government to cancel the power project and an antisuit injunction issued by Indian courts stalling the commercial arbitration initiated by the claimant. The dispute was eventually settled.[7] India lost its first investment arbitration in *White Industries* v. *Republic of India*, a case brought by an Australian investor.[8] There are approximately eight investment claims pending in various stages against India

[4] Ibid., 142–143. [5] Ibid., 143.

[6] Jagdish Bhagwati, "The Design of Indian Development," in Isher Judge *et al.*, *India's Economic Reforms and Development: Essays for Manmohan Singh*, 2nd ed. (New Delhi: OUP, 2012), 30–32.

[7] *The Tribune*, "GE Settles Dabhol Issue" (3 July 2005), www.tribuneindia.com/2005/20050703/biz.htm#1 (accessed 7 April 2015).

[8] *White Industries Australia Limited* v. *The Republic of India*, Final Award (30 November 2011).

currently.[9] These developments have generated interest in the subject of investor protection in India. The objective of this chapter is to study the regime of investment protection in India as reflected in the legal framework for entering the jurisdiction and the two levels of investment protection: the international level as found in India's investment treaties and the domestic level under municipal law. The rights granted under municipal law are larger in scope and are based on constitutional principles. The expediency and transparency of these proceedings is one plausible reason why investors may not have preferred the route of investment claims over domestic dispute resolution mechanisms. A study of India's investment protection regime shows that the standard of protection in municipal law is higher than the standard under India's investment treaties. This is a result of a vibrant judiciary and extensive protection under India's constitutional law jurisprudence.

This chapter is divided into seven sections. This brief section constitutes the Introduction. "Foreign investment and India" discusses the current trends in foreign investment and the rising role of India as a capital-importing and a capital-exporting country. The next section, "Legal framework for foreign investment", presents the legal regime for foreign investment, contained in the Foreign Direct Investment (FDI) Policy. The section titled "Protection under international law" discusses the protection of foreign investment under the regime of investment treaties. "Protection under municipal law" elaborates on the protection of foreign investment under municipal law. The penultimate section discusses "Recent developments", and the final section is the Conclusion to this chapter.

Foreign investment and India

The size of the inflow and outflow of investments plays a major role in shaping the investment policy of a country. It is, therefore, necessary to look at the magnitude of the investment received and exported from India.

India experienced significant investment inflows immediately after liberalization. Thereafter, the inflow of investments slowed. Investment inflow has continued to fluctuate over time; but overall, the flow has been on the rise in the last decade. The inflow was low prior to 2006 but dramatically increased thereafter. In 2000–2001, India received US $4

[9] Prabhash Ranjan, "India and Bilateral Investment Treaties – A Changing Landscape" (2014) 29 *ICSID Review-FILJ* 419, 443.

billion in foreign investment. This increased to US $9 billion in 2005–2006. In 2006–2007, it jumped to US $22.8 billion. India received the highest levels of total foreign investment during 2008–2009 and 2011–2012, with US $41.9 billion and US $46.6 billion, respectively.[10] India was ranked 14th on the list of recipients of foreign investments by the UNCTAD World Investment Report, 2014.[11] During 2012–2013, the overall inflow of capital into South East Asia had risen by 10 percent and is currently US $36 billion. The largest recipient of FDI in the subregion is India. The increase was 17 percent, and the FDI inflows stand at US $28 billion.[12] Globally, India has been the third most preferred investment destination since 2010.[13] It is expected that the inflow of capital will substantially rise in response to various measures adopted by the Government. As per the figures issued by the Ministry of Commerce of India, the FDI into India, estimated as the sum total of equity inflows, reinvested earnings, and other capital, was US $46,556 million in 2011–2012 and was US $34,298 million in 2012–2013. In 2013–2014, the figure stands at US $28,807 million for the period from April to January.[14] The total amount of FDI Inflow in India from April 2000 to December 2014 was US $355,415 million.[15]

Lately, there has been a slump in the inflow of capital. As an effort to attract foreign investment in the services sector, 100 percent FDI was permitted in the multibrand retail sector. However, this failed to attract adequate investments, mostly owing to macroeconomic problems.[16] As the fiscal stability of the economy is returning to normalcy, with a reduction in inflation and a promise to keep the fiscal deficit low, the inflow of investment is expected to rise. The new Government has introduced various measures in that direction.[17] The Prime Minister

[10] *RBI Bulletin*, February 2014.

[11] UNCTAD, World Investment Report, 2014, 4, http://unctad.org/en/PublicationsLibrary/wir2014_en.pdf (accessed 7 April 2015).

[12] Ibid., xx.

[13] Foreign Investment Promotion Board, Review 2011–2013 (Department of Economic Affairs, New Delhi), para. 2.6, www.fipb.gov.in/Forms/FIPBREVIEW2011-13.pdf (accessed 7 April 2015).

[14] Ibid., para. 1.1.

[15] Fact Sheet on Foreign Investment issued by the Ministry of Commerce, http://dipp.nic.in/English/Publications/FDI_Statistics/2014/india_FDI_December2014.pdf (accessed 7 April 2015).

[16] UNCTAD, World Investment Report, 2014, 56, available at: http://unctad.org/en/PublicationsLibrary/wir2014_en.pdf (accessed 7 April 2015).

[17] A dedicated website is created for inviting foreign investors (www.investindia.gov.in), and country-specific desk is created, especially keeping Asian countries and potential

has announced the "Make in India" campaign with the objective of converting India into a manufacturing hub. The Make in India campaign is a national program designed to facilitate foreign investment, foster innovation, and promote the development of skills. It promises to grant adequate protection to intellectual property rights.[18] These measures are aimed at presenting an investor-friendly image of the Government of India.[19]

With fluctuating but rapid gross domestic product (GDP) growth in the last decade, it is obvious that India has partially transformed itself into a capital-exporting state. Various measures have been taken by the Government and the central bank, the Reserve Bank of India (RBI), to sustain this trend.[20] Outward investment by Indian companies is on the rise, especially in the oil, gas, and natural resources sectors. Many manufacturing and service sector companies have acquired foreign companies through mergers and acquisitions.[21] Initially, the manufacturing sector was an important sector for the outflow of investments; but now, other sectors such as finance, insurance, real estate and business services, wholesale and retail trade, and restaurants and hotels have seen greater outflows.[22]

There are no verifiable data from the Government of India on the exact amount of investment outflows. According to UNCTAD, the outflow of

substantial investors in mind (http://dipp.nic.in/English/Investor/Foriegn_Desk.aspx). The FDI Policy of India has revised the extent to which investments can be made in various sectors in India; 100 percent investment is now allowed in defense.

18 The Make in India campaign is described on its website as: "A major new national programme. Designed to facilitate investment. Foster innovation. Enhance skill development. Protect Intellectual Property. And Build Best-in-Class Manufacturing Infrastructure. There's never been a better time to make in India." For the range of industries targeted, see www.makeinindia.com.

19 For example, the Government decided not to challenge a ruling to the higher court of appeal in a tax against Vodafone. *India Today*, "Govt Not to Challenge Bombay HC Rulings in Vodafone, Other Cases" (28 January 2015); http://indiatoday.intoday.in/story/govt-not-to-challenge-bombay-hc-rulings-in-vodafone-other-cases/1/415827.html (accessed 7 April 2015).

20 Harun Khan, "Outward Indian FDI – Recent Trends & Emerging Issues" http://rbi.org.in/scripts/BS_SpeechesView.aspx?Id=674 (accessed 7 April 2015).

21 For an analysis of this growth and the reasons for this trend, see Chaitra R. Beerannavar, "Indian Outward FDI: An Analysis" available at: http://ssrn.com/abstract=2268444 (accessed 7 April 2015); Premila Nazareth Satyanand and Pramila Raghavendran, "Outward FDI from India and Its Policy Context," *Columbia FDI Profiles*, http://academiccommons.columbia.edu/catalog/ac%3A128868 (accessed 7 April 2015).

22 Export Import Bank of India, "Outward Direct Investment from India: Trends, Objectives and Policy Perspectives," Occasional Paper No. 165, 15.

capital was between US $1 billion and US $9.9 billion in 2014.[23] The rising outflow was stunted owing to macroeconomic problems that have existed for the last few years. The ability of Indian investors to invest abroad has been reduced severely. In 2013, it dropped acutely to a mere US $1.7 billion.[24]

The Government is proposing policy interventions to reinvigorate the trend of outflow of investments. The RBI has issued certain guidelines relaxing the severe restrictions on investing abroad.[25] The Government is planning to acquire overseas assets.[26] As a holder of these overseas assets, the Indian Government becomes an investor and could raise investment claims in the future. There would be challenges as to whether these investments are "qualified investments" by "qualified investors" as per the definition of investors and investment in BITs. Professor Sornarajah has argued that the question of such sovereign wealth funds controlled by entities that are themselves under government control ought to be treated on par with multinational companies and granted protection under investment treaties.[27]

This shifting position, from predominantly a capital-importing country to a capital-exporting country, is bound to influence the approach and policy towards investor protection. It is suggested that as a policy tool the investment treaties of India ought to be aligned to give due consideration to inward and outward investment flows.[28] The difficult challenge is to protect investments made by Indian companies abroad and, simultaneously, ensure that the investment standards in investment treaties are not such that they excessively intrude into India's regulatory freedom. It is highly unlikely that India will return to the period of fervent nationalization that existed in the 1970s, but its concern would be to protect its regulatory space as it has always given due importance to reforms in the social sectors.[29] These could be the factors due to which the Indian Government has recently amended its Model BIT.[30]

[23] See note 11, 52. [24] Ibid., 53.

[25] For details see www.rbi.org.in/commonman/english/scripts/FAQs.aspx?Id=18 (accessed 7 April 2015).

[26] Indian in Business, Ministry of External Affairs, the Government to scout for overseas asset acquisition to reduce energy bills, http://indiainbusiness.nic.in/newdesign/index.php?param=newsdetail/11675(accessed 7 April 2015).

[27] M. Sornarajah, "Sovereign Wealth Funds and the Existing Structure of the Regulation of Investments" (2011) 1 *Asian Journal of International Law* 267, 272–273.

[28] See note 22, 22. [29] For example National Food Security Act, 2013.

[30] Available at: https://mygov.in/sites/default/files/master_image/Model%20Text%20for%20the%20Indian%20Bilateral%20Investment%20Treaty.pdf (accessed 7 April 2015).

Legal framework for foreign investment

An analysis of India's legal framework is necessary as it sets the contours for the entry and exercise of foreign investment. Professor Sornarajah has criticized the tendency to wrongly attribute the adoption of neoliberal policies for the success of the Asian economies. He has emphasized that Asian states have always controlled the inflow of investments and exercised regulatory control and governmental intervention in the entry and operation of foreign investments. The perception of liberalization is only in theory; as in practice, foreign investment has always been subject to control by the states. These controls are aimed at achieving economic goals.[31] The Indian investment treaties are noncommittal when it comes to liberalization. They protect investments only at the postestablishment stage.[32]

The Government of India, in the FDI Policy, announces the conditions of entry for foreign investment. This Policy imposes rigorous rules on the sectors, extent, manner, and the available vehicles for investing in India. The objective of the Policy is: "to attract and promote foreign direct investment in order to supplement domestic capital, technology and skills, for accelerated economic growth."[33] The Policy clearly states the central objective of "economic growth." Indian companies can receive foreign investment either directly or indirectly. An investment is direct if the investment is received directly by a resident entity, whereas if a resident Indian entity receives foreign investment from another resident entity that in turn already possesses a foreign investment, it is treated as an indirect foreign investment.[34] In all circumstances, the foreign investment has to be received by a resident Indian entity. The Policy insists that the investments must be through the form of equity in the Indian companies. This has been a popular route among developing states for receiving foreign investments.[35]

India follows a pattern of governmental control by permitting foreign investors to enter India but subject to conditions. The FDI Policy

[31] M. Sornarajah, "Review of Asian Views on Foreign Investment Law," in Vivienne Bath and Luka Nottage (eds.), *Foreign Investment and Dispute Resolution Law and Practice in Asia* (Oxford: Routledge, 2011), 243.

[32] See note 2, 145.

[33] Department of Industrial Policy and Promotion, "Consolidated FDI Policy," 17 April 2014, http://dipp.nic.in/English/Policies/FDI_Circular_2014.pdf (accessed 7 April 2015), para. 1.1.1.

[34] Ibid., para. 4.1.1.

[35] See generally M. Sornarajah, *Law of International Joint Ventures* (Singapore: Longman Singapore, 1992); See note 41, 116–118.

stipulates the sectors in which foreign investment can be made. It also imposes restrictions as to the extent to which foreign investors can hold a share in the Indian company. This restriction is called the "cap" on investment. Except for the sectors specifically mentioned, investment in any other section is not permitted. The permissible sectors and the permissible limit are specified in FDI Policy.[36] Furthermore, like China, India has resisted the imposition of restrictions on performance requirements in investment treaties, whereby conditions are imposed such as requirements to use local material and labor, locate industries in certain specified areas, and export certain percentages of production.[37] Certain conditions are imposed on foreign investments, such as a minimum capitalization requirement and a lock-in period.[38] These are intended to ensure that the investments serve the purpose of achieving economic development.

The foreign investment may be through the following instruments: "equity shares/fully, compulsorily and mandatorily convertible debentures/fully, compulsorily and mandatorily convertible preference shares of an Indian company."[39] Professor Sornarajah has expressed skepticism toward portfolio investment being treated as a qualified investment for protection under investment treaties.[40] These are unstable investments and may be withdrawn at any time.[41] The FDI Policy distinguishes portfolio investments from foreign investment for the purposes of coverage under the FDI Policy for protection. It mandates that the foreign investor should establish a "lasting interest" in an enterprise in India.[42]

The FDI Policy also specifies the permissible vehicles for receiving investments. These are investments in an Indian company, partnership firm or proprietary concern, venture capital fund, trusts, and LLPs.[43] Investment in any other form is not permitted.[44]

Foreign investment can be made through the automatic route or the government route. Under the automatic route, prior approval of the government is not required; but under the government route, prior approval is required.[45] If investment is made in the permitted sectors within the cap, the investment can be made through the automatic route,

[36] See note 33, para. 3.7.1. [37] See note 2, 150–151. [38] See note 33, para. 3.8.
[39] Ibid., 2014, para. 3.61.
[40] M. Sornarajah, "Portfolio Investments and the Definition of Investment" (2009) 24 *ICSID Review-FILJ* 516, 518–520.
[41] M. Sornarajah, *International Law on Foreign Investment*, 3rd ed. (Cambridge: CUP, 2010), 314.
[42] See note 33, para. 1.1.1. [43] Ibid., para. 3.2. [44] Ibid., para. 3.2.6. [45] Ibid.

that is, directly into the company.[46] It is mandatory to notify the RBI's regional office within 30 days from the receipt of foreign capital.[47] For the government route, a foreign investor can invest in an Indian company only with the prior approval of the Central Government.[48] There are three agencies of the Government involved in the approval process: the Foreign Investment Promotion Board (FIPB); the Finance Minister heading the Finance Ministry; and the Cabinet Committee on Economic Affairs (CCEA). The FIPB does background preparation on the proposals for foreign investment and makes recommendations. The Finance Minister or the CCEA, depending on the value of the transaction, takes the decision to approve the foreign investment. According to the existing rules, if the total foreign equity flow is Rs. 1,200 crores (approximately US $191 million) or less, the decision is taken by the Finance Minister after considering the recommendations of the FIPB.[49] For foreign equity inflow of more than Rs. 1,200 crores, the approval of the CCEA is required.[50] The financial limit might undergo change but the role of government in granting approval has not undergone major changes. Currently, there is a proposal to increase the threshold to 3,000 crores (approximately US $477 million).[51] Fresh approvals are not required if additional foreign investment is brought into entities, which have already been granted permission where the cap on investment is increased, the investment is within the limit of the cap, the sector has been converted into one in which the automatic route applies, or where prior approval of the Government or FIPB is not required for any other reason.[52] According to the survey of 2011–2013, almost 70 percent of the FDI has come through the automatic route, whereas 30 percent has come from the government approval route.[53] India was the world's thirteenth largest FDI host country in 2009. There are certain sectors of national and strategic importance, such as defense production, air transport services, ground handling services, asset reconstruction companies, private sector banking, broadcasting, commodity exchanges, credit information companies, insurance, print media, telecommunications, and

[46] Ibid., para. 3.7.1. For details of sector-wide caps see Chapter 6 of the FDI Policy. The sectors and the caps keep changing depending on needs of sectors and the priority of the Government.

[47] Ibid., para. 7.2.1. [48] Ibid., para. 2.1.17. [49] Ibid., para. 5.2.1. [50] Ibid., para. 5.2.2.

[51] *The Economic Times*, "DIPP Floats Draft Cabinet Note to Raise FDI Threshold to Rs. 3000 crores from Rs. 1200 crores," available at: http://economictimes.indiatimes.com/news/economy/finance/dipp-floats-draft-cabinet-note-to-raise-fdi-threshold-to-rs-3000-crore-from-rs-1200-crore/articleshow/46577157.cms (accessed 7 April 2015).

[52] See note 33, para. 5.3. [53] See note 13, para. 1.3.

satellites, which require government approval irrespective of the cap conditions. If the Indian company established with foreign investment is not owned or controlled by a resident entity or if the control of the existing Indian company currently owned by an Indian resident will be transferred to a nonresident entity as a consequence of a share transfer or fresh issue of shares, through amalgamation, or if merger/demerger, acquisition, and so on, takes place, then again, the permission of the government is required.[54]

In addition to the aforementioned requirements, it is mandatory that every Indian company receiving foreign investment must notify the concerned regulatory authorities, especially the RBI and Securities and Exchange Board of India (SEBI) (the regulator of the securities market).[55] The RBI and SEBI perform a dominant role in the setting-up and operation of a foreign investor by issuing various circulars from time to time. This facilitates monitoring of the amount of foreign investment that enters the economy. It also earmarks and distinguishes foreign investment from domestic investment. In addition to the FDI Policy, the RBI Act, SEBI Act, and Foreign Exchange Management Act (FEMA) regulate the entry and operation of foreign investments. Prior to the liberalization of 1991, the central bank's US dollar holdings was insignificant due to the lack of exports. This resulted in balance of payment issues. This was addressed through strict controls on the possession of foreign currency by private entities through the Foreign Exchange Regulation Act (FERA). As the inflow of capital into India started, it became necessary to loosen the restrictions on free movement of foreign currency. This was achieved by replacing the FERA with FEMA. Dealings in foreign currency are monitored and regulated by the RBI, while activities in the securities exchange are within the domain of SEBI. In addition to the legal provisions stated earlier, "the investment/investors are required to comply with all relevant sectoral laws, regulations, rules, security conditions, and state/local laws/regulations."[56]

The nationality of the investment is decided by the test of "residence." Only "nonresident" entities are permitted to invest in India.[57] The FDI Policy uses "nonresident company" to define foreign investors rather than the definition of nationality in the BITs. It defines foreign direct investment as "investment by non-resident entity/person resident outside India in the capital of an Indian company . . . ."[58] The term

[54] See note 33, para. 3.6.2. [55] Ibid., para. 7.2. [56] Ibid., 2014, para. 3.9.1.
[57] Ibid., para. 3.1. [58] Ibid., para. 2.1.11.

nonresident is not defined in the FDI Policy. It is defined in the FEMA instead.[59] That definition is negative, as it simply declares that a non-resident is a person who is not a resident in India.[60] Thereafter, the definition of a resident is provided. For individuals, a resident is a person who has spent more than 182 days in India during the course of the preceding financial year. In the case of incorporated bodies, a resident is: "any person or body corporate registered or incorporated in India" or "an office, branch or agency in India owned or controlled by a person resident outside India," or "an office, branch or agency outside India owned or controlled by a person resident in India."[61] The FDI Policy determines the nationality of an entity on the basis of actual control. This is also called the *siège social*, whereby the actual place of operation is used to decide nationality. It does not accept the place of incorporation as the appropriate test for determining the nationality of the entity. The BITs adopt the place of incorporation to determine nationality.[62] The FDI Policy deviates from the BITs to this extent. The interrelationship between the two is important, and the question is which shall prevail in the event of conflict. One view would be that, in case of conflict, the BIT would prevail over the FDI Policy, which is an internal law. In light of the ILC Draft Articles on State Responsibility, noncompliance with a treaty cannot be justified by referring to internal law.[63] This is a superficial interpretation. A nuanced approach suggests that the stage of operation of the FDI Policy and a BIT are different. The violation of conditions under the BIT would not arise until the conditions of FDI Policy are satisfied. The FDI Policy contains the conditions of entry and operation of foreign investment in India. BITs entered into by India specify that protection would be available for investments made in accordance with local laws and regulations.[64] The Policy declares that noncompliance with its conditions will result in penal consequences.[65] If a foreign investor fails to comply with these requirements, an investment claim may fail due to

[59] FDI Policy declares that relevant statutory provisions continue to apply. Ibid., para. 1.1.8.

[60] Article 2 (w), FEMA, 1999. [61] Article 2 (v), FEMA, 1999.

[62] Article 1(1)(b)(ii), India–Mauritius BIT, entered: 4 September 1998; came into effect: 20 June 2000.

[63] Article 3 and 32, Responsibility of States for Internationally Wrongful Acts 2001; Article 27, Vienna Convention on the Law of Treaties, 1969.

[64] Article 11, India–UK BIT entered on: 14 March 1994; came into effect: 6 January 1995; Article 10, India–Malaysia BIT entered: 3 August 1995; came into effect: 12 April 1997; http://finmin.nic.in/bipa/bipa_index.asp; accesses 7 April 2015. Most of the BITs entered into by India contain this clause.

[65] See note 33, para. 7.3.

illegality. In *Yaung Chi Oo Trading Corporation* v. *Myanmar*, the tribunal held that investments not made in accordance with the entry laws are illegal investments and, thus, not entitled to protection.[66] Even if the requirement of entry and operation of investments according to the laws of the host state is not mentioned in the BIT, it is always deemed to exist.[67] Noncompliance with mandatory conditions in the FDI Policy will result in illegality.[68]

As discussed earlier, Indian BITs follow the common law method of determining the nationality of an entity on the basis of its place of incorporation. This is exposed to the possibility of restructuring to secure benefits under a preferred treaty.[69] Often mailbox or shell companies are formed with nominal existence in a state where the investment treaty has the most convenient provisions. Professor Sornarajah has criticized the misuse of restructuring and round-tripping because it contravenes the obligation of good faith.[70] This misuse is undertaken for two purposes: forum shopping and round-tripping. The FDI Policy successfully addresses both these issues.

Forum shopping

A recurring problem in investment arbitration is the restructuring of companies to secure benefits under convenient investment treaties. Investment tribunals have held that restructuring companies with the objective of gaining the benefit of a liberal treaty is not barred in itself, as the determination of a company's nationality is based on the place of incorporation. However, if a company is restructured with a potential

[66] *Yuang Chi Oo Trading Pre Ltd* v. *Government of the Union of Myanmar*, Award, 31 March 2003 (2003) 42 ILM 540, paras. 59–63; *Philippe Gruslin* v. *Malaysia*, ICSID Case No. ARB/99/3, Award on Jurisdiction, 27 November 2000, paras. 25.5–25.7.

[67] *Plama Consortium Limited* v. *Bulgaria*, ICSID Case No. ARB/03/24, Award, 27 August 2008, para. 138; *Phoenix Action, Ltd.* v. *Czech Republic*, ICSID Case No. ARB/06/5, Award, 15 April 2009, para. 101.

[68] Ursula Kriebum, "Investment Arbitration – Illegal Investments," in Christian Klausegger *et al.* (eds.), *Austrian Yearbook on International Arbitration 2010* (Vienna: Manz'sche Verlags- und Universitätsbuchhandlung, 2010), 310; Stephan Schill, "Illegal Investments in Investment Treaty Arbitration" (2012) 11 *The Law & Practice of International Courts and Tribunals* 281, 309.

[69] Stephan Schill, *The Multilateralization of International Investment Law* (Cambridge: CUP, 2009), 197–240.

[70] M. Sornarajah, "Good Faith, Corporate Nationality, and Denial of Benefits," in Andrew D. Mitchell *et al.* (eds.), *Good Faith and International Economic Law* (Oxford: OUP, 2015), 117.

investment claim in mind, it would be a misuse of the provisions of a treaty.[71] According to Professor Sornarajah, allowing forum shopping defeats the object and purpose of investment treaties, that is, the "promotion of economic development of the states making the treaties."[72] The FDI Policy is close to reflecting Sornarajah's position. Its provisions ensure that the company through which foreign investment is routed is not merely a vehicle for investment. The FDI Policy stipulates that if an Indian resident company is incorporated only for the purpose of investment, then notwithstanding the contents of the FDI Policy prior approval of the Government will be required.[73] If indirect investment is made by a company into another, then it is called "downstream investment."[74] Foreign investment into an Indian company that is only a means of investing in another Indian company always requires prior approval of the Government and the FIPB, irrespective of the sector and the cap.[75] Purely financial companies are further expected to comply with the RBI regulations.[76] Furthermore, if foreign investment is to be made in an Indian company that does not have any assets or any downstream investments, approval of the Government is required irrespective of the sector and extent of investment. In addition, as and when such a company commences business or makes downstream investments, it will have to comply with sectoral requirements and caps on investments.[77] These provisions play an important role in determining the source of investment. As discussed, the FDI Policy stipulates that if an Indian resident company is incorporated only for the purpose of investment then notwithstanding the contents of the Policy prior approval of the Government will still be required.[78] This gives an opportunity to the Government at the stage of allowing entry and thereafter to ensure that the corporate vehicle is not intended to misuse the investment treaties.

Round-tripping

Round-tripping is a mechanism used by nationals of a state to create corporate structures to sue their own states. In *Tokios Tokelés*, the

[71] *Autopista Concesionada de Venezuela, C.A.* v. *Bolivarian Republic of Venezuela*, ICSID Case No. ARB/00/5, Decision on Jurisdiction, 27 September 2001, para. 126.

[72] See note 41, 327–328. [73] See note 33, para. 3.6.1. [74] Ibid., para. 3.10.2 (i).

[75] Ibid., para. 3.10.3.1.

[76] Ibid., 2014, para. 3.10.3.2. "Those companies, which are Core Investment Companies (CICs), will have to additionally follow RBI's Regulatory Framework for CICs."

[77] Ibid., para. 3.10.3.3. [78] Ibid., para. 3.6.1.

majority of the tribunal upheld such a transaction. In that case, 99 percent of the shares were owned, and two-thirds of the management was composed of Ukrainian nationals.[79] They incorporated a company in Lithuania and sued Ukraine under the Ukraine–Lithuania BIT. The majority took the view that actual control and ownership of the company is irrelevant. The only pertinent criterion is the place of incorporation as per the definition in the BIT.[80] The President of the Tribunal wrote a strong dissent, expressing the view that such an interpretation conflicts with the object and purpose of the ICSID Convention.[81] The Convention aims to resolve disputes between nationals of one party against the actions of another state.[82] Although India is not a party to ICSID, the underlying principle continues to apply. BITs are entered into to attract investments from another state. If nationals of the host state use restructuring to sue their own state, then it is an abuse of rights. The FDI Policy is an important tool to ensure that Indian nationals do not use corporate vehicles to invest in India and claim protection. It does not consider an investment by a company controlled by Indians to be a foreign investment.[83]

Protection under international law

India's BIT program is called the Bilateral Investment Promotion and Protection Agreements (BIPA) program. Since entering into India's first BIT with the United Kingdom in 1994, India now has BITs or FTAs with investment chapters with about 86 countries, 73 of which have come into force. From this, 69 are BITs and 4 are FTAs with investment chapters.[84] The BIPA program has been consistent, except for the shock suffered after India lost its first case against an Australian investor. The Government initially put further negotiations on hold, but now with

[79] *Tokios Tokelés* v. *Ukraine*, Decision on Jurisdiction, ICSID Case No. ARB/02/18, 29 April 2004, para. 21.

[80] Ibid., para. 30.

[81] Convention on Settlement of Disputes Between States and Nationals of Other States; https://icsid.worldbank.org/ICSID/StaticFiles/basicdoc/partA.htm (accessed 7 April 2015).

[82] Dissenting Opinion of Professor Prosper Weil, President, in *Tokios Tokelés* v. *Ukraine*, para. 1 (see note 79).

[83] See note 33, para. 4.1.3.

[84] A complete list with the text of treaties is available at Government of India, Ministry of Finance, Bilateral Investment and Promotion Agreement (BIPA) http://finmin.nic.in/bipa/bipa_index.asp?pageid=2 (accessed 7 April 2015).

a new Government, which is keen on foreign investment, the process has continued. Despite being a capital-importing country, most of the investment treaties entered into by India contain "capital-exporting" country features. The investment treaties contain fairly broad and vague treatment standards, except a liberal right of establishment. Exceptions and justifications are absent from most of these treaties. This is an outcome of the effect of the first BIT India entered into with the United Kingdom.[85]

The definition of "investment" in a BIT plays an important role in determining the jurisdiction of the tribunal. The definition of "investment" in India's BITs is broad and inclusive and contains a nonexhaustive lists of assets including direct and indirect investments, intellectual property rights, rights to money or to any performance under a contract having a financial value, and business concessions conferred under law or contract.[86] The open-ended texture of this definition makes it easy for tribunals to assert jurisdiction. In *White Industries*, the claimant argued that the right to receive money by enforcing a commercial arbitration award is an investment. The tribunal upheld the argument and held that since the definition of investment includes rights arising out of contract[87] and claims of money, the amounts receivable under the commercial arbitration award fall within the purview of the definition of investment.[88] The BITs do not provide any additional objective criteria for determining the notion of investment. The famous *Salini* test states that, in addition to the categories of investment included in the definition, additional objective criteria must be satisfied. These involve the contribution of the investor, duration, existence of operational risk, and contribution to the host state's development.[89] The tribunal in *White Industries* declined to extend this test as it took the view that the test is limited only to ICSID cases and India is not a party to the ICSID Convention.[90]

Most of the treaties contain an open-ended fair and equitable (FET) clause.[91] Tribunals have interpreted the FET clause broadly and exercised

[85] See note 9, 429–430.

[86] Article 1(b), India–Germany BIT, entered on: 10 July 1995; came into effect: 13 July 1998; Article 1(b), India–Vietnam BIT, entered on: 8 March 1997, came into effect 1 December 1999.

[87] See note 8, para. 7.4.7. [88] Ibid., para. 7.6.10.

[89] *Salini Construction SPA* v. *Kingdom of Morocco*, Decision on Jurisdiction, ICSID Case No. ARB/00/4 (23 July 2001), para. 52.

[90] See note 8, para. 7.4.9. See contra *Romak SA* v. *The Republic of Uzbekistan*, Award, PCA Case No. AA280 (26 November 2009), para. 207.

[91] Article 3.3, India-UK BIT.

powers of judicial review of governmental measures.[92] Even in situations where FET is tied to the international minimum standard (IMS), tribunals have taken the view that the IMS is also an evolving standard and have used it as a tool to review regulatory exercises by a state.[93] The lack of clarity on the content of the FET standard poses challenges to the Government's regulatory freedom and the actions of the judiciary. Likewise, the content of provisions guaranteeing full protection and security (FPS) is not clarified. These provisions are amenable to broad interpretations. Some tribunals have taken the view that FPS not only represents physical safety but also includes the obligation to maintain a stable legal environment.[94] The expropriation clauses include both direct and indirect expropriations.[95] The indirect expropriation clause includes effects "equivalent" to expropriation. There is a possibility that indirect expropriation could be interpreted according to the effect, ignoring the nature of the measure.[96] Consequently, a legitimate regulatory measure would be treated to amount to indirect expropriation if it causes substantial deprivation of property interests. The investment treaties contain an exceptions clause covering only emergency measures. They do not specify exceptions in the form of measures undertaken for the protection of the environment. Some treaties do not contain any exception clause.[97] All the treaties uniformly contain provision for repatriation without restrictions.[98] The national treatment and MFN clauses are defined in broad terms with sector-specific exceptions in limited circumstances.[99] All investment treaties contain a mandatory arbitration clauses.

In situations where investment treaties do not exist, the route of diplomatic protection remains. This route is crucial in India's case since it has entered into the compulsory jurisdiction of the

[92] UNCTAD, *Fair and Equitable Treatment: UNCTAD Series on Issues in International Investment Agreements II* (New York: United Nations, 2012), 61–88.

[93] *Mondev International Ltd* v. *United States of America*, ICSID Case No. ARB(AF)/99/2, Award (11 October 2002), para. 116; *Técnicas Medioambientales Tecmed, SA* v. *United Mexican States*, ICSID Case No. ARB(AF)/00/2, Award (29 May 2003), para. 153.

[94] *Compañiá de Aguas del Aconquija S.A. and Vivendi Universal* v. *Argentine Republic*, ICSID Case No. ARB/97/3, Award of 20 August 2007, paras. 7.4.13–7.4.17.

[95] Article 5, India–Germany BIT, see note 86.

[96] Ben Mostafa, "The Sole Effects Doctrine, Police Powers and Indirect Expropriation under International Law" (2008) 15 *Australian International Law Journal* 267.

[97] For example, India–Netherlands BIT, entered on: 6 November 1995, came into effect on 1 December 1996.

[98] Article 7, India–Switzerland BIT, entered on: 4 April 1997, came into effect on 16 February 2000.

[99] See note 9, 433–434.

International Court of Justice (ICJ).[100] Thus, if the foreign investor belongs to another state, which does not have an investment treaty with India, but which has agreed to the compulsory jurisdictional clause of the ICJ, the national state can take the dispute to the ICJ if it chooses to do so (of course, after satisfying the requirements of the exhaustion of local remedies and diplomatic protection). In a situation where states choose not to enter into investment treaties or enter into investment treaties without a compulsory arbitration clause, recourse to the ICJ remains.

Protection under municipal law

The Indian legal system is based on the common law and, therefore, is identifiable for foreign investors, especially from common law jurisdictions. According to Professor Sornarajah, the system is clumsy and slow, but it has a vibrant presence granting "meaningful protection for property and contract."[101] The separation of powers between the legislative, executive, and judicial branches is strongly entrenched in the jurisprudence and practice of the courts in India. There are no allegations of racial discrimination or other prejudice against the system. The concerns of foreign investors have arisen mostly out of delays in court proceedings or from a distinct interpretative approach toward certain legal provisions rather than from a bias against foreign investors. The writ jurisdiction continues to attract most of the disputes of corporations, including those of foreign investors. The higher judiciary provides fast justice at relatively low costs. This is one of the important reasons why India, which entered into its first BIT in 1994, did not have an investment treaty claim brought against it until 2009.

There is no specific statute that grants protection to foreign investors, but the interpretation and application of constitutional or public law jurisprudence applies to commercial matters and protects individuals from arbitrary and capricious actions of the state. The responsibility of the state to behave reasonably arises from a cumulative reading of Articles 14, 19, and 21 of the Constitution of India, which provide substantive protection. Article 14 is most well suited for protecting foreign investors. It says: "14. Equality before law: The State shall not deny to any person equality before the law or the equal protection of laws

[100] Article 36(2) of the Statute of the International Court of Justice. The text of the Declaration by India is available at: www.icj-cij.org/jurisdiction/?p1=5&p2=1&p3=3&code=IN (accessed 7 April 2015).

[101] See note 2, 138.

within the territory of India." This provision ensures national treatment for investors once they have validly entered and established their investments. They would also have to additionally satisfy the standing requirement elaborated later in this chapter.

In addition, Article 19 grants "fundamental freedoms" to citizens, such as: freedom of expression (which includes commercial speech such as in advertisements[102]); association; free movement throughout the country; and the right to carry out any occupation, trade, or business. Article 21 protects the right to life and personal liberty. Article 21 may appear irrelevant but the constitutional jurisprudence has developed in such a fashion that it sees all the three provisions comprehensively. They constitute different aspects of fundamental rights.[103] Fairness in action is a deeply embedded principle in the Constitution – "[a]rbitrariness is the very negation of the rule of law."[104] All arms of the state are to ensure that their behavior is devoid of arbitrariness, capriciousness, colorable conduct, and so on. These remedies are meant to prevent abuse of power and neglect of duties by public authorities. The Supreme Court has emphasized that the denial of a free trial amounts to violation of Article 14. It approved the standard of free trial of the European Convention for the Protection of Human Rights and Fundamental Freedoms, 1950.[105]

The mechanism for the enforcement of rights under Articles 14, 19, and 21 is through the writ jurisdiction of India's higher judiciary. The higher judiciary comprises the highest court in the province: the High Courts and the Supreme Court at the center. The Supreme Court also serves as the highest court of appeal. The courts at both levels possess the power to issue writs. However, the power of the Supreme Court is limited in comparison to that of the High Courts as the Supreme Court can only issue writs in cases of violation of fundamental rights.[106] The High Courts can issue writs in cases of violation of fundamental rights and also for "any other purpose."[107] The phrase "any other purpose" is wide and includes a range of legal rights.[108] These rights may not stricto sensu be

[102] *Tata Press Ltd.* v. *Mahanagar Telephone Nigam Ltd.* (1995) 5 Supreme Court Cases 139, paras. 17–23.

[103] *Maneka Gandhi* v. *Union of India* (1978) 1 Supreme Court Cases 248, paras. 4–7.

[104] *Kumari Srilekha Vidyarthi* v. *State of UP* (1991) 1 Supreme Court Cases 212, para. 35.

[105] *Dwarka Prasad Agarwal* v. *B D Agarwal* (2003) 6 Supreme Court Cases 230, para. 38.

[106] Article 32, Constitution of India. [107] Article 226, Constitution of India.

[108] Durga Das Basu, *Shorter Constitution of India*, 14th ed. (New Delhi: LexisNexis Butterworths Wadhwa Nagpur, Reprint 2010, vol. II), 1201–1204.

contractual or statutory rights.[109] Thus, a participant in a government procurement process can challenge the decision of the Government in the absence of a contractual relationship with the governmental agency. In this regard, the powers of an investment tribunal are limited.

In theory, purely contractual disputes may not be included within the scope of the public law remedies. In practice, the position of the state is such that it always has to adhere to public law principles. It does not matter that it is operating in a contractual sphere.[110] A breach of contract associated with the performance of public functions of the state would result into violation of legal right within Article 226.[111] The underlying principle is that the state cannot behave like a private individual. Its actions cannot be dictated by personal preferences and choices. It ought to be objective and impartial all the time, even if it is operating in a contractual or commercial sphere. Explaining this doctrine, the Supreme Court observed:

> **22.** There is an obvious difference in the contracts between private parties and contracts to which the State is a party. Private parties are concerned only with their personal interest whereas the State while exercising its powers and discharging its functions, acts indubitably, as is expected of it, for public good and in public interest. The impact of every State action is also on public interest. This factor alone is sufficient to import at least the minimal requirements of public law obligations and impress with this character the contracts made by the State or its instrumentality.[112]

Thus, even in contractual cases if the state fails to behave reasonably, the writ jurisdiction of the higher judiciary is available. This is a liberal approach toward contractual disputes as compared to investment tribunals. Tribunals have maintained a conscious distinction between breaches arising out of contract and breaches arising out of an investment treaty. The possibility of converting contractual disputes into treaty claims is possible only in cases of umbrella clauses. Tribunals are not consistent on the point that, in each case, the breach of contract would be converted into a treaty breach, independent of treaty breaches.[113] The prevailing view

[109] *Mahabir Auto Stores* v. *Indian Oil Corporation* (1990) 3 Supreme Court Cases 752, paras. 12, 18.

[110] See note 104, para. 28. [111] Basu, *Shorter Constitution of India*, 1218–1220.

[112] See note 104, para. 22.

[113] *SGS Société Génèrale de Surveillance S.A.* v. *Islamic Republic of Pakistan*, ICSID Case No. ARB/01/13, Jurisdiction (6 August 2003), para. 162. See contra *SGS Société Génèrale de Surveillance S.A.* v. *Republic of the Philippines*, ICSID Case No. ARB/02/6, Jurisdiction (29 January 2004), paras. 119–128.

does not favor a liberal interpretation of umbrella clauses. It retains the distinction between contractual breaches and treaty breaches and rejects the conversion of contractual breaches into treaty breaches, unless an independent treaty breach exists.[114] In treaties without an umbrella cause, breach of a purely contractual term would not result in a violation of treaty terms.[115] To this extent, the writ remedy is extensive and effective to subsume contractual breaches.

The writ remedies are available against the Government at the national level and regional level. It is available against different entities associated with the Government.[116] The Courts have liberally interpreted the other entities to include private entities performing public functions. These would include several corporations and companies constituted by the Government exclusively for trading purposes. Public functions are functions undertaken for the collective benefit of the public or a section of the public. Bodies may intervene in social and economic affairs in the public interest, and in such a case, they are accountable to public law principles.[117] The kind of authorities included within the writ jurisdiction is much wider in comparison to investment arbitration. For claiming responsibility of a state for the actions of its organs in investment arbitration, reference to the ILC Draft Articles on State Responsibility becomes necessary. Investment treaties do not stipulate rules of attribution. The actions of different organs of state can be attributed to a state.[118] The actions of persons or entities that are not an organ of the state may be attributable to the state if they are "empowered by the law of that State to exercise elements of the governmental authority" and if "the person or entity is acting in that capacity in the particular instance."[119] The number of authorities covered within these provisions is limited in comparison to those covered under the writ jurisdiction of the courts.

The requirement of standing is subsumed within the language of the substantive protection principles under the Constitution. A foreign

[114] *El Paso Energy International Company* v. *The Argentina Republic*, ICSID Case No. ARB/03/15, Jurisdiction (27 April 2006), paras. 85–88; *El Paso Energy International Company* v. *The Argentina Republic*, ICSID Case No. ARB/03/15, Award (31 October 2011), paras. 532–538. See further, Chapter 13 by C. L. Lim in this volume.

[115] *Waste Management Inc.* v. *United Mexican States*, Award, ICSID Case No. ARB(AF)/00/3 (30 April 2004), paras. 171–176. See further, Chapter 14 by Jean Ho in this volume.

[116] Article 12, Constitution of India.

[117] *Binny Ltd.* v. *V Sadasivan* (2005) 6 Supreme Court Cases 657, paras. 11, 29.

[118] Article 4, International Law Commission, "Responsibility of States for Internationally Wrongful Acts 2001" (2001), II *Yearbook of the International Law Commission*, 2001.

[119] Article 5, ibid.

investor can seek relief under the writ jurisdiction through Articles 14 and 21. The problem with Article 19 is that it applies only to citizens and an incorporated body cannot be treated as a citizen.[120] This does not mean that protection under Article 19 would not be available at all. In the matter of the protection of fundamental freedoms, the law does not distinguish between the rights of shareholders and the rights of a company. They are considered to be coextensive and a shareholder can bring proceedings on behalf of the company.[121] Articles 14 and 21 are available without any restrictions. In a situation involving a company in which the foreign investor has stakes along with Indian shareholders, the company may avail itself of protection under the writ jurisdiction if the petition is filed through its Indian shareholders. Moreover, because the company ultimately represents the interests of its shareholders, a writ petition would be maintainable by the company.[122] It is not necessary that Articles 14, 19, and 21 have to be invoked every time. The purpose of rights protection is adequately served by merely invoking Article 14. The availability of writ remedy does not depend on nationality. It is uniformly available for all. Since investments in India can be made only through Indian entities, they can approach the writ court. These remedies satisfy the national treatment requirements. In addition, they do not distinguish between two foreign investors; hence, this is in compliance with MFN requirements as well.

The power of the courts to grant relief is extensive. They may grant any appropriate order as is necessary in the circumstances of the case,[123] including monetary relief.[124] Normally, investment tribunals cannot strike down tax legislation except in the case where it is confiscatory and results in violation of one of the treatment standards in the investment treaty.[125] The taxing powers are protected as police powers under international law.[126] The higher judiciary is responsible, however, for safeguarding the Constitution. Thus, it possesses greater powers to check whether the authority imposing a tax possesses the necessary authority

120 *Tata Engineering and Locomotive Co. Ltd.* v. *State of Bihar* (1964) 6 SCR 885, 901–902.
121 *Delhi Cloth and General Mills* v. *Union of India*, AIR 1974 SC 937, 943.
122 *D.C.M.* v. *Union of India (1983) 4 SCC 166*, para. 12.
123 *Dwarka Nath* v. *ITO* All India Reporter 1966 Supreme Court 81, 85.
124 *ABL International Ltd.* v. *Export Credit Guarantee Corporation of India* (2004) 3 Supreme Court Cases 553, paras. 26–27.
125 *Marvin Feldman* v. *Mexico*, Award, ICSID Case No. ARB (AF)/99/1, 16 December 2002, para. 103.
126 *Link-Trading Joint Stock Company* v. *Department for Customs Control of Moldova*, Final Award (18 April 2002), paras. 69, 72.

and has strictly followed procedure. A tax regulation would be cancelled irrespective of the extent of its effect.[127] In the constitutional law jurisprudence, once a right is established, the subject matter of inquiry is the validity of the measure according to the touchstone of constitutional principles. The economic impact is not a supervening factor. The constitutional courts enjoy a liberal jurisdiction. The language of the treaties limits the jurisdiction of investment tribunals. The challenge to a measure becomes irrelevant unless it fits the frame of the standards of treatment. These would include improper exercise of governmental powers that affect investments made in India by foreign investors.

The protection under municipal law in most situations is higher than that provided by investment tribunals. Furthermore, the extent of discretion enjoyed by the municipal courts in granting and molding a relief to suit the circumstances of a case is peculiar. The attractive feature is their enforceability. Any non-compliance with the orders passed under the writ jurisdiction would amount to contempt of Court.[128] Government and government officials are extremely careful to ensure that they do not cross this line. The time taken to decide a writ case is much less than that required by an arbitral tribunal. The proceedings are mostly documents based. They involve only one level of appeal and in some cases two. This also reduces the time spent at different levels of appeals. The standard of protection available under public law is much higher than that of investment tribunals. Some issues cannot be effectively addressed under the writ jurisdiction. The writ court cannot decide complicated and heavily disputed questions of fact and would avoid situations where extensive oral testimony must be heard. The experience of *White Industries* shows that in situations where the order of the Court itself – including delays – is the basis of a cause of action in an investment claim, the protection under municipal law is futile. Denial of justice is bound to be a ground to challenge judicial decisions.

The writ remedy would be ineffective in cases of expropriation. The Constitution does not specify any requirements for valid acquisition, except that the acquisition has to take place under a statutory provision.[129] The standard of compensation in expropriation cases is not uniform in investment treaties. Different versions are used: "fair and

[127] *Mafatlal Industries Ltd.* v. *Union of India* (1997) 5 SCC 536.
[128] Articles 129 and 215, Constitution of India; Section 2, Contempt of Courts Act, 1961.
[129] Article 300-A, Constitution of India.

equitable" compensation;[130] "fair market value of the expropriated investments immediately before expropriation";[131] and "prompt adequate and effective" compensation.[132] The Constitution does not prescribe any standard of compensation. It does not even stipulate the necessity of compensation.

India has an effective system for ensuring the rule of law but has attracted lesser foreign investment in the past. As pointed out by Professor Sornarajah, the record of China may not be comparable to India on the rule of law, but China has still received much higher amounts of foreign investment. It is difficult to draw the connection between rule of law and flow of investments, and the "absence of a rule of law may indeed be a help in these matters rather than a hindrance."[133] To that extent, having the rule of law and a transparent judicial system has operated as a hindrance to India's single-minded implementation of foreign investment liberalization.[134]

Recent developments

A discussion on investment protection in India will be incomplete without the changes in thinking about the investment arbitration regime after the *White Industries* Award. The immediate reaction to the award was hostile. India put all further negotiations on hold. There were various options under consideration: termination of BITs and not entering into BITs in future; renegotiation or entering into new treaties without arbitration clauses; or "rebalancing" India's investment treaties.[135] After some trepidation and lack of clarity in recent years, India published its Model BIT in 2015. The Model BIT is in many respects a response to the *White Industries* Award and other pending claims. A raging concern regarding *White Industries* was the interpretation of a treaty most favored nation (MFN) clause. After finding India not responsible for denial of justice, the tribunal imported the standard of "effective means" from the India–Kuwait BIT, which did not exist in the India–Australia BIT. MFN was used as a tool to import the treatment standard of the claimant's

[130] Article 4(3), India–Egypt BIT, date of agreement: 9 April 1997; date of enforcement: 22 November 2000; Article 6(4), India–Spain BIT, date of agreement: 30 September 1997; date of enforcement: 16 October 1998; Article 6.3, India–Mauritius BIT.

[131] Article 5.2, India–South Korea BIT, date of agreement: 26 February 1996; date of enforcement: 7 May 1996.

[132] Article 6.3, India–UK BIT.

[133] See note 2, 138.

[134] Ibid., 138.

[135] See note 9, 446–449.

choice.[136] Thus, MFN clauses were bound to be a casualty in the Model BIT. The Model BIT does not contain an MFN clause. In line with the concerns regarding the FET standard,[137] the Model BIT gets rid of FET as well.

Many provisions in the Model BIT can be seen as a response to claims made against India. Tax legislation has been removed from the purview of consideration of arbitral tribunals. Any decision taken by the host state on taxation, before or after the commencement of arbitral proceedings, shall be nonjusticiable and outside the purview of arbitral tribunal.[138] It is mandatory to comply with all tax legislation.[139] These provisions are a response to the claim under the Netherlands–India BIT by Vodafone against retrospective tax amendment.[140] Another example is the freedom of the host state to "formulate, modify, amend or revoke its Laws in good faith" and specially conducting prosecutions and imposing penalties regarding the allocation of resources.[141] This is a response to notices received due to cancellation of the allocation of 2G licenses by the Supreme Court of India.[142]

The most sensitive factor in India is the review of judicial decisions by international arbitral tribunals. Indian courts have a revered tradition of independence and they have stood so through turbulent times in the constitutional history of India.[143] The courts are insulated by the Model BIT by removing them from the definition of investment:[144] the interpretation of the application of municipal laws that results in violation of national treatment.[145] An arbitral tribunal will not have jurisdiction to reexamine legal issues finally decided by the Indian judicial authorities.

The number and scope of treatment standards available have shrunk. The limited standards now contained are: denial of justice;[146]

[136] See note 8, paras. 11.29, 11.4.3, 11.4.19–11.4.20.

[137] The ASEAN Framework Agreement 1998 does not contain an FET clause.

[138] Article 2.6 (iv), India Model BIT, 2015. [139] Ibid., Article 11.

[140] Luke Eric Peterson, "As Vodafone Sues India – And Nokia Threatens the Same – Company Could Seek Interim Arbitral Order Blocking India from Pursuing Billions in Taxes," *Investment Arbitration Reporter* (13 May 2014).

[141] See note 138, Article 2.4.

[142] *Times of India*, "Sistema Threatens Arbitration in 2G Case" (28 February 2012), available at: http://timesofindia.indiatimes.com/business/india-business/Sistema-threatens-arbitration-in-2G-case/articleshow/12070637.cms; last visited: 8 July 2015. It appears that after notice there is no progress in the case.

[143] See Granville Austin, *Working a Democratic Constitution: The Indian Experience* (New Delhi: Oxford University Press, 2001).

[144] See note 138, Article 1.7 (vii). [145] Ibid., Article 4.4. [146] Ibid., Article 3.1(i).

"unremedied and egregious violations of due process";[147] "manifestly abusive treatment involving continuous, unjustified, and outrageous coercion or harassment";[148] national treatment postestablishment;[149] and expropriation.[150] The scope of each of these clauses has been substantially narrowed also when compared with the treaty practice of India in the past. For example, if losses are occasioned to the investor due to a competing business entity of the government, that will not be treated as direct or indirect expropriation,[151] and the compensation payable would be reduced after considering any mitigating factors.[152]

The Model BIT is long and detailed. It introduces many provisions for the first time, such as provisions on the obligations of the investor, investment and the home state,[153] challenges to the appointment of arbitrators and conflict of interest,[154] and transparency in arbitral proceedings.[155] A provision that impacts the dispute resolution clause the most is the mandatory exhaustion of local remedies clause. An investment claim cannot be filed unless there are no "reasonably available domestic remedies" or the relief cannot be obtained in a reasonable period of time.[156]

Conclusion

In conformity with Professor Sornarajah's views,[157] it is not just the Asian states but even the traditional capital-exporting states that are also moving toward treaties conserving greater regulatory space. India and China are both averse to loosing regulatory space.[158] Recent devel opments in India show that India is moving in that direction. The real challenge is how far India will stick to the proposed Model BIT and be successful in negotiating BITs based on the Model BIT. After a kneejerk reaction of suddenly putting all further investment treaty negotiations on hold, the Government is back at the negotiating table but with a guarded negotiating text.

The rise in outflow of investments from India, especially to Europe and Latin America, may result in greater claims by Indian investors against those countries.[159] An Indian national has filed a claim against the United

147 Ibid., Article 3.1(ii). 148 Ibid., Article 3.1(iii). 149 Ibid., Article 4.
150 Ibid., Article 5. 151 Ibid., Article 5.3. 152 Ibid., Article 5.6–5.7.
153 Ibid., Chapter III. 154 Ibid., Article 14.6. 155 Ibid., Article 14.8.
156 Ibid., Article 14.3.
157 Sornarajah, "Review of Asian Views on Foreign Investment Law," 252.
158 See note 2, 141–142. 159 Ibid., 139.

Kingdom under the India–UK BIT.[160] India faces the challenge of protecting its regulatory freedom by streamlining its investment treaties, while at the same time also ensuring that its investments abroad are adequately protected. It remains to be seen whether India succeeds in getting its counterparts to sign on to its Model BIT. If India does succeed, we will see how far those BITs retain the Model BIT's delicate balance between conserving India's regulatory space and protecting Indian investors abroad. With new zeal and policy changes, there is excitement and enthusiasm toward future investments in India. The Chinese economy is suffering from two economic problems, which reflect the limitations on its ability to absorb more investment: "overheating" and flat rate of growth. Overheating of the economy has occurred due to excessive inflow of investments, and flat rate of growth is due to expansion and growth in most prominent sectors of the economy.[161] In comparison, India has many sectors hungry for investment and large areas of the economy with the prospect of achieving a high growth rate. Two big sectors are power and railways, and the Government is aware of the potential of these sectors. With India becoming the fastest growing economy in the world,[162] careful application of investment protection along with conservation of regulatory freedom and judicial independence remain important considerations.

160 *Ashok Sancheti* v. *United Kingdom*, www.iisd.org/itn/2008/11/28/indian-lawyer-pursues-claim-against-the-united-kingdom-under-the-india-uk-bit/; last visited 11 December 2015.

161 *The Economist*, "China: The Economy: Go Slow" (7–13 March 2015), 29.

162 *The Telegraph*, "India to overtake China as fastest growing large economy, says IMF" (16 March 2015), available at: www.telegraph.co.uk/finance/globalbusiness/11474914/India-to-overtake-China-as-fastest-growing-large-economy-says-IMF.html (accessed 7 April 2015).

9

China–US BIT negotiation and the emerging Chinese BIT 4.0

WENHUA SHAN AND HONGRUI CHEN

Introduction

International investment law, a subject of international law to which Professor Sornarajah has made a significant contribution, has entered into an extremely interesting and exciting era.[1] On the one hand, investment treaties continue to grow,[2] with major investment players entering into mega-investment treaties. The rules in these treaties have also been converging, and this has brought about a shift toward a "global" bilateral investment treaty (Global BIT) 2.0.[3] On the other hand, the debate on the inclusion of investor-state dispute settlement (ISDS) in such treaties has captured extensive attention worldwide,[4] with the increasing number of

[1] M. Sornarajah, *The International Law on Foreign Investment*, 3rd ed. (Cambridge: CUP, 2010), 1.

[2] Statistics show that, as of 2014, the number of international investment agreements has reached 3268, intertwined to form a "Spaghetti bowl phenomenon." *UNCTAD, Recent Trends in IIAs and ISDS, IIA Issue Note, February 2015.*

[3] Wenhua Shan and Lu Wang, "The China–EU BIT and the Emerging 'Global BIT 2.0'" (2015) 30(1) *ICSID Review* 260–267.

[4] Most recent examples include the debate in the EU on whether or not there should be ISDS in the TTIP and a relevant debate in the US Congress in the context of the renewal of the Trade Promotion Authority (TPA, the so-called fast-track trade bill). See European Commission, Report on Online public consultation on investment protection and investor-to-state dispute settlement (ISDS) in the Transatlantic Trade and Investment Partnership Agreement (TTIP), http://trade.ec.europa.eu/doclib/docs/2015/january/tradoc_153044.pdf (accessed on 6 June 2015). See also the amendment to TPA bill introduced by Senator Elizabeth Warren, a Democrat from Massachusetts, to prohibit the use of trade authorities procedures to deals that include investor-state dispute settlement (ISDS) provisions failed, with 60 against and 39 in favor. See: US Senate Signs Off on Trade Legislation; House Fight Up Next, 28 May 2015. www.ictsd.org/bridges-news/bridges/news/us-senate-signs-off-on-trade-legislation-house-fight-up-next (accessed on 6 June 2015).

ISDS cases, which have been brought before international arbitration tribunals.[5]

As a major player in international investment and relevant treaty activities, China's approach to international investment treaties has attracted wide attention and interest. Recent years have seen dramatic changes in China's BIT practices, the most significant of which being China's acceptance of preestablishment national treatment and a "negative list" approach in the China–United States (US) BIT negotiations during the Fifth United States–China Strategic and Economic Dialogue in July 2013. As a result, a new "fourth generation" of Chinese BITs (Chinese "BIT 4.0") seems to be taking shape.[6]

This chapter attempts to discuss China's newly emergent fourth generation BIT by first exploring the background against which this new generation of treaties has developed. It will then discuss specific issues which China's new model BIT would need to address. These include the issues of investment liberalization, substantive protection (fair and equitable treatment (FET), expropriation, and umbrella clauses), social responsibility (environment and labor clauses), and dispute settlement (ISDS) reform. It concludes with an exploration of the would-be or should-be "Chinese characteristics" of China's BIT 4.0, including respect for a country's choice of political, social, and economic systems, allowances for countries in economic transition and accommodation of diverse local developmental needs inside the country.

The background: why a BIT 4.0 now?

China's recent move towards a new generation BIT is a result of a combination of economic, political, and international factors. Economically, China's shift from being mainly a capital-importing state to being both a capital-importing and a capital-exporting state now requires the country to play a more proactive role in promoting international investment. Politically, domestic reform has also reached a new stage under China's

[5] The number of arbitration cases that have been announced in the investor's host country at least reached 608, and the number of cases newly increased each year has remained at 50 or so in the recent years. See UNCTAD, IIA Issue Note, Feburary 2015.

[6] Since 1982, when China had signed the first international bilateral investment agreement with Sweden, China has signed more than 130 bilateral investment agreements and investment chapters in nearly 10 free trade agreements. During the last three decades, China has engaged in three generations of BITs, corresponding with the following periods of treaty activity: 1982–1989, 1990–1997 and from 1998 to the present time. For further details, see Norah Gallagher and Wenhua Shan, *Chinese Investment Treaties: Policies and Practice* (Oxford: OUP, 2009), 35–42.

so-called Reform Version 2.0, which in turn requires its investment regime to be looked at afresh. Finally, from an international perspective, the new generation Chinese BIT also demonstrates China's response to recent developments in investment treaty and arbitration practice in the rest of the world. The following discussion closely examines those factors in turn.

Economic factor: the changing role in international investment

The primary reason for China's adoption of BIT 4.0 was economic. The change in the role China plays in international investment demands a change in the approach China takes in its BIT regime.

Like other developing states, China started its BIT program in 1982 in the hope that it would help attract foreign investments. In other words, China started its BIT program as a capital-importing country. Accordingly, China's mindset when signing such BITs was defensive, aiming to preserve the interests of the host government as far as possible. Such mentality was vividly demonstrated by the contents of the first two generations of treaties, most prominently by the complete rejection or highly qualified acceptance of both a postestablishment national treatment standard and access to ISDS. For example, the China–Sweden BIT, the very first Chinese BIT, contained neither national treatment nor ISDS provisions. While there were a few BITs signed during that period which did grant national treatment, this was always substantially qualified by terms such as "in accordance with the laws and regulations" of the host state. Moreover, although most of the BITs provided for ISDS, such provision was restricted only to disputes concerning the "amount of compensation for expropriation." This was in sharp contrast to the approach taken by the capital-exporting states. For example, although ISDS was not included in the China–Sweden BIT, Sweden regularly included ISDS in its BITs. Article 6 of the Sweden–Egypt BIT (1978) requires that, "[I]n the event of a dispute arising between a national or a company of one Contracting State and the other Contracting State in connection with an investment on the territory of that other Contracting State, it shall upon the agreement by both parties to the dispute be submitted for arbitration . . . ." This was also stipulated in Article 9 of the Sweden–Sri Lanka BIT (1982).

China's mentality as a capital-importing state did not materially change until the late 1990s, when it started to seriously promote investment overseas. Consequently, China adopted its third generation BIT that tends now to include substantial national treatment and full access to

ISDS, including International Centre for the Settlement of Investment Disputes (ICSID) arbitration. The China–Barbados BIT of 1998, for example, was the first BIT signed following the third-generation prototype and included full access to ISDS. The China–Germany BIT of 2003, which is often cited as an example of China's third-generation BIT, goes further and offers both full access to ISDS and national treatment qualified only by a "grandfather" clause.

The third-generation BIT, however, was still drafted against the assumption of China as a net capital-importing state. In other words, although there was a rapidly growing amount of overseas investment, there was still far more inward foreign investment in China than outward investment from China. This is about to change very shortly if it has not already changed. According to some sources, China had already become a net capital exporter in 2014. However, Chinese official statements only confirmed that inward and outward investments were very close in 2014, and that China is expected to become a net capital exporter in the near future. In June 2014, the United Nations Conference on Trade and Development (UNCTAD) issued its World Investment Report for 2014, which reported Chinese overseas investments reaching USD 101 billion in 2013, making China the third largest foreign investor, next only to the United States and Japan.[7] China's foreign investment stock reached USD 613.6 billion by the end of 2013, making China eleventh in the world for foreign investment; by comparison, China was seventeenth in the world in 2011. According to the prediction of this report, China's foreign investment would most likely exceed the foreign investment it attracts in 2014, making China for the first time in modern history a net capital-exporting country. The trend in China's inward and outward foreign direct investment flows is presented in Figure 9.1 below. In early 2015, Zhong Shan, International Trade Representative and Vice-Minister of China's Ministry of Commerce (MOFCOM), stated in public that "China's outward foreign direct investment reached USD 102.9 billion in 2014, breaking the hundred billion dollar threshold for the first time and with a year-on-year growth of 14.1 percent, China continuously ranked third in the world in the same year." Zhong also predicted that China would become a net foreign exporter very soon.[8]

[7] UNCTAD, Overview, World Investment Report 2014, July 2015, xv.

[8] See the relevant report: http://finance.chinanews.com/cj/2015/01-16/6977506.shtml (accessed on 6 June 2015).

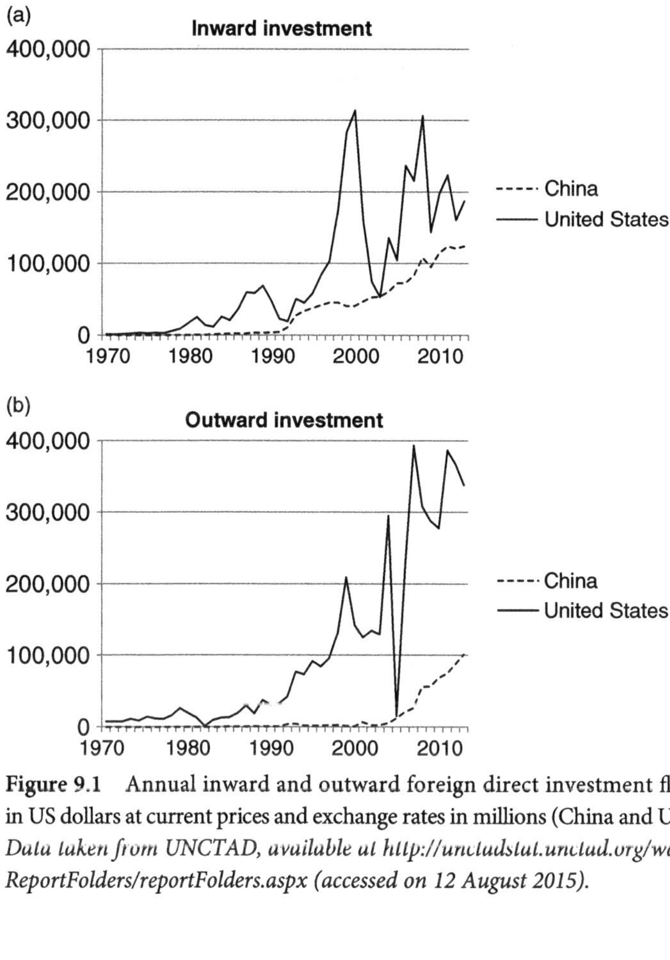

Figure 9.1 Annual inward and outward foreign direct investment flows measured in US dollars at current prices and exchange rates in millions (China and USA 1970–2013) *Data taken from UNCTAD, available at http://unctadstat.unctad.org/wds/ReportFolders/reportFolders.aspx (accessed on 12 August 2015).*

The fact that China is becoming a net capital-exporting state is a critical change that likely will have a transformative effect on China's international investment regime. Against this background, it is only natural for China to think more proactively about its BIT regime, just as other countries would if they were in China's position. It is, therefore, not surprising that China has accepted preestablishment national treatment coupled with a negative list for the areas open for foreign investment. China is rapidly going global, and its BITs should be upgraded to provide sufficient support and safeguards.

China, thinking from the perspective of a foreign investor, does not necessarily have a negative impact on other states, particularly, states receiving Chinese investments. This is because China will remain a top foreign investment recipient at the same time. Indeed, China's dual role in international investment should be welcomed by the rest of the world, as it means China has to go for a regime that balances the rights of foreign investors and the regulatory powers of the host states, which in turn should benefit capital-exporting and -importing countries alike.

In this connection, it is noted that some Chinese scholars have argued for two models of investment agreements for capital-exporting and capital-importing counterparts, respectively. However, such an approach should be rejected, as it is not only morally indecent but also practically problematic. Applying different standards of treaty protection to different states is a kind of discrimination. In practice, it is often difficult to distinguish one country's role as an investor from its role as a recipient; in most cases, it is a two-way street. The investment relationship between China and the United States is a good example. In 2013, China attracted USD 5.12 billion (contractual value) in investments from the US. In the same year, the nonfinancial direct investment of Chinese enterprises in the United States reached USD 4.23 billion. Obviously, this is a two-way investment relationship, in which each country has both "defensive" and "offensive" interests at the same time. To avoid conflict and maintain coherence, the best approach is to devise a well-balanced system. Indeed, a two-model BIT approach would be rendered meaningless, because all BITs have a most favored nation (MFN) provision, which would have the effect of leveling the standards of treatment, particularly with regard to substantive standards.

A political factor: the deepening reform agenda – China's reform 2.0

A second, equally important factor for China's BIT 4.0 is the deepening reform now taking place in China, which requires an upgraded and more open investment regime. Since 1978, economic reform and opening up have gone hand-in-hand. Indeed, they are two sides of the same coin, involving the marketization of the economy. Economic reform is the internal side, while opening up is the external side. This is particularly true given that the domestic and international markets have, by and large, been intergrated. Thus, in 1978 when China decided to commence economic reform, it decided to open up several special economic zones as "windows" to attract foreign investment and as "experimental fields" in order that China might have some practice in operating a market economy. The experiment, which was later practised throughout China, proved to be a great success and made China the second largest economy in the world. However, the new Chinese leadership is mindful of the challenges ahead. In particular, the leadership considers that the previously practised investment-driven economic growth model is not sustainable and has to be transformed. To effectuate such a transformation, economic- and other-related systems have to be reformed further. This new round of reform is now referred to as "China's Reform 2.0,"[9] suggesting that it is a grand reform endeavor comparable with the first version of the reform started in 1978 under the leadership of Deng Xiaoping. The reform is a systemic endeavor that covers a wide range of areas including economic, political, cultural, societal, and ecological systems.[10] But, the key lies in two areas: Economically, it intends to further strengthen the role of the market in resources allocation, from a "fundamental" to a "decisive" role. Politically, it intends to "promote modernization of the state governance system and governance capability," primarily, by implementing the "rule of law" in China.[11]

According to the reform agenda adopted in November 2013,[12] "establishing a unified, open, competitive and orderly market system is the basis for the market to play a decisive role in the allocation of resources." For this purpose, China determines that:

[9] Yang Jingjie, "'Reform 2.0' to be Unveiled," *Global Times*, 11 November 2013, available at: www.globaltimes.cn/content/823892.shtml (accessed on 26 May 2015).

[10] "China must: deepen economic system reform by centering on the decisive role of the market in allocating resources; deepen political system reform that features the organic unity of upholding the leadership of the Party; deepen cultural system reform by centering on building the core socialist value system and developing a strong socialist culture in China; deepen social structural reform by centering on safeguarding and improving the people's wellbeing and promoting social fairness and justice; deepen ecological environment management reform by centering on building a beautiful China; deepen the reform of the Party building system by centering on enhancing the Party's capacity to govern in a scientific and democratic way and in accordance with the law." Li Chengang, "China Has Lauchedan Era 2.0 of Reform and Opening-Up," *China Economic Times*, 13 November, http://theory.people.com.cn/n/2013/1114/c40531-23536137.html (accessed on 6 June 2015).

[11] Ibid., http://theory.people.com.cn/n/2013/1114/c40531-23536137.html (accessed on 6 June 2015).

[12] Decision of the Central Committee of the Communist Party of China on Some Major Issues Concerning Comprehensively Deepening the Reform (中共中央关于全面深化改革若干重大问题的决), adopted by the third Plenary Session of the 18th CPC Central Committee in Beijing on 12 November 2013. Chinese and English bilingual versions available at: www.china.org.cn/chinese/2014-01/17/content_31226494.htm (accessed on 26 May 2015).

> We will implement a unified market access system; and on the basis of making a negative list, all kinds of market players may enter areas not on the negative list on an equal basis and according to law. We will explore a management model for foreign investors with pre-establishment national treatment plus the negative list.

Clearly, this corresponds to the decisive aspect of the new generation BIT: the adoption of preestablishment national treatment combined with a negative list. However, what is more significant in the reform agenda is that it is not specific to foreign investment but rather seeks to reform the investment regime as a whole. In other words, the preestablishment national treatment plus negative list approach is only part of a larger-scale investment reform that aims to provide a unified level playing field for all categories of investors, foreign or domestic and public or private. As a matter of fact, China recently unveiled a new unified regime for inward foreign investment, which expressly adopts a system based on preestablishment national treatment plus a negative list approach.[13]

But reform of the investment regime goes further in having a direct impact on the reform of state governance. This is because the negative list system requires a change in the way in which the government functions. Previously, the Chinese government played an omnipotent role in Chinese society, including the economic life of society. Economic entities, particularly public companies, often turn to the relevant government department for a decision on matters that should be decided by the company itself, based upon an assessment of the relevant market. A negative list approach effectively requires the government to stay away from such matters and concentrate on what governments should do. To make sure that government does not extend a long arm into business activites, the Chinese Central Government adopted in March 2015 a Guiding Opinion[14] requiring all levels of local government to implement a "Power List System" under which local governments must sort out and publicize a list of the powers they have. Local governments are required to exercise their powers in strict compliance with the power list.[15] Local

[13] See Article 6 of Foreign Investment Law, available at: http://tfs.mofcom.gov.cn/article/as/201501/20150100871010.shtml (accessed on 6 June 2015).

[14] General Office of the CPC Central Committee and General Office of the State Council, Guiding Opinions on the Implementation of the Power List System of the Departments of Local Governments at All Levels, 24 March 2015. http://politics.people.com.cn/n/2015/0325/c1001-26744385.html (accessed on 6 June 2015).

[15] Ibid.

governments are also required to publish a list of responsibilitities, which is intended to enhance their accountability.[16]

Clearly, such a political reform agenda is evidence that China's BIT 4.0 has the necessary political support, which explains why it has emerged during this time in China.

An external factor: the mega BIT negotiations amid world BIT transformation

If the two factors mentioned earlier are the internal but most fundamental factors for the birth of China's BIT 4.0, the ongoing negotiations of mega BITs with the United States and the EU have provided a vital push for its implementation. Both the United States and the EU have pushed for "preestablishment national treatment" plus a "negative list" as one of their top priorities. Indeed, it was during the China–US BIT negotiations that these terms first entered into China's political and economic life. This might be an example of how the "opening-up" policy can push forward internal "reform" ("*Kaifang Cu Gaige*"). However, the internal factors have played the most fundamental role, because had there not been a strong political will to follow such a challenging path of reform, or the economic interest in a more liberal investment regime, one can hardly expect such a new BIT approach to have come about. As a matter of fact, the US government started re-negotiating the BIT with China in 2008, but the breakthrough on preestablishment national treatment and having a negative list did not occur until 2013, when China started to have a critical interest in overseas investments and the new leadership showed its determination to carry out the much-awaited but difficult reforms.

Beyond China's BIT negotiations with the United States and the EU, the world map of investment treaties is also under critical reform, which in turn requires the Chinese to respond in its latest BIT prototype. As written elsewhere, the recent world investment treaty practice, particularly the mega treaties such as the TPP and the TTIP and the Comprehensive Economic and Trade Agreement (CETA) between the EU and Canada, together with the Chinese BITs with the United States and the EU, have demonstrated a trend toward convergence around a "Global BIT 2.0."[17] This global trend has undoubtedly had an impact on the development of China's BIT 4.0.

[16] Ibid.

[17] Shan and Wang, "The China–EU BIT and the Emerging 'Global BIT 2.0,'" 265.

The issues: what has to be addressed?

China's BIT 4.0 has to address the issues of a new generation. In particular, it will have to tackle the sticky issues arising out of China's negotiations with the United States and the EU. Such issues may be categorized into four groups: investment liberalization, substantive standards, social responsibility, and dispute resolution.

Investment liberalization

Under customary international law, in the absence of overriding treaty obligations, the host state has the discretion in deciding whether and on what conditions a foreign investment project may be accepted in its territory.[18] In most IIAs, the host states do not undertake concrete commitments with regard to "the establishment, acquisition, [and] expansion" of investments, leaving those issues to be determined by local laws and regulations. This was the approach generally followed by Chinese BITs to date. Even the most recent and, probably, the most advanced Chinese BIT, the China–Canada BIT, states in Article 3 that "[E]ach Contracting Party shall encourage investors of the other Contracting Party to make investments in its territory and admit such investments in accordance with its laws, regulations and rules." The only exception seems to be that sometimes the national treatment standard is extended to the "expansion" of existing investments. The China–Korea BIT of 2007, for example, stipulates in Article 3(1) that "[E]ach Contracting Party shall in its territory accord to investors of the other Contracting Party and to their investments treatment no less favourable than the treatment it accords in like circumstances to its own investors and their investments (hereinafter referred to as 'national treatment') with respect to the expansion, operation, management, maintenance, use, enjoyment, and sale or other disposal of investments (hereinafter referred to as 'investment and business activities')." As "expansion" is often regarded as one form of "investment admission" (together with "establishment" and "acquisition"), the extension of the national treatment (NT) standard to cover "expansion" may be regarded as a relaxation of the Chinese position. But, it cannot be considered as a decisive breakthrough given the "expansion" only applies to invesments that are already established but simply have expanded in size. In other words, the

[18] Rudolf Dolzer and Christoph Schreuer, *Principles of International Investment Law* (Oxford: OUP, 2008), at 79–80.

"original establishment" is still free from the NT obligation. The same wording is used in the China–Canada BIT but with a further clarification. The third paragraph of the clause states that "[T]he concept of 'expansion' in this Article applies only with respect to sectors not subject to a prior approval process under the relevant sectoral guidelines and applicable laws, regulations and rules in force at the time of expansion. The expansion may be subject to prescribed formalities and other information requirements." It is, therefore, clear that no breakthrough was intended with regard to foreign investment market access by introducing the term "expansion" into the NT provision.

Although China did not offer general NT to foreign investments, China has sometimes offered most favored nation (MFN) treatment expressly or implicitly as shown in Table 9.1. Such treatment, nevertheless, does not require the host state to open up new areas to foreign investment.

Preestablishment national treatment was a significant issue in the China–US BIT negotiations. Preestablishment national treatment was also demanded by the EU in its BIT negotiaitons with China. To the surprise of many Chinese observers, China announced acceptance of this standard in 2013 at a relatively early stage in the China–US BIT negotiations. This demonstrates that China's acceptance of preestablishment national treatment was not primarily the result of pressure from the negotiating counterpart, but rather was based on domestic needs and circumstances. Further, reform and opening up is a determined policy of the current government, and preestablishment national treatment on the basis of a negative list could play a positive role in this process, as explored earlier.

More specifically, China benefits from preestablishment national treatment not only because this opens up the foreign markets of the treaty counterparts but also because this will attract more quality foreign investments by creating a more favorable and more transparent regulatory system. With the increase of labor and land costs, the attraction for foreign investment in China is gradually disappearing in the labor-intensive industries, particularly, in the rich eastern costal provinces. The transformation of the Chinese economy requires guiding foreign investment toward capital-intensive and technology-intensive industries. The Chinese government, thus, intends to gradually release its control over those industries. The 2015 catalog for the guidance of foreign investment in China, for example, completely opened up the real estate industry and, substantially, liberalized the financial sector and many manufacturing industries, including the pharmaceutical, petrochemical, petroleum, and equipment manufacturing industries.

Table 9.1 *MFN and preestablishment under Chinese BITs*

MFN not applied at pre-establishment stage	MFN applied at preestablishment stage	
	Express	Implied
China–Indonesia BIT (1994)	China–Canada BIT (2012)	China–Malaysia BIT (1998)
Article 4(2): Neither Contracting Party shall in its territory subject investors of the other Contracting Party, with regard to their management, use, enjoyment or disposal of their investment, and any activity connected with these investments, to treatment less favorable than that which it accords to investors of any third state.	Article 5(1): Each Contracting Party shall accord to investors of the other Contracting Party treatment no less favorable than that it accords, in like circumstances, to investors of a Noncontracting Party with respect to the establishment, acquisition, expansion, management, conduct, operation, and sale or other disposition of investments in its territory.	Article 3(1): Investments made by investors of either Contracting Party in the territory of the other Contracting Party shall not be subjected to a treatment less favorable than that accorded to investments made by investors of any third State.

Arguably, it is possible to liberalize the market with a positive rather than a negative list approach. However, the negative list approach certainly suggests a more open guesture given the default position is "open." Moreover, this approach better fits with the aforementioned administrative reform of cutting unnecessary governmental interference in business activites. The practice of China in the Shanghai Free Trade Zone, for instance, has demonstrated the Chinese government's determination to try out the negative list approach to investment governance with a view to solving the bottleneck problem encountered in the reform of China's system of administration.

Understandably, China faces significant challenges in adopting a negative list approach for the first time. First, China has to analyze each of its sectors and industries as to the feasibility and desirability of opening up. Obviously, this is a huge assignment. Second, China has to consider all of the relevant measures affecting such sectors and industries that are not completely open to foreign investment. Again, this is a tremendous undertaking as hundreds of thousands of measures might be affected. Finally, such sectors, industries, and measures would have to be carefully put together to form a comprehensive and coherent list, the negative list of nonconforming measures. Moreover, this is just the preparation of the list, which has to be exchanged and negotiated with the treaty counterparty. It is undoubtedly a very couragous move, for which the Chinese government should be commended. However, it is not impossible, as the long-established Guiding Catalogue of the Directions of Foreign Investment provides a starting point, and the negative lists of the Shanghai Pilot Free Trade Zone and other free trade zones are testing the effects of the potential national negative list.

Some further complications might arise in the adoption of preestablishment NT. For example, it might be difficult to use the conventional ISDS mechanism to deal with preentry disputes, as demonstrated in *Mexico* v. *United States*[19] and *CANACAR* v. *USA*.[20]

It should be noted that in the context of the China–EU BIT negotiations, the question of investment liberalization could go even further to include prohibition of certain nondiscriminary measure such as quotas and other forms of quantative restrictions on investment. While such requirements might not be as demanding as they appear, given that similar rules have already been included in GATS, it would be a further breakthrough in Chinese BIT negotiations. It merits a thorough and prudent investigation.[21]

[19] *Mexico* v. *United States* (in the Matter of Cross-Border Trucking Services), NAFTA Chapter 20 State-to-State arbitration, Final Report of the Panel, 6 February 2001.

[20] *CANACAR* v. *United States, Notice of Arbitration, United Nations Commission on International Trade Law and NAFTA (Chapter 11), ¶ 1 (2 April 2009)* [hereinafter *Canacar* v. *U.S.*], available at www.state.gov/documents/organization/121599.pdf (accessed on 6 June 2015).

[21] Also relevant are the performance requirement rules that are promoted by both the United States and the EU. Some of them go beyond the TRIMS agreement and require closer examination and careful assessment.

Substantive protection

The new-generation BIT would also have to address a number of substantive issues of investment protection in the form of the general and specific standards of treatment. The most important remaining issues for the new BIT to address include FET, expropriation and compensation, and umbrella clauses.

Fair and equitable treatment

The standard of FET has been the subject of intense debate over the last few decades in the field of international investment law and arbitration, mainly owing to its lack of precision and the high success rate of its invocation in investment treaty arbitration cases. Efforts have been made to further define the standard,[22] notably by the North American states by linking it to the international minimum standard under customary international law, as illustrated by the latest US Model BIT and by the exhaustive list approach developed by the European Union in its bilateral agreement with Canada (CETA).

Article 5 of the US Model BIT states:

Article 5: Minimum Standard of Treatment

1. Each Party shall accord to covered investments treatment in accordance with customary international law, including fair and equitable treatment and full protection and security.
2. For greater certainty, paragraph 1 prescribes the customary international law minimum standard of treatment of aliens as the minimum standard of treatment to be afforded to covered investments. The concepts of "fair and equitable treatment" and "full protection and security" do not require treatment in addition to or beyond that, which is required by that standard, and do not create additional substantive rights. The obligation in paragraph 1 to provide:
   (a) "fair and equitable treatment" includes the obligation not to deny justice in criminal, civil, or administrative adjudicatory proceedings in accordance with the principle of due process embodied in the principal legal systems of the world; and
   (b) "full protection and security" requires each Party to provide the level of police protection required under customary international law.

[22] More radical reactions include India's deletion of the FET from, e.g., its BIT with Singapore.

3. A determination that there has been a breach of another provision of this Treaty, or of a separate international agreement, does not establish that there has been a breach of this Article.

Moreover, the term "customary international law" is further defined in Annex A to the Model BIT, which states:

> The Parties confirm their shared understanding that "customary international law" generally and as specifically referenced in Article 5 [Minimum Standard of Treatment] and Annex B [Expropriation] results from a general and consistent practice of States that they follow from a sense of legal obligation. With regard to Article 5 [Minimum Standard of Treatment], the customary international law minimum standard of treatment of aliens refers to all customary international law principles that protect the economic rights and interests of aliens.

In contrast, Article X.9 of CETA reads:

> Article X.9: Treatment of Investors and of Covered Investments
>
> Each Party shall accord in its territory to covered investments of the other Party and to investors with respect to their covered investments fair and equitable treatment and full protection and security in accordance with paragraphs 2 to 6.
>
> A Party breaches the obligation of fair and equitable treatment referenced in paragraph 1 where a measure or series of measures constitutes: Denial of justice in criminal, civil or administrative proceedings; Fundamental breach of due process, including a fundamental breach of transparency, in judicial and administrative proceedings; Manifest arbitrariness; Targeted discrimination on manifestly wrongful grounds, such as gender, race or religious belief; Abusive treatment of investors, such as coercion, duress and harassment; or A breach of any further elements of the fair and equitable treatment obligation adopted by the Parties in accordance with paragraph 3 of this Article.
>
> The Parties shall regularly, or upon request of a Party, review the content of the obligation to provide fair and equitable treatment. The Committee on Services and Investment may develop recommendations in this regard and submit them to the Trade Committee for decision.
>
> When applying the above fair and equitable treatment obligation, a tribunal may take into account whether a Party made a specific representation to an investor to induce a covered investment, that created a legitimate expectation, and upon which the investor relied in deciding to make or maintain the covered investment, but that the Party subsequently frustrated.
>
> For greater certainty, 'full protection and security' refers to the Party's obligations relating to physical security of investors and covered investments.

> For greater certainty, a breach of another provision of this Agreement, or of a separate international Agreement, does not establish that there has been a breach of this Article.

It can be seen that in both instruments an attempt has been made to further clarify the FET standard. The difference appears to be that the approach taken by the United States is open-ended, while the EU's approach is a closed list. In other words, The US approach offers more flexibility while the EU's approach guarantees more certainty. However, a closer look reveals that the difference is not as significant as it appears. The US model attempted to achieve certainty by not only referring to the international minimum standard to define FET but also by explicitly referring to denial of justice as a demonstration of a breach of the standard. On the other hand, the EU approach also leaves significant room for flexibility, as terms such as "fundamental," "manifest," and "abusive" are not defined and are, therefore, subject to discretionary interpretation.

It is unclear which approach China will take for the new-generation BIT. The China–Canada BIT generally follows the US approach by referring to the minimum standard of treatment under international law, which effectively means customary international law, as defined under Article 38 of the ICJ Statute. The trilateral investment treaty (TIT) among China, Japan, and Korea also refers to international law but uses the term "generally accepted rule of international law." Such practices suggest that China is also qualifying the standard to make sure that it is not misused. It remains to be seen whether China adopts the EU approach in further defining the standard of treatment. The China–EU BIT presents the perfect opportunity to observe developments in this regard.

Expropriation and compensation

The question of expropriation and compensation remains a topic of controversy in international investment nowadays; not so much in relation to the amount of compensation owed, which has been generally standardized, but rather for the definition of expropriation and, particularly, of indirect expropriaiton. An effort has been made to clarify such indirect expropriation, which has also been adopted in the recent Chinese investment treaties. For instance, the China–Canada BIT stipulates in Annex B-10 that:[23]

> Annex B-10 Expropriation

[23] Similar stipulations can be found in China–Korean Free Trade Agreement, annex 12-B.

The Contracting Parties confirm their shared understanding that:

1. Indirect expropriation results from a measure or series of measures of a Contracting Party that has an effect equivalent to direct expropriation without formal transfer of title or outright seizure.
2. The determination of whether a measure or series of measures of a Contracting Party constitutes an indirect expropriation requires a case-by-case, fact-based inquiry that considers, among other factors:
   (a) the economic impact of the measure or series of measures, although the sole fact that a measure or series of measures of a Contracting Party has an adverse effect on the economic value of an investment does not establish that an indirect expropriation has occurred;
   (b) the extent to which the measure or series of measures interferes with distinct, reasonable, investment-backed expectations; and
   (c) the character of the measure or series of measures.
3. Except in rare circumstances, such as if a measure or series of measures is so severe in light of its purpose that it cannot be reasonably viewed as having been adopted and applied in good faith, a nondiscriminatory measure or series of measures of a Contracting Party that is designed and applied to protect the legitimate public objectives for the well-being of citizens, such as health, safety, and the environment, does not constitute indirect expropriation.

This definition is also found in the Protocol to the China–Japan–Korea investment agreement and can be taken as China's established new practice on this provision. It can be seen that China's recent BIT practice on the expropriation provision generally conforms to the practice of the United States (and the EU as demosntrated in the CETA), but with two closely related major differences. The first obvious difference is that Chinese BITs do not refer to the "Hull formula," and the second difference is that Chinese BITs do not expressly relate the treatment required to that required under customary international law. In Annex B of the US Model BIT, the first paragraph states:

> Article 6 [Expropriation and Compensation](1) is intended to reflect customary international law concerning the obligation of States with respect to expropriation.

Article 6(1) also sets out the conditions of a legal expropriation, including payment of "adquate, effective and prompt compensation" and treatment in accordance with the "minimum standard of treatment" as stipulated in Article 5. The US approach is understandable given that it coined the "Hull formula" in the 1930s and has insisted upon it ever since. However, the Chinese rejection of such a standard of compensation is equally understandable given that China has stood with other Third World countries to resist the "Hull formula" and has argued instead for "appropriate compensation" as the norm required under international law. It can be expected that China would stick to that position given the continued controversy over the customary international law standard of compensation, although that may not prevent China from agreeing on actual standards of compensation that are not different from those under a US-style BIT. In this connection, it should be noted that the North American Free Trade Agreement does not explicitly refer to the Hull formula, probably due to Mexico's historical resistance to it.

Umbrella clause

Umbrella clauses present another area of intense controversy in international investment law, having resulted in "parallel proceedings" and other problems and complications. At least 50 Chinese BITs contain an umbrella clause and a further six BITs contain a preservation of rights clause that has a similar and perhaps even a stronger effect.[24] Among the 50 BITs, most BITs adopt the standard formulation requiring the host state to observe any or all obligations/commitments it undertakes toward foreign investors.[25] The China–Nigeria BIT, for instance, stipulates in Article 10(2) that "[E]ach Contracting Party shall observe any commitments it may have entered into with the investors of the other Contracting Party as regards to their investments." It is observed that a considerable number of Chinese BITs specifically adopt a more restrictive approach, imposing substantive limitations on the scope of application of the umbrella clause: Some subject such obligations or commitments to the laws of the host state, while others confine the obligations or commitments to only "written obligations," obligations relating to "specific investments," "contractual obligations" concerning "approved investments," or "approved investment contracts." On the other hand, the Sino–Singapore BIT requires the host state to "observe" "any commitment" entered into between two private parties of the two

[24] Wenhua Shan, "Umbrella Clauses and Investment Contracts under Chinese BITs: Are the Latter Covered by the Former" (2010) 11(2) *The Journal of World Investment & Trade* 136.

[25] Ibid., 137.

contracting states and any commitment the host state has entered into with private parties of the other contracting party.

As written elsewhere, it is believed that purely commercial obligations are not covered by this clause, nor are legislative measures of general application that do not target any specific investment.[26] However, arbitration tribunals might take a different view, as demonstrated in cases such as the *SGS* v. *Philippines*[27] and *SGS* v. *Paraguay*.[28] The umbrella clause should, therefore, be rewritten in the new-generation BIT to make sure that its coverage is not excessively broad.

In this regard, it has to be admitted that the US Model BIT has achieved a marked progress. It does so in three steps. First, it clearly and carefully defines the term "investment agreement":

> "investment agreement" means a written agreement between a national authority of a Party and a covered investment or an investor of the other Party, on which the covered investment or the investor relies in establishing or acquiring a covered investment other than the written agreement itself, that grants rights to the covered investment or investor:
> (a) with respect to natural resources that a national authority controls, such as for their exploration, extraction, refining, transportation, distribution, or sale;
> (b) to supply services to the public on behalf of the Party, such as power generation or distribution, water treatment or distribution, or telecommunications; or
> (c) to undertake infrastructure projects, such as the construction of roads, bridges, canals, dams, or pipelines, that are not for the exclusive or predominant use and benefit of the government.

It is, therefore, clear that an investment agreement must meet three qualifications: (a) it must be in writing; (b) it must "grant rights to the covered investment or investor"; and (c) it must grant rights in one of three fields, namely natural resources, public utility, and infrastructure projects. This definition, therefore, excludes oral agreements or commitments and agreements that are not in one of the three fields mentioned earlier. Furthermore, although this definition might not necessarily or

[26] Ibid., 167.

[27] *SGS Société Générale de Surveillance S.A. (Claimant)* v. *Republic of the Philippines (Respondent)*, Decision of the Tribunal on Objections to Jurisdiction, ICSID Case No ARB/02/6, 29 January 2004.

[28] *SGS Société Générale de Surveillance S.A.* v. *The Republic of Paraguay*, ICSID Case No. ARB/07/2, Decision on Jurisdiction.

completely rule out purely commercial agreements (in the three fields),[29] it is more than likely that such agreements involve at least certain elements of governmental authority. In short, this definition should be commended for covering the key state contracts to be protected, while carving out all other unintended agreements and other forms of commitments.

Second, the US model text provides for a "fork in the road" requirement to prevent parallel or multiple proceedings, as can arise when an investor makes both a contractual and a treaty claim. Article 26(2) requires that any investor bringing a claim must produce a written waiver to exclude "any right to initiate or continue before any administrative tribunal or court under the law of either Party, or other dispute settlement procedures, any proceeding with respect to any measure alleged to constitute a breach referred to in Article 24."

Finally, the US model text designates a distinct set of laws to govern investment agreements. Article 30(2) reads:

2. Subject to paragraph 3 and the other terms of this Section, when a claim is submitted under Article 24(1)(a)(i)(B) or (C), or Article 24(1)(b)(i)(B) or (C), the tribunal shall apply:
   - (a) the rules of law specified in the pertinent investment authorization or investment agreement, or as the disputing parties may otherwise agree; or
   - (b) if the rules of law have not been specified or otherwise agreed:
     - (i) the law of the respondent, including its rules on the conflict of laws; and
     - (ii) such rules of international law as may be applicable.

Investment agreements are therefore generally governed by the law of "party autonomy." Failing that, the law of the host states and any applicable rule of international law should apply. Article 30(2) does not go any further to determine which law should apply if there is a conflict between the applicable domestic and international laws. However, arbitrators should be able to find a solution to such conflicts, perhaps with guidance from customary international law including commonly accepted rules reflected in the Vienna Convention on the Law of Treaties.

The US solution might be the best available solution so far and should, therefore, be a good starting point for China to design relevant provisions

[29] This would depend on the interpretation of the "rights" granted by the host state authority.

in the new model BIT. It might not, however, necessarily be the best or ideal model. For instance, it does not define the nature of the "right" conferred by such investment agreements, which could lead to diverse interpretations as to whether or not purely commercial contracts in the three areas are covered. Moreover, the list of the three covered areas of investment agreements might not necessarily be the best exhaustive list for each country, as countries might have different priorities for the areas of investment contracts to be protected. Finally, the US model does not clarify the relationship between the applicable domestic and international laws in the case of conflicts between the two, as noted earlier. Those aspects and the specific conditions of Chinese inward and outward investments should be taken into account when designing relevant clauses in the new Chinese model.

Social responsibility

Sustainable development has become a buzzword in the international investment law field and with good reason. More and more often, investment treaties or their models have included provisions addressing social concerns and requiring host states or foreign investors to understand certain social obligations. Among the most commonly found social clauses are those addressing environmental and labor protection.[30]

[30] Other social provisions include transparency provision as in the US Model BIT 2012 or corporate social responsibility as in Article 31 of the Norway new model BIT of 2015. The SADC Model BIT is special in that it includes in Article 10 "Common Obligation against Corruption." The provision reads: "10.1. Investors and their Investments shall not, prior to the establishment of an Investment or afterwards, offer, promise or give any undue pecuniary or other advantage, whether directly or through intermediaries, to a public official of the Host State, or a member of an official's family or business associate or other person in close proximity to an official, for that official or for a third party, in order that the official or third party act or refrain from acting in relation to the performance of official duties, in order to achieve any favour in relation to a proposed investment or any licences, permits, contracts or other rights in relation to an Investment.

10.2. Investors and their Investments shall not be complicit in any act described in Paragraph 10.1, including incitement, aiding and abetting, and conspiracy to commit or authorization of such acts.

10.3. A breach of this article by an Investor or an Investment is deemed to constitute a breach of the domestic law of the Host State Party concerning the establishment and operation of an investment.

10.4. The State Parties to this Agreement, consistent with their applicable law, shall prosecute and where convicted penalize persons that have breached the applicable law implementing this obligation."

As a major player in world investment, China has started to take the issue of investment social resposibility very seriously. There are two reasons for this. Internally, China has had to tackle significant environmental problems, as polution has gained prominence in Chinese life, both political and social. Externally, certain irresponsible investment activities by some Chinese investors have attracted criticism, which in turn impacts on domestic decision making. As a result, the Chinese government has determined to promote socially responsible inward and outward investments at the same time. In 2013, the Ministry of Commerce and the Ministry of Environmental Protection jointly promulgated the Environmental Protection Guidelines for Overseas Investment Cooperation, which was the first official document promoting corporate social responsibility of China's overseas investment enterprises.[31]

It is beyond doubt that the Chinese BIT 4.0 should help promote such societal values such as environmental and labor protection. However, China is mindful that the specific standards of environmental and labor protection should match the economic development of the countries concerned, and that there are specialized international instruments and organizations dealing with such matters. Hence, it would not be realistic or appropriate to expect investment treaties to take primary responsibility in tackling such issues. Rather, the role of IIAs should be supplementary to more specialized instruments and organizations. In this connection, China should observe that the relevant provisions in the US Model BIT have struck a good balance. Articles 12–13 read:

> Article 12: Investment and Environment
>
> 1. The Parties recognize that their respective environmental laws and policies, and multilateral environmental agreements to which they are both party, play an important role in protecting the environment.
> 2. The Parties recognize that it is inappropriate to encourage investment by weakening or reducing the protections afforded in domestic environmental laws . . .
>
> Article 13: Investment and Labor
>
> 1. The Parties reaffirm their respective obligations as members of the International Labor Organization ("ILO") and their commitments

[31] The document is avaible at: www.mofcom.gov.cn/article/b/bf/201302/20130200039930.shtml.

under the ILO Declaration on Fundamental Principles and Rights at Work and its Follow-Up.

2. The Parties recognize that it is inappropriate to encourage investment by weakening or reducing the protections afforded in domestic labor laws . . .

It can be seen that the US approach, although imposing a legal obligation to observe relevant existing domestic or international legal standards, does not create any new or additional substantive international obligations. Moreover, such obligations cannot be enforced by either the ISDS or state-to-state abitration mechanism. Such environmental provisions, therefore, serve more of an educational and hortatory function. As such, it should be possible for China to accept similar provisions. Indeed, some more recent Chinese BITs have already accepted similar obligations. For instance, Article 23 of the China–Japan–Korea investment treaty states that "[E]ach Contracting Party recognizes that it is inappropriate to encourage investment by investors of another Contracting Party by relaxing its environmental measures. To this effect each Contracting Party should not waive or otherwise derogate from such environmental measures as an encouragement for the establishment, acquisition or expansion of investments in its territory." Similar provisions can also be found in the China–Canada BIT.[32] The US model marks a step further in that it puts such commitments in a mandatory form by using the term "shall" rather than "should," but it is not dramatically different from the aforementioned Chinese practice given that such commitments are not enforceable under the BIT.[33]

Dispute resolution

China has traditionally adopted European-style dispute resolution clauses with certain adaptations. Thus, the provisions for the settlement of both state-to-state and investor-state disputes are rather short and lack detail. Recent treaties, however, have demonstrated a willingness to adopt more detailed dispute settlement rules, particularly, rules on ISDS. In the China–Canada BIT of 2012, for instance, there are 14

[32] Article 18 (3), China–Canada BIT 2012.

[33] Admittedly the labor provisions might be more of a challenge to China, as it has not yet accepted any concrete commitment on labor rights. However, China should view such provisions more positively now given that it has seriously commited to the improvement of the conditions of human rights including labor rights.

provisions devoted to ISDS, amounting to more than one-third of the treaty's provisions. Such new developments have certainly followed the world trend in including a "comprehensive" ISDS mechanism in BITs. However, there is no shortage of willingness for innovation. A case in point is the provision on the settlement of disputes relating to financial regulation. Article 20(3) reads:

(a) Where an investor submits a claim to arbitration under this Article, and the disputing Contracting Party invokes Article 33(3), the investor-State tribunal established pursuant to this Part may not decide whether and to what extent Article 33(3) is a valid defence to the claim of the investor. It shall seek a report in writing from the Contracting Parties on this issue. The investor-State tribunal may not proceed pending receipt of such a report or of a decision of a State-State arbitral tribunal, should such a State-State arbitral tribunal be established.
(b) Pursuant to a request for a report received in accordance with subparagraph (a), the financial services authorities of the Contracting Parties shall engage in consultations. If the financial services authorities of the Contracting Parties reach a joint decision on the issue of whether and to what extent Article 33(3) is a valid defence to the claim of the investor, they shall prepare a written report describing their joint decision. The report shall be transmitted to the investor-State tribunal, and shall be binding on the investor-State tribunal.
(c) If, after 60 days, the financial services authorities of the Contracting Parties are unable to reach a joint decision on the issue of whether and to what extent Article 33(3) is a valid defence to the claim of the investor, the issue shall, within 30 days, be referred by either of the Contracting Parties to a State-State arbitral tribunal established pursuant to Article 15. In such a case, the provisions requiring consultations between the Contracting Parties in Article 15(1) and (2) shall not apply. The decision of the State-State arbitral tribunal shall be transmitted to the investor-State tribunal, and shall be binding on the investor-State tribunal. All of the members of any such State-State arbitral tribunal shall have expertise or experience in financial services law or practice, which may include the regulation of financial institutions.

Thus, a special mechanism has been created to deal with disputes concerning the prudential regulation of financial institutions. Under this regime, if an investor intends to sue a host state, and the host state invokes the prudential regulation exception (Article 33 (3)) as a defense, then the issue of whether and to what extent Article 33(3) is a valid defense should first be decided by the financial services authorites of the two parties, and failing that by a state-to-state arbitral tribunal established under Article 15 of the treaty. The joint decision by the financial services authorties or the state-to-state arbitration tribunal is binding on relevant ISDS tribunals. To an extent, this mechanism is an innovation and can be regarded as a Chinese reflection on and contribution to the current worldwide debate on ISDS reform.

While the China–Canada BIT marks a step forward in the reform of the investment dispute settlement mechanism under the new-generation BITs, the BIT negotiations with the United States and the EU might bring about even further reform. At the very least, China needs to consider the following three major questions: First, how should disputes relating to preestablishment national treatment obligations be settled: local remedies, state-to-state arbitration, or ISDS? Second, should the BIT incorporate the new United Nations Commission on International Trade Law (UNCITRAL) rules on transparency in ISDS?[34] Finally, should China consider setting up an appeal mechanism or an investment court, and if so, should it be bilateral or multilateral? Such a mechanism has been conceived by the United States in its BIT practice and has been considered by the EU in its Concept Paper. In answering such questions, China should not only consider the general domestic and international factors explored earlier but also the special Chinese circumstances or "charateristics" as a major player in international investment markets.

The features: a model BIT with "Chinese Characteristics"

As China has become a major player in international investment, both as an investor and a recipient at the same time, its needs and concerns have become more and more aligned with those of other major players such as the United States, the EU, and Japan. As a result, it should not at all be surprising that the new Chinese BIT model by and large resembles the

[34] The UNCITRAL Rules on Transparency in Treaty-based Investor-State Arbitration (the "Rules on Transparency"), which come into effect on 1 April 2014, comprise a set of procedural rules that provide for transparency and accessibility to the public of treaty-based investor-state arbitration. See 2014 – UNCITRAL Rules on Transparency in Treaty-based Investor-State Arbitration, posted at www.uncitral.org/uncitral/en/uncitral_texts/arbitration/2014Transparency.html.

models of such other major players. However, each economy has its own special circumstances and, consequently, its special needs and concerns. Such needs and concerns have to a certain extent been addressed in previous BITs, albeit in a reactive manner (i.e. as a response to certain provisions that could or should not be accepted by China). For example, China has long rejected the adoption of the national treatment standard, mainly because China was in the process of market-oriented reform that made it impossible to grant foreign investors such treatment.

The mega-BIT negotiations and China's BIT 4.0 provide a great opportunity for China to take a more proactive and systematic approach to its BIT regime. In other words, as a major investment player worldwide, China should no longer just "follow the leader" but should start to "design" its own treaty models. In doing so, China should certainly take care of its own interests in international investment, while making a commensurate contribution to the design and development of a more desirable international investment regime for all stakeholders in the world.

Any treaty design has to be based on the circumstances and needs of the state concerned. In the case of China, as it is today, at least three major elements are likely to have a notable impact in shaping the new BIT model: that China is a "Socialist Country with Chinese Characteristics" (the political system); that China is still in transition from a planned economy to a fully fledged market economy (the economic transition); and that China is a huge country with regions and provinces at diverse stages of development and, hence, with different local needs and priorities (the local priorities issue).

The political system: a socialism with Chinese Charateristics

China is among the very few countries in the world that practise a socialist system, or, using the Chinese term, "Socialism with Chinese Characteristics." This is not only a label but also a fundamental political reality. Such a reality undoubtedly impacts on treaty drafting and inpterpretation.

When drafting BITs, Chinese negotiators have to be mindful of this reality and make sure that it is respected in its model and real BITs, as BITs were originally developed in the Western world based on the logic of the free market. For example, it might be advisable to include in the preamble the principle of mutual respect of fundamental political, social, and economic systems. Each country is entitled to choose its own fundamental political, social, and economic system, and such choice should be respected by other countries. Such respect is rooted in the principle of equal rights and self-determination of peoples and the principle of sovereign equality enshrined in the UN Charter.[35]

The inclusion of the principle of mutual respect of fundamental political, social, and economic systems should help prevent an "imaginative" interpretation of treaty provisions resulting in a breach, such as a finding that there has been a "denial of justice" simply because China has not adopted the Western system of separation of powers (and, therefore, lacks an independent judiciary) or because the Chinese communist party plays a role in the court system. Such interpretations might look far-fetched, but as a matter of fact there is no shortage of far-fetched or imaginative interpretations in ISDS awards.

The inclusion of such a principle should also have implications for the negotiation and interpretation of provisions relating to state-owned enterprises (SOEs); this is discussed in detail later.

The economic reality: an economy in transition

As we have mentioned, the Chinese economy has been under reform since 1978. However, the reform is still ongoing, with China's Reform 2.0 currently still being implemented. According to the decision on the deepening of the reform, "[C]hina's economic system is one with public ownership serving as its main body but allowing for the development of all types of ownership." Reform 2.0 requires further reform of SOEs to promote a "modern system for State-owned enterprises." Meanwhile, Reform 2.0 intends to complete the property rights protection system, while actively developing a diversified ownership economy. Efforts will also be made to build a market system that is unified but open, orderly, and competitive; this requires the government to effectively shift its role by building itself into a service-type government that bases its functions on the law.

It is beyond doubt that such profound and far-reaching reform takes not only resolve and wisdom but also time. Accordingly, it would only be reasonable for the new BIT regime to support the reform rather than distract or derail it. A case in point is the regulation of SOEs in BITs. Recent years have seen increasing demands from Western countries to introduce rules on SOEs in the name of "competitive neutrality." While

[35] See Article 1(2) and 2(1), respectively, of the Charter of the United Nations.

the concept of competitive neutrality is generally compatible with China's current reform agenda, it is not realistic to expect competitive neutrality to be realized in China overnight.

Indeed, for a country practicing a socialist system with "public ownership serving as its main body," it would only be natural for China to highlight its need to promote and protect the investments of its SOEs overseas. Statistics show that over half of China's total overseas investment is made by SOEs. If investments made by SOEs are not protected by the Chinese BITs, it can hardly be said that the BITs are fair or effective for China. Undoubtedly, Chinese SOEs should follow the rules of a market economy when investing abroad. But as long as they are doing so, they should be entitled to full protection and should not be discriminated against simply because of the nature of their ownership. The latter would effectively create a new type of discrimination: discrimination based on ownership.

Accordingly, provisions such as the definition of "investment" or "enterprise," non-discriminative treatment, and access to ISDS should be clarified to ensure that Chinese SOEs are fully protected.

The local priorities: a country of diversity

Although China is a unitary state, it is also a big country by all measurements. As in every big country, different local needs and priorities have to be taken into account and accommodated, BITs should not be an exception.

To start with, China has four jurisdictions: Mainland, Hong Kong, Macau, and Taiwan. The BIT must carefully define which jurisdiction(s) it applies to in order to avoid jurisdictional issues such as those that arose in *Tza Yap Shum* v. *Peru* and *Sanum* v. *Laos*, which were cases brought by investors located in Hong Kong and Macau, respectively.

Within the mainland, there are still a few Minority Autonomous Regions and various special economic areas such as the pilot free trade zones in Shanghai, Guangdong, Fujian, and Tianjin, and the Special Economic Zones in Guangdong, Fujian, Shanghai, and Hainan, where certain special policies and rules are being practiced without being extended to the rest of the country. How such special policies and rules can survive without being treated as a violation of the BIT deserves careful consideration. In this connection, it is recalled that the US Model BIT excludes the application of certain provisions to existing nonconforming measures maintained by local authorities;[36] this might be a way forward for China.

Conclusions

China's dramatic move towards a new generation BIT may come as a surprise to many, but is with good reason. China's changing role in international investment, coupled with the needs of deepening domestic reform and the demanding mega-BIT negotiations with the United States and the EU, requires China to rethink its investment regime, for both domestic and international investment activities.

China's BIT 4.0 will have to cover not only traditional issues of investment protection such as substantive protection (e.g. FET, expropriation, and umbrella clauses) and procedural standards (notably, ISDS) but also new issues including investment liberalization (such as preestablishment national treatment and a negative list), environmental and labor protection, etc. While it might not be possible or appropriate to predict which rules will ultimately be chosen on such matters, it can be expected that the Chinese investment market will be further opened up and the substantive and procedural rules further clarified and balanced.

China's BIT 4.0 is an opportunity for China to not only respond on the worldwide debate and reform of the investement treaty regime but also to think in a systematic and proactive manner on how a new-generation BIT should be designed to protect and promote the best interests of China, while promoting public goods in the international investment law sphere for the world at large. In particular, China and its counterparts should be mindful of the fact that China has chosen a somewhat unique political system ("Socialism with Chinese Characteristics"), that it is deep in economic transition and has significant differences between its different localities. Only when the global and national versions meet and fit with the local realities, can China's BIT 4.0 be a real success.

International investment law is at a time of change and uncertainty. While both the TPP and the TTIP are progressing, both the United States and the EU have their own work to do at home: the Obama administration at the time of writing is fighting for fast-track authority in the House of Representatives, and the EU has now adopted its widely discussed Concept Paper on ISDS reform. Australia has re-included ISDS in its

[36] US Model BIT 2012 Article 14 (1)(a)(iii).

recent treaty with Korea, and Norway published its new model BIT, which is more investment-friendly than its 2007 draft. Many developing countries have also been very active: Brazil just signed a couple of BITs after many years of inactivity, and India and South Africa have both adopted new model BITs. The world is now watching China for its response. While it is unclear what the exact answer will be, it is certain that China will have to decide its own course of action, taking into account its own local circumstances.

PART IV

10

Regulating foreign investment: *Methanex* revisited

KYLA TIENHAARA AND TODD TUCKER

Introduction

Professor Sornarajah has always been generous with his time, particularly when approached by young scholars who are new to the field. In 2006, a PhD student (who at that point had learned almost everything that she knew about international investment law from his canonical text *The International Law of Foreign Investment*[1]) invited him to a workshop on investment law and sustainable development in Amsterdam. The workshop was in honor of the late (great) Konrad von Moltke, who had previously sought Sornarajah's input on the International Institute for Sustainable Development (IISD)'s Model International Investment Agreement. Sornarajah kindly agreed to make the long journey from Singapore to Amsterdam and, subsequently, contributed an article to a special issue that emanated from the workshop. It is this article – "A law for need or a law for greed? Restoring the lost law in the international law of foreign investment"–that was the inspiration for this chapter.[2]

The article provides a scathing assessment of international investment law, which Sornarajah argues "is increasingly becoming bereft of the values of peace and justice" and has "been hijacked to serve public and private power."[3] Broad interpretations of the fair and equitable treatment standard (FET) are singled out for particularly harsh criticism. Sornarajah expresses concern that concepts like "legitimate expectations"

[1] M. Sornarajah, *The International Law of Foreign Investment*, 2nd ed. (Cambridge: CUP, 2004).

[2] M. Sornarajah, "A Law for Need or a Law for Greed?: Restoring the Lost Law in the International Law of Foreign Investment" (2006) 6(4) *International Environmental Agreements: Politics, Law and Economics* 329.

[3] Ibid., at p. 331.

and "transparency" are being "plucked out of the air" and incorporated into tribunal interpretations of the standard.[4] In hindsight, Sornarajah's concerns about FET seem very well placed. In the intervening years, interpretations of the standard have continued to diverge substantially rather than to stabilize, and even in the context of the North American Free Trade Agreement (NAFTA) – where FET has been expressly equated with the minimum standard of treatment under customary international law – controversial awards still occur.[5]

Sornarajah's article was not all doom and gloom. In addition to critiquing the system, he also identified where change was occurring that could help to shift away from a law of greed to a law of need. In particular, he expressed cautious optimism that the Final Award in *Methanex* v. *United States of America* (NAFTA) had "undermined the law on expropriation" and changed "the law in the area significantly."[6]

Historically, protection from expropriation was at the heart of the international investment regime.[7] However, direct takings of property have been a rarity for decades. As Sornarajah has noted, "The modern day reality is that states seldom adopt measures affecting property rights except when the interests of public welfare require it."[8] However, this reality has not rendered expropriation provisions obsolete; instead they took on a new significance, beginning in the mid-1990s, in protecting investors from "regulatory takings" or "indirect expropriation."

This evolution in the meaning of expropriation was made possible by the language in many investment treaties referring to measures having a "similar" or "equivalent" effect to expropriation. In the case of some treaties, such as NAFTA, reference is made to measures "tantamount" to expropriation; this language has been particularly contentious in investment arbitration, but it is now well established that it does not create a third category of expropriation.

[4] Ibid., at p. 346.

[5] As noted by dissenting arbitrator in a recent the *Clayton/Bilcon* v. *Canada* case, the majority of the tribunal found a potential violation of Canadian law to amount to a violation of the minimum standard/FET in NAFTA. See *Clayton/Bilcon* v. *Canada*, Dissenting Opinion of Professor Donald McRae, www.international.gc.ca/trade-agreements-accords-commerciaux/assets/pdfs/disp-diff/clayton-13.pdf.

[6] Sornarajah, "Law for Need", 343.

[7] C. Schreuer, "Introduction: Interrelationship of Standards", in August Reinisch (ed.), *Standards of Investment Protection* (Oxford: OUP, 2008), 1–8 at p. 2.

[8] M. Sornarajah, *Resistance and Change in the International Law on Foreign Investment* (Cambridge: CUP, 2015), 237.

It is generally accepted that indirect expropriation falls short of actual physical taking of property but results in "the effective loss of management, use or control, or a significant depreciation of the value of the assets of a foreign investor."[9] The key question plaguing various arbitral panels and numerous legal scholars for the past two decades is whether regulatory measures, adopted for a public purpose such as environmental protection, can be considered expropriatory and thus require the payment of compensation to the aggrieved investor.

In its Final Award, the *Methanex* tribunal essentially answered this question in the negative (with a caveat to be discussed further below) and thereby carved out nondiscriminatory regulatory measures from NAFTA's provision on expropriation. Sornarajah argues that the *Methanex* tribunal did not invent this regulatory exemption but rather "revived" a rule that had always existed but had been deliberately eschewed by other tribunals.[10]

The modest aim of this chapter is to track the impact of the *Methanex* decision on expropriation since it was promulgated a decade ago. In doing so, we endeavor to assess whether Sornarajah's optimism about the revival of a regulatory exemption from expropriation was well founded. This is a relevant objective not only in the framework of this book but also in the broader context of ongoing debates about investor-state dispute settlement (ISDS). As Lawrence has noted, the *Methanex* case has been used by supporters of NAFTA as evidence that there is no basis for public concerns about ISDS.[11] References to the case (by ISDS supporters and detractors) still emerge in contemporary debates about, for example, the Trans Pacific Partnership Agreement.[12] However, as Donald McRae (professor, sometime arbitrator, and counsel to the IISD in their intervention in the *Methanex* case) has argued, "in a system where investment agreements are interpreted by ad hoc tribunals with no provision for any wide ranging subsequent review or for an appellate process it is a pattern of decision-making rather than individual decisions

[9] UNCTAD, "Taking of Property", in *Issues in International Investment Agreements*, UNCTAD/ITE/IIT/15 (Geneva: UNCTAD, 2000), at p. 4.

[10] *El Paso Energy* v. *Argentina* (ICSID Case No. ARB/03/15) Legal Opinion of M. Sornarajah (2007), at p. 59, www.italaw.com/sites/default/files/case-documents/ita0970.pdf.

[11] J. Lawrence, "Chicken Little Revisited: NAFTA Regulatory Expropriations after Methanex" (2006) 41 *Georgia Law Review* 261.

[12] J. Weisman, "Trans-Pacific Partnership Seen as Door for Foreign Suits Against U.S.", *New York Times* (25 March 2015).

that count."[13] We seek to establish whether *Methanex* was a one-off "easy" case or instead has helped to establish a pattern of decision-making in investment arbitration that is deferential to states and thereby acts to preserve policy space.

To achieve this aim we first revisit the facts of the *Methanex* case and highlight how the tribunal's interpretation of indirect expropriation diverged from the case law up to that point. Then, with Sornarajah's concern that the "writings of 'highly qualified' publicists" have been overly influential in international investment law in mind, we assess the reaction to the *Methanex* decision in the academic literature.[14]

Subsequently, we ask whether there has been "less fervour in basing claims on expropriation" post-*Methanex*.[15] Related to this, we also address whether there has been a "shift to the other heads of liability under the investment treaties, namely treatment standards."[16] We further examine whether the *Methanex* decision has had a strong (informal) precedent effect by tracing references to it in subsequent awards. We disaggregate the data based on the development status of the country to address Sornarajah's concern that the benefits of the *Methanex* decision might be confined to powerful states like the United States.[17]

As noted by Sornarajah, at the time of the *Methanex* Award, some states were already beginning to "exclude" regulatory expropriation from their treaties. Such "safeguards" (in contemporary parlance) have proliferated in recent years, but there has not been a systematic study of their geographic reach or the extent to which they vary. We examine a large sample of treaties from the period immediately before and in the 10 years since the *Methanex* Award and compare the wording of the existing safeguards with the exemption for regulatory measures articulated by the tribunal.

We conclude that the *Methanex* case has not had the impact hoped for by Sornarajah and others. The enthusiasm of investors to claim indirect expropriation has not been dulled. While it is true that expropriation claims often fail, this is not attributable to an acceptance of the *Methanex* approach, which has actually been followed in very few subsequent cases.

[13] D. McRae, "Trade, Investment and the Environment: Closed Boxes?: Concluding Remarks" (2006) 100 *American Society of International Law Proceedings* 34, at 37.

[14] Sornarajah, "Law for Need", 348. [15] Ibid., 344. [16] Ibid. [17] Ibid., 349.

The Case: *Methanex* v. *United States of America*

The facts

Beginning in the late 1980s, various studies were undertaken in the United States to identify ways in which gasoline could be reformulated to help achieve certain air quality goals. These studies found that the addition of oxygenated organic compounds, such as alcohols and ethers, to conventional gasoline resulted in a reduction in the emissions of carbon monoxide and other products of incomplete combustion. The use of oxygenates in fuel subsequently became mandatory under US Federal law. In California, the "oxygenate of choice" was methyl tertiary-butyl ether (MTBE).

Thus, MTBE was initially brought into use in California (and in other locations) to bring about health and environmental benefits. However, improvements in the emission control technology used in cars significantly reduced emissions of air pollutants, and as a result, the impact of MTBE and other oxygenates on air quality has been rendered insignificant.[18] At the same time, oxygenates have been identified as potential groundwater contaminants. MTBE, for example, is highly soluble in water and will transfer readily to groundwater from gasoline leaking from underground storage tanks, pipelines, and other components of the gasoline distribution system.[19]

In 1997, the California Senate commissioned researchers at the University of California to conduct an assessment of the human health and environmental risks and benefits associated with the use of MTBE and other gasoline oxygenates.[20] In 1998, the researchers released their five-volume, 600-page report (the UC Report).[21] The UC Report concluded that California's water resources were being placed at risk by the use of MTBE in gasoline.

While the UC Report suggested that the risk of exposure to MTBE through ingestion or inhalation was low, they noted that there were significant gaps in the scientific understanding of the acute and chronic

18 "University of California Report: MTBE Fact Sheet", *UC Davis Website* (12 November 1998): 1, http://tsrtp.ucdavis.edu/public/mtbe/mtberpt/index.php.

19 Ibid.

20 *Methanex Corporation* v. *United States of America*, First Partial Award (7 August 2002), at para. 26.

21 Health & Environmental Assessment of MTBE, Report to the Governor and Legislature of the State of California, Volume I, Summary & Recommendations (November 1998), https://tsrtp.ucdavis.edu/public/mtbe/mtberpt/vol1.pdf.

toxicity of MTBE.[22] The UC Report also suggested that the potential treatment costs of MTBE-contaminated drinking water could be enormous. Furthermore, the costs associated with remediating leaks and spills from underground storage tanks and pipelines could be in the order of tens to hundreds of millions of dollars per year.[23]

The UC Report recommended that California phase out the use of gasoline oxygenates. In order to do so, it would have to seek a waiver from the Federal Environmental Protection Agency (EPA). A second-best option, suggested in the UC Report, was the use of ethanol in place of MTBE. The inadequate supply of ethanol in the state meant that an immediate ban on MTBE would have negative implications for consumers and disrupt gasoline production significantly, and the UC Report therefore recommended a scheduled phase-out, coupled with a careful study of the environmental and health impacts of alternative oxygenates, such as ethanol.[24]

Governor Gray Davis responded by issuing an Executive Order directing the relevant government bodies to implement the recommendations of the UC Report. California's request for a waiver from the Federal EPA was ultimately rejected, and, as such, the second-best option of using ethanol as a replacement oxygenate was adopted in the state.

The claims

In December 1999, Methanex Corp., a Canadian company that produces and markets methanol, served a Notice of Arbitration against the United States under NAFTA Chapter 11 and the UNCITRAL Rules of Arbitration.[25] The company supplied the vast majority of methanol in California, which has no methanol industry of its own.[26] While Methanex Corp. did not produce or sell MTBE, approximately one-third of the company's methanol production at the time was directed at the fuel sector, principally for use in the production of MTBE.[27]

The claims put forward in the company' subsequent pleadings included that NAFTA Article 1102 on national treatment, Article 1105 on the minimum standard of treatment (including FET), and Article 1110 on expropriation (including measures "tantamount" to expropriation) had

[22] Ibid. [23] Ibid. [24] Ibid., at 13–14.

[25] *Methanex Corporation* v. *United States of America*, Notice of Arbitration (3 December 1999).

[26] *Methanex Corporation* v. *United States of America*, Rejoinder to US Reply Memorial on Jurisdiction, Admissibility and the Proposed Amendment (25 May 2001), at p. 27.

[27] *Methanex* First Partial Award, at para. 24.

been breached by California's measures.[28] Methanex sought compensation in the order of US$970 million (plus interest and costs).[29]

The United States argued that the claims were not admissible and that the tribunal had no jurisdiction over the case.[30] One of the jurisdictional challenges laid out by the United States focused on the fact that NAFTA Article 1101.1 requires that measures subject to a dispute "relate to" an investor or investment. The United States asserted that the Californian ban on MTBE did not relate to Methanex Corp. because it was not directed at methanol or methanol producers. The United States contended that the phrase "relating to" requires a legally significant connection between the disputed measure and the investor.[31] This excludes measures of general application, especially measures aimed at the protection of human health and the environment, which are likely to affect a vast range of actors and economic interests. The United States argued that, if such general measures were not excluded from consideration by tribunals, the NAFTA Parties could be subject to claims based on untold numbers of local, state, and federal measures that merely have an incidental impact on an investor or investment.[32]

Methanex Corp., on the other hand, suggested that it should be sufficient that government measures affect an investor or its investment.[33] Furthermore, the company argued that the "relating to" requirement is easily satisfied if there is discriminatory intent behind a measure.[34]

The First Partial Award

In its First Partial Award, the tribunal found that several of the arguments in the US pleading were not actually jurisdictional challenges and that, even if they were, the issues were so tied up in the facts of the case that they would have to be dealt with in the merits phase of arbitration.

[28] *Methanex Corporation* v. *United States of America*, Amended Statement of Claim (12 February 2001).

[29] *Methanex Corporation* v. *United States of America*, Statement of Claim (3 December 1999), at p. 13.

[30] *Methanex Corporation* v. *United States of America*, Statement of Defense (10 August 2000).

[31] Ibid., at p. 28.

[32] *Methanex Corporation* v. *United States of America*, US Memorial on Jurisdiction (13 November 2000), at pp. 48–49.

[33] *Methanex Corporation* v. *United States of America*, Counter-Memorial on Jurisdiction (12 February 2001), at pp. 47–48.

[34] Ibid., at pp. 51–52.

However, the tribunal did extensively discuss the argument concerning the connection required between a measure and an investment. The tribunal noted:

> If the threshold provided by Article 1101(1) were merely one of "affecting," as Methanex contends, it would be satisfied wherever any economic impact was felt by an investor or an investment . . . As such, Article 1101 (1) would provide no significant threshold to a NAFTA arbitration . . . Methanex's interpretation would produce a surprising, if not an absurd, result. The possible consequences of human conduct are infinite, especially when comprising acts of governmental agencies; but common sense does not require that line to run unbroken towards an endless horizon.[35]

The tribunal determined that it would only have jurisdiction over the claims presented if Methanex Corp. could prove that there was discriminatory intent underlying the Californian regulations. The claimant was invited to submit a fresh pleading setting out its specific factual allegations related only to the issue of intent, and the decision on jurisdiction was postponed pending the conclusion of the merits phase of the arbitration.

In November 2002, Methanex Corp. submitted a fresh pleading outlining allegations that the MTBE ban was not motivated by the Government of California's desire to protect the environment but that this was merely a convenient cover for measures that would significantly benefit the powerful US ethanol industry.[36] A conspiracy theory involving Archer Daniels Midland (ADM – the company that produces more than 70 percent of US ethanol) and Governor Davis was proposed in the document.

The Final Award

The Final Award was issued on August 3, 2005. As the majority of the claimant's arguments had focused on discriminatory treatment and the First Partial Award had largely limited the case to an analysis of the motivation behind the Californian measures, the bulk of the Final Award also dealt with these issues.

In the tribunal's view, there was significant evidence that California's MTBE regulations were motivated by legitimate concern for the environment and the health and welfare of the population of the state: "This

[35] *Methanex* First Partial Award, at para. 137.

[36] *Methanex Corporation* v. *United States of America*, Second Amended Statement of Claim (5 November 2002).

policy was motivated by the honest belief, held in good faith and on reasonable scientific grounds, that MTBE contaminated groundwater and was difficult and expensive to clean up."[37]

In particular, the tribunal found that the UC Report reflected "a serious, objective and scientific approach to a complex problem in California."[38] They also rejected the conspiracy theory about ADM and Governor Davis, pointing out that the Senate Bill that had mandated gubernatorial action regarding MTBE was passed by the California legislature prior to his election and that once he was Governor, Davis had no discretion to deviate from the results and recommendations of the UC Report.[39]

Furthermore, the tribunal noted that the evidence suggested that the Government of California, far from favoring ethanol, aimed to receive a waiver from the US EPA so that it could prohibit the use of all gasoline oxygenates.[40] The tribunal, therefore, found no breach of Article 1102. The tribunal went on to address the issue of whether a breach of Article 1102 (had a breach been found) would have constituted a further breach of Article 1105. The tribunal decided that the claimant's argument was untenable, even in the absence of the NAFTA Free Trade Commission Notes of Interpretation,[41] because the plain meaning of the minimum standard does not support the contention that it precludes discrimination.[42] As this was the entire basis of the claimant's Article 1105 claim, it also failed.

Finally, the tribunal made its noteworthy decision on Article 1110, finding that

> as a matter of general international law, a non-discriminatory regulation for a public purpose, which is enacted in accordance with due process and, which affects, inter alios, a foreign investor or investment is not deemed expropriatory and compensable unless specific commitments had been given by the regulating government to the then putative foreign investor

[37] *Methanex Corporation* v. *United States of America*, Final Award of the Tribunal on Jurisdiction and Merits (3 August 2005), at para. III.A.102.2.

[38] Ibid., para. III.A.101. [39] Ibid., para. III.B.54. [40] Ibid., para. III.B.55.

[41] In 2001, the United States submitted a copy of the Notes of Interpretation issued by the NAFTA Free Trade Commission to the tribunal. The Notes of Interpretation clarified that Article 1105 did not require treatment beyond that prescribed in customary international law and stipulated that the determination that there had been a breach of another provision of NAFTA did not establish a breach of Article 1105. Methanex Corp. challenged the submission, arguing that the Notes of Interpretation had been made with a clear purpose of affecting the outcome of the case.

[42] *Methanex* Final Award, at para. IV.C.14.

> contemplating investment that the government would refrain from such regulation.[43]

The tribunal concluded that the California regulations met all these requirements and, therefore, did not constitute an indirect expropriation of Methanex Corp.'s investment.

Having dealt with the merits of the claim, the tribunal returned to the issue of jurisdiction, which it had delayed in order to assess the issue of intent. Having found no evidence of intent, the tribunal concluded that there was no legally significant connection between the Californian regulations and the claimant's investments. Thus despite having determined that all the claims had failed on the merits, the tribunal subsequently found that it lacked the jurisdiction to consider these claims and dismissed the case accordingly.

Finally, the tribunal ordered the losing party (Methanex Corp.) to pay all of the costs of the arbitration (nearly US$1.1 million) as well as close to US$3 million that the United States had incurred in legal fees.[44]

The significance of the decision on expropriation

As noted earlier, Sornarajah celebrated the *Methanex* decision at the time, claiming that it constituted a "redefinition of regulatory takings as not amounting to expropriation."[45] Sornarajah contrasted the *Methanex* decision with previous awards on expropriation, particularly in *Santa Elena* v. *Costa Rica* where the tribunal (considering a direct expropriation) stated:

> Expropriatory environmental measures – no matter how laudable and beneficial to society on the whole – are, in this respect, similar to any other expropriatory measures that a state may take in order to implement its policies; where property is expropriated even for environmental purposes, whether domestic or international, a state's obligation to pay compensation remains.[46]

The *Methanex* decision was also in sharp contrast to that found in *Metalclad* v. *Mexico* where the tribunal had adopted an approach that only focused the impact of government measures on the investment. Methanex Corp. had relied quite heavily on *Metalclad* in its pleadings.

There was also divergence from the approach in *Pope and Talbot* v. *Canada*, where the tribunal stated that a "blanket exception for

[43] Ibid., para. IV.D.7. [44] Ibid., para. V.13. [45] Sornarajah, "Law for Need", 343.

[46] *Compañía del Desarrollo de Santa Elena, S.A.* v. *Costa Rica*, ICSID Case No. ARB/96/1, Final Award (17 February 2000), at para. 72.

regulatory measures would create a gaping loophole in international protection against expropriation."[47] Similarly, in *TecMed* v. *Mexico*, the tribunal stated:

> We find no principle stating that regulatory administrative actions are *per se* excluded from the scope of the Agreement, even if beneficial to society as a whole – such as environmental protection – particularly if the negative economic impact of such action on the financial position of the investor is sufficient to neutralize in full the value, or economic or commercial use of its investment without receiving any compensation whatsoever.[48]

While there were certainly cases prior to *Methanex* that indicated some deference to regulatory intervention in the activities of investors (e.g. *Feldman* v. *Mexico*, *Lauder* v. *The Czech Republic*, *S.D. Myers* v. *Canada*, *Azinian* v. *Mexico*), *Methanex* was viewed by many as the clearest statement of a "police powers carve-out."[49]

Explaining the outcome

The ad hoc tribunal in *Methanex* was led by V.V. Veeder, who was joined by J. William Rowley (selected by the claimant) and former US Secretary of State Warren Christopher (selected by the respondent). However, Christopher resigned from the panel in 2002 following a challenge to his independence and impartiality.[50] While Christopher cowrote the First Partial Award, it was his replacement – Michael Reisman – who helped pen the Final Award.

Veeder, Rowley, and Reisman are counted among the most active arbitrators in the field of ISDS.[51] This was not a panel of newcomers to the field or radical thinkers out to redefine international investment law. In fact, Jan Paulsson (an arbitrator and past-President of the London Court of International Arbitration) described the *Methanex* panel as

[47] *Pope & Talbot* v. *Government of Canada*, Interim Award on Damages (31 May 2002), at para. 99.

[48] *Técnicas Medioambientales Tecmed, S.A.* v. *United Mexican States*, ICSID Case No. ARB (AF)/00/2, Award (unofficial English translation from Spanish original) (29 May 2003), at para. 121.

[49] J. Bonnitcha, *Substantive Protection under Investment Treaties: A Legal and Economic Analysis* (Cambridge: CUP, 2014), at p. 256.

[50] IISD, "Warren Christopher Steps Down as Arbitrator in Methanex Case", *Investment Law and Sustainable Development Weekly News Bulletin* (25 October 2002), www.iisd.org/itn/wp-content/uploads/2010/10/investment_investsd_oct_2002.pdf.

[51] "Arbitrator Profiles", www.iareporter.com/categories/profiles.

"comprised of well-known arbitrators at the height of their personal authority and intellectual powers."[52]

While Veeder and Rowley are primarily arbitrators (that also act as counsel or expert witnesses in some cases), Reisman is a Professor of International Law at the Yale Law School who has published widely on investment law. In a 2004 article on indirect expropriation, Reisman (and his coauthor Robert Sloane) argued that "while a host state is not, of course, precluded from regulating foreign investments, some regulations, and equally importantly, failures to regulate, may rise to the level of expropriatory action."[53] As Sornarajah has noted, the article "took the law beyond the already expansionist meaning of indirect expropriation into an area yet to be charted."[54] The authors argued that the economic effects of a government's actions are critical in the determination of an indirect expropriation.[55] It seems very surprising that only a year later Reisman would agree to an effective exemption for nondiscriminatory public interest measures from the expropriation provision of NAFTA.

It remains an open question as to why the tribunal made such a strong statement on regulatory powers, especially when it was not critical to their finding on jurisdiction. In hindsight, given subsequent decisions that have been made by members of the panel in other cases (see further below), it is even more puzzling. Some observers have suggested that the tribunal was preoccupied with the concept of national treatment, and this colored the decision on expropriation.[56] Others have speculated that perhaps this section of the Final Award was written in haste and without much thought put into the wording.[57] Given that the bulk of the case focused on discrimination and the claimant's far-fetched conspiracy theory, it is certainly understandable that the tribunal might have devoted less time to the question of expropriation. Nevertheless, it is hard to believe that the tribunal would not have been cognisant of the

[52] J. Paulsson, "Indirect Expropriation: Is the Right to Regulate at Risk?", in *Making the Most of International Investment Agreements: A Common Agenda* (Paris: OECD, 12 December 2005), at p. 3.

[53] M. Reisman and R. Sloane, "Indirect Expropriation and Its Valuation the BIT Generation" (2004) 74(1) *British Yearbook of International Law* 115, at p. 129.

[54] Sornarajah, *Resistance and Change*, at p. 211.

[55] Reisman and Sloane, "Indirect Expropriation", at p. 121.

[56] R. Dolzer and C. Schreuer, *Principles of Investment Law* (Oxford: OUP, 2012) at p. 121.

[57] OGEMID, "Methanex – Erroneous on Expropriation? (An OGEMID Discussion)" (2005) 5 *Transnational Dispute Management*, www.transnational-dispute-management.com/article.asp?key=680.

potential weight of their words on the topic given the level of discussion about indirect expropriation in academic and policy circles at the time.

An alternative explanation is that the tribunal was influenced by the attention the case had garnered and the public scrutiny of ISDS it had aroused. As noted by Barton Legum (lead counsel for the United States in *Methanex*), the case had "attracted the attention of the public in a way that disputes before international tribunals rarely do."[58] Schneiderman points out that the case (when it was ongoing) had a significant impact on the 2002 Congressional debate on whether to provide President Bush with ("fast track") Trade Promotion Authority.[59]

Van Harten has hypothesized that tribunals might choose to limit state liability in cases where a damages award could stoke controversy with decision-makers and the public, particularly in developed states.[60] More than one observer has suggested that a large award against the United States in *Methanex* would have been "politically unpalatable for the arbitrators" even if they had found evidence of discrimination.[61] Canadian lawyer Steven Shrybman is less diplomatic in his suggestion that "the adjudicators who make a pretty penny arbitrating these cases understand that there are certain places they shouldn't go if they want to continue to have these files."[62]

The *Methanex* tribunal certainly seemed conscious of the public attention that the case had garnered when it made its decision on allowing amicus curiae, noting that

> the Chapter 11 arbitral process could benefit from being perceived as more open or transparent; or conversely be harmed if seen as unduly secretive. In this regard, the Tribunal's willingness to receive amicus submissions might support the process in general and this arbitration in particular, whereas a blanket refusal could do positive harm.[63]

58 B. Legum, "Introductory Note to *Methanex Corporation* v. *United States of America*" (2005) 44 *ILM* 1343, at p. 1343.

59 Quoted in A. Vasil, "Toxic Tyranny: Americans Freaked by NAFTA Section That Lets Canuck Polluter Sue Them for Protecting Water", *Now Toronto Magazine* (24 June 2004), https://nowtoronto.com/news/toxic-tyranny/.

60 G. Van Harten, *Investment Treaty Arbitration and Public Law* (Oxford: OUP, 2007), at p. 147.

61 M. Endicott, "Remedies in Investor-State Arbitration: Restitution, Specific Performance and Declaratory Awards", in P. Kahn and T. Wälde (eds.) *New Aspects of International Investment Law* (Leiden: Brill, 2007), 517–552, at 540. See also the discussion in Vasil, "Toxic Tyranny".

62 Quoted in Vasil, "Toxic Tyranny".

63 *Methanex* v. *United States of America*, Decision on Petitions from Third Persons to Intervene as *Amici Curiae* (15 January 2001), at para. 49.

Perhaps, equally important as the fact that the case had generated controversy was the growing evidence that decision-makers were taking public concerns about ISDS seriously. Ortino argues that at a political level there was a "reorientation" of investment law taking place at the time that the *Methanex* tribunal was deliberating.[64] The issuance of the FTC Notes of Interpretation in 2001 and the development of new model bilateral investment treaties (BITs) by Canada and the United States in 2004 (see further below) are cited as prime examples of this shift. Ortino argues that the reorientation "has undoubtedly influenced investment tribunals practice and the *Methanex* award . . . is the *clearest example of such influence*."[65]

There is one final explanation worth considering, which is that the *Methanex* decision has been widely misinterpreted and was not actually intended by its authors to be a strict police powers carve-out. It is possible that the standard reading of the Final Award puts too much emphasis on the words "is not deemed expropriatory," rather than the battery of qualifications that follow ("non-discriminatory," "public purpose," "due process" and "specific commitments"). These qualifications create a playground for the enterprising claimant lawyer. Moreover, shortly after the famous and oft-quoted paragraph from the *Methanex* decision, the tribunal goes on to discuss the fact that the claimant had not established "that the California ban manifested any of the features associated with expropriation" and quotes *Feldman* v. *Mexico* on the level of deprivation required for a measure to be deemed expropriatory. The tribunal concludes that "[f]or *all* the above reasons", Article 1110 was not breached.[66]

Read in context, the expropriation finding appears more hedged, allowing either a police powers carve-out reading or a degree-and-qualities of deprivation reading. This has not been how the decision has been viewed in the literature, but it could help to explain the seemingly inconsistent views expressed by members of the *Methanex* panel in subsequent awards and expert opinion reports (see further below).

Academic reaction to the decision

As noted in the introduction, Sornarajah has expressed a concern that certain academics (and other "highly qualified" publicists) have an undue

[64] F. Ortino, "The Impact of *Amicus Curiae* Briefs in the Settlement of Trade and Investment Disputes", in K. Meessen (ed.), *Economic Law as an Economic Good: Its Rule Function and Its Tool Function in the Competition of Systems* (Munich: Sellier, 2009), 301–316 at 315.

[65] Ibid., at 316, emphasis added.

[66] *Methanex* Final Award, at para. IV.D.18.

influence on the development of investment law. Of course there is no standard definition of what makes a "highly qualified" publicist and while we may have some hunches about which individuals are most likely to be cited as authorities by a tribunal, we have not studied this systematically. Furthermore, it is possible that the reaction to a decision within the academy and investment arbitration community will have an impact in shaping how that decision is perceived by arbitrators that cannot be captured by measuring direct citations to the literature. As such, we have not placed any boundaries on our literature review.

Reactions to the *Methanex* decision can be categorized into four groups. First, there are those that accept/approve of the decision broadly speaking and express some hope that the decision will represent a turning point in investment arbitration. Most scholars within this group remain concerned that regulatory measures will continue to be challenged because of the lack of formal precedent in investment arbitration.[67] Many authors, including Sornarajah in his more recent writing on the case, while approving of the tribunal's deference to a state's police powers, find fault in the exception that the tribunal made for instances where a state had made "specific commitments" to the investor.[68] Sornarajah notes:

> The formulation of an exception to regulatory expectations on the basis of commitments to putative investors is an intervention to conserve the protection of the stabilization clause, and foreshadows commitments made to the investors giving rise to legitimate expectations. It is an infusion of a neoliberal thought, seeking to preserve what could be preserved for the cause of investment protection.[69]

The second group finds no fault with the decision and emphasizes that it proves that there was never any basis for the widespread concern about investment treaties encroaching on regulatory space in the first place.[70]

[67] H. Mann, *The Final Decision in Methanex v. United States: Some New Wine in Some New Bottles* (Winnipeg: IISD, 2005); R. Edsall, "Indirect Expropriation Under NAFTA and DR-CAFTA: Potential Inconsistencies in the Treatment of State Public Welfare Regulations" (2006) 86 *Boston University Law Review* 931; Lawrence, "Chicken Little Revisited".

[68] See also Mann, *Final Decision*, and M. Orellana, "Science, Risk and Uncertainty: Public Health Measures and Investment Disciplines", in Philippe Kahn and Thomas W. Wälde (eds.) *New Aspects of International Investment Law* (Leiden: Martinus Nijhoff, 2007), 671–790.

[69] Sornarajah, *Resistance and Change*, at p. 218.

[70] Paulsson, "Indirect Expropriation"; J. Marlles, "Public Purpose, Private Losses: Regulatory Expropriation and Environmental Regulation in International Investment Law" (2007) 16 *Journal of Transnational Law & Policy* 275.

The third group does not explicitly criticize the decision but suggests its application may be problematic.[71] For example, Schreuer notes that it has become very difficult for investors to succeed in a claim of indirect expropriation partly as a result of "growing sympathy on the part of tribunals for regulatory measures in the public interest" (specifically citing *Methanex* as an example). The consequence of decisions to carve out public policy measures from the category of compensable expropriation, Schreuer argues, is that "the investor gets nothing," which is an "unsatisfactory state of affairs and has led to a more balanced approach that would abandon the current 'all or nothing' situation between full compensation and zero compensation".[72] Schreuer argues that it "is no exaggeration to say that the current law on expropriation is in a state of crisis."[73]

The fourth and final group finds fault with the decision. In a discussion on the Oil-Gas-Energy-Mining Investment Disputes (OGEMID)[74] forum shortly after the publication of the Final Award, numerous commentators expressed the opinion that the decision on expropriation was wrong and did not reflect customary international law.[75] Notably, some scholars in this group expressed the view that the tribunal did get one thing right – the statement on specific commitments (the precise matter that the first group believes the tribunal got wrong).

Several published works espouse similar arguments to those found in the OGEMID discussion. Hoffman simply dismisses the *Methanex* decision and the existence of a general exemption from compensation for regulatory measures, citing *Santa Elena* for support.[76] Anzorena *et al.* suggest that the decision "seems to oversimplify the far from cohesive

[71] For example, Newcombe suggests that the decision "is generally correct" but "nevertheless overly broad." A. Newcombe, "The Boundaries of Regulatory Expropriation in International Law", in P. Kahn and T. Wälde (eds.), *New Aspects of International Investment Law* (Leiden: Brill, 2007), 391–446 at 442. Anzorena *et al.* also suggest that "critics" find the decision "unduly restrictive." C. Anzorena, R. Wisner, J. Coe, and C. Salomon "International Commercial Dispute Resolution" (2006) 40 *International Lawyer* 251.

[72] Schreuer, "Introduction", at p. 2. [73] Ibid.

[74] According to its website "OGEMID brings together most of the world's experienced professionals in the field of international dispute management, mainly arbitration, mediation, negotiation, with a particular emphasis on investment disputes." www.transnational-dispute-management.com/ogemid/.

[75] OGEMID, "Methanex – Erroneous".

[76] A. Hoffmann, "Indirect Expropriation", in A. Reinisch (ed.), *Standards of Investment Protection* (Oxford: OUP, 2008), 151–171 at 165.

authority addressing regulatory takings."[77] Dolzer and Schreuer conclude that "regulatory rules and the measures based on them are subject to the same standards of protection that have been developed for all other instances" and suggest that the tribunal in *Methanex* (as well as the tribunals in other cases that have adopted a similar approach) was (inappropriately) influenced by the concept of national treatment.[78]

Escarcena argues that the *Methanex* tribunal confused "the constitutive elements of a taking with the requirements of a lawful expropriation."[79] In other words, the "three requirements set out by Methanex for a regulatory, nonexpropriatory measure duplicate three out of the four criteria for compensable expropriations in Article 1110(1)."[80] Elcombe concludes:

> The "sole-effect" approach applied in *Metalclad* represents a valid interpretation of Article 1110(1), even if critics are correct in claiming that it restrains the governments' freedom to protect the environment and public health. The analysis used in *Methanex*, although celebrated for its public policy ramifications, is incompatible with the category of compensable expropriations established by the NAFTA text. Recent decisions, in particular the *Glamis Gold* judgment, point to the frailty of the *Methanex* precedent.[81]

In a published case comment, Weiler similarly notes "the Tribunal staked a position that will have undoubtedly delighted the NGOs that made submissions before it while confounding most experts on the customary international law of expropriation".[82] He further points out that the *Methanex* tribunal only cited two previous awards in support of its finding on expropriation and that neither award actually supported its position. He concludes that the text of NAFTA "simply cannot be reconciled with the Tribunal's finding" and will be unlikely to have a significant impact on the jurisprudence.[83]

77 Anzorena *et al.*, "International Commercial Dispute Resolution", at p. 256.
78 Dolzer and Schreuer, *Principles*, at p. 122
79 S. Escarena, *Indirect Expropriation in International Law* (Cheltenham: Elgar, 2014) at p. 170.
80 J. Elcombe, "Regulatory Powers vs. Investment Protection Under NAFTA's Chapter 1110: Metalclad, Methanex and Glamis Gold" (2010) 68 *University of Toronto Faculty Law Review* 71, at p. 85.
81 Ibid., at p. 98.
82 T. Weiler, "*Methanex Corp.* v. *U.S.A.*: Turning the Page on NAFTA Chapter Eleven?" (2005) 6 *Journal of World Investment & Trade* 903, at 918.
83 Ibid., at 921.

Interestingly, in a more recent document written for a nongovernmental organization (NGO), Weiler cites *Methanex* as evidence that there is a "commonly accepted position" that legitimate, nondiscriminatory public welfare measures do not require compensation "except in rare circumstances."[84] In a footnote, he acknowledges that this contradicts his previous writing on the decision but states that "both State practice and arbitral decisions have moved away from my position, such that it could not be safely assumed by any claimant that advancing my position would result in success before a BIT tribunal."[85]

Before turning to the question of whether state practice and arbitral decisions have in fact shifted post-*Methanex*, it is worth noting that in addition to the variety of reactions to *Methanex* in the literature there is also a notable absence of reference to it in some key law texts. For example, Brownlie's *Principles of Public International Law* (7th edition) devotes an entire page to quoting from *Pope and Talbot* on indirect expropriation,[86] but *Methanex* is not mentioned anywhere in the text.

The legacy of *Methanex*

*Investor claims post-*Methanex

As noted in the introduction, Sornarajah predicted that there would be "less fervour in basing claims on expropriation" after the *Methanex* decision. However, the available data suggest that this has not been the case. Out of 137 investment treaty cases where public merits awards are available from 1990 (the first award made) through 2013,[87] nearly all involve claims for both expropriation and FET. The change in expropriation claiming patterns since *Methanex* has been slight, dropping from 86 percent of 36 cases concluded prior to *Methanex* to 83 percent in the 101 cases since. There has been a more noticeable increase in FET claims, going from 78 percent pre-*Methanex* to 89 percent after.

This lack of major variation suggests that investors are more than willing to claim violations under multiple provisions irrespective of any possible doctrinal shifts occurring within the case law (although, as noted

[84] T. Weiler "*Philip Morris vs. Uruguay:* An Analysis of Tobacco Control Measures in the Context of International Investment Law" (2010) Report #1 for Physicians for a Smoke Free Canada, at p. 28, www.italaw.com/sites/default/files/case-documents/ita0345.pdf.

[85] Ibid., at footnote 79.

[86] I. Brownlie, *Principles of Public International Law*, 7th ed, (Oxford: OUP, 2008), at pp. 532–533.

[87] Note that this figure does not include the Methanex case itself, as, under this apples-to-apples definition, cases where tribunals declined jurisdiction over all claims are excluded.

below, the issue of indirect expropriation is also far from settled in the case law). This approach is quite rational given that the only additional cost associated with including an expropriation claim is the time spent by counsel in preparing the case.

Tribunal citations of the Methanex *decision*

What of *Methanex*'s influences among arbitrators? As a formal matter, investment treaty awards do not constitute binding precedent, and their determinations are not binding on parties outside the case. However, in practice, many arbitrators consult past cases for their persuasive value and extend or distinguish their reasoning.[88] Indeed, an early empirical study found that arbitrators cite each other more than any other source.[89]

Barton Legum (lead US counsel in *Methanex*) has suggested that the tribunal's decision on national treatment would "likely be a landmark in the field" and "its application of the international law concept of indirect expropriation to an environmental regulation will no doubt be cited by counsel and tribunals for years to come."[90] *Methanex* has certainly been widely cited, with 32 subsequent cases mentioning various aspects of the tribunal's reasoning. That is a third of the 101 finalized (and public) merits awards rendered since *Methanex* through 2013. However, citation is not the same as influence, and the tribunal's three main determinations (on expropriation, the relationship between FET and national treatment, and jurisdiction) have gotten little-to-no traction in subsequent cases – including from the award's own authors.

Out of the 32 cases, 6 have awards that make explicit reference to some form of police powers doctrine or class of noncompensable public policy measures in their determination on expropriation.[91] In *Saluka*, there was a direct citation of *Methanex*:

> In the opinion of the Tribunal, the principle that a State does not commit an expropriation and is thus not liable to pay compensation to a

[88] G. Kaufmann-Kohler, "Arbitral Precedent; Dream, Necessity or Excuse" (2007) 23 *Arbitration International* 357.

[89] J. Commission, "Precedent in Investment Treaty Arbitration – A Citation Analysis of a Developing Jurisprudence" (2007) 24 *Journal of International Arbitration* 129.

[90] Legum, "Introductory Note", at p. 1344.

[91] *Saluka* v. *Czech Republic* (2006) on a forced administration of a bank; *Continental Casualty* v. *Argentina* (2008)/*Suez/AWG* v. *Argentina* (2010)/*Total* v. *Argentina* (2010) on Argentina's 2001–2002 crisis measures; *EDF* v. *Romania* (2009) on the elimination of duty-free shops at airports out of concerns about corruption; and *Chemtura* v. *Canada* (2010) on the deregistration of a pesticide.

> dispossessed alien investor when it adopts general regulations that are "commonly accepted as within the police power of States" forms part of customary international law today. There is ample case law in support of this proposition. As the tribunal in *Methanex Corp.* v. *USA* said recently in its final award, "[i]t is a principle of customary international law that, where economic injury results from a bona fide regulation within the police powers of a State, compensation is not required."[92]

However, the tribunal went on to note:

> That being said, international law has yet to identify in a comprehensive and definitive fashion precisely what regulations are considered "permissible" and "commonly accepted" as falling within the police or regulatory power of States and, thus, non-compensable. In other words, it has yet to draw a bright and easily distinguishable line between non-compensable regulations on the one hand and, on the other, measures that have the effect of depriving foreign investors of their investment and are thus unlawful and compensable in international law.[93]

In *Continental Casualty*, the tribunal (which included Veeder) noted that a category of noncompensable measures exists and that different tribunals have come to different conclusions about how to determine whether a measure fits in that category, citing *Methanex* as one example.[94] In *Suez*, the tribunal noted the doctrine of police powers and cited *Methanex* and *Saluka*, and extended this approach with respect to Argentina's macroeconomic policies. With respect to Argentina's specific treatment of the water concessionaire, the tribunal determined that an expropriation had not occurred because "they did not constitute a permanent and substantial deprivation of the Claimants' investments."[95] In *Total*, macroeconomic policies were also excused under police powers doctrines, but here the tribunal does not cite *Methanex* on expropriation.

In *Chemtura*, the tribunal also looked at whether there had been a substantial deprivation (and found that there had not been), but then noted that they considered "in any event that the measures challenged by the Claimant constituted a valid exercise of the Respondent's police

[92] *Saluka Investments BV* v. *The Czech Republic*, Partial Award (17 March 2006), at para. 262.

[93] Ibid., at para. 263.

[94] *Continental Casualty* v. *Argentine Republic* (ICSID Case No. ARB/03/9) Award, 5 September 2008, at paras. 276–278. 129.

[95] *AWG Group Ltd.* v. *The Argentine Republic* (UNCITRAL), Decision on Liability (30 July 2010), at paras. 139–148. The same tribunal heard a virtually identical case under ICSID for other investors in Argentina's water systems and issued a virtually identical award.

powers."[96] However, the tribunal made a reference to *Saluka* rather than *Methanex* to support this finding.

In *EDF*, there is reference to one of the government's regulations being a "noncompensable police power measure" but *Methanex* is not cited as an authority.[97]

In addition, it is worth noting that *Teco* v. *Guatemala* – a case that did not deal with an expropriation claim specifically – cited the *Methanex* decision on expropriation in full and followed it with the note that "The Tribunal agrees."[98]

In other instances, tribunals took an assorted number of other qualitative approaches to the question of indirect expropriation and did not order states to pay damages.[99]

However, a substantial number of cases post-*Methanex* do not identify a category of noncompensable measures and instead take an approach to assessing state liability that focuses on the degree of deprivation, and in some cases whether the public benefit of the measure is proportionate to the harm caused to the investor. There were 15 of these cases in our sample. Most notable is *Vivendi* v. *Argentina*[100] because the President of that tribunal was J. William Rowley, who also sat on the *Methanex* panel. Without citing the *Methanex* award he signed 2 years prior, Rowley and the other Vivendi II arbitrators argued:

> the Treaty directs the Tribunal first to consider whether the challenged measures are expropriatory, and only then to ask whether they can comply with certain conditions, ie public purpose, non-discriminatory, specific commitments, et cetera. If we conclude that the challenged

96 *Chemtura Corp.* v. *Government of Canada*, Award (2 August 2010), at para. 266.

97 *EDF Services Ltd.* v. *Romania* (ICSID CASE NO. ARB/05/13), Award (8 October 2009), at para. 308.

98 *Teco Guatemala Holdings LLC* v. *Republic of Guatemala* (ICSID Case No. ARB/10/17), Award (9 December 2013), at para. 491.

99 *Biwater* v. *Tanzania* (2008) found that political acts were expropriatory (even if they did not reduce value but merely impaired rights), while contractual acts were not expropriatory (even if they sharply reduced value). The tribunal did not end up ordering any compensation for the investor, however. Other tribunals also found that total deprivation could be excused if it was pursuant to contractual behavior (*Bayindir* v. *Pakistan* (2009) on a highway contract, *Suez/AWG* v. *Argentina* (2010) on Argentina's water concessions, *Ulysseas* v. *Ecuador* (2012) on an electricity generation contract). Still others found that regulations would not be expropriations by other qualitative criteria: *EDF* v. *Romania* (2009) on financial police seizing a company's assets; *Merrill* v. *Canada* (2010) on a logging regime; *Iberdrola* v. *Guatemala* (2012) on electric utility regulations.

100 *Compania de Aguas del Aconquija S.A. and Vivendi Universal S.A.* v. *Argentine Republic*, (ICSID Case No. ARB/97/3), Award (20 August 2007).

> measures are expropriatory, there will be violation of Article 5(2) of the Treaty, even if the measures might be for a public purpose and non-discriminatory, because no compensation has been paid. Respondent's public purpose arguments suggest that state acts causing loss of property cannot be classified as expropriatory. If public purpose automatically immunises the measure from being found to be expropriatory, then there would never be a compensable taking for a public purpose. As the tribunal in *Santa Elena* correctly pointed out, the purpose for which the property was taken "does not alter the legal character of the taking for which adequate compensation must be paid".[101]

This and four other tribunals have taken similar analytical approaches and found expropriations.[102] In the other cases, no expropriation was found, but not because of an exemption for police powers.[103]

Although no tribunals in our sample explicitly denounce the *Methanex* decision on expropriation, the panel in *BG Group* v. *Argentina* comes close.[104] While the main focus of the panel's displeasure is on the *Methanex* approach to jurisdiction, they also suggest that following *Methanex* would "largely nullify the prohibition of indirect expropriation and measures tantamount to expropriation" and that they could find "no basis for adopting an interpretation that would render the substantive rights and obligations of the Argentina-U.K. BIT ineffective."[105]

Success of expropriation claims versus FET

The data show that claimants unable to prove expropriation or discrimination are able to win under the looser FET standard, something that Sornarajah himself predicted. In the 32 cases we examined for the purposes of this article, this happened on 6 occasions.[106] Additionally, *Teco* v. *Guatemala* (which did not deal with an expropriation claim)

[101] Ibid., at para. 7.5.21.

[102] *Fuchs* v. *Georgia* (2010) on pipeline development; *Tza Yap* v. *Peru* (2011) on tax collection; *Unglaube* v. *Costa Rica* (2012) on park and turtle protection; *Burlington* v. *Ecuador* (2012) on oil policy and potential environmental impacts.

[103] *Firemans Fund* v. *Mexico* (2006) on bank bailouts; *ADM* v. *Mexico* (2007)/*CPI* v. *Mexico* (2008)/*Cargill* v. *Mexico* (2009) on HFCS taxes; *BG Group* v. *Argentina* (2007)/*National Grid* v. *Argentina* (2008)/*El Paso* v. *Argentina* (2011)/and *Mobil* v. *Argentina* (2013) on utility regulation and crisis measures; *Glamis Gold* v. *USA* (2009) on gold mining and conservation; *Grand River* v. *USA* (2011) on Native cigarette sales.

[104] *BG Group PLC* v. *Republic of Argentina*, Final Award (24 December 2007).

[105] Ibid., at paras. 232–233.

[106] *Saluka* v. *Czech Republic*, *BG Group* v. *Argentina*, *National Grid* v. *Argentina*, *Suez/AWG* v. *Argentina*, *El Paso* v. *Argentina*, and *Mobil* v. *Argentina*.

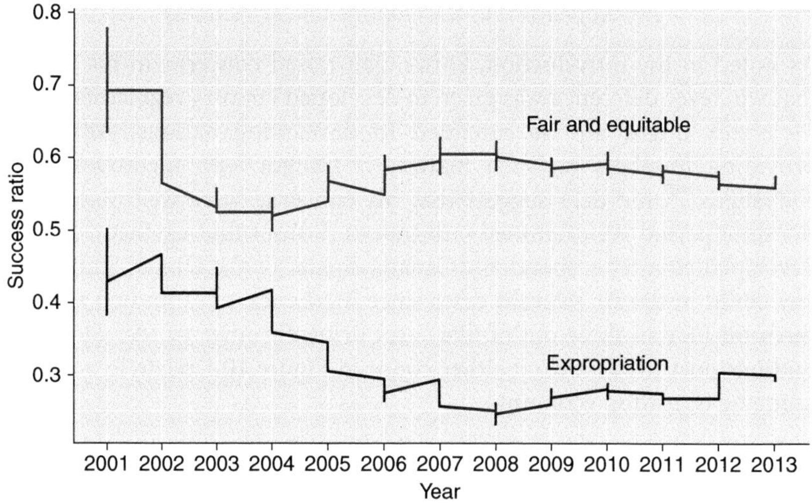

Figure 10.1 Investor success under distinct treaty provisions
Source: Tucker *(2015). Data represent all 274 times a tribunal made a determination on either fair and equitable treatment (118) or expropriation (115). Population is the 137 cases 1990–2013 for which a public merits award is available. Cumulative rates of success for each provision are shown on the y-axis.*

found an FET violation despite a favorable citation of the *Methanex* regulatory carve-out. *Continental Casualty* v. *Argentina* and *Total* v. *Argentina* (written by the same chair, Giorgio Sacerdoti) both left open whether a part of the claim (that was found to violate FET) might not also violate expropriation rules – an approach also taken in *Anatolie Stati* v. *Kazakhstan* and *Ioan Micula* v. *Romania.*

More systematic quantitative analysis yields a similar conclusion. As shown in Figure 10.1, after having relatively similar rates of success in the early years of investment treaty arbitration, a gulf emerged even before *Methanex.* Thereafter, FET claims were successful close to 60 percent of the time, while expropriation claims were successful at half that rate. However, this lesser success rate can clearly not be attributed to the widespread adoption of the *Methanex* approach. It more likely reflects the fact that other thresholds, such as the requirement for substantial deprivation, are high enough that the majority of claims will not meet them.

Developed versus developing country success

As noted in the introduction, Sornarajah raised concerns in his article that whatever deference was given to developed country regulators post-*Methanex* might not be extended to developing nations. Although providing numbers on such matters is fraught with methodological challenges,[107] the data suggest that his concerns were well placed. In the time period we examined, arbitrators did not find against a highly developed country respondent (Canada, Spain, or the United States) on any count in the six relevant cases since *Methanex*, after finding against them on FET in three out of five cases prior. In other words, all of the findings post-*Methanex* on either count in Figure 10.1 relate to a developing or transition economy.

Beyond *Methanex*: treaty safeguards

Treaty practice on expropriation began to shift prior to the *Methanex* decision. Both Canada and the United States released new model BITs in 2004, containing annexes on expropriation. In both models the annex had two distinct elements. The first element is a three-part test (which was first formulated in domestic case law in the United States) that addresses the effect of a measure, its character, and the extent to which it interferes with the investor's reasonable expectations. The second element is a statement that "except in rare circumstances" nondiscriminatory regulatory measures are not considered expropriations. The Canadian model includes an additional note clarifying what "rare circumstances" might entail: "such as when a measure or series of measures is so severe in the light of its purpose that it cannot be reasonably viewed as having been adopted and applied in good faith."

Some countries adopted identical or near identical provisions in their own models (e.g. Colombia's 2007 model BIT follows Canada on

[107] The definition of "developing country" in these exercises has been contested, and it is difficult to know whether investors are more likely to bring claims against developing countries in the first place – which could be a source of selection bias in assessing the true posture of arbitration vis-a-vis development. See S. Franck, C. Garbin, and J. Perkins, "Through the Looking Glass: Understanding Social Science Norms for Analyzing International Investment Law" (2011) *2010–2011 Yearbook of International Investment Law and Policy* 859; G. Van Harten, "The Use of Quantitative Methods to Examine Possible Bias in Investment Arbitration" (2011) *2010–2011 Yearbook of International Investment Law and Policy* 859.

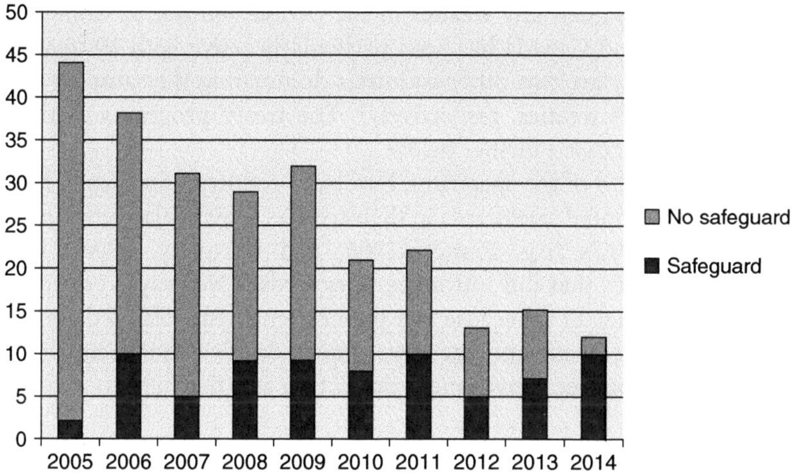

Figure 10.2 Number of treaties signed containing expropriation safeguards

expropriation[108]), while other countries have adapted them or adopted distinctive safeguards of their own.

In the period 2005–2014, there were 257 treaties in the UNCTAD repository[109] (based on date of signature) that had the full text of the investment chapter available in English and contained provisions on expropriation. As shown in Figure 10.2, while the number of treaties with an expropriation safeguard has fluctuated between five and ten since 2006, the proportion of treaties with a safeguard has increased as the number of treaties signed in a given year has steadily declined. In total, 29 percent of the treaties reviewed contained some form of safeguard on expropriation.

Of the 257 treaties, 85 were signed between two or more non-OECD countries, 156 were signed between one or more OECD countries and one or more non-OECD countries, and 16 were signed between two or more OECD countries.[110] However, a small number of countries appear to be behind the proliferation of safeguards. Canada and the United

[108] Model BIT of Colombia (2007), www.italaw.com/documents/inv_model_bit_colombia.pdf.

[109] UNCTAD's database contains 2922 BITs and 345 other international investment agreements, see: http://investmentpolicyhub.unctad.org/IIA.

[110] Over the period of study, four countries (Israel, Slovenia, Estonia, and Chile) joined the OECD. Here they are classified as OECD or non-OECD based on whether they were members at the time the relevant treaty was signed.

States have not signed any treaties in the period without an annex on expropriation, and Canada has been particularly active with 20 treaties. India and Turkey are two other countries dominating the sample (with 16 treaties and 9 treaties, respectively). The treaty programs of these countries are discussed further below.

At the other end of the spectrum, European countries and Japan have generally not adopted safeguards in their treaties. This is also reflected in recent model BITs (e.g. France, 2006, and Germany, 2008). One European country that did introduce safeguards – Norway – ended up shelving its model BIT because the public remained polarized on the value of the agreement and the government decided that achieving a proper balance between investment protection and the right to regulate was too difficult.[111]

For members of the European Union, model BITs are now redundant in any case as the European Commission was given competence for investment treaties under the Lisbon Treaty in 2009. In the first investment treaty that the EU has negotiated – the Comprehensive Trade and Economic Agreement (CETA) with Canada (which was not part of the sample studied for this chapter because it has not yet been signed) – the Canadian model expropriation annex is adopted with some changes. It seems this approach will also be the starting position for the EU in its negotiations with the United States for a Transatlantic Trade and Investment Partnership (TTIP).[112]

The vast majority (83 percent) of treaties that do contain safeguards include some version of the three-part test laid out in the US Model BIT. A small number of treaties contain a provision (usually stated before the three-part test) that stipulates the level of deprivation that must have occurred for a measure to be considered a possible expropriation. For example, the Taiwan–New Zealand BIT (2013) states that "In order to constitute indirect expropriation, the Party's deprivation of the investor's property must be: (a) either severe or for an indefinite period." The Canada–Korea Free Trade Agreement (FTA) (2014) states: "an action or series of actions by a Party cannot constitute an expropriation unless it interferes with a tangible or intangible property right in an investment and eliminates all or nearly all of its value."

[111] D. Vis-Dunbar, "Norway Shelves Its Proposed Model Bilateral Investment Treaty", *Investment Treaty News* (June 2009), www.iisd.org/investment/itn.

[112] European Commission, "Public Consultation on Modalities for Investment Protection and ISDS in TTIP", http://trade.ec.europa.eu/doclib/docs/2014/march/tradoc_152280.pdf.

Another variation is found in the China–India BIT (2006):

> A measure of expropriation includes, apart from direct expropriation or nationalization through formal transfer of title or outright seizure, a measure or series of measures taken intentionally by a Party to create a situation whereby the investment of an investor may be rendered substantially unproductive and incapable of yielding a return without a formal transfer of title or outright seizure.

This last example also introduces the requirement of intent on the part of the state to cause harm. This is rare, but not unique – the Saudi Arabia–India BIT (2006) also makes reference to intent: "any action of a Contracting Party taken as a part of normal business activities would not, by itself, constitute an indirect expropriation unless the *prima facie* intention to create adverse impact on the economic value of the investment is apparent."

These types of provisions appear to be hierarchical: if the deprivation does not rise to the level stipulated (or for a small number of treaties, no intent is found), no further analysis is required. However, the majority of treaties have very limited preamble before moving into the three-part test.

In terms of the specific content of the three-part test, there is very little variation between treaties on the first part of the test on economic impact. There is universal agreement that economic impact is relevant in determining whether an indirect expropriation has occurred but that the "sole effects" approach should be rejected.

There is far more variation with the second part of the three-part test. While 77 percent of IIAs with the three-part test refer to investor expectations, a small subset of these (9 percent) provide further clarification that, in determining whether or not an investor's expectations are "reasonable," a tribunal should look at how stringently regulated the sector was when the investment was made. An additional 8 percent of IIAs adopting a three-part test opt for the language "specific commitments" rather than expectations.

There is also significant variation on the third part of the test on the "character" of the government measure. Nearly half (43 percent) of the IIAs adopting a three-part test expand on the definition of character, usually in a manner that suggests that a proportionality approach should be adopted by the tribunal. For example, the Australia–Malaysia FTA (2012) suggests that the tribunal should consider "the character of the government action, including, its objective and whether the action is disproportionate to the public purpose."

All treaties in the safeguard sample included a statement about regulatory measures. The majority of these statements (76 percent) included the "except in rare circumstances" caveat. In half of the 18 treaties that did not contain any reference to rare circumstances, Turkey was a party to the treaty. There were also three major regional treaties in this group.[113]

One might ask why Turkey's treaty practice appears to differ so substantially from the norm? The answer possibly lies in the assistance that the country received in updating its model BIT by UNCTAD and the IISD.[114] Turkey's 2009 Model BIT states:

> Non-discriminatory legal measures designed and applied to protect legitimate public welfare objectives, such as health, safety and environment, do not constitute indirect expropriation and are not subject, therefore, to any compensation requirements.

The 2005 IISD Model Investment Agreement has a very similar provision:

> Consistent with the right of states to regulate and the customary international law principles on police powers, bona fide, non-discriminatory regulatory measures taken by a Party that are designed and applied to protect or enhance legitimate public welfare objectives, such as public health, safety and the environment, do not constitute an indirect expropriation under this Article.

Indian treaties in the sample were notable for frequently including an additional statement following the statement on regulation to the effect of carving out court decisions:

> Actions and awards by judicial bodies of a Contracting Party that are designed, applied or issued in public interest including those designed to address health, safety and environmental concerns, do not constitute expropriation or nationalization.

[113] Association of South-East Asian Nations (ASEAN) Comprehensive Investment Agreement (in force 29 March 2012), ASEAN–Australia–New Zealand FTA (in force 10 January 2012), Investment Agreement for the Common Market for Eastern and Southern Africa (COMESA) Common Investment Area (signed 23 May 2007).

[114] H. Akpinar, *Bilateral Investment Treaties as a Tool to Improve Investment Climate* (Republic of Turkey, 2011), at p. 9, www.yoikk.gov.tr/upload/IDB/20111013_BilateralTreaties_HasanAslan$Akpinar.pdf.

India has recently released a draft of a new model BIT for public comment that radically diverges from its prior practice, which was to adopt a variation on the three-part test.[115] The draft model states:

5.2 The determination of whether a Measure or a series of Measures have an effect equivalent to expropriation requires a case-by-case, fact-based inquiry, and usually requires evidence that there has been:
  (i) permanent and complete or near complete deprivation of the value of Investment; and
  (ii) permanent and complete or near complete deprivation of the Investor's right of management and control over the Investment; and
  (iii) an appropriation of the Investment by the Host State which results in transfer of the complete or near complete value of the Investment to that Party or to an agency or instrumentality of the Party or a third party;

5.3 For the avoidance of doubt, the Parties agree that an action taken by a Party in its commercial capacity shall not constitute expropriation or any other measure having similar effect.

5.4 For the avoidance of doubt, the parties also agree that, non-discriminatory regulatory actions by a Party that are designed and applied to protect legitimate public welfare objectives such as public health, safety and the environment shall not constitute expropriation.

Compensation can also be affected by a number of "mitigating factors" laid out in the model. The model is further notable for its exclusion of any reference to FET or most favored nation treatment and the requirement of investors to both meet a number of obligations and exhaust local remedies before making use of the ISDS provisions. As Peterson notes, "the draft model text goes well beyond the incremental reforms seen in the investment treaty programs of countries like Canada and the United States, and offers a radical departure from past agreements – Indian or otherwise."[116]

[115] Model Text for the Indian Bilateral Investment Treaty (2015), https://mygov.in/sites/default/files/master_image/Model%20Text%20for%20the%20Indian%20Bilateral%20Investment%20Treaty.pdf.

[116] L. Peterson, "Analysis: India Invites Comments on Draft Model Investment Treaty", *Investment Arbitration Reporter* (24 March 2015), www.iareporter.com/articles/20150324_1.

How do safeguards compare to the Methanex *decision?*

There are several commonalities between the safeguards typically found in treaties and the *Methanex* decision on expropriation. First, both reject the "sole effects" approach made famous in the *Metalclad* case. However, while *Methanex* did not even mention the effect on an investor in its expropriation analysis, the three-part test found in many treaties does include it as a factor that must be considered.

Second, both *Methanex* and those safeguards employing the three-part test consider the investor's expectations. However, it could be argued that "specific commitments" are narrower than "reasonable investment-backed expectations," even if we agree with Sornarajah that neither belongs in the analysis of whether a regulatory measure is an expropriation.

Third, there is the question of the character test. While the US Model BIT fails to elaborate on what a tribunal should consider in this part of the test, as noted earlier, other treaties have more specifically proposed a form of proportionality analysis. No such analysis was presented in *Methanex*, and we agree with Sornarajah that the "importation of the proportionality doctrine into investment law is intended to keep alive the idea that compensation is possible even in the case of regulatory expropriations."[117]

Finally, there is the second element found in most safeguards – the exemption for nondiscriminatory regulation. This is obviously where the similarities to the *Methanex* decision are the strongest. However, two issues arise. First, there is the question of how the exemption relates to the three-part test if, as in most treaties, it is present. It could be argued that there is a hierarchy. If the measure fits within the category of being a nondiscriminatory measure taken in the public interest, it does not have to undergo the three-part test. Alternatively, one could view the two elements as nonhierarchical, and, thus, that a nondiscriminatory public interest measure might be considered an expropriation if it failed to pass the three-part test.[118] In this reading, the safeguards are much weaker than the *Methanex* decision. Second, the vague qualifier – "rare circumstances" – further weakens the majority of safeguards in comparison to the *Methanex* decision.

Mann argues that it is not surprising that the US treaty language (and by proxy, that of many other countries) is weaker than the *Methanex* decision because it

117 Sornarajah, *Resistance and Change*, 211.

118 Edsall, "Indirect Expropriation", at p. 957.

> derives from a series of highly political inter-departmental negotiations dominated by economic agencies like [the US Trade Representative] with close ties to industry, and stakeholder dialogues. These discussions sought, at the same time, to push the limits on protections for U.S. investors abroad and to limit its application in the U.S. to the forever debated U.S. domestic law on expropriation.[119]

How do tribunals treat expropriation safeguards?

There have been at least ten cases involving expropriation claims that have been brought under treaties with the US Model expropriation safeguards. Of these, six cases are pending, two have been dismissed on jurisdictional grounds, and one has been settled.

The only case with a decision on expropriation is *Railroad* v. *Guatemala*. In this case, the tribunal went through the three-part test and found that an expropriation had not occurred because the economic impact of the government measures did not amount to a substantial deprivation.[120] It is worth noting that Michael Reisman (one of the arbitrators in *Methanex*) gave an expert opinion on behalf of the claimant in this case. In it, he argues that the

> critical element in determining whether an indirect expropriation has occurred is the impact of the actions on the investor's rights and whether there has been a "substantial loss of control or economic value of a foreign investment without a physical taking," (or, in this case, a "serious economic harm").[121]

He makes no reference to the *Methanex* decision in his report.

The exemption for nondiscriminatory regulatory measures was not discussed in the *Railroad* Award, but it is the subject of the pleadings in the ongoing *Spence* v. *Costa Rica* case. In this case, the claimants' lawyers (including Todd Weiler) have argued that Paragraph 4(a) of the annex on expropriation in the Central American Free Trade Agreement (CAFTA) (covering the three-part test) indicates that "on rare occasions a governmental measure that substantially interferes with the exercise of property rights by a foreign investor in her investment will constitute an indirect expropriation" and further that "[t]he instant case represents just such an

[119] Mann, *Final Decision*, at pp. 9–10.

[120] *Railroad Development Corp.* v. *Republic of Guatemala* (ICSID Case No. ARB/07/23), Award (29 June 2012).

[121] *Railroad Development Corp.* v. *Republic of Guatemala* (ICSID Case No. ARB/07/23) Opinion of W. Michael Reisman (11 June 2009).

occasion."[122] The claimant further argues that Paragraph 4(b) (the "except in rare circumstances" clause) "is not the general exemption clause Respondent would like it to be."[123] The claimant argues that the two subparagraphs are neither "sequential nor ranked in order of importance."[124] Interestingly, the parties also disagree on whether a measure has to actually be effective at protecting a public good (e.g. sea turtles) in order to be covered under subparagraph (b) of the annex or instead simply has be designed with that objective in mind.[125]

Outside of the case law dealing with treaties that have safeguards, there is at least one case (*Continental Casualty*) that cites the annex of US Model BIT as an authority on distinction between compensable and noncompensable regulatory takings.[126] In *Glamis Gold*, the tribunal noted that the parties to the case had cited the 2004 Model BIT in making an argument for the employment of a three-part test but then limited its analysis to "the foundational threshold inquiry of whether the property or property right was in fact taken."[127]

Given the limited experience with safeguards in arbitration, it remains an open question whether the more widespread adoption of safeguards could shift the pattern of arbitral decision-making on expropriation in a positive way. One could argue that the greater number of words in the safeguards makes them more precise than the *Methanex* decision[128] and that, all else being equal, greater precision equates to less arbitrator

[122] *Spence International Investments LLC et al.* v. *Republic of Costa Rica* (ICSID Case No. UNCT/13/2), Claimants' Memorial on the Merits (26 April 2014), at para. 208.

[123] *Spence International Investments LLC et al.* v. *Republic of Costa Rica* (ICSID Case No. UNCT/13/2), Claimants' Reply on Merits and Counter-Memorial on Jurisdiction (4 October 2014), at para. 179.

[124] Ibid.

[125] *Spence International Investments LLC et al.* v. *Republic of Costa Rica* (ICSID Case No. UNCT/13/2), Respondent's Reply on Jurisdiction and Rejoinder on the Merits (22 December 2014), at paras. 102–103.

[126] Award, para. 276. [127] Award, para. 356.

[128] Blake (2010, 2013) and Manger and Peinhardt (2014) have argued this point more generally on the theory that a greater number of words or provisions in treaties makes it clearer what states are (and are not) committing to. See: D. Blake, *Thinking Ahead: Time Horizons and the Legalization of International Investment Agreements*, PhD diss. (Ohio: Ohio State University, 2010), http://etd.ohiolink.edu/view.cgi?acc_num=osu1284993123; D. Blake, "Thinking Ahead: Government Time Horizons and the Legalization of International Investment Agreements" (2013) 67 *International Organization* 797. M. Manger and C. Peinhardt, "Learning and Diffusion in International Investment Agreements", in *PEIO Conference* (Princeton University, 2014), http://147.142.190.246/joomla/peio/files2014/papers/Manger,%20Peinhardt%2026.08.2013.PDF.

discretion and more protection for a state's right to regulate. However, we would suggest that the clarity of words, rather than their number, matters more. As such, it is unfortunate that more safeguards do not follow the "modified *Methanex*" approach (i.e. a regulatory carve-out with no exception for "specific commitments") of Turkey and the IISD Model.

Furthermore, having "pockets of precision" in treaties is problematic because investors and arbitrators can simply shift to the less precise standards.[129] Although we have not discussed FET safeguards in this chapter, others have noted that the common practice of equating the standard with customary international law has not prevented a number of tribunals from making expansive interpretations.[130] Furthermore, very few states have introduced the greater precision in the most favored nation treatment standard that is required to prevent investors from accessing looser standards in older treaties and, thereby, circumventing safeguards on expropriation and FET.

Conclusions

It has been a decade since the *Methanex* case ended. While the case will undoubtedly continue to have an impact in debates about expropriation in the future, it seems fair to conclude at this stage that while the tribunal's decision on expropriation was not insignificant, it also did not inspire a new pattern of decision-making among arbitrators. For their part, states (when they have altered their approach to expropriation) have been more influenced by US and Canadian practice in drafting safeguards than by the reasoning in *Methanex*.

In hindsight, it was probably overly optimistic for Sornarajah to declare that the *Methanex* award had substantially tamed the law on expropriation. His more recent writing reflects an acknowledgment of this:

> The neo-liberal ideas do not die out altogether. They are kept alive. No idea gets finally vanquished. The end of history never occurs ... The evidence of that is provided in this area by the resurgence of arbitral

[129] T. Tucker, "Institutions and Development Ideologies in Investment Treaty Arbitration" PhD diss. (Cambridge: CUP, 2015).

[130] M. Porterfield, "A Distinction Without a Difference? The Interpretation of Fair and Equitable Treatment under Customary International Law by Investment Tribunals", *Investment Treaty News* (22 March 2013). See also *Clayton/Bilcon* v. *Canada*, Dissenting Opinion of Professor Donald McRae.

> competence over regulatory expropriation through the application of the proportionality test. The pendulum keeps swinging. It does not stop.[131]

We agree that the area remains contested. The *Methanex* decision was never going to build a bridge across the grand expanse that divides supporters and critics of ISDS, if indeed that was their intention. The award has been strongly critiqued by scholars that are influential in the community, has not had a strong impact on subsequent case law (including on the *Methanex* arbitrators' later decisions), and has certainly not prevented investors from challenging regulatory measures in arbitration.

So long as arbitrators can pick and choose from past decisions (including their own) the question of what constitutes an indirect expropriation will not be definitively resolved. Some argue that this question cannot and should not be resolved because decisions on expropriation must be decided on a "case-by-case" basis.[132] This leaves regulators in a precarious position, unsure of whether their measures will be defensible in arbitration. Furthermore, the jurisprudence makes it clear that cases are not just distinguishable by the particular "facts" in contest but by the very different approaches (underpinned by different ideologies) that are adopted by panels.

This leads us to conclude that a systematic reshaping of investment treaty arbitration is far more important than the introduction of "safeguards" that are not only costly in terms of diplomatic resources but also may ultimately be insufficient to protect policy space. Mature legal systems have clear procedural safeguards (long tenures, set salaries, no revolving door, and centralized appeals) and greater clarity about applicable law (something difficult if not impossible in a system with chaotic interpretations of precedent, most favored nation rules, and FET). If arbitration is to be saved from itself (indeed, if it is to survive at all), the lawyers' sandbox must be left behind and maturation heartily embraced.

[131] Sornarajah, *Resistance and Change*, 206. [132] Paulsson, "Indirect Expropriation", 1.

11

The new frontier: economic rights of foreign investors versus government policy space for economic development

HOWARD MANN

Introduction

The rationale for the development of investment treaties was very clearly stated by the original developers of the first model bilateral investment treaty (BIT):

> Since it is now widely recognized that major steps must be taken to buttress the economic position of the free-world nations, both as a measure against Soviet moves and as a means of resolving some of the demands being made by the peoples of the underdeveloped nations of the world, the notion of greater protection under international law for private investment takes on added importance.[1]

As the present author has argued elsewhere, this rationale, when seen in its political context of the time, had a compelling ring to it.[2] Hungary had been invaded by the Soviet Union. The Cold War was the dominant political motif in the world, followed closely at the time by the nascent process of decolonization. Initial nationalizations had already taken place in the natural resources sector, in particular oil and gas. Future relationships between the emerging states and existing capital owners from the former colonial masters were unclear. The protection of capital from nationalization and expropriation was a rational issue to consider addressing.

The author would like to thank Kirsten Mikadze, LL.M., for her outstanding research support.

[1] Introduction to "The Proposed Convention to Protect Private Foreign Investment: A Roundtable" (1960) 9 *J. Pub. L.* 115, 115. The project was led by Lord Shawcross of the United Kingdom and Herman Abs of Germany.

[2] Howard Mann, "Reconceptualizing International Investment Law: It's Role in Sustainable Development" (2013) 17 *Lewis & Clark Law Review* 521–544.

Since these early days, there have been few new developments in the direction of international investment treaties. The principle thesis of this chapter is that the only significant additional direction since then has been the development of independent economic rights for capital owners, distinct in nature and application from the traditional notions of investment protection rights. Specifically, that expansion has been almost uniquely directed toward creating an international law right under a growing number of treaties to invest capital across borders and, importantly, to maximize the profits from such investments as a matter of legal right. This expansion, as documented in the following, comes at a specific cost: the equivalent loss of government rights to put in place economic and social development policies and tools that can help eliminate poverty, create greater diversity in economic development, and support intragenerational as well as intergenerational economic equity.

The issue of the government policy space that is left for governments under many international investment agreements (IIAs), often phrased as the right to regulate, is a predominant theme in the discourse between those who promote the expansion of the regime and those who question its role and direction in an age of globalization. Indeed, a significant amount of this Festschrift in honor of Professor Sornarajah is devoted to this question.

In most, if not all instances, this discourse is framed in terms of policy space for environmental protection, human health issues, worker safety, basic labor rights, and so on. In other words, the focus is on the environmental, social, and human rights issues that prevail in Western political debates about investment treaties.[3] What is often absent in the discourse is the question of policy space for promoting economic development, or

[3] Some examples elsewhere include Suzanne Spears, "The Quest for Policy Space in a New Generation of International Investment Agreements" (2010) 13(4) *J Intn'l Econ L* 1037; Luke E. Peterson, *Bilateral Investment Treaties and Development Policy Making* (2004), online: www.iisd.org/sites/default/files/pdf/2004/trade_bits.pdf; Jorge E. Vinuales, *Foreign Investment and the Environment in International Law* (Cambridge: CUP, 2012); Kevin P. Gallagher, *Policy Space to Prevent and Mitigate Financial Crises in Trade and Investment Agreements*, G-24 Discussion Paper (Geneva: UNCTAD, 2010); Gus van Harten, *Investment Treaty Arbitration and Public Law* (Oxford: OUP, 2007); Catherine Titi, *The Right to Regulate in International Investment Law* (Oxford: Hart Publishing, 2014); and contra see, e.g. Michael Waibel, Asha Kaushal, Kyo-Hwa Liz Chung, and Claire Balchin, (eds.), *The Backlash Against Investment Arbitration: Perceptions and Reality* (Alphen aan den Rijn: Kluwer Law International, 2010); Stephan Schill, "Private Enforcement of International Investment Law: Why We Need Investor Standing in BIT Dispute Settlement", in Waibel *et al.*, (eds.), *The Backlash Against Investment Arbitration*; Susan D. Franck, "Development and Outcomes of Investment Treaty Arbitration" 50

economic development rights.[4] In part, this may be because the largely Western framers of the debate start from a perspective of the right to property as a human right, despite the fact many other cultures do not adopt the same view, and many states within the "West" do not protect property as a human right.

But even if one puts aside any debate over this starting point, what is at the core of the issue in this chapter is not the protection of the right to property per se, but the creation of a fundamentally different type of international economic law right for capital owners to deploy their capital outside of their own country, and the right to maximize the profits from that capital when it is so deployed. These are not issues concerning the protection of capital from nationalization or expropriation, but reflect a set of far broader economic rights for existing capital owners in a globalizing context, even when these expanding rights limit or negatively impact the rights of others to social and economic developments.

The policy space discussed in this chapter therefore concerns the rights of governments to take measures to promote broad-based and equitable economic and social developments within their territory in so far as this relates to foreign investment and foreign investors. This includes the use of instruments designed to multiply the economic benefits of foreign direct investment (FDI) such as requirements to purchase goods and services locally, undertake certain levels of research and development, enhance employment skills and higher-value work opportunities, ensure local equity ownership at minimum levels, and require joint venture partnerships. In investment treaty terms, these issues can be understood as the ability of governments to impose performance requirements on foreign investors and/or market access restrictions on the full ownership of investments.

The issue matters very much in its own right. But it also matters from a different perspective enunciated several years ago by Professor Sornarajah when he lectured about the law of need versus the law of greed.[5] For, if investment treaties are being deployed now to create the

(2009) *Harv Int'l LJ* 435; and Daniel S. Myers, "In Defence of the International Treaty Arbitration System" (2008–2009) 31 *Hous. J Int'l L* 47.

[4] An excellent example of the smaller literature in this regard is Daniel Aguirre, "Corporate Liability for Economic, Social and Cultural Rights Revisited: The Failure of International Cooperation" (2011) 42 *California Western International Law Journal* 123.

[5] M. Sornarajah, "A Law for Need or a Law for Greed? Restoring the Lost Law in the International Law of Foreign Investment" (2006) 6 *Int'l Env'l Agmts* 329. The article

rights of existing capital owners to deploy their capital abroad and maximize their profit at the expense of governmental ability to generate a greater diversity in wealth and economic equity, then the law of greed over the law of need becomes an even more cogent concept as a description of the potential or actual direction of the international investment, and by extension, economic law, and regime.

Sustainable development, economic development, and income equity

Economic equity, FDI, and sustainable development

It is now axiomatic that the concept of sustainable development comprises three equally relevant and coequal pillars: economic development, social development, and environmental development. Within the economic development pillar, two elements are essential. The first is the base level of economic development, often phrased as lifting people out of poverty. At a minimum, this is an essential national goal among all developing countries as well as for most developed countries.

The second element is the equitable distribution of wealth between and within states. In the early days of writings on the economic pillar this was often phrased as intragenerational equity: that income distribution between and within states had to be equitable for achieving sustainable development:

> A corollary concept to the concept of intergenerational equity is intragenerational equity. This term can be formulated as the obligation "to ensure a just allocation of the utilisation of resources among human members of the present generation, both at the domestic and global levels". Intragenerational equity is directed at the serious socioeconomic asymmetry in resource access and use within and between societies and nations that has exacerbated environmental degradation and the inability of a large part of humanity to adequately meet its most basic needs.[6] (Footnote omitted)

followed from a conference at the Vrije Universiteit Amsterdam in honor of the author's late colleague at IISD, Konrad von Moltke. The present author was a discussant for Prof. Sornarajah's presentation at the conference.

[6] Marie-Claire Cordonier Segger and Ashfaq Kalfan, "Principles of International Law Relating to Sustainable Development", in Marie-Claire Cordonier Segger and Ashfaq Kalfan (eds.), *Sustainable Development Law: Principles, Practices, and Prospects* (Oxford: OUP, 2004), 125. See also, e.g., The Commonwealth, *Colombo Declaration on Sustainable, Inclusive and Equitable Development*, online: http://thecommonwealth.org/media/news/colombo-declaration-sustainable-inclusive-and-equitable-development; International Law Association, *New Delhi Declaration on the Principles of*

The notion that intragenerational equity is directed at serious asymmetries in resources access, be they physical, environmental, or economic resources, focuses the mind on the need to reduce such asymmetries. However, by establishing private economic rights that prevail over government rights to do just this, the greater likelihood is that investment treaties are far more likely to expand than contract these asymmetries.

Thomas Piketty, in his recent and influential book *Capital in the Twenty-First Century*, suggests an additional issue directly related to investment and intra- and intergenerational equities. In related passages, he notes first as follows:

> Generally speaking, the global income distribution is more unequal than the output distribution, because the countries with the highest per capita output are also more likely to own part of the capital of other countries and therefore to receive a positive flow of income from capital originating in countries with a lower level of per capita output. In other words, the rich countries are doubly wealthy: they both produce more at home and invest more abroad, so that their national income per head is greater than their output per head. The opposite is true for poor countries.[7]

Piketty then addresses the argument that investment-led growth promoted by market access liberalization is likely to be the key part of the answer to economic and social developments in low- and middle-income countries and, hence, moving toward greater internal and external economic equities. He notes the theory:

> Thus the wealthy countries – or at any rate the residents of wealthy countries with capital to spare – will obtain a better return on their investment by investing abroad and the poor countries will increase their productivity and thus close the gap between them and rich countries. According to classical economic theory, this mechanism, based on the free flow of capital and equalization of marginal productivity of capital at the global level, should lead to convergence of rich and poor countries and an eventual reduction of inequalities through market forces and competition.[8]

International Law Related to Sustainable Development (London: ILA, 2002), Principle 2; and more recently ASEAN, *The ASEAN Framework for Equitable Economic Development: Guiding Principles for Inclusive and Sustainable Growth*, ASEAN online: www.asean.org/news/item/the-asean-framework-for-equitable-economic-development.

7 Thomas Piketty, *Capital in the Twenty-First Century* (Cambridge, MA: The Belknap Press of Harvard University Press, 2014) at 67–68.

8 Ibid., at 69.

Piketty then debunks this classical approach:

> Furthermore, if we look at the historical record, it does not appear that capital mobility has been the primary factor promoting convergence of rich and poor nations. None of the Asian countries that have moved closer to the developed countries of the West in recent years has benefited from large foreign investments, whether it be Japan, South Korea, or Taiwan and more recently China. In essence, all of these countries themselves financed the necessary investments in physical capital and, even more, in human capital, which the latest research holds to be the key to long-term growth. Conversely, countries owned by other countries, whether in the colonial period or in Africa today, have been less successful, most notably because they have tended to specialize in areas without much prospect of future development and because they have been subject to chronic political instability.[9]

Piketty does not conclude that openness to investment is bad for developing countries. Quite the contrary, he is clear in stating that pursuing a desire for economic self-sufficiency ("autarky") is not a way to promote development. Rather, it is the manner in which FDI is harnessed for what it can bring in terms of its impact on employment, training, education, economic spin-offs, community development, technology transfer, skills transfer, etc., that is key to determining if the FDI received will increase or decrease economic disparities. The mere fact of the foreign ownership is not positive in itself for development benefits. Only if the "foreign" capital holder actually applies the ingredients to promote economic and social developments will it be positive. This is not a macroeconomic question, of balance of payments or assumptions that investment equals development, but a question of regulations and policies that ensure these ingredients are applied in practice.

In other words, it is the quality of the investment rather than the quantity that is critical for development purposes. This is precisely the position taken in this paper, with the key issue being how international law enables or constrains governments from addressing these quality-related issues.

A note on economic development rights, human rights, and business

The issues discussed earlier are also legally related directly to the implementation of the UN International Covenant on Economic, Social, and

[9] Ibid., at 70.

Cultural Rights.[10] This chapter is not the place to undertake a review of this Covenant. What can be noted is that it requires, in relation to economic development rights, their progressive realization by states. The need to understand and incorporate the state duties under the European Convention on Human Rights (ECHR) Covenant into the relationship between transnational business actors and host states in relation to human rights was confirmed by Professor John Ruggie is his capacity as the Special Representative of the Secretary General on Business and Human Rights:

> 13. The State duty to protect against third party abuse is grounded in international human rights law. The specific language employed in the main United Nations human rights treaties varies, but all include two sets of obligations. First, the treaties commit States parties to refrain from violating the enumerated rights of persons within their territory and/or jurisdiction. Second, the treaties require States to "ensure" (or some functionally equivalent verb) the enjoyment or realization of those rights by rights holders.[11]

The footnote to this passage expressly refers to the ESCR Covenant:

> In the International Covenant on Economic, Social and Cultural Rights, States parties undertake "to take steps ... achieving progressively the full realization of rights", while its rights-specific provisions, such as those dealing with labour, refer to States "ensuring" those rights.[12]

The differences Professor Ruggie noted in the form of the states' obligations did not reduce or eliminate his view that the ESCR Covenant sets out an important part of the core human rights that lie at the heart of the relationship of business to human rights. Indeed, Professor Ruggie went on to state in relation to the scope of the corporate responsibility to respect human rights:

> For the substantive content [of due diligence,] then, companies at a minimum should look to the International Bill of Human Rights – the

[10] An excellent discussion of the fuller relationship of the ESCR Covenant to investment issues, state rights, and corporate responsibilities is found in Daniel Aguirre, *supra*.

[11] Textual footnote omitted. Report of the Special Representative of the Secretary-General on the issue of human rights and transnational corporations and other business enterprises, PROMOTION OF ALL HUMAN RIGHTS, CIVIL, POLITICAL, ECONOMIC, SOCIAL AND CULTURAL RIGHTS, INCLUDING THE RIGHT TO DEVELOPMENT Business and human rights: Toward operationalizing the "protect, respect, and remedy" framework A/HRC/11/13, 22 April 2009, para. 13.

[12] Ibid., footnote 20.

> Universal Declaration and the two Covenants – as well as the ILO Declaration on Fundamental Principles and Rights at Work.[13]

The inclusion of economic and social developments rights by Professor Ruggie, who also noted in broad terms the linkages of these issues to investment law and treaties, is thus clear.[14] While he did not set out prescriptive standards, it is hard to imagine how treaty provisions that set out private economic rights for transnational investments while prohibiting the use of critical tools for promoting economic development in the host state from those investments fit the duty to protect and responsibility to respect framework of Professor Ruggie. This raises serious questions of whether states who draft the treaties, or corporations who enforce these rights, are meeting their respective duties and responsibilities.

Investment policy and the 1%

The promotion of the right to development in the context of inter- and intragenerational equities, and the role of business in this regard, is increasingly seen as a critical global economic problem. The World Economic Forum, in its top 10 trends of 2015, states:

> At the top of this year's list is worsening income inequality. As the world's rich continue to accumulate wealth at record rates, the middle class is struggling. Today, the top 1% of the population receives a quarter of the income in the United States. Over the last 25 years, the average income of the top 0.1% has grown 20 times compared to that of the average citizen. Last year, this trend ranked second place in the Outlook; this year, it rises to the top.[15]

Credit Suisse reports that the numbers are increasingly stark: in 2014, *Global Wealth Report* finds that 0.7 percent of the global population controls 44 percent of global wealth, while 69 percent exist on just 2.9 percent of global wealth.[16]

The issues of income inequality and economic development policy are closely tied together. Economic development policy instruments include those designed both to promote the distribution of existing capital to

[13] Ibid., para. 53. [14] Ibid., paras. 28–33.

[15] World Economic Forum, *Outlook on the Global Agenda 2015* (2015), 7. Retrieved from www3.weforum.org/docs/GAC14/WEF_GAC14_OutlookGlobalAgenda_Report.pdf.

[16] Credit Suisse Research Institute, *Global Wealth Report 2014* (October 2014), 24. Retrieved from www.credit-suisse.com/ch/en/news-and-expertise/research/credit-suisse-research-institute/publications.html.

possible new owners through different forms of equity-related requirements, and the use of existing capital to promote greater economic benefits for others besides the current capital owners. While economic spillovers have long been presumed to be an associated benefit of FDI, economic development instruments seek to directly mandate such spillover benefits, including, for example, local purchasing or training of higher-skilled labor.

While the issue at the center of this paper is the growing set of rights of capital owners to make transboundary investments and the related restrictions on economic development policy space for governments in new investment treaties, the relationship of this issue to the broader "1%" issue cannot be ignored.[17]

FDI and economic development: from assumptions to policy action

While the literature on FDI is rather recent compared to other economic processes, much of the thinking around FDI has been infused with assumptions, often related to similar assumptions around trade liberalization. In the broadest of terms, economic liberalization processes are assumed to provide a synonym for development: more trade equals more development, or higher levels of investment equals more development. Focusing on the investment side, the thinking has assumed benefits of FDI in the form of employment, technology transfer, higher wages paid by foreign-owned companies, higher tax revenues for governments, increased access to global markets, and more competitive industries. While all of these are potential benefits of FDI, what has become increasingly evident is that not all of them, or indeed any of them, are certain benefits of FDI. The likelihood of achieving these benefits will vary based on sector, investments through mergers and acquisitions versus greenfield investments, capacity to absorb the potential benefits, and other factors. For developing countries, where FDI can have a bigger positive or negative impact on economic development due to the scale of the investments in proportion to the local economy, moving toward greater certainty of benefits has led to a changing focus. As UNCTAD recently noted:

> [The] new generation of investment policies has been in the making for some time, and is reflected in the dichotomy in policy directions over the

[17] See Howard Mann, "Investment Law and the 1%: On Which Side of the Divide?" (May 2015) 6(2) *Investment Treaty News* 12–13.

> last few years – with simultaneous moves to further liberalize investment regimes and promote foreign investment, on the one hand, and to regulate investment in pursuit of public policy objectives on the other. It reflects the recognition that liberalization, if it is to generate sustainable development outcomes, has to be accompanied – if not preceded – by the establishment of proper regulatory and institutional frameworks.[18]

This reflects the basic reality that the assumed benefits of FDI for developing countries are not automatic. Indeed, not only are they not automatic, but in many cases it is becoming even more clear that their achievement is in doubt. Employment levels may increase or decrease based on the nature of the investment, with mergers and acquisitions potentially leading to job losses rather than gains. Even in the natural resource sectors, employment benefits are becoming a small fraction of what they used to be, with knowledge-based technologies now replacing labor in more and more cases. Higher technology-based processes may also not lead to broad-based technology transfer, as companies move to protect intellectual property rights more deeply prior to entering a market, and the manufacturing of the technologies is increasingly concentrated in fewer and fewer companies.

The net impact of this is that the thinking on economic development from FDI has shifted from quantity to quality and from making assumptions of benefits to policy-making to seek enhanced benefits. The necessary implication of this is a related shift from macroeconomic understandings of these linkages to a microeconomic approach: the development benefits of FDI come at a project-by-project level that, when operating at its best, will add up to more than the sum of the parts. But to achieve this, there must be a greater capacity of governments to seek to enhance the potential benefits of individual investments. This is the direction that underlies the UNCTAD passage quoted earlier. Yet, it is precisely in this policy space that the risk of collision between the expanding economic rights of transboundary investors and the role of government policy space is found.

[18] UNCTAD, *Investment Policy Framework for Sustainable Development* (2012), 5. Retrieved from http://unctad.org/en/PublicationsLibrary/diaepcb2012d5_en.pdf. A similar approach is found in J. Anthony VanDuzer, Penelope Simons, and Graham Mayeda, *Integrating Sustainable Development into International Investment Agreements: A Guide for Developing Countries* (London: Commonwealth Secretariat, 2013).

Economic development and policy tools

From an investment law and policy perspective, the key economic development tools can be seen as falling into four broad categories:

1. regulating the establishment of investments;
2. requiring certain levels of ownership of foreign investments by nationals or entities within the host state;
3. protecting infant industries or promoting local economic actors, either private or public sector; and
4. requiring foreign investors to generate local economic linkages.

Concomitantly, each of these areas also relates to the increased rights of capital owners to make transnational investments free of encumbrances by governments.

Each of these categories can be filled in with a range of specific and proactive economic development tools. It is important to note here that the use of any of these tools requires careful analysis in order to have a sound basis for applying them to a specific sector or proposed investment. Simply put, none of these tools will work effectively in all circumstances, and in some cases they may even produce negative development impacts. Nothing in this paper seeks to suggest a blanket application of these tools by government, nor do we take any position on their use in any given circumstance. But, because careful analysis is needed in applying and implementing any of these tools does not create a rationale for their outright prohibition or restriction at the international level when, as is amply understood, they can be of value when applied carefully and appropriately. Consequently, when one does see such restrictions being applied, it is especially appropriate to ask why and for the benefit of whom? The answer appears to be, increasingly, in order to create greater economic rights for investors in a transboundary context.

Some of the specific tools that help fill out the four categories noted earlier are set out in Table 11.1. There is some overlap among the categories here, as some tools may have more than one objective.[19] These tools cannot be ranked for preferred use or in terms of risk. As noted earlier, each can only be used successfully based on careful analysis of the circumstances involved. In this sense, the growing resurgence of

[19] For a fuller discussion of possible roles for each see A. Cosbey, H. Mann, and M. Cunningham, *Bilateral Investment Treaties, Mining and National Champions: Making It Work* (IISD, 2014). Available at www.iisd.org/publications/bilateral-investment-treaties-mining-and-national-champions-making-it-work.

Table 11.1 *Sample economic development tools*

Category	Specific economic development tool
Regulating the establishment of investments	– Not granting rights of entry or establishment to foreign investors in general or in specified sectors – Net-benefit tests for entry
Requiring certain levels of ownership of foreign investments by nationals or entities within the host state	– Minimum levels of local equity ownership – Joint venture requirements – National champion monopolies or near monopolies (other than in public service sectors)
Protecting infant industries or promoting local economic actors, either private or public sector	– Joint venture requirements – Technology transfer requirements – National champion monopolies or near monopolies (other than in public sectors services)
Requiring foreign investors to generate local economic linkages	– Local purchasing of goods and services – Training programs to enhance local purchasing opportunities (improve absorption capacity of host state) – Requirements for downstream value-added processing or other work (often tied to export restrictions) – Employment at higher skill levels – Training programs for employees – Technology transfer requirements – Research and development obligations

industrial policy in developing countries in the wake of the failure of the Washington Consensus merges well with the need for an investment policy that seeks to maximize the benefits of FDI in the local economy.

In the sections that follow, these tools are discussed in relation to the private economic rights being created for investors and the potential role for government policy space in relation to them.

Tracking the development of international law in respect to the economic development tools and economic rights of transboundary investors

Customary international law

The starting point for the analysis of how international investment law addresses the notion of economic rights of transboundary investors and the use of these economic development tools is customary international law (CIL). The analysis here, however, is remarkably short in nature: CIL granted no rights to investors to make transboundary investments. Rather, customary international law unequivocally allowed states to limit entry of foreign investors as they chose and impose the conditions they chose to apply when foreign investment was permitted. States could distinguish and discriminate between domestic and foreign investors and between investors of different foreign states. Postestablishment treatment does have some limitations under CIL, relating in particular to expropriation of investments. Certain of the measures set out earlier, such as requiring JV partners or an allowance for local equity ownership after an investment has been made, can in the extreme, constitute an expropriation under CIL. But when imposed clearly as a condition on making an investment before it has been made, no issue of expropriation under CIL could arise.[20]

This is a critical element in the analysis: newer economic treaties are not just "protecting" a pre-existing property right of an investor here, nor are they just protecting existing property in a foreign state. They are, rather, creating new economic rights to establish property and economic interests in a foreign state by undertaking a specific type of economic activity, FDI, and then significantly limiting the manner in which host states can regulate that activity. Consequently, it is to the treaties governing international economic matters that one must turn to find the

[20] See, e.g., M. Sornarajah, *The International Law of Foreign Investment*, 2nd ed. (Cambridge: CUP, 2004).

essential trends toward expanding the economic rights of capital owners by expanding rights to make transnational investments and the limitations on the use of economic development tools by governments relating to these investments.

Constraints under trade law

The first source of treaty law comes in the World Trade Organization (WTO) Uruguay Round texts in two agreements that entered into force in 1995: Trade-Related Investment Measures Agreement (TRIMS), and General Agreement on Trade in Services (GATS).[21]

GATS

For the purposes of the present issues, the GATS provides a list of service sectors and subsectors that states commit to allowing market access for foreign investors on an equal footing to domestic investors. This non-discrimination provision requires, in the case of the GATS, for the sectors or subsectors to be expressly listed in an Annex. There are no liberalization or nondiscrimination requirements under GATS for nonlisted sectors. The flip side of this, of course, is that investors gain a right to make the transnational investment within the listed sectors of any state.

For developing countries, one finds a range of listed sectors under GATS, from many to very few and even none. In many cases, the demands for liberalization commitments from developed countries were weak in this early stage of investment liberalization commitments. The result is a narrow set of international law rights for investors in services in developing countries. The effect of this is not that investors have no opportunity to invest in the broader array of service sectors. Rather, the effect is simply that the right of a foreign investor to invest is left to the domestic law and policy of the host state rather than addressed as a matter of international treaty law. Investments take place every day in sectors and countries not covered by treaty rights to make such investments.

The GATS did, however, go beyond the identification of sectors for national treatment for investment. It also established limitations on the imposition of other forms of entry or equity requirements on listed

[21] Treaty texts available at www.wto.org/english/docs_e/legal_e/final_e.htm; See summaries in, e.g. Michael Trebilcock and Robert Howse, *The Regulation of International Trade*, 3rd ed. (London: Routledge, 2005).

sectors. Article XVI.2 of the GATS on Market Access precludes, inter alia,

- limitations on the number of service suppliers in any listed sector;
- limitations on the total number of service operations or on the total quantity of service output;
- measures which restrict or require specific types of legal entity or joint venture through which a service supplier may supply a service;
- limitations on the participation of foreign capital in terms of maximum percentage limit on foreign shareholding; or
- limitations on ownership based on the total value of individual or aggregate foreign investment.[22]

These international law prohibitions on governments on creating equity ownership limitations or joint venture requirements appear to be the first of their type in international law. While applying only to listed services sectors, they now provide the model for what one sees becoming applied to investments in all sectors and on a negative list rather than positive list basis.

TRIMS

Trade-Related Investment Measures Agreement (TRIMS) starts from a different perspective. Its focus is on preventing trade restrictive and distorting effects of investment measures, based on the overall mission of the WTO to reduce and eliminate trade barriers. But TRIMS itself does not create new law. Rather, it provides an illustrative list of measures that would constitute a violation of Articles III and XI of the General

[22] The full text of the relevant paragraphs of GATS Article XVI, para. 2: In sectors where market-access commitments are undertaken, the measures which a Member shall not maintain or adopt either on the basis of a regional subdivision or on the basis of its entire territory, unless otherwise specified in its Schedule, are defined as:

> (a) limitations on the number of service suppliers whether in the form of numerical quotas, monopolies, exclusive service suppliers or the requirements of an economic needs test; . . . (c) limitations on the total number of service operations or on the total quantity of service output expressed in terms of designated numerical units in the form of quotas or the requirement of an economic needs test; . . . (e) measures which restrict or require specific types of legal entity or joint venture through which a service supplier may supply a service; and (f) limitations on the participation of foreign capital in terms of maximum percentage limit on foreign shareholding or the total value of individual or aggregate foreign investment.

Agreement on Tariffs and Trade (GATT).[23] The Annex to TRIMS contains the "Illustrative list" of measures that are enforceable under law or administrative processes, or are required of an investor in order to obtain an advantage:

- local purchase requirements for products as inputs into their operations;
- limiting an enterprise's purchases or use of imported products by relating it to the volume or value of local products it exports;
- measures that restrict the importation of products used in or related to its local operations in general or by relating it to the amount of products it exports, or by restricting its access to foreign exchange;
- restricting the export or sale for export by an enterprise of the products it produces.[24]

These measures clearly seek to limit the imposition of local purchase requirements on foreign investors, as well as impacting the ability to require local downstream processing or value addition to natural resources or other products, whether for domestic consumption or later higher-value exports. These are two critical elements in the performance requirement category and are especially central to benefit maximization for development in the natural resources sector. They provide governments with tools to enhance the economic spillovers of FDI. Their prohibition, by contrast, enhances the profit maximization opportunities of the investors, by creating, in effect, profit maximization rights for the investor on trade-related issues.

TRIMS and GATS are much more limited in scope than newer texts in investment treaties. They also have three features that limit their potential negative impact on the use of economic development policy tools.

First, the GATS requires a positive list, so states have full control over what is included in a very direct manner. Negative lists, of the type that now seems to predominate in newer agreements, risk greater degrees of error and difficulties in negotiations owing to the reverse starting point of all sectors being included except what a state lists out.

Second, TRIMS has no new obligations over those in the GATT. The illustrative list requires a clear nexus with trade. It is also specific to products and thus does not include services. While it enumerates illustrative violations of the GATT when they originate in investment-related

[23] TRIMS, Article 2. [24] TRIMS, Annex.

measures, they do not add to the GATT restrictions and thus do not create additional rights for investors when in the form of TRIMS.

Third, and importantly, the WTO Agreements are only enforceable by states taking action against other states. Since the entry into force of these agreements, 40 cases have raised issues related to TRIMS in the initial requests for consultations, though many are actually simply supplicate cases relating to the same facts. Of these, only nine separate issues (adjusting for consolidated cases on the same facts) have been subject to any decision in the dispute settlement process.[25]

Cosbey notes that one reason for the relatively small number of cases is that, despite the provisions of TRIMS, most states employ these types of measures at either the national or subnational levels, which makes it difficult to initiate actions against other states at the WTO.[26]

Bilateral Investment Treaties[27]

The European approach

Early Bilateral Investment Treaties (BITs) imposed few limitations on the ability of governments to impose restrictions on the entry of foreign investors or limitations on governments to impose equity or performance-based obligations on investors. Indeed, early treaties were focused only on the post establishment treatment of investors, not pre-establishment rights of entry. At most, the provisions on national treatment or most-favored nation treatment may have impacted the ability of governments to implement obligations just on foreign investors.

Post 1994, two approaches developed. The European-based treaties largely continued to eschew pre-establishment rights issues and focus on post establishment protection. After the adoption of the WTO Agreements, a number of European investment treaties began to include provisions affirming TRIMS, but they rarely went beyond this. While these provisions would allow individual investors to take measures

[25] Data based on WTO website on dispute settlement, searched by Agreement, on 4 June 2015. www.wto.org/english/tratop_e/dispu_e/dispu_agreements_index_e.htm?id=A25#.

[26] Aaron Cosbey, "Everyone's Doing It: The Acceptance, Effectiveness, and Legality of Performance Requirements", *Investment Treaty News* (19 February 2015), online: www.iisd.org/itn/2015/02/19/everyones-doing-it-the-acceptance-effectiveness-and-legality-of-performance-requirements/.

[27] For a detailed review of the historical development of related provisions in BITs, see S. Nikiema, *IISD Best Practice Series: Performance Requirements in Investment Treaties* (2014), available at www.iisd.org/publications/best-practices-series-performance-requirements-investment-treaties.

directly to investor-state arbitration, there appears to be just one arbitration so far of this happening under the European model. This is the case of *Lemire* v. *Ukraine*, where a claim that a requirement to play 50% Ukrainian music at a Ukrainian radio station was a breach of the provisions in the UK–Ukraine BIT. The claim did not succeed on this point.[28] The very low number of cases to date is probably explainable by the relatively recent uptake of broader performance requirement (PR) prohibitions in European-based treaties.[29]

However, the European model did provide a basis for challenging one of the initial national equity requirements under the expropriation and fair and equitable treatment (FET) provisions common to most investment treaties. This was South Africa's Black Economic Empowerment Act (BEE), in the rather well-known *Foresti* v. *South Africa*.[30] The BEE was a major plank in the response of the post-apartheid South African government to the economic disequilibrium created by the apartheid regime. Its focus was clearly on internal income distribution within South Africa for both economic and social development reasons. In the post-apartheid context, as in many other post-colonial contexts, intragenerational economic equity was and remains a critical issue to address. The *Foresti* case was essentially withdrawn by the claimant after permits necessary for ongoing operations of the claimants quarry were obtained from the government. However, while there was no decision on the merits in this case, it demonstrates the ability of investors to challenge essential economic and social development measures under the more general and traditional rights they are granted under investment treaties.

The North American model takes hold

The *Foresti* case took place under the Italian–South Africa BIT, a typical European type agreement. It did not take place under the more aggressive form of post-1994 North American model championed by the United States and Canada. This model adopted an aggressive pre-establishment rights regime, as well as TRIMS+ performance requirement prohibitions.

Unlike the European state's approach, post-1994 saw the development of a distinct North American approach to investment agreements that included pre-establishment rights, or rights to national treatment, for

[28] *Joseph Charles Lemire* v. *Ukraine*, Decision on Liability and Jurisdiction, 14 January 2010, ICSID Case No. ARB/06/18.

[29] Nikiema, *IISD Best Practice Series*, at 16.

[30] *Piero Foresti, Laura de Carli & Others* v. *The Republic of South Africa*, 4 August 2010, Award, ICSID Case No. ARB(AF)/07/01.

would-be foreign investors, a well as a set of "TRIMS+" performance requirement prohibitions.

The North American Free Trade Agreement (NAFTA)-based pre-establishment rights model differs significantly from the GATS services liberalization approach in that it starts from the premise of full liberalization of all investment in all sectors, including services in many instances, except for what is listed out in a specific annex that identifies the excluded sectors or subsectors. Thus, rights to invest on a nondiscriminatory basis are provided to foreign investors under such provisions, and conversely the right to preclude investors from entering into a sector is constrained, unless that sector is expressly excluded through the annex listing. The NAFTA language for this is deceptively simple:

> **Article 1102: National Treatment**
>
> 1. Each Party shall accord to investors of another Party treatment no less favorable than that it accords, in like circumstances, to its own *investors with respect to the establishment, acquisition, expansion*, management, conduct, operation, and sale or other disposition of investments. (emphasis added)

The simple inclusion of the words "with respect to the establishment, acquisition, expansion" of investments is sufficient to create the market access rights and the limitations on governments being able to constrain such rights. No special provision has been needed for this purpose. In this way, the NAFTA model provides a broad-based prohibition on managing the entry of foreign investors, save for the excluded sectors. Moreover, it does so in a manner that does not allow for unilateral amendment in the future: the policy of the day is effectively locked in as a matter of international law unless the other treaty party agrees to modifications.

It is worth noting again here that no international treaty commitments are required to liberalize investment into a national economy. This can be done at any time to any degree by the use of domestic law and policy instruments. Indeed, as noted earlier, the great majority of transboundary investments have been made solely on the basis of domestic law and policy provisions, with no international treaty provision being involved. The legal impact of the treaty is, therefore, not the liberalization of investment per se, but the locking in of that commitment unless the treaty is later amended by agreement or terminated by one of the states parties. Thus, longer-term control over inward investment policy is essentially forfeited by making this type of commitment. But from the perspective of granting economic rights to foreign investors, these liberalization provisions do just that for investors of the other treaty party. Moreover, they make these rights virtually irreversible.[31]

In addition, the above type of formulation includes all general laws relating to inward investment that (a) place a foreign investor in a less favorable position than domestic investors, and (b) are not expressly exempted in a special annex relating to excluded legal or policy measures. Thus, general foreign investment laws that include, for example, a net benefit test for foreign investors would not be treaty compliant unless expressly excluded. And, of course, the ability to adopt such a law would be precluded if one did not exist at the time and a reservation for the future was not taken. In this manner, the future reliance on such tools as a net benefit test can be proscribed without any actual policy deliberation having taken place on generating such a permanent result.

The TRIMS+ approach can also be seen as becoming increasingly broad in terms of precluding government measures that seek to enhance the economic benefits to the host state after an investment has been made. The "plus" elements begin by expanding the introductory language of the TRIMS illustrative list:

> TRIMs that are inconsistent with the obligation of national treatment provided for in paragraph 4 of Article III of GATT 1994 include those which are mandatory or enforceable under domestic law or under administrative rulings, or compliance with which is necessary to obtain an advantage, and which require: . . .[32]

The similar introductory language to Article 1106, titled Performance Requirements, states:

> 1. No Party may impose or enforce any of the following requirements, *or enforce any commitment or undertaking*, in connection with the establishment, acquisition, expansion, management, conduct or operation of an investment of an investor of a Party or of a non-Party in its territory: (emphasis added)

Two major things are of note here. First, the language goes beyond obligations of a host state toward investors of the other state party. The language states specifically: *operation of an investment of an investor of a party or of a non-party in its territory*. While this does not extend dispute

[31] The present author is unaware of any reversal of a commitment post entry into force of an investment treaty.

[32] World Trade Organization, Agreement on Trade-Related Investment Measures, Annex, Para 1.

settlement rights to non-state party investors, this could create legally binding obligations for a government related to even its own investors if the treaty is legally incorporated into domestic law. No other provision in NAFTA does this. Second, the highlighted language would seem to include any undertakings made, for example, in a natural resource exploitation contract between a government and a potential investor or in connection with a net benefit test required in many foreign investment laws, unless the sector or enabling legislation is expressly exempted in an Annex.

In making this extension over TRIMS clear, the NAFTA model goes in the opposite direction of good industry practice in key areas of investment, in particular, in the extractives sector. The International Bar Association's Model Mine Development Agreement, for example, specifically expresses the need to include local purchasing and other performance requirements as part of the benefit sharing in a fair and equitable resource development project.[33] The precision of the NAFTA would seem to stand in the way of following this type of good industry practice. The International Bar Association's document recognizes the need for value sharing though economic development associated with the making of international investments in the natural resource sector. The TRIMS+ NAFTA model, by contrast, seeks to preclude requirements for such benefit sharing.

In addition to the extension of the introductory language, the list of elements found in Article 1106 of NAFTA, titled Performance Requirements, prohibits technology transfer requirements:

> **Article 1106 (1)** . . .
>
> . . .
>
> (f) to transfer technology, a production process or other proprietary knowledge to a person in its territory, except when the requirement is imposed or the commitment or undertaking is enforced by a court, administrative tribunal or competition authority to remedy an alleged violation of competition laws or to act in a manner not inconsistent with other provisions of this Agreement;
>
> . . .

[33] International Bar Association, Mining Law Committee, *Model Mine Development Agreement*, Articles 20 (development obligations), 21 (Use of Local Goods and Services), 22 (Local Community Development), 22.1 (Community Development Agreement), 22.3 (Local Business Development Plan), *inter alia*. Available at www.mmdaproject.org/.

NAFTA does allow governments to impose some performance requirements, when conditioned to the receipt of an advantage:

> Article 1106.4. Nothing in paragraph 3 shall be construed to prevent a Party from conditioning the receipt or continued receipt of an advantage, in connection with an investment in its territory of an investor of a Party or of a non-Party, on compliance with a requirement to locate production, provide a service, train or employ workers, construct or expand particular facilities, or carry out research and development, in its territory.

What is meant by "an advantage" is not clarified, or whether this requires some form of monetary benefit or whether receipt of a permit to operate constitutes in itself receipt of an advantage. However, the implication of this is that research and development requirements or employment training requirements may not be permissible unless accompanied by an advantage in some form for the investor.

Since 1994, the NAFTA model has spread through the adoption of agreements by the United States and Canada with European, African, Latin American, and Asian states. In addition to the content of these provisions, the model also makes all of these issues subject to investor-state dispute settlement (ISDS). This right to initiate arbitrations over performance requirements has been acted on in the NAFTA context, with eight decided cases to date[34] and at least one other pending case which raises this point directly.[35]

Thus, there are nine arbitrations under the more developed provisions of NAFTA, which suggests the potential for a very significant number of arbitrations when the provisions are expanded through other treaties, especially regional and interregional treaties, as described further. As Dr. Suzy Nikiema notes, these cases have already, like other provisions

[34] On the basis of Nikiema, *IISD Best Practice Series*, note 27, these cases are: These are: *Pope & Talbot Inc.* v. *Government of Canada*, UNCITRAL, Interim ruling of 26 June 2000; *S.D. Myers Inc.* v. *Canada*, UNCITRAL, partial award of 13 November 2000; *ADF Group Inc.* v. *United States of America*, ICSID Case No. ARB (AF)/00/1, award of 9 January 2003; *Archer Daniels Midland Company and Tate & Lyle Ingredients Americas, Inc.* v. *United Mexican States*, ICSID Case No. ARB (AF)/04/5, award of 21 November; *Corn Products International, Inc.* v. *United States of America*, ICSID, Case No. ARB (AF)/04/1, award of 15 January 2008; *Cargill Incorporated* v. *United Mexican States*, ICSID Case No. ARB(AF)/05/2, award of 18 September 2009; *Merrill & Ring Forestry L.P.* v. *Government of Canada*, UNCITRAL, ICSID, award of 31 March 2010; *Mobil Investments Canada Inc. and Murphy Oil Corporation* v. *Government of Canada*, ICSID Case No. ARB(AF)/07/4, Decision of 22 May 2012. All the awards are available at http://italaw.com.

[35] *Mesa Power Group, LLC* v. *Government of Canada*, UNCITRAL, PCA Case No. 2012-17, ongoing.

of investment treaties, spawned at least two different schools of interpretation of the PR provisions, showing the difficulties for states in seeking clarity when attempting to draft or implement such provisions.[36]

Ultimately, the summary by Cosbey is especially clear and cogent:

> There are good reasons for the widespread use of performance requirements, even in situations where the implementing country is legally obliged to shun them. For one thing, all states are looking for ways to have investment contribute more pervasively to their economic development. For another thing, even though performance requirements are hard to get right, they sometimes work.
>
> Two conclusions stem from those widely understood realities. First, investment policy-makers need more guidance on the successful employment of these tools. Second, either the law or the practice should change (taking into account the evidence on effectiveness, among other things). As it stands now, the international community has agreed to ban tools that everyone continues to use.[37]

Alternative regional views

Intraregional investments agreements within developing country regions have taken alternative views on some of these issues. The South African Development Community (SADC) Agreement on Cooperation on Investment includes no mandatory investment liberalization provisions, and hence no independent economic rights to invest for foreign investors. Thus, it does not impact the ability of governments to differentiate between domestic and foreign investors for establishing different conditions on their entry or ownership.[38] While the region moves progressively toward more integrated economic outlooks, the Investment agreement does not create binding obligations in this regard, leaving the process of regional liberalization to the coordination of domestic law rather than the international level.

Article 3 of the agreement expressly provides for the need to encourage upstream and downstream economic linkages, in other words local purchasing of goods and services and value addition to products prior to consumption or export.[39] The international agreement therefore

[36] Nikiema, *IISD Best Practice Series*, at 13–15. [37] Cosbey, "Everyone's Doing It".

[38] South African Development Community, Protocol on Finance and Investment, Annex 1, Cooperation on Investment. Entered into force in 2013.

[39] Ibid., Art. 3.

empowers governments to take such measures for development purposes rather than prohibiting them from doing so.

This is further supported by Article 7, which provides a general exception in favor of development measures, as opposed to additional constraints:

> Notwithstanding the provisions of Article 6, State Parties may in accordance with their respective domestic legislation grant preferential treatment to qualifying investments and investors in order to achieve national development objectives.[40]

Unlike the performance requirements prohibition approach of the NAFTA that prohibits most PRs, even if attached to a benefit for the investor, the SADC agreement allows incentives of benefits tied to achieving development benefits.

The SADC Model Bilateral Investment Treaty template, drafted after the negotiation of the Agreement on Cooperation on Investment,[41] provides an agreed template for member states who decide to pursue additional bilateral investment treaty negotiations with non-regional states. It includes no pre-establishment rights for foreign investors, relying instead on a more traditional provision: "The State Parties shall promote and admit investments in accordance with their applicable laws, and shall apply such laws in good faith."[42] (It may be noted that the recent Canada-China agreement includes similar language rather than pre-establishment rights.[43])

In relation to the general national treatment obligation, it follows the pattern of allowing for exclusions of measures for post establishment treatment. But this general approach is reframed by an express set of development-related rights for states in additional Article 21, on the Right to Pursue Development Goals, that recognizes the right to take measures to promote economic development:

[40] Ibid., Article 7.1.

[41] South African Development Community, *Model Bilateral Investment Treaty Template* (June 2012). The Model Template is not a legally binding document but seeks to set out standards and suggestions to member states.

[42] Ibid., Article 3.

[43] Agreement between the Government of Canada and the Government of the People's Republic of China for the Promotion and Reciprocal Protection of Investments, Article 3: Promotion and Admission of Investment *Each Contracting Party shall encourage investors of the other Contracting Party to make investments in its territory and admit such investments in accordance with its laws, regulations, and rules.*

21.1. Notwithstanding any other provision of this Agreement, a State Party may grant preferential treatment in accordance with their domestic legislation to any enterprise so qualifying under the domestic law in order to achieve national or sub-national regional development goals.

21.2. Notwithstanding any other provision of this Agreement, a State Party may

(a) support the development of local entrepreneurs, and

(b) seek to enhance productive capacity, increase employment, increase human resource capacity and training, research and development including of new technologies, technology transfer and other benefits of investment through the use of specified requirements on investors made at the time of the establishment or acquisition of the investment and applied during its operation.

21.3. Notwithstanding any other provision of this Agreement, a State Party may take measures necessary to address historically based economic disparities suffered by identifiable ethnic or cultural groups due to discriminatory or oppressive measures against such groups prior to the signing of this Agreement.

Collectively, these exclusions provide, in a sense, an antidote to provisions that prohibit performance requirements, equity requirements or the use of other economic development instruments. Equally important, they would preclude the deployment of general obligations, such as for national treatment or FET against the use of economic development tools if the text were to be applied in a context with the potential for ISDS.

The investment agreement of the Common Market for Eastern and Southern Africa (COMESA) includes a general obligation to promote intraregional investment liberalization.[44] This is supplemented with a general national treatment that includes the establishment, acquisition and expansion of investments, and language drawn from NAFTA. However, the states parties also have the right to list out sectors or subsectors, and nonconforming legislative measures, in special annexes for this purpose.[45] However, unlike NAFTA and its related agreements, each member state of COMESA can unilaterally amend its annex to add or remove sectors or subsectors and future legislative measures, thus maintaining flexibility to adjust economic development policies.[46] The impact of this is that potential investors can know what sectors are open or closed and under what conditions, but they are not permanently locked in as under the NAFTA approach. Future policy space is thus

[44] Common Market for Eastern and Southern Africa, Investment Agreement for the COMESA Common Investment Area, Article 5(b).

[45] Ibid., Articles 17 and 18. [46] Ibid., Article 9(2).

preserved, while supporting liberalization policies for those states that adopt them.

The ASEAN investment agreement also has a mixed approach, which includes a general direction toward investment liberalization within the region.[47] At present, it provides for a positive list of sectors for pre-establishment liberalization, set out in Article 3:

- manufacturing
- agriculture
- fishery
- forestry
- mining and quarrying
- services incidental to manufacturing, agriculture, fishery, forestry, mining, and quarrying.[48]

This list is subject to reservations under Article 9 of the ACIA, in which reservations have included specific measures and broader approaches to exclusions of sectors and subsectors.[49] In addition, governments had the right to modify the schedules unilaterally for 1 year after their submission. They can be amended by agreement thereafter.[50]

On PRs, the Agreement reaffirms TRIMS.[51] It then has an interesting internal requirement calling for further review of the provision to determine, 2 years after entry into force, whether it should be expanded. To date, this review process has been initiated but not, as yet, concluded.[52]

ASEAN does not appear to include limits on the government capacity to impose equity ownership or joint venture requirements, other than through the general national treatment obligations, subject again to reservations being taken.

Future directions: some recent negotiations

The past is not always the guide to the future. A big question is where the European Commission will lead European negotiations given that it now has jurisdiction to negotiate investment treaties instead of the member states. Two recently concluded negotiations suggest they will seek to elaborate new directions compared to the traditional European state's

[47] ASEAN Comprehensive Investment Agreement, entered into force in 2011.
[48] Ibid., Article 3.3.
[49] On the basis of a review of the Schedules included as annexes to the Agreement on the ASEAN website.
[50] Ibid., Article 10. [51] Ibid., Article 7.1. [52] Ibid., Article 7.2.

model. This is likely to include more extensive provisions on performance requirements and on equity or ownership requirements. The two recent agreements are the Canada–Europe Comprehensive Economic and Trade Agreement (CETA), and the EU–Singapore FTA.

CETA

The Canada-Europe Comprehensive Economic and Trade Agreement, commonly known as CETA, includes perhaps the most extensive set of limitations on economic development tools ever pulled together in one instrument, at least to the knowledge of the present author. While this treaty is between two developed country regions, the impact if the same provisions were to be applied in a developing country, or developing region, context would be even more significant.

CETA contains the extensive pre-establishment rights typically found in the NAFTA-based model since 1994. It is the basic negative list model, allowing for exclusions from the general principle of investment liberalization by sector or for noncompliant measures.[53] The nondiscrimination provisions, as is common, extend to the postestablishment phase.

CETA includes the extensive range of prohibitions on PRs found in recent NAFTA-based texts and the TRIMS+ model discussed earlier.[54] This was the first time such a broad text appeared in the European context, however, making its role as a model text of increasing importance. The combination of extensive pre-establishment rights and broad prohibitions on PRs marked the first European agreement with such extensive economic rights for foreign investors.

However, the CETA goes still farther. It adopts extensive provisions, based on the GATS text discussed earlier, that prohibit conditioning the entry of investments on ownership or equity level requirements. Unlike GATS, Article X.4 applies a priori to all sectors, services and nonservices.[55] It also applies on a negative list basis as opposed to a positive list

[53] CETA, Article X.6. [54] CETA, Art. X.5.

[55] As the broadest such provision of its kind, this Article is set out in full here: CETA, Article X.4: Market Access:

1. Neither Party shall adopt or maintain with regard to market access through establishment by an investor of a Party, either on the basis of its entire territory or on the basis of the territory of a national, provincial, territorial, regional or local level of government, measures that:

   (a) impose limitations on:

requirement found in the GATS.[56] These two differences expand the scope of GATS market access provisions in a very significant way and broaden the economic rights of foreign investors beyond, as far as this author is aware, any other existing international treaty.

All three of the above CETA provisions are subject to a negative list for existing measures and for sectors excluded by negative lists in an Annex.[57] Notionally, this allows for the exercise of policy decisions at the time of the negotiation of the treaty. However, it effectively precludes any subsequent expansion of this policy space at a later time. For highly developed and liberalized economies, this may be less of a problem, but for smaller economies and those states with less negotiating and implementation capacity, this approach can become very difficult to manage, despite the very significant implications for economic development policy space.

Unusually for Canadian treaties, the CETA excludes the pre-establishment rights, PR prohibitions, and market access rules from ISDS, allowing only for state-to-state dispute settlement in relation to these provisions. Presumably, this will allow for some degree of flexibility for states in pursuing any disputes that might not be present for investor-initiated proceedings. Nonetheless, the existence or not of an international obligation on states limiting economic development policy space, or the concomitant economic right of a potential foreign investor, is not dependent on the form of dispute settlement associated with the treaty provision. Other than the Canada–China Investment treaty, which does not include pre-establishment rights or other economic rights for investors beyond reaffirming TRIMS, this appears to be the only post-NAFTA

(i) the number of enterprises that may carry out a specific economic activity whether in the form of numerical quotas, monopolies, exclusive suppliers or the requirement of an economic needs test;
(ii) the total value of transactions or assets in the form of numerical quotas or the requirement of an economic needs test;
(iii) the total number of operations or the total quantity of output expressed in terms of designated numerical units in the form of quotas or the requirement of an economic needs test;
(iv) the participation of foreign capital in terms of maximum percentage limit on foreign shareholding or the total value of individual or aggregate foreign investment;
(v) the total number of natural persons that may be employed in a particular sector or that an enterprise may employ and who are necessary for, and directly related to, the performance of economic activity in the form of numerical quotas or the requirement of an economic needs test.

[56] CETA, Article X.14. [57] CETA, Article X.14.

Canadian investment treaty to exclude pre-establishment rights from the ISDS process.

Singapore–EU Free Trade Agreement

The Singapore–EU FTA was concluded in two tranches: the free trade and other economic components in September 2013 and the Investment Protection chapter in October 2014.[58] However, unlike most agreements of this type, the market access rights for investment – pre-establishment rights in other words – were completed in 2013 under Chapter 8 entitled Services, Establishment, and Electronic Commerce. This division makes clear the actual distinction in the nature of the rights and obligations being negotiated. The original goal of investment treaties, the protection of existing investments, is seen in Chapter 9 on Investment Protection. The economic rights of foreign investors – as distinct from the protection rights – are found in a totally separate chapter (Chapter 8) that addresses establishment rights, equity ownership, and forms of partnerships, concluded a year ahead of the following chapter.

Chapter 9, on investment protection, does not address any of the types of issues being discussed here directly. PRs are not expressly addressed in any fashion, and there are no explicit economic or social development rights for government set out. Thus, it is possible that, unless excluded in the Schedule of Specific Commitments, the general post establishment national treatment provisions could be used by an investor to seek redress for any PRs imposed on it. A review of the Singapore schedule revealed no such exceptions, but in principle another state adopting this approach could do so.[59]

The primary source of text germane to this Chapter is found in Chapter 8. In relation to pre-establishment rights, Chapter 8 employs a positive list-in requirement for sectors to be covered, with the opportunity to then exclude specific subsectors of existing measures from the commitment. It is expressly stated in the text that the Establishment section applies to all sectors, not just services sectors.[60] For Singapore, the schedule is extensive, both in the services and nonservices sectors, with few excluded

[58] The full text of the EU–Singapore Free Trade Agreement and schedules is found at http://trade.ec.europa.eu/doclib/press/index.cfm?id=961.

[59] Singapore Schedule of Specific Commitments, Appendix 8-B-1 of the FTA.

[60] Article 8.8.

Table 11.2 *Development tools versus private economic rights in recent treaties*

Category	Specific economic development tool	Constrained by
Regulating the establishment of investments	– Not granting rights of entry or establishment to foreign investors in general or in specified sectors – Net benefit tests for entry	– CETA – Singapore
Requiring certain levels of ownership of foreign investments by nationals or entities within the host state	– Minimum levels of local equity ownership – Joint venture requirements – National champion monopolies or near monopolies (other than in public service sectors)	– CETA – Singapore
Protecting infant industries or promoting local economic actors, either private or public sector	– Joint venture requirements – Technology transfer requirements – National champion monopolies or near monopolies (other than in public sectors services)	– CETA – Singapore
Requiring foreign investors to generate local economic linkages	– Local purchasing of goods and services – Training programs to enhance local purchasing opportunities (improve absorption capacity of host state) – Requirements for downstream value-added processing or other work (often tied to export restrictions) – Employment at higher skill levels – Training programs for employees – Technology transfer requirements – Research and development obligations	– CETA – Singapore, only in part

measures set out on the nonservices side. The extension of economic rights to EU investors as a matter of international law is, therefore, extensive.[61]

Among the rights granted are national treatment rights for making an investment,[62] as commonly seen in many NAFTA-type models with pre-establishment national treatment rights. Article 8.11.2 goes further, however, to set out prohibitions on equity or ownership limitations, and joint venture requirements, as part of the rights given to foreign investors. This parallels the market access provisions in the CETA text. Article 8.12 of the FTA makes it clear that the rights granted cannot be revised to lower levels of rights later on. They are locked in.

What is absent in the Singapore FTA compared to CETA is the express limitation on the imposition of PRs In addition, these provisions, like CETA, are not subject to ISDS.[63]

However, the EU–Singapore FTA includes one additional, interesting Chapter 7: Non-Tariff Barriers to Trade and Investment in Renewable Energy Generation. What makes this chapter of interest is the clear identification of local purchase requirements and joint venture requirements – typical performance or equity-related development requirements – as nontariff barriers to trade and investment in the sector. This takes us back to the key linkage of TRIMS to trade in the WTO negotiations, but in a sector-specific application here. The first two principles set out in this chapter are

> **Article 7.4: Principles**
>
> A Party shall:
>
> (a) refrain from adopting measures providing for local content requirements or any other offset affecting the other Party's products, service suppliers, investors or investments.
>
> (b) refrain from adopting measures requiring the formation of partnerships with local companies, unless such partnerships are deemed necessary for technical reasons and the Party can demonstrate such technical reasons upon request by the other Party;

Given the unusual definition of local content and ownership requirements as technical barriers to trade and investment, one may well wonder what the implications of this would be for enhanced avenues of state-state dispute settlement.

[61] Undoubtedly, many of the sectors were covered in previous GATS commitments, and so will not be new to Singapore.

[62] Singapore–EU FTA, Art. 8.11.1.

[63] Article 9.14 of the FTA limits ISDS to the investor protection provisions in Chapter 9.

It is noteworthy that the EU–Singapore and EU–Canada agreements do not come to the same set of rights and obligation, as it relates to the economic rights of investors, with the provision against performance requirements absent from the Singapore text. But on the other elements, they are indeed very similar.

Mapping the development tools and the trends

At a conference in Montreux, Switzerland, in October 2014, Dr. Yilmaz Akyüz, former Director of the Division on Globalization and Development Strategies at the United Nations Conference on Trade and Development (UNCTAD), suggested a list of 10 key policies to promote stronger development benefits from FDI in developing countries, seven of which are germane to this discussion:[64]

- encourage greenfield FDI, but selective;
- caps over acquisitions in stock markets;
- go for joint ownership with local firms and pay attention to crowding-out;
- no incentives unless significant technological benefits;
- impose conditions to generate spillovers, local employment, and supply links with firms;
- nurture domestic firms to compete with TNCs; and
- embed FDI policy in the overall industrial strategy.

If one were to apply the range of constraints on government economic policy space put in place in CETA to support the economic rights of investors to make and maximize profits from FDI, each of these seven tools would be blocked. In a previous analysis by the International Institute for Sustainable Development on economic development tools in Africa, a similar mapping exercise of economic development tools against existing investment treaties with African states as at least one party produced a similar result.[65] If we return to the original four categories and illustrative lists of development tools in Table 11.1, the result of the above-mentioned analysis mapped against CETA and the EU–Singapore FTA is clear, as seen in Table 11.2. To be clear, not all treaties have included such measures within them. As we have seen, the

[64] Powerpoint presentation by Dr. Yilmaz Akyuz, on file with the author.
[65] Cosebey, Mann, and Cunningham, *Bilateral Investment Treaties, Mining and National Champions*.

ASEAN CIA does not go beyond TRIMS and does not include broad ownership prescriptions. Whether the CIA gets expanded further in this regard is still under consideration, with no clear direction being public as yet. African regionally based approaches generally do not extend significant economic rights either. But the growth in this area of treaty-making is still remarkable for its deliberate expansion of economic rights for investors that are very distinct in nature and application from the original purpose of investment treaties.

Additional factors in investment treaties

There are additional factors embedded within investment treaties that tend to support this result. One is the ability in many cases for investors to directly initiate ISDS proceedings. The NAFTA model is clearest on this, with nine separate cases, though three relate to a similar set of measures in Mexico. Discount for this and that still provides an interesting comparison to TRIMS, with nine instances going to decisions in the WTO dispute settlement system, on a global basis compared to seven different situations solely among Canada, Mexico, and the United States. Canada has now relented on the application of ISDS rights to these issues in the CETA. Whether the United States will insist on maintaining full ISDS applicability to these investor economic rights provisions in its negotiations with the EU remains to be seen. However, as noted earlier, the issue of direct enforcement of these rights is a secondary issue to their granting in the first place. Not being directly enforceable by investors does not make them less noteworthy as economic rights for private sector actors and concomitant constraints on economic development rights in the host states.

An additional element is the provision protecting investors from capital controls. While some exceptions articles to safeguard governments in the event of major economic crises are emerging, by and large, the right to repatriate capital is deeply embedded in the investment treaty regime.

Finally, one may note the inclusion of broader economic rights for investors is especially growing in the context of bilateral, regional, and interregional FTAs. From a policy space perspective, this actually imposes additional constraints on governments who later find economic development tools unavailable. In the case of pure investment treaties, withdrawal or termination is a possibility, and some states have begun to exercise this right now, including South Africa, Indonesia, and Italy. But when investment agreements, be they protection or investment liberalization and market access rights, are embedded in broad FTAs, the risk of losing trade rights or market access for goods is likely to preclude any serious discussion of termination for investment-related reasons. Thus, the FTA-type negotiation may weigh heavily to foreclose the final policy space options for states, withdrawal, or termination.

Conclusion

This chapter starts from the perspective that FDI can be a good thing. From an environmental perspective, the need to distribute new technologies that reduce environmental impacts on climate, water, and other concerns is self-evident. FDI is a principal mechanism for doing so. From a social and economic development perspective, FDI has much potential for positive impacts on employment, human resource development, microeconomic development, and social enhancement. But none of these potentials are simply guaranteed by the fact of FDI: these results come from good policy measures correctly applied, at the right time in the investment cycle. This chapter is about whether the development of private economic rights to make investments and maximize the profits from FDI, at the expense of government policy space to seek to ensure broader economic development benefits from FDI, is a good policy choice. Moreover, one should be under no illusion: while this should not have to be a trade-off, the current approach does make it one.

The trade-off is not necessarily the only option. States can maintain policy flexibility but still grant clear investment rights under their domestic law, for example, with or without any treaty provisions. Treaty provisions can be made more flexible on PR prohibitions, at a minimum allowing states to impose them prior to an investment being made. This would allow the market to discipline states rather than a treaty text. States would have to act in a mature way to balance the goals of maximizing benefits, with the fact that investors cannot be compelled to make investments if they do not wish to. The market does apply such discipline. Equity ownership or joint venture requirements, when clear up front, also leave market disciplines fully intact, while allowing states to find levels of ownership in sensitive situations that can help address major social issues and historical situations. In short, options exist.

The broader concern with the expansion of the NAFTA+ model into CETA and in a different way the EU–Singapore FTA is that it is not designed to promote sustainable development. Rather, it goes back two and three decades to the same failed assumptions that liberalization and deregulation are the answers to economic development needs. As UNCTAD have noted, this is not the primary global view today. Yet the growth in investment treaty provisions that start from this view continues.

It is clear from the earlier review that the only significant expansion of the substantive content of investment treaties in their 50-plus years of existence has been to extend investor rights from the protection of existing foreign investments to the right to establish investments in a foreign state, and then to maximize the profits from these investments – even when at the expense of social and economic development rights in the host states. The broad result is that investment treaties are becoming more supportive of the rights of existing capital owners to extend and expand their capital base, while precluding governments from adopting policies and tools aimed at broadening the base of economic development and intergenerational equity. If the World Economic Forum is correct that the concentration of wealth in the top 1% of individuals is the number one global economic issue today, then the policy metric behind the expansion of capital owners' rights is surely the wrong approach to help address it.

So to return to the starting point of this chapter: Is Professor Sornarajah right that, now more than ever, international investment treaties have become the international economic law support to the law of greed over the law of need?

12

Giving arbitrators *carte blanche* – fair and equitable treatment in investment treaties

NATHALIE BERNASCONI-OSTERWALDER

Introduction

Most investment treaties incorporate language requiring states to accord fair and equitable treatment (FET) to foreign investors and their investments. The language appears almost colloquial, and any state will readily sign on to it to confirm that, of course, it commits to treating foreign investors fairly and equitably. That these words may have serious legal implications, however, was rarely well understood in the past and continues to be misunderstood and underestimated today. Professor Sornarajah addressed the vagueness of the term in response to a 2004 report by the Organisation for Economic Cooperation and Development (OECD) on the FET standard. In an article published in 2007, he contends the idea set out in the report that the vagueness of the formulation of the fair and equitable standard was intentional to give "the arbitrator the facility to articulate the necessary principles," noting that "[t]he explanation assumes that in a document that contains limitation on their sovereignty, the state parties agreed to a casually appointed arbitrator should have the capricious discretion as to how their sovereignty should be limited in the future."[1]

Over a decade after the 2004 OECD report, many tribunals have indeed exercised broad discretion over the years, as investors used the FET provision as a kind of catch-all guarantee to challenge a wide range of government measures, including laws and regulations adopted in the public interest, ranging from health and safety measures, such as tobacco regulation, environmental regulation and permit refusals, taxation

[1] M. Sornarajah, "The Fair and Equitable Standard of Treatment: Whose Fairness? Whose Equity?," in F. Ortino *et al.* (eds.), *Investment Treaty Law: Current Issues. II, Nationality and Investment Treaty Claims; Fair and Equitable Treatment in Investment Treaty Law* (London: BIICL, 2007), 168.

measures, and water and electricity tariffs, to name a few. Accordingly, the FET standard has become the most popular legal ground relied upon by foreign investors for asserting treaty violations in investor-state arbitration, as compared to other types of investor guarantees, such as the right to compensation in case of expropriation or the right to nondiscrimination.[2] Not only has it become the most invoked standard, but it is also the standard pursuant to which tribunals have arguably been most activist, applying extensive discretion. As a response, in an attempt to rein in this arbitrator discretion, states have tried to clarify the meaning of FET and continue to test and provide new language to guide tribunals – but with limited success so far: investment tribunals continue to expand the scope and meaning of the FET standard to their liking. Today, arbitrators sitting in investment treaty cases have asserted their power to strike down not only arbitrary measures by governments against investors that appear unacceptable to the general public but also measures with legitimate policy objectives, struck down primarily based on the argument that they violated the investors' expectations. This article provides an account of how the concept of FET has evolved in treaty practice in recent years and how tribunals are responding. It concludes that the attempts of states to guide tribunals and to rein in the reach of the standard have failed in many instances. They have not stopped investment tribunals from continuing to develop their own autonomous standard based only on what they consider "fair and equitable" for the investor, often based on the concept of the investor's legitimate expectations. Newer, still untested, approaches and formulations of the FET standard, such as the one developed by the European Union (EU), are not likely to be much more successful due to the uncontrolled decision making power of arbitral tribunals.

States need to reassess this situation and find new ways to draw the line between legitimate actions of the state as the guarantor of the public interest, on the one hand, and specific unacceptable state conduct that should engage host state responsibility, on the other. This may not be possible as long as this line is interpreted through the arbitration system we know today.

[2] UNCTAD, *Fair and Equitable Treatment, UNCTAD Series on Issues in International Investment Agreements II* (New York and Geneva, 2012), UN Doc UNCTAD/DIAE/IA/2011/5, 39.

The fair and equitable treatment standard in treaties, their interpretation, and state reaction

While some treaties do not include any FET clauses at all,[3] the vast majority of investment treaties do. The drafting of the standard can be broadly categorized into four broad approaches. These include (1) FET without any reference to international law or any further criteria, simply requiring that host states provide FET; (2) FET linked to international law; (3) FET linked to the minimum standard of treatment of aliens under customary international law (CIL); and (4) FET with additional substantive content, in the form of either an exhaustive or exemplary list of requirements falling under the FET standard. Whether states originally had different standards in mind is questionable. It could be argued that they had a high threshold in mind, one that would lead to a finding of a violation of the standard only in the context of extraordinary and egregious state acts vis-à-vis the investors. This issue is addressed further below.

Whatever the intent of states may have been in the past, today states are having intense discussions about the wording of the clause if it is to be included in the first place. To some extent, it is hard to argue today that different language does not lead to different standards. States need to anticipate that a nonqualified FET clause negotiated today will likely be interpreted broadly, leaving little space to argue that the threshold for a violation of the standard is a high one. What is less clear is the extent to

[3] A number of treaties, particularly those signed by Singapore and Turkey, do not contain the FET standard, e.g. Comprehensive Economic Cooperation Agreement between the Republic of India and the Republic of Singapore (the India–Singapore CECA) (signed 29 June 2005); Agreement between New Zealand and Singapore on a Closer Economic Partnership (the New Zealand–Singapore free trade agreement (FTA)) (signed 14 November 2000); Agreement between the People's Republic of China and the Republic of Turkey Concerning the Reciprocal Promotion and Protection of Investment (the Turkey–China bilateral investment treaty (BIT)) (signed 13 November 1990); Agreement between the Government of the Republic of Turkey and the Government of the Republic of Indonesia Concerning the Promotion and Protection of Investment (the Turkey–Indonesia BIT) (signed 25 February 1997); Agreement between the Government of the Republic of Albania and the Government of the Republic of Croatia for the Encouragement and Reciprocal Protection of Investments (the Albania–Croatia BIT) (signed 10 May 1993); Agreement between the Government of the Republic of Croatia and the Government of Ukraine for the Promotion and Reciprocal Protection of Investments (the Croatia–Ukraine BIT) (signed 15 December 1997); and Agreement between the Government of Malaysia and the Government of the Republic of Chile on the Promotion and Protection of Investments (the Chile–Malaysia BIT) (signed 11 November 1992).

which tribunals will consider the newer and more qualified FET clauses. Will they nevertheless apply a low threshold to alleged violations? As discussed further below, some recent cases indicate that tribunals will apply a standard based on legitimate expectation considerations leading to a low threshold, despite the use of language that would seem to lead to an opposite approach.

An unqualified FET standard is the approach most often used in investment treaties – this is particularly true for the older treaties, i.e. those treaties that were signed before tribunals began to interpret the standard in the early to mid-2000s. A typical example would read as follows: "Each Party shall guarantee in its territory fair and equitable treatment of investments made by investors of the other Party."[4] This language makes the standard potentially very open-ended, giving little or no guidance to tribunals on how it should be interpreted and just as little guidance to countries as to what the standard implies in terms of obligations. Other treaties link FET to international law: "Investments or returns of investors of either Contracting Party in the territory of the other Contracting Party shall be accorded fair and equitable treatment in accordance with international law and provisions of this Agreement."[5] The language in the North American Free Trade Agreement (NAFTA) similarly requires "treatment in accordance with international law, including fair and equitable treatment and full protection and security."[6] The reference to international law provides some additional guidance, suggesting that the provision is to be interpreted by reference to international law, including customary law, but the case law resulting from this formulation does not make the standard any clearer or more predictable. Both of these approaches therefore leave much room for interpretation through tribunals. Whether states originally intended to give this much space to tribunals remains questionable, but case law shows that when the FET provision is formulated without any additional reference or simply refers to international law or international law

[4] See, e.g. Agreement between the Argentine Republic and the Kingdom of Spain on the Reciprocal Promotion and Protection of Investments (the Argentina–Spain BIT) (signed 3 October 1991), art. 4.1.

[5] See, e.g. Agreement between the Government of the Republic of Croatia and the Government of the Kingdom of Thailand on the Reciprocal Promotion and Protection of Investments (the Croatia–Thailand BIT) (signed 18 February 2000), art. 3.2.

[6] North American Free Trade Agreement (NAFTA) (adopted 17 December 1992, entered into force 1 January 1994) 32 ILM 289 (1993), art. 1105(1).

principles, tribunals have mostly not tried to ascertain the standard's status as a CIL standard.

Increasingly therefore – and primarily in response to broad interpretations of the FET standard through arbitral tribunals – states began to clarify what they meant with the FET standard, explicitly stating that the standard goes no further than what is required by CIL. These developments go back to early experience with NAFTA. As noted earlier, the NAFTA clause does not explicitly link FET treatment to CIL. As would become clear later on, it was the CIL threshold standard nevertheless that the three NAFTA parties had in mind when they drafted NAFTA. CIL was not the standard applied in the early NAFTA cases, however. In *Metalclad*, the tribunal found that a Mexican municipality's denial of a permit for the construction of a hazardous waste landfill by an investor from the United States violated the FET provision because it violated NAFTA's transparency provisions.[7] Likewise, in *S.D. Myers*, the tribunal found that, because Canada's ban on the export of polychlorinated biphenyls (PCBs) violated Chapter 11's national treatment provision, this also established a breach of the FET provision.[8]

In reaction to the interpretations in these early cases under NAFTA's Chapter 11 and out of fear that the FET concept could be used in case of a violation of any other obligation within or outside NAFTA (for example the WTO), the three NAFTA parties (Canada, Mexico, and the United States) issued a binding interpretation through the NAFTA Free Trade Commission, stating that "the concepts of 'fair and equitable treatment' and 'full protection and security' do not require treatment in addition to or beyond that which is required by the customary international law minimum standard of treatment of aliens."[9] They also noted "[a] determination that there has been a breach of another provision of the NAFTA, or of a separate international agreement, does not establish that there has been a breach of Article 1105."[10]

Professor Sornarajah rightly pointed to this development early on, concluding that this was evidence that the FET standard was no different

[7] NAFTA (ICSID), *Metalclad Corporation* v. *The United Mexican States*, Award, 30 August 2000, ICSID Case No. ARB(AF)/97/1, paras. 70–101.

[8] NAFTA (UNCITRAL), *S.D. Myers, Inc.* v. *Government of Canada*, Partial Award, 13 November 2000, para. 266.

[9] NAFTA Free Trade Commission, *Notes of Interpretation of Certain Chapter 11 Provisions* (Washington, DC, 31 July 2001), available at www.international.gc.ca/trade-agreements-accords-commerciaux/topics-domaines/disp-diff/NAFTA-Interpr.aspx (last visited 6 May 2015).

[10] Ibid.

than the international minimum standard under customary law. He wrote:

> The practice under NAFTA has involved a reinterpretation of the fair and equitable standard as no different from the international minimum standard. Given that the treaties contain the equally amorphous international minimum standard, the room for the view that there is need for a fair and equitable standard vanishes unless the argument that the fair and equitable standard is a higher standard than the international minimum standard is accepted. But, this view has been rejected by the NAFTA parties. The NAFTA Commission reinterpreted the fair and equitable standard as nothing more than a reference to the international minimum standard. Since then, the American Model Bilateral Investment Treaty, as well as its Canadian counterpart contain a statement that the fair and equitable standard is nothing more than a reference to the "customary principles" on the international minimum standard.
>
> [. . .]
>
> Unless it be argued that the law for the United States is different—and this is a distinct possibility—there is little life left in the fair and equitable standard after the reinterpretation of it by the United States, despite the continuing efforts of arbitrators, writers and the OECD to breath life into it. It would now be difficult to argue with any credibility for the existence of an independent fair and equitable standard.[11]

Professor Sornarajah points to the fact that, based on the clarification and "reinterpretation" provided by the NAFTA parties, there was no room for an autonomous standard of FET that would be different, i.e. higher and more stringent for states, than the CIL standard. But what happened after this reinterpretation was a two-way track for drafting FET clauses. On the one hand, the NAFTA interpretation had a significant impact beyond NAFTA itself. Not only has it had a binding effect on the arbitral tribunals in the subsequent NAFTA cases, but it has also affected the drafting of the FET provision in investment treaties in North America and beyond. A wide range of states began to add clarifications in their FET clauses along the lines of the NAFTA interpretation. On the other hand, some states, including European member states and countries of the Middle East, continued to include unqualified FET clauses in the treaties they negotiated. This paper does not examine whether these states intended to adopt an autonomous, higher standard, independent of CIL and how the clauses were interpreted. It will instead look at the evolution and treatment of those FET clauses that are explicitly linked to CIL based on the examination of a number of selected cases.

[11] Sornarajah, "The Fair and Equitable Standard of Treatment," 168–170.

Fair and equitable treatment standard explicitly linked to customary international law

The understanding elaborated by the NAFTA Free Trade Commission has now been included in the US and Canadian model bilateral investment treaties (BITs) and post-2004 investment treaties. Article 5 of the US Model BIT of 2012 (which replaced the 2004 Model) reads:

> **Article 5: Minimum Standard of Treatment [footnote 9]**
>
> 1. Each Party shall accord to covered investments treatment in accordance with customary international law, including fair and equitable treatment and full protection and security.
> 2. For greater certainty, paragraph 1 prescribes the customary international law minimum standard of treatment of aliens as the minimum standard of treatment to be afforded to covered investments. The concepts of "fair and equitable treatment" and "full protection and security" do not require treatment in addition to or beyond that which is required by that standard, and do not create additional substantive rights.
>
> [. . .]
>
> [Footnote 9]: Article 5 [Minimum Standard of Treatment] shall be interpreted in accordance with Annex A.
>
> **Annex A Customary International Law**
>
> The Parties confirm their shared understanding that "customary international law" generally and as specifically referenced in Article 5 [Minimum Standard of Treatment] and Annex B [Expropriation] results from a general and consistent practice of States that they follow from a sense of legal obligation. With regard to Article 5 [Minimum Standard of Treatment], the customary international law minimum standard of treatment of aliens refers to all customary international law principles that protect the economic rights and interests of aliens.[12]

Many countries have followed suit and adopted similar language in their bilateral and regional instruments,[13] explicitly expressing their

[12] *The 2012 U.S. Model Bilateral Investment Treaty (Treaty Between the Government of the United States of America and the Government of [Country] Concerning the Encouragement and Reciprocal Protection of Investment)*, available at www.state.gov/documents/organization/188371.pdf (last visited 6 May 2015).

[13] E.g. the Japan–Philippines FTA (2006); the China–Peru FTA (2009); the China–Colombia BIT (2008), the China–Mexico BIT (2008); the Agreement Establishing the ASEAN–Australia–New Zealand FTA (2009); the Malaysia–New Zealand FTA (2009); the India–Republic of Korea Comprehensive Economic Partnership Agreement (2009); the Investment Agreement for the COMESA Common Investment Area (2007).

understanding that FET is linked or equated to the customary international law minimum standard of treatment of aliens in order to make clear that the standard is not without limits but is defined and confined by CIL and requires that the standard is based on state behavior arising out of a sense of legal obligation. States appeared to be of the view that anchoring the FET standard in CIL would shield them from attacks to legitimate legislation and government action and that only intolerable, shocking, and egregious state behavior should amount to a breach of international law. Moreover, this formulation would ensure that FET is not interpreted as an autonomous treaty standard that could lead to overly expansive interpretations. While CIL standards must be objectively manifested through state behavior arising out of a sense of legal obligation (also referred to as *opinio juris*), a *mere* treaty standard does not. An independent treaty standard is therefore potentially much more open-ended and unpredictable, as it would be up to the tribunal to determine what is fair and what is equitable.

Differing interpretations of the fair and equitable treatment standard explicitly linked to customary international law

Several tribunals have examined FET provisions that were linked to CIL.[14] Tribunals have come to contradictory opinions on the scope and meaning of these. They have not been consistent in examining state practice and *opinio juris*, with some foregoing the examination altogether.[15] Moreover, tribunals' views differ as to the status of CIL today. While tribunals consistently accepted that CIL is evolutionary in nature, they have differed on the question as to whether the standard laid out in a 1926 dispute between the United States and Mexico, referred to as the *Neer* case, was still the CIL standard applicable.[16] That case looked at

[14] E.g., NAFTA (ICSID), *Mondev International Ltd.* v. *United States of America*, Award, 11 October 2002, ICSID Case No. ARB(AF)/99/2, paras. 114–119; NAFTA (ICSID), *ADF Group Inc* v. *United States of America*, Award, 9 January 2003, ICSID Case No. ARB(AF)/00/1, paras. 179–181; NAFTA (UNCITRAL), *Glamis Gold* v. *United States of America*, Award, 8 June 2009, paras. 600–627; NAFTA (UNCITRAL), *Merrill & Ring Forestry L. P.* v. *The Government of Canada*, Award, 31 March 2010, paras. 182–210.

[15] E.g., ICSID, *Waste Management* v. *The United Mexican States*, Award, 30 April 2004, ICSID Case No. ARB(AF)/00/3 (*Waste Management II*), paras. 89–99.

[16] Ibid.

whether Mexico had failed to take adequate steps to investigate and prosecute the assassination of an American citizen, which amounted to a denial of justice.[17] The General Claims Commission in that case had found that CIL prohibits egregious or outrageous behavior by a state toward a foreign citizen:

> [T]he treatment of an alien, in order to constitute an international delinquency, should amount to an outrage, to bad faith, to wilful neglect of duty, or to an insufficiency of governmental action so far short of international standards that every reasonable and impartial man would readily recognize its insufficiency.[18]

This is the threshold applied in *Glamis Gold* v. *United States (2009).*[19] In that case, a Canadian mining company challenged California's new mining legislation, in particular the requirement to backfill the mine and the associated costs.[20]

The *Glamis Gold* tribunal's analysis centered on the following central question:

> The question thus becomes: what does this customary international law minimum standard of treatment require of a State Party vis-à-vis investors of another State Party? Is it the same as that established in 1926 in *Neer v Mexico*? Or has Claimant proven that the standard has "evolved"? If it has evolved, what evidence of custom has Claimant provided to the Tribunal to determine its current scope?[21]

The tribunal ultimately concluded that, notwithstanding the evolution of CIL, the level of scrutiny of the *Neer* standard still applied, that is, it concluded that, to violate the FET standard, an act must be sufficiently egregious or shocking. Thus, while accepting the evolutionary nature of CIL, the tribunal held that the investor had not succeeded in proving that the standard had evolved beyond the standard set out in *Neer.*

[17] Mexico/USA General Claims Commission, *L. F. H. Neer and Pauline Neer (U.S.A.)* v. *United Mexican States*, Opinion, 15 October 1926 (1927), 4 RIAA 60 (2006).

[18] Mexico/USA General Claims Commission, *L. F. H. Neer and Pauline Neer (U.S.A.)* v. *United Mexican States*, Opinion, 15 October 1926 (1927), 4 RIAA 60 (2006), 61–62.

[19] NAFTA (UNCITRAL), *Glamis Gold* v. *United States of America*, Award, 8 June 2009.

[20] NAFTA (UNCITRAL), *Glamis Gold, Ltd.* v. *United States of America*, Award, 8 June 2009.

[21] NAFTA (UNCITRAL), *Glamis Gold, Ltd.* v. *United States of America*, Award, 8 June 2009, para. 600, footnotes omitted.

Other tribunals have also endorsed the application of the high threshold of the *Neer* standard.[22] What they have differed on is the question as to what is needed to prove an evolution in CIL. In particular, the question has arisen as to whether previous investment treaties and arbitral tribunal decisions create or prove CIL. Some tribunals have claimed that the practice of states to sign treaties with FET provisions was evidence of an evolving standard.[23] Tribunals have also referred to previous arbitral decisions to define the meaning of FET.[24] By contrast, the *Glamis Gold* tribunal found that arbitral awards could not create or prove CIL and that the burden was on the claimant to establish the relevant standard of protection under CIL based on state practice and *opinio juris*.[25] It held as follows:

> Claimant did provide numerous arbitral decisions in support of its conclusion that fair and equitable treatment encompasses a universe of "fundamental" principles common throughout the world that include "the duty to act in good faith, due process, transparency and candor, and fairness and protection from arbitrariness." Arbitral awards, Respondent rightly notes, do not constitute State practice and thus cannot create or prove customary international law. They can, however, serve as illustrations of customary international law if they involve an examination of customary international law, as opposed to a treaty-based, or autonomous, interpretation.[26]

A 2012 decision, *RDC* v. *Guatemala (2012)*,[27] applying the same type of FET provision, seemed to steer in the opposite direction. Giving much more weight to previous arbitral decisions as opposed to the *Glamis Gold* tribunal, the *RDC* tribunal, in deciding the content of the FET provision in the United States–Dominican Republic–Central America Free Trade Agreement (CAFTA), simply adopted the test applied in the *Waste*

[22] NAFTA (UNCITRAL), *International Thunderbird Gaming Corporation* v. *The United Mexican States*, Award, 26 January 2006, para. 194; NAFTA (ICSID), *Cargill, Incorporated* v. *United Mexican States*, Award, 18 September 2009, ICSID Case No. ARB(AF)/05/2, para. 272.

[23] E.g., NAFTA (ICSID), *Mondev International Ltd.* v. *United States*, Award, 11 October 2002, ICSID Case No. ARB (AF)/99/2, paras. 117 and 125.

[24] E.g., NAFTA (ICSID), *Waste Management* v. *The United Mexican States*, Award, 30 April 2004, ICSID Case No. ARB(AF)/00/3 (*Waste Management II*), para. 98.

[25] NAFTA (UNCITRAL), *Glamis Gold* v. *United States of America*, Award, 8 June 2009, para. 605.

[26] NAFTA (UNCITRAL), *Glamis Gold* v. *United States of America*, Award, 8 June 2009, para. 605, footnotes omitted.

[27] ICSID, *Railroad Development Corporation (RDC)* v. *Republic of Guatemala*, Award, 29 June 2012, ICSID Case No. ARB/07/23.

Management II decision, noting that earlier arbitral awards were "efficient" to define CIL.[28] The tribunal held that:

> Regarding the content of the standard, the Tribunal refers to and adopts the conclusion reached by the tribunal in *Waste Management II* in considering NAFTA Article 1105 standard of review and after surveying NAFTA arbitral awards: "[. . .] the minimum standard of treatment of fair and equitable treatment is infringed by conduct attributable to the State and harmful to the claimant if the conduct is arbitrary, grossly unfair, unjust or idiosyncratic, is discriminatory and exposes the claimant to sectional or racial prejudice, or involves a lack of due process leading to an outcome which offends judicial propriety—as might be the case with a manifest failure of natural justice in judicial proceedings or a complete lack of transparency and candor in an administrative process. In applying this standard it is relevant that the treatment is in breach of representations made by the host State which were reasonably relied on by the claimant." The Tribunal finds that *Waste Management II* persuasively integrates the accumulated analysis of prior NAFTA Tribunals and reflects a balanced description of the minimum standard of treatment. The Tribunal accordingly adopts the *Waste Management II* articulation of the minimum standard for purposes of this case.[29]

The dispute between RDC (a US investor) and the Guatemalan government arose over RDC's operation of Guatemala's railway system. RDC had won a concession and concluded several key contracts with the governmental railway agency to operate the country's privatized railways. After 10 years of slow progress, the Guatemalan government initiated an administrative process for several reasons to declare the contracts to be *lesivos* (or injurious) to the interests of the state. The tribunal had to examine if this government action amounted to a violation of CAFTA's FET provision.

To ensure that the tribunal would not adopt an overly expansive interpretation of the treaty, the nondisputing CAFTA parties submitted their understanding of CAFTA's FET clause. The United States explained that the content of FET in CIL should be ascertained by state practice and *opinio juris* of states rather than by "interpretations of similar but differently worked treaty provisions."[30] The United States argued that the

[28] ICSID, *Railroad Development Corporation (RDC)* v. *Republic of Guatemala*, Award, 29 June 2012, ICSID Case No. ARB/07/23, para. 217.

[29] ICSID, *Railroad Development Corporation (RDC)* v. *Republic of Guatemala*, Award, 29 June 2012, ICSID Case No. ARB/07/23, para. 219, footnote omitted.

[30] ICSID, *Railroad Development Corporation (RDC)* v. *Republic of Guatemala*, Award, 29 June 2012, ICSID Case No. ARB/07/23, para. 207.

burden was on the claimant to establish the existence and applicability of a relevant obligation under CIL that meets state practice and *opinio juris*. El Salvador agreed with the United States on state practice and *opinio juris*, noting that international awards were relevant to the determination of the appropriate interpretation under CAFTA, but only if and to the extent they actually examined state practice resulting from a sense of legal obligation. It considered that the interpretation and reasoning given by the *Glamis Gold* tribunal correctly reflected the interpretation of the requirement to provide FET as part of the minimum standard of treatment under CIL.[31] According to El Salvador, the standard articulated in *Neer* had not changed significantly over time. Honduras also agreed in substance with the United States and El Salvador.

The tribunal, however, largely ignored the views of the treaty parties and drafters of CAFTA. It noted that the *Neer* standard was not an expression of CIL because the alleged reflection of CIL was not based on state practice and *opinio juris* but on the opinions of commentators.[32] It, therefore, did not examine whether the high threshold of the *Neer* standard still applied. In respect of the relevance of case law for establishing CIL, the tribunal noted:

> [A]rbitral awards do not constitute State practice, but it is also true that parties in international proceedings use them in their pleadings in support of their arguments of what the law is on a specific issue. [. . .] It is an efficient manner for a party in a judicial process to show what it believes to be the law.[33]

Without looking at the issue of who needed to prove the status of CIL, the tribunal simply concluded that the *Waste Management II* tribunal had persuasively integrated the accumulated analysis of prior NAFTA tribunals and reflected a balanced description of the minimum standard of treatment. The tribunal, therefore, adopted the *Waste Management II* articulation of the standard.[34]

31 ICSID, *Railroad Development Corporation (RDC)* v. *Republic of Guatemala*, Award, 29 June 2012, ICSID Case No. ARB/07/23, para. 209.

32 ICSID, *Railroad Development Corporation (RDC)* v. *Republic of Guatemala*, Award, 29 June 2012, ICSID Case No. ARB/07/23, para. 216.

33 ICSID, *Railroad Development Corporation (RDC)* v. *Republic of Guatemala*, Award, 29 June 2012, ICSID Case No. ARB/07/23, para. 217.

34 ICSID, *Railroad Development Corporation (RDC)* v. *Republic of Guatemala*, Award, 29 June 2012, ICSID Case No. ARB/07/23, para. 219. For a discussion on the case, see M. Porterfield, *A Distinction Without Difference? The Interpretation of Fair and Equitable Treatment under Customary International Law by Investment Tribunals*, *Investment Treaty News*, 3 (3) (Geneva, 2013), available at www.iisd.org/itn/2013/03/

Relying on the previous NAFTA case, the *RDC* tribunal, without establishing state practice, ruled against Guatemala and found a violation of the FET provision.

This was not the first time tribunals took this approach. A few years prior to the *RDC* award, the *Merrill & Ring* tribunal also refused to apply the *Neer* standard on the grounds that it was not established in the context of business, trade, or investment and was not supported by the evolved state practice and *opinio juris*.[35] That tribunal went even further, holding that the FET standard had itself become an independent principle anchored in CIL. It held that "fair and equitable treatment has become a part of customary law"[36] because "a requirement that aliens be treated fairly and equitably in relation to business, trade and investment [. . .] has become sufficiently part of widespread and consistent practice so as to demonstrate that it is reflected today in customary international law as *opinio juris*."[37] The tribunal did little, however, to explain the content of FET, noting that it entailed "a sense of fairness, equity, and reasonableness."[38]

These past cases leave unclear the legal situation and level of exposure risks of states. Will the types of interpretative statements and clarifications introduced by NAFTA parties and other states shield them from activist tribunals creating their own standard? A recent case brought by Bilcon against Canada leads to the conclusion that the answer is "no," and that tribunals will readily apply an expansive interpretation of the FET concept under NAFTA.

Bilcon *v.* Canada *(2015): continued broad interpretations of FET clauses – the issue of arbitrariness and investors' legitimate expectations*

The *Bilcon* dispute involved a proposal by American investors to operate a quarry and a marine terminal in Nova Scotia. Beginning in 2002, the

22/a-distinction-without-a-difference-the-interpretation-of-fair-and-equitable-treatment-under-customary-international-law-by-investment-tribunals/ (last visited 5 May 2015).

35 NAFTA (UNCITRAL), *Merrill & Ring Forestry L. P.* v. *The Government of Canada*, Award, 31 March 2010, paras. 182–213.

36 NAFTA (UNCITRAL), *Merrill & Ring Forestry L. P.* v. *The Government of Canada*, Award, 31 March 2010, para. 211.

37 NAFTA (UNCITRAL), *Merrill & Ring Forestry L. P.* v. *The Government of Canada*, Award, 31 March 2010, para. 210.

38 NAFTA (UNCITRAL), *Merrill & Ring Forestry L. P.* v. *The Government of Canada*, Award, 31 March 2010, para. 210.

project underwent an extended environmental assessment (EA) by Nova Scotia and the Canadian Federal Government.[39] Ultimately, both governments rejected the project on environmental grounds, in line with the recommendations of a Joint Review Panel (JRP) at the end of 2007. In response, the investors brought a claim under NAFTA for violation of Article 1105 on FET and a violation of Article 1102 on national treatment. They contended that "the treatment they received at every stage of the EA was unfair, politically biased and discriminatory."[40]

The tribunal in that case agreed with the investors, finding a violation of both the FET provision and the national treatment standard. With respect to FET, the tribunal found itself "guided" by earlier NAFTA cases, "particularly the formulation of the international minimum standard by the [*Waste Management II*] Tribunal."[41] The tribunal began by stating that "fair and equitable treatment" and full protection and security could not be regarded as "autonomous" treaty norms that impose additional requirements above and beyond what the minimum standard requires[42] and then went on to examine the content of the minimum international standard. It stated:

> NAFTA Article 1105 is, then, identical to the minimum international standard. The crucial question—on which the Parties diverge—is what is the content of the contemporary international minimum standard that the tribunal is bound to apply. NAFTA awards make it clear that the international minimum standard is not limited to conduct by host states that is outrageous. The contemporary minimum international standard involves a more significant measure of protection.[43]

In defining the content of the minimum standard, the tribunal avoided analyzing the state of CIL, the burden of proof, and like the *RDC* tribunal described earlier, simply referred to earlier NAFTA decisions ("NAFTA awards make it clear . . ."), suggesting that NAFTA tribunals can create and shape CIL without examining state practice and *opinio juris*. In particular, the tribunal cited the *Merrill & Ring* decision which "referred

[39] NAFTA (UNCITRAL), *Bilcon of Delaware et al.* v. *Government of Canada*, Award on jurisdiction and liability, 17 March 2015, PCA Case No. 2009-04.

[40] NAFTA (UNCITRAL), *Bilcon of Delaware et al.* v. *Government of Canada*, Award on jurisdiction and liability, 17 March 2015, PCA Case No. 2009-04, para. 5.

[41] NAFTA (UNCITRAL), *Bilcon of Delaware et al.* v. *Government of Canada*, Award on jurisdiction and liability, 17 March 2015, PCA Case No. 2009-04, para. 427.

[42] NAFTA (UNCITRAL), *Bilcon of Delaware et al.* v. *Government of Canada*, Award on jurisdiction and liability, 17 March 2015, PCA Case No. 2009-04, para. 432.

[43] NAFTA (UNCITRAL), *Bilcon of Delaware et al.* v. *Government of Canada*, Award on jurisdiction and liability, 17 March 2015, PCA Case No. 2009-04, para. 433.

to practice, decisions, and commentary within both NAFTA and in the wider world conduct" to support a trend "towards the view that the international minimum standard has evolved over the years towards greater protection for investors."[44] The tribunal stated:

> Many NAFTA tribunals have shared the emerging consensus that the *Neer* standard of indisputably outrageous misconduct is no longer applicable, but there is no consensus yet on a formulation that best suits the modern evolution of the standard.[45]

It then went on to rely on the *Waste Management II* as the most apt to capture the meaning of Article 1105,[46] concluding a breach must be of a serious nature and that "there is a high threshold for the conduct of a host state to rise to the level of a NAFTA Article 1105 breach, but that there was no requirement in all cases that the challenged conduct reaches the level of shocking or outrageous behaviour."[47] It noted that the *Waste Management II* formulation also recognized "the potential relevance of reasonably relied-on representations by a host state, and a recognition that injustice in either procedures or outcomes can constitute a breach."[48]

In line with the latter aspect of *Waste Management II* on representations by the host state, much of the *Bilcon* decision on FET centered on the issue of the investors' legitimate expectation. The tribunal wrote at length about how various officials, including at the highest level, assured the investors that Nova Scotia "was open for business" and supportive of the project.[49] It was always clear, however, that several approvals were still needed under federal and provincial environmental protection laws.[50] In this case, a panel of experts was appointed to review the environmental study and gather comments. The expert

[44] NAFTA (UNCITRAL), *Bilcon of Delaware et al.* v. *Government of Canada*, Award on jurisdiction and liability, 17 March 2015, PCA Case No. 2009–04, para. 435.

[45] NAFTA (UNCITRAL), *Bilcon of Delaware et al.* v. *Government of Canada*, Award on jurisdiction and liability, 17 March 2015, PCA Case No. 2009–04, para. 440.

[46] NAFTA (UNCITRAL), *Bilcon of Delaware et al.* v. *Government of Canada*, Award on jurisdiction and liability, 17 March 2015, PCA Case No. 2009–04, para. 443.

[47] NAFTA (UNCITRAL), *Bilcon of Delaware et al.* v. *Government of Canada*, Award on jurisdiction and liability, 17 March 2015, PCA Case No. 2009–04, para. 444.

[48] NAFTA (UNCITRAL), *Bilcon of Delaware et al.* v. *Government of Canada*, Award on jurisdiction and liability, 17 March 2015, PCA Case No. 2009–04, para. 444.

[49] NAFTA (UNCITRAL), *Bilcon of Delaware et al.* v. *Government of Canada*, Award on jurisdiction and liability, 17 March 2015, PCA Case No. 2009–04, paras. 467–470.

[50] NAFTA (UNCITRAL), *Bilcon of Delaware et al.* v. *Government of Canada*, Award on jurisdiction and liability, 17 March 2015, PCA Case No. 2009–04, para. 447.

panel recommended that the project not proceed, among other things, because of the project's inconsistency with "core community values." On the basis of these recommendations, the relevant federal and provincial authorities rejected the project. The investors had found this review process flawed and not in accordance with the applicable Canadian laws, in particular because the panel considered "core community values" as part of its duty to consider impacts on the "human environment" and failed to propose mitigating measures. The tribunal agreed with the investors and found that Canadian law was applied incorrectly and that the investors should have been able to reasonably expect its proper application.[51] It concluded that, as a consequence, the government was in breach of its FET commitment.[52]

One of the tribunal members issued a dissenting opinion and took issue precisely with this point of reasoning. In his dissent, Professor Donald McRae agreed with the majority that "the well-known statement in *Waste Management II* as encapsulating the standard to be applied under Article 1105 and acknowledged that it was a 'high threshold.'"[53] But he disagreed with the way the majority had applied that standard, namely, meeting the threshold by simply alleging a breach of the domestic law.[54] In particular, McRae pointed to the majority's approach to legitimate expectations, which led to the conclusion that "the Claimant had 'legitimate' or 'reasonable' expectations based on encouragement by the government of Nova Scotia to invest in mining in the province."[55] He pointed out that, although the investors had been encouraged to invest, it was clear to them that they would obtain environmental permission only if the project satisfied the requirements of the laws of federal Canada and Nova Scotia. In the hope they would ultimately get permission, the investors spent substantial sums of money developing the project.

51 NAFTA (UNCITRAL), *Bilcon of Delaware et al.* v. *Government of Canada*, Award on jurisdiction and liability, 17 March 2015, PCA Case No. 2009–04, para. 470.

52 NAFTA (UNCITRAL), *Bilcon of Delaware et al.* v. *Government of Canada*, Award on jurisdiction and liability, 17 March 2015, PCA Case No. 2009–04, para. 591.

53 NAFTA (UNCITRAL), *Bilcon of Delaware et al.* v. *Government of Canada*, Dissenting Opinion of Professor Donald McRae, 10 March 2015, PCA Case No. 2009–04, paras. 2 and 32, footnotes omitted.

54 NAFTA (UNCITRAL), *Bilcon of Delaware et al.* v. *Government of Canada*, Dissenting Opinion of Professor Donald McRae, 10 March 2015, PCA Case No. 2009–04, para. 3, citing NAFTA (UNCITRAL), *Bilcon of Delaware et al.* v. *Government of Canada*, Award on jurisdiction and liability, 17 March 2015, PCA Case No. 2009–04, para. 448.

55 NAFTA (UNCITRAL), *Bilcon of Delaware et al.* v. *Government of Canada*, Dissenting Opinion of Professor Donald McRae, 10 March 2015, PCA Case No. 2009–04, para. 4.

In this context, McRae indicated that the encouragement of public officials to invest was in fact irrelevant and that all the investors could legitimately expect was that the law would be applied in order to determine whether their project would be approved or not. He wrote:

> With respect, the actions of Nova Scotia officials in encouraging investment in mining and any consequent "legitimate expectations" are simply irrelevant to whether the JRP has met the standards of Article 1105. Any investor would have the expectation that if the requirements of Canadian law (federal and provincial) regarding environmental assessment were met its investment could go ahead. Assurances or encouragement by provincial officials have nothing to do with the expectation that an investor will have Canadian law applied properly to it. That is an expectation that an investor would have independently of any assurances or encouragement. Thus, the long excursus by the majority into the actions of provincial officials, apart from creating an aura of mistreatment of the Claimant, simply has no bearing on the alleged violation of Article 1105.[56]

In sum, the threshold that the majority of the tribunal applied in the *Bilcon* case to determine whether there was an FET violation was low, despite the tribunal's claims that it was applying the high threshold set out in *Waste Management II*. If there was in fact a violation of Canadian law, nothing would indicate that this should be equated to a violation of NAFTA in accordance with the standard set out in *Waste Management II*. But that is what the majority did.

Looking for new approaches

The EU approach

States cannot find a safe harbor by explicitly anchoring the FET standard in CIL. The broad reference to CIL is increasingly circumvented as tribunals apply standards formulated by other tribunals to determine what amounts to a violation of FET and what does not. Although some tribunals have explicitly stated that the CIL-linked FET standard is not a so-called autonomous standard, the manner in which they treat the standard has been very much up to their discretion.

In order to take back some control, the EU – after the competence shifted from EU member states to the Union in 2009 – introduced yet

[56] NAFTA (UNCITRAL), *Bilcon of Delaware et al.* v. *Government of Canada*, Dissenting Opinion of Professor Donald McRae, 10 March 2015, PCA Case No. 2009–04, para. 5, footnote omitted.

a new way of drafting the FET clause. In its negotiations of the Comprehensive Economic and Trade Agreement (CETA) with Canada,[57] the EU proposed to define the FET standard through a list of instances that amount to a breach of the standard. The earlier versions of the EU proposal in those negotiations proposed a merely illustrative and non-exhaustive list of such situations.[58] The final clause agreed by the CETA parties, however, contains a closed list of instances that amount to breach of the standard. The list reflects some of the approaches taken by various tribunals and reads as follows:

> **Article X.9: Treatment of Investors and Covered Investments**
>
> Each Party shall accord in its territory to covered investments of the other Party and to investors with respect to their covered investments fair and equitable treatment and full protection and security in accordance with 2 to 6.
>
> A Party breaches the obligation of fair and equitable treatment referenced in paragraph 1 where a measure or series of measures constitutes:
>
> Denial of justice in criminal, civil or administrative proceedings;
> Fundamental breach of due process, including a fundamental breach of transparency, in judicial and administrative proceedings;
> Manifest arbitrariness;
> Targeted discrimination on manifestly wrongful grounds, such as gender, race or religious belief;
> Abusive treatment of investors, such as coercion, duress and harassment; or
> A breach of any further elements of the fair and equitable treatment obligation adopted by the Parties in accordance with paragraph 3 of this Article.
>
> The Parties shall regularly, or upon request of a Party, review the content of the obligation to provide fair and equitable treatment. The Committee on Services and Investment may develop recommendations in this regard and submit them to the Trade Committee for decision.

[57] See more information about the Canada–EU Comprehensive Economic and Trade Agreement (CETA) at www.international.gc.ca/trade-agreements-accords-commerciaux/agr-acc/ceta-aecg/index.aspx?lang=eng (last visited 6 May 2015).

[58] See, e.g. Draft CETA Investment Text dated 31 May 2013, available at www.tradejustice.ca/wp-content/uploads/2013/10/Investment-chapter-annotated-consoldated-text-31-May-2013.doc (last visited 6 May 2015). For a discussion on an earlier draft dated 7 February 2013, see, N. Bernasconi-Osterwalder, *Commentary to the Draft Investment Chapter of the Canada–EU Comprehensive Economic and Trade Agreement (CETA)*, IISD Report (May 2013), available at www.iisd.org/sites/default/files/pdf/2013/commentary_investment_chapter_CETA.pdf (last visited 6 May 2015).

> When applying the above fair and equitable treatment obligation, a tribunal may take into account whether a Party made a specific representation to an investor to induce a covered investment, that created a legitimate expectation, and upon which the investor relied in deciding to make or maintain the covered investment, but that the Party subsequently frustrated.
>
> For greater certainty, "full protection and security" refers to the Party's obligations relating to physical security of investors and covered investments.
>
> For greater certainty, a breach of another provision of this Agreement, or of a separate international Agreement, does not establish that there has been a breach of this Article.[59]

Interestingly, the final version, as seen above, no longer includes references to CIL, although Canada until the end had demanded variations of this to be included until the final stages of the negotiations – something EU member states from early on opposed. For Canada, therefore, the CETA represents a major deviance from its decade-long and consistent practice of defining FET in relation to the minimum standard of treatment under CIL on the treatment of aliens. What Canada expects from this new approach is unclear. Both Canada and the EU appear to have wanted to achieve a clarification of a standard that had evolved to become very open-ended despite its linkage to CIL. With this in mind, they opted for a list of those breaches that according to them would amount to a breach of FET. In so doing, the parties opted for language that sets a fairly high threshold, indicating the gravity of the government act by using strong qualifiers, such as "fundamental" breach of due process, "manifest" arbitrariness, and discrimination on "manifestly" wrongful grounds.

The language indicates that the parties, as they claim, wish to make the standard more predictable and less restrictive on legitimate policy-making. The question then is whether a tribunal, such as the *Bilcon* tribunal, applying this standard would have come to a different conclusion than under NAFTA. A careful analysis of the *Bilcon* decision indicates that this would not be the case. This is because the language used in the CETA list reflects, in large part, the language of the *Waste Management II* decision – the determining threshold applied in *Bilcon*. In particular, the CETA speaks of "manifest arbitrariness"

[59] Consolidated text of the Canada–EU Comprehensive Economic and Trade Agreement (published on 26 September 2014), available at http://trade.ec.europa.eu/doclib/docs/2014/september/tradoc_152806.pdf (last visited 6 May 2015).

and notes that "when applying the above fair and equitable treatment obligation, a tribunal may take into account whether a Party made a specific representation to an investor to induce a covered investment, that created a legitimate expectation, and upon which the investor relied in deciding to make or maintain the covered investment, but that the Party subsequently frustrated."[60] In *Bilcon*, the majority of the tribunal found a violation of FET precisely because it estimated the conclusions of the review panel arbitrary and in violation of the investors' legitimate expectations. As required in the CETA text, a violation of legitimate expectations could only be taken into account in the context of making the determination of whether there was a violation of FET, for example through arbitrary behavior. This was also the case in *Bilcon*, where the tribunal found arbitrary behavior on behalf of the state in that it allegedly did not comply fully with what was required under Canadian law and therefore frustrated the investors' legitimate expectations.

The loose concept of arbitrariness, even if qualified with the adjective "manifest," combined with the clarification that tribunals could consider the legitimate expectations of the investors, continues to leave the FET standard open-ended and unpredictable under the CETA language.

The 2015 Draft Indian model

The most recent Draft Indian model investment treaty attempts to address the problem that remains unresolved from a policy space objective under CETA and the CIL approach traditionally used in Canada and the United States. While it continues to include a state obligation relating to the standard of treatment, it explicitly ties it to a high-threshold understanding of the FET standard, by relating it to (i) denial of justice under CIL; (ii) egregious violations of due process; and (iii) abusive treatment and coercion. Strong qualifiers accompany each of these instances that amount to FET violations. They read as follows:

> **Article 3: Standard of Treatment**
>
> 3.1 Each Party shall not subject Investments of Investors of the other Party to Measures which constitute:

[60] Article X.9 of Section 4.

(i) Denial of justice under customary international law[61]
(ii) Un-remedied and egregious violations of due process; or
(iii) Manifestly abusive treatment involving continuous, unjustified and outrageous coercion or harassment.[62]

Not only does it move away from the "fair and equitable" terminology, but it also avoids references to "arbitrariness" or "legitimate expectations." These concepts have become a hook for tribunals to develop autonomous arbitrator-made standards, which go well beyond what most states expected or may expect in the future. The Draft Indian model, if appropriately applied, significantly reduces the risk incorporated in the CETA language.

Concluding remarks

Investment treaties and investment chapters in free trade agreements routinely contain a provision on FET. This guarantee has been problematic for states, because of the way tribunals have interpreted the standard more broadly than state parties expected and the fact that they have applied different interpretations, making the content of the standard difficult to predict. Originally, this standard was meant to provide a floor to shield foreign investors from unacceptable, egregious treatment. However, today some tribunals have decided that the standard is much more. In particular, it has been used to protect so-called legitimate expectations of investors, a development that has contributed significantly to the degree of unpredictability of the standard owing to the subjective nature of "legitimate expectations." As a response, states have again and again tried to rein in the tribunals' attempts to transform what was originally a baseline standard anchored in CIL into a self-standing, autonomous investment protection standard. However, time and time again, arbitral tribunals have largely disregarded the guidance given by states and instead created their own "autonomous" law. As an example, when the NAFTA parties explained that the minimum standard FET provision went no further than CIL, some tribunals simply ignored this, saying that CIL was evolutionary and that, in the absence of a clear

[61] For greater certainty, it is clarified that "customary international law" only results from a general and consistent practice of states that they follow from a sense of legal obligation.

[62] *Draft Model Text for the Indian Bilateral Investment Treaty (Bilateral Investment Treaty between the Government of the Republic of India and –)*, available at https://mygovin/sites/default/files/master_image/Model%20Text%20for%20the%20Indian%20Bilateral%20Investment%20Treaty.pdf (last visited 6 May 2015).

understanding of what constitutes CIL, the body of investment decisions could provide a basis for determining the contours of the FET standard. In short, instead of looking at state practice and *opinio juris*, the arbitrators decided instead to look at what their peers had held in other investment cases. If states were looking to find a safe haven in CIL, they were mistaken.

That is why some states are adopting yet a new approach, which so far has not been tested in case law. The CETA, for instance, includes a provision to accord FET to investors and investments. Here, the parties agreed to a closed list of situations that amount to a breach of FET. Given recent case law, it is likely that this approach will also develop to be seen as a *carte blanche* for activist investment arbitrators, despite its attempt to bring in more specificity. The recent *Bilcon* decision indicates just that. The tribunal in that case played lip service to "a high threshold" pointing to a formulation developed in an earlier NAFTA case (*Waste Management II*), which resembles the new CETA language. This did not prevent the majority of the tribunal from applying a rather low threshold revolving around the concept of the investor's legitimate expectations that ultimately resulted in the finding of a violation of the NAFTA minimum standard based for an alleged violation of national law that could have been reviewed easily through domestic administrative procedures. The widely respected dissenting arbitrator went so far as to see this development as contributing to regulatory chill and as "a remarkable step backward for environmental protection."[63]

If states truly wish to rein in the tribunals' ability to develop the law of FET to their own liking, they will have to be clear-cut in moving away from the concepts developed by tribunals to date. The 2015 Draft Indian model investment treaty might have achieved this. It includes a standard that aims at capturing egregious state behavior but contains no references to "fair and equitable" and does not mention "arbitrariness" as a basis for breach or "legitimate expectations" as elements for tribunals to consider. Whether India will be successful at defying the *carte blanche* syndrome will have to be tested – as long as investment tribunals remain unreviewable, one can never be certain.

[63] NAFTA (UNCITRAL), *Bilcon of Delaware et al.* v. *Government of Canada*, Dissenting Opinion of Professor Donald McRae, 10 March 2015, PCA Case No. 2009–04, para. 51.

PART V

13

Is the umbrella clause not just another treaty clause?

C.L. LIM

> The issue of the validity of the umbrella clause as a basis of claims requires more detailed analysis in light of the divisions that are apparent in the awards.
>
> M. Sornarajah[1]

Introduction

Today, the 'umbrella clause'[2] continues to divide legal opinion. Its basis and effects remain unsettled.[3] The clause is often said to 'internationalise' state contracts by rendering them effective under international law. This chapter challenges the idea of internationalisation.

Much of the controversy surrounding umbrella clauses has had to do with the idea of the internationalisation of contractual commitments. Professor Sornarajah called the idea of internationalisation a 'myth',[4] not least because the argument has tended to rely upon the 'low-order sources' of international law as the basis for claiming the sanctity of contracts under international law. However, umbrella clauses, too-long

1 M. Sornarajah, *The International Law on Foreign Investment*, 3rd ed. (Cambridge: CUP, 2010), 216.

2 The term is sometimes credited to Ignaz Seidl-Hohenveldern, see T.W. Wälde and K. Hobér, "The First Energy Charter Treaty Arbitral Award", in Charles Leben (ed.), *Le contentieux arbitral transnational relatif à l'investissement* (Paris: LGDJ, 2006), 307, 318 at footnote 13. Others credit Prosper Weil, see T. Waalde, "The 'Umbrella' (Or Sanctitiy of Contract/Pacta Sunt Servanda) Clause in Investment Arbitration", (October 2004) 1(4) *TDM* 1, 30. Yet, others credit Sir Elihu Lauterpacht's recommendation given in respect of the Anglo-Iranian Oil Company's claim against Iran in 1954, which was subsequently adopted in art. 2 of the Abs/Shawcross Draft Convention, discussed further below; see (e. g.) J.W. Salacuse, *The Law of Investment Treaties* (Oxford: OUP, 2010), 276.

3 E. Gaillard, "Treaty-Based Jurisdiction: Broad *Dispute Resolution* Clauses", *NY Law Journal*, 6 October 2005.

4 Sornarajah, *International Law on Foreign Investment*, 3rd ed., 304. Sornarajah also links the intended effects of umbrella clauses to those of stabilisation clauses, *Id.*

ignored, have always had a sound basis in treaty law. These clauses do not have to rely upon the low-order sources of international, but the straightforward application of the doctrine *pacta sunt servanda* between states.

This chapter argues against the widespread idea that the underlying contract is itself, necessarily, 'elevated' by the umbrella clause to the international plane.[5] Instead, such a treaty clause simply purports to treat breaches of certain contractual and other undertakings as straightforward treaty violations. Viewed in this way, umbrella clauses should be treated like any other garden-variety treaty clause, requiring only the ordinary methods of treaty interpretation to be applied to their construction.

This is one way of approaching criticism of the supposedly 'automatic, sweeping and unqualified' effect of umbrella clauses, in the words of the *SGS* v. *Pakistan* tribunal;[6] precisely because the umbrella clause in that Award was argued to have had the supposed effect of elevating the underlying contract itself to the international plane. Similar objections by critics of the umbrella clause have, in practice, lent support to a restrictive reading of umbrella clauses. It is thought that the notion that we can turn every contractual commitment into an equivalent treaty commitment would allow private parties to 'expand' the content of the treaty commitments undertaken by the host state.[7] As such, in *SGS* v. *Pakistan*, the tribunal required 'clear and compelling' evidence for saying that such an elevation had originally been intended by the treaty parties.

Today, opposed to *SGS* v. *Pakistan* and its progeny is a separate line of authorities constituted by the Awards in cases such as *SGS* v. *Philippines*,[8] and *Noble Ventures* v. *Romania*.[9] These Awards would require only the interpretation of the plain words of the treaty. No theory of internationalisation is involved.

However, more recent cases which have taken the kinds of concern expressed in *SGS* v. *Pakistan* seriously have sought to rely on some form of decisive contractual, private law or other factor in seeking to limit or deny the application of umbrella clauses. They include the idea that much

5 See further, J.O. Voss, *The Impact of Investment Treaties on Contracts between Host States and Foreign Investors* (Hague: Nijhoff, 2010), 238.

6 *SGS* v. *Pakistan*, ICSID Case No. ARB/01/13, Decision on Objections to Jurisdiction, 6 August 2003.

7 It could be argued in response that this was precisely what the contracting states envisaged, and had intended.

8 *SGS* v. *Philippines*, ICSID Case No. ARB/02/6, Decision on Jurisdiction, 29 January 2004.

9 *Noble Ventures* v. *Romania*, ICSID Case No. ARB/01/11, Award, 12 October 2005.

could depend upon whether the state's contractually violative acts took the guise of *acta jure imperii*, giving voice to the neglected role of contractual forum selection clauses and to the doctrine of privity of contract. There is also the suggestion that fair and equitable treatment (FET) clauses already operate as 'de facto umbrella clauses',[10] or even that umbrella clauses ought to be rendered effective only in tandem with other treaty standards.

The origin and definition of the umbrella clause

Origins and rationale

An early and influential illustration of an umbrella clause may be found in the Abs/Shawcross Draft Convention,[11] a privately sponsored joint-initiative by the former Deutsche Bank chairman, Hermann Abs, and Sir Hartley (later Lord) Shawcross.[12]

Historically, the notion of the international sanctity of contracts might be viewed in light of the attempt by the United States to promote that idea, in tandem with that of international arbitration, before the United Nations General Assembly in the early 1960s.[13] That attempt was a prelude to the modern bilateral investment treaty (BIT) movement, which, at the same time, had incorporated umbrella clauses early on. Umbrella clauses were also part of a two-fold project – not only to secure recognition of the international sanctity of private contracts but also to subject investment contract disputes to binding international arbitration. The reason treaty law ultimately became the preferred source of

[10] I.A. Laird *et al.*, "International Investment Law and Arbitration: 2012 in Review", in A.K. Bjorklund (ed.), *Yrbk Int'l Investment Law & Policy 2012–2013* (Oxford: OUP, 2014), 109, 150.

[11] Draft Convention on Investments Abroad, 1959, Article II; reproduced in A. Newcombe and L. Paradell, *Law and Practice of Investment Treaties: Standards of Treatment* (Netherlands: Kluwer, 2009), 441.

[12] See UNCTAD, International Investment Instruments: A Compendium, vol. 3 No. 159; also, *cf.* the 1967 OECD Draft Convention on the Protection of Foreign Property (12 October 1967) C(67)102, 14. For the background to the Abs/Shawcross and OECD draft conventions, see R. Dolzer and C. Schreuer, *Principles of International Investment Law*, 2nd ed. (Oxford: OUP, 2012), 8; Newcombe and Paradell, *Law and Practice of Investment Treaties*, 20–22 and the sources cited therein.

[13] UNGA resolution 1803 (XVII), 14 December 1962, para. 8. See further, A. Lowenfeld, *International Economic Law*, 2nd ed (Oxford: OUP, 2008), 487, and more generally 486–493; C.L. Lim, "The Strange Vitality of Custom in the International Protection of Contracts, Property and Commerce", in C. Bradley (ed.), *Custom's Future: International Law in a Changing World* (Cambridge: CUP, in press).

international law for securing the international sanctity of private contracts was precisely because other alternative bases for internationally enforcing contractual commitments had been controversial.[14]

Definition

An umbrella clause may be defined broadly. It is a treaty clause which extends the scope of the independent protection of the treaty to breaches of contractual and other domestic commitments relating to the foreign investor's investment.

Sceptics might ask why, when there is such widespread substantive treaty protection today, umbrella clauses might be thought to perform any function at all without making these other treaty forms of protection redundant. One answer is that the umbrella clause does not simply provide parallel protection in tandem with other treaty rights. Rather, it expands the scope of the treaty protection by including contractual commitments which do not always fall within the FET, full protection and security and expropriation clauses. That is the gravamen of the matter. Umbrella clauses are controversial precisely because they are not superfluous.

But are they as expansive as the tribunal in *SGS* v. *Pakistan* suggested? To use a well-worn example from trade law regulation, it might be thought that in their construction such clauses are akin to an accordion[15] and may be stretched widely or squeezed narrowly. That recent attempts have been made to revisit the language of these clauses only reinforces the point by showing that there is a wide variety of such clauses today.[16] However, one line of authorities – following *SGS* v. *Pakistan* – has insisted that, if permitted, umbrella clauses would effectively allow private parties to negotiate and infinitely expand the scope of protection given under a treaty deal struck between two or more sovereign

[14] *SGS* v. *Pakistan,* ICSID Case No. ARB/01/13, Decision on Objections to Jurisdiction, 6 August 2003, footnote 108 at para. 98, citing the Claimant's argument which had relied upon R. Dolzer and M. Stevens, *Bilateral Investment Treaties* (Hague: Nijhoff, 1995), 81–82, a comment expressed by the late Ibrahim Shihata and Professor Christoph Schreuer's opinion.

[15] Trade lawyers know this analogy, see *Japan – Alcohol*, WT/DS8/AB/R, 1 November 1996.

[16] See the definition of "investment agreement" as defined in Article 1 of the 2012 US Model BIT, which is also discussed in Chapter 9. That definition curtails the operation of the current version of a US umbrella clause contained in Article 24 of the 2012 Model BIT. *Contra* the earlier example of such a clause in Article II(2)(c) of the US–Argentina BIT.

contracting parties. In a similar vein, Sornarajah has argued that such clauses are in effect 'catch-all statements'.[17]

Sornarajah's scepticism

As we have seen, umbrella clauses purport to achieve what theories about the internationalisation of contracts have long sought – the international sanctity of private law contracts. The tribunal in *SGS* v. *Philippines* acknowledged this,[18] although – unlike the tribunal in *SGS* v. *Pakistan* – it refused to decide whether an umbrella clause would necessarily elevate or internationalise every contractual breach. As we shall see, the notion of internationalisation also became a point of criticism in the subsequent Award in *Noble Ventures* v. *Romania.*[19]

Sornarajah, who had begun his career by writing on investment contracts, has been a long-standing, well-known critic of the notion of internationalised state contracts.[20] He explains two broad historical versions of the idea. The first had to do with the importance, from the viewpoint of investors, of effecting some choice or selection of international or at least neutral, non-national law to govern contracts between host states and foreign investors.[21] The second and more 'extreme' theory, often associated with the view of the arbitrator in *Texaco* v. *Libya,*[22] does away altogether with the need for party choice and asserts that objectively viewed contracts can become 'internationalised' where

[17] The phrase appears in Sornarajah's *International Law on Foreign Investment*, 3rd ed., 215 (in which the term "umbrella clause" is also used). For the second edition, see *The International Law on Foreign Investment*, 2nd ed. (Cambridge: CUP, 2004), 248.

[18] *SGS* v. *Philippines*, ICSID Case No. ARB/02/6, Decision on Jurisdiction, 29 January 2004, para. 126; see also A.C. Sinclair, "The Umbrella Clause Debate", in A.K. Bjorklund, I.A. Laird, and S. Ripinsky (eds.), *Investment Treaty Law – Current Issues III* (London: BIICL, 2009), 275, 290.

[19] *Noble Ventures* v. *Romania*, ICSID Case No. ARB/01/11, Award, 12 October 2005.

[20] See M. Sornarajah, "The Myth of International Contract Law", (1981) 15 *Jo World Trade Law* 187. See also his other works discussing internationalisation which are cited at the outset of Chapter 14.

[21] Sornarajah, *International Law on Foreign Investment*, 3rd ed., 289 ("The removal of the foreign investment transaction from the sphere of the host state's law and its subjection to an immutable system is seen as essential for the protection of foreign investment under the theory of internationalisation.") See also his treatment of this point in Sornarajah, "Myth", 187, 202.

[22] *Texaco Overseas Petroleum Company/California Asiatic Oil Company* v. *The Government of the Libyan Arab Republic,* Award on the Merits, 19 January 1977, 17 International Legal Materials 1, paras. 44–45.

the intent of the parties may be shown through arbitration and stabilisation clauses too in long-term, high value contracts.[23]

Sornarajah has dismissed the whole idea as a myth[24] and wrote of that seemingly 'mystical quality' which, it is alleged, somehow enables state contracts 'to levitate'.[25] Sornarajah argues that contracts are valid by virtue of some domestic legal system, not by virtue of international law. There are treaty rights, rights under customary international law, and then there are private law contractual rights. But there is no such beast as an 'international contractual' right in the fauna of municipal and international rights.

His is no semantic quibble. It has been the conventional view. The *Serbian Loans* case had long been standard authority,[26] in which the Permanent Court of International Justice had considered contracts to be mere creatures of municipal, not international, law. Lord Radcliffe had held a similar view in the English case of *Kahler* v. *Midland Bank*.[27]

Umbrella clauses are, however, different. They at least observe the confines of conventional international legal doctrine. The question which such clauses pose is not whether the underlying contracts are in the end analysis only creatures of municipal law or whether they might have become 'international' contracts, but rather, whether the *breach* of the underlying contract ought in certain circumstances to be considered a treaty violation as a matter involving the ordinary construction of a treaty clause. Recall that a decade ago in *Noble Ventures* v. *Romania*, the

[23] Sornarajah, *International Law on Foreign Investment*, 3rd ed., 294 ("The more extreme variety of the theory of internationalisation is that the very nature of the foreign investment contract gives rise to the inference that it is subject to a supranational system of law".)

[24] Sornarajah, "Myth", *op. cit.* Sornarajah has been especially critical of F.A. Mann's view of the existence of a "commercial law of nations", based in part upon Mann's reading of one of the well-known arbitral Awards from the 1950s – the *Abu Dhabi Arbitration* (1951) 19 ILR 144 – for which Lord Asquith is commonly cited in favour of the existence of such a body of laws; F.A. Mann, *Studies in International Law* (Oxford: OUP, 1972), 143; *contra* Sornarajah, "Myth", 199, 201, 202. Where Mann criticised the defenders of the developing country viewpoint for being subjective, Sornarajah countered by criticising Mann and others for their thinly disguised efforts to serve the interests of Western capital; F.A. Mann, "Wrong in National and International Law", (1977) 48 *BYbIL* 1; *contra* Sornarajah, "Myth", 199.

[25] That is, out of the sphere of domestic law into that of international law; M. Sornarajah, *Law of International Joint Ventures* (Spore: Longman, 1992), 298.

[26] PCIJ No. 14, Ser. A, No. 20 at 41 ("Any contract which is not a contract between states in their capacity as subjects of international law is based on the municipal law of some country".)

[27] [1950] AC 24, 56 *per* Lord Radcliffe.

tribunal there had considered that a contractual breach has of itself nothing to do with international law unless it *also* amounts to a *violation* of a treaty standard. That Award is now cited for its support of umbrella clauses, but its chief value lies in the important distinction drawn between questions about the source of contractual validity and international treaty clauses which purport to govern the consequences of contractual breach.

Similarly, a controversy arose when the *Vivendi* tribunal upheld a contractual stipulation which required the dispute to be resolved locally before the Tucuman administrative courts. That tribunal had found the rights in question under the French–Argentine BIT to have been 'inseparable' from the contractual rights under a 30-year provincial concession contract. The Annulment Committee,[28] however, considered treaty and contractual rights to be separate and distinct. Thus, for the Annulment Committee, the contractual choice of the Tucuman courts did not mean that Vivendi's treaty rights could then be ignored or extinguished.[29] Each source of law – contract and treaty – existed within its own proper sphere.

Likewise, the Annulment Committee in *CMS* v. *Argentina* had emphasised that 'The effect of the umbrella clause is not to transform the obligation which is relied upon into something else; the content of the obligation is unaffected, as is its proper law'.[30]

The source of contractual validity remains the applicable law of the contract. The contract continues to be governed by that law in respect of the usual incidents of contract notwithstanding any treaty consequences which may apply to its breach.[31]

[28] *Compañia de Aguas del Aconquija SA and Vivendi Universal* v. *Argentina*, ICSID Case No. ARB/97/3, Decision on Annulment, 3 July 2002 (hereafter, *Vivendi*, Annulment).

[29] *Id.*, para. 96.

[30] ICSID Case No. ARB/01/8, Decision on Annulment, 25 September 2007, para. 95(c).

[31] In addition to *Serbian Loans*, PCIJ No. 14, Ser. A, No. 20 at 41 and *Kahler* v. *Midland Bank* [1950] AC 24, 56, this view also has the benefit of distinguished support in the sphere of academic commentary. H. Lauterpacht, *Private Law Sources and Analogies of International Law* (London: Longman, 1927), 156. Writers who compare treaties to contracts merely draw an analogy, and indeed the proposition was that treaties between states are "as binding" under international law as contracts between individuals under municipal law, see e.g. B. Cheng, *General Principles of Law as Applied by International Courts and Tribunals*" (London: Stevens, 1953), 112 (on the doctrine of *pacta sunt servanda*). Successive editions of Brownlie treated the *Serbian Loans* case under the rubric of "Issues of Municipal Law before International Tribunals", notwithstanding the fact that the contract in that case was between French bondholders and the Serb-Croat-Slovene Government. Brownlie never wavered from the view that: "The rules of public international law accept the normal

Observing the language of the umbrella clause

Let us then assume that umbrella clauses do not, or at least do not necessarily, presuppose any theory of internationalisation, elevation, transformation or similar notion. The treaty clause would presuppose the need for strict contractual analysis – of the validity of the contract, its terms, and breach – but what kinds of treaty clauses would be required to create such hybrid treaty rights?

The Abs/Shawcross formula and its progeny

As an example, the clause in the 1990 UK–Argentina BIT states:[32]

> Each Contracting Party shall observe any obligations it may have entered into with regard to the investments of investors of the other party.

This resembles the clause in the Abs/Shawcross Draft Convention on Investments Abroad today,[33] as opposed, for example, to the clause in

operation of rules of private international law and when a claim for a breach of contract between an alien and a government arises, the issue will be decided according to the applicable system of municipal law designated by the rules of private international law". This was what *Serbian Loans* had been about. The position would be no different even if the contractual parties were to choose public international law as the applicable law. In practice, international law would be chosen alongside municipal law where "in the face of such clauses arbitrators have a certain discretion in selecting the precise role of public international law." But, the view that the contractual selection of public international law as the applicable law places the contract on the international plane "cannot be correct". See I. Brownlie, *Principles of Public International Law*, 7th ed. (Oxford: OUP, 2008), 37, 549–550. Though seemingly plausible since a sovereign intention to be bound by law transpires, the argument that this makes that binding law international law has been criticised by Sornarajah as a political invention born of the fears of the "European club of States" during the post-colonial era. See M. Sornarajah, *International Commercial Arbitration: The Problem of State Contracts* (Spore: Longman, 1990), 123. To be sure, internationalisation had been advanced by equally distinguished commentators, counting McNair, Verdross, Mann and von Mehren among them; A. McNair, "The General Principles of Law Recognised by Civilised Nations", (1957) 33 *BYIL* 1; I. Seidl-Hohenveldern, "Recollections of Alfred Verdross", (1994) 5 *EJIL* 98, 102; Mann, *Studies*, 143; A. von Mehren, "Special Substantive Rules for Multistate Problems", (1974) 88 *Harv. L. Rev.* 347. Sornarajah's response was that if there had ever been cause for gap-filling by such low-order sources of law as the general principles of law recognised by civilized nations, or the general principles of law, this lasted for only so long as there were no comprehensive national rules on the part of developing nations on foreign direct investment; Sornarajah, *Joint Ventures*, 299.

32 United Kingdom–Argentina Bilateral Investment Treaty, 11 December 1990, Article 2(2).

33 Art. 2, Draft Convention on Investments Abroad, 1959, Article II; reproduced in Newcombe and Paradell, *Law and Practice of Investment Treaties*, 441, states that: "Each Contracting Party shall at all times ensure the observance of any undertakings, which it may have given in relation to investment made by nationals of any other party".

Article 2(4) of the Italy–Jordan BIT in *Salini* v. *Jordan*, which is worded entirely differently:[34]

> Each Contracting Party shall create and maintain in its territory a legal framework apt to guarantee to investors the continuity of treatment, including the compliance, in good faith, of all obligations assumed with regard to each specific investor.

Observe, in particular, the phrase 'any obligations' in the above-mentioned British–Argentine example. That lends itself to an expansive reading, but it is then qualified by the phrase 'it may have entered into', suggesting that the clause applies only to specific undertakings. Compare that with the absence of any stipulation at all in the Italian–Jordanian example about the observance of commitments. As the International Centre for the Settlement of Investment Disputes (ICSID) tribunal in *Salini* went on to explain, Italy and Jordan had failed to commit themselves in plain terms to the observance of 'any obligation' in respect of investments, let alone the 'specific' investments of investors of the other party.[35]

Thus, one starts with the treaty clause itself.

The two 'SGS' cases

Salini had been decided after two well-known cases – *SGS* v. *Pakistan* and *SGS* v. *Philippines*. Most discussions of the subject of umbrella clauses today begin by recalling how the *SGS* v. *Pakistan* tribunal had rejected the purported umbrella clause in the Switzerland–Pakistan BIT, while the *SGS* v. *Philippines* tribunal subsequently upheld the umbrella clause in the Switzerland–Philippines BIT. This rendition places too much emphasis on outcome alone.

Article 11 of the Switzerland–Pakistan BIT in *SGS* v. *Pakistan* had been drafted in the following way. It begins, with my emphasis, by stating that 'Either Contracting Party *shall constantly guarantee the observance of the commitments it has entered into*'. Notice the absence of the more expansive Abs/Shawcross phrase 'any undertakings'. The tribunal in *SGS*

The use of the word "any" before the word "obligations" in the UK–Argentine BIT earlier, and before the word "undertakings" in the Abs/Shawcross version, is considered significant today; see *Noble Ventures* v. *Romania*, discussed further below, para. 62.

[34] ICSID Case No. ARB/02/13, Decision on Jurisdiction, 9 November 2004.

[35] Discussed also in *Noble Ventures* v. *Romania*, ICSID Case No. ARB/01/11, Award, 12 October 2005, para. 49.

v. *Pakistan* emphasised, in what is now a famous statement, that the underlying contractual claims were not to be assumed to have automatically been 'elevated' to the level of a treaty claim.[36] This must be correct, since the violation of a commitment to constantly guarantee the observance of commitments is not the same thing as the violation of the guarantee itself.

The tribunal's use of the metaphor that the contractual commitment might have become 'elevated' goes to the heart of the issue. It had seemingly originated in counsel's (Monsieur Gaillard's) submission that:[37]

> … I myself prefer to call it a mirror effect clause, because in fact it is a mirror effect which it creates.
>
> You have a violation of the contract, and the Treaty says, as if you had a mirror, that this violation will also be susceptible to being characterised as a violation of the Treaty. So the same facts, the same breach will be a violation of the contract in itself, and a violation of the Treaty.

And that:[38]

> If I am the government and if I breach a contract, by the same token I will breach a treaty, so the useful effect of this is to create this mirror effect, to say that I will elevate in essence, and that's what it does, it may be far-reaching but that's what it does, to elevate breaches of contract as breaches of a treaty.

As it turned out, learned counsel had risked putting the argument at its highest.

Voss, who has devoted discussion to the matter, shows how all this might have occurred. Admittedly, the 'elevation' theory has had a long pedigree in the scholarly literature; beginning with Prosper Weil's 1969 Hague Academy Lectures, where Professor Weil then spoke of an 'umbrella treaty' between the host and home state 'which turns the obligation to perform the contract into an international obligation of the contracting state' and which 'transforms contractual obligations into international obligations'.[39] Monsieur Gaillard had himself written about

[36] *SGS* v. *Pakistan*, ICSID Case No. ARB/01/13, Decision on Objections to Jurisdiction, 6 August 2003, paras. 166–173; also discussed by the tribunal in *Noble Ventures*, ICSID Case No. ARB/01/11, Award, 12 October 2005, para. 47.

[37] *Id.*, para. 99. [38] *Id.*

[39] P. Weil, "Problèmes relatifs aux contrats passés entre un Etat et un particulier", (1969) 128 *Recueil des Cours* 95, 130.

a 'mirror effect' of the contractual commitments in the treaty realm.[40] But while these metaphors – of elevation, transformation or a mirror effect between the two worlds of contract and treaty – have exercised a painful hold on our imagination, in *SGS* v. *Pakistan* it was an especially generous way of reading the words 'shall constantly guarantee the observance of the commitments it has entered into'.

In contrast, the Switzerland–Philippines BIT's umbrella clause in *SGS* v. *Philippines* had stated – again with added emphasis – as follows:

> Each Contracting Party *shall observe any obligation it has assumed* with regard to *specific investments* in its territory by investors of the other Contracting Party.

The tribunal in *SGS* v. *Philippines* duly observed that the word 'shall' suggested the existence of a legal obligation, and that the phrase 'any obligation' (which is similar to the Abs/Shawcross phrase 'any undertakings' and which was missing from the Swiss–Pakistani BIT) included future obligations which the host state will assume. It considered that the principle of effectiveness in treaty interpretation requires effect to be given to the clause within the framework of a treaty whose object and purpose was to be 'the promotion and reciprocal protection of investments.' It was perfectly consistent with the BIT therefore that contractual commitments which were intended to be binding under their own applicable law should also have been brought within the scope of the BIT umbrella clause's protection,[41] and that disputes concerning the scope and application of that protective umbrella will be subsumed within the investor-state arbitration clause in the BIT.

However, as I shall go on to discuss further, the *SGS* v. *Philippines* tribunal refused to adopt the theoretical view urged by Monsieur Gaillard in *SGS* v. *Pakistan* earlier. While the outcomes in the two cases were opposed, it is not without irony that the tribunal in *SGS* v. *Pakistan* had ended up assuming the more expansive view of the basis and effects of umbrella clauses even if it did not support the existence of an umbrella clause in the Swiss–Pakistani BIT.

[40] E. Gaillard, L'arbitrage sur le fondement des traités de protection des investissements – Les Etats dans le contentieux économique international, I. Le contentieux arbitral (2003) *Rev. Arb.* 853, 868; cited and translated in Voss, *The Impact of Investment Treaties on Contracts between Host States and Foreign Investors*, 240.

[41] *SGS* v. *Philippines*, ICSID Case No. ARB/02/6, Decision on Jurisdiction, 29 January 2004, paras. 115–116, 127; discussed in *Noble Ventures*, ICSID Case No. ARB/01/11, Award, 12 October 2005, para. 48 and *Eureko BV* v. *Republic of Poland*, Ad Hoc Arbitration, 19 August 2005 (Partial Award), para. 255.

Noble Ventures v. *Romania*

Then came the tribunal in *Noble Ventures* v. *Romania* whose attention having been directed to the two *SGS* cases considered that the clause in that dispute should be construed according to its plain meaning.[42] Art. II (2)(c) of the US–Romania BIT of 1994 had stated, again I add emphasis, as follows:

> Each Party *shall observe any obligation it may have entered into* with regard to investments.

The tribunal applied Art. 31 of the Vienna Convention on the Law of Treaties[43] looked to the ordinary meaning of the treaty language in light of the treaty's object and purpose and proceeded to interpret those terms in good faith. Supplementary materials may be consulted, said the tribunal, in order to confirm the meaning arrived at as a result of an interpretation of the ordinary meaning of the treaty clause. The principle of effectiveness – once described eloquently as that principle which would make treaty terms 'a means of fulfillment rather than an exercise in futility'[44] – should also be observed.

Proceeding in the manner described, the tribunal considered, first, that the word 'shall' denotes the existence of a treaty obligation.[45] Secondly, it considered that the phrase 'any obligations it may have entered into' could not but refer to anything other than obligations which were contained in investment contracts, since states do not usually enter into investment agreements with other states. The treaty clause is thereby 'specific', not broad or general, for investment contracts after all contain specific rights.[46] The words 'entered into' likewise suggested an intention to include specific commitments, rather than general commitments undertaken by way of legislative acts.[47] As the tribunal then put it:[48]

> ... a clause that is readily capable of being interpreted in this way and which would otherwise be deprived of practical applicability is naturally to be understood as protecting investors also with regard to contracts with the host state generally in so far as the contract was entered into with regard to an investment.

42 *Noble Ventures,* ICSID Case No. ARB/01/11, Award, 12 October 2005, paras. 46–62.
43 *Id.*, para. 50.
44 "World Court and the United Nations Charter: The Principle of Effectiveness in Interpretation", (1962)11 *Duke LJ* 85, at 85.
45 *Noble Ventures,* ICSID Case No. ARB/01/11, Award, 12 October 2005, para. 51.
46 *Id.* 47 *Id.* 48 *Id.*, para. 52.

Analysing this 'plain meaning' approach According to the *Noble Ventures* tribunal, therefore, one should look closely at the language and formulation of the specific clauses. The tribunal offered a useful analysis of the different forms of treaty language in prior cases. It considered that the *Salini* tribunal had reached the correct result since the words 'shall create and maintain in its territory a legal framework apt to guarantee to investors the continuity of treatment, including the compliance, in good faith, of all obligations' simply did not suggest the existence of an umbrella clause.[49] According to the *Noble Ventures* tribunal, the word 'guarantee' in the BIT in *SGS* v. *Pakistan* suggests a similar reading. What Pakistan had undertaken to do was to take the requisite steps to protect contractual commitments under its municipal law. The clause in the Switzerland–Pakistan BIT therefore contained a general, rather than a specific, obligation.[50]

In contrast, however, the treaty clause in *SGS* v. *Philippines* stated that each party 'shall observe any obligation it has assumed with regard to specific investments made by investors of the other party'. The wording of the clause makes the breach of the investment contract itself a treaty violation.[51] In particular, the *Noble Ventures* tribunal observed the 'directness' of the reference in the Switzerland–Philippines BIT umbrella clause to investment contracts – i.e. 'any obligation it has assumed with regard to specific investments'. In *Noble Ventures*, the US–Romania BIT's reference to 'any obligation' the host state 'may have entered into' was considered to be equally direct, or explicit, in its reference to all forms of investment contracts because of the words 'obligation' and 'entered into'.[52]

This 'plain meaning' approach was subsequently adopted by the tribunal in *Eureko* v. *Poland* which also cited the tribunal's view in *SGS* v. *Philippines* that the treaty in that case 'means what it says' and should be given its 'plain meaning'.[53] This approach has the benefit of simplicity if not elegance. Even if it cannot settle all cases of doubt, it does present a useful device for weeding out such generally worded clauses which

[49] *Id.*, para. 57. [50] *Id.*, para. 58.

[51] Although the tribunal in *SGS* v. *Philippines* had also considered the clause in the Swiss–Pakistan BIT "arguably similar" to that in the Swiss–Philippine BIT; *SGS* v. *Philippines*, paras. 97, 199; discussed in Sinclair, "The Umbrella Clause Debate", 286.

[52] Even if the tribunal's choice of words in its reference to the clause as one falling into the category of "the most general and direct formulations" is an unhappy one. See para. 60.

[53] *Eureko* v. *Poland*, paras. 256, 258. However, the *Eureko* tribunal criticised the Award in *SGS* v. *Pakistan, Id.*, para. 257.

cannot, on their proper construction, be taken to qualify as umbrella clauses at all. Clearly, clauses which undertake to 'create and maintain' in the host state's territory an appropriate 'legal framework' cannot qualify as umbrella clauses.

'Plain meaning' versus 'sweeping and unqualified meaning'

But what about clauses which, like the clause in the Swiss–Pakistani treaty, require that the host State 'shall constantly guarantee the observance of the commitments it has entered into'? While the *Noble Ventures* tribunal considered such a 'guarantee' of 'observance' to be substantially similar to the commitment in the BIT in *Salini* (i.e. merely guaranteeing the existence of effective domestic laws for the continued enforcement of legal commitments), the tribunal in *Eureko* saw no essential difference between a 'guarantee of observance' and an 'undertaking to observe' a host state's commitments under the traditional Abs/Shawcross formulation.

The reasoning of the tribunal in *SGS* v. *Pakistan* had been especially complex. While the tribunal rejected the umbrella clause, as the subsequent *Noble Ventures* tribunal apparently would have done, it did so for entirely different reasons. Like the *Eureko* tribunal, the *SGS* v. *Pakistan* tribunal took the Swiss–Pakistani clause seriously; so seriously that it reasoned that treaty clauses requiring the host state to 'constantly guarantee the observance of the commitments it has entered into' would not be limited to the observance of contractual obligations. It did not view the words 'constantly guarantee' and 'commitments entered into' as qualifying words at all. Rather, they would be 'so far-reaching in scope, so automatic and unqualified and sweeping in their operation, and so burdensome in their potential impact upon a Contracting Party' that 'clear and convincing evidence' would be required to show such actual treaty intent.[54] An unlimited number of state contracts would be protected, rendering other treaty protective standards 'substantially superfluous'.[55] Freely negotiated contractual forum selection clauses would be

[54] *SGS* v. *Pakistan*, ICSID Case No. ARB/01/13, Decision on Objections to Jurisdiction, 6 August 2003, paras. 166–173.

[55] However, umbrella clauses that only apply to specific commitments are unlike other treaty standards in a BIT which are general in nature. The latter being general rather than specific are not thereby rendered superfluous by the existence of an umbrella clause. See Sornarajah, *International Law on Foreign Investment*, 3rd ed., 215.

nullified,[56] while the treaty clause was not even located together with the other protective treaty standards. These factors led the tribunal to doubt, as a matter of construction, that the treaty parties intended to create such a 'sweeping and unqualified' effect.

Problems of construction are especially fraught. Yet, the true cause of all this confusion is not that it involves the problem of treaty construction. The true cause might well be thought to lie in Gaillard's and Weil's invocation of that phantasm – the 'internationalisation' of the entire underlying contract by an umbrella clause.

El Paso: the myth of the 'internationalised' contract lurks still

There the matter could have ended; it was all simply a confusion over the construction of different terms, but for the fact that the tribunal in *SGS* v. *Philippines* also viewed the Award in *SGS* v. *Pakistan* to have been fundamentally mistaken. According to the tribunal in *SGS* v. *Philippines*, an umbrella clause need not mirror, transform, elevate or internationalise the underlying contract at all. In the words of the *SGS* v. *Philippines* tribunal, umbrella clauses address 'not the scope of the commitments entered into with regard to specific investments, but the performance of these obligations once they are ascertained'. An umbrella clause 'does not convert the issue of the extent or content of such obligations into an issue of international law'.[57] Similarly, the *Noble Ventures* tribunal had considered it unnecessary to answer the question whether 'any' breach of 'any obligation' would perfectly assimilate to a treaty breach.[58]

The odd theory that umbrella clauses were capable of internationalising entire underlying contracts had led the tribunal in *SGS* v. *Pakistan* to apply a strict evidentiary presumption against umbrella clauses. In this manner, a boundless theoretical view became a justification for prudence in respect of a practical legal issue,[59] resulting in a strong presumption against the very existence of umbrella clauses.[60]

[56] See the discussion in "Problems with the contractual forum selection clause" section.

[57] *SGS* v. *Philippines*, paras. 121–128, cited in *Eureko* v. *Poland*, Partial Award, 19 August 2005, para. 256.

[58] *Noble Ventures*, ICSID Case No. ARB/01/11, Award, 12 October 2005, para. 61.

[59] Sinclair, "The Umbrella Clause Debate", 287.

[60] *SGS* v. *Pakistan*, ICSID Case No. ARB/01/13, Decision on Objections to Jurisdiction, 6 August 2003, para. 173 ("The Tribunal is not saying that States may not agree with each other in a BIT that henceforth, all breaches of each State's contracts with investors of the other State are forthwith converted into and to be treated as breaches of the BIT. What the

But then came *El Paso* v. *Argentina*,[61] a case in which Professor Sornarajah served as an expert, only to re-confirm this original theoretical conceit. Like *SGS* v. *Pakistan*, the *El Paso* tribunal concluded that the phrase 'any obligations' is so broad that it could include the breach of any obligation by the host state, thereby rendering the whole treaty superfluous.[62] According to the tribunal, 'the smallest obligation of a state with regards to investment falls to be protected by the BIT and could give rise to an ICSID obligation'.[63] The tribunal in *El Paso* then criticised the incoherence of the view taken in *SGS* v. *Philippines*, which, as we saw earlier, had considered that while the contractual breach may be brought as a treaty claim under the umbrella clause, the contractual obligations themselves are governed separately by ordinary contractual principles. According to the *El Paso* tribunal, this would require investment tribunals to rule on contractual claims.

It is difficult to understand the *El Paso* tribunal's reservation. After all, a tribunal can engage in contractual analysis if the parties have mandated the tribunal to do so, and even in the absence of party agreement, various institutional rules (e.g. ICSID and UNCITRAL) typically accord the tribunal the discretion to apply domestic contract law either directly or

Tribunal is stressing is that in this case, there is no clear and persuasive evidence that such was in fact the intention of both Switzerland and Pakistan in adopting Article 11 of the BIT").

61 *El Paso* v. *Argentina*, ICSID Case No. ARB/03/15, Decision on Objections to Jurisdiction, 27 April 2006.

62 *Id.*, para. 76. No attempt was made to distinguish between the treaty protections that are of general application and umbrella clauses, which apply only to specific commitments.

63 *El Paso* v. *Argentina*, ICSID Case No. ARB/03/15, Decision on Objections to Jurisdiction, 27 April 2006, paras. 76–77. Curiously, the *El Paso* tribunal appeared to have considered that *Eureko* and *Noble Ventures* supported its view. But see, however, *Eureko*, *op. cit.*, para. 256, and *Noble Ventures*, ICSID Case No. ARB/01/11, Award, 12 October 2005, para. 61. *El Paso*'s (and *SGS* v. *Pakistan*'s) theory of the internationalised contract was, however, shared by other recent Awards. See *BIVAC* v. *Paraguay*, ICSID Case No. ARB/07/9, Decision on Jurisdiction, 29 May 2009, para. 142 ("it must have imported into the BIT all of the obligations owed … under the Contract"); *PanAm* v. *Argentina*, Decision on Preliminary Objections, ICSID Case No. ARB/03/13, ARB/04/8, para. 105. I do not read *SGS* v. *Paraguay*, ICSID Case No. ARB/07/29, Decision on Jurisdiction, 12 February 2010, to suggest such internationalisation. In fact, the tribunal went to great lengths to show that it did not need to decide whether the claims were merely contractual and not based upon treaty; which under a theory of the internationalised contract would be one and the same. In any event, the tribunal considered that the umbrella clause operated independently of the underlying contract was not solely reliant upon the contents of the contract and may in fact have been broader in scope than the contract; see *Id.*, paras. 125–142. Likewise, in *Duke Energy* v. *Ecuador*, ICSID Case No. ARB/04/19, Award, 18 August 2008, the tribunal had left the question of internationalisation open – see *Id.*, para. 319.

by first applying the choice of law rules of the appropriate domestic legal system in order to determine the proper law of the contract.[64]

If *El Paso* is somehow correct, the most ordinary contractual commitment could become an investment-treaty commitment. In this way, the *El Paso* tribunal saw a need to discuss the proliferation of devices which have been intended to limit the supposedly wide effect of umbrella clauses.[65]

Distinguishing commercial from investment commitments

The *El Paso* tribunal cited a wide variety of approaches, starting with that adopted by the tribunal in *Joy Mining* v. *Egypt*.[66] That latter dispute had concerned the potential application of an umbrella clause in the UK–Egypt BIT to certain performance guarantees regarding the proper functioning of equipment used at an Egyptian phosphate mine. The Egyptian agency, IMC, had alleged defective performance. Joy Mining submitted the dispute to ICSID arbitration. Egypt's argument was that this was a purely commercial dispute involving the sale of equipment, paid for by a confirmed irrevocable letter of credit, and that Joy Mining had therefore already been paid in full. As for the performance guarantee, it too was an ordinary commercial agreement and Egypt had not after all drawn on the guarantee. According to Egypt, the dispute only concerned its refusal to release the guarantees according to the agreed schedule because of the existence of the dispute about Joy Mining's allegation of mismanagement by Egypt's IMC, while IMC alleged that it had been supplied with defective equipment.

All of this, according to Egypt, has nothing whatsoever to do with an 'investment'. Joy Mining, however, contended that a guarantee which represents 97% of the contract price amounts therefore to an 'investment'.

The tribunal did not automatically preclude sales disputes from becoming investment disputes, but held that such situations would be

64 A.K. Bjorklund, "Applicable Law in International Investment Disputes", in C. Giorgetti (ed.), *Litigating International Investment Disputes: A Practitioner's Guide* (Leiden: Nijhoff, 2014), 261, 271–272. Consent to these rules, therefore, amounts to consent to the tribunal's application of domestic laws.

65 Professor Jeswald Salacuse has classified the cases into those which support the plain meaning approach and others which "seem to be influenced by the consequences to states and to the arbitral system of giving too broad an interpretation to the clause"; Salacuse, *Law of Investment Treaties*, 280.

66 *Joy Mining* v. *Egypt*, ICSID Case No. ARB/03/11, Award on Jurisdiction, 6 August 2004.

exceptional.[67] This, incidentally, reflects a long-standing view advanced by F.A. Mann: 'difficulties may arise in the event of the sale of goods', Mann once wrote, but 'where a very expensive machine or ship is supplied, this may well constitute an "investment".[68] According to the tribunal in *Joy Mining*, a dispute over a performance guarantee was, however, an inherently commercial dispute, because there was only a peripheral relationship with the underlying 'investment'.[69] The tribunal presided over by Professor Francisco Orrego-Vicuna considered that:[70]

> Disputes about the release of bank guarantees are a common occurrence in many jurisdictions and the fact that a State agency might be a party to a Contract involving a commercial transaction of this kind does not change its nature. It is still a commercial and contractual dispute ...

The tribunal went on to explain that had there been an investment, the purported umbrella clause was in any case akin to that in *SGS* v. *Pakistan* – ill-placed in the treaty and thereby lacking 'prominence'. As for the language of the clause, Article 2(2) of the BIT had stated in a final sentence at the end of a long paragraph that:[71]

> Each Contracting Party shall observe any obligation it may have entered into with regard to investments of nationals or companies of the other Contracting Party.

In any event, the nature of the underlying contract now become a key issue in the evolving jurisprudence on umbrella clauses. The *SGS* cases had concerned contracts for pre-shipment inspection services, while the *Noble Ventures* and *Eureko* cases had concerned the terms of share purchase agreements which had been employed as the preferred vehicle under various national privatisation policies. Much now turns upon what a tribunal, going through the facts, understands by an 'investment'.

Notice, however, that had the tribunal in *Joy Mining* adopted the internationalisation theory, there would have been no distinction between commercial and investment disputes. In this way, the tribunal's

[67] *Joy Mining* v. *Egypt*, ICSID Case No. ARB/03/11, Award on Jurisdiction, 6 August 2004, para. 58.

[68] F.A. Mann, "British Treaties for the Promotion and Protection of Investments", (1981) 52 *BYIL* 241, 243.

[69] *Joy Mining* v. *Egypt*, ICSID Case No. ARB/03/11, Award on Jurisdiction, 6 August 2004, paras. 78–79.

[70] *Id.*, para. 79. [71] *Id.*, para. 81.

view is at least consistent with the rejection of internationalisation[72] and is on that basis sound. Suppose, we had a construction contract in which the host State is the employer and the contractor alleges that it is an investor; can one simply say that the breach of a payment clause by virtue of a small, delayed payment would automatically amount to a treaty breach? In contrast, the unlawful repudiation or termination of a contract presents a clearer case of the breach of the umbrella clause where the very existence of the contract might be said to constitute the whole basis of the investor's investment.

Although phrases like 'any commitment' suggest a wider meaning, they are typically also qualified by words such as 'in relation to investments'. One might then, as the *El Paso* tribunal did subsequently, look to the definitions clause in the treaty. This would still be entirely consistent with a 'plain meaning' approach to umbrella clauses. Another way may be to rely upon the '*Salini* criteria' derived from ICSID jurisprudence.[73]

The *El Paso* tribunal canvassed a third method, to which we now turn. It involves distinguishing between a host state acting in its sovereign capacity and in a merchant capacity.[74] It is suggested, according to this third method of limiting the effect of umbrella clauses, that purely private acts of the host state have nothing to do with the host state's investment commitments.

Acta jure imperii

The *El Paso* tribunal cited *CMS* v. *Argentina*, which had adopted another device for containing the effect of umbrella clauses.[75] CMS had bought into a new company, TGN, which had been granted a gas transportation licence. The dispute concerned the tariff adjustment formula for gas transportation after Argentina's dismantlement of the tariff regime in the wake of the 1999 Argentine financial crisis. Article II(2)(c) of the US–Argentina BIT stipulated that the Contracting Parties: 'shall observe any obligation it may have entered into with regard to investments'. According to the tribunal (the President was, again, Professor Orrego-Vicuna):[76]

72 However, we will never know for sure as the arbitrator also rejected the clause as an umbrella clause.
73 See J. Ho, "The Meaning of 'Investment' in ICSID Arbitrations", (2010) 26 *Arb Int'l* 633.
74 *El Paso*, para. 79.
75 The Award was subsequently annulled but not, I think, on this point.
76 *CMS* v. *Argentina*, ICSID Case No. ARB/01/8, Decision on Annulment, 25 September 2007, para. 299.

> Purely commercial aspects of a contract might not be protected by the treaty in some situations, but the protection is likely to be available when there is significant interference by government or public agencies with the rights of the investor.

Notice that the Tribunal's requirement of 'significant interference by government or public agencies' is presumably only a necessary but insufficient requirement. In *Joy Mining*, the tribunal there had said that 'the fact that a State agency might be a party to a Contract involving a commercial transaction of this kind does not change its nature', and that the nature of the underlying contract in *Joy Mining*, being purely commercial, precluded its treatment as an investment.[77]

The *El Paso* Award and the Award in *Joy Mining* are now cited as authority for the proposition that states 'entering into such obligations must be acting as sovereigns and not as merchants'.[78] Such a view at least accommodates the internationalisation theory. The argument would go something like this. The contract is internationalised, but an ordinary commercial breach of the contract would not fall within the scope of the umbrella clause, as opposed to a breach by the sovereign acting in its sovereign capacity.

The effort to distinguish between sovereign and merchant acts has not met with universal acceptance. It had been argued by the Respondent in *SGS* v. *Paraguay*, but the argument was dismissed by that tribunal, which considered that where the plain language of the treaty does not distinguish between a governmental or other act, then no such distinction ought to be imposed.[79] For the sake of completeness, it is also worth mentioning that in *El Paso* and *Vivendi*, it had been said that the sovereign host state at least possesses an international legal personality which an independent state agency may not possess.[80] Yet, quite arguably, no reliance can be placed on

[77] *Joy Mining* v. *Egypt*, ICSID Case No. ARB/03/11, Award on Jurisdiction, 6 August 2004, para. 79.

[78] *CMS* v. *Argentina*, ICSID Case No. ARB/01/8, Decision on Annulment, 25 September 2007; *Joy Mining*, ICSID Case No. ARB/03/11, Award on Jurisdiction, 6 August 2004, para. 81; also *Impregilo* v. *Pakistan*, ICSID Case No. ARB/03/3, Decision on Jurisdiction, 22 April 2005, para. 260 (on the distinction between sovereign and merchant acts). See further, Salacuse, *Law of Investment Treaties*, 283.

[79] *SGS* v. *Paraguay*, ICSID Case No. ARB/07/29, Decision on Jurisdiction, 12 February 2010, paras. 164, 167–168.

[80] *Vivendi*, Annulment, para. 96; *El Paso*, para. 79.

this factor where the act of the agency is, in any event, attributable to the state under the normal rules of state responsibility.[81]

Overlap with fair and equitable treatment and other substantive treaty standards

However, the *El Paso* tribunal itself concluded, ultimately, that an umbrella clause's scope ought to be limited by the existence of a concurrent violation of some other substantive treaty standard. Where there has been such a concurrent breach which is attributable to the state, the jurisdiction of the investment tribunal will be established.[82] This highlights a new front in the debate – the potential operation of FET clauses as 'de facto umbrella clauses'.[83] This link with the FET standard was also drawn in *SGS* v. *Paraguay*, and in *EDF* v. *Argentina*, the tribunal observed that the FET clause and the umbrella clause operated 'in tandem'.[84]

Problems with the contractual forum selection clause

The rules of treaty interpretation

These various ways of limiting the effect of umbrella clauses which we have discussed stem from the 'public international law side' of the analysis. Other tools have also emerged from the 'contractual side' of the equation. The most serious challenge from the contractual side concerns the effect which ought to be given to the contractual forum selection clause. As the *SGS* v. *Pakistan* tribunal saw it:[85]

> A third consequence [of sweeping umbrella clauses] is that an investor may, at will, nullify any freely negotiated dispute settlement clause in a State contract. On the reading of Article 11 urged by the Claimant, the benefits of the dispute settlement provisions of a contract with a State also

[81] Article 4–11, ILC Articles on Responsibility of States for Internationally Wrongful Acts, UNGA res. 56/83, 14 December 2001. See further, J. Crawford, "Treaty and Contract in Investment Arbitration", (2008) 24 *Arb Int'l* 351, 356, for a clarification of this point.

[82] *El Paso* v. *Argentina*, ICSID Case No. ARB/03/15, Decision on Objections to Jurisdiction, 27 April 2006, paras. 82, 84.

[83] Laird *et al.*, *International Investment Law and Arbitration*, 150.

[84] *Id.*, 150–151. See further *SGS* v. *Paraguay*, ICSID Case No. ARB/07/29, Decision on Jurisdiction, 12 February 2010, paras. 160–161; *EDF* v. *Argentina*, ICSID Case No. ARB/03/23, Final Award, 11 June 2012, paras. 994, 999, 1022.

[85] *SGS* v. *Pakistan*, ICSID Case No. ARB/01/13, Decision on Objections to Jurisdiction, 6 August 2003, para. 168. The reference to "differing legal orders" is interesting, and casts some doubt on the tribunal's complete adherence to a theory of internationalisation.

> a party to a BIT, would flow only to the investor. For that investor could always defeat the State's invocation of the contractually specified forum, and render any mutually agreed procedure of dispute settlement, other than BIT-specified ICSID arbitration, a dead letter, at the investor's choice ... The Tribunal considers that Article 11 of the BIT should be read in such a way as to enhance mutuality and balance of benefits in the inter-relation of different agreements located in differing legal orders.

However, recall the *Vivendi* Annulment Committee's view that, although the sentiment expressed by the *SGS* v. *Pakistan* tribunal is appealing, contractual clauses cannot extinguish an investor's treaty rights as a matter of international legal principle.

In treaty terms, the circumstances in which contractual rights might extinguish or affect treaty rights would require the contractual right to supersede, amend or at least condition the interpretation of the treaty right. From the perspective of the hierarchy of legal norms, it is difficult to see how this could occur unless the contractual right itself somehow came to possess the status of international law – i.e. unless it is 'elevated' to the level of a treaty right – failing which a domestic law contractual right cannot serve as an excuse for the breach of a treaty right.[86]

There are ways under the rules of treaty interpretation by which BIT rights may be conditioned by contract. One thing seems clear, however; the contract cannot be said to constitute a 'subsequent agreement' between the Contracting Parties under Article 31(3)(a) of the Vienna Convention on the Law of Treaties of 1969 (VCLT) because the investment contract is only a contract with the foreign investor, not its home state.[87] However, under Article 31(3)(b), a 'subsequent practice which establishes the agreement of the Parties' could affect the reading of a treaty right. One would have to argue that the conclusion of the investment contract is a subsequent practice of the host state, one which the home state accepts implicitly, and that the home state's acceptance establishes – either alone or in combination with other facts – the 'agreement' of the treaty parties themselves. In such a case, the contractual forum selection clause would, as a matter of the proper

86 There was the suggestion, to the contrary, that a subsequent contract would simply supersede the BIT, but it is difficult to understand how that could occur unless, as I have argued here, the contract itself is elevated to the level of a subsequent international agreement; see *BIVAC*, Decision on Jurisdiction, 29 May 2009, para. 146; discussed also in *SGS* v. *Paraguay*, Decision on Jurisdiction, 12 February 2010, para. 178.

87 It is well known that the home state in *SGS* v. *Pakistan* subsequently expressed dissatisfaction with the tribunal's construction of Article 11 of the Switzerland–Pakistan BIT.

interpretation of the BIT, be able to condition the reading of a BIT umbrella or arbitration clause or both.

A second possible way, under Article 31(3)(c) of the VCLT, may be if the contract had become internationalised.[88] It could then become a 'rule of international law', which is 'relevant' and 'applicable' to the state parties, and, therefore, ought to be taken into account in the interpretation of the BIT. The very difficult idea that such a contract is also 'applicable' to the home state would have to be argued further.

The view in SGS *v.* Philippines

The problem occurs because the BIT stipulates recourse to investment arbitration.[89] In *SGS* v. *Philippines*, the tribunal upheld the umbrella clause while, at the same time, upholding the contractual forum selection clause. It pays to attend to how this occurs in the tribunal's view. The tribunal treated the contractual forum selection clause as a form of *lex specialis*, because the BIT arbitration clause did not refer to any specific investment or contract, while the contractual forum selection clause in fact did.[90]

This approach drew criticism from the *El Paso* tribunal, as well as in academic commentary.[91] The *El Paso* tribunal asked how the forum selection clause could have survived if the umbrella clause had already 'overridden' the contract.[92] The dissenting arbitrator in *SGS* v. *Philippines*, Professor Crivellaro, offered one possible answer – the BIT having been concluded after the contract expanded the rights of the investor by giving the investor a choice of a further forum in addition to the options stipulated in the contractual forum selection clause.[93]

[88] In *BIVAC* v. *Paraguay*, the tribunal reasoned that, once all the terms of the contract are elevated to treaty status, then the forum selection clause must – as with any BIT provision – be given effect to within that treaty setting; ICSID Case No. ARB/07/9, Decision on Jurisdiction, 29 May 2009, paras. 142–158, cited in *SGS* v. *Paraguay*, Decision on Jurisdiction, 12 February 2010, para. 172.

[89] For the separate regimes of treaty and contract, see again *Vivendi*, Annulment, ICSID Case No. ARB/97/3, Decision on Annulment, 3 July 2002, paras. 95, 96.

[90] *SGS* v. *Philippines*, ICSID Case No. ARB/02/6, Decision on Jurisdiction, 29 January 2004, para. 141.

[91] J. Wong, "Umbrella Clauses in Bilateral Investment Treaties: Of Breaches of Contract, Treaty Violations, and the Divide between Developing and Developed Countries in Foreign Investment Disputes", (2006) 14 *Geo Mason L Rev* 135, 137, 156 *et seq.*

[92] *El Paso* v. *Argentina*, ICSID Case No. ARB/03/15, Decision on Objections to Jurisdiction, 27 April 2006, para. 76.

[93] *SGS* v. *Philippines*, ICSID Case No. ARB/02/6, Decision on Jurisdiction, 29 January 2004, Declaration of Arbitrator Crivellaro. 2–4, 10.

But, what if the contract came after the BIT? There is no reason to suppose that in such event the umbrella clause could not, on its proper construction, direct the tribunal to the contractual forum selection clause itself by way of *renvoi.*[94] In fact, the reasoning in *SGS* v. *Philippines* that the contractual forum clause amounts to *lex specialis* might already suggest such an approach. As we have seen, the forum selection clause could also be given effect, notwithstanding the BIT's provision for investor-state arbitration, if in the circumstances the contractual right even if it did not supersede or amend the treaty right has nonetheless conditioned the interpretation of the latter. This, as we have already seen (in the section "The rules of treaty interpretation") might be done by applying the treaty interpretation rules under Article 31(3)(b) or (c) of the VCLT.[95]

The doctrine of privity of contract

Another challenge from the contractual side of the equation has emerged in the form of the privity doctrine. Gallus has shown that there are two aspects to the problem. The first occurs where a subsidiary that the state has harmed was not a party to the contract, while the second occurs

[94] In other words, if the treaty clause, properly interpreted, points to the application of the forum selection clause by way of *renvoi*, or if on its plain meaning the umbrella clause is taken not to have been intended to interfere with the contractual balance between the investor and the host state (thereby presenting both investor and state equal options in respect of forum selection). The fear of an expansion of the scope of treaty commitments remains, however, and this view could be treated as just another species of internationalisation. Conceptually, it is different from the elevation or internationalisation theory because the tribunal will employ ordinary forms of contractual analysis to the forum selection clause itself.

[95] We should beware that the problem also concerns the enforcement of such clauses by *municipal* courts. It is not entirely unimaginable that some courts, such as the English courts, may be slow to interfere with investment arbitration, especially ICSID arbitration particularly due to the perception that the ICSID process is "self-contained". Even matters connected with investment arbitration are justiciable (*Occidental* v. *Ecuador* [2005] EWCA Civ. 116, esp. paras. 41–42 *per* Mance L.J.), but there is *dicta*, which suggests that where the matter is properly remitted to the jurisdiction of an ICSID tribunal, special considerations raised by the ICSID Convention's largely self-contained arbitration procedures could arise (*E.T.I. Euro Telecom* v. *Bolivia* [2008] EWCA Civ. 888 at paras. 99–109 *per* Collins L.J). Conversely, a tribunal is bound to take an investment treaty right seriously; see *SGS* v. *Paraguay*, Decision on Jurisdiction, 12 February 2010, para. 172 ("risk of failing to carry out its mandate"), citing (at para. 171) *Vivendi*, Annulment, ICSID Case No. ARB/97/3, Decision on Annulment, 3 July 2002, para. 112.

where a sub-state entity responsible for the breach was not party to the contract entered into by the host state.[96]

Beginning with the first,[97] the *CMS* Annulment Committee had reasoned that where the treaty clause itself allows the parent to enforce the rights of a subsidiary the privity issue is irrelevant.[98] Much will depend upon whether a tribunal would treat the treaty analysis separately from the contractual analysis, as the *SGS* v. *Philippines* tribunal apparently did and which the *El Paso* tribunal rejected.

As for the second aspect, the problem may be overcome where the sub-state entity's actions are attributable to the host State under the international law rules of state responsibility.[99]

There is a broader objection to the privity doctrine where the underlying contract is considered to have become elevated or internationalised. Once all the contractual terms are elevated to the status of treaty terms, it becomes difficult to see how any room is left for contractually based limitations such as the privity doctrine. There appears neither room nor need left for any contractual analysis. One would have to argue that there is an equivalent treaty doctrine which applies to internationalised contracts.

The problem with elevating or internationalising the contractual terms under an umbrella clause

At bottom, however, the idea that all the contractual terms could become elevated or internationalised by an umbrella clause is problematic. Sornarajah's complaint has been that '[t]he process of this transformation has not been explained'.[100] As he put it in his Opinion in *El Paso* v. *Argentina*:[101]

> Being domestic contracts, contracts of foreign investment create obligations only in domestic law. It is without doubt that, through the use of appropriate language, the rights so created can be lifted up and subjected to an international regime of protection. But, the extent of those rights

[96] N. Gallus, "An Umbrella Just for Two? BIT Obligations Observance Clauses and the Parties to a Contract", (2008) 24 *Arb Int'l* 157, 158.

[97] See *Id.*, 159–162 for a survey of the split authorities.

[98] *CMS* v. *Argentina*, ICSID Case No. ARB/01/8, para. 95.

[99] Gallus, "An Umbrella Just for Two?", 166.

[100] *Id.*, para. 14.

[101] Legal Opinion of M. Sornarajah in *El Paso* v. *Argentina*, ICSID Case No. ARB/03/15, 5 March 2007, para. 12.

> must depend on domestic law … they can be protected only to the extent that they exist in domestic law.

F.A. Mann's view, on the contrary, was that we should turn to 'the commercial law of nations', which drew an unhappy retort from Sornarajah.[102] In essence, such reliance upon the 'low order sources of international law' is a retreat to the realm of private law analogies in the absence of a formal, as opposed to only a material, source of international legal justification.

The greatest difficulty may not be how internationalisation occurs, but what it means to admit the theory of the internationalised contract. In the umbrella clause debate, it presupposes that treaty law has doctrines that are equivalent to domestic contract law. Even outside the umbrella clause debate, if we were simply to rely on some low-order source such as Mann's 'commercial law of nations' as the basis for saying that a contract has become an 'internationalised' contract, that would almost presuppose that private international law practice has become irrelevant.

Conclusion

According to Sornarajah, a principal difficulty concerns the need to, first, ascertain the theoretical implications of umbrella clauses.[103] This chapter has tried to do that by showing how the extent or degree to which umbrella clauses might expand host state commitments depends ultimately upon whether or not we adopt the theory of the 'internationalised contract'.

I have discussed how *SGS* v. *Philippines* gave effect to the umbrella clause without elevating all the contractual commitments to some unexplained treaty status. That Award struck an intermediate position, but it was fiercely criticised by the *El Paso* tribunal, whose analysis was based upon the earlier view taken in *SGS* v. *Pakistan* that the contractual commitments would be elevated – a view which both the *El Paso* and *Pakistan* tribunals considered to be a logical consequence of upholding umbrella clauses.

Tribunals have adopted the ideas of elevation or internationalisation, or what Gaillard calls the mirror theory, as a result of certain influential scholarly writings in the field. To this extent, we might say that internationalisation has been the dominant view all along. However, an umbrella clause could – as this chapter has tried to argue – simply

[102] Sornarajah, "Myth", 199, 201, 202.
[103] Sornarajah, *International Law on Foreign Investment*, 3rd ed., 304.

require, as a matter of plain treaty construction, that the breach of some contractual commitments should be treated as breaches of the overlying BIT but that other contractual breaches should not. The *SGS* v. *Philippines* tribunal had explained this view forcefully by stating that an umbrella clause 'does not convert the issue of the extent or content of such obligations into an issue of international law'.[104]

The illustration given earlier in this chapter is that of a construction contract in which delayed payment by the host state could be treated as a simple contractual breach but that unlawful termination of the contract itself, which is the basis of the whole investment, would prima facie rise to the level of a treaty breach.

Despite the dominant scholarly view, the arbitral jurisprudence today contains strong suggestions that an umbrella clause should be construed as if it were just another treaty clause, does not require always the conversion of every contractual term into a treaty term, that the distinction between treaty and contract should be observed and that in applying umbrella clauses one ought to focus only upon whether the breach of the specific contractual or other commitment amounts also to a treaty breach.[105] Taking such an approach would neither result in a broader nor narrower reading than what ordinary treaty construction would require. If this plain view is adopted, there would also be less urgency in seeking to limit the operation of umbrella clauses.[106] It might make no

[104] *SGS* v. *Philippines*, paras. 121–128, cited in *Eureko* v. *Poland*, para. 256.

[105] This is the fourth of James Crawford's four-fold classification; "Treaty and Contract", 368; see also A.R. Sureda, *Investment Treaty Arbitration: Judging under Uncertainty* (Cambridge: CUP, 2012), 33.

[106] In some cases, a difficult question might arise about the need to imply elements of the host state's regulatory framework into the terms of the contract. In such cases, the contention is that subsequent regulatory changes have breached implied contractual terms. According to Sornarajah, in his Opinion in *El Paso*, Legal Opinion of M. Sornarajah in *El Paso* v. *Argentina*, ICSID Case No. ARB/03/15, 5 March 2007, para. 96, the tribunal in *LG & E* v. *Argentina*, ICSID Case No. ARB/02/1, Decision on Liability, 3 October 2006, had (erroneously) read the host state's regulatory provisions into the contract. If so, in such cases, it is not the treaty commitments of the host state, which have necessarily been expanded, but the host state's contractual commitments. Similarly, the question would have less to do with the construction of the umbrella clause as such, once it is accepted that the treaty clause encompasses breaches of contractual commitments. With respect, however, it is not obvious that this was necessarily what had transpired in *LG & E*. Rather, Argentina had made promises to which it bound itself under general legislation or regulations, and these legally binding promises fell within the scope of the 'obligations' which the BIT umbrella clause sought directly to protect. It was the Respondent itself, Argentina, which had contended that the promises were merely domestic contracts. See *Id.*, paras. 164–175.

great difference ultimately in practice,[107] but as Sornarajah once observed, it is important to be clear about what we are talking about.

[107] Since some of the factors relied upon to limit the scope of umbrella clauses – such as asking whether a sovereign act was involved, or whether the host state government was itself party to the contract – might still play an evidential role in determining whether the particular contractual breach ought to be considered a breach of the treaty in light of the particular language of the umbrella clause.

14

Internationalisation and State contracts: are State contracts the future or the past?

JEAN HO

Introduction

Many foreign investment disputes are contractual in origin. The cause of grievance is usually a breach of contract committed against the foreign investor by the host State. As claimant investors often plead that their contractual rights benefit from the protection of international law, arbitral tribunals must determine whether a breach of contract constitutes a violation of international law. The possibility of State responsibility being engaged for a breach of contract is well known, but the law on State responsibility for contractual breaches remains unsettled. Much of the uncertainty stems from persistent support for, and persistent objections to, the internationalisation of State contracts. Supporters posit that the effect of internationalisation is to transform contractual obligations into international obligations, thereby turning every breach of contract into a violation of international law. Opponents doubt the purported effect of internationalisation since the proper law of State contracts tends to be host State law, not international law.

Sornarajah is a staunch opponent of the internationalisation of State contracts. The constant admonition in his extensive writings on the topic is the absence of any legal basis to transform contractual obligations into international obligations in the name of investment protection.[1] It is, therefore, fitting to revisit Sornarajah's trenchant criticism of internationalisation in a volume of essays dedicated to his academic career. I argue

[1] M. Sornarajah, 'The Myth of International Contract Law' (1981) 15 *Journal of World Trade Law* 187; *The Pursuit of Nationalized Property* (Hague: Kluwer Law International, 1986); *International Commercial Arbitration: The Problem of State Contracts* (Singapore: Longman, 1990); *Law of International Joint Ventures* (Singapore: Longman, 1992); *The International Law on Foreign Investment*, 1st to 3rd eds. (Cambridge: CUP, 1994, 2004, 2010); *Resistance and Change in the International Law on Foreign Investment* (Cambridge: CUP, 2015).

in this chapter that Sornarajah's three main objections to the internationalisation of State contracts foreshadowed three contemporary developments in the law on State responsibility for contractual breaches. The first is the assimilation of State contracts to treaties, which most modern-day arbitral tribunals are reluctant to accept (State contracts as treaties). The second is the use of stabilisation clauses to internationalise State contracts and the subsequent disappearance of stabilisation clauses from modern-day State contracts (Stabilisation clauses as tools of internationalisation). The third is the association of investor protection with immutable State contracts, which has been weakened by the modern-day preference for renegotiating and adapting State contracts to changing circumstances (Investment protection and immutable contracts). The upshot of these developments is that Sornarajah's distinct vision for a world of investment protection without internationalisation may one day become a reality.

State contracts as treaties

The analogy between contracts and treaties is not new. It was drawn by Lauterpacht in 1927 in a discussion on the 'legal nature of private law contracts and international law treaties'.[2] However, the analogy there is one between two private contracting individuals and two sovereign contracting States. State contracts, as the very name implies, are not contracts between private individuals. They are contracts between a private entity and a State or State entity. State contracts are not concluded by parties in a horizontal relationship, such as two individuals or two States. Instead, they are concluded by parties in a vertical relationship. State contracts are, in a sense, mixed contracts because they are neither archetypal private law contracts nor treaties. Moreover, the analogy between contracts and treaties is qualified. The law governing private law contracts and the legal consequences of breaching private law contracts are very different from that of treaties. According to Lauterpacht, '[i]t is the law of the State which gives objective force to a contract in private law, and it is the rule *pacta sunt servanda*, one of the fundamentals of international law, which imparts objective force to international treaties'.[3] A breach of a private law contract amounts at

[2] H. Lauterpacht, *Private Law Sources and Analogies of International Law* (London: Longmans Green & Sons, 1927), 156.

[3] Lauterpacht, *Private Law Sources and Analogies of International Law*, 156.

most to a violation of State law, whereas a breach of a treaty is a violation of international law. In order for State contracts to be internationalised, their identity to treaties both in nature and in 'objective force' must be justified.

To those who claim that State contracts concluded with developing countries are 'economic development agreements'[4] and, therefore, identical in nature to treaties owing to their importance, Sornarajah has two responses. First, he notes that conscious effort was made to allot one regime for State contracts concluded with developed countries and another for State contracts concluded with developing countries. For the former category of State contracts, 'there had been little doubt that contracts between [S]tate and foreign private parties were governed by the law of the [S]tate'.[5] But for the latter category of State contracts, '[t]here was a sudden need for a change as the European club of [S]tates was losing it[s] power in Africa and Asia . . . [and] that the new [S]tates that emerged could evolve laws unfavourable to European interests'.[6] Whether a State contract was identical in nature to a treaty and, thus, internationalised depended entirely on the developmental status of the contracting State. Sornarajah calls this a 'particularly obnoxious feature' of internationalisation.[7] Second, whatever State contracts are called, labelling is not a substitute for robust legal reasoning. The identification of 'economic development agreements' with treaties stemmed from the initiative of some arbitrators and publicists. Sornarajah maintains that 'the creation of international law takes more than the repetition of views of individuals, singly in academic articles and in individual arbitral awards or collectively by bodies of scholars which meet in conferences'.[8]

To those who claim that State contracts are identical in 'objective force' to the treaties because of applicability of *pacta sunt servanda* to both types of agreements, Sornarajah counters that because international law does not recognise the absolute sanctity of treaties, neither does it recognise

4 A. Verdross, 'Quasi-International Agreements and International Economic Transactions' (1964) 18 *Yearbook of World Affairs* 230, 234; W. Wengler, 'Les accords entre Etats et entreprises étrangères sont-ils des traités de droit international?' (1972) 76 *Revue Générale de Droit International Public* 313, 343–345.

5 Sornarajah, *International Commercial Arbitration: The Problem of State Contracts*, 123.

6 Sornarajah, *International Commercial Arbitration: The Problem of State Contracts*, 123.

7 Sornarajah, *International Commercial Arbitration: The Problem of State Contracts*, 128.

8 Sornarajah, *International Commercial Arbitration: The Problem of State Contracts*, 131–132.

the absolute sanctity of State contracts.[9] While publicists like Wehberg are content assuming that incanting *pacta sunt servanda* internationalises State contracts and confers on them the 'objective force' of treaties,[10] Sornarajah spots and impugns this leap of logic. The true sting in Sornarajah's retort is not so much recourse to *pacta sunt servanda* by the proponents of internationalisation but the characterisation of *pacta sunt servanda* as the guardian of absolute contractual sanctity. While the principle of *pacta sunt servanda* does urge the keeping of promises, it does not urge the keeping of promises at all costs. When applied in the context of private law contracts, *pacta sunt servanda* is qualified by doctrines such as frustration, change of circumstances and supervening impossibility of performance, which permit the discharge or modification of the original contractual bargain.[11] When applied in the context of treaties, *pacta sunt servanda* is qualified by the doctrine *rebus sic stantibus*, or fundamental change in circumstances, which permits a contracting State to withdraw from or terminate a treaty.[12] Even if States have the 'objective force' of treaties, incanting *pacta sunt servanda* accords State contracts the same degree of sanctity that international law accords to treaties, not more. One would have to agree with Sornarajah that invoking *pacta sunt servanda* simply 'does not secure the foreign investment agreement to the extent desired by the proponents of … internationalisation'.[13]

The potential identity between State contracts and treaties is also a topical issue in investment treaty arbitration. This is because, in investment treaty arbitration, foreign investors can bring claims against host

[9] Sornarajah, *International Commercial Arbitration: The Problem of State Contracts*, 137–142; Sornarajah, *Law of International Joint Ventures*, 295–296; Sornarajah, *The International Law on Foreign Investment*, 3rd ed., 297–298.

[10] H. Wehberg, 'Pacta Sunt Servanda' (1959) 53 *A.J.I.L.* 775, 786: 'We have described above the rule of *[p]acta sunt servanda* as a general principle of law that is found in all nations. It follows, therefore, that the principle is valid exactly in the same manner, whether it is in respect of contracts between [S]tates or in respect of contracts between [S]tates and private companies'; see also Verdross, 'Quasi-International Agreements and International Economic Transactions', 234; Wengler, 'Les accords entre Etats et entreprises étrangères sont-ils des traités de droit international?', 343–345; J.-F. Lalive, 'Les Contrats d'Etat: Développements Récents et Perspectives d'Avenir' (1983) 181 *R.D.C.* 163, 192.

[11] R. Geiger, 'The Unilateral Change of Economic Development Agreements' (1974) 23 *I.C.L.Q.* 73, 87–99.

[12] Vienna Convention on the Law of Treaties (adopted 23 May 1969, entered into force 27 January 1980) 1155 UNTS 331, Art. 62.

[13] Sornarajah, *The International Law on Foreign Investment*, 3rd ed., 296.

States for a breach of contract.[14] There is a sizeable number of such claims. A contract claim is distinct from a treaty claim,[15] although the two may sometimes overlap. The former alleges a breach of contract while the latter a breach of an applicable investment treaty. As not every breach of contract gives rise to a breach of treaty according to investment treaty arbitral jurisprudence, the evolving law on State responsibility for contractual breaches confirms that State contracts cannot be assimilated to treaties. Sornarajah already argued against the assimilation more than 30 years ago. The manner in which the potential overlap between contract claims and umbrella clause (A) and fair and equitable treatment (FET) claims (B) has been addressed by investment treaty tribunals suggests that Sornarajah's view is the better one. It also suggests that any overlap between a contract claim and a treaty claim is better assessed on a case-by-case basis.

When a breach of contract breaches an umbrella clause

Around half of the investment treaties currently in force contain umbrella clauses. Notwithstanding some textual variation, these call for the respect or observance of obligations undertaken by the host State towards the foreign investor. If a host State is found to have breached an umbrella clause, its international responsibility will be engaged for violating a treaty obligation. What is far less certain is whether the breach of a contractual obligation by a host State breaches an umbrella clause. Umbrella clauses receive incisive treatment by C.L. Lim in Chapter 13, which I had the benefit of reading in preparation for this chapter. While Lim and I agree that the presence of an umbrella clause in an applicable investment treaty does not necessarily entail the internationalisation of State contracts (what I will call umbrella clause internationalisation), we part company on the reading of certain key awards that have fuelled the interpretive controversy over umbrella clauses.

14 Z. Douglas, 'Investment Treaty Arbitration and ICSID', in J. Crawford, A. Pellet, and S. Olleson (eds.), *The Law of International Responsibility* (Oxford: Oxford University Press, 2010), 815, 817.

15 The leading award on the contract–treaty distinction holds that '[e]ach of these claims will be determined by reference to its own proper or applicable law – in the case of the BIT, by international law; in the case of the Concession Contract, by the proper law of the contract', see *Compañia de Aguas del Aconquija SA and Vivendi Universal* v. *Argentina*, Decision on Annulment (Fortier, Crawford, Fernández Rozas), 3 July 2002 (ICSID Case No. ARB/97/3), para. 96.

Recourse to the canons of treaty interpretation in Articles 31 and 32 of the Vienna Convention on the Law of Treaties of 1969 (VCLT) to decipher the effect of umbrella clauses on contractual rights is an optimal starting point. However, the interpretation of an umbrella clause arguably poses a greater challenge than a garden variety treaty clause.[16] There are several reasons for this. First, the debut of an umbrella clause in the 1959 Abs-Shawcross Draft Convention on Investments Abroad provoked intense disagreement among commentators on the viability of umbrella clause internationalisation. Umbrella clauses, thus, carry the stigma of internationalisation, making it nearly impossible to interpret umbrella clauses without taking a position on the internationalisation of State contracts (2.1.1). Second, although ascertaining the intent of States lies at the heart of treaty interpretation,[17] *SGS* v. *Pakistan* is a valuable case study on just how elusive State intent with respect to the effect of an umbrella clause on contractual rights can be (2.1.2). Third, the *SGS* v. *Philippines* approach to umbrella clauses – enhanced protection to State contracts without internationalisation – is regularly misunderstood by both its adherents and its critics. The resulting confusion is another hurdle to the interpretation of umbrella clauses (2.1.3). Fourth and finally, differences in the categorisation of key awards and their progeny on umbrella clauses go beyond mere semantics. The differences change the level of support in arbitral *jurisprudence* for umbrella clause internationalisation (2.1.4). The remainder of this section elaborates on each of these reasons.

Early resistance to umbrella clause internationalisation

Article II of the Abs-Shawcross Draft Convention alluded to the possibility of contractual breaches engaging the international responsibility of States:

> Each Party shall at all times ensure the observance of any undertakings, which it may have given in relation to investments made by nationals of any other Party.

In the official commentary to the Abs-Shawcross Draft Convention, the drafters averred that Article II represented one of the 'fundamental principles of international law regarding the treatment of the property, rights, and interests of aliens' whereby no distinction was drawn 'between

[16] See Chapter 13 by C.L. Lim.

[17] E. Bjorge, *The Evolutionary Interpretation of Treaties* (Oxford: OUP, 2014), 56–141.

the rule [of *pacta sunt servanda*] applicable to treaties and that applicable to contracts with aliens'.[18] This led one commentator to infer that '[t]he purpose of [Article II] is to dispel whatever doubts may possibly exist as to whether a unilateral violation of a concession contract is an international wrong'[19] and another to challenge the accuracy of Article II as a restatement of international law as its drafters claimed.[20] It is generally accepted that a breach of contract per se does not violate international law.[21] Schwarzenberger captured the anti-internationalisation sentiment in his observation that Article II represented '[a] far-reaching departure from the law as it stands and may tilt the balance too far in favour of the investor'.[22]

Most modern day tribunals resist umbrella clause internationalisation. Crawford helpfully identified four 'schools of thought' on umbrella clauses in his 2008 Freshfields lecture.[23] To date, there are only four awards – *Noble Ventures* v. *Romania*,[24] *BIVAC* v. *Paraguay*,[25] *Duke*

[18] H. Abs and Lord H. Shawcross, 'The Proposed Convention to Protect Private Foreign Investment' (1960) 9 *Journal of Public Law* 115, 119–120; also Lord H. Shawcross, 'The Problems of Foreign Investment in International Law' (1961) 102 *R.D.C.* 335, 351–355.

[19] I. Seidl-Hohenveldern, 'The Abs-Shawcross Draft Convention to Protect Private Foreign Investment: Comments on the Round Table' (1961) 10 *Journal of Public Law* 100, 104.

[20] S.D. Metzger, 'Multilateral Conventions for the Protection of Private Foreign Investment' (1960) 9 *Journal of Public Law* 133, 137.

[21] C.C. Hyde, *International Law Chiefly as Interpreted and Applied by the United States*, 2nd rev ed. (Boston: Little, 1945), vol. II, 988, s. 303; F.A. Mann, 'State Contracts and State Responsibility' (1960) 54 *A.J.I.L.* 572, 574; R.Y. Jennings, 'State Contracts in International Law' (1961) 37 *B.Y.I.L.* 156, 165–168; C.F. Amerasinghe, 'State Breaches of Contracts with Aliens and International Law' (1964) 58 *A.J.I.L.* 881, 897; H. Pazarci, 'La responsabilité internationale des Etats à l'occasion des contrats conclus entre Etats et personnes privées étrangères' (1975) 79 *Revue Générale de Droit International Public* 354, 371–372; G.R. Delaume, 'State Contracts and Transnational Arbitration' (1981) 75 *A.J.I.L.* 784, 806; G. Sacerdoti, 'State Contracts and International Law: A Reappraisal' (1986–1987) 7 *Italian Yearbook of International Law* 26, 46; S.M. Schwebel, 'On Whether the Breach by a State of a Contract with an Alien is a Breach of International Law', in Stephen Myron Schwebel (ed.), *Justice in International Law: Selected Writings of Stephen M Schwebel* (Hague: Grotius, 1994), 425, 434.

[22] G. Schwarzenberger, 'The Abs-Shawcross Draft Convention on Investments Abroad: A Critical Commentary' (1960) 9 *Journal of Public Law* 147, 154–155.

[23] J. Crawford, 'Treaty and Contract in Investment Arbitration' (2008) 24(3) *Arbitration International* 351, 367–370.

[24] Award (Böckstiegel, Lever, Dupuy), 12 October 2005 (ICSID Case No. ARB/01/11), paras. 53–54.

[25] Decision of the Tribunal on Objections to Jurisdiction (Knieper, Fortier, Sands), 29 May 2009 (ICSID Case No. ARB/07/9), paras. 141–142.

Energy v. *Ecuador*,[26] and *SGS* v. *Paraguay* – where the tribunals endorsed umbrella clause internationalisation.[27]

SGS v. *Pakistan*

The dispute in *SGS* v. *Pakistan* arose from outstanding payment owed by Pakistan to SGS under a customs inspection services contract and the termination of the said contract by Pakistan. After unsuccessfully seeking redress from Swiss courts, SGS filed a request for arbitration with ICSID pursuant to the dispute settlement provision in the Switzerland–Pakistan investment treaty. One of the claims submitted to the ICSID tribunal by SGS was that Pakistan, in committing a breach of the contract, violated Article 11, the umbrella clause in the Switzerland–Pakistan investment treaty:

> Either Contracting Party shall constantly guarantee the observance of commitments it has entered into with respect to the investments of the investors of the other Contracting Party.[28]

Counsel for SGS argued that the wording of Article 11 was sufficiently clear for the tribunal to find that '[i]f I am the government and if I breach a contract, by the same token I will breach a treaty, so the useful effect of this is to create this mirror effect, to say that I will elevate in essence, and that's what it does, it may be far-reaching but that's what it does, to elevate breaches of contract as breaches of a treaty'.[29] Without commenting on Pakistan's apparent acquiescence in SGS' reading of Article 11, the tribunal opined that Article 11 could not be construed in the way suggested by SGS without '[c]lear and convincing evidence that such was indeed the shared intent of the Contracting Parties' to the investment treaty.[30] The tribunal added that while States are free to conclude umbrella clauses that elevated all contractual obligations into international obligations, there has to be 'clear and persuasive evidence' that

[26] Award (Kaufmann-Kohler, Pinzón, van den Berg), 18 August 2008 (ICSID Case No. ARB/04/19), para. 325.

[27] Award (Alexandrov, Donovan, Mexia), 10 February 2012, incorporating the Decision on Jurisdiction (Alexandrov, Donovan, Mexia), 12 February 2010 (ICSID Case No. ARB/07/29), paras. 168–169.

[28] Decision of the Tribunal on Objections to Jurisdiction (Feliciano, Faurès, Thomas), 6 August 2003 (ICSID Case No. ARB/01/13), para. 97.

[29] Decision of the Tribunal on Objections to Jurisdiction (Feliciano, Faurès, Thomas), para. 99.

[30] Decision of the Tribunal on Objections to Jurisdiction (Feliciano, Faurès, Thomas), para. 167.

such an expansive interpretation was intended.[31] In the case of Article 11, this evidence was missing.

In rejecting SGS' reading of Article 11 without proposing an alternative interpretation, the award in *SGS* v. *Pakistan* appeared to strip Article 11 of all legal effect. Crawford criticises the tribunal's insistence on 'clear and convincing evidence' and 'clear and persuasive evidence' before the consequences of invoking an umbrella clause can be spelt out, as 'effectively depriv[ing] the umbrella clause of any content, contrary to the principle of *effet utile* and to the apparent intent of the drafters'.[32] But what could the drafters of the Switzerland–Pakistan investment treaty have intended for Article 11 if its meaning was still obscure after an examination of the text and the treaty's object and purpose?

Considering that disputes submitted to investment treaty arbitration always involve a respondent State that was party to the applicable investment treaty, States should reproduce and rely on records of the drafting history of umbrella clauses in their written submissions to the tribunal. Yet, despite some tribunals highlighting the pertinence of the '*travaux* of the BIT' to the interpretation of an umbrella clause,[33] publicly available written submissions of host States generally do not contain any discussion of the *travaux* on an umbrella clause. In *SGS* v. *Pakistan*, Pakistan did not supply the *travaux* of the Switzerland–Pakistan investment treaty, and the tribunal neither pressed Pakistan for it, nor requested its production by Switzerland. After the award in *SGS* v. *Pakistan* was issued, Switzerland wrote a letter to the Deputy-Secretary General of ICSID, objecting to 'the very narrow interpretation given to the meaning of Article 11 by the Tribunal, which ... runs counter to the intention of Switzerland'.[34]

However, pre- or post-award elucidations by States on how an investment treaty provision should be interpreted are rare.[35] '*Traxaux* of the

[31] Decision of the Tribunal on Objections to Jurisdiction (Feliciano, Faurès, Thomas), para. 173.

[32] Crawford, 'Treaty and Contract in Investment Arbitration', 368.

[33] *CMS Gas Transmission Company* v. *Argentina*, Decision on Annulment (Guillaume, Elaraby, Crawford), 25 September 2007 (ICSID Case No. ARB/01/8), para. 95(f).

[34] Letter from the Swiss Secretariat for Economic Affairs to the ICSID Secretary-General, 'Umbrella Clauses in Bilateral Investment Agreements', 1 October 2003, 19 Mealey's International Arbitration Reports E1.

[35] There are two other instances of post-award elucidations. The first is the series of meetings between representatives of the Netherlands and the Czech Republic in 2002 after the Partial Award in *CME* v. *Czech Republic* (Kühn, Schwebel, Háandl), 13 September 2001 (UNCITRAL) was rendered. In the Final Award, the tribunal was guided by the common position reached by Dutch and Czech officials on the interpretation of the Netherlands–Czech Republic investment treaty, 14 March 2003 (UNCITRAL), paras.

BIT' may not exist. Relying on extensive interviews conducted with government officials intimately connected with the conclusion of BITs in their respective countries, political scientists Poulsen and Aisbett discovered that many countries have traditionally viewed the signing of investment treaties as 'photo opportunities' with visiting heads of State and pay significantly less attention to the terms of the treaty.[36] They have rarely bothered to keep records of the negotiations, if negotiations indeed took place. Some countries draw up a model investment treaty and adopt it as a template.[37] A new investment treaty can be swiftly concluded if treaty negotiators are content to import provisions from the model treaty. In *SGS* v. *Pakistan*, Pakistan was unable to point the tribunal to any *travaux* on the umbrella clause for a good, yet unsettling, reason:

> [T]he claim in 2001 took everyone within the Pakistani bureaucracy by complete surprise. When learning of the dispute, Pakistan's attorney

87–93, 400, 437, 504. The second and more recent is the exchange of letters between Laos and China in 2014 over the applicability of the China–Laos investment treaty to investments made in Macau. In *Sanum Investments Ltd.* v. *Laos*, the tribunal found that investments made in Macau, a Portuguese protectorate until 1999, after which it became a Special Administrative Region of China, were protected by the China–Laos investment treaty concluded in 1993, Award on Jurisdiction (Sureda, Stern, Hanotiau), 13 December 2013 (PCA Case No. 2013–13), paras. 219–300. On 7 January 2014, the Laotian Ministry of Foreign Affairs wrote to the Chinese Embassy in Vientiane, expressing the view that the China–Laos investment treaty did not extend to Macau and seeking Chinese views on the same matter. The Chinese Embassy agreed with Laos' interpretation of the scope of the treaty. This exchange of letters was pivotal to the decision of the High Court of Singapore to grant Laos' application to set aside the Award on Jurisdiction, see *Government of the Lao People's Democratic Republic* v. *Sanum Investments Ltd.* [2014] SGHC 15.

[36] L. Poulsen and E. Aisbett, 'When the Claim Hits: Bilateral Investment Treaties and Bounded Rational Learning' (2013) 65(2) *World Politics* 273, 280, 296 (Table 6). Officials from the following 29 countries participated in the study: Cambodia, Canada, Chile, China, Costa Rica, Croatia, Czech Republic, Denmark, Dominican Republic, Democratic Republic of Congo, Ecuador, Finland, Germany, Ghana, Estonia, Jamaica, Japan, Lebanon, Malaysia, Mexico, Netherlands, Pakistan, South Africa, Sri Lanka, Sweden, Switzerland, Thailand, United Kingdom and United States. This ground-breaking research appears to defeat the view that there is solid 'evidence of the origins of the umbrella clause, including the intentions of the drafters involved in producing the first formulations of the umbrella clause … [to] suggest[] that the umbrella clause had been intended effectively to ensure that [S]tate contracts (and other "obligations" of the host State) are lifted out of the domain of the host State's legal system so that, at least, the obligation to perform such obligations is not governed exclusively by the proper law', A. Sinclair, State Contracts in Investment Treaty Arbitration, PhD thesis (University of Cambridge, 2013), 163.

[37] See chapter contributions in Chester Brown (ed.), *Oxford Commentaries on International Law – Commentaries on Selected Model Investment Treaties* (Oxford: OUP, 2013).

general – one of the top experts on international public law in South Asia – actually had to look up 'BITs' and 'ICSID' on Google. And when inquiring with the relevant ministries, there were almost no records of Pakistan's past BIT negotiations with Switzerland. There were no files or documentation in any of the responsible ministries and no indication that the treaty had ever been discussed in Parliament. In fact, the treaty itself was nowhere to be found, and the government had to request a copy from Switzerland through formal channels.[38]

In light of Pakistan's unfamiliarity with the circumstances under which the Switzerland–Pakistan investment treaty was concluded, Switzerland's post-award elaboration on Article 11 more likely reflected Swiss intent, rather than the joint intent of Switzerland and Pakistan. Therefore, even after applying the canons of treaty interpretation found in Articles 31 and 32 of the VCLT, it is still not entirely clear if Article 11 of the Switzerland–Pakistan investment treaty directs a tribunal to endorse umbrella clause internationalisation.

SGS v. *Philippines*

When a breach of contract is the basis for an umbrella clause claim but will be judged by the tribunal in accordance with the proper law of the contract and not international law, every contractual obligation attracts the protection of an umbrella clause, but no contractual obligation is assimilated to an international obligation. By this approach, a breach of contract is far more likely to engage a host State's liability under national law and not its international responsibility even when an umbrella clause is invoked. As explained by the tribunal in *SGS* v. *Philippines*:

> [The umbrella clause] makes it a breach of the BIT for the host State to fail to observe binding commitments, including contractual commitments, which it has assumed with regard to specific investments. But it does not convert the issue of the extent or content of such obligations into an issue of international law . . . It is a conceivable function of a provision such as Article X(2) of the Swiss-Philippines BIT to provide assurances to foreign investors with regard to the performance of obligations assumed by the host State under its own law with regard to specic investments – in effect, to help secure the rule of law in relation to investment protection.[39]

[38] Poulsen and Aisbett, 'When the Claim Hits', 280.

[39] Decision of the Tribunal on Objections to Jurisdiction (El-Kosheri, Crawford, Crivellaro (partially dissenting)), 29 January 2004 (ICSID Case No. ARB/02/6), para. 128 (original emphasis). Art. X(2) provides: 'Each of the Contracting Parties shall observe all obligations entered into with respect to an investment in its territory made by an investor of the other Contracting Party.' Author's translation from the original French.

Stressing that the logic applied by the *SGS* v. *Philippines* tribunal to umbrella clauses was a straightforward one, one member of the tribunal subsequently added the clarification that:

> The purpose of the umbrella clause is to allow enforcement without internationalisation and without transforming the character and content of the underlying obligation.[40]

According to the *SGS* v. *Philippines* award therefore, the protection conferred by umbrella clauses on contractual rights is the enforcement of contractual obligations against host States by investment treaty tribunals. This reading of an umbrella clause complements the leading and unchallenged pronouncement of the first ad hoc Committee in *Vivendi* v. *Argentina* on the difference between a contract claim and a treaty claim. According to this tribunal, '[e]ach of these claims will be determined by reference to its own proper or applicable law – in the case of the BIT, by international law; in the case of the Concession Contract, by the proper law of the contract'.[41] The endgame of arguing that a breach of contract simultaneously violates an umbrella clause is, therefore, to bring a contract claim within the purview of investment treaty arbitration. Umbrella clauses, thus, authorise investment treaty tribunals to decide contract claims by applying the proper law of the contract.

Although one commentator claims that the interpretive approach of the tribunal in *SGS* v. *Philippines* is the approach that other tribunals interpreting umbrella clauses are converging towards,[42] the rationale adopted by the *SGS* v. *Philippines* has been a source of confusion. Some tribunals endorse the *SGS* v. *Philippines award*, and yet fail to appreciate what the tribunal was saying. The erroneous reading of the *SGS* v. *Philippines* award has occurred with worrying regularity.

The dubious honour for the most severe mischaracterisation probably goes to the *Noble Ventures* v. *Romania* tribunal:

> [I]n SGS v. Philippines, supra, the treaty clause was formulated so as to assimilate the host State's contractual obligations to its treaty obligations under the bilateral investment treaty . . .[43]

[40] Crawford, 'Treaty and Contract in Investment Arbitration', 370.

[41] Decision on Annulment (Fortier, Crawford, Fernández Rozas), para. 96.

[42] J. Antony, 'Umbrella Clauses since *SGS v Pakistan* and *SGS v Philippines* – A Developing Consensus' (2013) 29(4) *Arbitration International* 607, 618, 638.

[43] Award, *op. cit.*, para. 59.

The *SGS* v. *Philippines* tribunal, and one of its members in a subsequent publication, expressly rejected umbrella clause internationalisation. Occasions of mischaracterisation may multiply. To date, only three tribunals[44] and three commentators have fully grasped the firm resistance of the tribunal in *SGS* v. *Philippines* to umbrella clause internationalisation.[45]

The *SGS* v. *Philippines* award has also been wrongly criticised. According to the tribunals in *El Paso* v. *Argentina* and *PanAm* v. *Argentina*, the tribunal in *SGS* v. *Philippines* had drawn 'contradictory conclusions':

> [T]he Tribunal stated that, although the umbrella clause transforms the contract claims into treaty claims, first 'it does not convert the issue of the extent or content of such obligations into an issue of international law' (Decision, [para] 128, original emphasis), which means that the 'contract claims/treaty claims' should be assessed according to the national law of the contract and not the treaty standards . . . In other words, the Tribunal asserts that a treaty claim should not be analysed according to treaty standards, which seems quite strange . . .[46]

Upon closer inspection, the two tribunals appear to have missed the point that the tribunal in *SGS* v. *Philippines* was making. First, the *SGS* v. *Philippines* tribunal did not state that 'the umbrella clause transforms the contract claims into treaty claims'. On the contrary, it found that an umbrella clause '*does not* convert questions of contract law into questions of treaty law'.[47] Secondly, the purpose of maintaining a distinction

[44] *Eureko* v. *Poland*, Partial Award (Fortier, Schwebel, Rajski (dissenting)), 19 August 2005, paras. 256–257; *CMS* v. *Argentina*, Decision of the ad hoc Committee on the Application for Annulment of the Argentine Republic (Guillaume, Elaraby, Crawford), 25 September 2007 (ICSID Case No. ARB/01/8), paras. 95–97; *Toto Construzioni Generali SpA* v. *Lebanon*, Decision on Jurisdiction (van Houtte, Feliciani, Moghaizel), 11 September 2009 (ICSID Case No. ARB/07/12), para. 202.

[45] C. Schreuer, 'Travelling the BIT Route: Of Waiting Periods, Umbrella Clauses and Forks in the Road' (2004) 5 *J.W.I.T.* 231, 255; M. Sasson, *Substantive Law in Investment Treaty Arbitration – The Unsettled Relationship between International and Municipal Law* (Hague: Kluwer Law International, 2010), 184–185, 192; Sinclair, *State Contracts in Investment Treaty Arbitration*, 145–147. It may be useful, as Schreuer suggests, to think of the *SGS* v. *Philippines* approach as extending '[t]he range of remedies . . . from redress for violations of international law to relief for breach of domestic law'.

[46] *El Paso Energy International Company* v. *Argentina*, Decision on Jurisdiction (Caflisch, Stern, Bernadini), 27 April 2006 (ICSID Case No. ARB/03/15), para. 76; *Pan American Energy & BP Argentina Exploration Company* v. *Argentina*, Decision on Preliminary Objections (Caflisch, Stern, Bernadini), 27 July 2006 (ICSID Case No. ARB/03/13, ARB/04/8), para. 105.

[47] Decision of the Tribunal on Objections to Jurisdiction (El-Kosheri, Crawford, Crivellaro (partially dissenting)), para. 126 (emphasis added).

between contract claims and treaty claims is to ensure that contractual claims are subjected to the proper law of the contract. According to the *SGS* v. *Philippines* tribunal, the function of an umbrella clause is to 'provide assurances to foreign investors with regard to the performance of obligations *assumed by the host State under its own law*'.[48] Nowhere is it suggested that 'treaty claims should be assessed according to the national law of the contract'. Finally, after pointing out that an umbrella clause 'does not change the proper law of the [investment contract] from the law of the Philippines to international law', it is hardly strange that a contractual claim 'should not be analysed according to treaty standards'.

Differences in categorisation

Even for opponents of umbrella clause internationalisation, the relevant awards cannot be neatly bifurcated into those that categorically reject umbrella clause internationalisation and those that try to mitigate umbrella clause internationalisation. The latter category refers to awards where the tribunal accepts that an umbrella clause internationalises State contracts, but tries nonetheless to circumvent treaty language by devising ways to suppress internationalisation. If the outcome of applying Articles 31 and 32 of the VCLT is umbrella clause internationalisation, then any attempt to alter this outcome subverts the spirit of treaty interpretation. The tribunal in *SGS* v. *Pakistan* came close to exemplifying this approach by its refusal to uphold umbrella clause internationalisation in the absence of 'clear and persuasive evidence' that this was what Switzerland and Pakistan intended for Article 11 of the Switzerland–Pakistan investment treaty. As pointed out earlier, the tribunal was subsequently chided by Switzerland for its excess of caution in interpreting Article 11. It should come as no surprise that later tribunals have steered clear of the *SGS* v. *Pakistan* tribunal's approach of reducing treaty interpretation to a matter of evidence.

The rest of the awards reflect three different interpretive approaches. The first, pioneered by *SGS* v. *Philippines*, rejects umbrella clause internationalisation (see *SGS* v. *Philippines*). The second, pioneered by *Joy Mining* v. *Egypt*, also rejects umbrella clause internationalisation but for a different reason.[49] The *Joy Mining* v. *Egypt* line of awards holds that only

[48] Decision of the Tribunal on Objections to Jurisdiction (El-Kosheri, Crawford, Crivellaro (partially dissenting)), para. 128 (emphasis added).

[49] Award on Jurisdiction (Orrego Vicuña, Craig, Weeramantry), 6 August 2004 (ICSID Case No. ARB/03/11), paras. 79, also 72, 75, 81.

contractual breaches committed in a State's sovereign, and not commercial, capacity can ever amount to a violation of an umbrella clause.[50] The third, spearheaded by *Noble Ventures* v. *Romania*, recognises umbrella clause internationalisation. Together with the abandoned *SGS* v. *Pakistan* approach, these three approaches make up the four 'schools of thought' that Crawford identified. When categorised in this manner, the sum of the awards on umbrella clauses evince an unmistakeable resistance to umbrella clause internationalisation. A bifurcated categorisation forces the awards into one of two extremes – the wholesale rejection or acceptance of umbrella clause internationalisation. The reality, as the foregoing discussion has tried to show, is more nuanced.

When a breach of contract breaches a fair and equitable treatment clause

The projected exclusion of umbrella clauses from newer investment treaties[51] has led some to regard FET clauses as 'de facto' umbrella clauses.[52] If a host State reneges on 'specific commitments' given to the foreign investor, this in itself may amount to a violation of FET.[53] Should 'specific' commitments' cover contractual commitments, then those in favour of umbrella clause internationalisation of State contracts would just as readily accept FET internationalisation of State contracts.

[50] Cf. Chapter 13 by C.L. Lim in this volume. Contrary to what Lim suggests, the tribunal in *El Paso* v. *Argentina*, which cited the *Joy Mining* v. *Egypt* award with approval, does not support umbrella clause internationalisation. Like the tribunal in *Joy Mining* v. *Egypt* (paras. 79, 81), the tribunal in *El Paso* v. *Argentina* adopted the *acta jure imperii/acta jure gestionis* distinction, with only the former capable of triggering a treaty violation, as the interpretive lens through which umbrella clauses should be viewed. According to the tribunal in *El Paso* v. *Argentina* (para. 81), 'the umbrella clause in Article II of the [United States–Argentina] BIT . . . will not extend the Treaty protection to breaches of an ordinary commercial contract entered into by the State or a State-owned entity, but will cover additional investment protections contractually agreed by the State as a sovereign – such as a stabilization clause – inserted in an investment agreement'. If umbrella clauses elevate only sovereign contractual breaches to treaty violations, there is no umbrella clause internationalisation. There is at best partial internationalisation.

[51] 2012 United States Model Bilateral Investment Treaty, online: www.state.gov (accessed 2 March 2015).

[52] L. Johnson and L. Sachs, 'International Investment Agreements, 2011–2012: A Review of Trends and New Approaches', in Andrea Bjorklund (ed.), *Yearbook on International Investment Law and Policy 2012–2013* (New York: Oxford University Press, 2014), 219, 229.

[53] *Metalpar* v. *Argentina*, Award on the Merits (Blanco, Cameron, Chabaneix), 6 June 2008 (ICSID Case No. ARB/03/5), paras. 185–186; *Glamis Gold* v. *USA*, Award (Young, Caron, Hubbard), 8 June 2009 (NAFTA-UNCITRAL), paras. 766–767.

However, it is questionable if an FET clause is so expansive that it encompasses an umbrella clause. If this were so, umbrella clauses would be rendered superfluous. States that deliberately exclude umbrella clauses from their treaties in order to avoid internationalising State contracts would have their actions nullified by the presence of an FET clause. Moreover, reading an umbrella clause into an FET clause imports the ongoing interpretive controversy over the nature of protection conferred by umbrella clauses to the interpretation of FET clauses, making it even harder to determine the content of FET.

Using FET clauses to internationalise State contracts is novel. Contractual breaches per se do not violate FET. Based on existing awards, only contractual breaches that are committed in a sovereign capacity ('Acta jure imperii'), that involve forced renegotiation ('Forced renegotiation') and that amount to an unjustified cancellation of the contract ('Unjustified cancellation') are more likely to violate FET. These awards confirm once again that Sornarajah's reservations towards the internationalisation of the State contracts are shared by the modern day-arbitral tribunals.

Acta jure imperii

Some tribunals have found that, in order for a breach of contract to violate FET, the host State had to be acting in its sovereign capacity. The *Duke Energy* v. *Ecuador* tribunal held that a violation of FET called for 'a violation different in nature from a contract breach, in other words a violation which the State commits in the exercise of its sovereign power'.[54] In this case, the commitment by the Ministry of Finance to establish a payment guarantee to discharge Ecuador's payment obligations under an electricity distribution contract 'entailed the exercise of sovereign power as it implied that funds would be drawn from the Ministry and Public Credit's account'.[55] The subsequent failure to establish this payment guarantee was, therefore, a violation of FET.[56]

[54] Award (Kaufmann-Kohler, Pinzón, van den Berg), para. 345; see also *Impregilo SpA* v. *Pakistan*, Decision on Jurisdiction (Guillaume, Cremades, Landau), 22 April 2005 (ICSID Case No. ARB/03/3), para. 260.

[55] Award (Kaufmann-Kohler, Pinzón, van den Berg), para. 360.

[56] Award (Kaufmann-Kohler, Pinzón, van den Berg), paras. 361, 364; see also *Siemens AG* v. *Argentina*, Award (Sureda, Brower, Janeiro), 6 February 2007 (ICSID Case No. ARB/02/8), para. 308: 'The Tribunal also finds that when a government awards a contract, which includes among its critical provisions an undertaking of that government to conclude agreements with its provinces, the same government cannot argue that the

However, not every exercise of sovereign authority entails the violation of FET. In *AES* v. *Hungary*, although the tribunal agreed with the claimants that legitimate expectations are part of the content of FET, it found that the claimants had no legitimate expectation that the original terms of their energy supply contract could not be modified by legislation.[57] As Hungary never assumed any undertaking, contractual or otherwise, towards the claimants relating to the exercise of its sovereign powers, there were no self-imposed constraints on its sovereign prerogative to legislate. The claimants' FET claim failed because no legitimate expectations were breached. The tribunal was also unsympathetic to the claimants' argument that its legitimate expectations with respect to the stability of the Hungarian legal framework were frustrated by the subsequent legislative amendments. It stressed that the expectations of stability 'will always depend on the specific circumstances that surrounds the investor's decision to invest and the measures taken by the [S]tate in the public interest'.[58] The tribunal reiterated that the absence of any express undertaking by Hungary to refrain from changing its laws was the deciding factor in the dismissal of the FET claim.

Forced renegotiation

The few awards where the conduct of a host State during contractual renegotiations has been challenged as a violation of FET highlight how a genuine attempt at renegotiation cannot be about the host State imposing its will on the foreign investor. A host State that initiates a renegotiation of an investment contract, only to ride roughshod over the investor during the negotiation process will most likely violate FET.

In *Desert Line* v. *Yemen*, the Omani claimant signed a total of eight road construction contracts with Yemen. Yemen defaulted on various progress payments, and the matter was referred to arbitration in Yemen. The arbitrators held that the Yemeni government owed a substantial debt to the claimant, but despite the binding validity of this arbitral award on Yemen, no payment was forthcoming. Yemen subsequently concluded a settlement agreement with the reluctant claimant, where the amount judged owing in the earlier arbitral award was reduced by half. When

structure of the State does not permit it to fulfil such undertaking. This runs counter to the principle of good faith underlying fair and equitable treatment.'

57 Award (von Wobeser, Stern, Rowley), 23 September 2010 (ICSID Case No. ARB/07/22), paras. 9.3.6–9.3.35.

58 Award (von Wobeser, Stern, Rowley), 23 September 2010 (ICSID Case No. ARB/07/22), para. 9.3.30.

the matter was submitted to investment treaty arbitration, the tribunal noted that Yemen relied on a potent mix of financial duress – refusal to pay, which brought the claimant to the brink of bankruptcy just prior to the signing of the settlement and physical duress – harassment of the claimant's work sites by armed men, arrests and threats to the personal safety of the claimant's employees, to coerce the claimant into signing the settlement agreement.[59] The settlement agreement, procured through coercion and harassment of the claimant, evinced Yemen's violation of its treaty obligation to accord FET to protected investments.[60]

The facts of *Desert Line* v. *Yemen* are extreme. A claimant need not be physically intimidated in order for a tribunal to find that its consent to a renegotiated investment contract was vitiated by coercion. In *Suez* v. *Argentina*, AASA, an Argentinian company formed by a consortium which included the claimants, was awarded a 30-year concession to operate water distribution and waste water services in the City of Buenos Aires. One of the most important changes Argentina made to its regulatory framework in response to the economic crisis of the early 2000s was the abolition of automatic tariff adjustments in the public utilities sector in accordance with international indices. This gravely affected the profitability of the Suez concession. It is against this backdrop of economic instability and depressed profits that Argentina broached the renegotiation of the concession with AASA. The tribunal noticed a marked difference in the way the concession was renegotiated and revised pre- and post-crisis. The post-crisis renegotiation process challenged by the claimants as a breach of FET 'had an extremely forceful character quite different from what the legal framework provided and from the way previous negotiations had taken place'.[61] The numerous changes demanded by Argentina of the concession, which were already secured by newly enacted legislation, led the tribunal to question if 'Argentina sought to structure the "renegotiation" process in such a way as to severely limit or indeed curtail the contractual freedom of AASA in order to arrive at a predetermined result desired by

[59] Award (Tercier, Paulsson, El-Kosheri), 6 February 2008 (ICSID Case No. ARB/05/17), paras. 181–186.

[60] Award (Tercier, Paulsson, El-Kosheri), 6 February 2008 (ICSID Case No. ARB/05/17), para. 179.

[61] Decision on Liability (Salacuse, Kaufmann-Kohler, Nikken), 30 July 2010 (ICSID Case No. ARB/03/17), para. 241.

Argentina'.[62] A renegotiation procured through threats clearly falls short of FET. However, as the tribunal in *Suez* v. *Argentina* pointed out, a renegotiation that leaves no room for compromise is no different from the coerced acceptance of one-sided terms and, therefore, equally illustrative of host State conduct that violates FET.

Unjustified cancellation

A cancellation may violate FET if the host State is, in the tribunal's view, unable to justify why the investment contract was cancelled. In *Gemplus* v. *Mexico*, the tribunal was sceptical that having a foreign concessionaire run a national vehicle registry in Mexico, with the aim of lowering the frequency of car thefts and criminal activity, posed 'imminent peril to national security', thereby warranting a takeover by the Mexican government.[63] By invoking national security, Mexico displayed 'a clear intention . . . to terminate the Concession and Concession Agreement without due regard to the Claimants' legal rights'.[64] In light of this overt intent, the list of deficiencies supplied by Mexico with respect to the claimants' performance of the concession prior to its termination came across as afterthoughts, cobbled together to give the impression that there were many good reasons for termination. The way by which Mexico orchestrated the termination of the concession in *Gemplus* v. *Mexico* was criticised by the tribunal as 'irrational, perverse and tainted with bad faith towards the Concessionaire'[65] and found to be a violation of FET.[66]

When a host State is contractually obliged to give the investor an opportunity to cure the defects in its performance of the contract and to exercise the right of termination only when the investor refuses to do

[62] Decision on Liability (Salacuse, Kaufmann-Kohler, Nikken), 30 July 2010 (ICSID Case No. ARB/03/17), para. 242.

[63] *Gemplus SA et al.* v. *United Mexican States* & *Talsud SA* v. *United Mexican States*, Award (Fortier, Gomez, Veeder), 16 June 2010 (ICSID Case No. ARB(AF)/04/3) & (ICSID Case No. ARB(AF)/04/4), paras. 7–25.

[64] Award (Tercier, Paulsson, El-Kosheri), 6 February 2008 (ICSID Case No. ARB/05/17), paras. 7–70.

[65] Award (Tercier, Paulsson, El-Kosheri), 6 February 2008 (ICSID Case No. ARB/05/17), paras. 4–183, 4–187.

[66] See also *Rumeli* v. *Kazakhstan*, Award (Hanotiau, Boyd, Lalonde), 29 July 2008 (ICSID Case No. ARB/05/16), para. 615; *Metalclad* v. *Mexico*, Award (Lauterpacht, Civiletti, Siqueiros), 30 August 2000 (ICSID Case No. ARB(AF)/97/1), para. 99; *Wena Hotels Ltd.* v. *Egypt*, Award (Leigh, Fadlallah, Wallace), 8 December 2000 (ICSID Case No. ARB/98/4), para. 84; *Compañia de Aguas del Aconquija SA & Vivendi Universal* v. *Argentina*, Award (Kaufmann-Kohler, Verea, Rowley), 20 August 2007 (ICSID Case No. ARB/97/3), para. 7.4.19.

so, denying the investor the opportunity of making amends can amount to a violation of FET. Conversely, when a host State exercises a contractual right to cancel the contract in response to breaches committed by the investor, there is no violation of FET.[67]

Stabilisation clauses as tools of internationalisation

There is always the risk that a host State may unilaterally modify or terminate rights found in State contracts, to the detriment of the foreign investor. Therefore, the most savvy among them (or their legal team) have devised a clause that expressly forbids the host State from modifying any aspect of the contract without the consent of the foreign investor. Such a clause freezes contractual rights at the date of the making of the contract and is commonly referred to as a stabilisation clause.

The idea that a stabilisation clause in a State contract can effectively insulate the contract from all host State legislative activity surfaced in the *Anglo-Iranian Oil Co Case*, which concerned the nationalisation of an oil concession by the Iranian government. The United Kingdom, espousing the claim of the Anglo-Iranian Oil Company before the ICJ in 1952, argued that the stabilisation clause in an oil concession was 'inserted with the specific object of making it legally impossible for the Government of Iran to put an end to the concession by some such measure of nationalization'.[68] The ICJ found that it had no jurisdiction over the dispute between the United Kingdom and Iran and, as a result, did not pronounce on the legal effect of a stabilisation clause.[69]

The UK pleadings in the *Anglo-Iranian Oil Co Case* did not articulate a clear link between stabilisation clauses and the internationalisation of State contracts. This was accomplished by Dupuy sitting as sole arbitrator in the highly controversial *Texaco* v. *Libya* award:

> [Stabilisation] clauses tend to remove all or part of the agreement from the internal law and to provide for its correlative submission to sui generis rules . . . or to a system which is properly an international law system.[70]

[67] See *Vannessa Ventures Ltd.* v. *Venezuela*, Award (Lowe, Brower, Stern), 16 January 2013 (ICSID Case No. ARB(AF)/04/6), paras. 221–222.

[68] (*United Kingdom* v. *Iran*) [1952] I.C.J. Rep 93, Observations and Submissions Presented by the Government of the United Kingdom of Great Britain and Northern Ireland in Regard to the Preliminary Objection Lodged by the Imperial Government of Iran, para. 12.

[69] (*United Kingdom* v. *Iran*) (Jurisdiction) [1952] I.C.J. Rep 93.

[70] Award on the Merits, 19 January 1977, 53 I.L.R. 389.

According to Dupuy, a stabilisation clause turns every contractual obligation into an international obligation, the breach of which violates international law. Although some favour this reading of stabilisation clauses,[71] Sornarajah does not:

> It may not be possible, as a matter of constitutional theory, for a [S]tate to bind itself by a contract made with a private party, particularly a foreign party, to fetter its legislative power. It is trite law that a legislature is not bound by its own legislation and has the power to change it. That being so, a provision in a contract cannot bind the [S]tate.[72]

Sornarajah's doubts are well-founded. While a stabilisation clause in a State contract is arguably enforceable against the State in the same way as any garden variety contractual clause, its intended effect – suspending an essential attribute of sovereignty – is so far-reaching that its legitimacy cannot be understood in terms of the private law of contract. A State can exercise its public powers in the public interest. In contrast, an individual has no public powers, which it can exercise in the public interest. Foreign investment contracts involving the undertaking of large-scale infrastructural, utilities, resource exploration and mining works, or the provision of services that benefit the public, require the screening, approval, participation and overall supervision of the contracting State *qua* sovereign. Given how a State's regulatory function is likely to dominate in State contracts, these contracts hardly resemble typical private law contracts concluded between individuals. The distinction is pronounced in France where some contracts between individuals and the administration are known as '*contrats administratifs*' and governed by French public law, not French private law.[73] As the private law of contract, whether in France or elsewhere, generally, does not contain any mechanism for assessing the legitimacy and enforceability of a contractual undertaking given by a contracting party *qua* sovereign, recourse must be had to a body of law that does.[74]

[71] *AGIP* v. *Congo*, Award (Trolle, Dupuy, Rouhani), 30 November 1979 (ICSID Case No. ARB/77/1), 67 ILR 318, 338; also dissenting opinion of G. Fitzmaurice in *Kuwait* v. *American Independent Oil Co. (Aminoil)*, Award (Reuter, Sultan, Fitzmaurice (partially dissenting)), 24 March 1982 (1982), 21 I.L.M. 976.

[72] Sornarajah, *The International Law on Foreign Investment*, 3rd ed., 282.

[73] P.-L. Frier and J. Petit, *Droit Administratif*, 9ème ed. (Paris: LGDJ 2014), 379 *et seq.*

[74] *Niger Delta Development Commission v. Nigeria Liquefied Natural Gas Company Ltd.*, commented in B. Adaralegbe, 'Stabilizing Fiscal Regimes in Long-Term Contracts: Recent Developments from Nigeria' (2008) I(III) *Journal of World Energy Law and Business* 239, 239–242.

A stabilisation clause is unique because it embodies an assurance that only a State may be in a position to give. Doubts over the enforceability of a stabilisation clause cannot be resolved simply by asking if a stabilisation clause is like any other contractual clause. The more fundamental question is whether the State has the capacity to limit the future exercise of its sovereignty by contract? The United Kingdom, notwithstanding its pro-stabilisation stance in the *Anglo-Iranian Oil Co Case*, consistently maintains that the power of the Crown to vary contracts via legislation cannot be circumscribed by contract.[75] In 1975, the United Kingdom passed the Petroleum and Submarine Pipe Lines Act, imposing new licensing and tax regulations on oil production in the North Sea.[76] This resulted in substantial changes to existing licences between the United Kingdom and both local and foreign contractors. The Act did not provide for compensation for any loss suffered as a result of the legislative changes. To criticisms that the Act gave the UK *carte blanche* to unilaterally rewrite its contractual obligations, the United Kingdom insisted that it was within the legitimate exercise of its sovereign powers to alter contractual obligations without prior consultation and without compensation.[77]

The vacillating stance of some States on the ability of stabilisation clauses to neutralise the sovereign prerogative to legislate only serves to deepen existing doubts over the enforceability of stabilisation clauses.[78] If a State lacks the capacity to conclude stabilisation clauses in the first place, a stabilisation clause is *ultra vires* the constitutional powers of the State and cannot be enforced. If it is within a State's constitutional mandate to conclude stabilisation clauses, but the State can still unilaterally modify contractual obligations via legislation at a later date, then a stabilisation clause is not a tool of internationalisation because it does not

[75] *Rederiaktiebolaget Amphitrite* v. *The King* [1921] K.B. 500, 503 (*per* Rowlatt J); *Cugden Rutile (No. 2) Pty Ltd. & Anor* v. *Gordon William Wesley Chalk* [1975] A.C. 520, 534 (*per* Lord Wilberforce); also *Williams & Humbert* v. *W & H Trade Marks (Jersey)* (1985) 75 I.L.R. 268, 314–15 (*per* Lord Templeman).

[76] c.74. The Act was repealed on 15 February 1999.

[77] For an overview of the impact of the Petroleum and Submarine Pipe Lines Act on North Sea oil concessions concluded with the United Kingdom, see D.W. Bowett, 'State Contracts with Aliens: Contemporary Developments on Compensation for Termination or Breach' (1988) 58 *B.Y.I.L.* 49, 58–59, fn 40.

[78] O. Schachter, 'International Law in Theory and Practice: General Course in Public International Law' (1982) 178 *R.D.C.* 1, 314; T. Wälde and G. Ndi, 'Stabilizing International Investment Commitments: International Law versus Contract Interpretation' (1996) 31 *Texas International Law Journal* 215, 220–236, 242; R. Dolzer and C. Schreuer, *Principles of International Investment Law*, 2nd ed. (Oxford: Oxford University Press, 2012), 75–77.

shield the contract from legislative changes. Persistent objections to using and viewing stabilisation clauses as tools of internationalisation[79] may explain why support for Dupuy's theory of internationalisation has sharply dwindled over the years.[80]

Even if stabilisation clauses are effective tools for the internationalisation of State contracts, the days of investors relying on stabilisation clauses to shield State contracts from legislative changes are probably over. A 2009 study of 76 modern investment contracts found that a full stabilisation clause, namely one that purports to insulate all contractual rights from all manner of interference by the host State, does not appear in contracts concluded with the governments of 'South Asia, Eastern Europe, Southern Europe, Central Asia or OECD countries'.[81] Developing States that have achieved economic progress and are keen to preserve or recover their regulatory autonomy would be extremely wary of stabilisation clauses.[82] When States are no longer willing to trade sovereignty for foreign capital injection, contractual rights carved in stone will gradually become a thing of the past. Today, 'stabilization clauses are highly speculative in terms of contract stability'.[83]

Investment protection and immutable contracts

Internationalisation was devised to confer maximum protection on State contracts. By using international law to sanction any breach of contract by the host State, so the proponents of internationalisation argue, the risk

[79] I echo Sornarajah's objections in 'Unraveling the Lex Causae in Investment Claims' (2014) 15 *J.W.I.T.* 757, 764–765.

[80] A lone contemporary supporter is J. Cantergreil, 'The Audacity of the Texaco/Calasiatic Award: René-Jean Dupuy and the Internationalization of Foreign Investment Law' (2011) 22(2) *E.J.I.L.* 441.

[81] A. Shemberg, 'Stabilization Clauses and Human Rights' (A research project conducted for IFC and the United Nations Special Representative of the Secretary-General on Business and Human Rights), 27 May 2009, online: www.ifc.org (accessed 1 March 2015), 21.

[82] Separate Opinion of Judge Padilla Nervo in the *Case Concerning the Barcelona Traction, Light and Power Company, Limited* (*Belgium* v. *Spain*) Second Phase (1970) I.C.J. Rep 3, 250: 'Perhaps modern international business practice has a tendency to be soft and partial towards the powerful and the rich, but no rule of law could be built on such flimsy bases. Investors who go abroad in search of profits take a risk and go there for better or for worse, not only for better. They should respect the institutions and abide by the national laws of the country where they chose to go.'

[83] W. Peter, *Arbitration and Renegotiation of International Investment Agreements* (Hague: Kluwer Law International, 1995), 230; cf. generally P. Cameron, *International Energy Investment Law: The Pursuit of Stability* (New York: Oxford University Press, 2010), paras. 2.19–2.56.

of the foreign investor being adversely affected by unilateral host State activity would be reduced to a minimum. The overriding objective of internationalisation is to make State contracts immutable. However, Sornarajah has always questioned if the key to investment protection necessarily lies in immutable contracts. Even if State contracts cannot be assimilated to treaties and even if stabilisation clauses do not beget internationalised contracts, this does not mean that the investor is deprived of protection. While some may consider protection found in host State laws transient since a State can alter its own laws,[84] there are two reasons why internationalisation has fallen from favour as a response to legislative change.

First, the possibility of bringing a claim for expropriation against the State when contractual rights are violated is a far more established method of vindicating contractual rights than internationalisation. An expropriation claim can be brought even if a State alters its legislation to the detriment of a State contract. The protection of property rights, and by extension contractual rights, is a constitutional guarantee in many countries. Unless the State takes the drastic step of amending its constitution, investors can be assured of constitutional protection for expropriated contractual rights, under domestic law.[85] In the event where there is no domestic constitutional protection for contractual rights, foreign investors who have the option of submitting their disputes with host States to international arbitration can still bring a claim for expropriated contractual rights under general international law[86] or under investment treaty law.[87] A claim for expropriated contractual rights avoids the controversy typically associated with a claim for internationalised contractual rights because both national and international laws on expropriation are relatively stable. Expropriation is lawful unless it is not accompanied by compensation, does not pursue a public purpose or is conducted without due process. Therefore, not every breach of contract will amount to an unlawful expropriation. A claim for expropriated contractual rights does not demand absolute protection for contractual

[84] R. Kreindler, 'The Law Applicable to International Investment Disputes', in N. Horn and S.M. Kröll (eds.), *Arbitrating Foreign Investment Disputes, Procedural and Substantive Legal Aspects* (Hague: Kluwer Law International, 2004), 401, 417.

[85] A.J. van der Walt, *Property and Constitution* (Cape Town: Pretoria 2012), 124.

[86] *Norwegian Shipowners' Claim* (*Norway* v. *United States*), Award, 13 October 1922 (1922) R.I.A.A. vol. I 307, 334.

[87] *Emmis International Holding BV & Ors* v. *Hungary*, Award (McLachlan, Lalonde, Thomas), 16 April 2014 (ICSID Case No. ARB/12/2), para. 169.

rights, while a claim for internationalised contractual rights does. The notion of inviolable contractual rights has never been recognised in international law. Support for internationalisation was bound to dissipate once it became apparent that its proponents were asking for the one thing that recourse to international law cannot deliver.

Second, over time, the appeal of immutable State contracts has been eclipsed by adaptable State contracts. Long-term State contracts are likely to experience changed circumstances. The renegotiation of contractual terms to accommodate changed circumstances is more likely to preserve the contractual relationship than a rigid insistence on the performance of the original contractual bargain. The tribunal in *Aminoil* v. *Kuwait* saw the benefits of renegotiation back in the early 1980s (even though attempts at renegotiation between Aminoil and Kuwait ultimately failed), and since then, more have championed the adaptation of State contracts to changed circumstances. Instead of a stabilisation clause, State contracts should contain a renegotiation clause. In 1992, Sornarajah counselled that 'the better strategy is to introduce in the contract clauses which provide for the renegotiation of the contract when circumstances upsetting the equilibrium of the contract occur'.[88] In 2013, Salacuse, an experienced negotiator of State contracts, offers the same advice to the investors. If a contractual relationship is worth maintaining, then 'it may be more realistic and wiser to think of an international deal as a *continuing negotiation* between the parties to the transactions as they seek to adjust their relationship to the rapidly changing international environment in which they must work together'.[89]

Conclusion

As laudable as investment protection is, it cannot, and this is a central tenet in Sornarajah's writings, be taken to extremes. Immutable State contracts are anathema to international law and international business practice. One does not need to adopt Sornarajah's developmental perspective to appreciate how incompatible the internationalisation of State contracts is with recent developments in the law of State responsibility on contractual breaches.

[88] Sornarajah, *Law of International Joint Ventures*, 306.

[89] J.W. Salacuse, *The Three Laws of International Investment – National, Contractual, and International Frameworks for Foreign Capital* (New York: Oxford University Press, 2013), 297 (original emphasis).

1. Early indications that State contracts could be assimilated to treaties have been disproved by the vast majority of arbitral tribunals interpreting umbrella and FET clauses. Both clauses are perceived to be investor-friendly and harboured the potential to internationalise State contracts. Yet, arbitral jurisprudence on these clauses leans heavily against internationalisation.
2. Stabilisation clauses, once a powerful tool of internationalisation, appear to have outlived their usefulness. The gradual disappearance of stabilisation clauses from modern-day State contracts may turn them from 'one of the most complex issues in international economic law',[90] into a non-issue.
3. The dubious legal basis for internationalisation makes it a poor safeguard against legislative change. Rather than running the futile argument that their contractual rights are inviolable, investors may be better off pursuing other options. Investors who decide to end their contractual relationship with the host State may bring a claim for expropriation. Those who decide to preserve the contractual relationship will renegotiate and adapt their contract to accommodate the changed circumstances.

State contracts have been and will continue to be one of the most common ways foreign investment enters a host State's territory. How State contracts and the rights arising therefrom are best protected will continue to be debated. Sornarajah's objections to the internationalisation of State contracts reveal his scepticism towards the availability of enhanced protection for contractual rights under international law. He is not alone.

[90] Wälde and Ndi, 'Stabilizing International Investment Commitments', 238.

PART VI

15

State capitalism and sovereign wealth funds: finding a "soft" location in international economic law

JIANGYU WANG

Introduction

State capitalism has become a formidable force in the international economy. As described in a Special Report of *The Economist*, state capitalism, which attempts to meld "the powers of the state with the powers of capitalism," is posing a potent alternative to liberal capitalism, which rests mainly upon free markets and private ownership.[1]

The magic of state capitalism lies in its ability to marry government control to market forces. "It depends on government to pick winners and promote economic growth. But, it also uses capitalist tools such as listing state-owned companies on the stock market and embracing globalization."[2] With such characteristics, Ian Bremmer asserts that state capitalism can take many forms, the most important being "national oil (and gas) corporations (NOCs), other state-owned enterprises (SOEs), privately owned national champions, and sovereign wealth funds (SWFs)."[3]

State capitalism, in its various forms, has been an international concern since the early days of its creation. As has been noted, state enterprises are the "new masters of the universe," thanks to their rapid spread at the global level.[4] The simplest and most straightforward activities of state enterprises are that they are swallowing resources overseas. National

[1] See, "The Visible Hand", in *Special Report: State Capitalism, The Economist*, 21 January 2012, available at www.economist.com/node/21542931 (visited 15 June 2015).

[2] *Id.*

[3] I. Bremmer, *The End of the Free Market: Who Wins the War between States and Corporations*, Kindle version (New York: Portfolio, 2010), Kindle location 841–851.

[4] See, "State Capitalism's Global Reach: New Masters of the Universe", in *Special Report: State Capitalism, The Economist*, 21 January 2012.

energy companies "are increasingly venturing abroad in order to lock up future energy supplies or forming alliances with private-sector specialists to increase their access to expertise and ideas."[5] They are also proactively engaged in cross-border mergers and acquisitions. In finance, SWFs are used by state capitalists to earn profits overseas or to promote economic growth at home.[6]

With such internationally oriented characteristics, one of the imperative questions about state capitalism is where to place it in the legal and regulatory frameworks of international (economic) law. Professor M. Sornarajah asks this question in his only, but significant, paper on SWFs.[7] Noting that SWFs are "emblematic of a more profound change taking place within international relations," Sornarajah wonders what impact SWFs will have on the dynamism of international law:[8]

> A major issue is whether the newly emerging states would conform to the rules that the developed states devised for investment protection or whether they would want to ensure that the rules they had sought to advance as erstwhile developing countries are reflected. Another issue is how the developed world itself would respond. It could respond by changing the rules to protect its interests, by advocating the very rules that the developing countries had advanced in the past by seeking refuge in sovereignty-centred, protectionist norms that it has hitherto revisited. The emergence of new and competing trends would provide interesting contexts in which change in international law could be studied.

Indeed, although state capitalism exists in both developed and developing countries, it is the state-related companies in the non-Western emerging economies that have caused concerns in the West. Norway has the world's largest SWF, "estimated to be worth $1 [trillion] by 2020."[9]

5 *Id.*

6 SWFs are classified into two varieties by *The Economist*: "'savings" funds intended to find productive homes for investments and 'development' funds that also promote economic development". See *id.*

7 See generally, M. Sornarajah, "Sovereign Wealth Funds and the Existing Structure of the Regulation of Investments" (2011) 1 *Asian Journal of International Law* 267.

8 *Id.*, 268.

9 M. Price, "Norway: Is the World's Largest Sovereign Wealth Fund Too Big?", *BBC News*, 12 September 2013, available at www.bbc.com/news/world-europe-24049876 (visited 23 April 2015). According to the Sovereign Wealth Fund Institute, the world's fifteen biggest SWFs in 2014 were Government Pension Fund – Global (Norway), Abu Dhabi Investment Authority (UAE–Abu Dhabi), SAMA Foreign Holding (Saudi Arabia), China Investment Corporation (China), SAFE Investment Company (China), Kuwait Investment Authority (Kuwait), Hong Kong Monetary Authority Investment Portfolio (Hong Kong, China), Government of Singapore Investment Corporation (Singapore), Qatar Investment

However, according to the definitional statement in *The Economist*'s 2012 Special Report, "[i]t is possible for a country to have any or all of these [state capitalist] institutions in place without being a member of the state capitalist club."[10] The reason for making such a distinction is simple but domineering: although Norway owns one of the world's largest oil companies and its biggest SWF, the Government Pension Fund, it "requires both of them to behave like regular companies."[11]

However, although state enterprises and the governments behind them maintain that they operate on a commercial basis, it is simply not correct to assume that state enterprises can move freely around the world. The world is not short of stories of how China's state-owned companies have been denied access to markets in the United States and Europe.[12]

International law, or, more precisely, international economic law, has not formed firm rules about state capitalism. This paper aims to examine this issue by looking for a regulatory framework for state capitalism, particularly SOEs and SWFs, at the international level. It argues that a soft law approach is, at this stage, the best way to put state capitalism under a legal umbrella at the international level.

This chapter proceeds as follows: The section "Hard and soft law in international [economic] law" introduces the concept of soft law in international economic law and explains the advantages of the soft law approach. "State capitalism under 'hard' international economic law: WTO regulation of state enterprises" examines the effect of current regulatory regimes on state enterprises, focusing, in particular, on the relevant rules of the World Trade Organization (WTO). "The Santiago Principles and their discontents: the developing soft law framework for SWFs" offers a critical analysis of the development of the Santiago Principles, which embody a soft law approach to regulating SWFs. "Concluding remarks: an 'inclusive soft law approach'" proposes an "inclusive soft law" approach and ends the chapter with some remarks which look to the future.

Authority (Qatar), National Social Security Fund (China), Temasek Holdings (Singapore), Australian Future Fund (Australia), Abu Dhabi Investment Council (UAE–Abu Dhabi), and Reserve Fund (Russia).

10 See "State Capitalism's Global Reach", *Supra* note 4. 11 *Id.*

12 Another article in *The Economist* noted that "Australia and Canada, once open markets for takeovers, are creating hurdles for China's state-backed firms, particularly in natural resources, and it is easy to see other countries becoming less welcoming too". See "Chinese Acquisitions: China Buys Up the World", *The Economist*, 11 November 2010, available at www.economist.com/node/17463473 (visited 15 June 2015).

Hard and soft law in international [economic] law

International economic law, arguably as a branch of international law, identifies its sources by making reference to Article 38(1) of the Statute of the International Court of Justice (ICJ), which covers international conventions/treaties, international custom, general principles of law, judicial decisions, and the writings of publicists.[13] Conventional wisdom holds that different branches of international economic law follow the same framework, though with limited variations. For instance, the sources of the law of the WTO include the WTO's "covered agreements," reports of panels and the Appellate Body as a form resembling judicial decisions, customary international law, teachings of the most highly qualified publicists, general principles of law, and other international instruments such as agreements referred to in the WTO agreements and the agreements between WTO members.[14]

According to Moshe Hirsch, the sources of international investment law are even more traditional; these include multilateral and bilateral investment treaties (BITs), international customary law, general principles of law, judicial decisions, and scholarly writings.[15] However, Hirsch observes that "binding legal rules and influential non-binding norms complement each other in the fabric of international investment law," which makes it "almost impossible to disentangle between 'soft' and 'hard' rules in the real life of international investment law."[16]

The notion of soft law is first of all a useful conceptual tool to capture "norms that are neither law, nor mere political or moral statements, but lie somewhere in between."[17] The rise of normative instruments or arrangements in the past few decades, which are not law (because they are not legislated according to formal law-making procedures) but are above what is not law, has posed challenges to international lawyers with respect to the applicability and binding force of these instruments.

[13] Statute of the International Court of Justice, 26 June 1945, 59 Stat. 1055, T.S. No. 993 (1945). For a systemic examination of the sources of international law, see I. Brownlie, *Principles of Public International Law* (Oxford: OUP, 2008), 3–29.

[14] See M. Matsushita, T.J. Schoenbaum, and P.C. Mavroidis, *The World Trade Organization: Law, Practice and Policy* (Oxford: OUP, 2003), 53–76.

[15] M. Hirsch, "Sources of International Investment Law", in A.K. Bjorklund and A. Reinisch (eds.), *International Investment Law and Soft Law* (Cheltenham: Edward Elgar, 2012), 9–33.

[16] *Id.*, 38.

[17] M.G. Desta, "Soft Law in International Law: An Overview", in A.K. Bjorklund and A. Reinisch (eds.), *International Investment Law and Soft Law* (Cheltenham: Edward Elgar, 2012), 40.

Professor W Michael Reisman has opposed the use of soft law in the activities of international judges and arbitrators on the ground that it introduces uncertainty into a regulatory regime. "Uncertainty about the law is a very effective *disincentive* for investing wealth . . . The cultivation of uncertainty is a favoured technique of intimidation by authoritarian governments."[18] However, certain advantages of soft law make it a rather effective tool for solving certain problems in international governance. As a matter of fact, as Abbott and Snidal have argued, "most international law is 'soft' in distinctive ways," and "hard law is not the typical international legal arrangement."[19] This current state of affairs featuring frequent use of soft law is simply a result of the fact that "softer forms of legalized governance ... offer superior institutional solutions."[20] Specifically:[21]

> Soft law offers many of the advantages of hard law, avoids some of the costs of hard law, and has certain independent advantages of its own. Importantly, because one or more of the elements of legalization can be relaxed, softer legalization is often easier to achieve than hard legalization. This is especially true when the actors are states that are jealous of their autonomy and when the issues at hand challenge state sovereignty. Soft legalization also provides certain benefits not available under hard legalization. It offers more effective ways to deal with uncertainty, especially when it initiates processes that allow actors to learn about the impact of agreements over time. In addition, soft law facilitates compromises, and thus mutually beneficial cooperation, between actors with different interests and values, different time horizons and discount rates, and different degrees of power.

This chapter argues that a soft form of regulatory approach for state capitalism is a more effective way to address the relevant conflicts and achieve consensus. To the extent that state capitalism, especially its cross-border activities, should be regulated at the international level, a soft law approach helps to alleviate the concerns of the powerful owners of state enterprises, who are in most cases rapidly growing emerging economies that are rather sensitive with respect to almost anything concerning state sovereignty. They also need a transition period to get used to a new state of affairs in which their state enterprises are governed by a set of new

18 M.W. Reisman, "Soft Law and Law Jobs" (2011) 2(1) *Journal of International Dispute* 25–26.

19 K.W. Abbott and D. Snidal, "Hard and Soft Law in International Governance" (2000) 54(3) *International Organization* 421.

20 *Id.* 21 *Id.*, 423.

rules, as the old and existing regulatory regime under the umbrella of the World Trade Organization (WTO), to the limited extent it governs state enterprises, is largely ownership-neutral. In addition, at the current stage, no international organization possesses sufficient legitimacy to make hard rules for state capitalism.

State capitalism under "hard" international economic law: WTO regulation of state enterprises

Discussions of international regulation of state capitalism should begin with world trade law, namely WTO law, as this is possibly the only place in international economic law that has hard rules on state enterprises. It is important to emphasize that the world trading system (under the auspice of the WTO and the General Agreement on Tariffs and Trade (GATT) that is now part of the WTO regime) has adopted an ownership-neutral philosophy since its inception following the Second World War (WWII). Although the world trading system is conventionally understood as one based on market economies, this understanding has not prevented it from granting nonmarket economies, ranging from Eastern Europe to Latin America, GATT/WTO membership. As a matter of fact, the whole system is premised on the assumption that governments are impartial regulators that should treat all economic actors equally. In other words, the GATT/WTO does not have compulsory rules regarding property ownership for members to comply with. Accordingly, a "WTO member is free to establish and maintain SOEs if it wishes to do so."[22] In this light, two groups of rules in the GATT/WTO system apply to state capitalism.

State trading enterprises

To a limited extent, state capitalism is regulated. Article XVII of the GATT 1994 is the principal rule in the GATT/WTO system dealing with state trading enterprises (STEs) and their operations. In essence, Article XVII "sets out that such enterprises – in their purchases or sales involving either imports or exports – are to act in accordance with the general principles of *non-discrimination*, and that commercial considerations

[22] M. Du, "China's State Capitalism and World Trade Law" (2014) 63(2) *International and Comparative Law Quarterly* 409–427.

only are to guide their decisions on imports and exports."[23] In other words, the original parties to the GATT only wanted to ensure that SOEs, or private enterprises with special privileges granted by their government, were not given a safe haven as a result of the privileged situation, so that they may escape the GATT rules of nondiscrimination.[24]

Article XVII is, however, of limited use in regulating the booming industry of state capitalism today.[25] This is primarily because of definitional difficulties and failures. As noted by the WTO Secretariat, in the history of Article XVII, "a major lacuna has been the absence of any clear definition of what a State trading enterprise is, or what State trading is."[26] As a result, modern SOEs, the visible hands of state capitalism that recently exploded onto the international economic scene, can actually be excluded from this definition if they prove that they do not engage in state trading or are not granted special rights or privileges. The coverage of the requirement of nondiscrimination is also not clear. Numerous GATT/WTO decisions have suggested that STEs possess full freedom to act, as long as their behavior does not violate the obligation of nondiscrimination.[27] In short, very few SOEs, apart from those explicitly granted special rights or privileges for state trading, would find they are subject to the legal obligations of Article XVII.

WTO rules on government subsidies

More meaningful, and with a more focused scope of coverage of SOE activities, are those GATT rules on subsidies provided by governments to their state enterprises. The WTO's Agreement on Subsidies and Countervailing Measures (ASCM), together with GATT Articles VI and XVI, form the legal framework for the provision of subsidies by governments to enterprises. In brief, "it disciplines the use of subsidies,

[23] "The Regulation of State Trading under the WTO System", available at www.wto.org/english/tratop_e/statra_e/statrad.htm (visited 1 April 2015).

[24] World Trade Organization Secretariat, *Guide to Uruguay Round Agreements* (Geneva: World Trade Organization, 1998), 54.

[25] Du, "China's State Capitalism and World Trade Law", *supra* note 22, 428.

[26] "Technical Information on State Trading Enterprises", available at www.wto.org/english/tratop_e/statra_e/statra_info_e.htm (visited 1 April 2015).

[27] Du, "China's State Capitalism and World Trade Law", *supra* note 22, 429 (examining the WTO Appellate Body Report, *Canada-Measures Relating to Export of Wheat and Treatment of Imported Grain*, WT/DS276/AB/R (30 August 2004)).

and it regulates the actions countries can take to counter the effects of subsidies."[28]

One could easily appreciate the significance of the WTO's subsidies law from its efforts to define subsidies. An actionable subsidy, which may entitle other members to initiate dispute settlement proceedings against the government that allegedly provided the subsidy, contains three constituting elements: (i) a financial contribution (ii) provided by a government or a public body within the territory of a WTO member (iii) which confers a benefit.[29] Because subsidies can be provided not only by a government but also by a public body, subsidies law's reach extends beyond the actions of governments to bodies such as SOEs.[30] Consequently, the WTO could treat SOEs as providers of subsidies, which can potentially render transactions between SOEs and other enterprises illegal under WTO law. This was something of a nightmare for countries with many SOEs, not least China itself.

The issue was litigated in a recent WTO case, *United States – Definitive Anti-Dumping and Countervailing Duties on Certain Products from China*, or *US – AD & CVD* (China), the final binding report of which was adopted in 2011.[31] In this case, China, the plaintiff (officially called the Complainant), faced "ice and fire," to use a Chinese expression,[32] since the Appellate Body ultimately reversed the initial, hostile panel ruling on this point.

Pursuant to the WTO's procedure for dispute settlement, a dispute between members is first adjudicated at the panel level; then, it can be appealed to the Appellate Body. It was the panel report in this case that put China in a rather risky situation.[33] The case involves China's complaint concerning definitive antidumping and countervailing duties imposed by the US on importation of certain Chinese products. One of the key issues in China's complaint concerns how to define subsidies in

[28] "Anti-Dumping, Subsidies, Safeguards: Contingencies, etc.", in *Understanding the WTO*, available at www.wto.org/english/thewto_e/whatis_e/tif_e/agrm8_e.htm (visited 1 April 2015).

[29] ASCM, Article 1.1.

[30] World Trade Organization Secretariat, *Guide to Uruguay Round Agreements*, *supra* note 24, 98.

[31] WTO Appellate Body Report, *United States – Definitive Anti-Dumping and Countervailing Duties on Certain Products from China*, WT/DS379/AB/R, adopted 25 March 2011.

[32] The Chinese expression being "冰火两重天".

[33] WTO Panel Report, *United States – Definitive Anti-Dumping and Countervailing Duties on Certain Products from China*, WT/DS379/R, issued 23 July 2010.

the unique economic, political, and legal structure of China. Specifically, it was about whether China's SOEs and state-owned commercial banks (SOCBs) are public bodies under the ASCM.

The panel report generated fear among many Chinese because it ruled that the United States had not violated or acted inconsistently with any WTO rules by treating Chinese SOEs and SOCBs as public bodies. The panel concluded that a "public body" under the ASCM "is any entity controlled by a government."[34] Specifically, the panel noted that:[35]

> [W]e consider that interpreting "any public body" to mean any entity that is controlled by the government best serves the object and purpose of the SCM Agreement. This reading ensures that whatever form a public entity takes (whether agency, Ministry, Board, corporation, etc.) the government that controls it is directly responsible for those of its actions that are relevant under the Agreement ... To read "any public body" in Article 1.1(a)(1) as excusing from a Member government's direct responsibility a wide swathe of government controlled entities engaging in exactly the sorts of transactions listed in Article 1.1(a)(1)(i)-(iii) of the SCM Agreement would fundamentally undermine the Agreement's logic, coherence and effectiveness, and thus would be at odds with its object and purpose.

On this basis, the panel concluded, from the perspective of international economic law, that all China's SOEs and SOCBs are public bodies. Were the panel report adopted, the hundreds of thousands of SOEs, which form the most important pillar of China's economy, would become public bodies in WTO law with respect to the determination of subsidies (and, possibly, many other purposes under the WTO's covered agreements), and their transactions would most likely be regarded as activities providing actionable subsidies.

Fortunately, for China, the Appellate Body reversed most of the crucial elements in the panel's ruling, especially the one concerning the definition of public body. The Appellate Body rejected the panel's interpretation of public body as lacking a proper legal basis.[36] As noted above, the panel's interpretation follows a "government control approach," believing that majority state ownership in an enterprise renders that enterprise a public body.[37] The Appellate Body found this a troublesome approach

[34] Panel Report, *U.S. – AD & CVD (China)*, para. 8.94.
[35] Panel Report, *U.S. – AD & CVD (China)*, para. 8.79.
[36] Appellate Body Report, *U.S. – AD & CVD (China)*, para. 322.
[37] See also R. Ding, "'Public Body' or Not?: Chinese State-owned Enterprises" (2014) 48(1) *Journal of World Trade* 167, 173–174.

that misunderstood the meaning of the relevant rules and the object and purpose of the ASCM. In the Appellate Body's view, "the performance of government functions, or the fact of being vested with, and exercising, the authority to perform such functions are core commonalities between government and public body."[38] It concludes that:[39]

> We see the concept of "public body" as sharing certain attributes with the concept of "government." A public body within the meaning of Article 1.1.(a)(1) of the SCM Agreement must be an entity that possesses, exercises or is vested with government authority. Yet, just as no two governments are exactly alike, the precise contours and characteristics of a public body are bound to differ from entity to entity, State to State, and case to case. Panels or investigating authorities confronted with the question of whether conduct falling within the scope of Article 1.1.(a)(1) is that of a public body will be in a position to answer that question only by conducting a proper evaluation of the core features of the entity concerned, as its relationship with government in the narrow sense.

In short, the Appellate Body substantially limited the scope of SOEs that may be subject to the WTO's discipline on subsidies. According to the panel report, all the SOEs in which the government has a majority control would automatically become public bodies, thus making it impossible – or at least extremely risky – for those SOEs to do business at the international level as ordinary commercial entities. The ruling of the Appellate Body cleared an immediate threat for China (and other countries with SOEs) but has also created uncertainty insofar as how to determine the nature of SOEs under international economic law. This will be further analyzed in the section "Concluding remarks: an 'inclusive soft law approach.'"

The Santiago Principles and their discontents: the developing soft law framework for SWFs

The rise of SWFs and international responses

The term "sovereign wealth fund" was first coined by Andrew Rozanov in 2005, when it received little attention.[40] In 2007 and 2008, SWFs suddenly became the focus of innumerable media headlines in both the

[38] Appellate Body Report, *U.S. – AD & CVD (China)*, para. 290.

[39] Appellate Body Report, *U.S. – AD & CVD (China)*, para. 317.

[40] See generally, A. Rozanov, "Who Holds the Wealth of Nations?" (2005) 15 *Central Banking Journal* 1. See also A. Rozanov, "Definitional Challenges of Dealing with Sovereign Wealth Funds" (2011) 1 *Asian Journal of Comparative Law* 249.

developed and the developing world and the subject du jour of international meetings such as the World Economic Forum. The term was on the tongues of politicians, economists, and lawyers around the world, though the name itself was the only new thing. According to Joaquin Almunia, the European Commissioner for Economic and Monetary Policy,

> Sovereign Wealth Funds have been with us for more than half a century since the very first fund was established by the Kuwait Investment Office in 1953. And during the oil price increases of the 70s and 80s, a major wave of funds was set up by oil producers. But it is only in the last 10 to 15 years that we've seen a dramatic increase in the number of sovereign wealth funds worldwide.[41]

However, the term was coined at a time just before the SWFs erupted onto the international financial scene and created both joy and fear. Some of the more prominent funds were growing significantly in size, new funds were being established, and others that had previously been domestically focused were turning outward. It is the practice of many SWFs that they do not disclose the total amount of assets they manage, and therefore it is not possible to determine the total amount of assets held by these funds worldwide. Just prior to the 2007 Global Financial Crisis, the International Monetary Fund (IMF) released an estimate regarding the amount of wealth held by SWFs. While sovereigns held upward of US$7 trillion in reserves worldwide, between US$2 and US$3 trillion of that was in the hands of SWFs. The IMF explained, "SWFs exceed[ed] the size of hedge funds (US$1.7 trillion), but the latter tend to be heavily leveraged, so that the comparison is somewhat misleading."[42] Today, according to the latest update of the Sovereign Wealth Fund Institute, the world's established SWFs own US$7.1 trillion in total assets, of which US$4.2 trillion is oil and gas related.[43]

There is, thus, no longer any doubt that the SWFs have become a major presence in the global economy and major players in the global markets. Flush with reserves from escalated oil prices, export surpluses, changes in the global economic fundamentals, and new opportunities, an "intensive

[41] J. Almunia, "The EU Response to the Rise of Sovereign Wealth Funds", Speech at the Crans Montana Forum, Brussels, 2 April 2008, available at http://europa.eu/rapid/press-release_SPEECH-08-165_en.htm (visited 25 March 2015).

[42] International Monetary Fund (IMF), *Sovereign Wealth Funds – A Work Agenda* (Washington, DC: IMF, 2008), 5.

[43] Sovereign Wealth Fund Institute (SWFI), *Sovereign Wealth Fund Ranking* (2015), www.swfinstitute.org/fund-rankings/ (visited 16 April 2015).

SWF shopping spree" began. These changes in growth, number, and strategy have caused many to take note and begin to ask questions.

The SWFs have sparked heated debates worldwide. Broadly speaking, critics of SWFs can be categorized into two groups: (1) those who believe that SWFs pose a threat to the national security of host states and the international relations in general and (2) those who believe SWFs present a danger to the global financial markets specifically and to capitalism more generally. These concerns about SWFs, in particular, and state capitalism in general were lucidly summarized in *The Economist*'s 2012 Special Report on State Capitalism.[44] Underlying all of these fears is a common concern: SWFs present unique risks and dangers because of their inherent mix of political and economic motivations. Lawrence Summers observed:[45]

> The logic of the capitalist system depends on shareholders causing companies to act so as to maximize the value of their shares. It is far from obvious that this will over time be the only motivation of governments as shareholders. They may want to see their national companies compete effectively, or to extract technology or to achieve influence.

On the other hand, however, all those concerns expressed by politicians, economists, and lawyers in the West have not been backed by any substantial evidence that SWFs have actually acted in ways so as to damage the national security or economic system of host states. Nevertheless, much was said about how the governments in North America and Europe took preemptive actions to stop transactions involving foreign SOEs or SWFs, even though on many occasions, it could be proven that those firms were actually doing business on the basis of commercial considerations. One of the leading examples is the Foreign Investment and National Security Act of 2007 (FINSA), adopted by the US Congress to give stronger powers to the Committee on Foreign Investment in the United States (CFIUS) to restrict the inflow of suspicious foreign investment into the US.[46]

Nevertheless, the marriage of state ownership and market systems on such a global scale is indeed a new phenomenon that warrants reasonable concerns. It has grown out of the changing global economic

[44] See "The Visible Hand", *The Economist, supra* note 1.

[45] L. Summers, "Funds That Shake Capitalist Logic", *Financial Times* (30 July 2007), available at http://ft.com/economistsforum (visited 23 April 2015).

[46] M. Bellis, "Global Standards for Sovereign Wealth Funds: The Quest for Transparency" (2011) 1(2) *Asian Journal of International Law* 349, 350.

fundamentals and may reshape the international economic and even political order in the long run.

The traditional self-proclamation of the Western-dominated international economic system is that it is open to international trade and investment. For example, Article 56 of the European Community Treaty prohibits not only restrictions to free movement of capital and payments between Member States but also between Member States and third countries. In other words, the EU is committed to be a favorable place for foreign investment irrespective of the home state of the investors.[47] This liberal commitment makes it an original sin to put restrictions on foreign investment, be it done by SOEs or private investors. On the other hand, as discussed earlier, critics of SWFs have argued that SWF investment presents a variety of specific dangers that warrant specific and binding regulations.

It is against this background that several rounds of calls for international regulation of SWFs have been issued. For sure, it is not true that such entities were unregulated. Rather, they were exposed to a variety of different forms of regulation at the national and international levels. One has to admit that they are at least governed by all the same regulations as any other investor.[48] A joint international response to the calls for regulating SWFs, featuring home and host states and some international organizations, has led to the drafting of the Santiago Principles (published in October 2008), which is the most significant development in this regard. The Principles and their drafting process and effects are critically examined in the next section.

The development of the Santiago Principles

The Santiago Principles, officially known as the Generally Accepted Principles and Practices (GAPP) for SWFs, is the resulting document of the International Working Group of Sovereign Wealth Funds (IWG),

[47] The Commission of the European Communities has stated that "The Commitment to openness to investments and free movement of capital has been a long standing principle of the EU and is key to success in an increasingly globalized international system". See Commission of the European Communities, *A Common European Approach to Sovereign Wealth Funds*, COM (2008) 115 provisional, available at http://ec.europa.eu/internal_market/finances/docs/sovereign_en.pdf (visited 10 April 2015).

[48] Professor Sornarajah has examined the treatment of SWFs under the traditional legal and regulatory framework of international law. See Sornarajah, "Sovereign Wealth Funds and the Existing Structure of the Regulation of Investments", *supra* note 7, 271–288.

which was eventually adopted in Santiago, Chile.[49] The establishment of the IWG was mandated by a 2007 meeting of the International Monetary and Financial Committee (IMFC), a committee of the Board of Governors of the IMF.[50] With the IMF serving as its secretariat, the IWG brought together 26 countries, the Organization for Economic Cooperation and Development (OECD), and the World Bank and, within 6 months, announced the completion of the Santiago Principles in October 2008.[51]

The document itself comprises twenty-four principles with a short explanation to each and subprinciples to some of the main principles. The principles are divided into three groups: (i) legal framework, objectives, and coordination with macroeconomic policies (five principles); (ii) institutional framework and governance structure (12 principles); and (iii) investment and risk management framework (seven principles).

Specifically, the first group of principles asks the SWF to have a sound legal framework, disclose its policy purpose, sources of funding and financial relationship with the government, and report statistical data to its owner. The second group of principles asks the SWF to establish a sound governance framework. The owner should set objectives, appoint governing members, and exercise oversight over the SWF. The governing bodies of the SWF have a fiduciary duty to act in the best interest of the SWF. The operational management should perform its responsibilities independently. Furthermore, the SWF's accountability should be clearly defined in the country's law or other legal enactments, and its financial documents should be audited regularly. The management personnel of the SWF should be subject to clearly defined professional and ethical standards. The SWF's dealing with third parties should be based on economic and financial grounds and follow clear rules and procedures. The SWF's operations are fully subject to all the relevant laws of the host countries. The governance framework and objectives of the SWF should

[49] *Sovereign Wealth Funds: Generally Accepted Principles and Practices. "Santiago Principles"*, October 2008, published by the International Working Group for Sovereign Wealth Funds (IWG), available at www.iwg-swf.org/pubs/eng/santiagoprinciples.pdf (visited 26 April 2015).

[50] "*Santiago Principles*", "Introduction", *supra* note 49, 1.

[51] IWG members are Australia, Azerbaijan, Bahrain, Botswana, Canada, Chile, China, Equatorial Guinea, Islamic Republic of Iran, Ireland, Korea, Kuwait, Libya, Mexico, New Zealand, Norway, Qatar, Russia, Singapore, Timor-Leste, Trinidad and Tobago, the United Arab Emirates, and the United States. Permanent observers of the IWG include Oman, Saudi Arabia, Vietnam, the OECD and the World Bank. See "*Santiago Principles*", "Introduction".

be publicly disclosed. The Principles also ask for financial information regarding the SWF to be publicly disclosed.

Regarding the investment policy of SWFs, the Principles ask the relevant policy to be clear and consistent with the SWF's defined objectives, risk tolerance, and strategy. They should always be disclosed. The SWF's investment decisions should aim to maximize risk-adjusted financial returns. If the investment decisions are subject to other economic and financial considerations, these should be clearly set out in the publicly disclosed investment policy. The SWF should not seek or take advantage of privileged information or inappropriate influence by the broader government in competing with private entities. If the SWF exercises its shareholder ownership rights, it should do so in a manner that is consistent with its investment policy and its aim to maximize the financial value of its investments.

Regarding risk management and performance measurement, SWFs are asked to have a framework that identifies, assesses, and manages the risks of its operations, which should be publicly disclosed. Finally, the assets and investment performance of the SWF should be measured and reported to the owner according to clearly defined principles or standards.

The soft law approach of the Santiago Principles

Impracticability of the hard law approach

The Santiago Principles have generated disappointments for those who desire greater regulation of SWFs. Among the criticisms leveled at the Principles is that the language is excessively vague and undefined, that the voluntary and non-binding nature makes it a nullity, that they do little in respect of SWF activity, which had raised suspicion that they give too much leeway to national law, and that they lack discussion of the need for a supervising or disciplinary body to pressure SWFs into compliance.[52]

These criticisms are, probably, all correct only from the perspective of hard legalization of the SWFs globally. A hard law approach is, however,

[52] See Y. Lee, "A Reversal of Neo-Colonialism: The Pitfalls and Prospects of Sovereign Wealth Funds" (2009) 40 *Geo. J. Int'l L.* 1103 at 1140; S. Firth and D. Juric, "Common Ground", *The Deal*, 3 October 2008, available at www.thedeal.com; and S. Behrendt, "Sovereign Wealth Funds: The Governance Challenge", *Carnegie Middle East Center*, 21 January 2010, available at http://carnegieendowment.org/sada/index.cfm?fa= show. . .article=24757. . .solr_hilite= (visited 15 June 2015).

misguided. It is motivated by idealism and seeks a solution that is unrealistic in the present environment for the following reasons:

First, no international organization, or group of international organizations, possesses the historical and contemporary political legitimacy to make hard rules for SWFs, in particular, or state capitalism in general.

An early episode in the debate between the developed and developing countries regarding the regulation of multinational corporations (MNCs) is telling about the lack of full credibility on both sides. The following is an account of the episode by Professor Sornarajah, who witnessed the debate:[53]

> During the NIEO days, the developing countries were intent on setting up a code of conduct for MNCs to curb what was considered conduct that was deleterious to their economic development . . . The excessive power of the MNCs caused general concern, but more so among developing countries which saw that their enormous economic power had the capacity for good as well as for bad and that the bad aspects should be subject to binding international codes.
>
> The multinationals did not like binding codes and the principal home states of these corporations were often intent on wrecking the project to create binding codes. Thus, one of the arguments that the US advanced was that if the private MNCs were to be subject to binding obligations at the international level, so should their counterparts, the state entities of the socialist and the developing worlds. These state entities, the US argued, were in no different a position from the MNCs and should be subject to the same code. The US and its allies proceeded to draft a code of conduct that would apply to these state entities as well as to MNCs. The idea was that there had to be parity of status between MNCs and the state entities.

Nothing is new under the sun. Today, the same debate exists only in a different form. Eventually, no binding code was created for the MNCs. It is accordingly difficult to persuade the owner-states of SWFs, most of them belonging to the developing world, to easily accept a binding code for SWFs. At the same time, the developing world would look unreasonable if they still want to treat MNCs differently. "Coupled with the situation of sovereign immunities, the idea that the state entity should be treated exactly like the MNC has received acceptance in the practice of states."[54]

[53] Sornarajah, "Sovereign Wealth Funds and the Existing Structure of the Regulation of Investments", *supra* note 7, 272–273.

[54] Sornarajah, "Sovereign Wealth Funds and the Existing Structure of the Regulation of Investments", *supra* note 7, 273.

The lack of institutional legitimacy is even more obvious. The IMF seems to be most suitable for governing SWFs, as it has the mandate to foster global monetary cooperation and secure financial stability in the international economic system. However, it is not likely that the increasingly powerful economies which own most of the largest SWFs would subscribe to the IMF's legislative process to make hard international law, as they are severely underrepresented in the IMF's voting mechanism.[55] Furthermore, the SWFs emerged vehemently onto the international financial stage in about 2007–2008 and were initially welcomed by Western countries, which, undergoing the Financial Crisis, desperately wanted the new state funds to inject cash into their ailing financial institutions.

The fear of the emerging economies, which are home to the SWFs, is that the legitimacy deficit suffered by the Western-dominated international institutions, coupled with the eventual bias against SWFs in the West, would make it a mistake to create anything more concrete, binding, or definitive than a set of soft law rules such as the Santiago Principles.

It is also not in the interest of any party, be it the home state or host state to the SWFs, to wait for binding international law rules in the form of an international convention or agreement to be formed, at least at this stage. The experience of legislative activity in international economic institutions such as the WTO and IMF indicate that it could take a decade or longer to propose, draft, negotiate, and adopt a set of rules, which will have binding force under international law. Apart from the traditional fear of states, especially the weaker ones, of compromising their sovereignty by committing to hard rules and regulations at the international level, the making and implementation of those rules would be complicated by the commonly acknowledged truth about state behavior "that states do not always say what they mean, or mean what they say."[56]

Nevertheless, it has to be recognized that SWFs are now active players in the global markets, warranting their regulation in some form. The nature of the SWFs' position in global business should be clarified with impartiality and without bias. On the other hand, their state-owned

[55] For example, China's share in the voting power of the IMF is 3.81 percent. In the recent Second Asian-African Submit in Bandung, Indonesia, in April 2015, Singapore's Prime Minister Lee Hsien Loong remarked "It doesn't make sense" that China's weight in the IMF is less than that of a medium-sized European country. See Z. Hussain, "Indonesia President Jokowi Calls for New, More Equal Global Economic Order", *The Straits Times*, 23 April 2015.

[56] C.L. Lim and O. Elias, "Withdrawing from Custom and the Paradox of Censensualism in International Law" (2010–2011) 21 *Duke J. Comp. & Int'l L.* 143 at 153.

nature has also sparked debates caused by genuine concerns. It is important and in the interest of all affected states to have a loose framework that offers best practices or guidelines for the business operations of SWFs.

Advantages of the Santiago Principles' soft law approach

In this light, the soft law approach of the Santiago Principles appears to be indispensably valuable for the participating states to achieve consensus and, eventually, produce the first set of internationally agreed principles on the best practices for SWFs. Several features of the soft law approach in the Santiago Principles are worth examining here.

First, the Principles hold themselves out as "a voluntary set of principles and practices."[57] Not intending to be binding rules in international law, the Principles nevertheless "can be expected to guide existing and future SWFs in various aspects of their activities – most importantly investing professionally in accordance with their investment policy objectives – and to help inform any associated legal and institutional reform."[58] This means that those involved in making the Principles did not set out to constrain the activities of SWFs. Ironically, this approach actually makes it easier for the participating states to form consensus for accepting detailed rules with substantive norms rather than empty slogans.

Second, the inclusion of the major SWF countries and the OECD countries in the negotiating room for the Principles, who were then enticed by the soft law approach to agree to a set of common rules on SWFs (which they otherwise would not have done), has the advantage of quicker and more effective consensus-building. As a result, countries from both the developed and developing world swiftly reached, for the first time, an agreement on certain key principles for dealing with SWFs. For example, the Santiago Principles point out that the principles are underpinned by the following "guiding objectives":[59]

i. to help maintain a stable global financial system and free flow of capital and investment;
ii. to comply with applicable regulatory and disclosure requirements in the countries in which they invest;
iii. to invest on the basis of economic and financial risk and return-related considerations; and

[57] "*Santiago Principles*", "Objective and Purpose", *supra* note 49, 5.
[58] "*Santiago Principles*", "Objective and Purpose", *supra* note 49, 5.
[59] "*Santiago Principles*", "Objective and Purpose", *supra* note 49, 4.

iv. to have in place a transparent and sound governance structure that provides for adequate operational controls, risk management, and accountability.

One should not underestimate the significance of these "objectives" and the associated principles. With such a wide acceptance at the international level, those principles have formed a common discourse for guiding the activities of SWFs. If not incorporated into an international convention someday, it would not be surprising if they become part of customary international law. At least, they assist international and domestic judges or arbitrators, when confronted with disputes concerning SWFs, in interpreting BITs and relevant domestic laws. No doubt they will interpret those laws in the ways consistent with the spirit of the Santiago Principles.

The last two aforesaid objectives are, especially, worthy of mention. Together with the relevant substantive principles,[60] the Santiago Principles make it politically incorrect – and eventually illegal under international law sometime later – for SWFs to carry out noncommercial and strategic objectives for their home state. However, it might be true that some SWFs were indeed established to advance the country's strategic interests such as promoting economic development or to lock up a supply of energy or resources overseas. It is now legitimate for national governments to limit or even prohibit such activities of SWFs.[61]

However, the Santiago Principles do allow SWFs to invest in accordance with certain ethical standards, which are obviously noncommercial and noneconomic considerations, provided that those standards are clearly defined and made known to the members of the SWF's governing bodies, management, and staff (Principle 13). Norway's Government Pension Fund Global, which is now the world's largest SWF, has taken human rights performance into consideration and has even created a council to advise on the fund's investments in this regard. Not surprisingly, some have argued that it is hypocritical and unfair to allow SWFs to consider noncommercial and ethical standards such as human rights protection but not noncommercial considerations that advance the home state's other national interests. This might generate a battle of values in the international economic system. However, this is precisely

[60] GAPP 19 and the associated sub-principles, GAPP 19.1 and GAPP 19.2.

[61] See S. Chesterman, "The Turn to Ethics: Divestment from Multinational Corporations for Human Rights Violations – The Case of Norway's Sovereign Wealth Fund" (2008) 23 *Am. U. Int'l L. Rev.* 577, at 582–590.

why greater "hard" regulation for SWFs would be problematic, as so many strong disagreements remain.

Third, the Santiago Principles have clarified a [mis]understanding that has long plagued SWFs. Many in the West have voiced concern over the threat of SWFs to host states' national security; some have expressed concern that an SWF might become a means of pressuring the host state into a compromise with respect to its foreign policy in favor of the SWF's home state or that the SWF might become a vehicle for stealing defense-related sensitive information or technology. However, as observed by some commentators, these appear to be hypothetical dangers:[62]

> At least to date, SWFs have acted as model investors and have not sought to leverage their position to pursue political ends. That their track record is superior to many a domestic pension fund in this regard is not surprising: SWFs have strong natural incentives to avoid being perceived as strategic investors, so as to avoid a public backlash that could compromise their continued access to Western markets. In light of this, proposals for prophylactic regulations designed to save our capitalist system from a new "mercantilism" seem overly dramatic.

The Santiago Principles, after defining SWFs as "special purpose investment funds or arrangements that are owned by the general government,"[63] state that the IWG, the drafting committee of the Principles, "recognizes that SWF investments are both beneficial and critical to international markets."[64] On whether an SWF can indeed present dangers, the Principles maintain that it all depends on the setup of the SWF arrangements, the quality of information disclosure and the grounds on which the investment decisions are made.

In short, the common discourse resulting from the adoption of the Santiago Principles has set the minimum international standards for governing SWFs. A loose and rudimentary framework at this stage, its significance cannot be underestimated as it not only establishes an international consensus on certain key issues concerning SWFs but also has the potential to develop into binding rules of international law in the future. The advantage of the soft law approach is that it can be more effective in making workable rules for economic activity when the making of hard law is neither feasible nor desirable.

[62] R. Epstein and A.M. Rose, "The Regulation of Sovereign Wealth Funds: The Virtues of Going Slow" (2009) 76 *U. Chi. L. Rev.* 111 at 134.

[63] "*Santiago Principles*", "Objective and Purpose", *supra* note 49, 3.

[64] "*Santiago Principles*", "Objective and Purpose", *supra* note 49, 4.

Concluding remarks: an "inclusive soft law approach"

A profound implication of the current international effort to govern state capitalism is that a hard law approach, through binding rules and regulations of international law, is neither feasible nor desirable for many of the new areas in international economic activity. Hard legalization has many benefits and conforms to the developing trend of the international rule of law – or at least a rule-based international system.[65] However, while it may be a little ironic, a new international economic law landscape has made the hard law approach less desirable in many ways, as analyzed in the previous parts of this chapter. Indeed, the limited regulation of STEs and SOEs in the GATT/WTO has created more uncertainties and problems than solutions.

For emerging yet very controversial areas such as state capitalism, sovereign wealth funds, certain aspects of human rights, and electronic commerce, soft legalization is preferable. When countries are not politically ready to make credible commitments in the form of meaningful binding rules, negotiating and drafting of a set of soft law rules first succeeds in bringing these countries to the negotiating table. Second, eliminating the need to make firm commitments might entice the participating states to agree to principles and best practices being drafted that they otherwise would not agree to. As a Chinese saying goes, this is a process of *qiu tong cun yi* (meaning "to seek common ground while reserving differences"). Third, and perhaps most importantly, a project of soft legalization can change the prevailing political discourse, or even generate political discourse, and create incentives for both states and private actors to adjust in the direction of complying with soft law rules. As noted by Abbott and Snidal, "Soft law provides a basis for efficient international 'contracts', and it helps create normative 'covenants' and discourses that can reshape international politics."[66]

For the soft law approach to be successful in the contemporary context, it has to be inclusive, involving all stakeholders. With the obvious global shift in the balance of power, a few "Third World" countries, such as India, Brazil, and China, formerly colonies or semi-colonies, have now

[65] See L. Hsu, "The Rule of Law and Foreign Investment: Treaty Contexts and the Rule of Law", in J. Jowell, J.C. Thomas, and J.Z. Smit (eds.), *Rule of Law Symposium 2014: The Importance of the Rule of Law in Promoting Development* (Singapore: Academy Publishing, 2015), 129–150 (noting "trade and investment treaties may also promote international rule of law").

[66] Abbott and Snidal, "Hard and Soft Law in International Governance", *supra* note 19, 456.

become global powers with the kind of global bargaining power that is at least strong enough to block the formation of international consensus on many issues. In such a context, although "international law is predominantly Western,"[67] it is not always favorable to the West. As Tony Anghie has remarked, "[i]t is both ironic and telling that Western governments themselves are concerned about the operations of international investment regimes and instruments that they deployed in the past against developing countries."[68] Quite obviously, we are living in a world in which the weaker Third Word states are growing stronger, strong enough to block the formation of international agreements but not to make rules for the world, and the strongest states are declining, no longer able to dominate world affairs but still able to control the agenda of international negotiations. In such an increasingly multipolar world, no one is strong enough, and everyone is vulnerable. This is the "New Normal" state of global affairs, in which the way to make things work is through consensus-building. In such a world, legalized governance through soft law offers superior institutional solutions under some circumstances, at least as seen in the formation of the regulatory principles for SWFs.

Evaluated in this light, the Santiago Principles are the successful result of a soft legalization project. Given all the constraints, difficulties and different national aspirations, the "toothelessness" of the Principles is not a concern. What should be celebrated is the inclusiveness, albeit still very limited, of the Principles' drafting process, which brought the representatives of all the major SWF nations together with the Western powers and incorporated the views of both home states and host states alike. The text of the Principles is not as comprehensive as expected by some, but this is because there is no international consensus regarding some of the fundamental questions surrounding SWFs such as working definitions, acceptable and unacceptable commercial objectives, and the appropriate and fair levels of governance and disclosure. The Principles, however, lay a foundational framework, though still rudimentary, for more detailed provisions to be inserted. In the near future, further developments in the regulation of SWFs should still be soft law based, but this does not rule out the possibility of establishing a more binding international covenant on SWFs once conditions are more favorable for hard legalization.

[67] A. Anghie, "Imperialism and International Legal Theory", forthcoming in Anne Orford and Florian Hoffman (eds.), *The Oxford Handbook of International Legal Theory* (Oxford: OUP, 2015) (on file with the author).

[68] *Id.*

To conclude, the response to Professor Sornarajah's expectation that "SWFs have to be located somewhere in the law"[69] is that there should be a separate legal framework for SWFs, which may eventually be embodied in an independent international convention. But, this framework has to be developed through soft legalization. The logic of this approach largely applies to state capitalism in general.

[69] Sornarajah, "Sovereign Wealth Funds and the Existing Structure of the Regulation of Investments", *supra* note 7, 288.

PART VII

16

The many-headed hydra and laws that rage of gain, a chapter in conclusion

C.L. LIM

The privatisation of international state responsibility

This book has dealt with contextual issues, principally the backlash against modern bilateral investment treaty (BIT) negotiations and investor-state dispute settlement (ISDS), as well as practical and doctrinal legal issues involving points of treaty design, drafting and interpretation which are likely to be of interest to legal policy-makers, government practitioners and disputes lawyers.

However, the reader might also expect some discussion of M. Sornarajah's approach towards teaching and writing on his subject, his legal philosophy, how he defined his area of inquiry, picked his intellectual tools and defined the tasks which he then set out to perform. I had begun this story in Chapter 1. This concluding chapter sets out to complete that earlier account.

Sornarajah has always used conventional legal analysis, for the reasons earlier explained in Chapter 1, but his scholarly project is more ambitious and complex. He had embarked on that project apparently on the assumption that, as recently as 1994, the law could not be stated through use of a positivist methodology. Things were too fluid, at least under customary international law. Effort was required to foster or create acceptable norms for which an understanding of international investment law's shaping factors would first be necessary. This can in turn be accomplished by analysing past trends, projecting the law's future, appraising that future and formulating in its light the appropriate legal policy in a forward-looking manner. This policy-oriented approach, as Chapter 1 explained, is therefore a species of legal pragmatism. It treats the law fundamentally as a matter of prescription[1] rather than that which

[1] K. Llewelyn, "Some Realism about Realism – Responding to Dean Pound", (1931) 44 *Harv L Rev* 1222, 1252–1253.

is merely discoverable then applied, and constantly re-applied, to new and sometimes surprising factual situations.

In short, while in its outward appearance Sorna's legal method is conventional, he had from the very beginning counselled the importance of locating such conventional analysis firmly within the law's larger social context, keeping in mind, especially, the law's global policy aims. In this way, the law exists only to meet a social function. Sorna, however, always recognised the manipulability of legal policy prescriptions.[2] So, he is a legal pragmatist, moderate to the extent that he accepts that the conventional analysis of rules plays an important role, yet sceptical to the extent that he is suspicious of even widely accepted views of legal policy at any moment. This iconoclastic approach to the law he brought to bear, with all its force, on the international law on foreign investment.

Legal practice and legal practitioners have always prized legal creativity.[3] Pragmatism, that chief characteristic of American legal method and American law, has also always fostered creativity. In turn, the law schools do what it is believed that lawyers in practice do or ought to do. If the law is an instrument for the achievement of social ends, then one must be inventive even (or especially) in legal practice in adapting our existing doctrines to desirable social ends; not least when justifying new and controversial laws.[4] Of course, reasonable people may disagree about what those ends might be.

There has been much legal creativity in the practical world of international lawyering, and it was not always confined to the views of lawyers in the industrialised world. What legal advisors from the developing nations in the post-United Nations decolonisation era had attempted to do was to fashion the law towards the protection of their

[2] M. Tushnet, "Legal Scholarship: Its Causes and Cure", (1981) 90 *Yale LJ* 1205, 1209–1210. See the sudden remark in M. Sornarajah, *The Pursuit of Nationalised Property* (Dordrecht: Nijhoff, 1986), 315.

[3] In the Anglo-American tradition, which is what the present author understands, the idea that true mastery involves facility in applying legal doctrines to ever-unfolding situations has had a longer history. See for example, Langdell's famous remark that to have a mastery of legal doctrines is "to be able to apply them with constant facility and certainty to the ever-tangled skein of human affairs", and that "is what constitutes a true lawyer"; C.C. Langdell, *Selection of Cases on the Law of Contracts* (Boston: Little Brown, 1871), Preface. To the reader who wonders what that has to do with the subject of international investment law, see the discussion, *post*, on legal "inventiveness"; particularly, in prescribing a "contractual solution" to the declining relevance of customary international law following the post-war wave of expropriations of the twentieth century.

[4] R. Dworkin, *Taking Rights Seriously* (London: Duckworth, 1977), 3.

new-found sovereignty.[5] What they sought from international law was the furtherance of economic self-determination, expressed – among other ways – in a new doctrine of permanent sovereignty over their natural resources, a New International Economic Order including a Charter on the Economic Rights and Duties of States, a concept of the Common Heritage of Mankind in respect of the distribution of deep sea-bed resources under the 1982 Law of the Sea Convention and a right to development as an inalienable human right.[6]

However, the capital-exporting nations and their lawyers have viewed the law's chief purpose to be the protection of property rights. This view too required inventiveness, and as dicussed in Chapter 1, the device of contract was adapted to the international protection of foreign-owned property when it was realized that customary international law had become inadequate to its task as a new world order threatened to emerge.[7]

The new African and Asian nations were or at least intended to be a revolutionary force and had sought, consciously, to create a New International Economic Order. A new North–South divide between the prosperous North, and the fledgling, developing South meant that new law-ways had to be discovered, or invented, on both sides.[8] The terms of resource allocation were no longer so surely governed by custom's default rules on the protection of foreign-owned property. However, the industrialised West continued to adhere to the classical nineteenth-century conception of the inviolability of property rights. The debate had begun earlier, notably in that famous exchange between Secretary of State Hull and his Mexican counterpart. Secretary Hull had explained that, in essence, the United States did not seek specially favoured treatment for

[5] See *e.g.* C.L. Lim, "Neither Sheep Nor Peacocks: T.O. Elias and Post-Colonial International Law", (2008) 21 *Leiden Jo Int'l L* 295.

[6] This tale is well known. By far the best treatment concise treatment, see A. Cassese, *International Law in a Divided World* (Oxford: OUP, 1986), 356–375, esp. 364 *et seq.* For other condensed accounts, see (e.g.) Sornarajah, *Pursuit*, 14–21; R.P. Anand, *Studies in International Law and History* (Leiden: Brill, 2004), 252–256; Lim, "Neither Sheep Nor Peacocks", 297–301, and the sources cited therein.

[7] Sornarajah's account has been stated, and re-stated over time, see Sornarajah, *Pursuit*, 81–153; M. Sornarajah, *Law of International Joint Ventures* (Singapore: Longman, 1992), 294–302; M. Sornarajah, *The International Law on Foreign Investment*, 3rd ed. (Cambridge: CUP, 2010), 279–299.

[8] On law-ways, see K.N. Llewelyn and E.A. Hoebel, *The Cheyenne Way: Conflict and Caselaw in Primitive Jurisprudence* (Oklahoma: University of Oklahoma Press, 1941), 273 *et seq.*

its nationals or object to a national standard of treatment so long, however, as that standard of treatment also adhered to an international minimum standard of treatment for foreign-owned property.[9]

The debate shifted, as the old bilateral diplomacy came to be replaced by a new world wide parliamentary form of diplomacy.[10] It was to be shaped by the new diplomatic and legal technology of the nuclear age. What was only a couple of decades ago a matter of bilateral diplomatic correspondence became a subject for parliamentary-style debate in the United Nations General Assembly. In 1962, the United States, through a process resembling Senate-style legislative horse trading, secured recognition in General Assembly Resolution 1803 of the sanctity of State contracts and the international arbitration of disputes where the host State had consented to such arbitration. That story, as some readers will know, has been well told in Stephen Schwebel's writings.[11] In any event, Resolution 1803, ultimately, represented the views of the industrialised nations, adapted to the changing circumstances.[12] Resolution 1803 was a compromise admitting the need for inventiveness, and the arbitrator in *Texaco* v. *Libya* famously took the view that it represented customary international law.[13]

In truth, however, contrary to the hopes of the Third World and its lawyers, customary international law had become relegated to second place as a principal source of the international law on foreign investment.[14] To legal advisors in the West, where public international law had failed,[15] private law sources and analogies would now offer

[9] US Secretary of State to Mexican Ambassador, 22 August 1938, reproduced in A. Lowenfeld, *International Economic Law*, 2nd ed. (Oxford: OUP, 2008), 478,479.

[10] H. Nicolson, *The Evolution of Diplomacy* (New York: Collier Books, 1954), 99–125.

[11] UNGA res. 1803 (XVII), 1962, UN GAOR Supp (No. 17), 15–16, paras. 4, 8. See Lowenfeld, *International Economic Law*, 486–489 for an account of the history of the negotiations.

[12] These circumstances included, in Sornarajah's view, an inability to put pressure on the developing nations, as the developed nations could when they were colonies, owing in part also to the circumstances of the Cold War, the mood during the decolonisation era, and the restraint that the United Nations Charter effectively had, at the time, on the use of force in international relations; see Sornarajah, *Foreign Investment*, 280.

[13] *Texaco* v. *Libya* (1977) 53 ILR 389 (1978); 17 ILM 1 (Dupuy, sole arbitrator).

[14] See C.L. Lim, "The Strange Vitality of Custom in the International Protection of Property, Contracts, and Commerce", in Curtis A. Bradley (ed.), *Custom's Future: International Law in a Changing World* (Cambridge: CUP, in press).

[15] Notwithstanding that there had been attempts to uphold the international sanctity of investment contracts by citing international judicial support, e.g. an inapposite pronouncement in the *Wimbledon* case [1926] PCIJ Rep. Series A, No. 1, 25. See further Sornarajah, *Joint Ventures*, 295. See, however, Ole Spiermann's observation that "[i]t is not that investment contracts concluded between states and foreign investors derive their

answers.[16] Public international law was at least cognisant of private law principles where they took the form of the general principles of law recognised by the civilised nations.[17] Equally, the writings of the most highly qualified publicists provide material evidence of relevant public law principles and of the *lex mercatoria*,[18] which, together with the device of arbitration between private merchants, were also well recognised and could be adapted to provide a solution to a practical need.[19] Sornarajah has rejected the possibility that customary international law sanctioned the international protection of contractual rights. For, to him, resort to such 'low order sources' of international law was but a feeble justification for an attempted privatisation of the public international law principles of state responsibility.[20]

Ultimately, the turn to contract was only temporary, although it has had an enduring impact on investment law reasoning.[21] At first,

legal force from international; law", rather "if contractual rights held by the investor are affected in a way not in conformity with the principle *pacta sunt servanda*, and national law does not provide an adequate remedy, an arbitral tribunal is likely to resort to law other than national law", O. Spiermann, "Applicable Law", in P. Muchlinski *et al.* (eds.), *The Oxford Handbook of International Investment Law* (Oxford: OUP, 2008), 89, 94.

16 I have mentioned other practical attempts to affirm the international law sanctity of state investment contracts, such as in UNGA res. 1803 (XVII), para. 8; and the statement of the US Ambassador, quoted in Lowenfeld, *International Economic Law*, 488. On the status of UN General Assembly resolutions in law-making, see R.Y. Jennings, *The Acquisition of Territory in International Law* (Manchester: Manchester University Press, 1963) 84; F.B. Sloan, "The Binding Force of a 'Recommendation' of the General Assembly of the United Nations", (1948) 25 *BYIL* 1; D.H.N. Johnson, "The Effect of Resolutions of the General Assembly of the United Nations", (1956–1957) 32 *BYIL* 97; O. Asamoah, "The Legal Effect of Resolutions of the General Assembly", (1964) 3 *Columbia J Trans'l L* 210.

17 Sornarajah, *Joint Ventures*, 296.

18 M. Sornarajah, *International Commercial Arbitration* (Singapore: Longman, 1990), 116–117. See further, M.E. Basile *et al.* (eds.), *Lex Mercatoria and Legal Pluralism: A Late Thirteenth-Century Treatise and Its Afterlife* (Cambridge: Ames Foundation, 1998), 163–188.

19 See (e.g.) A. McNair, "The General Principles of Law Recognised by Civilised Nations", (1957) 33 *BYIL* 1; I. Seidl-Hohenveldern, "Recollections of Alfred Verdross", (1994) 5 *EJIL* 98, 102; F.A. Mann, *Studies in International Law* (Oxford: OUP, 1972), 143; A. von Mehren, "Special Substantive Rules for Multistate Problems", (1974) 88 *Harv. L. Rev.* 347.

20 This became his criticism of Mann, M. Sornarajah, "The Myth of International Contract Law", (1981) 15 *Jo World Trade Law* 187, 199, 201, 202; contra Mann's reading of the *Abu Dhabi Arbitration* (1951) 19 ILR 144, citing Lord Asquith in favour of the existence of such a body of laws; Mann, *Studies*, 143. For Mann's own criticism of the developing country viewpoint, see F.A. Mann, "Wrong in National and International Law", (1977) 48 *BYIL* 1.

21 See the case of the debate over umbrella clauses in Chapter 13 and Chapter 14 in this book.

that contractual turn manifested itself most loudly in the recognition by the arbitrator in *Texaco* v. *Libya* of the role of special purpose clauses – unusual choice of law clauses, stabilisation clauses and arbitration clauses, which could be said to evince an intent to effect the 'internationalisation' of the foreign investment contract.[22] In retrospect, this theoretical turn to contract was relatively short-lived,[23] even if its implications continue today. The complaint by Sorna and others has been that,[24] today, such commitments are instead being swept under the protective shield of international law in situations in which an international law commitment had plainly been unintended by the host state.

Sorna's early writings had, therefore, focused on the attempt to privatise the international law of state responsibility in the field of investment protection. To him, these new devices – contract and commercial arbitration – were anathema, not simply because they contradicted what the developing nations sought to achieve, which no doubt he sympathises with, but, primarily, because he viewed such inventive legal manoeuvres as a subversion of public international law doctrines and teachings. He was against the attempt to privatise such matters, which properly involved the public international law of state responsibility.

This inventive, creative and pragmatic legal turn was neither rooted in a doctrinal view of the law nor policy prescription. The contractualisation of public international law problems of state responsibility was a simple recasting of one side's perspective in the midst of a genuine clash in perspectives and interests between the North and South and between multinationals and the international non-governmental organisations (NGOs) during the later periods of economic globalisation.[25]

[22] *Texaco* v. *Libya* (1977) 53 ILR 389 (1978); 17 ILM 1 (Dupuy, sole arbitrator), paras. 40–45.

[23] It was overtaken the rise of BITs, but see also M. Sornarajah, *The Settlement of Foreign Investment Disputes* (Hague: Kluwer, 2000), 56–60. However, this is not to say that the contractual device has not been reinforced, some say "fully internationalised", by umbrella treaty clauses today; see Chapter 13 on umbrella clauses and Chapter 14 in this book.

[24] S. Asante, "International Law and Foreign Investment: A Reappraisal", (1988) 37 *ICLQ* 588, 612.

[25] This focus on the role of non-state actors in law-making, be they multinational corporations or the "transnational moral entrepreneurs" referred to in Chapter 1, is also a notable characteristic of New Haven scholarship. See, for example, the study of "aspirants" in W. M. Reisman and E. Suzuki, "Recognition and Social Change in International Law: A Prologue for Decisionmaking", in W.M. Reisman and B.H. Weston (eds.), *Toward World Order and Human Dignity: Essays in Honor of Myres S. McDougal* (New York: Free Press,

Sorna is still seen today by his critics to be casting the debate, perhaps unnecessarily, in North–South terms, but we would be remiss in failing to recall his early view of 'normlessness' as well as his view that the whole project of systematising and publicising the international law on foreign investment involves a search for acceptable norms.[26] To the question 'Acceptable to whom?', his answer would I imagine be 'to rich and poor alike'. It is not sufficient that one side's perspectives should prevail over the other. It is important to understand this aspect of his methodology. The very existence of normlessness had been due to a fierce clash between the North and South. The legal problem, properly defined as a social or sociological problem, is that rich nations/home States/multinationals and the poorer nations/host states/non-governmental organisations have different 'preferred events' in the language of the law and policy science approach. They have different values.[27]

Critics may recall how Antonio Cassese once quoted Bertolt Brecht. To the critic, Sorna was simply doing no more than 'painting still lives on the walls of a sinking ship',[28] at least once the Third World's efforts to reshape global economic rules began to wane. Three things, however, are worth remembering. The first, as described earlier, is the methodology Sornarajah acquired at Yale. He did not begin by advocating a Third World viewpoint, although he has ended up there. Rather, Sorna set out to define the legal problem as a clash of preferred events, expectations, values and interests. Those who believe that the analytical frame of a North–South divide is now

1976), 403; and also M.S. McDougal and G.C.K. Leighton, "The Rights of Man in the World Community: Constitutional Illusions Versus Rational Action (1949) 59 *Yale L.J.* 60, 84 on the task of "devising a world law appropriate for all the new participants such as international governmental organisations, transnational political parties, transnational private associations (cartels), and even the humble individual human being". See further, S. Charnovitz, "How Nongovernmental Actors Vitalise International Law", in M.H. Arsanjani *et al.* (eds.), *Looking to the Future: Essays on International Law in Honor of W. Michael Reisman* (Leiden: Brill, 2011), 135, 137–139.

26 See Chapter 1 of this book.

27 "Values", according to the New Haven method, are what people actually cherish; see L. Chen, *An Introduction to Contemporary International Law: A Policy-Oriented Perspective* (New Haven: Yale, 1989), 16. Sornarajah has said all this more-or-less in express terms, stating the very problem to be that "value systems of somewhat equal moral validity are in collision"; Sornarajah, *Foreign Investment*, 3. This position remains unaltered in the third edition; Sornarajah, *Foreign Investment*, 7.

28 Cassese, *International Law in a Divided World*, 375; citing Bertolt Brecht's "Fünf Schwierigkeiten beim Schreiben der Wahrheit" ("Five Difficulties with the Writing the Truth"), see B. Brecht, "Writing the Truth: Five Difficulties" (1935), available at roundtable.kein.org (translated as: "They are like a painter adorning the walls of a sinking ship with a still life").

stale are likely to miss this step in his sociological method,[29] which is to define the law job sociologically.[30]

Secondly, Sorna is an unapologetic believer in the progressive promise of our international institutions, rejecting the suggestion that '[t]he acceptance by the developed states of a legal obligation to eradicate poverty in the Third World is no longer seriously expected'. Or the notion that 'the very idea that economic injustice might be usefully dealt with by States, and public law, may now seem all-together old-fashioned and politically ambivalent'.[31] If such dejectedness is now true of the European tradition of international law, it would only make it 'necessary that lawyers belonging to TWAIL confront neo-liberal views so that the other side is heard'.[32]

Thirdly, Cassese's metaphorical ship did not sink, however perilously close it came.

Neo-conservatism

For a time, capital's triumph seemed assured.[33] Some international law practitioners and scholars may remember it also as a moment of

[29] S.W. Schill, "W(h)ither Fragmentation? On the Literature and Sociology of International Investment Law", (2011) 22 *European Journal of International Law* 875–908, available on Global Law Books at www.globallawbooks.org/reviews/detail.asp?id=712, to which the page references is here made, 8.

[30] On 'law jobs', see Llewelyn and Hoebel, *The Cheyenne Way: Conflict and Caselaw in Primitive Jurisprudence*, 290.

[31] M. Koskenniemi, *The Gentle Civiliser of Nations: The Rise and Fall of International Law 1870–1960* (Cambridge: CUP, 2002), 513.

[32] M. Sornarajah, "Mutations of Neo-Liberalism in International Investment Law", (2011), 3 *Trade, Law & Development* 203, 205. It is perhaps noteworthy in this regard that none of the writers Koskenniemi cites for "the new work . . . in describing international law as part of the colonialist project" had worked outside the West at the time, and with one exception, none were non-European; Koskenniemi, *The Gentle Civiliser of Nations*, 9.

[33] Sornarajah characterised this as the rise of private power in the post-Cold War context, associated with the expansion of the activities of multinational enterprises (MNEs) and their ability to shape public international law; M. Sornarajah, "Power and Justice: Third World Resistance in International Law", (2006) 10 *SYBIL* 19, 22–23. Previously, private power sought to adapt the tools of private law, and the device of contract law, in particular, to the needs of public international legal regulation, but now in the post-Cold War context, private power was shaping public international law in a more direct fashion. This is the triumph of private power in the form of global private capital, in the field of public international law. Of course, the seminal work on the transnational and international legal regulation of MNEs remains Peter Muchlinski's work, which in its first edition declared that the fear of MNEs dominating nation states had been replaced by a

professional soul-searching,[34] with heated debates on the permissibility of the pre-emptive use of force, and controversy over enhanced interrogation techniques. The *jus in bello* and *jus ad bellum* had both been seemingly up-ended by the War on Terror and the Second Gulf War. But, if so, it was otherwise with international economic law. In the trade law field, the Doha Round was launched in 2001 partly to reassure the world in the aftermath of 9/11 that it was to be business as usual.[35] International investment arbitration continued to grow as a dynamic area of international disputes practice with the world wide proliferation of cases following the arbitrations under Chapter 11 of the North American Free Trade Agreement (NAFTA).[36] It was left to the international NGOs based largely in the Western industrialised nations, less so in the developing nations, to mount a backlash with amicus briefs and calls for greater transparency in the manner in which international economic disputes are addressed.

For Sornarajah, there was a growing tension between demands for power and justice in the political sphere and between need and greed in the economic sphere.

Need and greed

These terms are not used in their ordinary sense. Knowledge of Sornarajah's methodology is required. In many ways, Sorna views the functions of legal practice separately from the role of law schools and professors. Admittedly, legal scholarship and law craft overlap. Notwithstanding his New Haven training, Sornarajah, as we have seen, takes the conventional criteria used for the professional identification of legal rules seriously. We have also seen how, in the first edition of *The International Law on Foreign Investment*, he had expressed the view that

more mature understanding, P. Muchlinski, *Multinational Enterprises and the Law* (Oxford: Blackwell, 1995), 11.

34 J.E. Alvarez, "The Closing of the American Mind", in "Reconciling Law, Justice and Politics in the International Arena", Proceedings of the 32nd Annual Conference of the Canadian Council on International Law, Ottawa, 16–18 October 2003, 74.

35 P. Blustein, *Misadventures of the Most Favored Nations* (New York: Public Affairs, 2009), 3. But, the success of the World Trade Organization (WTO) had been due, even earlier, to the success of the new dispute settlement system and what that meant for international trade litigation, see Thomas A. Zimmermann, *Negotiating the Review of the WTO Dispute Settlement Understanding* (London: Cameron, May 2006), 73 *et seq*.

36 See P. Eberhardt *et al.*, *Profiting from Injustice: How Law Firms, Arbitrators and Financiers are Fuelling an Investment Arbitration Boom* (Brussels/Amsterdam: CEO & TNI, 2012), 14–15.

the legal claims of all sides failed to meet the stringent criteria for the establishment of customary international law rules.[37] It is only if we accept that there are conventional legal criteria that we can understand his diagnosis of 'normlessness'.[38]

At the same time, it is the job of legal scholars to prescribe acceptable norms, but for Sorna, those who had claimed to have successfully applied the conventional criteria for legal discovery had been overstating their case. Many of these publicists, in his view, wrote in the service of capital.[39] Inventiveness in their advocacy had taken the form of attempts to privatise the rules of state responsibility and to subject non-contractual investment treaty disputes to private arbitration. Claims of legal discovery based upon such inventiveness required a response and where such claims support the capital-exporting nations and multinationals, they were to be properly appreciated as one-sided. Sorna's efforts have, therefore, been part, even a key part, of a larger project of scholarly resistance. But, what was the aim? The answer, according to Sorna, is to produce better policy prescriptions than have hitherto been expressed.

At this stage, it might be thought that the two legal-intellectual exercises are distinct. One set of arguments, based on what the contracts and arbitral tribunals say, reflects the preoccupations of the world of legal advisory and disputes practices. The other, the scholarly resistance

[37] See Chapter 1 of this book.

[38] M. Sornarajah, *The International Law on Foreign Investment* (Cambridge: CUP, 1994), 21. It must be appreciated, however, that the New Haven methodology does itself require something similar or analogous to conventional legal criteria, as it requires authoritative decisions in which social decision-makers formulate policy by "projecting desired consequences into living contexts as well as respond to words describing what prior decision-makers have done in earlier contexts"; See Chen, An Introduction to Contemporary International Law, 14. "What prior decision-makers have done in earlier contexts" resemble conventional legal criteria. *Contra* M. Koskenniemi, *From Apology to Utopia: The Structure of International Legal Argument* (Helsinki: Finnish Lawyers' Publishing Company, 1989), 175–178, arguing that the New Haven methodology blurs the distinction between law and politics or sociology. For a defence of our conventional legal criteria as social facts, see O.A. Elias and C.L. Lim, *The Paradox of Consensualism in International Law* (Hague: Kluwer, 1998), 264–268.

[39] Not only have certain claims been overstated from the viewpoint of the strict requirements of conventional criteria, but what is stated is a partial view, demonstrating a situation "where the existing principles of law, formulated at a time when they were kept in place by hegemonic control and dominance, are under attack", footnotes omitted; *id.* 3. For some, Sornarajah may have broken with scholarly convention in his latest characterisation of such scholars, see Sornarajah, *Resistance and Change*, 414. He would no doubt be able to point to the example of Grotius, for having been in the employ of the Dutch East India Company, as justification.

project, is something which textbook writers might properly, and harmlessly, occupy themselves and their law students with. The problem, however, is that the first set of arguments fail to meet the stringent, conventional criteria for law. The public international law on foreign investment is not made up of private contracts and private justice from private tribunals. Attempts to clothe such contractually based solutions – arbitration being also contractual – in the garb of public international law only end in desperate invocations of the low-order sources of international law (general principles of law, the writings of industrialised world publicists, the *lex mercatoria*, the common commercial law of nations and the list goes on).

For the conventionalist in him, close professional judgment is still required in determining the law. Properly measured and judged, contractually based claims to legal normative authority in tribunal practice ring hollow. These claims do not pass the threshold set by conventional legal criteria. They also do not pass the sociologically defined threshold that the tribunal Awards in question ought to be 'decisions made by those who are expected to make them, in accord with criteria expected by community members, in established structures of authority, with enough bases in power to secure necessary control, and by authorised procedures'.[40]

We imagine this to be a matter of philosophy, not the province of international law. But, the point of the New Haven-trained policy scholars has been that even philosophy cannot be the sole preserve of lonely philosophers where problems of the common interest, expressed in legal terms, represent social conflicts that require practical resolution.[41] Statements about legal rules, however, are couched at such high levels of abstraction that they soon reveal themselves to be ambiguous, and each application of a rule in a legal claim attracts a counterclaim.[42] The claims and counterclaims are only concealed behind a mirage of seemingly clear, abstract statements of rule.[43]

In the earlier phases of his career, Sornarajah's concern was almost purely doctrinal.[44] He was occupied with the task of providing detailed

[40] Chen, *An Introduction to Contemporary International Law*, 18.
[41] Chen, *An Introduction to Contemporary International Law*, 19. [42] *Id.*, 13.
[43] See further, B. Bix, *Law, Language and Legal Determinacy* (Oxford: Clarendon, 1993).
[44] All that I have described thus far draws from the history of Western jurisprudence from the late nineteenth century to the present time. The New Haven School had devoted itself to a Benthamite task. John Austin understood the relationship between law and sanction. Pound articulated a social theory of law. American legal realism was sceptical of

counterclaims to every new and inventive argument. In this, he eschewed grand theorising, saving him from what the late Thomas Wälde once described as the 'emotionalism' of many Third World scholars.[45] Instead, Sorna chose the path of 'hard law'.

However, what I have tried to show in Chapter 1, and in the past few pages, is that the conventional manner of Sorna's early writings stood upon a larger theoretical inquiry, which viewed the law in social and policy terms. But, even his underlying legal theory has become more dense and sophisticated over time, as his latest writings show. This has, in part, been the result of his interpretation of recent events.

Sociology and legal doctrine

This book has attempted to explain and assess the backlash against investment treaties and investment arbitration. It has also sought to address the question of reform and contemporary questions of treaty practice and doctrine. A brief recapitulation may be useful, as a prelude to an account of Sorna's own current writings in light of the recent concerns addressed by the several authors in this book.

According to Ken Vandevelde, the United States' (US) post-war Freedom, Commerce and Navigation (FCN) treaties have reflected a liberal orientation, both historically and philosophically. Liberalism consists of the economic ideas of investment neutrality, investment security and market facilitation and the corresponding political principles of liberty, the rule of law and regulatory necessity. Ken has distinguished liberalism from economic neo-liberalism, which had emerged in the 1970s and the 1980s and which, while fully capable of being promoted by arbitral tribunals, is not necessitated by treaties designed according to the liberal model.[46] Subsequent US treaty practice did not stray from the

legal claims made with Langdellian (Christopher Columbus Langdell) certitude and sought to take what Pound had begun to its logical conclusion. Hart and Dworkin argued over the question of certitude across the Atlantic. The Critical Legal Studies Movement led by Unger and Kennedy sought out arbitrary legal choices, and to uncover the underlying role of power. Critical Race Theorists understood the need to avoid philosophical parlour games in light of the tasks at hand (Critical Race Feminists challenged liberal Feminism). Public choice theory helped us to understand the logic of collective action, not least the political economy of international economic disputes.

45 T. Wälde, Book Review, *Int'l Bus Lawyer*, September 1996, 393, 394.

46 This is consistent with Sornarajah's view that "[o]ver the past few decades, international investment law has been increasingly used as an instrument for neo-liberalist ideals"; Sornarajah, "Mutations", 203.

liberal model notwithstanding the rise of neo-liberalism. Rather, neo-liberalism's effect has been on the treaty policy perspectives of the developing nations themselves who, at least prior to the recent backlash described by Trakman and Musayelyan, had become more receptive to US-style BITs.

Chapter 2 is an eloquent reminder that political liberalism permits the choice of social policy over economic productivity, just as economic liberals can differ about degrees of permissible market intervention. Ken's views come close to the ideas of reform and regulatory improvement expressed by Peter Muchlinski and Karl Sauvant. In contrast, Gus Van Harten has asked whether retrenchment ought to be preferred over piece meal reform, while David Schneiderman points out the problem of a legal industry which itself remains in denial.

These chapters, which I shall call the 'first tranche' in this book, are a collective effort, at the present time, to subject the current backlash to scholarly discussion; generating a range of assessments and proposals. Unsurprisingly, nations such as India, the subject of Chapter 8, have caught our attention, together with countries such as Egypt and Indonesia. India is proposing to revise its investment treaties, and there is now a new 2015 Draft Model BIT.[47] China's case is more intriguing. In its international economic relations, China has more than once found itself in two places at once in recent times. In the trade sphere, it is on the side of the developing nations, while seeking market access abroad.[48] In the investment sphere, it is now a capital importer and capital exporter, as Shan and Chen have pointed out in Chapter 9, in nearly equal measure. How China handles present-day treaty debates will be interesting to observe in the coming years. Sorna had once observed the 'cohesion' between China and India during the period of the Non-Aligned Movement and remarked on their potential to influence the international economic order today.[49]

The second tranche, comprising Chapters 10–14, have dealt with practical legal and doctrinal issues instead. They have dealt with

[47] For an unvarnished account of the controversies underlying the latest developments in India, see Mahdev Mohan, "Asian Perspectives in Investment Agreements and Arbitration", in *Yr'bk Int'l Investment Law & Pol, 2013–2014* (New York: OUP, in press, 5) (manuscript on file).

[48] See C.L. Lim and Jiangyu Wang, "China and the Doha Development Agenda", (2010) 44 *Jo World Trade* 1309.

[49] M. Sornarajah and J. Wang (eds.), *China, India and the International Economic Order* (Cambridge: CUP, 2010), 136–139, and Sornarajah, "Power and Justice", 19.

developments in treaty drafting and arbitral practice against the backdrop of concern over the restrictions which BITs and tribunals have threatened to impose upon sovereign, often democratic, decision-making on matters of domestic social policy. Together with Chapters 6 and 7, Chapters 10, 11, and 12 reflect Sorna's own long-standing concern with the remodelling of the existing international treaty framework governing foreign investment. The final set of chapters (Chapters 13–15) applies a conventional analysis to other legal-doctrinal issues in which Sornarajah had also expressed a special interest. They do so, because the issues themselves have raised intriguing doctrinal questions. Sorna has devoted close attention to attempts to protect foreign-owned property through contract and Chapter 14 revisits that debate, while Chapter 13 explores the relevance of that debate over 'internationalised contracts' to treaty umbrella clauses. Jiangyu Wang has dealt with a relatively new phenomenon – SWFs, their proper conceptualisation and international regulation.

In sum, the first tranche of the chapters in this book has dealt with the politics, economics and sociology of the law, while the second tranche has addressed doctrinal issues. Let us address Sornarajah's thoughts in that same order, beginning with his views about the politics, economics and sociology of the subject in the period roughly coinciding with the period from the end of Western colonialism to the present day. In his latest book, Sorna divides that period into the 'second', 'third' and 'fourth phases' of the law; the first phase having occurred much earlier with the nineteenth-century emergence of the Calvo Doctrine and subsequent events on the American Continent which had lasted until the twentieth-century pre-war period. That earlier history of the subject, culminating in the *Lena Goldfields* arbitration, is already well known, and our reader might wish to turn to the usual sources instead.[50] In the next two sections – Power and justice and The many-headed hydra – I propose to address Sorna's views about the politics, economics and sociology of the international law on foreign investment,[51] taking the reader to his 'fourth phase', which is currently represented by today's global backlash and signs of a return to

[50] See, for example, A. Nussbaum, "Arbitration between the Lena Goldfields Ltd. and the Soviet Government", (1950) 36 *Cornell LQ* 31. See further, Sornarajah, *Resistance and Change*, 32.

[51] See also Sornarajah, *id.*, 35, 43.

normlessness.[52] We will conclude with Sorna's views on the state of contemporary legal doctrine.[53]

Power and justice

According to the New Haven method of the Yale Law School, the scholar working in the present views international law as an on-going social process. Briefly described, our scholar draws on past trends of actual social behaviour, in situations where both control is exercised and legal authority invoked, in order to project the future.[54] Such projections are not an end in themselves but are intended to be appraised against other alternative policy goals.[55] The method, therefore, involves a forward-looking, yet evaluative, 'policy science' exercise.

9/11, the War on Terror, the Second Gulf War, the Global Financial Crisis and subsequent Global Economic Crisis have been some of the major events in the past 15 years. Sorna's implicit theory, nay his instinctive method, would have required him to analyse these unfolding events while framing an agenda for a forward-looking legal-scholarly inquiry. This he did. According to his account, these years saw capital (what he

[52] *Id.*, 45. See further, M. Sornarajah, "Toward Normlessness: The Ravage and Retreat of Neoliberalism in International Investment Law", in K. Sauvant (ed.), *Yearbook on International Investment Law & Policy (2009–2010)* (New York: Oxford University Press, 2010), 595.

[53] "Privateers bearing letters of marque", below.

[54] Chen, *An Introduction to Contemporary International Law*, 20–21.

[55] This is the final step of New Haven methodology, but it is also the most contentious; see J. Stone, *Visions of World Order* (Baltimore: Johns Hopkins, 1984), 29–30; Sornarajah, *Pursuit*, 315. Part of the controversy surrounding the New Haven method, and perhaps one reason it has not taken off, especially among developing world legal scholars, in stark contrast today to the TWAIL (Third World Approaches to International Law) Movement, which grew later out of the Harvard Law School or the more moderate and progressive voice of the Columbia School, had to do with the Cold War values which Lasswell and McDougal promoted; H.D. Lasswell and M.S. McDougal, "Legal Education and Public Policy: Professional Training in the Public Interest", (1942) 52 *Yale LJ* 203, reproduced in McDougal *et al.*, *Studies in World Public Order* (New Haven: Yale, 1960), 53, 55. They themselves considered that "the lead must of course be taken by scholars and public figures physically located in the non-Soviet world"; Myres S. McDougal and Harold D. Lasswell, "The Identification and Appraisal of Diverse Systems of Public Order" (1959) 53 *AJIL* 1, 5, 8. That would have excluded large parts of the developing world at that time, realistically understood. This also made Sornarajah a rare voice from the Third World in promoting, even if only implicitly, the Yale method in the study of the international law of foreign investment during the ensuing, tumultuous period. For the policy conclusions these legendary American patriots of Yale would tend to draw always seemed so politically partial in the eyes of Third World scholars.

calls 'greed') become more closely allied to power. At the same time, however, 'pre-emptive strike', 'extraordinary rendition' and 'waterboarding' became near-household terms just as a new round of global trade talks was launched. The answer, in part, nations had decided was to have more liberalisation of trade and investment in order to stimulate growth and address poverty as a perceived cause of global terrorism.[56] A neo-liberal economic prescription was proposed for curing terror.[57]

These events brought Sorna out of the relative seclusion of the international investment law field, what he preferred to call the 'international law on foreign investment' if only to emphasise the field's subordinate status as only one part of the larger system of public international law. There was no legal-professional incentive for others to do so, for the investment law field was booming, its appearance of self-containment near complete. The 1997 Asian financial crisis having now been long forgotten, finance, trade and investment expanded as did investment disputes practices in the international law firms.[58] During this period, Sorna embarked upon a research programme quite different from that during the years in which he had focused on doctrinal questions. This time there would be the entire canvas of the international law field to work on. Resistance to his own future projections – the policy scientist's task of formulating, evaluating and presenting alternative policies – also required a more abstract kind of scholarship. Thus, he began to craft the arguments for an 'international law of justice', his preferred policy, against its jural opposite, which he called the international law of 'power'. Events were forcing an implicit theory out into the open.

The expression 'international law of justice', what Sorna has more recently called 'cosmopolitan global justice',[59] became the new shorthand for that political morality he once called 'the law of need'. His now overt terminology brought Sornarajah to the attention of the present generation of the critical Third World Approaches to International Law Movement (TWAIL). Sorna argued that colonialism was European international law's principal product – being in large part a subversion of justice to ensure 'the enslavement of the larger part of humanity'.[60] This

[56] Blustein, *Misadventures of the Most Favored Nations*, 3.

[57] See also C.L. Lim, "Regional Trade Agreements and the Poverty Agenda" in J. Linarelli (ed.), *Research Handbook on Global Justice and International Economic Law* (London: Elgar, 2013), 96.

[58] See Y. Dezalay and B. Garth, *Dealing in Virtue* (Chicago: University of Chicago Press, 1996).

[59] Sornarajah, *Resistance and Change*, 417.

[60] Sornarajah, "Power and Justice", 20.

is a 'radical view' when it is considered that contemporary writing still rues the passing of a 'gentle' or 'civilising' mission of international law.[61] In any event, the Third World had long sought to articulate new organising or constitutive principles, including the doctrine of self-determination for colonial peoples. According to Sorna, now 'power had to find new forms of expression through the assertion of new philosophies and the adoption of new strategems'.[62] What the Third World nations had tried to articulate were norms of justice to speak truth to power,[63] and they certainly managed to disrupt the operation of the West's investment norms, at least for a while, during the 1960s and 1970s. Then, the pendulum swung anew when the Cold War ended, giving rise eventually to a unipolar world and the momentary but seemingly near-total triumph of a global and globalised species of capitalism.

Neo-liberalism as economic thought had owed much to the Reaganomics and Thatcherism of the 1980s and early 1990s, but it was the Clinton administration's clinching of the NAFTA deal which became the true embodiment of Reaganomics in the international economic field. NAFTA's creation in 1994 was to give ISDS a real boost through the commencement of Chapter 11 arbitrations during the late 1990s. But, just as soon as that began, a backlash against globalisation also emerged, pitting non-governmental pressure groups against what Sorna calls 'the transnational class'.[64]

From a political economy perspective, there were also changes occurring within the Hyper-Power itself, and we began to see the emergence of corporate influence not just domestically but in the form of considerable transnational corporate influence. Declining aid at the time and sovereign defaults had led to the greater dependency by developing nations on foreign capital, which then broke the unity of the Third World and created Third World supporters for the Washington Consensus.[65]

That the Third World project had crumbled may be loosely illustrated by comparing two cases, a well-known 1964 judgment of the United States Supreme Court in *Banco Nacional de Cuba* v. *Sabbatino*,[66] and an English Court of Appeal decision in 2005 in *Occidental Exploration and Production Co.* v. *Republic of Ecuador*.[67] The former was a well-known

[61] See Koskenniemi, *The Gentle Civiliser of Nations.*

[62] Sornarajah, "Power and Justice", 20–21. [63] *Id.*, 22.

[64] Sornarajah, "Mutations", 205. [65] Sornarajah, "Power and Justice", 22–23.

[66] *Banco Nacional de Cuba* v. *Sabbatino* 376 US 398 (1964).

[67] [2005] EWCA Civ. 1116 [2006]; Q.B.432.

decision at the height of the Cold War and involved the Cuban expropriation of an American sugar factory. In the US Court of Appeals, Second Circuit, Judge Waterman had said that, 'until the day of capable international adjudication', municipal courts must be 'the custodians' of international law,[68] but Justice Harlan, writing for an eight-to-one Supreme Court majority, held that while the Respondent's:[69]

> ... basic contention is that United States courts could make a significant contribution to the growth of international law ... magnified by the relative paucity of decisional law by international bodies ... [but that] ... given the fluidity of present world conditions, the effectiveness of such a patchwork approach towards the formulation of an acceptable body of law is ... highly conjectural. Moreover, it rests on the sanguine proposition that the decisions of the courts of the world's major capital exporting country and principal exponent of the free enterprise system would be accepted as disinterested expressions of sound legal principle.

Hence, *Sabbatino* stood for the view that, where international law is in a state of flux, the US courts should treat questions concerning the validity of the acts of a foreign state in its own territory to be Acts of State and, therefore, non-justiciable. Be it even so that the allegation involved discriminatory, confiscatory and unlawful expropriation of American property. That was in 1964, prompting an outraged Congress to enact the Sabbatino Amendment.[70] However, by 2005, Christopher Greenwood QC (as he then was) would fail to persuade a three-judge English Court of Appeal in *Occidental Petroleum* that a dispute arising under the 1993 US–Ecuador BIT involving the right to a VAT refund should, likewise, be considered non-justiciable. The irony of an investor attempting to deny the availability of domestic judicial recourse in an investment dispute,[71] and failing, should not escape notice. Too much should not be read into passing comparisons, but these cases illustrate how times have changed and how the developing countries had themselves embraced BITs. Today, it is not simply that domestic courts are uninvolved in the backlash against the treaty protection of investments but are likely seen as in the current European debate to be a bulwark against the excesses of tribunals in their ability to set aside or refuse enforcement to particular Awards.

[68] *Banco Nacional de Cuba* v. *Sabbatino*, 307 F.2d 845 (1962).
[69] *Banco Nacional* v. *Cuba*, 376 US 398 (1964), at 428.
[70] Sornarajah has written on this, see Sornarajah, *Pursuit*, 282–285.
[71] Occidental had sought to argue that it would be wrong for an English Court to set aside an arbitral award in its favour.

Sorna had devoted considerable attention to domestic courts in his 1986 book.[72] His criticisms today, as we shall see, are confined, however, to patterns of international treaty behaviour, international tribunal conduct and international law writing.[73] According to Sornarajah, within these spheres, an international law of power had re-emerged; owing something to the policies of the George W. Bush administration, which had also sought to refashion other international law rules in far-reaching ways.[74]

The effect of the Bush years saw Sorna not in the least discouraged but waiting patiently for the pendulum which he knew would swing again.[75]

The many-headed hydra

The night grows dark and the road
lonely. Fireflies gleam among the
leaves.
Who are you that follow me with
stealthy silent steps?
Ah I know, it is your desire to rob
me of all my gains. I will not dis-
appoint you!
For I still have something left,
And my fate has not cheated me of
everything.

– Rabindranath Tagore[76]

[72] Sornarajah, *Pursuit*, 242–311.

[73] In neither case above, *Banco Sabbatino* or *Occidental*, would Sornarajah or the present author see much to criticise. The question of how domestic courts in international financial centres should deal not just with occasional changes in international law but the sheer fluidity of developments in the international investment field is however a subject which would be worthy of serious attention in its own right.

[74] For this author's views at least, see C.L. Lim, "The Great Power Balance, the United Nations and What the Framers Intended", (2007) 5 *Chinese Jo Int'l L* 307; C.L. Lim, "Inter Arma Silent Leges? Black Hole Theories of the Laws of War" in V.V. Ramraj (ed.), *Terrorism and the Rule of Law: Legal Theory in Times of Crisis* (Cambridge: CUP, 2008), 385; C.L. Lim, "Did Captain America Kill International Law?" in Marie-Luisa Frick and Andreas Oberprantacher (eds.), *Power and Justice in International Relations* (Farnham: Ashgate Press, 2009), 29. See further Alvarez's trenchant remarks in his lunch address, cited earlier, "Closing of the American Mind".

[75] Sornrajah credits the distinguished London University economist Edith Penrose and her colleagues with his idea of the cyclical nature of nationalisations, and the "decline and return" of ideas in politics and law; *Resistance and Change*, 68; see E. Penrose, G. Joffê, and J. Stevens, "Nationalisation of Foreign Owned Property for Public Purpose", (1992) 55 *MLR* 1.

[76] R. Tagore, *The Gardener* (London: MacMillan, transl. by the author from the original Bengali, 1920), 124.

The 2008 Global Financial Crisis and subsequent Global Economic Crisis has since done damage to economic neo liberalism,[77] while the backlash against economic globalisation, which had begun with the collapse of the Multilateral Agreement on Investment in 1998 and the Seattle demonstrations in 1999, has since been directed towards the device of ISDS. By century's end, the disparity between rich and poor in the West was such that the 'Third World' had emerged within the Western industrial societies themselves,[78] creating – in Sorna's view – more favourable conditions at least for a shift from a state-centric international law of power to a demand for law based upon 'ethical and justice-related notions'.[79]

However, neo liberalism's retreat will not be gracious but, rather, will be marked by renewed legal arguments and stratagems by its proponents. The former schoolboy who had excelled in Latin and Greek began, in his latest writings, to recall a beast of the ancient world from his youth. Neoliberalism is the many-headed hydra, a 'wounded beast trying to survive', whose adherents are already 'resorting to new arguments or rehashing old ones' with a familiar inventiveness. The new heads are fresh heads of legal claim. Equally grotesque are new 'mutations' in legal reasoning. The signs of such legal inventiveness are telling.[80]

Yet, the latest international developments and transformations have always proven ephemeral. There had been a consistent attempt, since the Second World War, to re-enact a classical nineteenth-century Lockean

[77] 2008 also damaged the standing of the West, see Julia Leung, *The Tides of Capital* (London: OMFIF, 2015).

[78] Sornarajah, "Power and Justice", 25, citing C. Thomas, "Where is the Third World Now?", in M. Cox *et al.* (eds.), *The Interregnum: Controversies in World Politics 1989–1999* (New York: Cambridge, 1999), 225. For the economic foundations of imperialism, and the pacifism of labour in creditor nations, see also H.H. Gerth and C. Wright Mills (eds.), *From Max Weber: Essays in Sociology* (London: Routledge, 1948), 162–171.

[79] Sornarajah, "Power and Justice", 25. See further, F. Teson, "The Kantian Theory of International Law", (1992) 92 *Columbia L Rev* 53. However, Sornarajah rejects Kant for he argues that a vision of the world order must be historically informed in this regard and must accept the history of colonialism; *id.*, 27. His position has at least the support of the New Haven insistence that values must be empirical even if, as we have seen, the derivation of values by the New Haven method has been a mystery to its critics, Stone, *Visions of World Order*, 29–30; and see further Koskenniemi, *Apology*, 175 (footnote 163 on that page). Koskenniemi's observation that McDougal and Lasswell seem to derive values from "an identification with the whole of humankind" seems correct, without detracting from the fact that the process of discovering those values remains shrouded in mystery. All that is clear is that the function of values in the New Haven methodology is to constrain power; Koskenniemi, *id.*

[80] Sornarajah, "Mutations", 204.

notion of property.[81] This notion paid little heed to international law's subsequent development in other spheres after the War, during which the search for an ethically grounded, just international legal order saw the emergence of the human rights movement, international labour standards, expressions of an international law right to development, and international environmental regulation.[82] These are also, at least potentially, higher-order norms in the international legal order. The proponents of the international legal protection of property rights, however, wished to break away from these inconvenient truths about the international legal order.[83] It is also for this reason, as I have said, that Sornarajah speaks of the 'international law on foreign investment', there being no such thing in his mind as a segregated or clinically isolated field of 'international investment law'.

The entire BIT-investor-state dispute settlement apparatus, so favoured by neo-liberals, now faces not only fierce attack by international non-governmental groups but also the rejection of host states. In one form, we have Bolivia's, Ecuador's, and Venezuela's withdrawals from the ICSID Convention. In another, we see Venezuela's, Ecuador's, the Czech Republic's, Bolivia's, South Africa's and Indonesia's BIT 'terminations'.[84] In his latest work, *Resistance and Change*, Sornarajah offers an account of how the cracks had earlier begun, in 2004, the year of the *Methanex* arbitration and new US and Canadian Model BITs, and widened during the 2004 to 2007 period just before the Global Financial and Economic Crisis.[85] By 2004, expansive arbitral interpretations of NAFTA protection meant that the shoe was now on the other foot and developed states themselves began to re-consider the importance of their own regulatory

[81] J. Locke, *Second Treatise of Civil Government*, C.B. McPherson, ed., (Indianapolis/Cambridge: Hackett, 1980), Ch. V.

[82] Much of which took the form of a right of peoples, see James Crawford (ed.), *The Rights of Peoples* (Oxford: Clarendon, 1988).

[83] See also T. Franck, *Fairness in International Law and Institutions* (Oxford: OUP, 1995), 455.

[84] R. Beckmann *et al.*, "BIT by BIT in Indonesia: Signs of a Pushback on Foreign Investment", *Norton Rose Fulbright*, October 2014; available at nortonrosefulbright.com. Brazil appears to adopt a distinct model by now putting faith into new state-to-state co-operation mechanisms, thereby allowing sovereign states to recover a lost role in the direct management of international investment relations. Brazilian investment abroad and the Brazilian model of capitalism present two explanations. See N. M. Perrone and G. R. Cerqueira César, "Brazil's Bilateral Investment Treaties: More Than a New Investment Treaty Model?", *Columbia FDI Perspectives*, No. 159. 26 October 2015.

[85] *Methanex* v. *US*, UNCITRAL (NAFTA), Ad Hoc Arbitration, Final Award, 3 August 2005.

space.[86] At roughly the same time, the BIT disputes resulting from the Argentine Financial Crisis of 2001/2002 saw investors asserting claims in reliance on their legitimate expectations, and unfair and inequitable treatment. Dissatisfaction with these and other Latin American cases, eventually, led to the fateful meeting of the Bolivarian Alliance of the Americas in 2007.[87] The two threads, North American and Latin American, foreshadowed what we think of presently as a more widespread, global backlash against the investment dispute system, which had been so successful since the 1990s. Following the Global Economic Crisis in 2008, the law has begun to revert to a new state of uncertainty,[88] while the backlash against ISDS and of regulatorily intrusive treaties has now spread to Egypt in the Middle East, India in South Asia, and Indonesia in Southeast Asia.

The pendulum swung wildly from one decade to the next, while Sornarajah attended to his scribblings.

Privateers bearing letters of marque

> The Oxford English Dictionary defines a privateer as "an armed vessel owned and officered by private persons, and holding a commission from the Government, called letters of marque, authorizing the owners to use it against a hostile nation, and especially in the capture of merchant shipping".
>
> – *Richard Pares*[89]

Sornarajah cautions that the use of conventional legal arguments by neo-liberal scholarship will continue, in an instrumental fashion, to develop and advance and that the current backlash only entrenches neo-liberals further. It will cause them to develop ever more innovative doctrines and arguments.[90] Doctoral theses spew from the elite universities in the industrialised world, while the institutions in the developing

86 Sornarajah, *Resistance and Change*, 399–400. The 2004 model treaties contained general exceptions and environmental and labour standards, and they at least attempted to limit the fair and equitable treatment standard to the minimum standard of treatment under customary international law; *id.*, 349. They were to usher in the new 'balanced treaties' which were also emerging elsewhere from Southeast Asia to the Southern African states; *id.*, 352 *et seq*.

87 *Id.*, 400–404. By late 2007, there were 40 cases against Argentina alone pending before ICSID arbitration.

88 *Id.*, 406.

89 R. Pares, *Colonial Blockade and Neutral Rights 1739–1763* (Oxford: Clarendon, 1938), 1.

90 Sornarajah, "Mutations", 205 ("[i]nstrumentalism becomes entrenched").

world lack the same capacity and resources. He observes that there has been the 'increasing publication of journal articles and books in the developed world by young scholars who are eager to join the neo-liberal bandwagon'.[91] They only needed to point to a lucrative industry.[92] To Sorna, this involves a misunderstanding of the protean nature of the subject, viewed against the backdrop of global events, and the direction of international law as a whole.

International events, reflected in other parts of international law, have long driven the subject of international investment law. Scholarship, which recognises the force of fundamental and increasingly rapid shifts, is required. A perspective which takes the social and political dynamics of the subject seriously does not deny the need for practitioner texts on tribunal case-law and procedure, but argues for a more comprehensive view which would also provide an account of trends over time, shaping factors, changing and multiplying actors, and the transience and instability of every new doctrine and set of opposing legal arguments. A narrow approach, as opposed to an 'integrative approach', towards the study of the subject through the 'analytical exposition of awards and the texts of treaties' would fail to comprehend fully the causes of divergence in the awards, which can only be explained by an adequate sociology of the discipline.

According to Sornarajah, the disciplinary techniques and professional orientation of international commercial arbitration practitioners, often sitting as arbitrators and producing a specialist practice-orientated narrative, are different from those of the scholars who study the subject as a 'system' with different 'hierarchies of interest and conflicting obligations'.[93] Neo liberalism's more perceptive proponents have not failed to observe the importance of legal hierarchies and now search for a renewed source of authority and prestige in an attempt to elevate the arbitration industry to the status of a global administrative apparatus, like privateers of old bearing letters of marque. Recall too that our metaphorical hydra has multiple heads.[94] Previously, considerable attention had been focused on the way in which the public law doctrine of legitimate

[91] *Id.*, 206. [92] Schill, W(h)ither Fragmentation?, 12–13.
[93] Sornarajah, "Mutations", 214.
[94] The "hydra" is a metaphor, as is the "twailing machine" referred to in the opening chapter of this book, which deciphers and counters the hydra's moves. In his latest writings as this book goes to print, he speaks of neo-liberalism's "adaptive capacity and its ability to morph into different forms when faced with criticism"; Sornarajah, *Resistance and Change*, 68.

expectations had become a new head of international treaty claim for unfair and inequitable treatment.[95] The impact of that doctrine is now also felt in cases where a contractual stabilisation clause operates to restrict the scope of the host state's regulatory powers.[96] Now, we see the extension of that argument to situations where there is no treaty at all, and no fair and equitable treatment clause, but only an internationalised contract.[97] Likewise, Sorna draws our attention to the adaptation of the public law doctrine of proportionality to the settlement of investment disputes as neo liberalism's latest ruse.[98]

For Sornarajah, the hydra's fresh heads beguile, because the new legal arguments show a post-modern sensibility towards reasoning driven by considerations of fact, degree and value. Precisely because counter-arguments have also been advanced to shrink the doctrine of legitimate expectations back to size,[99] while proportionality appears to involve a rational balancing of competing factors,[100] the new legal sensibility is deceptively even-handed in appearance. Sorna observes that his prey only behaves thus for it is wounded. Post-modern scholars would simply urge that where our legal appreciation gains sophistication, the old conception of 'all or nothing rules' tends to yield to a more nuanced form of reasoning based on judgments which depend on the facts of each case, judgments of degree, and explicit moral-political choices.[101] On this 'post-modern' view, use of the doctrines of legitimate expectation and proportionality merely recognises the open texture of rules, that the law produces conflicting results in particular cases and that value choices are therein involved. It is nothing more than a conceptual advance in modern legal thought. But, as I have explained, Sorna remains committed to a sociological, not simply a conceptual, explanation of legal developments. In his latest writings, he ascribes an almost Newtonian quality instead to the social process of legal development. Each legal action begets an equal

[95] See Chapter 12. [96] Sornarajah, *Resistance and Change*, 132–133. [97] *Id.*, 133.

[98] *Id.*, 371. [99] *Id.*, 272 *et seq.*

[100] See *Arif* v. *Moldova*, ICSID Case No. ARB/11/23, 8 April 2013, para. 537; *Yukos* v. *Russia*, PCA Case No. AA 227, 18 July 2014, paras. 1575–1578.

[101] See, in the context of the application of the fair and equitable treatment standard, *Rompetrol* v. *Romania*, ICSID Case No. ARB/06/3, 18 April 2008. I am indebted to Professor Richard Parker of the Harvard Law School for his lessons on judgments of "fact, degree and value" and the post-modern turn in US constitutional jurisprudence. For the post-interpretative stage of a legal society, see also Ronald Dworkin, *Law's Empire* (Cambridge, MA: Belknap, 1986), 62 *et seq.*; Stephen Guest, *Ronald Dworkin* (Edinburgh: Edinburgh University Press, 1992), 28–32.

and opposite reaction.[102] Not only are there logically opposed legal arguments, conceptually speaking, which mirror underlying tensions between power and justice, need and greed;[103] there are social forces too arrayed on each side in which any movement on either side begets an equal and opposite social reaction. As he puts it:[104]

> When a set of norms reaches acceptance, those adversely affected by the change will mount resistance to it, querying the wisdom of such acceptance in the context of the specific interests that they articulate.

For Sornarajah, opposing doctrines do not exist only conceptually as a part of a postmodern appreciation of legal logic. There are not only opposing meanings but opposing human agencies and clashing interests at work.

To spurn the rage of gain

The medium of a multi-authored work has allowed exploration of the complexities of Sornarajah's observations over time of key ideas, events, actors and doctrines. Doctrinally, his work has sought to anchor international investment law as a branch of the international law of state responsibility. He has always pursued 'joined-up writing' in the field by rejecting the fragmentation of investment treaty arbitration from the field of international investment law.[105]

Within investment arbitration itself, the schisms and tensions between awards, which exist presently will only deepen as normlessness, an unsettled state of law, again draws near. Viewing international law as a part of a global social process, the time has not come for Sornarajah to lay

102 Sir Isaac Newton's "Third Law of Motion";, in *Philosophiæ Naturalis Principia Mathematica* (Londini: Jussu Societatis Regiæ, 1686), 16, available at www.gutenberg.org.

103 See e.g. A.B., Rubin, "Does Law Matter? A Judge's Response to the Critical Legal Studies Movement", (1987) 37 *Jo Legal Educ* 307 ("One facet of Critical Legal Studies doctrine is that what we call 'law' is but a grab bag of legal rules, some diametrically opposed to others"); Jack Balkin, "Deconstructive Practice and Legal Theory", (1987) 96 *Yale LJ* 743. For "counterprinciples", see R.M. Unger, *The Critical Legal Studies Movement* (Harvard: Belknap, 1983), 60.

104 Sornarajah, *Resistance and Change*, 415.

105 *Id.*, 29. The phrase "joined-up writing" comes from C. McLachlan, "The Principle of Systemic Integration and Article 31(3)(c) of the Vienna Convention", (2005) 54 *ICLQ* 279, 284. Sornarajah has also kept an eye on the neighbouring field of international trade regulation, closely observing the Agreement on Trade-related Investment Measures (TRIMS) as a high-point for neo liberalism and the shelving of investment as one of the "Singapore issues" in the currently moribund Doha negotiations; Sornarajah, "Mutations", 209, 212.

down the 'twailing machine'.[106] The current backlash against investment treaties in their present form and investor-state tribunals is only the latest of a series of unfolding events. He knows that those who hold neo-liberalism to be true will likely behave like Oliver Goldsmith's village schoolmaster. Although vanquished, they would argue still.[107] Perhaps, the law will one day settle upon a more stable and lasting accommodation of the various clashing interests. For now, he intends to continue to write, his motivations best captured by his favourite poet.[108]

> . . . Still let thy voice, prevailing over time,
> Redress the rigours of th' inclement clime;
> Aid slighted truth; with thy persuasive strain
> Teach erring man to spurn the rage of gain . . .

[106] See Chapter 1 of this book.

[107] Sornarajah, "Mutations", 216; Oliver Goldsmith, *The Deserted Village, a Poem* (London: W. Griffin, 1770), reprinted in J. Wain (ed.), *The Oxford Library of English Poetry*, Vol. II, Sackville to Keats (Oxford: OUP, 1986), 155, 160.

[108] Wain (ed.), *id.*, 165.

INDEX

AUTHOR INDEX